CONSUMER GUIDE®

AUTOMOBILE BOOK

ALL NEW 1990 EDITION

CONTENTS

Acknowledgment

Contributing Writer
James M. Flammang
(Shopping Tips, Warranties and Service Contracts,
Consumer Complaints, Safety, and Insurance sections.)

HOW TO USE THIS BOOK

The *Automobile Book* contains the information you'll need to pick the right car, van, or light truck and to negotiate a fair deal. Begin with our introductory sections for buying strategies and pitfalls in today's car market, plus the latest on such issues as safety and warranties. Then turn to our analysis of the individual vehicles for an in-depth look at the 1990 models. Each report concludes with a price list. The price lists are the most valuable information we provide because they allow our readers to compare the costs of different models and options at home, away from the pressures of the new-car showroom.

Here's how the Auto Editors of CONSUMER GUIDE® have arranged each report:

What's New

This section spotlights changes to the car's styling, mechanical equipment, and options for 1990. It also gives an overview of the car itself, with a thumbnail sketch of its main features. Most of the information in this section is provided by the manufacturers several months before the '90 models go on sale. Once the car appears in the showroom, we occasionally find that some of the changes are not as the manufacturer promised. Therefore, some models and options mentioned in this section may not actually be offered to the public during the model year. Feel free to contact us if our report differs from what you find at the dealership.

For

A quick-reference list of the vehicle's key positive features and attributes.

Against

A quick-reference list of the vehicle's key negative features and shortfalls.

Summary

Here's where you'll learn how the car performs on the road and how it succeeds or fails in everyday use. The Auto Editors of CONSUMER GUIDE® road test scores of cars, vans, and light trucks each year. We don't conduct formal race-track tests of performance. Instead, we drive them the way you would: commuting to and from work, on pleasure trips, and over a mix of city and suburban routes, on freeways, and over rural roads. We scrutinize acceleration, braking, handling, driving position, instruments and controls, interior comfort, cargo space, and fuel economy. And we take note of the car's general assembly quality. Finally, we analyze the combination of options and equipment that works best, and determine which comparable cars might be worth considering.

Specifications

This table lists the car's major interior and exterior dimensions, weight, capacities, and other measurements. Our specifications table lists a standard sedan with a trunk as a notchback. A 2-door car with a rear liftgate is listed as a 3-door hatchback, the liftgate constituting the third door. Similarly, a 4-door car with a rear liftgate is listed as a 5-door hatchback. *Cargo Volume* expresses the vehicle's maximum possible luggage capacity; for example, the cubic-foot cargo capacity of a station wagon or a hatchback with its rear seat folded. Seating capacity is the maximum possible with all optional seats in place. The specifications are provided by the manufacturers.

Engines

This catalogs the displacement, fuel-delivery system type, and horsepower and torque ratings of every engine offered with the vehicle. The information is drawn from manufacturer data. The fuel economy estimates come from the Environmental Protection Agency and correspond to a specific transmission type. If no EPA number is listed, it means the transmission is not available for purchase with that engine.

Note that a key to these specifications appears on every two-page spread that has a chart.

Consumer Guide®
7373 N. Cicero Ave.
Lincolnwood, IL 60646

Prices

The *Retail Price* is the price suggested by the manufacturer for the vehicle and its options. This is the price that must appear on the federally mandated Monroney sticker posted in the window of each car. The dealer is not bound to honor these prices. Please see our Shopping Tips for a description of the Monroney sticker and a discussion of the second window sticker that's frequently posted by the dealer. The *Retail Price* is the latest available at publication time. Where an automaker has not yet announced a 1990 price, we list the 1989 price and note the fact. And in the case of a new car not yet on sale at the time of publication, there's no price to list. Prices labeled *Preliminary* are those the manufacturer has released to dealers with a caution that they may be changed.

The *Dealer Invoice* price is what the dealer pays to buy the car from the manufacturer. On most domestic cars, this includes the dealer's share of the cost of preparing the car for delivery, the dealer's share of the cost of advertising the car, and any other delivery-related expenses. Most import makers do not include such costs in their invoice price.

The *Low Price* constitutes a fair deal on a vehicle and its options. It is our estimate based on national market conditions. Supply, demand, and competition rule the market, and market conditions vary greatly for different cars in different parts of the country. Our *Low Price* is only a guide. You'll have to determine the best price in your area by shopping for the same car at three or more dealerships. Where dealer invoice and low price are unavailable, we print only retail prices.

Some important notes on pricing:

- The destination charge is the amount the manufacturer lists as the cost of transporting the vehicle from the final assembly point to the dealership. This fee is not negotiable.
- Car companies are free to change prices at any time, and frequently do. Market conditions and the fluctuating value of the U.S. dollar against foreign currencies are often the cause.
- If a dealer claims our prices are incorrect, contact us and we'll do our best to help you out.

SHOPPING TIPS

Buying a new car used to be mostly a matter of choosing a body style and color, but now that the price of a new car has topped $14,000, it's a tough decision packed with conflicts.

The first decision is should it in fact be a car. Maybe you should buy a compact van or a 4-wheel-drive off-road vehicle. Front-wheel drive or rear-drive? Small cars are generally cheaper to buy and to run, yet big ones tend to protect occupants better in collisions. Young drivers crave sporty cars—but not their high insurance premiums.

Then comes the ordeal of jousting with dealers. When a car is in high demand, the salesperson may only chuckle at your below-list-price offer. If a selling price does sound great, you have to be careful that the dealer isn't making up the difference elsewhere, such as in your loan terms or on the value of your trade-in. Do you need the $700 "protection package" that the salesman praises so highly? How about the $600 extended warranty? Who offers the best finance rate, the dealer or a bank?

Take heart. You've already begun to ease the anxiety surrounding the purchase of a new car by buying the *Automobile Book*. Indeed, doing preliminary research and then visiting as many dealerships as possible are essential before you put down your hard-earned money on a new set of wheels. Take the process in steps:

1. Choose a model and options that suit your needs. Consult the Buying Guide that follows to help you decide. Don't forget to consider resale value if you plan to sell the car in fewer than four years or so.

2. Use our Buying Guide to learn the suggested retail price and dealer-invoice price of the car with the options you want.

3. Decide how much you're willing to pay.

4. Shop at least three dealers to compare prices on the same car with the same equipment. Get written price quotes that spell out what's on the car. Be on the lookout for dealers that appear to give the best after-purchase service.

5. Compare financing costs from various sources.

6. Learn the value of your old car, then decide whether to trade it in or to sell it independently.

7. Buy the car you really want and need.

Choosing a Dealership

Dealers hope to lure your business by outdoing one another in advertisements on TV and in the newspaper. But beware of the dealer whose come-on sounds too good to be true. Chances are, it is, as these cases attest:

- Authorities in North Carolina recently filed charges against a dealer for advertising selling prices that were discounted from inflated, fictitious "sticker" prices.
- The Texas Motor Vehicle Commission issued a complaint alleging that a dealer advertised new vehicles for at or below the "factory invoice price" but did not honor the offer. The same dealer was also accused of high-pressure sales tactics and false "official fee" charges.
- A Pennsylvania dealer was sued by the state's Office of Consumer Protection for requiring buyers to sign documents waiving their "free" gift of a motor scooter or a lawn mower before negotiating a price on their new car.
- In New Jersey, a Christmas-time ad from one dealer said "Buy Now and Get $5000 Holiday Cash!" Only in the finest of fine print did it become evident that it wasn't a gift from Santa, but merely an opportunity to apply for a $5000 loan. The dealer and its advertising agency were fined $30,000 for false advertising.

There's at least one "gimmick," however, that has become a staple of today's auto market: the rebate. A rebate is not a price cut, but an offer by the manufacturer to return part of the purchase price of the car as an inducement to buy.

Cash rebates are great if they're offered on a car you want, but most are tip-offs of slow sellers. Chevrolet, for instance, was offering a $750 rebate on the new Lumina sedan within months of its debut. Rebates and their cousins, low finance rates, frequently apply only to certain models or require a large down payment. Be aware that many dealers advertise an attractive price on a car, only to note in the fine print that it's assumed the buyer will fork over the rebate.

Look twice: $109 per month is an attractive payment, but note in the fine print that your monthly bill quickly jumps to $188. This deal is based on a 60-month loan at 11.25 percent APR, so your payment of $109 holds for four months only. The total amount to be paid for this $8600 car comes to more than $11,000, plus your rebate.

Be Flexible

Narrow your choices to one or two models that fit your needs and budget. This makes it easier to compare prices

A typical come-on offers a $1000 cash rebate *or* 2.9 percent APR financing. Which is best? A $10,000 loan at 2.9 percent for 24 months costs $304.88 in interest. A $10,000 bank loan at 11.5 percent costs $1241.16 in interest. In this case, the low-rate financing would save you $936.28 ($1241.16 minus $304.88). Accept the rebate, and you'll end up ahead by $63.72. Always compare the rebate against the total cost of the loan.

among dealers. A shopping list that contains a sporty hatchback, a luxury sedan, and a 4-wheel-drive off-roader doesn't lend itself to meaningful comparisons.

Shop several dealers before starting price negotiations:

- Pick up brochures.
- Talk to salespeople; ask questions.
- Test drive several brands.

Rigidity doesn't pay. You won't get the best price if a salesperson knows you "must" have that particular red coupe with its sunroof and aluminum wheels. To save money, you must sometimes be willing to take a different color or equipment—even a different body style.

Take advantage of option packages. They may include a few more items than you want, but they can be cheaper than buying each option individually.

Special ordering the exact car and equipment you want is practical only with a domestic model. Import dealers can search other dealers for the model you want and can sometimes install or delete options once the car arrives, but seldom can they order a car from the factory. Be aware that some domestic dealers might be reluctant to order a car for you. Even though they'll require a deposit, they have no guarantee that you won't back out of the deal, leaving them with a car they might have trouble unloading. The dealer has a financial interest in getting you to buy a car that's in stock. He wants to retire the loan he took out to buy the car, and storing the car is costing him money. Use this knowledge as leverage in price negotiations.

Window Stickers

The Monroney sticker. Federal law requires that all cars sold in the U.S. post what is called a Monroney sticker. It's usually pasted to a window and shows:

- The manufacturer's suggested retail price for the vehicle and all its factory-installed options.
- A destination charge for shipping from final assembly point (or port of importation) to the dealer.
- EPA fuel economy estimates.

This law does not apply to light trucks, or to some passenger vans or to most 4-wheel-drive vehicles.

The dealer's sticker. Most dealers add a second window sticker that lists accessories installed at the dealership, as well as various other charges. Be wary. Many of these accessories or charges are no more than extra profit opportunities for the dealer. They typically include:

Federal law requires that every new car sold by a dealer must display a Monroney sticker. In the sticker's upper left corner is a list of the vehicle's standard equipment included at no extra cost. The column on the right lists all of the optional factory-installed equipment and its suggested retail price. At the bottom of the column is the destination/delivery charge and the manufacturer's total suggested retail price. In the lower left corner are EPA estimates of gas mileage and annual fuel cost. Information at the bottom includes the car's Vehicle Identification Number and city of manufacture. The label may be removed only by the purchaser.

- Pinstripes: Acceptable only if you want them. Same with door guards, fender moldings, and other doodads. Look askance at dealers who routinely apply such accessories to cars and then are reluctant to remove them or to drop them from the price of the car.

- Rustproofing: Most manufacturers who provide long factory corrosion warranties advise against additional rustproofing (see Warranty section). A car backed by a 6-year/100,000-mile corrosion warranty doesn't need extra-cost treatment.

- Protection packages: These usually consist of dealer-applied paint sealers and fabric protectants. They are of little or no value, or duplicate substances applied at the factory or those you can apply for a fraction of the cost.

- Burglar alarms: Useful, but investigate whether an aftermarket alarm might be better and cheaper.

- Dealer prep charge: Domestic manufacturers fold this expense into the retail price of the car; that's how they intend for the dealer to recover the cost of preparing the car for delivery to the customer. Don't pay for it as a separate item.

- Advertising fee: Some manufacturers allow regional dealer advertising groups to collect ad funds by assessing a one percent charge on the invoice price of new cars and trucks. This is a dealer expense, but one that should be considered part of the dealer's cost of doing business, not yours. Would any other kind of retailer dare to charge a separate fee to cover advertising costs?

- Documentary or Computer charges: These ostensibly cover the cost of the dealer's paperwork or computer operation. Again, these expenses are part of the dealer's cost of doing business and should not be borne as separate items by the customer. Less-scrupulous dealers are clever at coming up with terms that sound legitimate.

- Import tariff fee, Ocean freight fee: Dealers attempt to portray these as extra delivery costs. We know of no legitimate delivery costs other than the destination fee listed on the manufacturer's window sticker.

- Currency valuation fee: Some dealers have invented such fees or similar-sounding charges under the guise of authentic expenses related to the rise and fall of the dollar against foreign currency. Such fluctuations are taken into account by the manufacturer in setting the vehicle's suggested retail price and should not be assessed to the buyer as an independent charge.

- Additional Dealer Markup (ADM): Some dealers come right out and simply give this name to the profit they expect to make on top of that built into the wholesale-to-retail markup.

Negotiate the Price

No one has to pay the price shown on either the sticker posted by the manufacturer or the dealer. Those figures are points from which to bargain.

How much can you save by bargaining? Perhaps more than you think, though there are limits. A recent study found that dealers increased selling prices to take advantage of less knowledgeable customers. The same study found that prices quoted initially varied little between small and large dealers, and city and suburban dealers.

Settle on a firm price for the new car—and get it in writing—before talking to a dealer about financing or about trading in your old car. A dealer who offers you low-rate financing may be planning on recovering his discount elsewhere in the deal. And if the dealer asks early on whether you're trading, "maybe" is the prudent reply. Otherwise, you could wind up committed to a deal that sounds good but incorporates an inflated trade-in value.

Here are some terms to be aware of when negotiating price:

Invoice price: Manufacturer's initial charge to the dealer. Includes freight.

Base price: Cost of the vehicle without options, but including the factory warranty and freight charges.

Sticker price: Price on the Monroney sticker plus suggested retail of dealer-installed options usually listed on the second sticker.

Shop for a Loan

Early in your shopping, get a quote on a loan from at least one bank and, if possible, a credit union or other lending institution. This helps determine how expensive a car you can afford and gives a figure to compare against the dealer's financing proposal.

Loan interest is expressed as an "annual percentage rate" (APR). In addition to the APR, find out how much the monthly payments will be. And be certain you know the total amount to be paid over the life of the loan. Get all three figures in writing. Oral promises don't count.

Financing your purchase through the dealership might be convenient, but don't accept the dealer's financing unless you're sure it's the best deal. Financing and insurance (F&I) now amount to more than one-fifth of the average dealer's gross sales revenue, so the dealer has a strong incentive to furnish them at a profit.

Here are some financing points to remember:

Loan rates are negotiable. If you're not satisfied with the figure quoted, ask for something lower.

Credit life insurance is optional. Credit life insurance pays off the car loan if you die or become disabled, but usually carries an astronomical mark-up.

Keep the loan short. Loan periods are growing longer. The average in 1987 was 54 months. Longer loans reduce your monthly payment but they cost more in the end because they usually carry a higher interest rate, plus they frequently require a larger down payment. A short loan means higher monthly payments, but lower interest and smaller overall debt.

installed options usually listed on the second sticker.

Holdback: An amount domestic dealers receive periodically from the manufacturer. It usually amounts to 3 percent of the invoice price. Thus, a dealer can turn a profit even by selling a car at invoice price. Dealers may also receive rebates, allowances, discounts, and incentives from the manufacturer on certain models. There is no obligation to inform the customer of the holdback fee or any additional allowances.

Profit margin: Difference between suggested retail and invoice price. It's typically 12 to 15 percent, but varies considerably.

The difference between retail and invoice price varies from manufacturer to manufacturer, and from car to car. Supply and demand, not original cost, determine the final selling price. No magic formulas apply. A "good deal" on a slow-selling car might be $200 above dealer invoice; on a popular car, it might be full suggested retail price.

Don't succumb to myths. Dealers don't necessarily lower prices at the end of the month, or at a certain time of year. Neither can you walk in 20 minutes before closing time and expect to negotiate a great deal. An eager salesperson will stay as long as needed—or invite you to come back tomorrow.

Read Before Signing

A buyer who's in a hurry to complete the deal is asking to be taken advantage of and signed contracts are extremely difficult to get out of. Read and understand what you're signing before you sign.

The dealership is a poor place to study the sales papers. Take the contract home. Call the dealer with any questions. If the dealer doesn't want the contract to leave his office, get a written purchase agreement that spells out all the details. Once you're satisfied, it can be written into a contract.

Here's what to look for in any paperwork:

Sale price: The amount you've agreed to pay for the car and all factory- or dealer-installed optional equipment.

Down payment: The amount that must be paid in cash up front or in trade-in value.

Destination charge: Cost of shipping, as listed on the sticker. This is usually not negotiable, but don't pay it twice; some dealers hide the charge in the sale price, then add it again.

Trade-in value: The amount allowed for your old car. Trade-ins give dealers plenty of room for manipulation, so be sure you know exactly how much you're getting and that it's a fair value.

Sales tax: Some taxes are calculated on a net price after the trade-in value has been deducted; in most states, it's paid on the full purchase price of the new car. Check with your state or local governments to determine the rate, and how tax is assessed.

Loans: Federal regulations require lenders to disclose all charges to borrowers. Find out exactly how much you

Buy or Lease?

Leasing has become a popular alternative to buying. One attraction to buying had been the ability to deduct loan interest on income tax returns. But the deduction is fading. Taxpayers can deduct only 10 percent of the interest in 1990, after which the deduction disappears.

Leasing's major advantage is that a large down payment isn't needed, though some leases require a substantial initial payment. Also, monthly lease payments are often lower than the monthly loan payment for an equivalent car. But leasing is usually cheaper than buying in the long run only if you can deduct automobile costs as a business expense. Consult an accountant or the Internal Revenue Service for advice on applicable tax laws. Leasing usually benefits those who drive less than 15,000 miles a year, trade for a new model every three years or so, and maintain their cars well.

Here are some common lease terms and conditions:

Open versus Closed End Leases: A "closed-end" lease, also called a "walk-away" lease, simply lets you walk away from the deal at the end of the lease period. No additional payments are required unless the vehicle has serious damage or excessive wear.

With an "open-end" lease, you and the leaser estimate what the car will be worth at the end of the period. If the car winds up worth less than the estimate, you're responsible for the difference. In most cases, the amount for which you are responsible is no more than the equivalent of three monthly payments. Monthly payments are usually lower with an open-end lease, but the risks are greater. Best bet: pick a car likely to hold its value.

Monthly payments: Be certain of both the monthly payment and the total amount to be paid over the lease term. Because trade-in values have fallen recently, monthly payments have tended to rise.

Mileage limits: Most leases specify a limit of around 15,000 miles per year. Beyond that, you have to pay extra (usually 10 or more cents per mile). A lower high-mileage charge might be negotiated at the start of the lease.

Security deposit: Find out how much must be put down at the start of the lease, and whether you have to pay the first and/or last monthly payment in advance. Ask who pays for state sales tax, license, and title fees.

Insurance and maintenance: The lease must specify who provides insurance coverage and pays for maintenance. Generally, it's cheaper for the customer to pay both.

Early termination and purchase options: Before signing, learn whether you can terminate the lease early, and how much penalty must be paid. It could be modest, or thousands of dollars. Find out if you can buy the car after the lease ends. The purchase price or method of calculating it should be specified. This could be important if you move to another state.

End-of-lease costs: You might have to pay for excessive wear (make sure "excessive" is explained) or have the car prepped for resale.

Shopping for a lease is no different than shopping for a car. Compare price quotes from leasing agents for the same car and terms. Negotiate price first, then the terms. A 16-page booklet called "A Consumer Guide to Vehicle Leasing" is available from the Federal Trade Commission for 50 cents. Write:

Consumer Information Center
Department 458P
Pueblo, CO 81009

are actually borrowing, the Annual Percentage Rate (APR), monthly payment, length of the loan (48 months, for example) and total amount of money to be paid over the course of the loan.

Total cost: Be sure the bottom line is filled in, showing total price including everything above. Don't sign if it's blank, or you can end up paying more than you bargained for.

Selling versus Trading

Most new-car buyers trade in their old car. It's fast and easy, and it also frequently covers all or much of the down payment on the new vehicle. Because the new-car market is so competitive, though, dealers often realize a higher profit on the resale of used cars than on the sale of new ones. So dealers have a strong incentive to offer you as little as possible for your car. Particularly try to avoid trading a car before it's paid for. The dealer will gladly pay off your old loan, use any residual value as a down payment, and write another loan for the new car—all with ample profit for himself.

Selling the old car privately is likely to bring you more money. There are several ways to find how much your car is worth. Used-car price guides, so-called "blue books," are available at the public library, or at your lending institution. They'll tell you the price it's likely to fetch at retail, and the price a professional used-car dealer would pay at wholesale.

What a difference the rate makes...

Monthly payments and total price paid for a $15,000 loan at various interest rates and loan periods

Interest Rate	No. of Months	Monthly Payment	Total Amount	Total Interest
2.9	24	$644.05	$15457.20	$457.20
2.9	36	435.56	15680.16	680.16
5.9	36	455.64	16403.04	1407.04
5.9	48	351.59	16876.32	1876.32
8.9	48	372.56	17882.88	2882.88
8.9	60	310.65	18639.00	3639.00
9.9	60	317.96	19077.60	4077.60
11.25	60	328.01	19680.60	4680.60

Average bank loan rate as of September 1989 was 12.29 percent, according to the *Bank Rate Monitor*.

Also consult the CONSUMER GUIDE® *Used Car Book* and the classified section of the newspaper.

But be wary. Weigh the extra money you might get against the chance you might be taking in inviting a stranger to your home to view the car. Plus, there's the time you'll spend showing the car and negotiating price.

Patience Pays

Salespeople hate "be-backs." They want to sell a car today, before you have a chance to look elsewhere and comparison shop. Rarely is the deal offered to you really valid for one day only. Just say you'll be buying soon—and not necessarily from this person. If you can't get a price that's good tomorrow, or next week, or whenever *you* are ready, take your business elsewhere.

Buying Services

A conventional dealer's showroom isn't

Typical Trade-in Values (Wholesale versus Retail)		
	Wholesale	Retail
1984 Ford Escort	$1550	$2250
1985 Dodge Aries	2,600	3350
1986 Chev. Caprice	4850	5800
1987 Nissan Maxima	9000	10,350
1988 BMW 325	16,200	18,400

These wholesale and retail valuations are approximate and are based upon figures from used-car price guides. Wholesale value represents what you might get for your trade-in from a new-car dealer or a private buyer. Retail value is what a new-car dealer would expect to resell your trade-in for.

the only source for a new car. Auto brokers act as middlemen between the customer and dealer. Some operate as a referral service, locating the dealer who has the best price, then sending the customer there in return for a fee or a commission. Others are licensed dealers. Because there's no salesperson to earn a commission, and the broker can get good prices by handling large numbers of cars, customers can save a tidy sum. Before coming to terms with a broker, ask for names of former customers and check the Better Business Bureau—the same sort of advice to follow when selecting a car dealer.

Look for the fine print.
Not all of the facts and figures in ads mean quite what they appear to.

"From" indicates this is the lowest-priced model. Is that one actually available or will you be pushed toward a more expensive model?

Exactly what is included in the price shown? Are there add-on charges on top of this amount?

Are special qualifications required to get this price?

Make sure the car really is new, not a demonstrator or last year's model

Who qualifies for the low finance rate?

WARRANTIES AND SERVICE CONTRACTS

A warranty is the manufacturer's pledge to absorb certain repair or replacement costs over a specified period. Lengthy and encompassing warranties allow manufacturers to tout their car's quality and reliability. We don't recommend choosing a car for its warranty, but it is one factor in the decision.

Shoppers face a complex array of warranty packages, including expansive guarantees against corrosion and tricky extra-cost service contracts. No warranty comes free of loopholes and fine print. Look at any warranty with a critical eye. Detailed information should be available through the dealer or manufacturer.

1990 Highlights

Only a few of the companies selling cars in the U.S. have made significant changes in warranty coverage for 1990. The trend is toward longer "bumper-to-bumper" basic warranties, as well as toward added benefits beyond simply repairing the car. Here are some examples of the wide variety of warranties now offered:

Cadillac: Allante Assurance Plan covers most components for 7 years or 100,000 miles, in addition to basic 4-year/48,000-mile coverage.

Oldsmobile: Dissatisfied buyers can return the car within 30 days or 1500 miles for credit toward the purchase of another Oldsmobile. The program is called the "Oldsmobile Edge." Buyers now get 24-hour emergency roadside service.

Audi: Offers the "Audi Advantage," which absorbs charges for all routine maintenance, including oil changes, brake pads and wiper blades during the basic period, plus membership in U.S. Auto Club.

Infiniti: New for 1990. Roadside Assistance for the 4-year warranty period lets owners call a number to summon help.

Lexus: New for 1990 with 4-year, 50,000-mile basic coverage and 6-year, 60,000-mile powertrain warranty.

Porsche: Roadside Assistance program includes towing and trip insurance, plus locksmith allowance.

Sterling: Includes three years of road service.

Toyota: Adds 5-year, 60,000-mile powertrain coverage.

Yugo: Corrosion coverage extended to 3 years.

Factory Warranties

Here's an overview of how warranties and service contracts work and what they generally cover.

Basic warranty: Usually covers the entire car, except for tires and battery, which are warranted by their manufacturers. Other typical exclusions:

- Normal wear and maintenance items (oil, air filters, brake linings).
- Damage from the environment (hail, floods, other "acts of God").
- Damage due to improper maintenance (incorrect fuel or lubricants).
- Damage caused by the owner or vehicle occupants.

Extended warranty: Coverage for a specific period beyond the basic warranty. Usually applies to the car's powertrain, which consists of such major components as the engine, transmission or transaxle, fuel system, turbocharger, drive shafts and related parts, plus the transfer case on 4-wheel-drive vehicles. Like basic warranties, powertrain warranties usually exclude damage and maintenance items.

Deductible: Domestic manufacturers and Yugo charge owners for warranty work performed after the basic coverage has expired. The deductible generally is $100, meaning the owner pays the first $100 of each repair made under the extended warranty and the car manufacturer picks up the rest.

Corrosion: Warranty against perforation rust in which sheetmetal is eaten through. Most corrosion warranties last at least three years and some have no mileage limits. Typical exclusions include surface corrosion caused by hail, stone chips, and industrial pollution.

Transfers: Most manufacturers allow factory warranties to be transferred from owner to owner at no charge for as long as the warranty is in effect. Chrysler charges $100 to transfer warranties to subsequent buyers of most of its cars; Subaru charges $25. Specific second-owner exclusions may apply to leased and fleet vehicles.

Service Contracts

Once you've sealed the deal on your new car, the salesperson's likely to suggest an extra-cost service contract or extended warranty. The pitch makes it sound as if only a fool would take a chance on unexpected repair costs.

Beware. The manufacturers and independent companies that write these service contracts expect to make a sizable profit on them. It's insurance, not a warranty. They bet that they'll pay out less in repairs than you paid for the contract. The odds are in their favor. A recent study cited in *Automotive Marketing* magazine found the average price of an extended-service contract to be $473, with profit to the dealer of $280.

Extra-cost warranties usually extend coverage of the car's powertrain past the manufacturer's coverage. But while powertrain components are indeed among the most expensive to fix, they also are among the least likely to need repair or replacement during the warranty period. Some extra-cost warranties cover items not protected under extended factory warranties, such as electrical components. This is a positive feature of such contracts; so is the peace of mind they afford.

If you choose to purchase extended coverage, be aware that several car manufacturers offer their own. GM sells the General Motors Protection Plan. Ford has the Extended Service Plan. Dealers may offer the factory-sponsored plan, or one from another source—likely an independent underwriter who offers the dealer a higher profit margin.

All but the most expensive service contracts carry deductibles for each repair, usually $25 to $75. Some specify where the work must be done, which may make repairs more costly or inconvenient. Extra-cost contracts issued by automakers require that repairs be made at an authorized dealership. Not only may that be inconvenient, but some dealer service departments are less than eager to handle contract work. Also, some contracts require that you pay when repairs are made, then file for reimbursement. That takes time.

Before you buy, compare prices and coverage carefully. Make sure you know:

- Who is issuing the contract.
- Exactly what is covered by the regular warranty, and by the contract.
- Where the work must be performed.
- How to cancel the coverage and get a refund (and if a fee must be paid).

Our advice: give any service contract careful scrutiny. Think about it at home, not in the showroom. Get a copy of the contract, not just a brochure summarizing the coverage. It's not always necessary to buy a service contract at the time you buy the car. Later, you might receive mailed solicitations for service contracts from the manufacturer or an underwriter, and these offers might be priced lower than the dealer's plan.

Rustproofing

Modern anti-corrosion techniques allow automakers to provide rust warranties that often run five years or longer. Extensive use of two-sided galvanized steel, sealed body seams and joints, high-tech primer application, and anti-chip paint are among the steps taken by manufacturers to combat rust.

Despite these advances, many dealers continue to sell aftermarket rustproofing that may be unnecessary and, in some cases, cause harm. Dealers persist because rustproofing is hugely profitable, as the headline of an ad in a dealer trade publication attests: "Rustproofing only $4.95 per car! Paint shield and fabric protection at similar savings." The profit involved is sizable when retail buyers are charged $300 or more for the job. Worse yet, some dealers routinely rustproof new vehicles and add the cost to the selling price before the car hits the showroom floor.

J. Joseph Curran, Jr., Attorney General of Maryland, warned in early 1989 that "consumers are purchasing this after-manufacture rustproofing product without being fully informed of all the facts." He cited GM's advice that aftermarket rustproofing could plug body drain holes, possibly promoting corrosion; and Nissan's claim that the holes, drilled for the substance could cause premature rusting. Curran further advised his state's GM, Toyota, and Nissan dealers to inform consumers that manufacturers consider aftermarket rustproofing to be unnecessary.

To keep a car protected, wash and wax regularly, and touch up paint chips without delay. In high-salt areas, frequently spray the underside and wheel wells with water. These preventive measures do more good than dealer-applied rustproofing.

Fabric protection for which the dealer charges $100 or more can be accomplished at home with a $3.95 can of spray. And upholstery in many GM cars now comes with Scotchgard-brand fabric protection, so additional treatment isn't necessary.

1990 Manufacturers' Warranties

Make/Model	Basic Warranty (Months/Miles)	Extended Warranty (Months/Miles)	Deductible	Corrosion Warranty (Months/Miles)	Transferable?
Acura	36/36,000	none	none	36/unltd	Yes/no cost
Alfa Romeo	36/36,000	none	none	72/60,000	Yes/no cost
Audi	36/50,000	none	none	120/unltd	Yes/no cost
BMW	36/36,000	none	none	72/unltd	Yes/no cost
Buick	36/50,000	none	$100 after 12/12,000	72/100,000	Yes/no cost
Cadillac (exc Allante)	48/50,000	none	$100 after 12/12,000	72/100,000	Yes/no cost
Cadillac Allante	48/50,000	84/100,000 powertrain & major systems	$25 after 12/12,000	84/100,000	Yes/no cost
Chevrolet	36/50,000	none	$100 after 12/12,000	72/100,000	Yes/no cost
Chrysler (exc Imperial, New Yorker & Imports)	12/12,000	84/70,000 powertrain	$100 after 12/12,000	84/100,000	Yes/$100
Chrysler Imperial, New Yorker, TC Maserati	12/12,000	84/70,000 powertrain; 60/50,000 major systems[5]	$100 after 12/12,000	84/100,000	Yes/$100
Chrysler Imports	36/36,000	36/50,000 powertrain	none	72/unltd[1]	Yes/no cost
Daihatsu	36/36,000	none	none	36/unltd	Yes/no cost
Dodge	12/12,000	84/70,000 powertrain	$100 after 12/12,000	84/100,000	Yes/$100

Warranties and Service Contracts

Make/Model	Basic Warranty (Months/Miles)	Extended Warranty (Months/Miles)	Deductible	Corrosion Warranty (Months/Miles)	Transfer- able?
Eagle (exc Summit)	12/12,000	84/70,000 powertrain	$100 after 12/12,000	84/100,000	Yes/$100
Eagle Summit	36/36,000	84/70,000 powertrain	$100 after 36/36,000	84/100,000	Yes/$100
Ford	12/12,000	72/60,000 powertrain	$100 after 12/12,000	72/100,000	Yes/no cost
Geo	36/50,000	none	$100 after 12/12,000	72/100,000	Yes/no cost
Honda	36/36,000	none	none	36/unltd	Yes/no cost
Hyundai	36/36,000	none	none	36/unltd	Yes/no cost
Infiniti	48/60,000	none	none	84/unltd	Yes/no cost
Isuzu	36/36,000	none	none	36/unltd	Yes/no cost
Jaguar	36/36,000	none	none	72/unltd	Yes/no cost
Jeep	12/12,000	84/70,000 powertrain	$150 after 12/12,000[2]	84/100,000	Yes/$100
Lexus	48/50,000	72/60,000 powertrain	none	72/unltd	Yes/no cost
Lincoln	12/12,000	72/60,000 powertrain & major systems	$100 after 12/12,000	72/100,000	Yes/no cost
Mazda	36/50,000	none	none	60/unltd	Yes/no cost
Mercedes-Benz	48/50,000	none	none	48/50,000	Yes/no cost
Mercury	12/12,000	72/60,000 powertrain	$100 after 12/12,000	72/100,000	Yes/no cost
Merkur	12/12,000	72/60,000 powertrain & major systems	$100 after 12/12,000	72/100,000	Yes/no cost
Mitsubishi	36/36,000	36/50,000 powertrain[3]	none	60/unltd outer panels; 36/unltd all panels[4]	Yes/no cost
Nissan	36/36,000	none	none	60/50,000	Yes/no cost
Oldsmobile	36/50,000	none	$100 after 12/12,000	72/100,000	Yes/no cost
Peugeot	36/36,000	60/50,000 powertrain	none	36/36,000	Yes/no cost
Plymouth	12/12,000	84/70,000 powertrain	$100 after 12/12,000	84/100,000	Yes/$100
Pontiac	36/50,000	none	$100 after 12/12,000	72/100,000	Yes/no cost
Porsche	24/unltd	none	none	120/unltd	Yes/no cost
Range Rover	36/36,000	none	none	72/unltd	Yes/no cost
Saab	36/36,000	none	none	72/unltd	Yes/no cost
Sterling	36/36,000	none	none	72/unltd	Yes/no cost
Subaru	36/36,000	none	none	60/60,000	Yes/no cost
Suzuki	24/24,000	none	none	36/unltd	Yes/no cost
Toyota	36/36,000	60/60,000 powertrain	none	60/unltd	Yes/no cost
Volkswagen	24/24,000	none	none	72/unltd	Yes/no cost
Volvo	12/unltd	36/unltd powertrain & major systems	none	36/unltd surface; 60/unltd body; 96/unltd structure	Yes/no cost
Yugo	12/12,000	48/40,000 powertrain	$25 after 12/12,000	36/unltd	Yes/no cost

1. 84/100,000 on Dodge/Plymouth Colt.   2. $100 after 12/12,000 on 2-wheel drive models.   3. 36/36,000 on Precis.   4. 84/100,000 outer panels on Galant and Mirage, and for all panels on Eclipse; 36/unltd for all Precis panels.   5. 60/50,000 coverage for most systems, has no deductible and is transferable to second owner for $400.

CONSUMER COMPLAINTS

Prevention Is the Best Policy

There's no substitute for buying a car with a track record of reliability from a dealer with a good reputation for service after the sale. Dealers and manufacturers are putting more emphasis than ever on the importance of after-sale satisfaction. But how can the prospective buyer tell what kind of service the dealer will provide after the sale?

Good treatment during the sale doesn't guarantee that you'll get the same reception afterwards, but it's one predictor. On the other hand, if sparring with dealer personnel is less than thrilling during the sale, chances are it'll be no fun at all later on, when repairs are needed.

The best way to increase your chances of getting the conscientious attention you deserve after buying your car is to do some investigation.

Call your local Better Business Bureau. It can tell you whether a dealer has had an unusually large number of complaints and how they were resolved.

Ask friends and neighbors for recommendations:

- Did a particular dealer treat them fairly and courteously?
- If a problem recurred, did the staff grow nasty or remain patient? A quick, concerned response can be just as important as what's actually done to resolve the problem.
- Was the car ready when promised, with the repair made correctly?
- Were they ever overcharged, or given a part or service they didn't ask for?
- Would they buy from this dealer again?

Before You Take Delivery

Don't succumb to new-car fever. Make a thorough inspection of your car before you accept delivery. Cars can be damaged in transit, and dealer prep work isn't always perfect. Here are some suggestions:

- Take delivery in the daylight. Artificial lighting can hide scratches or blemishes in the finish.
- Make sure it's the car you paid for. Compare the Vehicle Identification Number (VIN) and the information on the window sticker to the title and other documents.

- Is every option you've purchased listed on the window sticker? Is it on the car and in working order?
- Inspect paint, trim, and body panels. Look for evidence of body repair, such as a color mismatch; glass fragments on the floor; loose or missing pieces.
- See that doors, hood, and trunk lid open and close easily.
- Check for such items as the spare tire and jack, cigar lighter, owner's manual.
- Examine upholstery and interior trim.
- Be sure you know how to start the engine properly.

Before driving off:

- Do you have copies of all documents, including the bill of sale, warranty papers, and the like?
- Do you know where to go and who to contact if servicing is needed?
- Do you have a copy of the recommended maintenance schedule?
- Do you know what kinds of maintenance work will void the warranty?
- The contract should include details of any problems with the car in case an initial minor flaw leads to something more serious.
- If a dealer-installed option isn't available at the time of delivery, get installation details in writing.
- Don't sign the sales contract until you're satisfied that everything you're paying for on the car is present and operating properly.
- ALWAYS test drive the car before taking final delivery.

Service Visits

Service advisors need complete information to deliver a successful fix. Be sure the advisor writes down a complete and correct description of each problem you've noted. Mechanics rely on that written service order.

Ordering parts is a sad fact of modern automotive life. Dealers can't stock every component, but many can be obtained overnight. Parts for low-volume import makes often take longer to obtain. Think about that when shopping for a car.

Don't leave until you're satisfied that all the work has been done correctly.

It often pays to let the dealer handle routine servicing, such as oil changes. Regular customers tend to get closer attention when a real problem comes up. Your car also will be up-to-date in the dealer's records, which is in your favor if a serious flaw develops.

Keep a detailed record of service visits, including all receipts. Always be prepared to provide full vehicle data (mileage, date of purchase, and Vehicle Identification Number); describe the problem and what's been done to correct it; and explain why you're dissatisfied. Above all, clarify exactly what action or solution you're seeking.

Step-by-Step Problem Solving

Some cars just don't stay fixed. Some problems defy the experts.

Here's a list of steps to take when a long-term or recurrent problem develops.

1. Two fruitless visits to the service department are enough. After that, speak to those in authority at the dealership. Go up the management one step at a time, all the way to the owner if necessary, until your problem is resolved.

2. The service manager should contact the manufacturer's service representative to consult on a recurring problem. Other cars may suffer the same malady, and the corporate computer might hold details on an appropriate fix.

3. Consider trying another dealer's service staff. A fresh approach might unearth a remedy.

4. After the mechanics run out of tricks, contact a customer-service or technical-support representative at the manufacturer's zone office. The zone-office phone number—frequently, it's a toll-free hotline—should be in your owner's manual. Jot down the names and numbers of all people with whom you speak.

5. Contact a third-party dispute-resolution program for mediation and, if necessary, arbitration.

6. Consult a lawyer about possible legal action.

Consumer Complaints
Intermittent Problems

Something in the drivetrain may have been grinding away all morning—but as you glide onto the dealer's driveway, it makes a miraculous recovery. Maybe the engine idles crazily after each morning's start-up, or stalls after two miles. By the time you arrive at the service entrance, all is well.

Don't be apologetic if you can't make the problem appear during a brief test drive with the service writer. Just describe the symptoms and explain the exact circumstances under which they occur. Insist that the service people examine the car under conditions in which the problem is likely to surface.

Mediation and Beyond

Some automakers mediate disputes with customers internally, but a majority participate in a program that allows dissatisfied owners to seek satisfaction through an independent third party. Ask your salesperson about the process used by the maker of the car in which you're interested.

Typically, third-party mediation and arbitration programs pit the consumer against the manufacturer, not the dealer. The consumer presents a complaint, along with any documentation, to a mediation or arbitration panel. The manufacturer's representative does the same, and the panel renders a decision or a recommendation.

With some findings binding on the manufacturers, consumers have been awarded remedies as "minor" as a new paint job or as major as a new vehicle. When the panel sides with the manufacturer, however, pursuing the complaint grows difficult.

How It Works

Here's a look at some mediation and arbitration services:

- The Council of Better Business Bureaus operates an Auto Line program that combines mediation and arbitration between consumers and automakers. Close to 200,000 consumers used it in 1988. A number of dealers also use the service to resolve disputes with customers that don't involve a manufacturer.
- Mediation alone is provided by the National Automotive Consumer Action Program (AUTOCAP), a service directed by the National Automobile Dealers Association (NADA) but per-

Customer Satisfaction Index

You probably have seen advertising in which an automaker touts the ranking it received in something called a Customer Satisfaction Index. The CSI has become an important new standard by which manufacturers and dealers measure themselves in the race to win business by pleasing the consumer. A number of private companies conduct CSI surveys of new-car owners, and some manufacturers have their own polls. But the most publicized CSI ranking is produced by J.D. Power & Associates, an automotive survey and consulting firm in Agoura Hills, California. The firm rates cars through its Initial Quality Survey, which contacts thousands of owners 60 to 90 days after they've bought a new car and quizzes them about 89 specific problem areas. Another J.D. Power survey polls thousands of new-car buyers who have owned their vehicles for 12 to 15 months. It measures how reliable their new car has been and how satisfied they are with the service and treatment they've received from their dealership.

Naturally, automakers who receive high rankings on such surveys are the ones who will advertise the findings. Furthermore, a sub-industry has sprung up to help dealers improve their rankings. They include employee bonuses if the dealer's CSI rating rises.

The surveys also are important for the wider picture they paint of customer satisfaction. For instance, one professional consultant to dealers says the surveys show that about 65 percent of the buyers who rate dealer service poorly are unhappy because they feel they've been treated poorly by an employee. Alan Wilbur of the National Automobile Dealers Association notes that customers want "convenience, courtesy and cost, perhaps even in that order."

Dealers talk about CSI a lot at their conventions, but there's a tendency to worry more about the rating number earned than the actual amount of special attention given. The auto business is traditionally a numbers industry.

Third-Party Dispute Programs

Manufacturer(s)	Arbitration Program Used
General Motors	Auto Line (BBB)
Ford/Lincoln/ Mercury	Ford Consumer Appeals Board (contact district office or call (1-800-241-8450)
Chrysler/Dodge/ Plymouth/Jeep/ Eagle/Maserati	Chrysler Customer Arbitration Board (contact any zone office or call National Owner Relations Manager at (313/956-5970 or 1-800-992-1997)
AMC/Jeep/Renault (before 1988 models)	Auto Line (BBB)
Audi, Volkswagen	Auto Line (BBB)
Honda/Acura, Nissan, Peugeot, Saab	AUTOCAP (also endorses BBB Auto Line)
Alfa Romeo, BMW, Isuzu, Jaguar, Mazda, Mitsubishi, Rolls-Royce, Sterling, Volvo, Yugo	AUTOCAP (non-exclusive)
Porsche	American Arbitration Association (call 212/484-4000)
Toyota	Complaint Arbitration Services of AAA (1-800-331-4331)

States with Major-Defect Legislation (Lemon Laws), as of October 1989

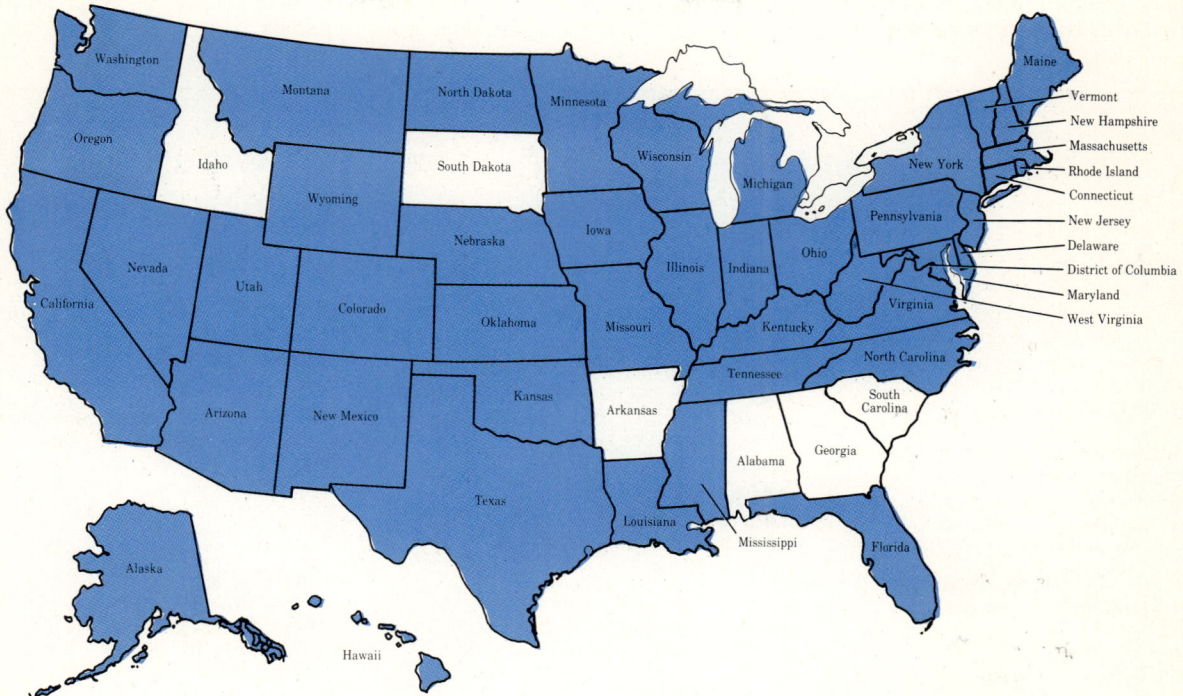

SOURCE: Center for Auto Safety

Lemon Laws

As of October 1989, 44 states and the District of Columbia have some form of "lemon law" that requires a manufacturer to refund the purchase price or to replace a car that's proven critically flawed. Few consumers actually gain such dramatic results, so here again, don't expect miracles.

In most lemon-law states, you must exhaust all other possible re-medies first. That means making a specified number of tries at the dealership, then passing through arbitration without successful resolution. A car might have to be inoperable for at least 30 days (not necessarily consecutive) during your first 12 months or 12,000 miles of ownership. Details vary, so obtain guidance from your state attorney general's office, a consumer protection agency, or the Center for Auto Safety. While you can handle arbitration alone, fighting under a lemon law requires a lawyer.

Lemon laws typically stipulate that a manufacturer be given one last chance to remedy the complaint. Even if you "win," the automaker nearly always is allowed to deduct a portion from your award to compensate for mileage you've put on the vehicle. If your state has no lemon law, you'll have to seek remedy in the courts.

formed by state or local dealer associations. Some automakers work only with Auto Line, others can be dealt with through either program. Several manufacturers operate their own programs.

With either Auto Line or AUTOCAP, the organization's staff will first try to settle the dispute informally. Recommendations are not binding on either party, but the vast majority of cases are resolved in this informal stage.

Unsettled complaints progress to panels made up of consumer volunteers and representatives of manufacturers or dealer organizations. The findings of these mediators are not binding on either party.

Arbitration and Lawsuits

If you're dissatisfied with the recommendation of mediators, the next option is arbitration. Of the 173,000 consumers who used the Better Business Bureau's Auto Line in 1987, 29,000 went as far as arbitration.

Ford and Chrysler run their own arbitration programs; Toyota works through the American Automobile Association. GM and other automakers that accept arbitration deal with BBB'S Auto Line. Your owner's manual should tell you which service to use.

Details differ, but in any of these programs you'll present your case orally or in writing. You'll need complete records, including work orders, receipts, letters, and notices. You must prove the car doesn't work properly, that both dealer and manufacturer have failed in several attempts to fix it, and that you've exhausted other avenues of complaint. The manufacturer and/or dealer will then present its case, assisted by a rep-

resentative familiar with repair problems.

The decision of the arbitration panel is binding only on the company. You can accept the verdict, or go on to the next step: formal legal action. You usually get 60 days to decide; but if you accept the arbitrator's decision, you

can't change your mind and take legal action.

Don't expect miracles from mediation or arbitration. About 30 percent of the consumers who complain have the dispute settled wholly their way, but in most cases, the decision satisfies both parties.

Government Agencies and Consumer Groups

The following list includes telephone numbers and addresses for auto arbitration programs, government agencies and consumer groups that may be able to help with car problems. In addition, many states and some local governments have their own consumer protection agencies that may be able to act faster than a federal agency.

American Automobile Association
8111 Gatehouse Road
Falls Church, VA 22047-0001
(703) 222-6000

AAA services Toyota's mediation/arbitration program.

Better Business Bureau

Check local phone book for the nearest office.

Center for Auto Safety
2001 S Street, NW
Washington, DC 20009
(202) 328-7700

Non-profit consumer group lobbies on behalf of consumer interests in vehicle safety and quality, highway safety and mobile home safety. It also provides information on lemon laws and provides a lawyer referral service.

Chrysler Motors Owner
Relations Department
P.O. Box 1718
Detroit, MI 48288-1718
(313) 956-5970 or (800) 992-1997

This department handles complaints not resolved at the dealer or zone-office level and provides information about Chrysler's regional customer arbitration boards.

Environmental Protection Agency
401 M Street, SW
Washington, DC 20460
(202) 382-2090

EPA publishes the EPA Gas Mileage Guide and enforces emissions control regulations.

Federal Trade Commission
6th & Pennsylvania Avenue, NW
Washington, DC 20580
(202) 326-2222

The FTC provides information on arbitration and other consumer complaints. Regional offices are in major cities.

Ford Consumer Appeals Board
1-800-241-8450

Call this number for information on Ford's arbitration program.

General Motors Arbitration
Handbook
1-800-824-5109

Your name and address will be taken on a recording and you will receive a handbook about GM's arbitration program.

General Motors Technical Bulletins
1-800-551-4123

Call for information on technical bulletins that might apply to your car.

Highway Loss Data Institute and
Insurance Institute for Highway
Safety
Watergate 600
Washington, DC 20037
(202) 333-0770

Insurance industry lobbying group compiles information on vehicle and highway safety.

National Automobile Dealers
Association
AUTOCAP
8400 Westpark Drive
McLean, VA 22102
(703) 821-7144

NADA headquarters will refer you to a local office to answer questions on the AUTOCAP arbitration system and tell you if your dealer is a member.

National Highway Traffic
Safety Administration
400 7th Street, SW
Washington, DC 20590
(202) 366-5972

NHTSA investigates safety defects and enforces safety regulations. NHTSA operates a consumer hotline for information on safety recalls and reporting a safety problem: 1-800-424-9393 (In Washington, D.C., 366-0123)

National Insurance
Consumers Organization
121 N. Payne Street
Alexandria, VA 22314
(703) 549-8050

Consumer-advocate group works to educate consumers on insurance issues, researches public policy and rate making, and does some lobbying.

U.S. Department of Justice
Office of Consumer Litigation
10th Street, NW
Washington, DC 20530
(202) 724-6786

This office enforces federal laws covering price labeling of new cars.

SAFETY

Safety is beginning to sell. Anti-lock brakes, which can help a driver maintain control in panic stops on wet pavement, are no longer found primarily on high-dollar high-performance cars; they're now offered on such family sedans as the Oldsmobile Eighty Eight Royale and the Ford Taurus. Prodded by government safety standards, automakers have installed passive restraints, such as air bags, and rear-seat shoulder belts on all 1990 cars. Even if it wasn't motivated by market demand, the addition of such items has given safety a higher profile than ever. You can be sure that manufacturers such as Ford will use as a sales tool the installation of both driver's- and passenger-side air bags in its Lincoln Continental and Town Car.

Government Crash Tests

The National Highway Traffic Safety Administration (NHTSA) establishes the federal government's auto safety regulations and investigates safety issues. It performs two major tests:

- The 30-mph crash test, which every automobile, light truck, and utility vehicle sold in the U.S. must pass. Each car is crashed head-on into a concrete barrier. Seat belted and wired dummies occupying the front seats transmit force signals to electronic monitoring devices. The tests do not predict a level of injury; they only measure an acceptable threshold of force as established by NHTSA.
- The 35-mph crash test. This is the same head-on barrier test, but the car is traveling at 35 mph. The dummies are monitored for forces on the head, chest, and upper legs.

While the 30-mph test is essentially a pass-fail exam, the 35-mph test provides a wider range of results and forms a basis for evaluating the relative safety of the cars tested. NHTSA subjects only about 35 cars per year to the 35-mph test, and while it publishes the results, the findings are not a basis for certifying a car for sale or for regulating its design.

NHTSA does not advise using its crash results to pick one car over another. They're intended only as a narrow comparison of vehicles of similar size and weight. Their ability to reflect real-world crashworthiness is limited: Actual crashes are rarely head-on into flat barriers; the dummies, though statistically representative of the average male, represent only a fraction of the population; and NHTSA crash results are often at odds with injury ratings compiled by insurance companies. Plus, critics charge that automakers can make changes in their cars that will boost their scores on NHTSA crash tests with no guarantee of a corresponding improvement in real-world crashworthiness. We conclude that while NHTSA testing is far from perfect, the results are important. Cars that fall far below acceptable levels of injury protection should be regarded warily by buyers interested in safety.

Injury and Collision Ratings

The Highway Loss Data Institute (HLDI), a trade association financed by insurance companies, ranks cars by the number of personal-injury insurance claims filed by their occupants. Its injury ratings typically show that the fewest number of claims are filed by occupants of large cars, while small, less expensive cars have more claims. These findings correspond to other data about vehicle size and auto safety. But it is important to remember that large cars used by families and older, wealthier drivers are driven differently than smaller cars. Smaller cars are more likely to be driven in congested urban areas by younger, less-experienced drivers who are statistically more likely to be involved in an accident than their older, wealthier counterparts.

Insurance-based data reflects only claims experience, and doesn't "prove" any particular design flaw. However,

The Decline in U.S. Motor Vehicle Deaths (1979-88)		
Year	Total Deaths	Deaths per 100,000 Population
1979	51,093	23
1980	51,091	22
1981	49,301	21
1982	43,945	19
1983	42,589	18
1984	44,257	19
1985	43,825	18
1986	46,087	19
1987	46,390	19
1988	47,093	19

Source: NHTSA and Insurance Institute for Highway Safety.

Types of Fatal Crashes (as a percentage of all fatal crashes)		
Impact type	Cars	Trucks & Vans
Frontal	40%	35%
Side	28	12
Rear	3	2
Rollover	24	47
All other	5	4
Total percent	100	100

Source: National Highway Traffic Safety Administration

Injury Ratings for 1986-88 Models
(Highway Loss Data Institute)

Best Injury Ratings	Worst Injury Ratings
41 Mercedes-Benz SDL/SEL	189 Hyundai Excel 4-dr
42 Saab 9000	182 Isuzu I-Mark 2-dr
50 Mercedes-Benz 560SL	178 Chevrolet Sprint 2-dr
53 Pontiac Safari wgn	176 Chevrolet Spectrum 4-dr
54 Olds Custom Cruiser wgn	167 Ford Escort
55 BMW 5-series	166 Chevrolet Spectrum 2-dr
55 Mercedes-Benz 260E/300D/E	164 Chevrolet Sprint 4-dr
56 Plymouth Grand Voyager	164 Isuzu I-Mark 4-dr
57 Dodge Grand Caravan	162 Mitsubishi Cordia/Mirage
58 Chevrolet Caprice wgn	162 Yugo
58 Ford Crown Victoria wgn	157 Hyundai Excel 2-dr
58 Mercury Grand Marquis wgn	155 Ford EXP

Note: HLDI injury ratings are based on frequency of injury claims filed under personal injury coverage for 1986-88 models. Ratings are expressed in relative terms: 100 represents the average of all cars. A rating of 41 is 59 percent better than average; a rating of 189 is 89 percent worse than average. Some of the models listed have been discontinued or redesigned since 1988, so these ratings may not apply to current models.

common sense suggests thinking twice about buying a car that regularly ranks near the bottom of the injury claims list. At least part of the reason could be due to design.

Copies of the HLDI brochure, "Injury and Collision Loss Experience," are available from:

**Highway Loss Data Institute
600 Watergate
Washington, DC 20037**

Restraint Systems

For 1990, every passenger car must have some form of passive restraint for the front seat outboard positions. A passive restraint is a device that protects the driver and passenger without their need to take any action.

Two types are in use: automatic seat belts and air bags. Cars with a driver's-side air bag may use a manual front passenger belt until 1994. Whether bags or belts, automatic protection should save 9,000 lives a year, NHTSA says. Light trucks are the next vehicles

likely to be fitted with mandatory passive restraints, probably for the 1993 model year.

Air Bags

An air bag is an inflatable crash protection device that remains concealed in the steering-wheel hub or the dashboard until it is activated by a crash. In a frontal impact of about 12 mph or more, sensors in the nose of the car send an electric signal that triggers the release of a non-toxic gas that inflates the fabric bag in less than one-tenth of a second. The inflated bag creates a protective cushion between the person and the steering wheel, dashboard, and/or windshield. The air bag is designed to deflate within fractions of a second, restoring visibility and allowing the driver to continue steering the car. The entire cycle takes less than one second from the time of impact.

Modern air bag technology has been around for more than a decade. But only in the last few years, as federal

passive-restraint regulations have become more stringent, have automakers used them widely. About 700,000 cars sold for 1989 had a bag, but nearly 3 million will have one available this year. A driver's-side air bag is standard equipment on all '90 Chrysler cars, on 13 GM models, and on nine Ford models. In addition, both driver's- and passenger-side air bags are standard on all '90 Porsches, on Mercedes-Benz models equipped with V-8 engines, and on the Lincoln Continental, Town Car, and the Merkur Scorpio. GM expects to phase passenger bags in on some of its models by 1992.

Some customers are naturally wary of the new technology, but the evidence is that air bags do indeed inflate when they are designed to, and there's little evidence of unintentional inflation.

Cases of inadvertent inflation are "extremely rare," according to NHTSA. Those few instances typically resulted from a car "bottoming out" when running into a ditch or otherwise suffering a severe jolt. Tests have demonstrated that even if a bag should "go off" accidentally, it happens so fast that the bag deflates before impairing forward vision. Although the explosive noise is loud, test drivers have maintained control of their cars.

To work as designed, however, air bags must be used in tandem with seat and shoulder belts. A NHTSA study of frontal collisions shows that a combination of three-point lap/shoulder belt and air bag offers the greatest chance of survival:

Restraint system used in frontal collision	Percent of passengers who survived
Manual lap belts	30-40%
Manual lap and shoulder belts	40-50
Automatic belts	35-50
Air bags alone	20-40
Air bags and lap belts	40-50
Air bags and lap/shoulder belts	45-55

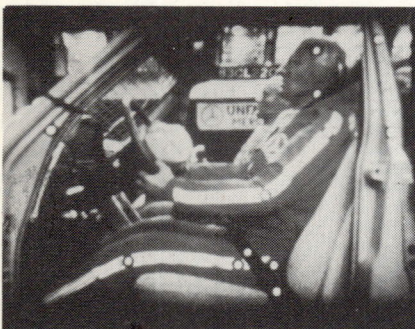
Crash sensors detect collision

Explosive charge generates nitrogen gas

Nitrogen inflates air bag

States with laws requiring the use of front-seat safety belts, as of October 1989

Two-point shoulder belt

Motorized shoulder belt

Three-point passive belts

It is also vital to note that air bags are designed to open only in frontal collisions, which amount to 40 percent of the total. Side or rear impacts have no effect and only a seat belt will help protect you in these types of crashes.

Air bags remain expensive. As options, they run about $950. As they become standard on more vehicles, their price is expected to drop below $300. Reinstalling a bag after it has deployed costs more than its original price, but it's just one of the repairs needed after a collision, and one that should be covered by insurance. And a number of insurance carriers now give personal-injury discounts for air bag-equipped cars.

Automatic Seat Belts

Many automakers have found automatic seat belts the most cost-effective way of meeting the government mandate for passive restraints.

- The most common system is a motorized arrangement that uses a shoulder belt with one side anchored at the inside of the seat and the other to a receptacle that slides on a track above the door. The belt locks into place around the torso when the ignition key is switched on and slides forward when the key is switched off. Since a separate lap belt has to be buckled manually, this system is not fully automatic. Plus, some motorists may ignore the lap belt and get only partial protection. The main drawback to this system is that the motorized belt can tangle arms, eyeglasses, hats, or packages the occupant may be carrying. Also, it may be frustrating to wait a few seconds for the belt to travel along its track to the buckled or unbuckled position.

- The next most frequently used system attaches the inboard shoulder and lap belt point at the inside of the front seat and anchors the outside points to the door frame. When the door is opened, you can slip behind the anchored lap and shoulder belts and into the seat. You can also use this as a manual system, detaching the inboard latch each time you leave the car and re-buckling it each time you enter. This form of automatic system is preferred by GM, but, as the system that's easiest to ignore, it also happens to be the system most likely

Bag inflates in 1/10 second

Occupant protected

Deflation in less than one second

CONSUMER GUIDE®

Safety

not to be used by owners. One problem is that, according to a recent NHTSA survey, owners find it the most uncomfortable and troublesome system for entry and exit. Another study found that most GM owners didn't know their car's belts were automatic.

• A few automakers use a shoulder belt that remains anchored to the door and at the inboard hip position. There is no lap belt used with this system; padding on the lower portion of the dashboard is designed to protect the occupant in a crash.

Seat Belt Slack

NHTSA advises that belts should fit snugly at all times. Shoulder belts should pass over the shoulder and across the chest with little or no slack. Unfortunately, some domestic automakers use shoulder belts that provide a few inches of slack around the shoulder and neck. The argument is that snug-fitting shoulder belts would discourage motorists from wearing belts at all. The shoulder belts are designed to snug up during sudden deceleration, but left unchecked as the passenger leans forward, then back, they can create a great deal of slack. Safety officials warn that no more than an inch or so of slack should be allowed at any time. Keeping belts properly snug is easy, in any kind of system. A quick tug on the belt, or pulling the belt out then letting go, should take up any excess slack.

For 1990, Ford has deleted its tension-relieving device from all models, and Chrysler from most. About half of GM's cars still have it. Most imports use an inertia reel to automatically take up any slack.

Rear Seat Belts

For 1990, all cars are required to have lap/shoulder belts at the rear outboard positions as standard equipment. Many vans and light trucks also now have this feature. And most older cars can be retrofitted using a kit that's available from dealers. Of course, seat belts are important for rear passengers; left unbelted, they can shoot forward in a frontal crash, seriously injuring themselves and the front-seat occupants. But a 1986 study of 26 frontal crashes suggested that rear-seat lap belts, when worn alone, caused as many injuries as they prevented. The findings indicated that a combination shoulder harness and lap belt is far safer than a lap belt alone.

Passive Restraints used in 1990 passenger cars

Vehicle	Air Bags Driver	Air Bags Passenger	Automatic Belts Motorized	Automatic Belts Non-Motor
ACURA				
Integra			Std	
Legend	Std			
ALFA ROMEO (not required; 1990 models built before 9/1/89)				
BUICK				
Century/Regal				Std
Electra/LeSabre				Std
Estate wagon				Std
Reatta/Riviera	Std			
CADILLAC				
Brougham				Std
All other Cadillac	Std			
CHEVROLET				
Camaro/Corvette	Std			
All other Chev. (also see Geo)				Std
CHRYSLER	Std			
DAIHATSU				
Charade hatchback			Std	
Charade sedan				Std
DODGE				
Colt			Std	
Monaco			Std	
All other Dodge	Std			
EAGLE			Std	
FORD				
Crown Victoria	Std			
Mustang	Std			
Taurus	Std			
Tempo	Opt		Std	
All other Ford			Std	
GEO				
Metro hdtp				Std
Metro conv.	Std			
Prizm			Std	
Storm	Std			
HONDA				
Accord			Std	
Civic sdn, wgn			Std	
Civic hatchback				Std
Prelude/CRX				Std
HYUNDAI			Std	
INFINITI	Std			
ISUZU	Std			
JAGUAR				
XJ6			Std	
XJ-S	Std			
LEXUS	Std			
LINCOLN				
Contin./Town Car	Std	Std		
Mark VII	Std			

Vehicle	Air Bags Driver	Passenger	Automatic Belts Motorized	Non-Motor
MASERATI			Std	
MAZDA				
RX-7 convertible	Std			
Miata	Std			
Other Mazda			Std	
MERCEDES-BENZ				
190	Std			
260E	Std	Opt		
300 (exc. rdstr.)	Std	Opt		
Other Mercedes	Std	Std		
MERCURY				
Cougar			Std	
Sable/Gr. Marquis	Std			
Topaz	Opt		Std	
NISSAN				
Axxess van			Std	
240SX/300ZX				Std
Sentra				Std
Maxima/Stanza			Std	
Pulsar	Opt			Std
OLDSMOBILE				
88 Royale	Opt			Std
98 Regency	Opt			Std
98 Touring sedan				Std
Toronado	Std			
Other Oldsmobiles				Std
PEUGEOT				
405			Std	
505				Std
PLYMOUTH				
Colt/Laser			Std	
Other Plymouths	Std			
PONTIAC				
Firebird	Std			
LeMans			Std	
Other Pontiacs				Std
PORSCHE	Std	Std		
SAAB	Std			
STERLING			Std	
SUBARU				
Justy		Std	Std	
Some Loyale models				Std
Other Subarus			Std	
SUZUKI				Std
TOYOTA				
Camry/Cressida			Std	
Celica/Supra	Std			
Corolla/Tercel				Std
VOLKSWAGEN				
Cabriolet	Std			
Corrado/Passat			Std	
Fox/Golf/GTI/Jetta				Std
VOLVO	Std			
YUGO				Std

Child Restraints

Every state has laws governing the use of child safety seats, though the statutes vary as to the ages of children who must use them. Your motor vehicle department or state police headquarters will be able to tell you the appropriate requirements in your state. In general, babies and children under four years of age or weighing under 40 pounds belong in an approved child's car seat. These children are too small for a standard lap or shoulder belt to protect them in a collision. It is the height of parental irresponsibility to allow children to ride in a vehicle if they are unbelted or unprotected by a car seat.

Child restraint systems vary in design and attachment. As a rule, the child is held to the carrier or seat by straps for each shoulder, and another between the legs. The seat itself is secured by the car's seat belts. Some car seats have a tether strap that bolts to the car at the rear parcel shelf and prevents the seat from falling forward or sideways in a serious crash.

Car shoppers with small children might want to investigate whether the vehicle they are considering offers an anchor point. Some automakers even offer an approved child seat as a new-car accessory.

Anti-lock Brakes

An anti-lock braking system (ABS) is a critically acclaimed safety feature designed to eliminate skids and to maintain steering control during braking in rain or snow or on icy pavement. With ABS, a computer on board the car controls braking force to prevent the wheels from locking. Locked brakes result in skids and rob the front tires of their steering forces. When ABS brakes are applied, the computer senses when a wheel is about to lock up and then "pumps" the brakes many times per second, applying them and releasing them far faster than any human could. It allows the wheels to continue rotating while slowing the car. The driver simply applies steady force to the brake pedal. Actual stopping distances may not be dramatically shorter with ABS, but the degree of control during deceleration is dramatically higher.

ABS was once the province of only very expensive cars. While Mercedes-Benz, Porsche, and BMW are among the automakers that offer ABS as standard equipment across the board, the system is now also available as standard or optional on such mid-priced cars as the Ford Probe, Dodge Dynasty, Olds-

1990 Cars with Anti-lock Braking

Standard	Optional
Acura Integra GS	Audi 80 Quattro
Acura Legend L/LS	Buick LeSabre
Audi (exec 80)	Buick Regal
BMW (all)	Buick Riviera
Buick Electra T Type/Ultra	Cadillac DeVille
Buick Reatta	Cadillac Eldorado
Cadillac Allante	Cadillac Seville
Cadillac Brougham	Chrysler New Yorker
Cadillac Fleetwood	Dodge Dynasty
Cadillac Seville STS	Ford Probe
Chevrolet Astro	Ford Taurus sedan
Chevrolet Corvette	Ford Thunderbird
Chrysler Imperial	Jeep Cherokee
Ford Bronco II	Jeep Wagoneer
Ford Thunderbird SC	Lincoln Town Car
GMC Safari van	Mazda 626/MX-6
Infinity (all)	Mazda 929
Jaguar (all)	Mercury Cougar LS
Lexus (all)	Mercury Sable sedan
Lincoln Continental	Mitsubishi Galant GS/GSX
Lincoln Mark VII	Mitsubishi Sigma
Mazda 929 S	Nissan Maxima SE
Mazda MPV (rear)	Nissan Stanza GXE
Mazda RX-7 Turbo	Nissan 240SX
Mercedes-Benz (all)	Oldsmobile Cutlass Supreme
Mercury Cougar XR7	Oldsmobile Eighty-Eight
Merkur Scorpio	Oldsmobile Ninety-Eight
Nissan 300ZX	Oldsmobile Touring Sedan
Oldsmobile Trofeo	Pontiac Bonneville
Peugeot Mi 16	Pontiac Grand Prix
Pontiac Grand Prix STE	Sterling 827 S
and Turbo coupe	Subaru Legacy L, LS
Porsche (all)	Toyota Camry LE
Range Rover	Toyota Celica GT-S, All-Trac
Saab (all)	Toyota Supra
Sterling 827 SL/SLi	Volkswagen Corrado
Toyota 4Runner (rear)	Volkswagen Jetta GLI 16V/Carat
Volvo 740 GLE/Turbo, 760, 780	Volvo 740/740 GL

mobile Cutlass Supreme, and Toyota Camry LE.

Unintended Acceleration

True unintended acceleration involves a car with automatic transmission that accelerates out of control suddenly and without warning. Such allegations go back more than 20 years and target a succession of makes and models, but a recent National Highway Traffic Safety Administration study casts doubt on the suspicion that unintended acceleration is the result of a mechanical defect. The typical unintended acceleration allegation has the car running away forward or backward as it's shifted from park into drive or reverse. Drivers insist they were unable to stop the car even by applying the brake pedal with all the force they

could. Consumer safety advocates cited a number of alleged causes, usually a design defect in the cruise control, the electronic idle-speed systems, or the computerized fuel/ignition system.

The controversy gained its widest public exposure with a 1986 segment on the CBS-TV news program *60 Minutes.* The report focused on unintended acceleration charges against the Audi 5000. NHTSA files showed the Audi 5000 to have the highest rate of unintended acceleration claims, some resulting in death and injury. Audi representatives retorted that the automaker could not duplicate true unintended acceleration in a controlled test environment and had concluded that the cause of actual crashes was driver error. Specifically, Audi said it believed the drivers had mistakenly depressed the accelerator pedal. It further maintained that even

with the throttle of an Audi 5000 jerry rigged to stay fully open, the car's brakes were still strong enough to bring it to a stop. Charges of unintended acceleration were also leveled at models from Chrysler, Ford, GM, Honda/Acura, Mercedes, Austin Rover (Sterling), Nissan, Toyota, Volvo, and Volkswagen.

Audi subsequently recalled all 1979-86 5000 models with automatic transmission to install a shift lock, which prevents the vehicle from being shifted into drive or reverse without first stepping on the brake. Nissan's 280ZX and 300ZX had a similar recall while other manufacturers recalled models to reposition the brake and gas pedals, or voluntarily install shift locks. Additional recalls involved cruise control units and poorly-positioned floor mats that might impair pedal action.

Early in 1989 NHTSA released the findings of its unintended acceleration investigation and concluded "the major cause appears to have been drivers unknowingly stepping on the accelerator instead of the brake pedal." NHTSA said the misapplication was aggravated by pedal design defects in some cars, namely that the brake and accelerator were too close to one another. But the agency could not uncover a mechanical glitch that would cause the cars to accelerate out of control. The agency's 435-page study, "An Examination of Sudden Acceleration," is available to the public through the National Technical Information Service of the Department of Transportation.

Many critics do not accept the NHTSA finding, however, and lawsuits against Audi remain in litigation, so the controversy isn't likely to evaporate.

If your car ever accelerates suddenly, hit the brake pedal—being certain that it is the brake pedal. Practice this maneuver so you'll be most familiar with the pedal positions if it has to be done in a hurry. Keep your foot on the brake whenever you shift into a drive gear. Be ready to shut off the ignition quickly, too.

Rollovers

Rollovers are directly related to a vehicle's stability in turns. This stability is influenced by the relationship between the vehicle's center of gravity and its track, or width between wheels on the same axle. A high center of gravity and a narrow track make a vehicle unstable in turns or sharp changes of direction and increase the chances it will tip over once it begins to skid sideways.

The problem is most pronounced in 4WD trucks and sport-utility vehicles.

Deaths by Body Style (1987)

Body Type	As a percent of all vehicles involved in fatal accidents	Percentage of all vehicle deaths
Convertible	0.4	0.5
2-dr sdn/htp/cpe	30.6	34.3
3-dr hatchback	1.7	2.3
4-dr sedan	19.0	20.6
5-dr hatchback	0.4	0.6
Station wagon	3.8	3.9
Auto-based pickup	0.3	0.3
Other/unknown	2.9	2.6

These vehicles need extra ground clearance to maneuver off-road. A narrow track also helps them slip through backwoods obstacles. But on dry pavement—where the majority of off-road vehicles spend most of their lives—these off-road advantages put the 4WD truck or sport-utility vehicle out of its element.

Sure enough, fatality rates tell the tale. NHTSA figures show the largest single share of fatal truck crashes—47 percent—are rollovers. By contrast, only 24 percent of fatal car crashes occur when the car turns over. The 1986 death rate in rollovers was 51 per one million cars, but a whopping 99 per one million trucks.

Other factors besides height and track are at work in rollover crashes, however, not the least of which is how a vehicle is typically driven. Large and medium-sized cars share with vans a rather conservative owner population: families, older drivers, much suburban and rural use. By contrast, small cars, small pickups, and 4WD vehicles are frequently purchased by younger, less-experienced drivers and are often driven in riskier ways. Once again, NHTSA's study of real-world crashes illustrates the point.

Vans had about the same rollover-fatality rate as mid-size cars, about 50 per million vehicles. But the death count grows frighteningly high for trucks with both a high center of gravity and with a particular attraction for younger buyers.

The rollover fatality rate for standard-size pickups was 91 per one million vehicles. It was 128 per million for small pickups. And it was 156 per million for all 4WD utility vehicles.

It was the rollover question that grabbed headlines in July 1988 when Consumers Union charged that the 4WD Suzuki Samurai tipped too easily. Additionally, the Center for Auto Safety petitioned NHTSA to order Suzuki to buy back about 140,000 Samurais. NHTSA responded that its studies show the Samurai behaves no differently from most other 4 × 4s and is, in fact, about in the middle of the pack in instances of reported rollovers. It declined to issue a recall. The real issue, NHTSA said, is that rollovers are a problem common to all 4WD vehicles—and not just because of their typically high center of gravity and narrow track, but because of the way they are driven.

Most fatal 4WD rollovers are single-vehicle accidents occurring on weekend nights, the agency says. The drivers are most frequently males under 25 years of age. Alcohol is usually involved. And in two of every three fatal rollover crashes, the person killed was ejected from the vehicle—indicating the victim was probably not wearing a seat belt.

How Safe Is Safe?

Even the experts can't agree upon which cars are safest. Government crash tests have been criticized as having little relevance to real-world collisions, while the variables associated with real accidents are too numerous to be of much value in comparing the safety of one vehicle against another.

Still, some important findings emerge from the spectrum of crash tests and the study of real-world collisions. We can discuss safety in terms of vehicle size or occupant protection, for instance. But the overriding fact is that no car is safe if driven recklessly or inattentively, if its driver is impaired by drugs, alcohol, illness, or fatigue, or if its occupants do not wear seat belts.

Safety, however, should be a factor in choosing a new car. Consider the vehicle's:

- Size and weight.
- Standard safety equipment.
- Optional safety features.

In general, large, heavy vehicles are safer than small, light ones. This is according to the laws of physics and the study of real-world fatality rates. Factors beyond size and weight have a strong bearing on safety, however. These factors include the structural soundness of the vehicle and the design of its safety equipment. Then there's the issue of a vehicle's ability to avoid a collision. Brakes, steering and handling prowess, even outward visibility, all play a role in accident avoidance.

NHTSA Auto Safety Hotline
1-800-424-9393
(In Washington, D.C., 366-0123)

The National Highway Traffic Safety Administration operates a toll-free Auto Safety Hotline for information on government crash tests, safety-related recalls, and government ratings of tires. Consumers can also call this number to report safety problems with their cars. The number is open between 8 a.m. and 4 p.m. Eastern time on regular business days. An answering machine is available after hours. Consumers can also write to:

National Highway Traffic Safety Administration
400 7th Street, NW
Washington, DC 20590

Motor Vehicle Deaths by Type of Vehicle (1988)

Persons & Vehicles Involved	Deaths	Percent
Passenger car occupants	25,700	55
Light trucks, vans, utility vehicles	8,404	18
Tractor-trailers	711	2
Other medium/heavy trucks	198	below 1
Motorcyclists	3,486	7
Bicyclists	900	2
Pedestrians	6,869	15
Other	825	2
	47,093	

Source: Insurance Institute for Highway Safety.

INSURANCE

California voters sparked a revolt against skyrocketing auto insurance premiums in 1988 when they approved Proposition 103. The mix of referenda mandated major rate rollbacks to 1987 levels, plus a host of reforms in the state's rate structure. Proponents said Prop 103 would trigger similar revolts in other states. Some insurers in California, however, staged a near-revolt of their own by refusing to write policies in California. Implementation of the proposition was delayed for review by the state's Supreme Court and then a subsequent ruling kept certain provisions alive but tossed out the rollback. The insurance industry said the Supreme Court had agreed that the companies were entitled to "a fair rate of return."

At this writing, the situation remains unresolved. In fact, a number of California insurers have boosted their premium rates, alleging that they'd been losing money in the state. So the California consumer revolt, after an initial frenzy, essentially fizzled before it could have an impact on other states. Nevada and New Jersey have similar referendums on the November 1989 ballot, but neither is expected to make a major difference.

Can't Do Without It

About 40 states require motorists to carry personal liability coverage. Even where it's not mandatory, no responsible motorist drives without proper coverage. Without it, all your property is put at risk for even a modest accident. *Best's Review*, an insurance trade magazine, says that one in five drivers has an accident each year.

While you may be required to have insurance, no company is compelled to sell it to you at a "fair" price. And the only motorists "guaranteed" insurance are those with very bad driving records. They're placed in a high-risk pool, where all companies share the risk, and they pay very high rates.

Higher and Higher They Go

Insurers set rates according to their own standards, exchanging information through "rate bureaus" and subject only to state regulation. Little has been done to halt rate hikes, however, and pre-

miums grew by an average of 9 to 13 percent in 1986 and 1987.

Insurers justify the increases by pointing out that the cost of buying and repairing cars goes up each year. Jury awards involving liability settlements are growing, and medical costs continue to skyrocket. The Insurance Information Institute says that between 1977 and 1986, average payments for bodily injury claims rose 156 percent and damage claims were up 139 percent, while premiums increased only 93 percent. Average payments edged up another four percent in 1988.

High insurance costs have even been blamed for the demise of some sporty and performance models, including the Pontiac Fiero. Sales slumps of such cars as the Toyota MR2 and Mazda RX-7 are attributed to high insurance rates. A Mazda spokesman said some RX-7 owners are saddled with insurance payments equal to 75 percent of their monthly car payments. Perfor-

mance-oriented cars appeal most to the young, of course, who are charged the most for insurance.

Setting Insurance Rates

Insurers insist they can't rely wholly on driving records as a factor in setting rates. They say the data available from states isn't consistent. Nor can they be sure a policy-seeker's claim of driving below a set number of miles is true. So they rely on factors that are easy to determine, but may or may not be the best predictors. Three basic factors are involved:

1. Where you live.
2. Who you are (age, gender, driving record, occupation, etc.).
3. Type and age of car insured (mainly for collision and comprehensive coverage).

Single males under the age of 25 pay the highest rates. Getting married

---

Types of Coverage

Six forms of coverage are included in most policies:

Bodily injury liability: Pays injury/death claims against you, and legal costs if your car injures or kills someone.

Property damage liability: Pays claims for property that your car damages in an accident.

Medical payments: Pays for injuries to yourself and occupants of your car.

Uninsured motorist protection: Covers you for injuries caused to you or the occupants of your car by an uninsured or hit-and-run driver; in some states, property damage is included. "Underinsured" coverage also is available, in case you're hit by a driver who has inadequate insurance.

Collision coverage: Pays for damage to your own car in an accident, up to its book value, unless covered by a liability claim against the other party.

Comprehensive (physical damage): Covers damage to your car from fire, wind, flood, theft, vandalism, and other causes unrelated to accidents.

Liability coverage is expressed

by three figures, for example, "$25/50/15" means $25,000 bodily injury coverage for one person, $50,000 total for a single accident, and $15,000 for property damage. Because it protects the other party, it's the coverage required by law in most states.

Collision coverage has a deductible: a specified amount that you have to pay before the coverage takes effect. Deductibles run as low as $50, or as high as $1000 ($2000 in a few states). Comprehensive may have a similar deductible but full coverage doesn't cost much more. Coverage for medical payments ranges from $1000 on up.

No-fault programs were supposed to pull down premium rates by reducing the number of lawsuits. Fourteen states have a form of no-fault, but that hasn't necessarily cut the rates. Regulations vary, but regardless of who "caused" an accident, each party can make all claims for collision and medical reimbursement to his or her own insurance company. Separate personal injury coverage, similar to medical payments, may be available or required.

24

Damage Repair Costs in Low-speed Crash Tests of Small Cars

Vehicle	Amount
Isuzu Impulse	$3444
Daihatsu Charade	3047
Honda CRX HF	3040
Chrysler Conquest TSi	2357
Pontiac LeMans	2144
Plymouth Sundance	2117
Volkswagen Jetta	2105
Honda CRX DX	2061
Nissan 240SX XE	1976
Volkswagen Fox	1887
Volkswagen GTI	1875
Ford Festiva L Plus	1849
Acura Integra LS	1763
Dodge Daytona ES	1754
Saab 900	1673
Volkswagen Golf	1655
Geo Metro coupe	1620
Ford Probe GL	1592
Mercury Tracer	1571
Dodge Daytona	1545
Nissan 240SX SE	1531
Ford Escort LX	1481
Mazda MX-6 DX	1465
Honda Civic 3-dr	1262
Nissan Pulsar NX XE	1248
Volkswagen Cabriolet	1144
Toyota MR2	1091
Toyota Tercel EZ	1001
Mazda 323	934
Hyundai Excel GL	842
Mitsubishi Mirage Turbo	824
Plymouth Colt	642
Toyota Corolla	495
Geo Spectrum	434

Amounts indicate the dollar cost of repairs after a 5-mph crash of 1988 models into four barriers: flat concrete (front and rear), front impact at an angle, and rear impact into a steel pole. Fourteen of the cars listed were tested in 1988, but their repair costs have been updated to reflect 1989 parts/labor prices. Damage to the Isuzu Impulse amounted to $238 for the front barrier alone, $507 for the rear barrier, $1254 for front-angle barrier, and $1445 for the rear pole damage. Several vehicles sustained little or no damage during front or rear barrier crashes, but significant damage in other tests. All cars were damaged in front-angle test, and only the Geo Metro survived the rear-pole crash without damage.

Source: Insurance Institute for Highway Safety.

usually but not always lowers the rate somewhat.

Statistics show that younger drivers, especially males, are involved in a higher rate of accidents. Hawaii and Massachusetts, however, do not allow insurance companies to set rates based on sex or age.

Because accident rates are high in urban areas, insurers charge much higher premiums to drivers who live in or near a major city. That New Jersey ranks as the state with the highest average premiums can be traced to the fact that 85 percent of its drivers live in densely populated areas.

Some companies boost premiums for a single traffic violation or minor accident. Some won't insure those with a blemished driving record.

Shopping for Insurance

Prices for the same coverage can differ vastly, even when buying from agents of the same company. Surveys have found people charged up to two or three times as much as others in the same area. Unless you're satisfied that your current premium is in line with those offered by other agencies, investigate a couple of others when buying a new car.

Shopping isn't easy. You actually have to read the fine print in your policy before attempting to compare it against another company's. Call or visit at least one agent for each company you have in mind. Explain exactly what you want. If quoted rates are far apart, call back to confirm that each agent is talking about the same coverage. Ask to see an itemized list. Don't be surprised if some won't quote a price on the phone, or put anything on paper. Focus on those who cooperate.

In addition to low price, you want a company that's ready to provide quick, efficient claims service. Contact your state insurance department or a consumer agency to see if the company you're considering has any serious complaints against it. Ask about price guides or other helpful information, too.

Basic rates are just the beginning. Ask about discounts that might apply. In addition to discounts and surcharges tacked onto certain car models, there might be a discount for:

1. Students with a B or better grade average (as much as 25 percent off), or away at college.
2. More than one car insured by the company.
3. Anti-theft alarms.

4. Safety devices on the vehicle, including air bags, automatic seat belts, anti-lock brakes.
5. Insuring car and home with the same company.
6. Good driving record.
7. Driving less than a set number of miles per year.
8. Driving only for pleasure instead of for business or commuting.
9. Taking a defensive-driving class.
10. Age over 50-55 (or retired).
11. Nonsmokers or nondrinkers.
12. No male drivers in household.
13. Drivers in specified professions.
14. Participation in a car pool.
15. Middle-aged female drivers only.

Most discounts apply only to one portion of the policy, so don't expect a dramatic price cut. Ironically, the one factor that seems most logically related

Six Ways To Cut Costs

1. Increase the deductible amount for collision and/or comprehensive. Switching from a $100 deductible to a $500 deductible could slash your premium cost by 30 percent. Going to $1000 might cut it in half. You're still covered for catastrophic incidents, but you bypass the fender-benders. Experienced motorists think twice about filing small claims anyway: Why risk earning a sharp rise in later premiums?

2. Drop collision coverage if your car is more than five or six years old. Claim payments are limited to book value, so you wouldn't get much in case of loss. In fact, unless a creditor demands collision coverage, you're free to skip it for any car.

3. Have your teenager share the family car instead of buying one for his or her use exclusively.

4. Investigate carefully whether your employee group health insurance has enough coverage that would allow you to eliminate the medical-payments portion of your auto policy.

5. Drop coverage for such extras as towing costs, or the cost of a rental car if yours is in the shop.

6. Before renewing your auto policy, read the fine print carefully to see whether anything has changed in the coverage. If it's weakened, another company might have a better offer waiting.

Insurance

to risk, your driving and accident record, doesn't always warrant as great a discount as those factors that have little to do with driving skill.

How Much Do You Need?

Minimum-level insurance is seldom enough. A state may require only 15/30/10 coverage, or even less. If there's anyway you can afford it, buy more insurance. Increased liability coverage, for instance, doesn't usually cost a whole lot more. A typical $10,000 maximum for property damage won't help if you collide with a new Mercedes-Benz.

The rule of thumb is that the more you have in assets and income at risk, the more insurance you need. Most insurance agents would recommend at least 100/300/50 ($100,000 per person, $300,000 per accident, $50,000 property damage) coverage, but evaluate your own circumstances, needs, and risks before settling upon a level of coverage. Better to save money on other parts of the policy than to cut corners on liability. A lawsuit could bring financial ruin. A million-dollar limit could cost as little as $100-$150 per year under an all-encompassing "personal liability umbrella" in conjunction with homeowner's coverage.

Some Cars Cost More

Collision coverage rates vary with the type of vehicle and are ostensibly based on how expensive the car is to repair. Plus, there are surcharges for certain cars that are involved in a high rate of accidents or suffer a high rate of theft. Only the insurer's experience sets the rates. Fred Cripe, a spokesman for Allstate Insurance Company put it simply: "cars which are less susceptible to serious damage in minor accidents and cost less to repair when they are damaged cost less to insure."

Since surcharges apply only to collision and comprehensive, they don't always amount to a large sum. State Farm Insurance Company, for instance, adds 10 to 30 percent to the basic rate for cars with a "bad" claims record, and lops off like amounts for those with claim rates lower than the norm. Domestic models—especially full-size sedans and wagons—are most likely to warrant a discount.

The Highway Loss Data Institute classifies cars by injury and collision loss experience and insurers use the data as a guide in setting rates. On the

Collision Ratings for 1987-88 Models
Highway Loss Data Institute

Lowest Payment per Claim	Highest Payment per Claim
45 GMC Safari van	305 Volkswagen Scirocco
49 Chevrolet Astro van	289 Plymouth Conquest
51 Dodge Grand Caravan	251 Porsche 944
52 Plymouth Voyager van	229 BMW 3-Series 2-dr
52 Plymouth Grand Voyager	206 Mitsubishi Cordia
53 Dodge Caravan	195 Chev. Corvette cpe
55 Pontiac Safari wagon	181 Toyota Supra
56 Chevrolet Caprice	179 Nissan 300ZX
56 Mercury Grand Marquis	178 Saab 900 2-dr
58 Dodge Diplomat	176 Mazda MX-6 & RX-7
58 Ford Crown Victoria	174 Chev. Corvette conv.

Note: HLDI collision ratings are based on average loss payments per claim for collision damage on 1987-88 models. Ratings are expressed in relative terms: 100 represents the average of all cars studied. A rating of 45 is 55 percent lower than average; a rating of 305 is 205 percent higher than average. Only models that rated much lower or higher than average are listed above. Some models in this list have been discontinued or structurally modified since the 1987-88 model years, so these ratings may not apply to 1990 models.

Insurance Surcharges and Discounts

Models That Might Get a Surcharge	Models That Might Get a Discount
Alfa Romeo	Buick (exc. Regal)
Chevrolet Camaro	Cadillac
Chevrolet Corvette	Chevrolet (mid/full)
Ford Escort/Mustang	Chrysler
Hyundai Excel	Dodge (full-size)
Nissan 240SX/300ZX	Ford (mid/full-size)
Pontiac Firebird	Jeep
Porsche	Lincoln
Suzuki Samurai	Mercury
Toyota MR2	Plymouth (full-size)
Volkswagen	Volvo
Yugo	Dodge/Plymouth vans

Chart lists examples of cars that are likely to be hit with a surcharge or earn a discount based upon an insurer's claims experience. High-performance models (Camaro IROC-Z, Firebird Trans Am) are hit the hardest.
Source: State Farm and Allstate insurance companies

Most Frequently Stolen Cars—1987 Models

Model	Number Stolen	Theft Rate (Per 1000)
Pontiac Firebird	2424	30.1
Chevrolet Camaro	3333	26.0
Chevrolet Monte Carlo	1516	20.3
Toyota MR2	381	19.3
Buick Regal	910	14.8
Mitsubishi Starion	100	14.6
Ferrari Mondial	2	13.6
Mitsubishi Mirage	357	12.8
Pontiac Fiero	563	12.7
Oldsmobile Cutlass Supreme	1338	11.7

Number Stolen is the total number of thefts per car line during calendar 1987. Theft Rate is the number of cars stolen for each 1000 cars manufactured for that car line during 1987. For example, 2,424 Pontiac Firebirds were stolen and 80,414 were produced in 1987. Only two Ferrari Mondials were stolen, but only 147 were imported.

Source: National Highway Traffic Safety Administration, based on data supplied by the National Crime Information Center.

whole, big cars have fewer injury claims, while high-performance, sporty, and luxury models have more claims.

Thieves Prefer Certain Cars

A car is stolen every 22 seconds—more than 1.4 million in 1988. The best way to hang onto yours? Move out of the city. More cars are stolen in New York, Boston, Chicago, and Los Angeles than in the rest of the country combined.

If moving isn't practical, you could forget that Chevrolet Corvette or Pontiac Firebird and buy a humdrum station wagon or nondescript, no-frills sedan. Thieves and their customers prefer sporty and luxury models.

It's also interesting to note that Volkswagens tend to head lists of theft-claim frequencies. That's not because Volkswagens themselves are in high demand among thieves. It turns out that VW mounts its "premium" stereo system high on the dashboard. The radio/cassette units are clearly visible to passersby and relatively easy to remove. Radios in Audi, BMW, Jaguar, Mercedes, Peugeot, and Saab models are also easy to pry out. Most of these European automakers have begun to put a disabling circuit into their stereo systems. When removed from the dash or disconnected from the battery, the radio/cassette unit will not operate again until a specific code—known only to the owner and the manufacturer—is punched into the system.

Automakers have been trying other measures to discourage theft. Theft alarms are now common as standard equipment among high-line models, and several manufactures have begun to etch identification numbers on body panels and windows to make it more difficult to disguise a stolen car. But despite these efforts, theft certainly hasn't ground to a halt. Investigate details of a factory- or dealer-installed alarm before buying a car with a high theft rate.

Protect Your Car

Anti-theft alarms are growing more sophisticated all the time, but unfortunately, some are more annoying than protective. The best alarms are simple to arm and disarm and do not activate unless the threat of theft is real. Some sporty GM models, including the Chevrolet Corvette and Camaro and the Pontiac Firebird, will not start unless a pellet imbedded in the ignition key matches an ignition code set at the factory. GM says the system has dramatically lowered theft rates for these cars.

Relative Average Theft Loss Payment 1988 Passenger Cars

Model	Payment per Claim
Jaguar XJ6	$8256
Chevrolet Monte Carlo	7919
Mercury Grand Marquis 4-dr	7413
Lincoln Town Car	7118
Lincoln Mark VII	5981
Ford Thunderbird	5602
Pontiac Firebird	5265
Nissan Maxima	4781
Chevrolet Camaro	4696
Dodge Shadow	4465
Mercury Cougar	4465

The average loss payment per insurance claim for 1988 models was $2106, up slightly from $2081 for 1987 models. Some models had insufficient claims to be included in this list. Corvette convertibles, for example, had a loss payment of $14,945 for the 1987 model year (more than 7 times the average). High payouts suggest cars that are never recovered but broken up for parts, the victims of "chop shops."

Source: based on data from Highway Loss Data Institute.

Other alarms can differentiate between dangerous sounds, a hammer breaking glass, for example, and ordinary street noises. Others cut off the ignition as the alarm blares. Some can be turned on or off from outside the car by remote control. Those with coded numbers that must be entered before a car can be started offer millions of possible combinations.

While a thief isn't likely to give up because a car has an alarm, he can at least be encouraged to pick an easier target. But which alarms work best? Ask your insurance company. It has to pay out the claims on auto thefts and can recommend the most effective units. Some insurers offer a discount if a car contains an acceptable alarm, but the discount applies only to comprehensive coverage. In a few states, such a discount is mandatory.

Most Frequent Theft Claims 1988 Passenger Cars

Model	Claim Frequency
Suzuki Samurai	875
Volkswagen Golf 2-dr	733
Volkswagen Jetta 4-dr	676
Volkswagen Fox 4-dr	468
Hyundai Excel 4-dr	411
Cadillac De Ville 2-dr	396
Cadillac Brougham	372
Pontiac Firebird	330
Hyundai Excel 2-dr	324
Jeep Wrangler	304
Cadillac De Ville 4-dr	301
Volkswagen Fox 2-dr	293
Chevrolet Camaro	279

Source: Highway Loss Data Institute. Theft claim frequency is expressed in relative terms, with 100 representing the average for all cars. A claim frequency of 875 is 8.75 times the average of all cars, and a claim frequency of 279 is 2.79 times the average of all cars. Theft claims include those for stolen parts and accessories, such as stereos, as well as vehicle thefts. This list covers only frequency of claims, not dollar value. Vehicles with low claim frequencies (well under half the average) include Buick Regal, Ford Escort wagon, Chevrolet Cavalier 4-door sedan, Dodge Omni/Plymouth Horizon, Mercury Topaz, Eagle Premier, Ford Aerostar van, and Toyota Camry wagon.

CAR BUYER'S GLOSSARY

If you're about to venture into a new-car showroom for the first time in several years, you may discover that your automotive vocabulary is out of date. Such terms as anti-lock brakes, 4-wheel steering, fuel injection, and multi-valve engines await the new-car shopper. The unprepared face an avalanche of high-tech double-talk. We've compiled a glossary of some recent technical innovations. This list will also help define many of the terms used to describe vehicles in the *Automobile Book*.

Airbags: A fabric bag that inflates in frontal collisions of around 12 mph or higher to prevent front-seat occupants from hitting the steering wheel, dashboard, or windshield. Airbags are designed to inflate within fractions of a second, then immediately deflate so the driver's ability to control the car isn't impeded. Most cars equipped with airbags have only one, for the driver, housed in the steering wheel hub. A few cars also have passenger-side airbags mounted in the dashboard. (See "Automatic seat belts" and "Passive restraints")

All-season tires: Tread designs that allow water and snow to escape from under the tire for better traction. Ordinary tread designs tend to trap water, causing "hydroplaning," in which the tire rides on a thin film of water. Most all-season tires are designed for a soft ride rather than good handling, though some tire companies now offer all-season radials that have a high-performance tread. (See "Tire sizes")

Anti-lock braking systems (ABS): A computer controls braking force to prevent the wheels from locking in a panic stop. This safety feature is designed to dramatically reduce stopping distances and improve steering control, especially in rain, snow, or on icy pavement. Locked brakes result in skids, in which the driver can neither stop nor steer the car. When ABS brakes are applied, the computer senses when a wheel is about to lock up and then "pumps" the brakes many times per second. The driver simply continues to apply steady force to the brake pedal, but the computer allows the wheels to rotate while slowing the car.

Automatic seat belts: Front seat belts that engage automatically upon entering a car or turning on the ignition. There

are two basic types. Motorized shoulder belts anchored to the door frame pivot around front-seat occupants when the front doors are closed and the ignition is on (separate lap belts usually have to be buckled manually). Non-motorized automatic belts can be left buckled, but will automatically extend or retract when the front doors are opened or closed. Automatic seat belts are part of a passive-restraint system. (see "Airbags," "Passive restraints")

Curb weight: The weight of the vehicle when ready for the road, including fuel and other fluids. Curb weights listed in this issue are for base models without optional equipment.

Direct ignition: Ignition coils, which supply the spark that ignites the air/fuel mixture inside the engine, are mounted directly atop the spark plugs, eliminating the ignition distributor and ignition wires to the plugs.

Disc brakes: Brake design in which a caliper squeezes two friction pads against a disc that's attached to the wheel. Considered more efficient than a drum brake, in which a drum-shaped iron casting is attached to the wheel. Curved brake shoes press against the inside of the drum to provide braking action.

Double overhead camshafts: Also called twin overhead cams. Two camshafts per cylinder bank, with one operating the intake valves and the other the exhaust valves. Double overhead-cam engines usually have four valves per cylinder, two intake, two exhaust. A V-type engine with one overhead camshaft per cylinder bank is still a single-cam engine. (See "Multi-valve engines" and "Overhead-camshaft and overhead-valve engines")

Driveability: Term used to describe a combination of mechanical and tactile impressions, often subjective. Includes how smoothly an engine runs and how quickly it to responds to the throttle. Also describes the ability of an automatic transmission to shift smoothly and to downshift promptly for passing, and the smoothness of a manual transmission's shift action and clutch movement.

Electronically adjustable suspension: A suspension system that changes

the ride quality to suit road or driving conditions, usually by altering shock-absorber damping or air-spring rates. Some electronically adjustable suspensions are designed to enhance ride comfort by softening settings for rough roads. Others stiffen settings to improve handling, at the expense of ride quality. Some systems are automatic, with microprocessors sensing inputs from the steering, brakes, throttle and other sources to determine the suspension setting. Others are adjustable by the driver from the cockpit. (See "Handling," "Ride quality," and "Suspension")

Four-wheel drive: Engine power is delivered to all four wheels. The chief advantage is added traction on slippery surfaces. Disadvantages include a higher purchase price, extra weight, and reduced fuel economy. The most common system is "part-time, on-demand" 4WD, which allows the driver to shift from 2WD into 4WD via a transfer-case lever or an electric switch in the interior. This system is meant for use only on slippery pavement or off road. "Full-time" 4WD can be used on any surface and is of two types: on-demand or permanent (it's always engaged). The most sophisticated full-time systems engage automatically, using a viscous, or fluid, coupling to sense which wheels need traction and then deliver engine power accordingly. The driver does nothing to engage or disengage the system. Some on-demand 4WD systems lack "shift-on-the-fly" capability. That is, they require that the vehicle be stopped and that the front-wheel hubs be locked by hand before 4WD can be engaged.

Four-wheel steering: Allows rear wheels to steer the vehicle in tandem with the front wheels. Introduced by Honda and Mazda in 1988, it's also offered on some Nissan products for 1990. With 4WS, the rear wheels steer opposite the fronts a few degrees at slow speeds to decrease the turning radius and increase maneuverability. At higher speeds, the rear wheels turn a few degrees in the same direction as the fronts to enhance cornering and stability.

Front-wheel drive: Engine power is transmitted to the front wheels. Effect is to pull the car by the front wheels, rather than push it by the rears. FWD eliminates the drive shaft extending from the transmission to the rear-mounted differential, resulting in more passenger and cargo room.

Fuel injection: Replaces the carburetor to supply fuel for combustion. Fuel injection is of two basic designs, both of which meter fuel more efficiently than a carburetor. One design is called port (or multi-point) fuel injection, in which fuel is squirted directly into each cylinder at its intake port. The other is throttle-body (or single-point) fuel injection, in which fuel is squirted from one or two injectors into an intake manifold on top of the engine and then distributed to the cylinders. Multi-point injection is more expensive, but also more precise; it provides more efficient combustion and thus more power, better mileage, and lower emissions. Computers turn the fuel injectors on and off based on signals from sensors that measure oxygen in the exhaust, coolant temperature, engine speed, and other operating conditions.

Handling: Refers to how a car responds to the driver's steering input. A good-handling car remains stable and holds the road well in turns and over rough surfaces. This is not the same as "ride," which is a judgment of a car's over-the-road comfort. (See "Oversteer," "Stabilizer bar," "Suspension," and "Understeer")

Hatchback: Sedan or coupe body with a rear liftgate that opens to a cargo area. Cars with two passenger doors and a liftgate are called 3-door hatchbacks; four passenger doors and a liftgate make it a 5-door hatchback. (See "Notchback")

Head-up display (HUD): HUDs use vacuum fluorescent displays to project information from the main instrument cluster, such as vehicle speed, onto the windshield in the driver's field of view so this information can be read without glancing away from the road. This new electronic feature is available on some General Motors and Nissan cars.

Horsepower: A measurement of an engine's ability to perform work, measured by a dynamometer and expressed as brake horsepower. Engines that produce most of their horsepower at low rpm (revolutions-per-minute of the crankshaft), say 3000 rpm, often provide better low-speed pickup than engines that develop more horsepower at higher rpm, 5000 rpm, for example. Horsepower is not the only measurement of an engine's overall strength. Its ability to produce torque—turning or twisting force—

is also a key factor. (See "Torque," "Redline," "Tachometer," and "RPM")

Intercooler: Found on some turbocharged and supercharged cars. Acts as a radiator to cool air before it enters the combustion chamber. Cooling makes the air denser and increases the power of the ignited fuel-air mixture. (See "Naturally-aspirated engine," "Supercharger," and "Turbocharger")

Liftover: The height of the rear sill of the trunk or cargo area.

Lockup torque converter: A fuel-saving device found on some automatic transmissions. Power is sent from the engine to the transmission through a viscous, or fluid, coupling. A lockup torque converter "locks" the engine crankshaft to the transmission input shaft so the two turn as one, eliminating the slippage, or power loss, of the viscous coupling. The lockup torque converter is usually activated at highway speeds. In most cars, the converter can be felt engaging and disengaging, much as when the transmission shifts gears.

Multi-valve engines: Engines with three or four valves per cylinder instead of the customary two. Multiple-valve cylinder heads move more air and fuel through the engine quickly, letting the engine "breathe" better. In all engines, separate valves open in sequence to allow air-fuel mixture into the combustion chambers and then out as exhaust gases. Instead of simply enlarging one intake valve and one exhaust valve, using three or four valves of smaller size and lighter weight allows higher engine speeds, more power, and more efficient combustion. (See "Double-overhead camshafts" and "Overhead-camshaft and overhead-valve engines")

Naturally aspirated engine: Engines that draw air/fuel mixture into their cylinders without aid of a supercharger or turbocharger. (See "Intercooler," "Supercharger," and "Turbocharger")

Nosedive: Front end of the car dips under hard braking, caused by weight shifting forward. With excessive nosedive, the front brakes will carry too much of the braking load, while the lack of weight in the tail increases chances the rear brakes will lock. (See "Anti-lock braking systems")

Notchback: A sedan or a coupe body with a separate trunk. (See "Hatchback")

Overdrive: Fuel-saving transmission gear that lowers engine speed to save fuel and reduce noise. Usually the fourth gear of an automatic transmission and the fifth gear of a manual transmission. "Overdrive" transmissions allow the driveshafts to spin at a faster speed than the engine; those without overdrive have a less-efficient "direct-drive" top gear, in which the engine and driveshafts turn at the same speed.

Overhead-camshaft and overhead-valve engines: Distinguishing feature is placement of the camshaft. The camshaft in either design activates the valves. In an overhead-valve engine (ohv), the camshaft is located in the engine block, below the valves. It activates the valves by means of pushrods and other components. In an overhead-cam (ohc) engine, the camshaft is located in the cylinder head, with the valves mounted below. The ohc design is more expensive to manufacture, but has fewer parts and acts more directly on the valves, thus allowing the engine to run more efficiently and at higher speeds. Some engines use double-overhead cams (dohc) for still more efficiency. (See "Double-overhead camshafts" and "Multi-valve engines")

Oversteer: Tendency for the rear wheels of a car to lose traction and skid sideways in a turn. Most common in high-performance, rear-wheel drive cars or in tail-heavy vehicles. (See "Handling," "Stabilizer bar," "Suspension," and "Understeer")

Passive restraints: Safety features designed to protect occupants in crashes without being actively engaged. The two kinds are automatic seat belts and airbags. Associated components may include under-dashboard knee bolsters. Federal regulations require passive restraints on all passenger cars sold in the U.S. as 1990 models. (See "Airbags" and "Automatic seat belts")

Performance: An overall evaluation of how a car accelerates, holds the road, corners, and brakes. Good performance is usable daily. It enables a driver to merge easily with expressway traffic, pass quickly on 2-lane roads, negotiate turns and bumpy roads with good control, and stop safely.

Powertrain: All items necessary to transmit power to the wheels: engine, transmission or transaxle, clutch (on manual-transmission cars), torque converter (on automatic-transmission cars), and drive shafts.

Rear-wheel drive: Only the rear wheels receive power. The most common configuration has the engine mounted in front. Advantages are simplicity and better front-rear weight balance than front-drive cars. Disadvantages include reduced wet-weather traction compared to front-wheel drive and less efficient use of space. Passenger room is reduced because the drive shaft that links the transmission with the rear-mounted differential runs the length of the interior, taking up passenger and cargo space. (See "Front-wheel drive" and "Four-wheel drive")

Redline: An engine's maximum recommended speed in revolutions per minute (rpm). Tachometers mark this maximum engine speed with a red line at the appropriate rpm. (See "Horsepower," "Torque," "Tachometer," and "RPM")

Ride quality: A subjective judgment of a car's over-the-road comfort. Because automotive suspensions are studies in design compromise, ride quality is often the antithesis of handling. A car with a taut suspension that provides high-speed stability and good handling may be too stiff to ride comfortably on a rough road. If the ride is too soft, the suspension may be so compliant that maneuverability, steering response, and overall control are impaired. (See "Handling" and "Suspension")

RPM (Revolutions per minute): A measurement of engine speed, based on how fast the crankshaft is rotating. RPM is displayed on a tachometer. (See "Horsepower," "Torque," "Redline," and "Tachometer")

Stabilizer (anti-roll) bar: A bar linking the left and right sides of a suspension system. Can be used at the front, rear, or both ends of a car. It reduces body roll by helping the suspension system resist the weight shift that occurs when a car changes direction. (See "Handling," "Oversteer," "Suspension," and "Understeer")

Steering response: Good steering response means there is an immediate, precise change in direction when you turn the steering wheel.

Supercharger: A supercharger is similar to a turbocharger in that it forces additional air/fuel mixture into the combustion chamber to produce more power. An important difference is that a turbocharger is driven by spent exhaust gases; a supercharger is driven by the engine's crankshaft, and thus reacts more directly to the throttle and without the lag in response found on many turbochargers. (See "Intercooler," "Naturally-aspirated engine," and "Turbocharger")

Suspension: The components that support the weight of the car, keep the tread of the tires on the road, absorb bumps and road shocks, and control forces produced during acceleration, braking, and cornering. Suspensions vary in design and components, but typical parts include springs, shock absorbers, control arms, and stabilizer bars. An independent suspension means each wheel operates independently of the others, so that when one tire hits a pot hole, the spring and shock absorber at that corner absorb the bump without affecting the rest of the suspension. (See "Handling," "Oversteer," "Ride quality," and "Understeer")

Tachometer: Dashboard gauge that displays engine speed in revolutions per minute (rpm) of the crankshaft. (See "Horsepower," "Torque," "Redline," and "RPM")

Tire sizes: A series of numerals and letters stamped into the sidewall that denote the tire's intended use, tread width, profile, construction, and wheel diameter. An example is a P185/70R14 tire. "P" stands for passenger car tire; "185" is the tread width in millimeters; "70" is the tire's "profile," meaning the height of the sidewall is 70 percent of the width of the tread; "R" stands for radial; and "14" is the wheel diameter in inches. Tire widths generally increase and decrease in increments of 10 millimeters (185, 195, 205). Tires with a 70-series profile or less (60, 50, 45) are called "low-profile" tires and are designed for better handling. Tires with a 75-series profile or taller (80, 85) are designed for ride comfort. Some tires have an "H," "V" or some other letter as part of the size description, such as "P185/70HR14." Those letters denote maximum speed ratings: "S" for up to 112 mph; "H" for up to 130 mph; "V" for up to 149 mph; and "Z" for over 149 mph. (See "All-season tires")

Torque: The amount of twisting force generated by an engine, measured at the crankshaft and expressed in pounds/feet. This is different from horsepower. The amount of torque an engine produces affects ability to accelerate and move heavy loads. As with horsepower, engine speed is a factor with torque. An engine that develops 250 pounds/feet at 2000 rpm, can accelerate well from low speeds. It also tends to work well with automatic transmission. An engine that produces 150 pounds/feet of torque at 4000 rpm will have to be revved much higher to accelerate well from low speeds and will have a harder time hauling heavy loads. An engine with poor low-end torque is probably better suited for use with a manual transmission, which gives the driver more control over engine speed. Engines that produce maximum horsepower at high rpm often have little torque at low rpm. (See "Horsepower," "Tachometer," and "RPM")

Turbocharger: An air compressor that delivers more air to an engine than could be drawn in naturally, thus increasing engine power. Exhaust gas is recirculated through a turbine, which in turn drives the compressor to force more air into the engine. The amount of pressure generated is described as "boost" and measured in terms of pounds per square inch. Turbos enable engineers to increase horsepower without increasing engine size. A major disadvantage is the lag between when the throttle pedal is depressed and when the turbo generates boost. (See "Intercooler," "Naturally aspirated engine," and "Supercharger")

Understeer: The tendency for a car to resist turning and for the front tires to lose grip in a turn before the rear tires. The result is that the car continues largely in a straight line, its front tires "plowing" rather than rolling. Many cars are designed to understeer when they are driven into a turn too quickly. Understeer is thought to be safer and easier to manage for the average driver than "oversteer," in which the rear wheels skid before the front ones do. Understeer is more prevalent on front-wheel drive cars because of their forward weight bias. (See "Handling," "Oversteer," "Stabilizer bar," and "Suspension")

VIN (vehicle identification number): A series of letters and numbers stamped onto a metal plate attached to the left front top side of the dashboard and visible from the outside of a car through the windshield. The VIN contains such coded information as the vehicle's model year, production series, and place of manufacture.

Wheelbase: The distance between the center of a car's front wheels and the center of its rear wheels.

BEST BUYS

The Auto Editors of CONSUMER GUIDE® have selected Best Buys in ten categories of passenger cars, compact vans, and 4-wheel-drive vehicles. Vehicles are assigned to one of these categories based on their size, price, and market position, so an $8000 subcompact competes against other low-priced small cars, not against a $38,000 luxury car, for example.

At least one Best Buy has been selected in each category. Most categories also include models labeled Recommended that are worthy of attention. Road-test results play a major role in the selections and the editors only consider cars they have driven. Other factors used to select Best Buys among cars include price, cost of ownership, warranties, reputation for reliability and durability, and safety record.

Subcompact Cars

The **Honda Civic** is a Best Buy among small cars because of its brisk acceler-

Honda Civic DX

ation, good fuel economy, quality, and durability. Civic's prices range from under $7000 for a base 3-door hatchback to nearly $12,000 for a loaded sedan, and even more for a 4-wheel-drive station wagon. The mid-level DX models offer plenty of value with prices ranging from $8695 for a 3-door hatchback to $10,370 for a 4-door with automatic transmission. Add another $1000 or so for air conditioning and a stereo, which are dealer-installed options that don't carry manufacturer's suggested retail prices (dealers are free to set their own prices). Civics are among the most expensive subcompacts, but they're also among the most dependable and they have exceptionally high resale value.

The **Toyota Corolla** and similar **Geo Prizm** are Best Buys among small cars because of their commendable reliabil-

Toyota Corolla

Geo Prizm LSi

ity, low maintenance costs, and high fuel economy. The Prizm is built from the same design as the Corolla, but has different exterior styling and is sold through Chevrolet dealers with Geo franchises. Prizms and some Corolla 4-door sedans are built at a General Motors-Toyota plant in California, and we don't see any difference in quality between U.S.-built Corollas and those imported from Japan. Since Corolla and Prizm share mechanical components, they should be equally reliable and durable. The only advantage to buying a Corolla might be higher resale value; the Toyota brand name is much better known than Geo. Corollas start at about $8800 and Prizms are over $10,000, so they're hardly cheap. In today's competitive market, you should be able to buy either a Corolla or a Prizm for less than suggested retail price, with bigger discounts available on Prizm.

The front-drive **Dodge Omni** and identical **Plymouth Horizon** are 12 years

Dodge Omni

old, but despite their age they are Recommended because they offer so much value for the money. This year, they have something new to boast about: They're the lowest priced cars with a driver's-side airbag, an important safety feature that a few years ago was available only on cars costing more than $25,000. Even with the standard airbag, Omni/Horizon is still priced at a modest $6995; with the optional air conditioning, automatic transmission, power steering, and a stereo radio, they're still under $9500, before any price discounts. Chrysler's warranties cover the powertrain for 7 years/70,000 miles and rust for 7 years/100,000 miles.

Compact Cars

Toyota Camry, a Best Buy, is a roomy, comfortable, economical, and reliable compact that offers buyers much to choose from: front-wheel or 4-wheel drive, 4-door sedan or 5-door wagon body styles, 4-cylinder or V-6 engines, and optional anti-lock brakes. Some

Toyota Camry LE V6

Camrys are imported from Japan, but Toyota also builds 200,000 Camry sedans a year at its Kentucky plant. That's good news for consumers, because Toyota has been giving its dealers incentives to discount prices on Camrys to boost sales, and keep the Kentucky plant running at capacity. Quality on the U.S.-built models appears to match that of the Japanese-built models. A Camry can be quite expensive: a top-line LE sedan with front-wheel drive, the V-6, anti-lock brakes, leather upholstery, and a few other options costs about $19,000. However, a Deluxe 4-door with the standard 115-horsepower 4-cylinder engine, automatic transmission, air conditioning, power windows and door locks, stereo, and cruise control is around $15,000, before any discounts. Low maintenance costs and high resale value are two more good reasons to buy a Camry.

Best Buys

Dodge Spirit LE

Plymouth Acclaim LE

The **Dodge Spirit** and nearly identical **Plymouth Acclaim,** introduced for 1989, are the best new models from Chrysler since the minivans came out five years ago. They're solid, comfortable, well-designed, well-built compacts that earn Best Buy honors. Spirit and Acclaim come only as 4-door sedans, but they have ample passenger space and roomy trunks that can be expanded by folding rear seats. We like the optional 3.0-liter V-6 engine best because it's the quietest and smoothest, but could live with either of the available 4-cylinder engines. A loaded Spirit or Acclaim with the V-6, air conditioning, power locks and windows, stereo with cassette player, and other extras will be less than $15,000 at suggested retail. A basic 4-cylinder model with fewer conveniences runs about $12,500. Actual selling prices should be hundreds of dollars lower because of factory incentives and/or dealer discounts. Add Chrysler's 7-year warranties, and you're getting a lot of car for the money.

The **Hyundai Sonata,** a Korean-built, front-drive 4-door, is Recommended because it has a roomy interior, a peppy

Hyundai Sonata GLS

2.4-liter 4-cylinder engine, and low prices. For 1990, a Mitsubishi-designed V-6 engine (the same one used in the Dodge Spirit and Plymouth Acclaim) is optional. The base Sonata starts at around $10,000; a top-line GLS with automatic transmission is about $13,000, and that includes power door locks and windows, cruise control, and a stereo with cassette player. Add air conditioning (about $800) and you're still under $14,000, considerably less than a Toyota Camry LE. With such attractive prices, Sonata stands as a good value among compact family sedans.

Mid-size Cars

The front-drive **Ford Taurus** and similar **Mercury Sable** were introduced four years ago, but no domestic or foreign manufacturer has yet produced a better mid-size, moderately priced family car.

Ford Taurus

Mercury Sable LS

Taurus and Sable remain Best Buys for their good acceleration, capable handling, roomy interiors, sound ergonomics, and reasonable prices. This year, there are two new features that makes us like these cars even more: A driver's-side airbag is standard and anti-lock brakes are optional. These are two safety features we highly recommend, and we're glad to see them available on cars in the $15,000-$19,000 price range. We recommend the 3.0-liter V-6 that's standard on all Sables and most Tauruses, or the 3.8-liter V-6 that's optional in both lines. The 4-cylinder engine standard in lower-priced Taurus models doesn't have enough power for a car this heavy. The front-drive Taurus and Sable are functionally the same and they're simi-

larly priced. The best deals are a Taurus GL or Sable GS with one of Ford's "preferred equipment" packages, which lump popular options into groups at discount prices. In addition, Ford and Mercury have been offering rebates and other sales incentives on these cars the past two years.

Redesigned for 1990, the front-drive **Honda Accord** is larger, more powerful, and more refined than the previous generation, and it is Recommended. Overall length on the new Accord is 185 inches,

Honda Accord LX

which is compact territory, but the wheelbase (distance between front and rear wheels) is 107 inches, which is mid-size territory. Whether you consider it a large compact or a small mid-size car, the new Accord offers ample room for four people and their luggage, plus solid construction, a comfortable ride, competent handling, and reasonably peppy acceleration. The lack of a V-6 engine, anti-lock brakes, or a driver's-side airbag—all of which are available on the Ford Taurus and Mercury Sable—prevent us from naming the Accord a Best Buy. Prices are $700-$800 higher this year, not a huge jump considering the larger dimensions. As with the previous generation, the mid-level LX models, at about $15,000 to $16,000, offer the most value.

Full-size Cars

The **Buick LeSabre, Oldsmobile Eighty Eight Royale,** and **Pontiac Bonneville** are built from the same design and they share Best Buy status in this class. All three have abundant passenger and cargo space, ample comfort,

Buick LeSabre Custom

Oldsmobile Eighty Eight Royale

Pontiac Bonneville SSE

and commendable quality, plus anti-lock brakes are available as a $925 option. A driver's-side airbag also is optional on the Eighty Eight for $850. Anti-lock brakes can help you avoid an accident, while an airbag reduces the chances of injury in case of an accident. All three models use a 165-horsepower 3.8-liter V-6 engine that delivers strong acceleration and good highway fuel economy. Their front-wheel drive design gives them better traction in snow than rear-drive rivals. All three are built with corrosion-resistant galvanized steel, eliminating the need for extra-cost rustproofing. Figure on a sticker price of at least $18,000 and more than $20,000 for plush versions, though dealers should be offering substantial discounts.

The rear-drive **Chevrolet Caprice** will be redesigned and introduced as an early 1991 model next spring, but until then you can still buy the 4-door sedan and 5-door wagon that date to the 1977 model year. Despite its age, the current Caprice is Recommended. Caprice comes with powerful V-8 engines and

1989 Chevrolet Caprice Classic

body-on-frame construction (as opposed to unit-body construction on newer cars). Fuel economy won't be as good as on General Motors' front-drive full-size cars, which use a V-6, but Caprice has room for six people and loads of luggage, and it ranks among the best in insurance statistics for occupant protection and collision damage. Best of all, the base Caprice sedan starts at less than $15,000, and that includes air conditioning. A fully equipped base or Classic 4-door sedan should still be less than $18,000, less than many mid-size cars, even some compacts. Caprice's low base prices give it a significant cost edge over the Ford LTD Crown Victoria and Mercury Grand Marquis. This year the Ford and Mercury come with a standard driver's-side airbag; Caprice makes do with automatic front shoulder belts.

Those who want a traditional full-size American family car with rear-wheel drive and body-on-frame construction should give strong consideration to the **Ford LTD Crown Victoria** and the

Ford LTD Crown Victoria

Mercury Grand Marquis

nearly identical **Mercury Grand Marquis,** which are Recommended. These cars historically rank among the best in insurance statistics for occupant protection and collision damage, and this year a driver's-side airbag is standard, providing even better injury protection. Both are available as 4-door sedans or 5-door wagons. A 150-horsepower 5.0-liter V-8 and 4-speed overdrive automatic transmission are standard. The engine delivers brisk acceleration with commendable refinement, though fuel consumption is higher than on General Motors' front-

drive full-size cars. Prices start at nearly $18,000 and can get up to $22,000 or so for either brand if you want more comfort and convenience features. Dealers should be selling these cars for well below suggested retail price.

Premium Coupes

With its reliable performance, generous amount of standard equipment, high quality, and good resale value the Honda-made **Acura Legend** remains a Best Buy among premium-priced coupes. All Legends come with a driver's-side airbag and the L and LS

Acura Legend Coupe LS

models also have anti-lock brakes standard. Base models start around $25,000 and the top-line LS goes for around $31,000. Because these cars are quite popular, most Acura dealers have been stingy about discounting prices. However, new competition from Lexus and Infiniti, the luxury-car divisions of Toyota and Nissan, respectively, should encourage Acura dealers to be more open to bargaining. Legend has a reputation for requiring little maintenance, so it won't cost an arm and a leg to keep it on the road. When you're ready to sell, there should be plenty of eager buyers ready to pay top dollar.

The front-drive **Cadillac Eldorado,** which is Recommended, offers satisfying acceleration, a generous helping of standard equipment (including a driver's-

Cadillac Eldorado

side airbag), luxurious accommodations, and impressive assembly quality. Anti-lock brakes are a $925 option that we highly recommend. Cadillac has made significant improvements in its en-

Best Buys

gines and quality control in recent years, a necessary step to compete in the luxury-car league. This year Eldorado's 4.5-liter V-8 has 180 horsepower, 35 more than last year's, for stronger acceleration and highway passing with little sacrifice in fuel economy. Eldorado's base price is nearly $29,000, and you can still add $2000-$3000 in options. Eldorado has been selling at large discounts, so you should be able to buy one for much less than suggested retail.

Also Recommended is the **Lincoln Mark VII,** a rear-drive luxury coupe with substantial power, a full load of luxury equipment, and fine quality. For 1990, a driver's-side airbag is standard equipment. The Mark VII comes two ways: the Bill Blass Designer Series and the sportier LSC; both use a 225-horsepower 5.0-liter V-8 that delivers outstanding acceleration and a smooth,

Lincoln Mark VII LSC

steady power flow. Standard anti-lock brakes provide commendable stopping ability. Base price for both is a little over $29,000 and since most everything is standard, there are only a few big-ticket options. The Mark VII hasn't been a hot seller recently, so you'll probably be able to buy one at an attractive discount.

Premium Sedans

The **Acura Legend** debuted in 1986 as the first $20,000 Japanese car sold in the U.S. Prices now start in the $23,000-$24,000 range for the base model and a top-line LS is just over $30,000, but we still rate Legend as a Best Buy in

Acura Legend Sedan LS

this class. Legend has a sporting personality that makes it a fine alternative to more expensive European luxury sedans. It is powered by a smooth, eager 2.7-liter V-6 engine that provides quick acceleration and relaxed cruising. A driver's-side airbag is standard on all Legends and anti-lock brakes are standard on L and LS versions. Legend has compiled an admirable record of reliability and durability in its four years, so trips to the dealer for repairs or service should be infrequent. Legend also commands high resale value, further lowering ownership costs.

The **Cadillac De Ville** and **Fleetwood** are front-drive sedans that differ only in the Fleetwood's more lavish standard furnishings and higher price. Both are

Cadillac Sedan de Ville

Cadillac Fleetwood

Best Buys. The 1990 models boast a 180-horsepower V-8 engine (25 more than last year) that moves these luxury cars with authority, and with commendable smoothness and refinement. De Ville/Fleetwood also boasts bountiful interior space (even back-seat passengers can stretch out), wide doorways for easy entry/exit, and ample cargo capacity. Cadillacs we've tested recently have been well assembled and virtually trouble-free. The De Ville starts at nearly $28,000, the Fleetwood at $33,000. Both have a driver's-side airbag as standard equipment; anti-lock brakes are standard on the Fleetwood and a $925 option on the De Ville. You can save money by buying a De Ville with the anti-lock brakes.

The **Infiniti Q45,** Nissan's new premium sedan entry, is Recommended. The Q45,

Infiniti Q45

the flagship of the new Infiniti division, is a rear-drive 4-door sedan powered by a 278-horsepower 4.5-liter V-8 engine. Base price is $38,000 and the lengthy standard equipment list includes a driver's-side airbag and anti-lock brakes. The engine is quiet, silky, and responsive. The ride is smooth and stable, while handling and braking are quite good. The Q45 has more of a European character than the Lexus LS 400 and shapes up as a good BMW and Mercedes alternative, especially at its price. It's also a strong challenger to the less-expensive Acura Legend and domestic cars such as the Cadillac De Ville/Fleetwood.

The **Lexus LS 400,** Toyota's new entry in the luxury-sedan league, also is Recommended. The LS 400 is the top model in the Lexus Division, carrying a $35,000 base price. The LS 400 is a

Lexus LS 400

rear-drive sedan with a 250-horsepower 4.0-liter V-8 and a 4-speed automatic transmission. Standard equipment includes anti-lock disc brakes and a driver's-side airbag; a traction-control system is optional. The LS 400 is one of the quietest cars we've driven and its powerful V-8 engine is incredibly smooth. The ride is stable at high speed yet absorbent over tar strips and bumps. There are several options available for the LS 400 that can push the price over $40,000, considerably higher than a Legend LS, but still cheaper than most BMW or Mercedes models. The LS 400 is an extremely rewarding car that provides comfortable, virtually vice-free motoring.

The **Nissan Maxima,** a front-drive 4-door redesigned for 1989, is a competent, pleasant, and accommodating sedan that is Recommended as a bargain among premium sedans. Maxima's base prices run from about $18,000 for the GXE to $20,000 for the sportier SE,

Nissan Maxima SE

handily undercutting most rivals. Both use a 160-horsepower V-6 engine that provides smooth, brisk acceleration. We prefer the SE for its better handling and 4-wheel disc brakes; you also have to buy the SE to get the optional anti-lock brakes ($995), which we highly recommend. Maxima offers a clean, modern design, more than adequate room, and quality workmanship. And, the price is right.

Sports Coupes

The Best Buy in this category is sold under three different brand names—**Eagle Talon, Mitsubishi Eclipse,** and **Plymouth Laser**—but there are only minor differences among them. We're

Eagle Talon TSi AWD

Mitsubishi Eclipse

Plymouth Laser RS

highly impressed by their intelligent design, sporty performance, and reasonable prices. All three are built by Diamond-Star Motors, a partnership between Mitsubishi and Chrysler. All three have front-wheel-drive models; in addition, Eclipse and Talon are available with permanently engaged 4-wheel drive. All models come with capable handling, a purposeful control layout, and long warranties. The 4WD Talon TSi and Eclipse GSX models have outstanding traction, sticking like glue even to wet roads, but they come only with a turbocharged engine that is not available with automatic transmission. Prices start at just under $11,000 and a fully-equipped front-drive version should be less than $15,000, no matter which brand you choose.

The 1990 **Acura Integra,** built from a new front-wheel-drive design that is larger than the 1986-89 original, is Recommended. It is available as a 3-door hatchback coupe and a new 4-door

Acura Integra GS

Acura Integra LS

sedan (instead of a 5-door hatchback). The new Integra feels more substantial than the old and has a more supple ride. In addition, anti-lock brakes are standard on the top-line GS models. The new Integras lack the frisky eagerness of the old models and rivals such as the Mitsubishi Eclipse, but they're refined, well-made sporty cars that should be reliable and have good resale value. Base models start in the $12,000-$13,000 range and the GS models top out at $17,000 or so.

Sports & GT Cars

The **Mazda Miata** became the star of the automotive world when it debuted as an early 1990 model. Many see it as the rebirth of the classic sports car: two seats, attractive styling, a convertible

Mazda Miata

top, spirited performance, and road-hugging handling. All that for a modest base price of $13,800, making it a Best Buy. If only you could buy a Miata for that little. Mazda dealers were reportedly getting $5000 or more above Miata's suggested retail price because so many eager buyers were clamoring to buy this new sports car. Only 40,000 Miatas are scheduled to be sent to the U.S. during 1990, so demand might continue to exceed supply. The rear-drive Miata comes with a 116-horsepower dual-cam 1.6-liter engine, and a 5-speed manual transmission. An automatic transmission is not available. Standard features include a driver's-side airbag and a manual folding top that can be raised or lowered by one person from inside the car. Miata is everything you ever liked about British and Italian roadsters of yore, but with none of the hassle. It should be reliable for many miles.

The **Ford Mustang GT,** which is Recommended, is a classic American muscle car that comes with a 225-horsepower 5.0-liter V-8, a driver's-side airbag, power steering, and a stereo radio for a low base price of $13,986. Even with air conditioning, power windows and locks, premium sound system, and

Ford Mustang GT

other amenities, a GT hatchback won't be much more than $16,000. A GT convertible is considerably more expensive at $18,805 base, but there aren't that many options available to push the price much higher. It's hard to find better value in a high-performance car. You can get the same 225-horsepower engine on the less expensive Mustang LX 5.0L, but the GT commands higher resale value and has greater potential for becoming a collectible car in the future.

Dodge Caravan ES

Plymouth Grand Voyager LE

Compact Vans

The **Dodge Caravan** and **Plymouth Voyager,** Chrysler's nearly identical minivans, are still the Best Buys in this class, despite new rivals from domestic and Japanese companies. They come in two sizes: 176-inch body/112-inch wheelbase and Grand Caravan/Grand Voyager with an extended 190-inch body/119-inch wheelbase. Two 4-cylinder engines and two V-6s are available. We recommend the V-6s; a 142-horsepower Mitsubishi-built 3.0-liter engine that's optional on the short-wheelbase models and a new 150-horsepower Chrysler-built 3.3-liter engine standard on the Grand models. The front-drive Caravan and Voyager have more traction in snow than rear-drive vans, and are more like cars than trucks to drive. For a short-wheelbase model with the V-6, air conditioning, and other popular options, plan on spending $17,000 or more. If you want a Grand model, brace yourself for a $20,000 sticker price, and don't expect a big discount from most dealers. These are still the most popular minivans, so dealers don't have to cut their prices to generate business. A luxury version of the Caravan/Voyager is now sold as the Chrysler Town & Country (base price is $25,000), with leather upholstery and other amenities, but no mechanical differences.

The **Mazda MPV** (Multi-Purpose Vehicle) is Recommended as a good choice in a compact passenger van. Unlike the other rear-drive compact vans, the MPV is quite car-like to drive, much like the Caravan/Voyager. A 4-wheel-drive model with a convenient, on-demand 4WD system also is available. The MPV's most unusual feature is its conventional, swing-out rear side door, instead of the sliding type found on most vans. A 121-

Mazda MPV

horsepower 2.6-liter 4-cylinder engine is standard on rear-drive MPVs, but we prefer the optional 150-horsepower 3.0-liter V-6, which generates sufficient power to safely merge with traffic and haul a full load of people and/or cargo. The V-6 is standard on the 4WD model. Seats for five are standard and seats for seven are optional. A rear-drive MPV with the V-6 should be $16,000-$18,000, while a 4WD model will run $19,000-$21,000.

4WD Vehicles

The **Jeep Cherokee** is the Best Buy in this class because it does more things than any competitor, and does them quite well. To start, Cherokee comes in

Jeep Cherokee Laredo

Jeep Cherokee Sport

3- and 5-door body styles, while many competitors (including Ford and Chevrolet) are just now adding 5-door models. Jeep offers the most powerful engine in this class, a 177-horsepower 4.0-liter 6-cylinder, and makes it available with two 4-wheel-drive systems. Both 4WD systems offer true shift-on-the-fly, meaning you can change in or out of 4WD while the vehicle is moving. Some Japanese rivals still don't offer that fea-

ture. And, Jeep's Selec-Trac 4WD system can be left permanently engaged, whether the roads are dry or wet. No rival has a similar feature. Jeep also offers an anti-lock brake system that works on all four wheels; most rivals have anti-lock systems that work only on the rear wheels. Jeep charges a high price for these features. The cheapest Cherokee 5-door with 4WD is nearly $16,000; a top-line Cherokee Limited with the optional anti-lock brakes is $27,000. Even if you go easy on the options, you'll be lucky to get out the door in a 4WD Cherokee for less than $18,000. A sluggish market and intense competition forced Jeep to offer rebates and other discounts on the 5-door models during 1989, and there are signs that sales incentives will continue in 1990. If you can live with a less-convenient 3-door model, you'll save more money.

The **Toyota 4Runner** was redesigned last spring and is a much improved vehicle, earning Recommended status. It is much quieter now and has a softer, comfortable ride for a more carlike feel. It also is available with four side doors, not just two, so it is much more convenient as an everyday family vehicle. A rear anti-lock braking system is standard on V-6-powered 4Runners and op-

Toyota 4Runner

tional on 4-cylinder models. We recommend the 150-horsepower V-6 over the 116-horsepower 4-cylinder, not only because it has more muscle, but also because it's so much quieter and more refined. V-6 4×4 models come with 4WDemand, a system that allows changing in or out of 4WD on the move at speeds up to 50 mph. 4WDemand is optional on some 4-cylinder models, but other 4Runners have to be stopped to engage or disengage 4WD. A 4Runner with the V-6, automatic transmission, 4WDemand system, and air conditioning will cost more than $20,000, in the same price range as a Jeep Cherokee. Cherokee has more horsepower, a choice of two convenient 4WD systems, and 4-wheel anti-lock brakes, but the 4Runner has a reputation for being more reliable.

Buying Guide

Acura Integra

Acura Integra LS

What's New

The 1990 Integra, which went on sale in May, is built from a new design that is visibly larger than the 1986-89 original and shares none of its major components. Model choices comprise a returning hatchback coupe and a new notchback 4-door instead of a 5-door hatchback. The Integra coupe has grown 3.9 inches in wheelbase, 4.2 inches longer overall, and 1.8 inches in width. Curb weights are up 190-235 pounds depending on model. As before, a dual-cam 4-cylinder engine drives the front wheels, but displacement is boosted from 1.6 to 1.8 liters and horsepower increases from 118 to 130. A 5-speed manual transmission remains standard; the optional 4-speed overdrive automatic now features a Sport mode with higher shift points, as on the larger Legend. All-disc brakes and power rack-and-pinion steering also continue, but the brakes are larger and steering assist now varies with road speed. A Honda-designed anti-lock brake system (ABS) is available only on GS models (as standard). Motorized front shoulder belts are standard on all Integras.

For

- Acceleration (5-speed)
- Handling/roadholding
- Anti-lock brakes (GS)

Against

- Acceleration (automatic)
- Rear-seat room (hatchback)

Summary

Integra's new 1.8-liter engine provides brisk pickup, at least with manual shift. We timed a 5-speed GS coupe at 9.0 seconds 0-60 mph. Informal clockings show the automatic sedan at 11.5 seconds—hardly great for a car with sporting intentions. Steep uphill grades betray a lack of low-end torque, and speed tails off noticeably unless you drop down a gear or two. The new Integra feels more substantial than the old and suffers less road noise. A small increase in suspension travel and improved damping make for a smoother, more supple ride than on earlier Integras. The new model has minimal body roll and impressive grip in turns, yet it doesn't feel quite as agile or responsive as the old one. The GS's standard ABS did its job in our test regimen of 10 simulated 60-mph panic stops, the coupe averaging a commendable 116 feet. Other models also have commendable stopping ability. The larger new Integras are roomier, but not everywhere. Honda's own tape measure says both body styles have less rear shoul-

der room than before, while the coupe loses almost 3/4-inch of rear leg room. Up front, the new models offer about two inches more leg room and an inch more head room. The sedan seats four adults without cramping, while the coupe is more of a 2+2, its back seat being best left to kids and cargo. The new Integras leave us a bit cold because they lack the frisky eagerness of the old models and rivals such as the Mitsubishi Eclipse. Still, they're refined, competent, well-made compacts that should be reliable and have good resale value.

Specifications

	3-door hatchback	4-door notchback
Wheelbase, in.	100.4	102.4
Overall length, in.	172.9	176.5
Overall width, in.	67.4	67.4
Overall height, in.	52.2	52.8
Turn diameter, ft.	33.1	33.7
Curb weight, lbs.	2544	2579
Cargo vol., cu. ft.	16.2	11.2
Fuel capacity, gals.	13.2	13.2
Seating capacity	5	5
Front headroom, in.	38.5	38.7
Front shoulder room, in.	52.7	52.5
Front legroom, max., in.	43.6	43.5
Rear headroom, in.	34.7	36.8
Rear shoulder room, in.	52.0	52.4
Rear legroom, min., in.	28.6	31.7

Powertrain layout: transverse front engine/front-wheel drive.

Engines

	dohc I-4
Size, liters/cu. in.	1.8/112
Fuel delivery	PFI
Horsepower @ rpm	130 @ 6000
Torque (lbs./ft.) @ rpm	121 @ 5000
Availability	S

EPA city/highway mpg

5-speed OD manual	24/28
4-speed OD automatic	23/27

Prices

Acura Integra	Retail Price	Dealer Invoice	Low Price
RS 3-door hatchback, 5-speed	$11950	$10038	$10967
RS 3-door hatchback, automatic	12675	10647	11632
LS 3-door hatchback, 5-speed	13725	11529	12596
LS 3-door hatchback, automatic	14450	12138	13261
GS 3-door hatchback, 5-speed	15825	13293	14523
GS 3-door hatchback, automatic	16550	13902	15188
RS 4-door notchback, 5-speed	12850	10794	11793
RS 4-door notchback, automatic	13575	11403	12458
LS 4-door notchback, 5-speed	14545	12217	13348
LS 4-door notchback, automatic	15270	12826	14013
GS 4-door notchback, 5-speed	15950	13398	14637
GS 4-door notchback, automatic	16675	14007	15303
Destination charge	295	295	295

> **KEY: ohv** = overhead valve; **ohc** = overhead cam; **dohc** = double overhead cam; **I** = inline cylinders; **V** = cylinders in V configuration; **flat** = horizontally opposed cylinders; **bbl.** = barrel (carburetor); **PFI** = port (multi-point) fuel injection; **TBI** = throttle-body (single-point) fuel injection; **rpm** = revolutions per minute; **OD** = overdrive transmission; **S** = standard; **O** = optional; **NA** = not available.

Prices are accurate at time of printing; subject to manufacturer's change.

Acura

Standard equipment:

RS: 1.8-liter DOHC 16-valve PFI 4-cylinder engine, 5- speed manual or 4-speed automatic transmission, power steering, 4-wheel disc brakes, reclining front bucket seats, split folding rear seat, rear shoulder belts, tinted glass, remote fuel door and hatch releases, dual manual mirrors, fog lights, rear defogger, rear wiper/washer (hatchback), tachometer, coolant temperature gauge, tilt steering column, intermittent wipers, door pockets, cargo cover (hatchback), 195/60R14 tires. **LS** adds: power mirrors, power locks (4-door), power sunroof (hatchback), AM/FM cassette with power antenna, driver's seat lumbar support adjustment, cruise control, map lights (hatchback). **GS** adds: anti-lock braking system, power windows, map lights, adjustable side bolsters on driver's seat, alloy wheels.

OPTIONS are available as dealer-installed accessories.

Acura Legend

Acura Legend Coupe LS

What's New

The Legend Coupe and Sedan are carried over with minor changes for what probably will be their final season in this form. The Sedan was introduced for 1986 when American Honda launched its Acura division and the Coupe arrived about a year later. New versions of both are expected for 1991, perhaps with a V-8 engine. Changes for 1990 include a restyled grille for Coupes and a rear spoiler for the LS Coupe; burled-walnut center console trim for the flagship LS Sedan and Coupe; and new front seats for all models. All Legends have front-wheel drive and a 160-horsepower 2.7-liter V-6 engine. A driver's-side airbag is standard on all models and anti-lock brakes are standard on L and LS models.

For

- Acceleration
- Handling/roadholding
- Airbag
- Anti-lock brakes
- Ride

Against

- Driveability (automatic transmission)
- Rear seat room (Coupe)

KEY: ohv = overhead valve; **ohc** = overhead cam; **dohc** = double overhead cam; **I** = inline cylinders; **V** = cylinders in V configuration; **flat** = horizontally opposed cylinders; **bbl.** = barrel (carburetor); **PFI** = port (multi-point) fuel injection; **TBI** = throttle-body (single-point) fuel injection; **rpm** = revolutions per minute; **OD** = overdrive transmission; **S** = standard; **O** = optional; **NA** = not available.

Summary

Legend has reigned for four years as the most expensive, most prestigious Japanese car sold in the U.S., but for 1990 it has been surpassed in price, performance, and panache by two newcomers: Infiniti Q45 and Lexus LS 400, the V-8-powered flagships of the new luxury-car divisions from Nissan and Toyota, respectively. The success of the Legend in particular and Acura in general helped inspire Nissan and Toyota to start their own luxury divisions. Acura expects to sell 150,000 cars in the U.S. in 1989, as many as Mercedes-Benz and BMW combined, though more than half of Acura's sales are of the under-$20,000 Integra, not the over-$20,000 Legend. Despite the new competition from Infiniti and Lexus, Legend still impresses us as an excellent all-around car, whether you want two doors or four. Acceleration is brisk from the smooth, eager V-6 engine; the ride is comfortable and the handling is competent; the anti-lock brakes on the L and LS provide short, safe stops; there's ample room inside for four adults; and assembly quality is top-notch. In addition, Acura has consistently scored at the top of customer-satisfaction surveys; Legend commands high resale value; and service and maintenance costs are low. All that makes Legend hard to beat, especially when the most expensive models top out at just over $30,000. Infiniti and Lexus offer V-8 engines and posher furnishings, while European rivals such as Mercedes and BMW offer greater prestige. Legend offers more value for less money.

Specifications

	2-door notchback	4-door notchback
Wheelbase, in.	106.5	108.7
Overall length, in.	188.0	190.6
Overall width, in.	68.7	68.9
Overall height, in.	53.9	54.7
Turn diameter, ft.	36.4	37.1
Curb weight, lbs.	3139	3170
Cargo vol., cu. ft.	14.7	16.6
Fuel capacity, gals.	18.0	18.0
Seating capacity	5	5
Front headroom, in.	37.2	38.4
Front shoulder room, in.	55.4	55.7
Front legroom, max., in.	42.9	43.4
Rear headroom, in.	36.3	36.5
Rear shoulder room, in.	54.3	55.4
Rear legroom, min., in.	30.3	34.5

Powertrain layout: transverse front engine/front-wheel drive.

Engines	ohc V-6
Size, liters/cu. in.	2.7/163
Fuel delivery	PFI
Horsepower @ rpm	160 @ 5900
Torque (lbs./ft.) @ rpm	162 @ 4500
Availability	S

EPA city/highway mpg

5-speed OD manual	19/24
4-speed OD automatic	18/22

Prices

Acura Legend	Retail Price	Dealer Invoice	Low Price
Sedan			
4-door notchback, 5-speed	$22600	$18532	$19532
4-door notchback, automatic	23400	19188	20188

	Retail Price	Dealer Invoice	Low Price
4-door notchback w/sunroof, 5-speed . . .	23485	19257	20257
4-door notchback w/sunroof, automatic . .	24285	19913	20913
L 4-door notchback, 5-speed	25900	21238	22238
L 4-door notchback, automatic	26700	21894	22894
L w/leather trim, 5-speed	26850	22017	23017
L w/leather trim, automatic	27650	22673	23673
LS 4-door notchback, 5-speed	29610	24280	25280
LS 4-door notchback, automatic	30410	24935	25935
Coupe			
2-door notchback, 5-speed	24760	20303	22532
2-door notchback, automatic	25560	20959	23260
L 2-door notchback, 5-speed	27325	22406	24866
L 2-door notchback, automatic	28125	23062	25594
L w/leather trim, 5-speed	28275	23185	25730
L w/leather trim, automatic	29075	23841	26458
LS 2-door notchback, 5-speed	30690	25195	27943
LS 2-door notchback, automatic	31490	25821	28656
Destination charge	295	295	295

Standard equipment:

Sedan: 2.7-liter SOHC 24-valve PFI V-6, 5-speed manual or 4-speed automatic transmission, power steering, 4-wheel disc brakes, driver's-side airbag, air conditioning, cruise control, power windows and locks, tilt steering column, remote fuel door and trunk releases, door pockets, lighted visor mirrors, rear defogger, map lights, illuminated entry system, reclining front bucket seats, moquette upholstery, driver's seat lumbar and thigh support adjustments, rear armrest, AM/FM ST ET cassette with EQ and power diversity antenna, maintenance interval reminder, tachometer, coolant temperature gauge, trip odometer, intermittent wipers, Michelin MXV 205/60HR14 tires on alloy wheels; coupe has power sunroof, V-rated tires. **L sedan** has: anti-lock braking system, memory power driver's seat, security system; coupe adds power driver's seat, heated mirrors, driver's seatbelt presenter, driver's information center. **LS** has: automatic climate control, power passenger seat, Bose sound system, driver's information center.

OPTIONS are available as dealer-installed accessories.

Acura NS-X

Acura NS-X prototype

What's New

Honda was the first Japanese car company to break the $20,000 price barrier in the U.S. with the Acura Legend luxury sedan. Now, it intends to be the first to crack $50,000 when it unveils a 2-seat, mid-engine sports car, code-named NS-X. The NS-X is scheduled to go on sale late next spring (under a different name) as an early 1991 model with a base price between $50,000 and $60,000. Lightweight aluminum is being used for the body, the double-wishbone suspension, and the block and cylinder heads on the engine, a new 3.0-liter V-6 with dual overhead cams, four valves per cylinder, and Honda's variable valve timing. Variable valve timing allows

stronger low-end performance without sacrificing top-end speed. Horsepower is projected at 270 and top speed at more than 155 mph. Acura estimates the NS-X will hit 60 mph in less than six seconds and do the quarter-mile sprint in less than 14. The NS-X's engine is mounted transversely behind the seats and drives the rear wheels. Other technical features include 4-wheel independent suspension, 4-wheel ventilated disc brakes with anti-lock control, and traction control. The traction-control system uses the anti-lock sensors at the rear wheels to detect wheelspin under acceleration, restricting the amount of power as needed to maintain traction. Initially, only a 5-speed manual transmission will be available; an automatic will be added later. A driver's-side airbag will be standard. So far, Honda has shown only hardtop prototypes, though the company says a convertible is possible in the future. All prototypes shown thus far have had black roofs. NS-X is intended to be a limited-production sports car, not a mass-market vehicle like the other Acuras. Production is pegged at a maximum of 5000 units per year, with 3000 of those destined for the U.S. We have not driven the NS-X, so we cannot comment on its performance.

Specifications

	2-door notchback
Wheelbase, in.	98.4
Overall length, in.	169.9
Overall width, in.	70.9
Overall height, in.	46.1
Turn diameter, ft.	38.1
Curb weight, lbs.	2850
Cargo vol., cu. ft.	8.0
Fuel capacity, gals.	18.5
Seating capacity	2
Front headroom, in.	NA
Front shoulder room, in.	NA
Front legroom, max., in.	NA
Rear headroom, in.	—
Rear shoulder room, in.	—
Rear legroom, min., in.	—

Powertrain layout: transverse mid engine/rear-wheel drive.

Engines	dohc V-6
Size, liters/cu. in.	3.0/182
Fuel delivery	PFI
Horsepower @ rpm	270 @ 7300
Torque (lbs./ft.) @ rpm	210 @ 5500
Availability	S
EPA city/highway mpg	
5-speed OD manual	NA

Prices not available at time of publication.

Alfa Romeo Spider and 164
What's New

Alfa Romeo, struggling to bolster its presence in the U.S., has two major changes planned for 1990. First, the front-drive 164 sedan is scheduled to go on sale next March as a replacement for the rear-drive Milano, which stays home in Italy this year. Second, Alfa's dealer network will be expanded through an agreement between Chrysler Motors and Fiat, which owns Alfa Romeo. About 300 Chrysler-Plymouth dealers who cur-

Alfa Romeo 164 (European model)

rently sell the Italian-made Chrysler's TC by Maserati will be able to sell and service the 164 as an Alfa Romeo model. The 164 is a 4-door notchback sedan derived from the same front-drive platform as the Saab 9000. Fiat and Lancia also build cars from this platform, the result of a design collaboration among these European car companies. The 164's wheelbase and overall length are slightly shorter than the Saab 9000's. Base engine for the 164 will be a 188-horsepower 3.0-liter V-6, previously offered in the Milano. A sport version of the 164 will have a dual-cam, 24-valve version of the V-6 making 210 to 220 horsepower. A driver's-side airbag will be standard on all 164s; anti-lock brakes will probably be standard as well. Also due next spring, about a month after the 164 arrives, is a facelifted Spider, Alfa's 2-seat sports car from the mid-1960s. The revised Spider will have new front and rear sheetmetal, integrated bumpers, and a driver's-side airbag standard. Until then, the Spider returns in three price ranges: Graduate, Veloce, and Quadrifoglio. All versions gain three horsepower from new electronic engine controls. Since the 164 will be a 1991 model, the Spider will be Alfa's only 1990 U.S. model.

For

● Handling

Against

● Driving position/control layout   ● Noise

Summary

We haven't driven the 164, so our comments here pertain only to the Spider, which is more than 20 years old—and shows it. For many years there were few alternatives to the Spider if you wanted a 2-seat, open sports car. For a few years, there were no alternatives, at least if you wanted to spend less than $25,000. Now, however, there's the Mazda Miata, a much more modern sports car that offers better overall performance, a more comfortable ride, and much better workmanship than the Spider. To top it off, the Miata is a few thousand dollars cheaper, using suggested retail prices

for comparison. High demand for the Miata and minimal demand for the Spider mean that you can probably buy the Alfa for less, but you should dig deeper into your pockets and pay more to get a Miata if this is the kind of car you want. In return, you'll get better quality and reliability, and higher resale value. A new Spider is scheduled to arrive in 1993; until then, look elsewhere.

Specifications

	Spider 2-door conv.	164 4-door notchback[1]
Wheelbase, in.	88.6	104.7
Overall length, in.	168.8	179.3
Overall width, in.	64.1	69.3
Overall height, in.	48.8	55.1
Turn diameter, ft.	34.5	35.4
Curb weight, lbs.	2550	2860
Cargo vol., cu. ft.	NA	NA
Fuel capacity, gals.	12.2	18.2
Seating capacity	2	5
Front headroom, in.	NA	38.2
Front shoulder room, in.	NA	NA
Front legroom, max., in.	NA	NA
Rear headroom, in.	—	36.6
Rear shoulder room, in.	—	NA
Rear legroom, min., in.	—	NA

1. European model.

Powertrain layout, Spider: longitudinal front engine/rear-wheel drive; **164:** transverse front engine/front-wheel drive.

Engines

	dohc I-4	ohc V-6
Size, liters/cu. in.	2.0/120	3.0/182
Fuel delivery	PFI	PFI
Horsepower @ rpm	120 @ 5800	188 @ 5800
Torque (lbs./ft.) @ rpm	117 @ 2600	181 @ 3000
Availability	S[1]	S[2]

EPA city/highway mpg
5-speed OD manual	23/30	NA
4-speed OD automatic	—	NA

1. Spider   2. 164

Prices

Alfa Romeo Spider	Retail Price	Dealer Invoice	Low Price
Graduate 2-door convertible	$16950	—	—
Veloce 2-door convertible	20950	—	—
Quadrifoglio 2-door convertible	23950	—	—
Destination charge	375	—	—

Dealer invoice and low price not available at time of publication.

Standard equipment:

Graduate: 2.0-liter DOHC PFI 4-cylinder engine, 5-speed manual transmission, 4-wheel disc brakes, limited-slip differential, tachometer, coolant temperature and oil pressure gauges, bronze tinted glass, power mirrors, mahogany steering wheel rim, intermittent wipers, reclining front bucket seats, remote decklid release, 185/70R14 tires. **Veloce** adds: power windows, AM/FM cassette, leather upholstery, alloy wheels. **Quadrifoglio** adds: air conditioning, hardtop with rear defogger, power antenna, leather-wrapped steering wheel, 195/60HR15 tires on alloy wheels.

Optional equipment:

Air conditioning, Graduate & Veloce	995	—	—
AM/FM cassette, Graduate	645	—	—
Metallic paint	275	—	—

KEY: **ohv** = overhead valve; **ohc** = overhead cam; **dohc** = double overhead cam; **I** = inline cylinders; **V** = cylinders in V configuration; **flat** = horizontally opposed cylinders; **bbl.** = barrel (carburetor); **PFI** = port (multi-point) fuel injection; **TBI** = throttle-body (single-point) fuel injection; **rpm** = revolutions per minute; **OD** = overdrive transmission; **S** = standard; **O** = optional; **NA** = not available.

Audi V8 Quattro

Audi V8 Quattro

What's New

The $47,450 V8 Quattro is Audi's new high-performance luxury sedan that challenges Mercedes, BMW, and Jaguar. On sale since July, the V8 Quattro has a 240-horsepower 3.6-liter aluminum engine with dual overhead cams and four valves per cylinder. Power is routed through a 4-speed overdrive automatic transmission to a permanently engaged all-wheel-drive (AWD) system. Normally, power is split 50/50 between front and rear. When there's wheel slip, more power is delivered to the axle with the most traction; in extreme situations all the power is temporarily sent to either the front or rear. This is the first Audi Quattro with an automatic transmission; it has three shift modes: E for higher fuel economy; S for sportier performance; and M for manual. A standard automatic shift lock requires that the brake pedal be applied to shift into a drive gear. Anti-lock brakes, a driver's-side airbag, 2-sided galvanized steel body panels, leather upholstery, cellular telephone, and a Bose sound system are among the standard features. While the V8's exterior styling resembles that of the Audi 100/200 (formerly called 5000), only the roof and front doors are shared.

For

- Handling/roadholding • Anti-lock brakes • Airbag
- Room/comfort

Against

- Ride • Road noise • Fuel economy

Summary

The V8 Quattro has some impressive qualities: Outstanding traction from its sophisticated all-wheel drive system; amazing stability at high speeds; precise, responsive steering; and strong brakes with anti-lock control. The V8 Quattro also has some qualities that may turn off prospective buyers. One is a stiff ride, the product of a firm suspension and wide Z-rated tires (designed for speeds over 149 mph). While this combination provides reassuring stability at ultra high speeds, it also produces too much impact harshness on bumpy roads taken at legal speeds. The tires also generate considerable noise, which is tiresome on long drives. Audi's dual-cam engine delivers strong, prompt passing response on the highway, but lacks brisk off-the-line acceleration, especially if the transmission is in the "economy" mode. We found around-town response better in the "sport" mode, but were annoyed that the

transmission reverted to "economy" every time the engine was started. Highway fuel economy is disappointing; we didn't even reach 22 mpg. The V8's well-designed interior offers plenty of room and comes with nearly every convenience feature known to man as standard equipment (a compact disc player is the main omission). On top of that, Audi's warranties cover scheduled maintenance for the first three years/ 50,000 miles. While all that sounds good, we think the new Lexus LS 400 and Infiniti Q45 are more tuned to American driving tastes, and are better values for the money.

Specifications

	4-door notchback
Wheelbase, in.	106.4
Overall length, in.	191.9
Overall width, in.	71.4
Overall height, in.	55.9
Turn diameter, ft.	34.4
Curb weight, lbs.	3946
Cargo vol., cu. ft.	17.0
Fuel capacity, gals.	21.1
Seating capacity	5
Front headroom, in.	37.8
Front shoulder room, in.	56.8
Front legroom, max., in.	41.7
Rear headroom, in.	37.5
Rear shoulder room, in.	55.3
Rear legroom, min., in.	35.0

Powertrain layout: longitudinal front engine/permanent 4-wheel drive.

Engines

	dohc V-8
Size, liters/cu. in.	3.6/217
Fuel delivery	PFI
Horsepower @ rpm	240 @ 5800
Torque (lbs./ft.) @ rpm	245 @ 4000
Availability	S

EPA city/highway mpg

4-speed OD automatic	14/18

Prices

Audi V8 Quattro	Retail Price	Dealer Invoice	Low Price
4-door notchback	$47450	—	—
Destination charge	335	—	—

Dealer invoice and low price not available at time of publication.

Standard equipment:

3.6-liter DOHC 32-valve PFI V-8, 4-speed automatic transmission, permanent 4-wheel drive, anti-lock 4-wheel disc brakes, power steering, driver's-side airbag, leather power front bucket seats, heatable front seats, automatic climate control, cruise control, power windows and locks, heated power mirrors, power sunroof, Audi-Bose AM/FM cassette with diversity antenna, tachometer, gauges (coolant temperature, oil pressure and temperature), trip odometer, 6-function trip computer, 10-function Auto Check System, cellular phone, headlamp washers, rear shoulder belts, seatback pockets, leather-wrapped steering wheel and shift knob, reading lamps, lighted visor mirrors, ski sack, anti-theft alarm, tinted glass, rear defogger, heated windshield washer nozzles and door locks, intermittent wipers, 215/60ZR15 tires on alloy wheels.

Optional equipment:

Pearl White metallic paint	450	—	—

Prices are accurate at time of printing; subject to manufacturer's change.

Audi

Audi 80/90 and Coupe Quattro

Audi 90 Quattro

Summary

The 80/90 sedans and the new Coupe suffer from the same problem: not enough engine to justify their high prices. We clocked a front-drive 90 with the 130-horsepower engine and automatic transmission at 10.4 seconds (slower than a Hyundai Sonata V-6) and a Coupe Quattro at 9.3 seconds (slower than a Mitsubishi Eclipse). We don't base all our conclusions on 0-60 times, but at these prices we expect to blow the doors off Hyundais and Mitsubishis. None of the three engines Audi offers here has enough low-end torque for brisk takeoffs, especially the 4-cylinder. On the plus side, the anti-lock brakes provide short, straight stops; on three different test cars we averaged between 121 and 126 feet in stops from 60 mph, an excellent showing. We've also been impressed by the assembly quality and paint finishes on the cars we've tested, which shows that Audi is trying hard to win back owners after surviving the sudden-acceleration issue. Our other major complaint is the skimpy cargo space on the sedans; you can carry four people in an 80/90, but only one or two will be able to squeeze their luggage into the tiny trunk. The Quattro models would be great if they cost about $20,000 or so, but that's where the front-drive 80 starts. The Quattros go from $24,000 up to nearly $30,000, which is the same range as the Acura Legend, a better value by far.

What's New

The all-wheel-drive Coupe Quattro, which went on sale in July, is built on the same platform as the 80/90 sedans, but introduces a new dual-cam, 20-valve version of Audi's 2.3-liter 5-cylinder engine. The 2-door Coupe's engine makes 164 horsepower, 34 more than the single-cam version used in the 80 Quattro and the front-drive 90. This fall, the 20-valve engine also becomes standard on the 90 Quattro. The front-drive 80 has a 108-horsepower 2.0-liter 4-cylinder. The Coupe uses the same permanently engaged AWD system as the 80/90 Quattros. It normally splits engine torque 50/50 between the front and rear axles. When there's wheel slip, a torque-sensing center differential automatically sends as much as 78 percent of the power to the axle with the most traction. As with the 80 and 90 Quattros, a 5-speed manual is the only transmission offered on the Coupe. Anti-lock brakes are standard on the Coupe and all 90 models, and optional on the 80 Quattro. All models now have a driver's-side airbag standard. Other new features this fall for the 80/90 models include: a stereo radio/cassette player with anti-theft circuitry is standard on the front-drive 80; a Sport Package is optional on the 80 Quattro (sport seats, trim computer, and additional gauges); a Luxury Package is optional on the front-drive 90 (Audi/Bose sound system, theft alarm, and trip computer); and an All-Weather Package is optional on the 90 Quattro.

For

- Handling/roadholding • Anti-lock brakes • Airbag
- 4WD traction (Quattros)

Against

- Acceleration (80) • Cargo space

KEY: ohv = overhead valve; ohc = overhead cam; dohc = double overhead cam; I = inline cylinders; V = cylinders in V configuration; flat = horizontally opposed cylinders; bbl. = barrel (carburetor); PFI = port (multi-point) fuel injection; TBI = throttle-body (single-point) fuel injection; rpm = revolutions per minute; OD = overdrive transmission; S = standard; O = optional; NA = not available.

Specifications

	2-door notchback	4-door notchback
Wheelbase, in.	100.4	100.4
Overall length, in.	176.0	176.3
Overall width, in.	67.6	66.7
Overall height, in.	54.3	55.0
Turn diameter, ft.	33.8	33.8
Curb weight, lbs.	3171	2612[1]
Cargo vol., cu. ft.	24.0	10.2
Fuel capacity, gals.	18.5	15.9
Seating capacity	5	5
Front headroom, in.	35.1	35.1
Front shoulder room, in.	51.7	51.7
Front legroom, max., in.	42.2	42.2
Rear headroom, in.	35.4	35.4
Rear shoulder room, in.	50.6	51.7
Rear legroom, min., in.	32.6	32.6

1. 2954 lbs., Quattro.

Powertrain layout: longitudinal front engine/front-wheel drive or permanent 4WD (Quattro).

Engines

	ohc I-4	ohc I-5	dohc I-5
Size, liters/cu. in.	2.0/121	2.3/141	2.3/141
Fuel delivery	PFI	PFI	PFI
Horsepower @ rpm	108 @ 5300	130 @ 5700	164 @ 6000
Torque (lbs./ft.) @ rpm	121 @ 3200	140 @ 4500	157 @ 4500
Availability	S[1]	S[2]	S[3]

EPA city/highway mpg

5-speed OD manual	22/30	20/26	18/24
3-speed automatic	23/27	19/22	

1. 80 2. 80 Quattro, 90 3. Coupe, 90 Quattro

Prices

Audi 80/90	Retail Price	Dealer Invoice	Low Price
80 4-door notchback	$18900	—	—
80 Quattro 4-door notchback	22800	—	—

	Retail Price	Dealer Invoice	Low Price
90 4-door notchback	23990	—	—
90 Quattro 4-door notchback	27500	—	—
Destination charge	335	335	335

Dealer invoice and low price not available at time of publication.

Standard equipment:

80: 2.0-liter PFI 4-cylinder engine, 5-speed manual transmission, power steering, 4-wheel disc brakes, driver's-side airbag, air conditioning, tinted glass, rear defogger, cruise control, power windows and locks, AM/FM cassette with diversity antenna, power mirrors, velour reclining front bucket seats with height adjusters, rear head restraints, rear shoulder belts, tachometer, coolant temperature gauge, trip odometer, digital clock, intermittent wipers, lighted right visor mirror, 175/70SR14 SBR tires. **80 Quattro** adds: 2.3-liter PFI 5-cylinder engine, close-ratio 5-speed, permanent 4-wheel drive, rear spoiler, 195/60VR14 tires on alloy wheels. **90** has: 2.3-liter 5-cylinder engine with 5-speed or 2.0-liter 4-cylinder with 3-speed automatic, anti-lock braking system, fog lights, clearcoat metallic paint, leather interior, wood dashboard trim, power sunroof, individual passenger reading lamps, Auto Check System, 195/60VR14 tires (H-rated on 4-cylinder). **90 Quattro** adds: DOHC 20-valve engine.

OPTIONS prices not available at time of publication.

Prices

Audi Coupe Quattro	Retail Price	Dealer Invoice	Low Price
3-door hatchback	$29750	—	—
Destination charge	335	—	—

Dealer invoice and low price not available at time of publication.

Standard equipment:

2.3-liter DOHC 20-valve PFI 5-cylinder engine, 5-speed manual transmission, permanent 4-wheel drive, power steering, anti-lock 4-wheel disc brakes, driver's-side airbag (late availability), leather reclining front bucket seats with lumbar support and height adjustments, split folding rear seat with armrest, automatic climate control, power windows and locks, cruise control, heated power mirrors, power sunroof, AM/FM cassette, tachometer, coolant temperature and oil pressure gauges, voltmeter, trip odometer, 6-function trip computer, 10-function Auto Check System, rear shoulder belts and head restraints, Zebrano wood inlays, leather-wrapped steering wheel and shift knob, lighted visor mirrors, anti-theft alarm system, tinted glass, rear defogger, intermittent wipers, ski sack, 205/60VR15 tires on alloy wheels.

Optional equipment:

Cold Weather Pkg.	350	—	—
Heatable front seats, headlight washers, heated windshield washer nozzles and door locks.			
Power front seats w/driver's-side memory .	825	—	—
Pearl White metallic paint	395	—	—
California equipment	125	—	—

Audi Coupe Quattro

Audi 100/200

1989 Audi 100

What's New

The 100 and 200 lines have been streamlined and all remaining models have a driver's-side airbag as standard equipment. Last year, the airbag was standard on 200 models and optional on 100 models. Last year's lowest-priced model, the 100E sedan, has been dropped. The 100 wagon also is gone. The 100 series now consists of a front-drive sedan with a 130-horsepower 2.3-liter 5-cylinder engine and 3-speed automatic transmission, and an all-wheel drive 100 Quattro sedan with the same engine and a 5-speed manual transmission. The 200 models are a front-drive sedan with a 162-horsepower 2.2-liter turbocharged 5-cylinder engine and 3-speed automatic transmission, and AWD Quattro sedan and wagon models, both with the turbo engine and 5-speed manual transmission. The front-drive 200 sedan now has leather upholstery standard, while the 200 Quattros gain heated front and rear seats and heated front door locks as standard.

For

● Acceleration (turbo engine) ● Handling/roadholding
● Airbag ● 4WD traction (Quattro) ● Anti-lock brakes
● Passenger room

Against

● Fuel economy ● Acceleration (2.3-liter engine)

Summary

Audi won a major victory last summer when the federal government ruled that unintended acceleration in the Audi 5000 (now called 100 and 200) was caused by drivers stepping on the wrong pedal, not by mechanical or electronic flaws in the cars. Now, Audi has an even greater obstacle to overcome: How to restore consumer confidence and regain sales momentum. That won't be easy in such a competitive market. Other European luxury-car makers are struggling to maintain their sales and two Japanese newcomers, Lexus and Infiniti, have made the competition even more cutthroat. The 100 and 200 models offer commendable ride and handling, standard anti-lock brakes, ample passenger room, and, with the Quattro models, an impressive permanently engaged all-wheel drive system. Acceleration from the 2.3-liter engine in the 100 models is tame compared to Japanese rivals such as the Acura Legend and Nissan Maxima. In addition, the automatic transmission lacks an overdrive top gear, which could improve the mediocre highway mileage (Audi plans to introduce an overdrive automatic on the 100 next summer). While the AWD Quattro models stick to roads like glue, even in rain and snow, they come only with a 5-speed manual transmission. That eliminates those models from consideration in most American

Prices are accurate at time of printing; subject to manufacturer's change.

1989 Audi 200 Quattro

households. Audi has been so busy fighting the battle over unintended acceleration the past few years that it hasn't kept its products current with American driving tastes. European-style luxury reigned during the Eighties, but Japanese-style luxury may well rule the Nineties. Try an Audi 100 or 200, and then drive the Lexus and Infiniti sedans and see which fits your style best.

Specifications

	4-door notchback	5-door wagon
Wheelbase, in.	105.6	105.6
Overall length, in.	192.7	192.7
Overall width, in.	71.4	71.4
Overall height, in.	55.9	55.9
Turn diameter, ft.	34.2	34.2
Curb weight, lbs.	2932[1]	3042[2]
Cargo vol., cu. ft.	16.7	75.4
Fuel capacity, gals.	21.1	21.1
Seating capacity	5	5
Front headroom, in.	37.5	36.5
Front shoulder room, in.	NA	NA
Front legroom, max., in.	NA	NA
Rear headroom, in.	36.5	36.5
Rear shoulder room, in.	NA	NA
Rear legroom, min., in.	NA	NA

1. 3306 lbs., Quattro.   2. 3439 lbs., Quattro.

Powertrain layout: longitudinal front engine/front-wheel drive or permanent 4WD (Quattro).

Engines

	ohc I-5	Turbo ohc I-5
Size, liters/cu. in.	2.3/141	2.2/136
Fuel delivery	PFI	PFI
Horsepower @ rpm	130 @ 5600	162 @ 5500
Torque (lbs./ft.) @ rpm	140 @ 4000	177 @ 3000
Availability	S	S
EPA city/highway mpg		
5-speed OD manual	18/24	17/25
3-speed automatic	18/22	18/22

Prices

Audi 100/200	Retail Price	Dealer Invoice	Low Price
100 4-door notchback	$26900	—	—
100 Quattro 4-door notchback	29470	—	—
200 4-door notchback	33405	—	—
200 Quattro 4-door notchback	35805	—	—
200 Quattro 5-door wagon	36930	—	—
Destination charge	335	335	335

Standard equipment:

100: 2.3-liter PFI 5-cylinder engine, 3-speed automatic transmission, power steering, anti-lock 4-wheel disc brakes, driver's-side airbag, automatic climate control, power windows and locks, heated power mirrors, velour reclining bucket seats with driver's-side height adjustment, folding rear armrest, rear shoulder belts, reading lamps, lighted visor mirrors, anti-theft alarm, ski/storage sack, tinted glass, rear defogger, cruise control, intermittent wipers, AM/FM cassette with diversity antenna, Zebrano wood inlays, rear head restraints, front seatback pockets, leather-wrapped steering wheel, power sunroof, 205/60VR15 SBR tires on alloy wheels. **100 Quattro** has 5-speed manual transmission, permanent 4-wheel drive. **200** adds to 100: 2.2-liter turbocharged PFI 5-cylinder engine, trip computer, leather upholstery, Audi/Bose music system.

OPTIONS prices not available at time of publication.

BMW 3-Series

What's New

All 3-Series models gain a driver's-side airbag as standard equipment this fall to satisfy the federal requirement for passive restraints. All other BMW models already have airbags. Next spring, BMW tries to recapture the spirit of former models such as the 2002 with a new entry-level model, the 318is, a 2-door with a 1.8-liter 4-cylinder engine. The 318is engine has dual overhead cams, 16 valves, and 134 horsepower, and is teamed only with a 5-speed manual transmission. The only other 4-cylinder model in recent years has been the high-performance, limited-production M3, which continues for 1990. The current 3-Series design debuted in 1983 as the 2-door, 4-cylinder 318i, but BMW switched to 6-cylinder engines for 1986. Other changes for the 3-Series this year are that all models will be prewired to accept a trunk-mounted compact-disc changer and a remote-control central locking system is a new option. The remote control system also arms a theft-deterrent system as it locks the doors. New options for the 325i and the 4-wheel-drive 325iX models are leather upholstery, an electric sunroof (a manual sunroof is standard), and a premium 8-speaker sound system. Both the 325i and the 325iX are available in 2- and 4-door styling; all other 3-Series models are 2-doors only. The M3 uses a 192-horsepower 2.3-liter 4-cylinder; all other carryover 3-Series model use a 168-horsepower 2.5-liter 6-cylinder.

For

● Acceleration ● Anti-lock brakes ● Airbag ● Handling ● 4WD traction (325iX)

Against

● Passenger room ● Cargo space

Summary

BMW is having a hard time selling 3-Series models these days, mainly because these cars have small, rather Spartan interiors, but big price tags. Mercedes-Benz has similar problems with its compact 190 models. Most 3-Series models are in the $25,000-$30,000 range, the same as the Acura Legend, which offers similar features in a roomier package. As Legend's sales have steadily increased, 3-Series sales have steadily dropped, perhaps an indication of a shift in American tastes in premium sedans. Aside from the cramped quarters, there's lots to like about the 3-Series cars. The smooth, high-revving 2.5-liter 6-cylinder delivers brisk acceleration; the firm suspension provides capable handling without a jarring ride;

1989 BMW 325i

and the standard anti-lock brakes have outstanding stopping power. Concerned that the rear-drive 3-Series won't have good traction in snow? Try a 325iX, whose permanent 4WD system easily handles winter weather. The BMW 3-Series may no longer be the dream car of Yuppies, but that doesn't mean it isn't worth owning. We wish there was a "325iL" model, with the "L" denoting a longer wheelbase for more interior room.

1989 Specifications

	2-door notchback	4-door notchback	2-door conv.
Wheelbase, in.	101.2	101.2	101.2
Overall length, in.	170.2	170.2	175.2
Overall width, in.	64.8	64.8	64.8
Overall height, in.	54.3	54.3	53.9
Turn diameter, ft.	34.4	34.4	34.4
Curb weight, lbs.	2811[1]	2855[2]	3055
Cargo vol., cu. ft.	14.3	14.3	11.0
Fuel capacity, gals.	16.4	16.4	16.4
Seating capacity	5	5	4
Front headroom, in.	37.7	37.7	NA
Front shoulder room, in.	52.0	52.0	NA
Front legroom, max., in.	NA	NA	NA
Rear headroom, in.	36.4	36.4	NA
Rear shoulder room, in.	52.4	52.4	NA
Rear legroom, min., in.	NA	NA	NA

1. 3010 lbs., 325iX. 2. 3054 lbs., 325iX.

Powertrain layout: longitudinal front engine/rear-wheel drive or permanent 4WD.

Engines

	ohc I-6	dohc I-4
Size, liters/cu. in.	2.5/152	2.3/140
Fuel delivery	PFI	PFI
Horsepower @ rpm	168 @ 5800	192 @ 6750
Torque (lbs./ft.) @ rpm	164 @ 4300	170 @ 4750
Availability	S	S[1]

EPA city/highway mpg

5-speed OD manual	18/23	17/29
4-speed OD automatic	18/22	

1. M3.

Prices

BMW 3-Series

	Retail Price	Dealer Invoice	Low Price
325i 2-door notchback	$24650	—	—
325i 4-door notchback	25450	—	—
325is 2-door notchback	28950	—	—
325i 2-door convertible	33850	—	—
325iX 2-door notchback	29950	—	—
325iX 4-door notchback	30750	—	—
M3 2-door notchback	34950	—	—
Destination charge	345	345	345

Dealer invoice and low price not available at time of publication.

Standard equipment:

325i: 2.5-liter PFI 6-cylinder engine, 5-speed manual transmission, power steering, anti-lock 4-wheel disc brakes, driver's-side airbag, air conditioning, cloth or leatherette reclining bucket seats with height/tilt adjustments, outboard rear lap/shoulder belts, power windows and locks, cruise control, power mirrors, AM/FM cassette, power antenna, tinted glass, Service Interval Indicator, Active Check Control, manual sunroof, toolkit, 195/65VR14 tires on alloy wheels. **Convertible** adds: leather upholstery, map lights, trip computer, premium sound system, cross-spoke alloy wheels. **325is** adds: limited-slip differential, front and rear spoilers, power sunroof. **325iX** has: permanent 4-wheel drive, sill extensions, leatherette upholstery, manual sunroof, folding rear armrest with ski sack, 205/55VR15 tires. **M3** has 325is equipment plus 2.3-liter DOHC PFI 4-cylinder engine, sport suspension, 205/55VR15 tires.

Optional equipment:

4-speed automatic transmission (NA M3)	700	—	—
Metallic paint	375	—	—
Leather upholstery, 325i exc. conv., iX	895	—	—
Power sunroof, 325i, 325iX	225	—	—
Glass sunroof, 325is	495	—	—
Limited-slip differential, 325i	400	—	—
Cross-spoke alloy wheels, conv.	500	—	—
Heated front seats	250	—	—
Not available on 325i hardtops.			
Premium sound system, 325is & iX	250	—	—
CD changer	780	—	—
Ski sack, 325is	160	—	—
Remote alarm system	515	—	—

BMW 5-Series

What's New

Traction control is a new option for the 535i and a driver's-side airbag is standard on the 525i this year. The 5-Series sedans were redesigned for 1989 and only the higher-priced 535i came with an airbag last year. The new traction-control system, called ASC by BMW (for automatic stability control) will be phased in as an option for the 535i during the model year. It uses the anti-lock brake sensors at the rear wheels to detect wheel slip during acceleration, and then it reduces power transmitted to the wheels as needed to maintain traction. ASC also will be optional on the larger 735i and 735iL sedans and standard on the 750iL. The high-performance M5, derived from the 5-Series sedan and already on sale in Europe, comes to the U.S. next spring. The M5 uses a dual-cam 3.6-liter inline 6-cylinder engine rated at 311 horsepower, 15 more than the V-12 engine used in the 750iL. The M5 will come only with a 5-speed manual transmission and will have seats for four. The 525i and 535i have seats for five and are available

> **KEY: ohv** = overhead valve; **ohc** = overhead cam; **dohc** = double overhead cam; **I** = inline cylinders; **V** = cylinders in V configuration; **flat** = horizontally opposed cylinders; **bbl.** = barrel (carburetor); **PFI** = port (multi-point) fuel injection; **TBI** = throttle-body (single-point) fuel injection; **rpm** = revolutions per minute; **OD** = overdrive transmission; **S** = standard; **O** = optional; **NA** = not available.

Prices are accurate at time of printing; subject to manufacturer's change.

1989 BMW 525i

with either a 5-speed manual or 4-speed automatic. A 168-horse-power 2.5-liter 6-cylinder powers the 525i and a 208-horse-power 3.4-liter 6-cylinder powers the 535i. Both models are now prewired for a cellular telephone and a trunk-mounted compact-disc changer. Newly optional is a remote-control feature for the central locking system that also activates a burglar alarm when it locks the doors. The 535i's interior, which came with leather and vinyl upholstery last year, gains more leather this year, plus new wood trim.

For

- Acceleration • Anti-lock brakes • Airbag • Handling
- Ride • Passenger room • Cargo space

Against

- Fuel economy • Driveability (automatic transmission)

Summary

We like the 535i a lot, but we also like the new Infiniti Q45 and Lexus LS 400, Japanese luxury sedans that are invading BMW's domain. We like the 525i somewhat less because its 2.5-liter 6-cylinder engine just doesn't have enough low-speed torque to move a 3400-pound sedan with the gusto you expect in this price range. We've only tested a 525i with a 5-speed manual transmission; we fear it will be more disappointing with automatic. At times, even the 535i with automatic balks at downshifting for prompt passing response. By comparison, the Q45 and LS 400 cost about the same, but come with V-8 engines that provide stronger passing power without delay. The 6-cylinder 535i virtually matches the V-8 LS 400 in standing-start acceleration (right around 8.0 seconds to 60 mph for both in our tests), a credit to BMW's engineering. However, the Lexus is quieter, has a cushier ride, and coddles its occupants a little more than the 535i. Where the LS 400 is soft and smooth, the 535i is firmer and even a little rough at times. The 535i is still a good car, but it's designed first for the German Autobahn, where the speed limit is set by the abilities of the driver and his car. We encourage you to compare the 535i to the LS 400 and Q45. You might find the 535i is everything you want. Or, you might find that Germany no longer builds the definitive premium sedan.

> **KEY: ohv** = overhead valve; **ohc** = overhead cam; **dohc** = double overhead cam; **I** = inline cylinders; **V** = cylinders in V configuration; **flat** = horizontally opposed cylinders; **bbl.** = barrel (carburetor); **PFI** = port (multi-point) fuel injection; **TBI** = throttle-body (single-point) fuel injection; **rpm** = revolutions per minute; **OD** = overdrive transmission; **S** = standard; **O** = optional; **NA** = not available.

1989 Specifications

	4-door notchback
Wheelbase, in.	108.7
Overall length, in.	185.8
Overall width, in.	68.9
Overall height, in.	55.6
Turn diameter, ft.	37.7
Curb weight, lbs.	3395[1]
Cargo vol., cu. ft.	16.2
Fuel capacity, gals.	21.1
Seating capacity	5
Front headroom, in.	38.5
Front shoulder room, in.	NA
Front legroom, max., in.	42.0
Rear headroom, in.	37.4
Rear shoulder room, in.	NA
Rear legroom, min., in.	25.5

1. 3530 lbs., 535i.

Powertrain layout: longitudinal front engine/rear-wheel drive.

Engines	ohc I-6	ohc I-6
Size, liters/cu. in.	2.5/152	3.4/209
Fuel delivery	PFI	PFI
Horsepower @ rpm	168 @ 5800	208 @ 5700
Torque (lbs./ft.) @ rpm	164 @ 4300	225 @ 4000
Availability	S	S
EPA city/highway mpg		
5-speed OD manual	18/24	15/23
4-speed OD automatic	18/23	15/21

Prices

BMW 5-Series	Retail Price	Dealer Invoice	Low Price
525i 4-door notchback	$33200	—	—
535i 4-door notchback	41500	—	—
Destination charge	345	345	345
Gas Guzzler Tax, 535i 5-speed	650	650	650

Dealer invoice and low price not available at time of publication.

Standard equipment:

525i: 2.5-liter PFI 6-cylinder engine, 5-speed manual transmission, power steering, anti-lock 4-wheel disc brakes, driver's-side airbag, air conditioning with individual temperature controls, leather power front bucket seats, folding center armrests, rear armrest with storage, rear shoulder belts, power windows and locks, heated power mirrors, fog lights, adjustable steering wheel, tinted glass, tachometer and coolant temperature gauge, rear defogger, seatback pockets, front and rear reading lights, dual LCD trip odometers, Service Interval Indicator, fuel economy indicator, trip computer, power sunroof, toolkit, 205/65VR15 tires on alloy wheels. **535i** adds: 3.4-liter engine, 5-speed manual or 4-speed automatic transmission, leather-wrapped steering wheel, automatic climate control, 225/60VR15 tires.

Optional equipment:

4-speed automatic transmission, 525i	700	—	—
Leather upholstery, 525i	1100	—	—
Limited-slip differential	400	—	—
Heated front seats	250	—	—
CD changer	780	—	—
Ski sack	160	—	—
Remote alarm system	515	—	—
Glass sunroof	810	—	—

BMW 7-Series

1989 BMW 735i

What's New

Traction control is standard on the 750iL and optional for the other 7-Series sedans as the major change for 1990. BMW calls its traction-control system ASC, for automatic stability control. The system uses the anti-lock brake sensors at the rear wheels to detect wheel slip. If either rear wheel slips during acceleration, ASC limits the amount of power to that wheel (or both) until it regains traction. ASC is optional on the 735i and 735iL, and also on the smaller 535i. The 735i and 735iL use a 208-horsepower 3.4-liter 6-cylinder engine; the 750iL has a 296-horsepower V-12. The "L" in the model names denotes a longer wheelbase, 116 inches instead of 111.5 on the 735i. No new 7-Series models are coming to the U.S. this year, but next June a new luxury coupe, the 850i, arrives to replace the 6-Series 2-door. The 6-Series, which had been sold in the U.S. since 1976, has ceased production. The 4-seat 850i will use the 750iL's V-12 engine, teamed with either a 4-speed automatic or new 6-speed manual transmission. The 850i also will be the first car with BMW's new Seat-Integrated Belt System, in which the front seat-belt anchors and guiding points are located on the seats themselves. BMW claims this system improves occupant protection and makes the belts more comfortable.

For

● Acceleration ● Anti-lock brakes ● Airbag ● Ride
● Handling ● Passenger room ● Cargo space
● Quietness

Against

● Fuel economy ● Price

Summary

BMW's flagship 750iL effortlessly devours long stretches of highway while nearly totally isolating its occupants from outside unpleasantries. Its only real competitor is the similarly priced, V-8-powered Mercedes 560SEL. It more than matches the 560 for acceleration, room, quietness, and snob appeal, plus, it's a newer design with a more sporting feel. The 735i is $21,000 or so cheaper than the 750iL but basically the same car except for slight sacrifices in acceleration, features, and back-seat space. Of course, you don't have to spend this much money to get a good luxury sedan. In fact, thrift-minded shoppers in the premium-sedan market can buy an Acura Legend for less than half the price of a 750iL. Or, there are the new Japanese luxury sedans, the Lexus LS 400 and Infiniti Q45, which start out in the $35,000 to $38,000 range.

How about one of those *and* a Legend, both for less than the 750iL. Besides the high prices and low fuel economy of the 750iL and its 6-cylinder brothers, there's really nothing to complain about. These cars do everything you expect, and then some. The trouble is, they cost as much as you'll pay for a 2-bedroom house in many parts of the country.

1989 Specifications

	735i 4-door notchback	735iL/750iL 4-door notchback
Wheelbase, in.	111.5	116.0
Overall length, in.	193.3	197.8
Overall width, in.	72.6	72.6
Overall height, in.	55.6	55.1
Turn diameter, ft.	38.1	39.4
Curb weight, lbs.	3835	4015[1]
Cargo vol., cu. ft.	17.6	17.6
Fuel capacity, gals.	21.5	24.0
Seating capacity	5	5
Front headroom, in.	38.3	38.3
Front shoulder room, in.	NA	NA
Front legroom, max., in.	44.3	44.3
Rear headroom, in.	37.2	37.2
Rear shoulder room, in.	NA	NA
Rear legroom, min., in.	NA	32.8

1. 4235 lbs., 750iL.

Powertrain layout: longitudinal front engine/rear-wheel drive.

Engines

	ohc I-6	ohc V-12
Size, liters/cu. in.	3.4/209	5.0/304
Fuel delivery	PFI	PFI
Horsepower @ rpm	208 @ 5700	296 @ 5200
Torque (lbs./ft.) @ rpm	225 @ 4000	332 @ 4100
Availability	S	S

EPA city/highway mpg

5-speed OD manual	15/23	
4-speed OD automatic	15/21	12/18

Prices

BMW 7-Series	Retail Price	Dealer Invoice	Low Price
735i 4-door notchback	$49000	—	—
735iL 4-door notchback	53000	—	—
750iL 4-door notchback	70000	—	—
Destination charge	345	345	345
Gas Guzzler Tax, 735i, 735iL	650	650	650
750iL	1500	1500	1500

Dealer invoice and low price not available at time of publication.

Standard equipment:

3.4-liter PFI 6-cylinder engine, 4-speed automatic transmission, power steering, anti-lock 4-wheel disc brakes, driver's side airbag, automatic climate control system with separate left and right controls, power front bucket seats with 3-position driver's-side memory (including outside mirrors), leather upholstery, rear shoulder belts, cruise control, fog lamps, speed-sensitive intermittent wipers, heated wiper parking area, heated windshield washer jets, heated power mirrors, heated driver's door lock, power windows and locks, leather-wrapped steering wheel, rear head restraints, front center armrests, rear armrest with storage compartment, Bubinga wood trim, time-delay courtesy light, map lights, rear reading lights, tinted glass, tachometer and coolant temperature gauge, LCD main and trip odometers, Service Interval Indicator, fuel economy indicator, Active Check Control, trip computer, rear defogger, power sunroof, AM/FM cassette, power antenna, toolkit, 225/60VR15 tires on cast alloy wheels. **735iL** adds: power rear seat,

Prices are accurate at time of printing; subject to manufacturer's change.

self-leveling rear suspension, remote alarm system. **750iL** adds: 5.0-liter PFI V-12, additional leather trim, Elmwood trim, cellular telephone, forged alloy wheels.

Optional equipment:

Limited-slip differential	400	—	—
Heated front seats, 735i, 735iL	250	—	—
Heated rear seats, 750iL	250	—	—
CD changer, 735i, 735iL	780	—	—
Ski sack	160	—	—
Roll-up rear sunshade, 735iL	140	—	—
Cellular telephone, 735i, 735iL	1205	—	—
Remote alarm system, 735i	515	—	—

Buick Century

Buick Century Custom

What's New

Century returns for its ninth season with few changes after undergoing an exterior facelift last year. Air conditioning is now standard and the front outboard seat belts can be left buckled to create a passive-restraint system. Top-line Limited models get a new seat design and, along with the base Custom versions, get new door trim panels with map pockets and new power window and lock controls. Power seat recliners are a new option and there's a new, smaller jack. There also are four new exterior colors: Ice Blue, Saddle Brown, Dark Maple red, and Flame red. The front-drive Century continues in 2-door coupe, 4-door sedan, and 5-door wagon body styles. A minor restyle for '89 brought a vertical-bar grille and flush composite headlamps. A new rear window and roof pillars gave the coupes and sedans a rounded appearance at the back, while full-width taillamps and a new trunk lid added a family resemblance to the Buick Regal. A 160-horsepower 3.3-liter V-6, which Buick calls the 3300, is optional in place of the standard 110-horsepower 2.5-liter four. A 3-speed automatic transmission is standard; a 4-speed overdrive automatic is optional with the V-6. Buick says it's improved the ride quality of the '90 Century, which uses the division's Dynaride suspension and its deflected disc shock absorber valving. Century is part of GM's A-body family, which includes the Chevrolet Celebrity, Oldsmobile Cutlass Ciera, and Pontiac 6000.

For

● Performance (V-6) ● Passenger room ● Trunk space
● Quietness

KEY: ohv = overhead valve; **ohc** = overhead cam; **dohc** = double overhead cam; **I** = inline cylinders; **V** = cylinders in V configuration; **flat** = horizontally opposed cylinders; **bbl.** = barrel (carburetor); **PFI** = port (multi-point) fuel injection; **TBI** = throttle-body (single-point) fuel injection; **rpm** = revolutions per minute; **OD** = overdrive transmission; **S** = standard; **O** = optional; **NA** = not available.

Against

● Performance (4-cylinder)   ● Handling (base suspension)

Summary

The 3.3-liter V-6 replaced a 3.8-liter V-6 as Century's most powerful optional engine in 1988. The car gained 10 more horsepower, but gave up some torque; the 3.3 has 185 pounds/feet, the 3.8 had 200. On the road, however, the 3.3 doesn't suffer a big performance deficit compared to the 3.8. In the Century, the 3.3, in fact, seems to rev more quickly and smoothly than did the 3.8. It gives this staid mid-size car a surprising kick under heavy throttle. It's also a fairly quiet engine that should serve Century owners better than the weaker, noisier standard four. Century's suspension isn't up to the spirit of its 3300 engine, however. Dynaride might improve ride comfort, but makes little apparent difference in handling ability. The base suspension and narrow standard tires are fine for gentle, everyday commuting, but spirited cornering sets the front end to plowing and exposes the tires' modest grip. The optional Gran Touring Suspension, with its fatter tires, improves cornering ability, but suffers a harsh ride and does little to keep the car from bounding dramatically over high-speed dips. On the whole, though, Century remains a roomy, comfortable intermediate priced competitively against the Ford Taurus/Mercury Sable.

Specifications

	2-door notchback	4-door notchback	5-door wagon
Wheelbase, in.	104.8	104.8	104.8
Overall length, in.	189.1	189.1	190.9
Overall width, in.	69.4	69.4	69.4
Overall height, in.	53.7	54.2	54.2
Turn diameter, ft.	38.5	38.5	38.5
Curb weight, lbs.	2754	2776	2924
Cargo vol., cu. ft.	16.2	16.2	74.4
Fuel capacity, gals.	15.7	15.7	15.7
Seating capacity	6	6	6
Front headroom, in.	38.6	38.6	38.6
Front shoulder room, in.	56.1	56.2	56.2
Front legroom, max., in.	42.1	42.1	42.1
Rear headroom, in.	37.9	38.0	38.9
Rear shoulder room, in.	57.0	56.2	56.2
Rear legroom, min., in.	36.1	35.9	34.8

Powertrain layout: transverse front engine/front-wheel drive.

Engines

	ohv I-4	ohv V-6
Size, liters/cu. in.	2.5/151	3.3/204
Fuel delivery	TBI	PFI
Horsepower @ rpm	110 @ 5200	160 @ 5200
Torque (lbs./ft.) @ rpm	135 @ 3200	185 @ 2000
Availability	S	O

EPA city/highway mpg

3-speed automatic	23/30	20/27
4-speed OD automatic		20/29

Prices

Buick Century	Retail Price	Dealer Invoice	Low Price
Custom 4-door notchback	$13150	$11348	$11548
Custom 2-door notchback	13250	11435	11635
Custom 5-door wagon	14570	12574	12774

Buick Electra/Park Avenue

	Retail Price	Dealer Invoice	Low Price
Limited 4-door notchback	14075	12147	12347
Limited 5-door wagon	15455	13338	13538
Destination charge	450	450	450

Standard equipment:

Custom: 2.5-liter TBI 4-cylinder engine, 3-speed automatic transmission, power steering, dual outside mirrors, tinted glass, map lights, instrument panel courtesy lights, cloth split bench seat, AM/FM radio, P185/75R14 all-season SBR tires. **Wagon** adds: split folding rear seatback, two-way tailgate. **Limited and Estate** add: 55/45 notchback cloth seat, armrest with storage, trunk trim (4-door).

Optional equipment:

3.3-liter V-6	710	604	639
4-speed automatic transmission (V-6 req.)	200	170	180
Popular Pkg. SB, Custom 2-door	410	349	369
Custom 4-door	420	357	378
Custom wagon	535	455	482
Rear defogger, tilt steering column, intermittent wipers, door edge guards, floormats, roof rack (wagon).			
Premium Pkg. SC, Custom 2-door	1218	1035	1096
Custom 4-door	1268	1078	1141
Custom wagon	1703	1448	1533
Pkg. SB plus power locks, cruise control, AM/FM cassette, styled steel wheels, 55/45 front seat with storage armrest. Wagon adds: remote tailgate lock release, air deflector, rear-facing third seat.			
Luxury Pkg. SD, Custom 2-door	1651	1403	1486
Custom 4-door	1766	1501	1589
Custom wagon	2201	1871	1981
Pkg. SC plus power windows, wire wheel covers, lighted right visor mirror.			
Prestige Pkg. SE, Custom 2-door	2124	1805	1912
Custom 4-door	2239	1903	2015
Custom wagon	2624	2230	2362
Pkg. SD plus power mirrors, power driver's seat, power antenna, remote decklid release.			
Premium Pkg. SC, Ltd 4-door	945	803	851
Ltd wagon	1125	956	1013
Tilt steering column, rear defogger, intermittent wipers, power locks, cruise control, styled steel wheels, floormats, door edge guards, roof rack and remote tailgate lock release (wagon).			
Luxury Pkg. SD, Ltd 4-door	1525	1296	1373
Ltd wagon	2093	1779	1884
Pkg. SC plus wire wheel covers, AM/FM cassette, power windows. Wagon adds: rear window air deflector, rear-facing third seat, lighted right visor mirror, power antenna.			
Prestige Pkg. SE, Ltd 4-door	2150	1828	1935
Ltd wagon	2500	2125	2250
Pkg. SD plus power driver's seat, power mirrors, reading lights, premium speakers, lighted right visor mirror, power antenna, remote decklid release.			
Cruise control, Custom w/SB	195	166	176
Power locks, Custom 2-door w/SB	175	149	158
Custom 4-door w/SB	215	183	194
AM/FM cassette	140	119	126
Power antenna	75	64	68
Power seatback recliners	110	94	99
Cloth 55/45 seat w/armrest, Custom w/SB	183	156	165
w/Empress cloth, Custom w/SB	551	468	496
w/Empress cloth, Custom w/SC/SD/SE	368	313	331
Leather & vinyl 55/45 seat, Ltd	450	383	405
Wire wheel covers, Custom w/SB	215	183	194
Custom w/SC	100	85	90
Styled steel wheels, Custom w/SB	115	98	104
Alloy wheels, Custom w/SB	270	230	243
Custom & Limited w/SC	155	132	140
Custom & Limited w/SD/SE	55	47	50
Rear wiper/washer, wagons			
Custom w/1SB, Limited w/SC	125	106	113
Custom w/1SC/SD/SE, Ltd w/SD/SE	85	72	77
Power windows, Custom 2-door w/SB/SC	230	196	207
Custom 4-door w/SB/SC, Ltd 4-door w/SC	295	251	266

Buick Electra T Type

What's New

Park Avenue Ultra, labeled by Buick as the most luxurious full-size sedan it's ever offered, enters its first full model year in 1990. Introduced in January 1989, the 4-door flagship has a leather interior and 20-way power adjustments for the driver and front passenger seats. Conventional 6-way power seat adjustments are controlled by switches on the front door armrests. A separate control panel folds out of the center armrest to reveal buttons for seatback recliners, thigh and lumbar supports, and power headrests. Anti-lock brakes, 2-tone paint and 15-inch aluminum wheels also are standard on Ultra. Limited, Park Avenue, and T Type Electras continue with few changes for '90. All get more body reinforcements that Buick says improve rough-road solidity and a revised power-steering valve designed to enhance road feel. Dove Gray, Gunmetal, Palomino Brown and Chestnut Brown are new exterior colors, brown and gray are new interior hues, and there are four new vinyl top colors. A compact disc player is a new option. A 165-horsepower 3.8-liter V-6 and a 4-speed overdrive automatic is the only available powertrain. Carried over are standard front seat belts that can be left buckled for automatic protection. The basic design for the front-drive Electra/Park Avenue also is used for the Buick LeSabre, Oldsmobile Ninety-Eight and Eighty-Eight, and Pontiac Bonneville.

For

• Performance   • Room/comfort   • Driveability
• Anti-lock brakes

Against

• Fuel economy   • Ride (T Type)

Summary

The main difference between Electra and the less-expensive LeSabre is Electra's mission as a luxury sedan instead of a family sedan. Thus, Electra offers plusher furnishings, more standard equipment, and a few options not available on LeSabre. However, Electra offers no advantages in its mechanical components, which are shared with LeSabre. The 3.8-liter V-6 provides brisk acceleration, though it uses too much gas (expect 15-18 mpg around town) and isn't the smoothest engine. The front-drive Electra is a traditional Buick in most respects, providing a soft ride, roomy and posh interior, and quiet highway cruising. The T Type has a more sporting personality, due to its firmer suspension and larger tires, which improve handling and roadholding, but at a noticeable loss

Prices are accurate at time of printing; subject to manufacturer's change.

in ride comfort. We highly recommend the anti-lock brakes, standard on the T Type and Ultra, optional on the others, for the extra safety margin they provide. However, since you can also get the anti-lock feature on the cheaper LeSabre, we recommend that car over this one.

Specifications

	4-door notchback
Wheelbase, in.	110.8
Overall length, in.	196.9
Overall width, in.	72.4
Overall height, in.	54.3
Turn diameter, ft.	39.4
Curb weight, lbs.	3288
Cargo vol., cu. ft.	16.4
Fuel capacity, gals.	18.0
Seating capacity	6
Front headroom, in.	39.3
Front shoulder room, in.	58.9
Front legroom, max., in.	42.4
Rear headroom, in.	38.1
Rear shoulder room, in.	58.8
Rear legroom, min., in.	41.5

Powertrain layout: transverse front engine/front-wheel drive.

Engines

	ohv V-6
Size, liters/cu. in.	3.8/231
Fuel delivery	PFI
Horsepower @ rpm	165 @ 4800
Torque (lbs./ft.) @ rpm	210 @ 2000
Availability	S

EPA city/highway mpg

4-speed OD automatic	19/28

Prices

Buick Electra	Retail Price	Dealer invoice	Low Price
Limited 4-door notchback	$20225	$17454	$17704
T Type 4-door notchback	23025	19871	20121
Park Avenue 4-door notchback	21750	18770	19020
Park Avenue Ultra 4-door notchback	27825	23735	23985
Destination charge	550	550	550

Standard equipment:

Limited: 3.8-liter PFI V-6 engine, 4-speed automatic transmission, power steering, air conditioning, 55/45 cloth front seat with storage armrest, power driver's seat, tilt steering column, power windows, intermittent wipers, cruise control, AM/FM cassette, rear defogger, left remote and right manual mirrors, trip odometer, remote fuel door release, tinted glass, front reading and courtesy lights, rear shoulder belts, automatic level control, wire wheel covers, 205/75R14 all-season SBR tires. **T Type** adds: anti-lock braking system, Gran Touring suspension, sport steering wheel, floormats, overhead console, quartz analog gauge cluster (includes tachometer, voltmeter, coolant temperature and oil pressure gauges, low-fuel warning), rear headrests, lighted visor mirrors, power mirrors, 45/45 front seat with console and armrest, leather-wrapped steering wheel, power antenna, remote decklid

KEY: ohv = overhead valve; **ohc** = overhead cam; **dohc** = double overhead cam; **I** = inline cylinders; **V** = cylinders in V configuration; **flat** = horizontally opposed cylinders; **bbl.** = barrel (carburetor); **PFI** = port (multi-point) fuel injection; **TBI** = throttle-body (single-point) fuel injection; **rpm** = revolutions per minute; **OD** = overdrive transmission; **S** = standard; **O** = optional; **NA** = not available.

release, 215/65R15 Goodyear Eagle GT+4 tires on alloy wheels. **Park Avenue** adds to base: cruise control, power locks, power mirrors, coach lamps, rear reading and courtesy lights, lighted right visor mirror, added sound insulation, floormats, upgraded carpet, WSW tires. **Ultra** adds: anti-lock braking system, 55/45 leather front seat with 20-way power adjustments, two-tone paint, rear armrest, 205/70R15 tires on alloy wheels.

Optional equipment:

	Retail Price	Dealer Invoice	Low Price
Anti-lock brakes	925	786	833
Premium Pkg. SB, Limited	398	338	358
Power antenna, floormats, door edge guards, lighted right visor mirror, power right seatback recliner, remote decklid release.			
Luxury Pkg. SC, Limited	1009	858	908
Pkg. SB plus automatic climate control, door courtesy/warning lights, power mirrors, power passenger seat.			
Prestige Pkg. SD, Limited	2199	1869	1979
Pkg. SC plus cornering lights, automatic power locks, Twilight Sentinel, remote keyless entry, illuminated entry, light monitors, automatic day/night mirror, lighted left visor mirror, driver's seatback recliner, self-sealing tires, upgraded radio (includes AM stereo, EQ and tape search/repeat).			
Premium Pkg. SB, T Type	690	587	621
Automatic climate control, door edge guards, power passenger seat with power recliner, Concert Sound speakers.			
Luxury Pkg. SC, T Type	1178	1001	1060
Pkg. SB plus cornering lights, Twilight Sentinel, illuminated entry, lamp monitors, door courtesy/warning lights, rear reading lights, low washer fluid indicator, power decklid pulldown.			
Prestige Pkg. SD, T Type	2099	1784	1889
Pkg. SC plus automatic power locks, remote keyless entry, automatic day/night mirror, heated left mirror, power driver's seatback recliner, two-position driver's seat memory, deluxe trunk trim, upgraded radio (includes AM stereo, EQ and tape search/repeat).			
Premium Pkg. SB, Park Ave	825	701	743
Ultra	410	349	369
Automatic climate control, door edge guards, Twilight Sentinel, Concert Sound speakers, power antenna, power passenger seat with power recliner.			
Luxury Pkg. SC, Park Ave	1500	1275	1350
Ultra	1050	893	945
Pkg. SB plus cornering lights, automatic power locks, four-note horn, illuminated entry, remote keyless entry, light monitors, low fuel and washer fluid indicators, lighted left visor mirror, power decklid pulldown.			
Prestige Pkg. SD, Park Ave	2306	1960	2075
Ultra	1596	1357	1436
Pkg. SC plus automatic day/night mirror, heated left mirror, two-position driver's seat memory, driver's seatback recliner, deluxe trunk trim, self-sealing tires, upgraded radio (includes AM stereo, EQ and tape search/repeat).			
Gran Touring Pkg., Ltd & Park Ave	272	231	245
Ltd & Park Ave w/SD	122	104	110
Gran Touring suspension, HD cooling, 2.97 axle ratio, leather-wrapped steering wheel, 215/65R15 Eagle GT tires on alloy wheels.			
2.97 axle ratio	NC	NC	NC
HD cooling (std. T Type)	40	34	36
Quartz analog gauge cluster (std. T Type)	126	107	113
Park Ave & Ultra w/SC/SD	110	94	99
Electronic instruments, Park Ave & Ultra	299	254	269
Park Ave & Ultra w/SC/SD	283	241	255
Decklid luggage rack	115	98	104
Firemist paint, exc. T Type	210	179	189
UX1 radio			
T Type, Park Ave & Ultra w/SB/SC	150	128	135
Includes AM stereo, EQ, tape search/repeat and Concert Sound speakers.			
Bose music system (NA Ltd)	773	657	696
w/SB/SC	703	598	633
w/SD	553	470	498
CD player	454	386	409
T Type, Park Ave & Ultra w/SB/SC	384	326	346
w/SD	234	199	211
Includes AM stereo, EQ and Concert Sound speakers.			
Astroroof	1230	1046	1107
Theft deterrent system	159	135	143

	Retail Price	Dealer Invoice	Low Price
Vinyl top, LTD & Park Ave	260	221	234
Ultra	895	761	806
Leather/vinyl 55/45 seat, Park Ave	450	383	405
T Type	395	336	356
Alloy wheels, Ltd & Park Ave	55	47	50
California emissions pkg.	100	85	90
Bodyside stripes, Ltd & T Type	45	38	41

Buick Estate Wagon

Buick Estate Wagon

What's New

Buick's full-size wagon is now offered in a single, luxury model called the Estate Wagon. The less plush LeSabre Estate is discontinued, and "Electra" has been trimmed from the surviving model's name. The standard equipment list is similar to that offered in the former LeSabre Estate Wagon, with the addition of delay windshield wipers and a tilt steering wheel. The seat design is similar to that in the former Electra Estate Wagon, in cloth or leather. New exterior color options include light maple and dark maple metallic. There's a new tri-shield hood ornament and a new Estate Wagon emblem on the front fenders. Imitation wood bodyside paneling remains standard. The only powertrain is a 140-horsepower 5.0-liter V-8 engine coupled to a 4-speed overdrive automatic transmission. Air conditioning and a two-way power tailgate with power window is standard, as is a third, rear-facing third seat, for 8-passenger capacity. A 5000-pound trailer-towing package is optional and includes heavy-duty engine and transmission cooling, automatic level control, limited slip differential, and a 3.23 final drive ratio. The Chevrolet Caprice wagon and Oldsmobile Custom Cruiser wagon share the Estate Wagon's design.

For

● Room/comfort ● Cargo room ● Trailer towing capacity

Against

● Fuel economy ● Size and weight
● Handling/maneuverability

Summary

This is Buick's largest car—its 115.9-inch wheelbase is five inches longer than the Park Avenue's—and it's the only one with a V-8 engine and rear-wheel drive. Its design dates to 1977. With substantial trailer-towing ability, 8-passenger seating, and nearly 90 cubic feet of cargo space, these big wagons exceed the capabilities of mid-size, front-drive rivals, and

nearly match the minivans. In addition, this traditional wagon may come out a little cheaper than a fully equipped minivan. GM's full-size wagons have impressive reputations for occupant protection. At well over 4000 pounds, they're too heavy for their carbureted V-8 engine, so fuel economy is poor and acceleration lackluster. They also have clumsy, boat-like handling and a mushy, poorly controlled ride—though the optional trailering package cures some of that. While these aren't our favorites, they serve a market niche that calls for a luxurious beast of burden in a traditional wagon format.

Specifications

	5-door wagon
Wheelbase, in.	115.9
Overall length, in.	220.5
Overall width, in.	79.3
Overall height, in.	59.3
Turn diameter, ft.	41.4
Curb weight, lbs.	4281
Cargo vol., cu. ft.	87.9
Fuel capacity, gals.	22.0
Seating capacity	8
Front headroom, in.	39.6
Front shoulder room, in.	60.9
Front legroom, max., in.	42.2
Rear headroom, in.	39.3
Rear shoulder room, in.	61.0
Rear legroom, min., in.	37.8

Powertrain layout: longitudinal front engine/rear-wheel drive.

Engines	ohv V-8
Size, liters/cu. in.	5.0/307
Fuel delivery	4 bbl.
Horsepower @ rpm	140 @ 3200
Torque (lbs./ft.) @ rpm	255 @ 2000
Availability	S

EPA city/highway mpg
4-speed OD automatic 17/24

Prices

Buick Estate Wagon	Retail Price	Dealer Invoice	Low Price
5-door wagon	$17940	$15482	$15682
Destination charge	505	505	505

Standard equipment:

5.0-liter 4bbl. V-8, 4-speed automatic transmission, power steering, air conditioning, 55/45 cloth front seat with manual passenger recliner, tinted glass, tilt steering column, trip odometer, intermittent wipers, front reading lamps, AM/FM radio, 2-way tailgate with power window, 225/75R15 WSW tires on alloy wheels.

Optional equipment:

Popular Pkg. SB	1150	978	1035
Floormats, cruise control, rear defogger, power locks, remote tailgate lock release, roof rack, woodgrain vinyl applique, door edge guards.			
Preimum Pkg. SC	1965	1670	1769
Pkg. SB plus air deflector, bodyside moldings, power driver's seat, power windows, AM/FM cassette.			
Luxury Pkg. SD	2208	1877	1987
Pkg. SC plus lighted right visor mirror, Exterior Molding Pkg., power antenna.			

Prices are accurate at time of printing; subject to manufacturer's change.

	Retail Price	Dealer Invoice	Low Price
Prestige Pkg. SE	2766	2351	2489
Pkg. SD plus automatic climate control, cornering lights, Twilight Sentinel, illuminated entry, power mirrors, front light monitors, power passenger seatback recliner.			
AM/FM cassette	150	128	135
AM/FM cassette w/AM ST & EQ, w/SA/SB .	300	255	270
w/SC/SD/SE	150	128	135
Power antenna	75	64	68
Power passenger seat	270	230	243
Delete third seat (credit)	(215)	(183)	(183)
Trailer Towing Pkg.	215	183	194
Leather/vinyl 55/45 seat	450	383	405
Limited-slip differential	100	85	90
Requires Trailer Towing Pkg.			
Wire wheel covers	215	183	194

Buick LeSabre

Buick LeSabre

What's New

Buick's perennial best seller gets a facelift for '90. There's a new vertical-bar grille, composite headlamps, integrated park and turn lamps, and body-colored fascia and bumper guards. At the rear are new full-width taillamps. The sporty T Type has been discontinued as a separate model, but most of its features are optionally available in the Gran Touring package, which for '90 has added automatic level control. The full-size, front-drive LeSabre is built from the same design as the luxury Electra/Park Avenue, but has less standard equipment and a lower price. LeSabre uses the same 165-horsepower 3.8-liter V-6 as Electra/Park Avenue. LeSabre also shares its design with the Oldsmobile Eighty-Eight Royale and Ninety-Eight and Pontiac Bonneville. This year's lineup includes a base LeSabre 2-door coupe, Custom 4-door sedan, and Limited coupe and sedan. Driver and right-side front passenger seat belts can be left buckled as a passive restraint system.

For

- Performance • Room/comfort • Driveability
- Anti-lock brakes

> **KEY: ohv** = overhead valve; **ohc** = overhead cam; **dohc** = double overhead cam; **I** = inline cylinders; **V** = cylinders in V configuration; **flat** = horizontally opposed cylinders; **bbl.** = barrel (carburetor); **PFI** = port (multi-point) fuel injection; **TBI** = throttle-body (single-point) fuel injection; **rpm** = revolutions per minute; **OD** = overdrive transmission; **S** = standard; **O** = optional; **NA** = not available.

Against

- Fuel economy • Ride (T Type)

Summary

This is a stellar family automobile, with front-wheel drive, a responsive engine, standard air conditioning, optional anti-lock brakes, and a big-car ride and feel. The 1989 LeSabre was the top domestic model and ranked No. 2 among 154 domestic and imported models in J.D. Power and Associates' independent study of the most trouble-free cars produced for the U.S. market. We favor LeSabre over the similar but more expensive Electra simply because there are no substantive differences between the two. While Electra is clearly plusher, LeSabre is hardly a stripped econocar by comparison. In addition, all body panels except the roof are made of two-sided galvanized steel (same as Electra) for long corrosion resistance. LeSabre's V-6 has ample low-end power for quick get-aways and brisk passing response, though the EPA estimates (19 mpg city and 28 mpg highway) are optimistic; we usually average 15-18 mpg in urban driving and 22-24 mpg on the highway. The Gran Touring package offers better handling than LeSabre's base suspension and tires, but at considerable sacrifice in ride comfort. We recommend the optional anti-lock brakes, which are available on all models. LeSabre isn't cheap, but it doesn't cost as much as some smaller imported cars, and that helps make it a good value. The Buick trods a traditional path in its conservative styling, soft, flat bench seats that can hold six people, and adequate trunk space. Overall, it shares with its corporate cousins—the Oldsmobile Eighty-Eight Royale and Pontiac Bonneville—a combination of size, comfort, and refined road manners that's hard to match in this price class.

Specifications

	2-door notchback	4-door notchback
Wheelbase, in.	110.8	110.8
Overall length, in.	196.5	196.5
Overall width, in.	72.4	72.4
Overall height, in.	54.2	54.9
Turn diameter, ft.	40.0	40.0
Curb weight, lbs.	3242	3269
Cargo vol., cu. ft.	15.7	16.4
Fuel capacity, gals.	18.0	18.0
Seating capacity	6	6
Front headroom, in.	38.1	38.9
Front shoulder room, in.	59.0	59.5
Front legroom, max., in.	42.4	42.4
Rear headroom, in.	37.6	38.3
Rear shoulder room, in.	57.8	59.5
Rear legroom, min., in.	37.4	38.7

Powertrain layout: transverse front engine/front-wheel drive.

Engines

	ohv V-6
Size, liters/cu. in.	3.8/231
Fuel delivery	PFI
Horsepower @ rpm	165 @ 4800
Torque (lbs./ft.) @ rpm	210 @ 2000
Availability	S

EPA city/highway mpg

4-speed OD automatic	19/28

Prices

Buick LeSabre

	Retail Price	Dealer Invoice	Low Price
2-door notchback	$16145	$13933	$14133
Custom 4-door notchback	16050	13851	14051
Limited 4-door notchback	17400	15016	15216
Limited 2-door notchback	17300	14930	15130
Destination charge	505	505	505

Standard equipment:

Base and Custom: 3.8-liter PFI V-6, 4-speed automatic transmission, power steering, air conditioning, tilt steering column, cloth split bench seat with armrest, trip odometer, tinted glass, AM/FM radio, automatic front seatbelts, rear shoulder belts, 205/75R14 all-season SBR tires. **Limited** adds: 55/45 front seat with storage armrest, reclining seatbacks, wide lower bodyside moldings.

Optional equipment:

Anti-lock brakes	925	786	833
Popular Pkg. SB, base & Custom	714	607	643

Floormats, cruise control, rear defogger, 55/45 seat with storage armrest, intermittent wipers, white-stripe tires.

Premium Pkg. SC, base	1254	1066	1129
Custom	1294	1100	1165

Pkg. SB plus power locks, AM/FM cassette, wire wheel covers.

Luxury Pkg. SD, base	1859	1580	1673
Custom	1974	1678	1777

Pkg. SC plus power driver's seat, power windows, door edge guards, manual seatback recliners.

Prestige Pkg. SE, base	2218	1885	1996
Custom	2333	1983	2100

Pkg. SD plus lighted right visor mirror, power mirrors, power antenna, remote decklid release, Concert Sound speakers.

Popular Pkg. SB, Ltd 2-door	1356	1153	1220
Ltd 4-door	1461	1242	1315

Floormats, cruise control, rear defogger, power windows and locks, power driver's seat, AM/FM cassette, intermittent wipers, white-stripe tires.

Premium Pkg. SC, Ltd 2-door	1769	1504	1592
Ltd 4-door	1884	1601	1696

Pkg. SB plus door edge guards, lighted right visor mirror, power antenna, remote decklid release, wire wheel covers.

Luxury Pkg. SD, Ltd 2-door	2261	1922	2035
Ltd 4-door	2376	2020	2138

Pkg. SC plus automatic climate control, door courtesy light and reflector, front and rear reading lights, power mirrors, power passenger seatback recliner, deluxe trunk trim.

Prestige Pkg. SE, Ltd 2-door	2766	2351	2489
Ltd 4-door	2881	2449	2593

Pkg. SD plus power passenger seat, upgraded radio (includes AM stereo, EQ, tape search/repeat).

Gran Touring Pkg.	738	627	664
w/SB	662	563	596
w/SC/SD/SE	447	380	402

Gran Touring suspension, 2.97 axle ratio, HD cooling, leather-wrapped steering wheel, automatic level control, 215/65R15 tires on alloy wheels.

2.97 axle ratio	NC	NC	NC

Requires HD cooling.

HD cooling	40	34	36
Power locks, base	175	149	158
Custom	215	183	194
Gauge pkg.	110	94	99

Tachometer, coolant temperature and oil pressure gauges, voltmeter.

Decklid luggage rack	115	98	104
AM/FM cassette, Custom w/SA/SB	150	128	135
AM/FM cassette w/EQ & AM ST	385	327	347
Custom w/SC/SD, Ltd w/SB/SC/SD . . .	235	200	212
Custom w/SE	150	128	135
Power antenna	75	64	68
Automatic level control	175	149	158
Vinyl top, 4-doors	200	170	180
55/45 seat w/storage armrest, base & Custom	183	156	165

	Retail Price	Dealer Invoice	Low Price
Leather/vinyl 55/45 seat, Ltd	450	383	405
Alloy wheels, w/SA/SB	270	230	243
s/SC/SD/SE	55	47	50
Wire wheel covers, w/SA/SB	215	183	194
Power windows, 2-doors	230	196	207
4-doors	295	251	266
California emissions pkg.	100	85	90
Bodyside stripes	45	38	41

Buick Reatta

Buick Reatta

What's New

A convertible version of Buick's luxury 2-seater is scheduled to bow in showrooms this spring. A companion to the front-wheel-drive Reatta coupe introduced in January 1988, this is the first convertible offered by Buick since the 1982-85 Riviera. It's also the first Buick ragtop built "in house" since the '75 LeSabre. Production will take place alongside the coupe at the Reatta Craft Centre in Lansing, Michigan. Reatta's convertible top must be raised and lowered by hand, but it does feature a power pulldown to snug it against the hard rear tonneau cover. Powered by the same 165-horsepower 3.8-liter V-6 that drives the coupe, the ragtop will share the hardtop's long list of standard equipment, including anti-lock brakes, automatic climate control system, a tilt steering column, and power six-way leather bucket seats. All Reatta dashboards for '90 come without the controversial Electronic Control Center video screen. Introduced on the 1986 Riviera and carried over to the Reatta, the touch-sensitive video screen had taken the place of conventional switch controls and gauge readouts for the climate system, stereo, and other functions. Gone also is the Reatta's previous digital instrumentation. It's replaced by vacuum-fluorescent readouts that mimic analog gauges. Among new standard equipment for '90 are revised interior door panels with floodlit power mirror and window toggles. A driver's-side air bag is standard on both coupe and convertible.

For

● Performance   ● Handling/roadholding   ● Anti-lock brakes

Against

● Ride   ● Noise

Summary

Reatta is an attractive luxury 2-seater that can sprint to 60 mph in about 10 seconds and deliver strong passing power on the highway. Its brakes are strong, and it corners with

Prices are accurate at time of printing; subject to manufacturer's change.

Buick

more athletic skill than you expect from a Buick, thanks partly to high-performance tires that have an all-season tread design, making for good traction even in rain or snow. However, these tires also are stiff and noisy, and Reatta's short chassis has two-thirds of its weight at the front. As a result, there's marked body pitch on wavy roads, and the suspension feels too stiff over bumpy pavement, creating a jiggly ride. Inside, there's adequate passenger and cargo room for a 2-seater, and the dashboard is improved significantly now that the distracting Electronic Control Center has been dropped. The car's climate system and stereo controls are located close at hand, and the vacuum-fluorescent instrumentation is an easy-to-read compromise between digital and analog gauges. Reatta sales so far haven't reached the 10,000 per year Buick had anticipated. But Buick expects demand for the Reatta convertible to be high.

Specifications

	2-door notchback	2-door conv.
Wheelbase, in.	98.5	98.5
Overall length, in.	183.7	183.7
Overall width, in.	73.0	73.0
Overall height, in.	51.2	51.2
Turn diameter, ft.	38.0	38.0
Curb weight, lbs.	3379	3562
Cargo vol., cu. ft.	10.5	10.5
Fuel capacity, gals.	18.2	18.2
Seating capacity	2	2
Front headroom, in.	36.9	36.9
Front shoulder room, in.	57.0	57.0
Front legroom, max., in.	43.1	43.1
Rear headroom, in.	—	—
Rear shoulder room, in.	—	—
Rear legroom, min., in.	—	—

Powertrain layout: transverse front engine/front-wheel drive.

Engines

	ohv V-6
Size, liters/cu. in.	3.8/231
Fuel delivery	PFI
Horsepower @ rpm	165 @ 4800
Torque (lbs./ft.) @ rpm	210 @ 2000
Availability	S

EPA city/highway mpg

4-speed OD automatic	18/27

Prices

Buick Reatta	Retail Price	Dealer Invoice	Low Price
2-door notchback	$28335	$24170	$25612
2-door convertible	NA	NA	NA
Destination charge	550	550	550

Standard equipment:

3.8-liter PFI V-6 engine, 4-speed automatic transmission, power steering, 4-wheel disc brakes, anti-lock braking system, driver's side airbag, automatic

KEY: **ohv** = overhead valve; **ohc** = overhead cam; **dohc** = double overhead cam; **I** = inline cylinders; **V** = cylinders in V configuration; **flat** = horizontally opposed cylinders; **bbl.** = barrel (carburetor); **PFI** = port (multi-point) fuel injection; **TBI** = throttle-body (single-point) fuel injection; **rpm** = revolutions per minute; **OD** = overdrive transmission; **S** = standard; **O** = optional; **NA** = not available.

climate control, power windows and locks, power front bucket seats with recliners, leather upholstery, remote keyless entry, electronic instruments (tachometer, coolant temperature and oil pressure gauges, voltmeter, trip odometer), tinted glass, intermittent wipers, AM/FM cassette with EQ and power antenna, full-length console, lighted visor mirrors, intermittent wipers, tilt steering column, leather-wrapped steering wheel, rear defogger, digital clock, cruise control, remote fuel door and trunk releases, cornering lamps, fog lamps, Pass Key theft deterrent system, map lights, illuminated driver's door lock and interior light control, 215/65R15 Goodyear Eagle GT + 4 tires on alloy wheels.

Optional equipment:	Retail Price	Dealer Invoice	Low Price
CD player	396	337	356
Sliding sunroof	895	761	806
16-way driver's seat	680	578	612
California emissions pkg.	100	85	90

Buick Regal

Buick Regal Gran Sport

What's New

Along with the Pontiac Grand Prix and the Oldsmobile Cutlass Supreme, Buick's Regal was redesigned from a rear-drive car to a front-wheel drive coupe for the 1988 model year. For '90, all three divisions finally get 4-door sedan versions of those cars. Regal, however, is the only one with exterior styling that differs significantly from that of its coupe counterpart. The sedan shares the coupe's chassis, 4-wheel independent suspension, and standard 4-wheel disc brakes. But in addition to the obvious changes brought about by the addition of two doors, the sedan has a smoother nose with a more horizontal grille and a more tapered tail and smaller rear lights. Like the coupe, the Regal sedan is offered in Custom trim with a 55/45 split front bench seat or in Limited and Gran Sport models, which can be outfitted with four bucket seats. A 4-speed overdrive automatic is the only available transmission. The standard engine is a 135-horsepower 3.1-liter V-6. A 170-horsepower 3.8-liter V-6 is optional and is exclusive to the Regal line for '90. Also unique to Regal for '90 are optional dual temperature controls for the driver and front-seat passenger. The instrument panel and front-door control switches are now illuminated for up to 30 seconds after either front door is opened. Seeking a quieter ride at no sacrifice to handling, Buick uses high-performance touring tires in place of the previous Goodyear Eagle GT + 4s as part of the optional Gran Touring package.

For

- Ride   • Passenger room   • Trunk space
- Anti-lock brakes

Against

- Performance   • Instrumentation   • Engine noise

Summary

Given a rather substantial 107.5-inch wheelbase, a car with four doors makes more sense than one with two and, indeed, the Regal is far more appealing as a sedan than as a coupe. Its rear seat is now as accessible as a family car's ought to be. Once back there, passengers will find sufficient head and leg room, though the lower cushion itself feels puny and un-substantial. The coupe's cumbersome doors are eliminated with the sedan, but unfortunately, the 4-door's front shoulder belts are anchored to its center pillar, a position that allows them to ride on the neck of shorter occupants. Buick's done nothing to improve the poorly designed Regal instrument cluster. You get a fuel gauge and a ribbon-speedometer laid out in a narrow, hard-to-read strip; an optional electronic cluster can be substituted, but it's squeezed into the same small space and has poorly designed graphics. On the bright side, the Regal seems to drive a little better than its W-body cousins. Its suspension strikes a fine compromise between ride and handling, and the mid-year availability of the slightly stronger 3.8 V-6 promises to usher the 3200-pound sedan along with some verve. Available anti-lock brakes are a major plus.

Specifications

	2-door notchback	4-door notchback
Wheelbase, in.	107.5	107.5
Overall length, in.	192.2	194.6
Overall width, in.	72.5	70.9
Overall height, in.	53.0	54.3
Turn diameter, ft.	40.0	40.0
Curb weight, lbs.	3108	3163
Cargo vol., cu. ft.	15.5	15.6
Fuel capacity, gals.	16.5	16.5
Seating capacity	6	6
Front headroom, in.	37.8	38.8
Front shoulder room, in.	57.6	57.6
Front legroom, max., in.	42.3	42.4
Rear headroom, in.	37.1	37.7
Rear shoulder room, in.	56.8	58.1
Rear legroom, min., in.	34.8	36.2

Powertrain layout: transverse front engine/front-wheel drive.

Engines

	ohv V-6	ohv V-6
Size, liters/cu. in.	3.1/191	3.8/231
Fuel delivery	PFI	PFI
Horsepower @ rpm	135 @ 4400	170 @ 4800
Torque (lbs./ft.) @ rpm	180 @ 3600	220 @ 3200
Availability	S	O

EPA city/highway mpg

4-speed OD automatic	19/30	19/28

Prices

Buick Regal	Retail Price	Dealer Invoice	Low Price
Custom 2-door notchback	$15200	$13118	$13318
Limited 2-door notchback	15860	13687	13887
Destination charge	455	455	455

Prices for 4-door models not available at time of publication.

Standard equipment:

3.1-liter PFI V-6, 4-speed automatic transmission, power steering, 55/45 cloth front seat with armrest and recliners (bucket seats are available at no charge), tilt steering column, tinted glass, digital speedometer, left remote and right manual mirrors, black lower bodyside moldings, AM/FM radio, automatic front seatbelts, rear shoulder belts, 205/70R14 all-season SBR WSW tires. **Limited** adds: upgraded carpet, bright wide bodyside moldings, 55/45 seat with storage armrest.

Optional equipment:	Retail Price	Dealer Invoice	Low Price
3.8-liter V-6	395	336	356
Anti-lock braking system, Ltd & GS	925	786	833
Popular Pkg. SB, Custom	306	260	275
Rear defogger, intermittent wipers, door edge guards, white-stripe tires.			
Premium Pkg. SB, Custom	861	732	775
Pkg. SB plus AM/FM cassette, cruise control, power locks, floormats.			
Luxury Pkg. SD, Custom	1574	1338	1417
Pkg. SC plus power windows, power antenna, lighted right visor mirror, wire wheel covers, courtesy and reading lights, remote decklid release.			
Prestige Pkg. SE, Custom	2416	2054	2174
Pkg. SD plus power driver's seat, power mirrors, Concert Sound speakers, steering-wheel-mounted radio controls, electronic instrumentation.			
Premium Pkg. SC, Limited	626	532	563
Rear defogger, AM/FM cassette, intermittent wipers, cruise control, white-stripe tires.			
Luxury Pkg. SD, Limited	1814	1542	1633
Pkg. SC plus power windows and locks, power driver's seat, power antenna, remote decklid release, wire wheel covers, lighted right visor mirror, floormats, door edge guards.			
Prestige Pkg. SE, Limited	2581	2194	2323
Pkg. SD plus power mirrors, Concert Sound speakers, electronic instrumentation, steering-wheel-mounted radio controls, dual air conditioning controls, upgraded radio (includes AM stereo, EQ and tape search/repeat).			
Gran Sport Popular Pkg. SM	1624	1380	1462
Gran Touring Pkg., Gran Sport exterior trim, cloth reclining seats, floorshift, AM/FM cassette, cruise control, rear defogger, intermittent wipers, floormats.			
Gran Sport Prestige Pkg. SF	2969	2524	2672
Pkg. SM plus power windows and locks, electronic instrumentation, front reading/courtesy lights, power mirrors, power antenna, power driver's seat, Concert Sound speakers, remote decklid release, lighted right visor mirror.			
Gran Touring Pkg., w/SC	531	451	478
w/SD	271	230	244
w/SE	175	149	158
Gran Touring suspension, leather-wrapped steering wheel (exc. w/SE), 215/60R16 tires on alloy wheels.			
Cruise control, Custom w/SB	195	166	176
Power locks	175	149	158
Electronic instrumentation, Ltd w/SD	299	254	269
Tachometer, coolant temperature and oil pressure gauges, voltmeter, trip odometer, low fuel indicator.			
Remote keyless entry, Ltd & GS	125	106	113
Requires SE or SF.			
Decklid luggage rack	115	98	104
Wide black molding, Custom	70	60	63
Custom w/SB/SC/SD/SE	55	47	50
Lower accent paint, w/SB/SC	205	174	185
w/SD or SE	160	136	144
AM/FM cassette, Custom w/SB	140	119	126
AM/FM cassette w/EQ & AM stereo	150	128	135
Available on Custom w/SE and Gran Sport.			
CD player, Custom w/SE, GS	274	233	247
Ltd w/SE	124	105	112
Power antenna	75	64	68
Power glass sunroof	650	553	585
Steering-wheel-mounted radio controls, GS	29	25	26
Leather/vinyl 55/45 seat, Ltd	450	383	405
Leather/vinyl bucket seats, Ltd & GS	450	383	405
Four Seater Pkg., GS	409	348	368
Cloth bucket seats, floorshift, rear bucket seats with head restraints.			
Styled steel wheels, w/SB/SC	115	98	104
Wire wheel covers, w/SB/SC	215	183	194
Alloy wheels (14"), w/SB/SC	270	230	243
Alloy wheels w/205/70R15 tires, w/SB/SC	244	207	220
w/SD/SE	29	25	26
Power windows, w/SB/SC/SD	240	204	216

Prices are accurate at time of printing; subject to manufacturer's change.

Buick Riviera

Buick Riviera

What's New

Buick's personal luxury coupe builds upon last year's exterior restyling with a revamped interior. The highlight is a new dashboard that uses conventional buttons and slide levers instead of a touch-sensitive video screen to control the climate and stereo systems. Critics had denounced the video screen as a distraction for the driver. The digital speedometer, tachometer, and other engine gauges have been replaced by vacuum-fluorescent readouts made to look like analog instrumentation; a switch lets the driver choose a speedometer that's analog, digital, or both. A new center console and revised door panels complete the cabin's cosmetic make over, while a standard driver's-side air bag is an added safety feature for '90. A new 16-way power driver's seat is optionally available, as are two new stereo radio/compact disc systems. The "pass key" anti-theft system is now standard. A 165-horsepower 3.8-liter V-6 and 4-speed overdrive automatic transmission comprise the only available drivetrain. A Gran Touring suspension with wider tires and faster-ratio power steering is optional.

For

● Anti-lock brakes ● Quietness

Against

● Fuel economy

Summary

Buick sold 11,773 Rivieras during the first seven months of '89, more than double the total by the same time in '88. Buick credits a 1989 reskin that added 11 inches to the car's overall length, even though it didn't increase interior room. Sales had sagged in the wake of a 1986 downsizing. Riviera shares its basic design with the Cadillac Eldorado and Oldsmobile Toronado luxury coupes, both of which have sold better than the Buick. Despite its enhanced styling, Riviera does nothing exceptional. You get plenty of luxury and convenience features

for the $23,000 base price, and adequate space for four people and their luggage. Acceleration is only adequate, however, while ride and handling are at least competent. The optional anti-lock brakes give it commendable stopping ability. We do applaud the elimination of the Riviera's electronic control center. The new instrumentation and controls are far more logical, and placement of the climate and audio-systems—high on the dash and within easy reach of the driver—is welcome.

Specifications

	2-door notchback
Wheelbase, in.	108.0
Overall length, in.	193.3
Overall width, in.	71.7
Overall height, in.	53.6
Turn diameter, ft.	37.5
Curb weight, lbs.	3464
Cargo vol., cu. ft.	14.4
Fuel capacity, gals.	18.2
Seating capacity	5
Front headroom, in.	37.8
Front shoulder room, in.	57.9
Front legroom, max., in.	42.7
Rear headroom, in.	37.8
Rear shoulder room, in.	57.4
Rear legroom, min., in.	35.6

Powertrain layout: transverse front engine/front-wheel drive.

Engines

	ohv V-6
Size, liters/cu. in.	3.8/231
Fuel delivery	PFI
Horsepower @ rpm	165 @ 4800
Torque (lbs./ft.) @ rpm	210 @ 2000
Availability	S

EPA city/highway mpg

4-speed OD automatic	19/28

Prices

Buick Riviera	Retail Price	Dealer Invoice	Low Price
2-door notchback	$23040	$19653	$19853
Destination charge	550	550	550

Standard equipment:

3.8-liter PFI V-6, 4-speed automatic transmission, power steering, 4-wheel disc brakes, driver's side airbag, power windows and locks, automatic level control, cloth reclining bucket seats, power driver's seat, AM/FM cassette, power antenna, rear shoulder belts, floormats, full-length console, cruise control, rear defogger, intermittent wipers, Pass Key theft deterrent system, door edge guards, electronic instrumentation (tachometer, coolant temperature and oil pressure gauges, voltmeter, trip odometer), remote fuel door and decklid releases, tinted glass, tilt steering column, leather-wrapped steering wheel, illuminated driver's door lock and interior light control, cornering lamps, coach lamps, door courtesy and warning lights, power mirrors, lighted visor mirrors, 205/70R15 all-season SBR tires, locking wire wheel covers.

Optional equipment:

Anti-lock brakes	925	786	833
Prestige Pkg. SE	865	735	779

Twilight Sentinel, remote keyless entry, automatic power locks, heated left mirror, power decklid pulldown, power passenger seat with power recliner.

KEY: **ohv** = overhead valve; **ohc** = overhead cam; **dohc** = double overhead cam; **I** = inline cylinders; **V** = cylinders in V configuration; **flat** = horizontally opposed cylinders; **bbl.** = barrel (carburetor); **PFI** = port (multi-point) fuel injection; **TBI** = throttle-body (single-point) fuel injection; **rpm** = revolutions per minute; **OD** = overdrive transmission; **S** = standard; **O** = optional; **NA** = not available.

	Retail Price	Dealer Invoice	Low Price
Gran Touring Pkg.	104	88	94

Gran Touring suspension, 2.97 axle ratio, leather-wrapped steering wheel and shift handle, fast-ratio power steering, 215/65R15 Goodyear Eagle GT + 4 tires on alloy wheels.

Riviera Appearance Pkg.	205	174	185

Firemist lower accent paint, bodyside stripe, painted alloy wheels.

Firemist or pearlescent paint	210	179	189
Lower accent paint	190	162	171
Delco/Bose Gold music system w/CD player	1399	1189	1259
CD player w/EQ	516	439	464
Astroroof	1230	1046	1107

Buick Skylark

Buick Skylark

What's New

A new Luxury Edition sedan tops a revamped Skylark range for '90. Its standard features include a full formal vinyl top, wire wheel covers, two-tone paint, bodyside moldings, and bright exterior trim. Inside are a reclining cloth split front bench and split rear folding seats. It shares with the rest of the Skylarks a new instrument panel that uses analog gauges instead of digital readouts. The windshield-wiper controls have been relocated from the dashboard to a steering-column stalk. A new vertical grille and a turn-signal chime that sounds if the signal has been left on for one-half mile also is standard across the board. Gone from the Skylark line is the Limited 4-door sedan and 2-door coupe. The Skylark Custom returns, one step up from the new "premium value" base coupe and sedan, which feature 13-inch steel wheels and a split bench seat. A Gran Sport Coupe rounds out the new models with its Gran Touring suspension, 14-inch Shelby aluminum wheels, Eagle GT tires, reclining bucket seats, leather-wrapped steering wheel, and blackout exterior trim. Standard on all these front-drive compacts is a 110-horsepower 2.5-liter 4-cylinder engine. Optional on all but the base car is a 160-horsepower 2.3-liter Quad 4 or the 160-horsepower 3.3-liter V-6. Buick's N-body compact Skylark is similar to the Oldsmobile Cutlass Calais and Pontiac Grand Am.

For

● Performance (V-6, Quad 4) ● Visibility

Against

● Noise (Quad 4) ● Rear seat room ● Trunk space

Summary

Buick's front-drive compact doesn't lack for horsepower with a choice of three engines offering 110, 150 or 160. Too bad all of them have to work through a 3-speed automatic that's incapable of tapping all the available power and is slow to downshift when you need more power for passing. Even so, the V-6 gives Skylark ample pickup and smooth, quiet cruising. Sadly, the potent Quad 4 also suffers even more with the 3-speed automatic since it requires higher engine speeds to produce maximum horsepower and torque. The Quad 4 also has a loud, nasty growl when worked hard. The standard 2.5-liter 4-cylinder is adequate for this car. Skylark's interior and trunk space aren't as generous as some Japanese rivals, such as the Honda Accord and Toyota Camry. With a flat front bench seat, column-mounted shift lever and foot-operated parking brake, the base and Skylark Custom models have a conservative American flavor. The Gran Sport has a sporty flair that falls well short of serious performance, while the new Luxury Edition offers pint-size plushness that's actually quite appealing in its way. There's nothing special here to make us want to buy a Skylark, yet prices are reasonable and dealers should be discounting.

Specifications

	2-door notchback	4-door notchback
Wheelbase, in.	103.4	103.4
Overall length, in.	180.0	180.0
Overall width, in.	66.6	66.6
Overall height, in.	52.1	52.1
Turn diameter, ft.	37.8	37.8
Curb weight, lbs.	2568	2636
Cargo vol., cu. ft.	13.4	13.4
Fuel capacity, gals.	13.6	13.6
Seating capacity	5	5
Front headroom, in.	37.7	37.7
Front shoulder room, in.	54.6	54.3
Front legroom, max., in.	42.9	42.9
Rear headroom, in.	37.1	37.1
Rear shoulder room, in.	55.2	54.1
Rear legroom, min., in.	34.3	34.3

Powertrain layout: transverse front engine/front-wheel drive.

Engines
	ohv I-4	dohc I-4	ohv V-6
Size, liters/cu. in.	2.5/151	2.3/138	3.3/204
Fuel delivery	TBI	PFI	PFI
Horsepower @ rpm	110 @ 5200	160 @ 6200	160 @ 5200
Torque (lbs./ft.) @ rpm	135 @ 3200	150 @ 5200	185 @ 2000
Availability	S	O	O

EPA city/highway mpg
3-speed automatic	23/30	22/31	20/27

Prices

Buick Skylark	Retail Price	Dealer Invoice	Low Price
4-door notchback	$10465	$9659	$9859
2-door notchback	10565	9752	9952
Custom 4-door notchback	11460	10234	10434
Custom 2-door notchback	11460	10234	10434
Luxury Edition (LE) 4-door notchback	13145	11738	11938
Gran Sport (GS) 2-door notchback	12935	11551	11751
Destination charge	425	425	425

Standard equipment:

2.5-liter TBI 4-cylinder engine, 3-speed automatic transmission, power steering, cloth split bench seat, tinted glass, trip odometer, AM/FM radio, 185/80R13 tires. **Custom** adds: front and rear center armrests, remote fuel door

Prices are accurate at time of printing; subject to manufacturer's change.

release, split folding rear seat, upgraded trunk trim. **Luxury Edition** adds: vinyl top, two-tone paint, wire wheel covers, reclining split bench seat, wide bodyside moldings, left remote and right manual mirrors. **Gran Sport** adds to Custom: Gran Touring suspension, AM/FM cassette, left remote and right manual mirrors, leather-wrapped steering wheel, wide black bodyside moldings, 215/60R14 Goodyear Eagle GT + 4 tires on alloy wheels.

Optional equipment:	Retail Price	Dealer Invoice	Low Price
2.3-liter Quad 4 engine	660	561	594
3.3-liter V-6	710	604	639
Popular Pkg. SB, base 2-door	831	706	748
Base 4-door	921	783	829
Air conditioning, front center armrest, right visor mirror, upgraded trunk trim, remote fuel door release, seatback recliners (4-door).			
Premium Pkg. SC, base	856	728	770
Air conditioning, bodyside moldings, wheel opening and rocker panel moldings.			
Luxury Pkg. SD, base 2-door	967	822	870
Base 4-door	1057	898	951
Pkgs. SB and SC.			
Prestige Pkg. SE, base 2-door	1155	982	1040
Base 4-door	1245	1058	1121
Pkg. SD plus tilt steering column, left remote and right manual mirrors.			
Elite Pkg. SF, base 2-door	1534	1304	1381
Base 4-door	1599	1359	1439
Air conditioning, power windows, cruise control, intermittent wipers, tilt steering column, left remote and right manual mirrors, bodyside moldings, wheel opening and rocker panel moldings.			
Popular Pkg. SB, Custom	1178	1001	1060
Air conditioning, rear defogger, tilt steering column, left remote and right manual mirrors, bodyside moldings, wheel opening moldings.			
Premium Pkg. SC, Custom	1473	1252	1326
Pkg. SB plus cruise control, intermittent wipers, floormats.			
Luxury Pkg. SD, Custom	1893	1609	1704
Pkg. SC plus AM/FM cassette, wire wheel covers, white-stripe tires, 4-way seat adjuster.			
Prestige Pkg. SE, Custom 2-door	2308	1962	2077
Custom 4-door	2413	2051	2172
Pkg. SD plus power windows and locks.			
Elite Pkg. SF, Custom 2-door	2786	2368	2507
Custom 4-door	2891	2457	2602
Pkg. SE plus power driver's seat, power antenna, lighted visor mirror, remote decklid release, front reading lamps, wide rocker panel moldings.			
Popular Pkg. SB, LE	1015	863	914
Air conditioning, rear defogger, tilt steering column.			
Premium Pkg. SC, LE	1485	1262	1337
Pkg. SB plus cruise control, intermittent wipers, AM/FM cassette, 4-way seat adjuster, floormats.			
Luxury Pkg. SD, LE	2005	1704	1805
Pkg. SC plus power windows and locks.			
Prestige Pkg. SE, LE	2433	2068	2190
Pkg. SD plus power driver's seat, power antenna, lighted visor mirror, remote decklid release, front reading lamps.			
Premium Pkg. SB, GS	1015	863	914
Air conditioning, tilt steering column, rear defogger.			
Luxury Pkg. SC, GS	1345	1143	1211
Pkg. SB plus intermittent wipers, cruise control, 4-way seat adjuster, floormats.			
Prestige Pkg. SD, GS	1835	1560	1652
Pkg. SC plus power windows and locks, power antenna.			
Gran Touring Pkg., Custom w/SA/SB/SC .	565	480	509
Custom w/SD/SE/SF	320	272	288
Gran Touring suspension, leather-wrapped steering wheel, 215/60R14 tires on alloy wheels.			
WSW tires, base	68	58	61

	Retail Price	Dealer Invoice	Low Price
185/75R14 WSW tires, Custom w/SA/SB/SC	68	58	61
Bucket seats & floorshift, base & LE	210	179	189
Wire wheel covers, Custom w/SA/SB/SC . .	177	150	159
Alloy wheels, Custom w/SA/SB/SC	346	294	311
Custom w/SD/SE/SF	101	86	91
Engine block heater	18	15	16
Decklid luggage rack	115	98	104

Cadillac Allante

Cadillac Allante

What's New

Allante, Cadillac's most expensive model, becomes the first front-drive car with traction control, a new standard feature for 1990. The traction-control system uses the sensors for the anti-lock brakes to detect wheel slip during acceleration or steady cruising. When one of the front wheels starts to slip, the system applies the brakes to that wheel to prevent excessive slippage. If both front wheels are slipping, enough braking force is applied to both sides to optimize traction. In addition, if the traction-control system is engaged for more than three seconds, the engine computer cuts fuel delivery to one of the cylinders. If traction control remains engaged, the computer cuts fuel to as many as four cylinders to minimize stress on the brakes, engine, and transmission. There is no audible warning when the system is engaged, but a dashboard warning light appears during prolonged operation. Cadillac has added a lower-priced model that comes only with a folding convertible top; the higher-priced version comes with the convertible top and a removable aluminum hardtop. Other changes for Allante are that a driver's-side airbag is now standard and the electronically controlled shock absorbers have been retuned to improve ride quality. The shock absorbers now remain in a soft mode up to 40 mph instead of 25 mph; at 40 mph, damping switches to "normal" and at 60 it changes to firm. With an airbag now standard, Allante's steering column loses its telescoping feature, but retains a tilt feature. A compact disc player has been added to the standard sound system, which includes a cassette player.

For

● Acceleration ● Anti-lock brakes ● Airbag

Against

● Price ● Fuel economy

Summary

Cadillac made a slew of major changes to Allante last year to try to generate more sales, including a larger, more powerful engine and a revamped suspension. The result: 1989 sales

---

KEY: ohv = overhead valve; **ohc** = overhead cam; **dohc** = double overhead cam; **I** = inline cylinders; **V** = cylinders in V configuration; **flat** = horizontally opposed cylinders; **bbl.** = barrel (carburetor); **PFI** = port (multi-point) fuel injection; **TBI** = throttle-body (single-point) fuel injection; **rpm** = revolutions per minute; **OD** = overdrive transmission; **S** = standard; **O** = optional; **NA** = not available.

dropped slightly. This year, Cadillac adds traction control and an airbag, but Allante has another problem to face. That's the new Mercedes-Benz SL, which offers as much luxury equipment, more horsepower, and greater prestige. Allante's main advantage over the Mercedes SL remains its lower price, but that hasn't helped before, so it probably won't matter much now. Allante's 4.5-liter V-8 delivers brisk acceleration, but with too much noise and a crude nature that is out of place in a car this expensive. We haven't been able to road test a 1990 model yet, so we can't say how much this year's ride has been improved. Our initial impression is that this year's suspension changes haven't made a huge difference. Allante still rides too firmly for our tastes, partly because of its wide, stiff, high-performance tires. The 1990 Allante is a much better car than the original version, which debuted for 1987. We're still not convinced there's enough here to justify spending so much money.

Specifications

	2-door conv.
Wheelbase, in.	99.4
Overall length, in.	178.7
Overall width, in.	73.5
Overall height, in.	52.2
Turn diameter, ft.	40.2
Curb weight, lbs.	3466
Cargo vol., cu. ft.	16.2
Fuel capacity, gals.	22.0
Seating capacity	2
Front headroom, in.	37.2
Front shoulder room, in.	57.7
Front legroom, max., in.	43.2
Rear headroom, in.	—
Rear shoulder room, in.	—
Rear legroom, min., in.	—

Powertrain layout: transverse front engine/front-wheel drive.

Engines

	ohv V-8
Size, liters/cu. in.	4.5/273
Fuel delivery	PFI
Horsepower @ rpm	200 @ 4400
Torque (lbs./ft.) @ rpm	270 @ 3200
Availability	S

EPA city/highway mpg

4-speed OD automatic	15/22

Prices

Cadillac Allante	Retail Price	Dealer Invoice	Low Price
2-door convertible	$51500	$44068	$45068
2-door convertible w/hardtop	57813	48873	49873

Price includes $650 Gas Guzzler Tax and $550 destination charge.

Standard equipment:

4.5-liter PFI V-8 engine, 4-speed automatic transmission, power steering, anti-lock 4-wheel disc brakes, traction control system, driver's-side airbag, removable hardtop, folding convertible top, ten-way power Recaro seats with leather upholstery and driver's-side position memory, Delco-GM/Bose Symphony music system with cassette and CD player, tilt steering column, power mirrors, intermittent wipers, automatic day/night mirror, power decklid pulldown, theft deterrent system, 225/55VR16 Goodyear Eagle VL tires on alloy wheels.

OPTIONS prices not available at time of publication.

Cadillac Brougham

Cadillac Brougham

What's New

Anti-lock brakes are a new standard feature and a 5.7-liter V-8 engine is a new option for Brougham, Cadillac's rear-drive luxury sedan. The Brougham also wears revised exterior styling, though the changes aren't nearly as dramatic as on the arch rival Lincoln Town Car. At 221 inches overall, the 4-door Brougham edges the redesigned Town Car by less than an inch to remain the longest production car built in the U.S. Major appearance changes include composite front headlamps, new bumper covers and rub strips, and a padded vinyl roof. The new standard anti-lock feature regulates braking force to the front disc brakes individually and to the rear drum brakes jointly to keep the wheels from locking, which can cause skidding. The optional 175-horsepower 5.7-liter V-8 has single-point fuel injection and is available only with the Coachbuilder or Trailer Towing packages. With EPA fuel-economy estimates of 14 mpg city and 21 highway, the 5.7 V-8 carries an $850 gas-guzzler tax. A 140-horsepower 5.0-liter V-8 with a 4-barrel carburetor and no guzzler tax remains standard. Other new standard features include front shoulder belts that can be left buckled for automatic deployment, an electronic instrument cluster, rear-window defogger, a cassette player and preset graphic equalizer for the stereo system, and black walnut burl trim for the interior. A revamped climate-control system now has three automatic settings and two manual settings. A compact disc player is a new option.

For

● Acceleration (5.7-liter) ● Anti-lock brakes ● Quietness ● Passenger and cargo room

Against

● Fuel economy ● Acceleration (5.0-liter) ● Size and weight

Summary

Prodded by the imminent arrival of a redesigned Town Car, Cadillac has made some major—and overdue—changes on the Brougham, whose design dates to the 1977 model year. The standard anti-lock brakes fill a big void in the safety department, while the optional 5.7-liter V-8 gives Brougham the power to keep up with traffic, though it still lags behind most other sedans in this price range. Cadillac estimates Brougham does 0-60 mph in 10.5 seconds with the 5.7, versus 14.3 seconds with the standard 5.0-liter engine, a dramatic improvement. Even so, we're not recommending you buy a Brougham because of this year's new brakes and larger engine, or a Town Car either, for that matter. Both these cars

Prices are accurate at time of printing; subject to manufacturer's change.

Cadillac

are still overweight and clumsy compared to most other luxury sedans, including domestic cars such as the Cadillac De Ville/Fleetwood, Lincoln Continental, and Chrysler Imperial and New Yorker Fifth Avenue.

Specifications

	4-door notchback
Wheelbase, in.	121.5
Overall length, in.	221.0
Overall width, in.	76.5
Overall height, in.	56.7
Turn diameter, ft.	40.5
Curb weight, lbs.	4283
Cargo vol., cu. ft.	19.5
Fuel capacity, gals.	25.0
Seating capacity	6
Front headroom, in.	39.0
Front shoulder room, in.	59.4
Front legroom, max., in.	42.0
Rear headroom, in.	38.1
Rear shoulder room, in.	59.4
Rear legroom, min., in.	41.2

Powertrain layout: longitudinal front engine/rear-wheel drive.

Engines

	ohv V-8	ohv V-8
Size, liters/cu. in.	5.0/307	5.7/350
Fuel delivery	4 bbl.	TBI
Horsepower @ rpm	140 @ 3200	175 @ 4200
Torque (lbs./ft.) @ rpm	255 @ 2000	295 @ 2000
Availability	S	O

EPA city/highway mpg

4-speed OD automatic	17/24	14/21

Prices

Cadillac Brougham	Retail Price	Dealer Invoice	Low Price
4-door notchback	$27400	$23372	$24767
Destination charge	550	550	550
Gas Guzzler Tax, w/Trailer Towing or Coachbuilder Pkg.	850	850	850

Standard equipment:

5.0-liter 4bbl. V-8, 4-speed automatic transmission, power steering, anti-lock braking system, 55/45 cloth front seat with power driver's side (including recliner), storage armrest, seatback pockets, automatic climate control, power windows and locks, cruise control, automatic level control, AM/FM cassette with EQ and power antenna, rear defogger, power mirrors, illuminated entry, digital instruments, trip odometer, automatic parking brake release, tilt/telescopic steering column, remote decklid release, tinted glass, door edge guards, floormats, front and rear lamp monitors, cornering lights, right visor mirror, Uniroyal Royal Seal 225/75R15 tires.

Optional equipment:

Trailer Towing Pkg.	549	461	387

5.7-liter TBI V-8, 3.08 axle ratio, HD suspension, oil cooler, HD transmission and driveshaft, trailer wiring harness.

> **KEY: ohv** = overhead valve; **ohc** = overhead cam; **dohc** = double overhead cam; **I** = inline cylinders; **V** = cylinders in V configuration; **flat** = horizontally opposed cylinders; **bbl.** = barrel (carburetor); **PFI** = port (multi-point) fuel injection; **TBI** = throttle-body (single-point) fuel injection; **rpm** = revolutions per minute; **OD** = overdrive transmission; **S** = standard; **O** = optional; **NA** = not available.

	Retail Price	Dealer Invoice	Low Price
Coachbuilder Pkg.	(139)	(117)	(117)

Same content as Trailer Towing Pkg. less trailer wiring harness.

| d'Elegance Pkg. w/cloth | 2171 | 1824 | 1532 |
| w/leather | 2731 | 2294 | 1927 |

50/50 front seat, power passenger seat, lighted visor mirrors, illuminated entry, rear reading lamps.

| Option Pkg. B | 768 | 645 | 542 |

Lighted visor mirrors, rear reading lamps, power passenger seatback recliner, power passenger seat, power decklid pulldown, Twilight Sentinel.

| Option Pkg. C | 1243 | 1044 | 877 |

Pkg. B plus automatic power locks, remote fuel door release, theft deterrent system.

| d'Elegance Pkg. C | 475 | 399 | 335 |

Automatic power locks, remote fuel door release, theft deterrent system.

Astroroof	1355	1138	956
Gold Ornamentation Pkg.	395	332	279
Livery Pkg.	299	251	211
Leather seating area	560	470	395
Automatic day/night mirror	80	67	56
Firemist paint	240	202	169
CD player	296	249	209
Leather-wrapped steering wheel	115	97	81
Wire wheel covers	445	374	314
Wire wheels	1000	840	706
California emissions pkg.	100	84	71

Cadillac De Ville/Fleetwood

Cadillac Sedan de Ville

What's New

The front-drive De Ville and Fleetwood have 25 more horsepower this year, thanks to multi-point fuel injection and other changes to their 4.5-liter V-8 engine. A driver's-side airbag and GM's Pass Key theft-deterrent system are new standard features. Last year's 5-model lineup returns: base Sedan de Ville and Coupe de Ville, plusher Fleetwood sedan and coupe, and top-shelf Fleetwood Sixty Special, available only as a 4-door. All now have 180 horsepower and one fuel injector serving each cylinder; last year's 155-horsepower V-8 had two injectors mounted atop the engine. Torque has increased by five to 245 pounds/feet. The compression ratio has been bumped to 9.5:1 from 9.0:1 and the 4.5-liter V-8 now requires premium unleaded fuel, plus the EPA city fuel-economy estimate has dropped by one to 16 mpg; the highway estimate is unchanged at 25. With an airbag now standard across the board, all models lose the telescoping feature for the steering column, but a standard tilt feature returns. Anti-lock brakes remain standard on the Fleetwoods, optional on the De Villes.

CONSUMER GUIDE®

For

- Acceleration • Driveability • Airbag
- Anti-lock brakes • Quietness
- Passenger and cargo room

Against

- Fuel economy • Electronic instruments

Summary

We were impressed with the acceleration provided by last year's 4.5-liter V-8, and we're even more impressed with the 1990 version, which moves these luxury cars with even more authority. There's ample power for brisk takeoffs from stoplights and for quick, safe highway passing. Cadillac estimates a 0-60 mph time of 9.5 seconds, about half a second quicker than last year. In addition, the 4-speed overdrive automatic transmission enhances driveability by staying out of overdrive until the car reaches a cruising speed over 40 mph, and by downshifting quickly in passing situations. The engine feels a little rough when the throttle is floored, but otherwise delivers power smoothly and promptly. Fuel economy was disappointing last year (we averaged just 15.7 mpg from a mix of city and highway driving), and we don't look for any improvement this year, plus you now have to buy more expensive premium gas. There are other reasons why we like the De Ville and Fleetwood. The wheelbase on the sedans was stretched three inches last year and they boast bountiful interior space, so even back-seat passengers can stretch out, wide doorways for easy entry/exit, and ample cargo capacity. We wish the standard electronic instrument cluster offered more information besides vehicle speed, fuel level, and trip mileage, but we can live with it. In fact, we think we could live happily with a De Ville or Fleetwood because of their strong, refined engine, comfort and convenience features, and overall quality.

Specifications

	2-door notchback	4-door notchback
Wheelbase, in.	110.8	113.8
Overall length, in.	202.7	205.6
Overall width, in.	71.7	71.7
Overall height, in.	54.9	55.2
Turn diameter, ft.	39.8	41.0
Curb weight, lbs.	3466	3546
Cargo vol., cu. ft.	18.1	18.4
Fuel capacity, gals.	18.0	18.0
Seating capacity	6	6
Front headroom, in.	39.3	39.3
Front shoulder room, in.	59.0	59.0
Front legroom, max., in.	42.4	42.4
Rear headroom, in.	38.0	38.1
Rear shoulder room, in.	57.6	59.3
Rear legroom, min., in.	40.3	43.6

Powertrain layout: transverse front engine/front-wheel drive.

Engines

	ohv V-8
Size, liters/cu. in.	4.5/273
Fuel delivery	PFI
Horsepower @ rpm	180 @ 4300
Torque (lbs./ft.) @ rpm	240 @ 2600
Availability	S

EPA city/highway mpg

4-speed OD automatic	16/25

Prices

Cadillac De Ville/Fleetwood	Retail Price	Dealer Invoice	Low Price
Coupe de Ville 2-door notchback	$26960	$22997	$23297
Sedan de Ville 4-door notchback	27540	23492	23792
Fleetwood 2-door notchback	32400	27637	27937
Fleetwood 4-door notchback	32980	28132	28432
Fleetwood Sixty Special 4-door notchback	36980	31544	31844
Destination charge	550	550	550

Standard equipment:

De Ville: 4.5-liter PFI V-8, 4-speed automatic transmission, power steering, driver's-side airbag, 45/45 front seat, power driver's seat, storage armrest, seatback pockets, automatic climate control, power windows and locks, cruise control, power mirrors, intermittent wipers, automatic level control, Fuel Data Center (instantaneous and average fuel economy, distance to empty), automatic parking brake release, Pass Key theft deterrent system, AM/FM cassette with EQ and power antenna, tilt steering column, trip odometer, remote decklid release, tinted glass, door edge guards, retainer for garage door opener, visor mirrors, leather-wrapped steering wheel, 205/70R15 tires. **Fleetwood adds:** anti-lock brakes, power passenger seat, digital instruments, walnut appliques, fender skirts, remote fuel door release, power decklid pulldown, illuminated entry, rear overhead mirrors (4-door), opera lamps (2-door), formal cabriolet roof (2-door), padded vinyl roof (4-door), Twilight Sentinel, lace alloy wheels. **Sixty Special adds:** leather interior, heated front seats with power lumbar, thigh, and lateral supports, automatic day/night mirror, rear passenger foot rests, rear overhead console, vinyl top.

Optional equipment:

	Retail Price	Dealer Invoice	Low Price
Anti-lock brakes, De Ville	925	777	823
De Ville Option Pkg. B	356	299	317
Floormats, power passenger seat, trunk mat.			
De Ville Option Pkg. C	771	648	686
Pkg. B plus illuminated entry, lighted visor mirrors, power decklid pulldown, Twilight Sentinel.			
De Ville Option Pkg. D	961	807	855
Remote fuel door release, automatic day/night mirror, trumpet horn.			
De Ville Option Pkg. E	1146	963	1020
Pkg. D plus automatic power locks.			
Fleetwood/Sixty Special Option Pkg. B	410	344	365
Automatic power locks, theft deterrent system.			
Astroroof (NA Sixty)	1355	1138	1206
Rear defogger	195	164	174
Gold Ornamentation Pkg.	395	332	352
Digital instruments, De Ville	250	210	223
Leather seating areas (std. Sixty)	560	470	498
Memory power driver's seat, Fleetwood & Sixty	235	197	209
Automatic day/night mirror, Fleetwood & Sixty	80	67	71
Firemist paint	240	202	214
Delco-Bose sound system	576	484	513
w/CD player	872	732	776
Power recliners (each), Fleetwood	95	80	85
Formal cabriolet roof, De Ville	825	693	734
Vinyl roof delete (credit), Fleetwood 4-door & Sixty	(374)	(314)	(314)

Cadillac Fleetwood

Prices are accurate at time of printing; subject to manufacturer's change.

	Retail Price	Dealer Invoice	Low Price
Theft deterrent system, De Ville	225	189	200
Wire wheel covers (credit), Fleetwood & Sixty	(115)	(97)	(97)
Lace alloy wheels, De Ville	480	403	427
ElectriClear windshield	250	210	223
Accent striping, De Ville	75	63	67
California emissions pkg.	100	84	89
Engine block heater	45	38	40

Cadillac Eldorado/Seville

Cadillac Seville STS

What's New

More horsepower, a standard driver's-side airbag, and new exterior styling touches are the major changes for the Eldorado coupe and the Seville sedan, which are built on the same front-drive platform. Both use a 4.5-liter V-8 that gains multi-point fuel injection this year (one injector for each cylinder) instead of throttle-body injection (two injectors mounted on top of the engine). Horsepower increases from 155 to 180, while torque grows from 240 pounds/feet to 245. The compression ratio has increased from 9.0:1 to 9.5:1, so the 4.5 now requires premium unleaded gas. The EPA city fuel-economy estimate has dropped one mpg to 16, while the highway estimate is unchanged at 25. To accommodate the standard airbag, the telescoping feature for the steering column has been dropped, but a tilt feature returns. Last year the Seville Touring Sedan (STS) was an option package; this year it's a regular model. Both Seville and Eldorado have new bumper moldings, taillamps, and other minor styling changes. A new feature for the optional automatic door locks is "central unlocking"; all doors are unlocked if the key is held in a turned position for 1.5 seconds in either front door. A rear window defogger, heated outside mirrors, and illuminated entry system are now standard on all models, while the standard climate-control system this year has three automatic settings and two manual settings. Anti-lock brakes are standard on the STS, optional on the other models.

For

- Acceleration • Driveability • Airbag
- Anti-lock brakes • Quietness

KEY: **ohv** = overhead valve; **ohc** = overhead cam; **dohc** = double overhead cam; **I** = inline cylinders; **V** = cylinders in V configuration; **flat** = horizontally opposed cylinders; **bbl.** = barrel (carburetor); **PFI** = port (multi-point) fuel injection; **TBI** = throttle-body (single-point) fuel injection; **rpm** = revolutions per minute; **OD** = overdrive transmission; **S** = standard; **O** = optional; **NA** = not available.

Against

- Fuel economy • Electronic instruments • Trunk space

Summary

We're enthused about this year's more powerful 4.5-liter V-8, based on our brief exposure to it at Cadillac's preview. One of our recent long-term test cars was a 1988 Eldorado with a 155-horsepower 4.5; this Eldo could sprint smartly away from traffic signals, easily merge into fast-moving traffic, and quickly pass other cars on the highway. With 180 horsepower, the 1990 models promise even better performance, though you'll pay a higher price for fuel, since premium gas is now required. We averaged 18 mpg over about 14,000 miles in our 1988 Eldo, ranging from 11 mpg in the city to an impressive 27.5 mpg over one stretch of flat interstate highway. The 1990 models may be less economical. We were impressed by the lasting quality of our 1988 Eldorado, which suffered virtually no mechanical problems during our test, but Eldorado and Seville share some design deficiencies. Their digital instrument cluster conveys little information (vehicle speed, fuel level, and odometer reading) and both models could use more rear-seat and trunk space. In addition, the STS' suspension (optionally available on the Eldorado) is quite stiff, so try it over rough roads before you buy. On balance, though, Eldorado and Seville have plenty to offer those seeking luxury and performance and we recommend you include them on your shopping list.

Specifications

	Eldorado 2-door notchback	Seville 4-door notchback
Wheelbase, in.	108.0	108.0
Overall length, in.	191.4	190.8
Overall width, in.	72.4	72.0
Overall height, in.	53.7	53.7
Turn diameter, ft.	39.4	39.4
Curb weight, lbs.	3426	3480
Cargo vol., cu. ft.	14.0	14.0
Fuel capacity, gals.	18.8	18.8
Seating capacity	5	5
Front headroom, in.	37.8	37.8
Front shoulder room, in.	57.6	57.2
Front legroom, max., in.	42.4	42.5
Rear headroom, in.	37.8	37.9
Rear shoulder room, in.	57.5	57.2
Rear legroom, min., in.	36.1	36.1

Powertrain layout: transverse front engine/front-wheel drive.

Engines

	ohv V-8
Size, liters/cu. in.	4.5/273
Fuel delivery	PFI
Horsepower @ rpm	180 @ 4300
Torque (lbs./ft.) @ rpm	240 @ 2600
Availability	S

EPA city/highway mpg

4-speed OD automatic	16/25

Prices

Cadillac Eldorado/Seville	Retail Price	Dealer Invoice	Low Price
Eldorado 2-door notchback	$28885	$24613	$24913
Seville 4-door notchback	31830	27151	27451

	Retail Price	Dealer Invoice	Low Price
Seville STS 4-door notchback	36320	30981	31281
Destination charge	550	550	550

Standard equipment:

Eldorado: 4.5-liter PFI V-8, 4-speed automatic transmission, power steering, 4-wheel disc brakes, driver's-side airbag, cloth and leather reclining front bucket seats, power front seats, automatic climate control, power windows and locks, cruise control, heated power mirrors, intermittent wipers, tilt steering column, rear defogger, Driver Information Center (outside temperature, engine data, instantanious and average fuel economy, distance to empty), oil life indicator, trip odometer, automatic level control, remote fuel door and decklid releases, power decklid pulldown, AM/FM cassette with EQ and power antenna, illuminated entry, automatic parking brake release, Pass Key theft deterrent system, lighted visor mirrors, front and rear reading lamps, floormats, cornering lights, front and rear lamp monitors, retainer for garage door opener, door edge guards, tinted glass, leather-wrapped steering wheel, Twilight Sentinel, 205/70R15 tires on alloy wheels. **Seville** adds: birdseye maple trim, two-tone paint. **Seville STS** adds: anti-lock brakes, 3.31 axle ratio, leather interior with elm burl accents, rear console, automatic power locks, theft deterrent system, 215/65R15 tires.

Optional equipment:

Anti-lock brakes (std. STS)	925	777	823
Option Pkg. B, exc. STS	410	344	365
Automatic power locks, theft deterrent system.			
Biarritz Pkg., Eldo	3180	2671	2830
Leather upholstery, power front recliners and lumbar support adjusters, power passenger seat, seatback pockets, walnut on instrument panel, console and door panels, cabriolet roof with opera lamps, two-tone paint, closed-in backlight treatment, wire wheel discs, accent molding, reversible floormats.			
Birdseye maple appliques, Eldo	245	206	218
Astroroof	1355	1138	1206
Gold Ornamentation Pkg.	395	332	352
Leather seating area, Seville	450	378	401
Eldo	545	458	485
Eldo includes power passenger seatback recliner.			
Automatic day/night mirror	80	67	71
Firemist paint, Seville & STS	240	202	214
Firemist primary paint, Eldo & Seville			
w/2-tone	190	160	169
Secondary	50	42	45
White diamond paint, Eldo & Seville	240	202	214
Two-tone paint, STS	225	189	200
Delco-Bose sound system	576	484	513
w/CD player	872	732	776
Padded vinyl roof, Eldo	1095	920	975
Cabriolet roof, Seville	1095	920	975
Phaeton roof, STS	1195	1004	1064
215/65R15 WSW tires, Eldo & Seville . . .	76	64	68
Touring suspension, Eldo & Seville	155	130	138
Wire wheel covers, Eldo & Seville	235	197	209
Alloy wheels, Eldo	115	97	102
California emissions pkg.	100	84	89

Chevrolet Astro/GMC Safari

What's New

A full-time 4-wheel-drive system is now available on these compact-van twins and 4-wheel anti-lock brakes have been added as standard equipment. Plus, an extended-length model is due in January 1990, along with a more powerful optional engine. Astro, sold by Chevrolet dealers, and Safari, sold by GM dealers with GMC truck franchises, are identical except for names and series designations. Their optional new 4WD system augments the standard rear-wheel drivetrain by transferring power to the axle with the best grip when a loss of traction is sensed. The driver does nothing; a viscous cou-

Chevrolet Astro RS

pling inside a transfer case handles the chore automatically. The 4WD system is available on both passenger and cargo models of the vans and on both the standard- and new extended-length versions. The extended model increases cargo capacity nearly 19 cubic feet by adding 10 inches behind the rear wheels. It rides the standard 110-inch wheelbase. Astro and Safari retain front-disc and rear-drum brakes for '90, but now all have better stopping power on slippery surfaces thanks to the 4-wheel anti-lock system. (Rear anti-lock brakes were added as standard for '89.) Standard on all Astros and Safaris is a 4.3-liter V-6 rated at 150 horsepower. In January, 2WD passenger models will be available with a 175-horsepower version of that engine. The 5-speed manual transmission is no longer available, so all Astros and Safaris have a 4-speed overdrive automatic as standard. Content of the various trim levels has been adjusted slightly for '90, but the major change common to all is a restyled instrument panel with a larger glove box. Base payload of the 2WD models is 1000 pounds and they can be equipped to tow up to 6000 pounds.

For

- Anti-lock brakes   • Passenger and cargo room
- Towing capacity   • Extended-length availability
- High-output optional engine

Against

- Fuel economy   • Entry/exit   • Ride

Summary

Astro/Safari is similar to the Ford Aerostar in design and concept: a modern, smaller interpretation of the traditional van, well suited to heavy-duty and light-commercial use. That's in contrast to the new front-drive vans marketed by Chevrolet, Pontiac, and Oldsmobile which, like the Dodge Caravan, Plymouth Voyager, and Mazda MPV, are designed to replace the family station wagon. The extended-length Astro/Safari body will add to already good passenger and cargo room. But these vehicles still suffer a truck-like ride and subpar handling. Four-wheel drive should correct the 2WD model's poor traction in rain and snow, though its added weight won't do much for fuel economy. The 4WD models will get an acceleration-enhancing axle ratio to offset some of that weight, but they'll add another ¾ of an inch to the body's already high step-up. The standard V-6 engine has plenty of torque for hauling heavy loads and towing, but that muscle doesn't translate into brisk acceleration. The optional high-output six should help in this regard.

Prices are accurate at time of printing; subject to manufacturer's change.

Specifications

	4-door van	4-door van
Wheelbase, in.	110.0	110.0
Overall length, in.	177.0	187.0
Overall width, in.	77.0	77.0
Overall height, in.	74.1	74.1
Turn diameter, ft.	39.5	39.5
Curb weight, lbs.	3084	NA
Cargo vol., cu. ft.	151.8	170.4
Fuel capacity, gals.	27.0	27.0
Seating capacity	8	8
Front headroom, in.	39.2	39.2
Front shoulder room, in.	64.0	64.0
Front legroom, max., in.	41.6	41.6
Rear headroom, in.	37.9	37.9
Rear shoulder room, in.	67.8	67.8
Rear legroom, min., in.	36.5	36.5

Powertrain layout: Longitudinal front engine/front-wheel drive or full-time 4-wheel drive.

Engines

	ohv V-6	ohv V-6
Size, liters/cu. in.	4.3/262	4.3/262
Fuel delivery	TBI	TBI
Horsepower @ rpm	150 @ 4000	175 @ 4600
Torque (lbs./ft.) @ rpm	230 @ 2400	230 @ 2800
Availability	S	O[1]

EPA city/highway mpg

4-speed OD automatic	17/22	16/20

1. Two-wheel drive models only.

Prices

Chevrolet Astro/GMC Safari Passenger Van	Retail Price	Dealer Invoice	Low Price
Astro CS	$13790	$12314	$12514
Astro CL	14830	13243	13443
Astro LT	16325	14088	14288
Safari SLX	14003	12505	12705
Safari SLE	15043	13433	13633
Safari SLT	16538	14768	14968
Destination charge	500	500	500

Standard equipment:

CS/SLX: 4.3-liter TBI V-6 engine, 4-speed automatic transmission, 4-wheel anti-lock brakes, coolant temperature and oil pressure gauges, voltmeter, trip odometer, tinted glass, intermittent wipers, AM radio, highback bucket seats, 5-passenger seating, rubber floor covering, remote fuel door release, 205/75R15 tires. **CL/SLE** adds: air dam with fog lamps, floormats, visor mirror, custom steering wheel, auxiliary lighting, carpet, wide bodyside moldings, rally wheels. **LT/SLT** adds: velour seat and door panel trim, upgraded front bucket seats with recliners, integrated armrests and adjustable headrests, split-back center bench seat with integrated armrests, headrests, recliners and fold-down center console with convenience tray and cup pockets; right-hand seat folds forward for access to rear, deep-tinted glass.

Optional equipment:

Air conditioning, front	820	697	738
Front & rear	1343	1142	1209

KEY: ohv = overhead valve; **ohc** = overhead cam; **dohc** = double overhead cam; **I** = inline cylinders; **V** = cylinders in V configuration; **flat** = horizontally opposed cylinders; **bbl.** = barrel (carburetor); **PFI** = port (multi-point) fuel injection; **TBI** = throttle-body (single-point) fuel injection; **rpm** = revolutions per minute; **OD** = overdrive transmission; **S** = standard; **O** = optional; **NA** = not available.

	Retail Price	Dealer Invoice	Low Price
Optional axle ratio	38	32	34
Locking differential	252	214	227
Sport Pkg., CL/SLE	905	769	815
Others	1309	1113	1178
Sport suspension, sport steering wheel, color-keyed bumpers, wide bodyside molding.			
Convenience Group ZQ2	411	349	370
Power windows and locks.			
Convenience Group ZQ3	346	294	311
Cruise control and tilt steering column.			
Power door locks	211	179	190
7-passenger seating, CS/SLX	1069	909	962
CL/SLE	981	834	883
LT/SLT	878	746	790
8-passenger seating, CS/SLX	344	292	310
CL/SLE	396	337	356
LT/SLT	878	746	790
Custom vinyl bucket seats, w/8-pass.	158	134	142
w/5-pass.	106	90	95
Custom cloth bucket seats, w/8-pass.	158	134	142
w/5-pass.	106	90	95
Deluxe bumpers, CS/SLX	128	109	115
Others	76	65	68
Cold Climate Pkg.	46	39	41
Engine block heater, antifreeze protection to −32 degrees F.			
Roof console	83	71	75
Includes dome and reading lights, two storage compartments.			
Engine oil cooler	135	115	122
HD radiator	56	48	50
HD radiator & trans oil cooler	118	100	106
w/F&R A/C	63	54	57
Complete body glass	157	133	141
Deep tinted glass, w/o body glass	161	137	145
w/body glass	290	247	261
Rear heater	267	227	240
Electronic instruments	88	75	79
Auxiliary lighting	129	110	116
Deluxe outside mirrors	52	44	47
Power mirrors	150	128	135
AM/FM radio	151	128	136
AM/FM cassette	273	232	246
AM/FM cassette w/EQ	423	360	381
AM radio delete (credit)	(95)	(81)	(81)
Seatback recliner & armrests	241	205	217
Power driver's seat	240	204	216
HD shock absorbers	40	34	36
Sport suspension, CS/SLX	509	433	458
Others	417	354	375
HD Trailering Special Equipment	564	479	508
w/F&R A/C	507	431	456
LD Trailering Special Equipment	109	93	98
Alloy wheels, CS/SLX	325	276	293
Others or w/sport suspension	233	198	210
Argent rally wheels, CS/SLX	92	78	83
Deluxe two-tone paint, CL/SLE	172	146	155
Others	334	284	301
Special two-tone paint	172	146	155
Custom two-tone paint, CS/SLE	187	159	168
Others	329	280	296

Chevrolet Beretta

What's New

Chevy's front-wheel-drive sports coupe gets two new model variations: a convertible and the high-performance GTZ. Meanwhile, the standard engine in the base model increases from 2.0-liters to 2.2, while the V-6 that's standard in the GT and convertible versions goes from 2.8 liters to 3.1. The convertible features a manual-folding top with a heated glass backlight. Chevy says the roof bar that arcs over the passen-

Chevrolet Beretta GTZ

ger area is not designed to protect occupants in a rollover, but that it does help minimize body shake, improve window-glass sealing, and cut top-down wind draft into the cabin. It also allows the convertible to use an interior dome lamp and to retain the Beretta coupe's door handles and shoulder-belt anchors. The GTZ replaces the GTU as the sport entry in the front-drive Beretta line. It sees Chevy's first use of the Quad 4, a double-overhead-cam, 16-valve 2.3-liter 4-cylinder engine developed by Oldsmobile. This is the High Output Quad 4, rated at 180 horsepower. The GTZ comes standard with its own grille and rocker-panel extensions and exclusive 16-inch alloy wheels. A 5-speed manual transmission is standard on all Berettas. A 3-speed automatic is optional on all but the GTZ. A new molded, non-metallic 15.6-gallon fuel tank replaces a 13.5-gallon tank on all models.

For

- Performance (V-6, Quad 4) • Handling/roadholding

Against

- Performance (4-cylinder) • Rear seat room

Summary

Beretta was already appealing as a sporty car with decent road manners and an attractive price that benefited from frequent dealer discounts. Now, the GTZ takes the performance a serious step forward, while the convertible should interest a whole new spectrum of buyers. Revved into its power band in older GM compacts such as the Pontiac Grand Am and Oldsmobile Cutlass Calais, the Quad 4 tends to feel quite coarse. It seems much smoother and more isolated in the GTZ, a Beretta that welcomes spirited driving more than the Beretta GT did. And even if its sport suspension and 205/55R16 tires can't prevent the GTZ from getting week-kneed in really fast driving, the $13,750 base price (which includes air conditioning) should put it on many sports-sedan shopping lists. The convertible shares the GTZ suspension and tires, and is available with a V-6 and automatic transmission. It replaces the Cavalier Z24 convertible as Chevy's compact ragtop offering. One attractive feature is that the back seat retains the three-passenger capacity of the coupe. We're happy to see the 2.2-liter four, with its 95 horsepower and 120 pounds/feet of torque, replace the 2.0 four, which was wimpy at 90 horsepower and 108 pounds/feet of torque. And though the 135-horsepower 3.1 has only 5 more horsepower than last year's 2.8, its torque advantage is 180 pounds/feet to 160.

Specifications

	2-door notchback	2-door conv.
Wheelbase, in.	103.4	103.4
Overall length, in.	187.2	187.2
Overall width, in.	68.0	68.0
Overall height, in.	52.6	NA
Turn diameter, ft.	37.8	37.8
Curb weight, lbs.	3000	NA
Cargo vol., cu. ft.	13.5	NA
Fuel capacity, gals.	15.6	15.6
Seating capacity	5	5
Front headroom, in.	38.0	NA
Front shoulder room, in.	55.3	NA
Front legroom, max., in.	43.4	NA
Rear headroom, in.	36.6	NA
Rear shoulder room, in.	55.1	NA
Rear legroom, min., in.	34.6	NA

Powertrain layout: transverse front engine/front-wheel driuve.

Engines

	ohv I-4	ohv V-6	dohc I-4
Size, liters/cu. in.	2.2/133	3.1/191	2.3/138
Fuel delivery	TBI	PFI	PFI
Horsepower @ rpm	95 @ 5200	135 @ 4200	180 @ 6200
Torque (lbs./ft.) @ rpm	120 @ 3200	180 @ 3600	160 @ 5200
Availability	S	O[1]	S[2]

EPA city/highway mpg

5-speed OD manual	NA	NA	NA
3-speed automatic	NA	NA	

1. Standard GT and Convertible. 2. GTZ.

Prices

Chevrolet Beretta	Retail Price	Dealer Invoice	Low Price
2-door notchback	$10320	$9216	$9416
GT 2-door notchback	12500	11163	11363
GTZ 2-door notchback	13750	12279	12479
2-door convertible	NA	NA	NA
Destination charge	425	425	425

Standard equipment:

2.2-liter TBI 4-cylinder engine, 5-speed manual transmission, power steering, cloth reclining front bucket seats, console with storage armrest, rear shoulder belts, tachometer, coolant temperature and oil pressure gauges, voltmeter, trip odometer, left remote and right manual mirrors, AM/FM radio, console, tinted glass, F41 sport suspension, 195/70R14. **GT** adds: 3.1-liter PFI V-6, air conditioning, FE3 sport suspension, sport steering wheel, 60/40 split folding rear seatback, custom cloth trim, overhead consolette, remote decklid release, 205/60R15 Goodyear tires on styled steel wheels. **GTZ** adds: 2.3-liter DOHC 16-valve PFI Quad 4 engine, FE7 performance suspension, air conditioning, front air dam with fog lights, rear spoiler, leather-wrapped steering wheel, 205/55R16 Goodyear Eagle GT+4 tires on alloy wheels. **Convertible** has base equipment plus 3.1-liter V-6, FE3 sport suspension, 205/55R16 tires on alloy wheels.

Optional equipment:

3.1-liter V-6, base	685	582	617
3-speed automatic transmission	540	459	486
Air conditioning, base	780	663	702
Preferred Group 1, base	112	95	101
Intermittent wipers, floormats, map lights, consolette.			
Preferred Group 2, base	1222	1039	1100
Group 1 plus air conditioning, cruise control, tilt steering column.			
Preferred Group 3, base	1817	1544	1635
Group 2 plus AM/FM cassette, power windows and locks, remote decklid release.			

Prices are accurate at time of printing; subject to manufacturer's change.

Chevrolet

	Retail Price	Dealer Invoice	Low Price
Preferred Group 1, GT	442	376	398
Cruise control, tilt steering column, intermittent wipers, floormats, map lights, consolette.			
Preferred Group 2, GT	1037	881	933
Group 1 plus AM/FM cassette, power windows and locks, remote decklid release.			
Preferred Group 1, GTZ	363	309	327
Cruise control, tilt steering column, floormats.			
Preferred Group 2, GTZ	958	814	862
Group 1 plus AM/FM cassette, power windows and locks, remote decklid release.			
Rear defogger	160	136	144
Power locks	175	149	158
Electronic instruments	156	133	140
Removable sunroof	350	298	315
Alloy wheels	210	179	189
AM/FM cassette	140	119	126
AM/FM cassette w/EQ	290	247	261
Sound system prices are for base models; prices vary with option package content.			
Two-tone paint	123	105	111
Decklid luggage rack	115	98	104
California emissions pkg.	100	85	90

Chevrolet Camaro

Chevrolet Camaro IROC-Z

What's New

This rear-drive pony car heads into its eighth model year with a larger standard engine for its base RS version and driver's-side air bags for all models. Both the RS and IROC-Z are available as a 3-door hatchback or 2-door convertible. A 3.1-liter V-6 replaces a 2.8-liter V-6 as standard on the RS models. Horsepower is up by only 5, to 140, but torque increases by 20 pounds/feet, to 180. Other engine choices are unchanged, though Chevrolet says a new underhood control system improves the reliability of all Camaro engines. Camaros equipped with the 4-speed automatic get a tighter torque converter with higher lockup points designed to improve the driving feel and fuel economy. Added to the standard-equipment list on all models are such items as a tilt steering wheel, tinted glass, intermittent wipers, and halogen headlamps. The IROC-Z gets a standard limited-slip differential and new 16-inch alloy wheels are standard on the IROC-Z convertible and optional on the IROC-Z coupe. In addition to the air bag, the cabin

---

KEY: ohv = overhead valve; **ohc** = overhead cam; **dohc** = double overhead cam; **I** = inline cylinders; **V** = cylinders in V configuration; **flat** = horizontally opposed cylinders; **bbl.** = barrel (carburetor); **PFI** = port (multi-point) fuel injection; **TBI** = throttle-body (single-point) fuel injection; **rpm** = revolutions per minute; **OD** = overdrive transmission; **S** = standard; **O** = optional; **NA** = not available.

---

features new, yellow, instrument-panel graphics and Scotch-gard-brand fabric protection. Leather upholstery is a new option. Camaros are among the nation's most frequently stolen vehicles, and Chevy continues to offer as standard equipment its "pass-key" theft deterrent system. A resistor pellet in the ignition key must match special coding in the ignition lock or the starter is temporarily disabled. Chevrolet says the system has helped lower theft rates and reduce insurance premiums on Corvettes and Camaros so equipped. Camaro and the similar Pontiac Firebird are due for a minor front- and rear-end restyle about the middle of the 1990 model year.

For

● Performance (V-8s) ● Handling ● Resale value

Against

● Fuel economy ● Ride ● Interior room

Summary

Ford's Mustang outsells Camaro nearly 2-1 in the pony car field, but the Chevy's still a siren to performance fans and younger drivers (who also help keep resale values high by eagerly buying used Camaros). The appeal is extroverted styling and V-8 muscle. Before you succumb, however, check with your insurance agent. Despite the standard anti-theft system, we suspect insurance rates will still be quite high for most buyers. V-8 Camaros hold to the muscle-car ethic with quick acceleration, lousy gas mileage, a burbling exhaust note, a punishingly stiff ride, and poor wet-weather traction. Passenger and cargo room are skimpy for the car's size, and rattles and squeaks are familiar companions. Newer, tamer coupes, such as the Chevy Beretta and Acura Integra are easier to live with as everyday vehicles. But if macho-style performance is your meat, then we suggest you also shop Camaro before committing to the Mustang GT.

Specifications	3-door hatchback	2-door convt.
Wheelbase, in.	101.1	101.1
Overall length, in.	192.0	192.0
Overall width, in.	72.8	72.8
Overall height, in.	50.0	50.3
Turn diameter, ft.	36.9	36.9
Curb weight, lbs.	3077	3263
Cargo vol., cu. ft.	31.0	5.2
Fuel capacity, gals.	15.5	15.5
Seating capacity	4	4
Front headroom, in.	37.0	37.1
Front shoulder room, in.	57.5	58.6
Front legroom, max., in.	43.0	42.9
Rear headroom, in.	35.6	36.1
Rear shoulder room, in.	56.3	48.1
Rear legroom, min., in.	29.8	28.3

Powertrain layout: longitudinal front engine/rear-wheel drive.

Engines	ohv V-6	ohv V-8	ohv V-8	ohv V-8
Size, liters/cu. in.	3.1/190	5.0/305	5.0/305	5.7/350
Fuel delivery	PFI	TBI	PFI	PFI
Horsepower @ rpm	144 @ 4400	170 @ 4000	220 @ 4400	230 @ 4400
Torque (lbs./ft.) @ rpm . . .	180 @ 3600	255 @ 2400	290 @ 3200	330 @ 3200
Availability	S[1]	S[2]	O[3]	O[3]

EPA city/highway mpg	ohv V-6	ohv V-8
5-speed OD manual	NA	17/25
4-speed OD automatic . . .	NA	17/26

1. RS Coupe. 2. RS convt., IROC-Z; optional RS coupe 3. IROC-Z.

Prices

Chevrolet Camaro	Retail Price	Dealer Invoice	Low Price
RS 3-door hatchback	$10995	$9819	$10019
RS 2-door convertible	16880	15074	15274
IROC-Z 3-door hatchback	14555	12998	13198
IROC-Z 2-door convertible	20195	18034	18234
Destination charge	439	439	439

Standard equipment:

RS: 3.1-liter PFI V-6 engine (hatchback; convertible has 5.0-liter TBI V-8), 5-speed manual transmission, power steering, driver's-side airbag, AM/FM radio, left remote and right manual mirrors, cloth reclining front bucket seats, folding rear seat, rear shoulder belts, tilt steering column, intermittent wipers, tinted glass, Pass Key theft deterrent system, power hatch pulldown, tachometer, coolant temperature and oil pressure gauges, voltmeter, 215/65R15 tires on alloy wheels. **IROC-Z** adds: 5.0-liter TPI V-8 engine, limited-slip differential, right visor mirror, fog lamps; convertible has 245/50ZR16 tires.

Optional equipment:

5.0-liter TBI V-8, RS hatchback	350	298	315
5.7-liter PFI (TPI) V-8, IROC	300	255	270
4-speed automatic transmission	515	438	464
Air conditioning	805	684	725
Performance axle ratio & dual exhaust . . .	466	396	419
Preferred Group 1, RS hatchback	1410	1199	1269
Air conditioning, AM/FM cassette, power locks, cruise control, bodyside moldings, floormats.			
Preferred Group 2, RS hatchback	1782	1515	1604
Group 1 plus power windows and locks, remote hatch release, cargo cover, reading lamps.			
Preferred Group 1, IROC hatchback	865	735	779
Air conditioning, bodyside moldings.			
Preferred Group 2, IROC hatchback	1759	1495	1583
Group 1 plus AM/FM cassette, power windows and locks, cruise control, remote hatch release, cargo cover, floormats.			
Preferred Group 3, IROC hatchback	2143	1822	1929
Group 2 plus power driver's seat, power mirrors, reading lamps.			
Preferred Group 1, RS convertible	1040	884	936
Air conditioning, AM/FM cassette, bodyside moldings, floormats.			
Preferred Group 2, RS convertible	1640	1394	1476
Group 1 plus power windows and locks, cruise control.			
Preferred Group 1, IROC convertible	865	735	779
Air conditioning, bodyside moldings.			
Preferred Group 2, IROC convertible	1640	1394	1476
Group 1 plus AM/FM cassette, power windows and locks, cruise control, floormats.			
Preferred Group 3, IROC convertible	2001	1701	1801
Group 2 plus power driver's seat and power mirrors.			
Custom cloth bucket seats	327	278	294
Leather bucket seats	800	680	720
Rear defogger	160	136	144
Power locks	175	149	158
Remote hatch release	50	43	45
Rear window louvers	210	179	189
Power mirrors	91	77	82
Removable glass roof panels	866	736	779
245/50ZR16 tires on alloy wheels	520	442	468
AM/FM cassette	140	119	126
Delco-Bose audio system	1015	863	914
Sound system prices are for base models; prices vary with option package content.			
Engine block heater	20	17	18
California emissions pkg.	100	85	90

Chevrolet Caprice

1989 Chevrolet Caprice Classic Brougham

What's New

Chevy's full-size rear-drive Caprice has been around since 1977, but a swoopy new bodystyle is due for '91. The current car's boxy styling will be replaced by flowing lines and a steeply sloped windshield and backlight. The new Caprice will remain full-size, with plenty of interior room for six, a huge trunk, and a V-8 engine powering the rear wheels. Those attributes are available today as the Caprice carries over into '90 with minimal changes. The 4-door sedan comes in base, Classic, Brougham, and Brougham LS trim. A 3-seat, 8-passenger wagon comes in Classic trim only. Sedans are again powered by a throttle-body fuel-injected 5.0-liter V-8; wagons get a carbureted version of that engine. Both are available only with a 4-speed overdrive automatic transmission. The only underhood change is new quick-connect, nylon fuel lines for easier servicing. Front disc brakes have new linings and insulators to reduce brake noise. Interior refinements include new front passive seat belts and Scotchgard-brand fabric protection. Two new metallic red exteriors and a color-coordinated deep red interior are offered. Buick, Oldsmobile, and Pontiac offer similar wagons, but Caprice is the only rear-drive family sedan in the GM stable.

For

● Passenger and cargo room ● Quietness ● Trailer towing

Against

● Fuel economy ● Size and weight
● Handling/maneuverability

Summary

Caprice's only direct rivals are the Ford LTD Crown Victoria and Mercury Grand Marquis. Slightly more refined V-8s make the Ford products a little more pleasant to drive, but the choice is mostly one of brand loyalty. Beyond its large size and traditional bearing, Caprice pluses include very high ratings for collision damage and occupant protection, according to insurance-industry statistics. Among the negatives are ponderous handling and little road feel for the driver. Fuel economy also suffers. Expect 15-17 mpg around town, 21-23 mpg on the highway. We've seen a prototype of the '91 car, which seems to blend the old and the new in some of its details. For example, the rounded overall shape might appeal to younger shoppers, while buyers with traditional tastes might be attracted by such touches as the rear fender skirts or the chrome grille that dominates the nose. The cabin is updated with a

Prices are accurate at time of printing; subject to manufacturer's change.

dashboard that uses a gently curving hood over the instrument pod reminiscent of that in the current Pontiac Bonneville. Today's Caprice continues to offer big-car room and comfort and V-8 power at a price lower than some Japanese compacts. Dealers should be willing to offer even larger-than-usual discounts on the '90 Caprice as the '91 changeover approaches.

Specifications

	4-door notchback	5-door wagon
Wheelbase, in.	116.0	116.0
Overall length, in.	212.2	215.7
Overall width, in.	75.4	79.3
Overall height, in.	56.4	58.2
Turn diameter, ft.	38.7	39.7
Curb weight, lbs.	3693	4192
Cargo vol., cu. ft.	20.9	87.9
Fuel capacity, gals.	24.5	22.0
Seating capacity	6	8
Front headroom, in.	39.5	36.9
Front shoulder room, in.	60.5	60.9
Front legroom, max., in.	42.2	42.2
Rear headroom, in.	38.2	39.3
Rear shoulder room, in.	60.5	60.9
Rear legroom, min., in.	39.1	37.2

Powertrain layout: longitudinal front engine/rear-wheel drive.

Engines

	ohv V-8	ohv V-8
Size, liters/cu. in.	5.0/305	5.0/307
Fuel delivery	TBI	4 bbl.
Horsepower @ rpm	170 @ 4000	140 @ 3200
Torque (lbs./ft.) @ rpm	255 @ 2400	255 @ 2000
Availability	S[1]	S[2]

EPA city/highway mpg

4-speed OD automatic	17/24	17/24

1. Sedans   2. Wagon.

Prices

Chevrolet Caprice	Retail Price	Dealer Invoice	Low Price
4-door notchback	$14525	$12535	$12735
Classic 4-door notchback	15125	13053	13253
Classic Brougham 4-door notchback	16325	14088	14288
Classic Brougham LS 4-door notchback	17525	15124	15324
Classic 5-door wagon	15725	13571	13771
Destination charge	505	505	505

Standard equipment:

5.0-liter (305-cid) TBI V-8 engine (4-doors; 307-cid 4bbl. on wagon), 4-speed automatic transmission, power steering, air conditioning, left remote and right manual mirrors, tinted glass, rear shoulder belts, AM/FM radio, knit cloth bench seat, 205/75R15 all-season SBR tires (4-doors; wagon has 225/75R15). **Classic** adds: wheel opening moldings, Quiet Sound Group, vinyl door pull straps, bright wide lower bodyside moldings, hood ornament, carpeted lower door panels. **Brougham** adds: upgraded carpet, front door courtesy lights, vinyl roof, 55/45 cloth front seat with center armrest. **LS** adds: Landau-style vinyl roof, sport mirrors, tinted glass.

KEY: ohv = overhead valve; **ohc** = overhead cam; **dohc** = double overhead cam; **I** = inline cylinders; **V** = cylinders in V configuration; **flat** = horizontally opposed cylinders; **bbl.** = barrel (carburetor); **PFI** = port (multi-point) fuel injection; **TBI** = throttle-body (single-point) fuel injection; **rpm** = revolutions per minute; **OD** = overdrive transmission; **S** = standard; **O** = optional; **NA** = not available.

Optional equipment:	Retail Price	Dealer Invoice	Low Price
Limited-slip differential	100	85	90
Performance axle ratio	21	18	19
Vinyl bench seat, base 4-door	28	24	25
Wagon (credit)	(172)	(146)	(146)
Vinyl 50/50 seat, base 4-door	305	259	275
Wagon	103	88	93
Cloth 50/50 seat	275	234	248
Leather 45/55 seat	550	468	495
Preferred Group 1, base 4-door	170	145	153
Bodyside moldings, floormats, extended-range speakers, wheel opening moldings.			
Preferred Group 2, base	820	697	738
Group 1 plus power locks, cruise control, tilt steering column, intermittent wipers, auxiliary lighting.			
Preferred Group 1, Classic 4-door	713	606	642
Cruise control, tilt steering column, 205/75R15 white-stripe tires, bodyside moldings, intermittent wipers, remote decklid release, auxiliary lighting, floormats, extended-range speakers, remote mirrors.			
Preferred Group 2, Classic 4-door	2087	1774	1878
Group 1 plus AM/FM cassette with power antenna, power windows and locks, power front seats, deluxe luggage compartment trim, intermittent wipers, remote decklid release, lighted right visor mirror.			
Preferred Group 1, wagon	211	179	190
Bodyside moldings, auxiliary lighting, load floor carpet, remote mirrors.			
Preferred Group 2, wagon	1556	1323	1400
Group 1 plus AM/FM cassette with power antenna, power windows and locks, cruise control, tilt steering column, luggage rack, intermittent wipers, floormats.			
Preferred Group 3, wagon	2475	2104	2228
Group 2 plus AM/FM cassette with EQ, power front seats, deluxe rear compartment decor, gauge package with trip odometer, Twilight Sentinel, cornering lamps, lighted right visor mirror.			
Preferred Group 1, Brougham	470	400	423
205/75R15 white-stripe tires, gauge package with trip odometer, bodyside moldings, Twilight Sentinel, remote decklid release, lighted right visor mirror, floormats, extended-range speakers, remote mirrors.			
Preferred Group 2, Brougham	2384	2026	2146
Group 1 plus AM/FM cassette with power antenna, power windows and locks, power front seats, cruise control, wire wheel covers, tilt steering column, deluxe luggage compartment trim, intermittent wipers, cornering lamps.			
Preferred Group 1, LS	2270	1930	2043
AM/FM cassette with power antenna, power windows and locks, power front seats, cruise control, wire wheel cdovers, tilt steering column, 205/75R15 white-stripe tires, gauge package with trip odometer, bodyside moldings, Twilight Sentinel, intermittent wipers, remote decklid release, lighted right visor mirror, floormats, remote mirrors.			
Preferred Group 2, LS	2494	2120	2245
Group 1 plus AM/FM cassette with EQ, deluxe luggage compartment trim, cornering lamps.			
Rear window air deflector, wagon	65	55	59
Trunk cargo net	30	26	27
HD cooling	40	34	36
Rear defogger	160	136	144
Power locks, 4-doors	215	183	194
Wagon	290	247	261
AM/FM cassette	175	149	158
AM/FM cassette w/EQ	285	242	257
Sound system prices are for base models; prices vary with option package content.			
Estate equipment, wagon	307	261	276
F40 HD suspension, 4-doors	26	22	23
F41 sport suspension	49	42	44
Inflatable rear shock absorbers	64	54	58
205/75R15 white-stripe tires, 4-doors	76	65	68
225/70R15 white-stripe tires, 4-doors	188	160	169
Wheel covers, base & Classic	65	55	59
Wire wheel covers, Brougham	150	128	135
Others	215	183	194
Custom 2-tone paint	141	120	127
Vinyl roof	200	170	180
California emissions pkg.	100	85	90
Engine block heater	20	17	18

Chevrolet Cavalier

1989 Chevrolet Cavalier Z24

What's New

Chevy sends its front-drive compact into its ninth model year with larger engines but without a convertible model. Cavalier again comes as a coupe, a sedan, or a wagon. The stripper VL (Value Leader) package, offered previously only on the coupe, is now available on all body styles, as is the mid-level RS package. The convertible, introduced in 1984 and available last year only in sporty Z24 guise, has been supplanted in the Chevy line by the new Beretta ragtop. Cavalier's standard engine, the 2.0-liter 4-cylinder, has been replaced by a 2.2-liter four. Horsepower is bumped from 90 to 95, while torque jumps from 108 pounds/feet to 120. Optional on the wagon and standard on the Z24 is a 3.1-liter V-6. It replaces a 2.8-liter V-6. Horsepower increases to 140, from 130, and torque is up to 180 pounds/feet, from 160. Both engines come standard with a 5-speed manual transmission; the 2.2's is built by Isuzu, the 3.1's is a Muncie-Getrag unit. A 3-speed automatic is optional with either engine. All except VL models get power steering and tinted glass as standard for '90, while all Cavaliers are given new seats, passive front seat belts, Scotchgard-brand fabric protection, and a stainless steel exhaust system. Cavalier was introduced for the 1982 model year, as were similar J-body subcompacts at the other four GM divisions. Cavalier and the Pontiac Sunbird are the only ones still offered.

For

- Performance (V-6) • Fuel economy (4-cylinder)
- Handling/roadholding (Z24) • Prices

Against

- Performance (4-cylinder/automatic) • Rear seat room

Summary

Cavalier isn't as roomy or technically sophisticated as newer Japanese subcompacts, yet it offers good value for the money. While imports have jumped in price the past few years, Cavalier has inched higher by comparison. A base Cavalier 4-door with automatic transmission, air conditioning, power steering, and several other comfort and convenience features lists for less than $10,700. That undercuts most comparably equipped Japanese sedans. Cavalier's performance isn't as competitive, though. This year's larger standard 4-cylinder should keep it economical and deliver decent performance with manual transmission, but don't expect much zip with the more popular automatic transmission. Note also that Cavalier's automatic is a 3-speed, while most Japanese rivals offer automatics with an overdrive fourth gear for quieter, more economical cruising. The V-6 is a different story. The Z24 is a mini-muscle car with brisk performance and a reasonable price, while the 3.1 will give the wagon enough muscle to handle a full load of passengers or cargo. Cavalier shows its age, but deserves consideration.

Specifications

	2-door notchback	4-door notchback	5-door wagon
Wheelbase, in.	101.2	101.2	101.2
Overall length, in.	178.4	178.4	174.5
Overall width, in.	66.0	66.3	66.3
Overall height, in.	52.0	52.1	52.8
Turn diameter, ft.	34.7	34.7	34.7
Curb weight, lbs.	2436	2444	NA
Cargo vol., cu. ft.	13.2	13.7	64.4
Fuel capacity, gals.	13.6	13.6	13.6
Seating capacity	5	5	5
Front headroom, in.	37.9	39.7	38.3
Front shoulder room, in.	53.7	53.7	53.7
Front legroom, max., in.	42.9	42.2	42.2
Rear headroom, in.	36.1	37.9	38.8
Rear shoulder room, in.	52.0	53.7	53.7
Rear legroom, min., in.	30.5	34.3	33.7

Powertrain layout: transverse front engine/front-wheel drive.

Engines

	ohv I-4	ohv V-6
Size, liters/cu. in.	2.2/133	3.1/190
Fuel delivery	TBI	PFI
Horsepower @ rpm	95 @ 5200	135 @ 4500
Torque (lbs./ft.) @ rpm	120 @ 3200	180 @ 3600
Availability	S	S[1]

EPA city/highway mpg

5-speed OD manual	26/36	19/28
3-speed automatic	25/32	NA

1. Z24; optional, wagon.

Prices

Chevrolet Cavalier	Retail Price	Dealer Invoice	Low Price
VL 2-door notchback	$7577	$7145	$7345
VL 4-door notchback	7777	7334	7534
VL 5-door wagon	8165	7700	7900
2-door notchback	8620	7956	8156
4-door notchback	8820	8141	8341
5-door wagon	9195	8487	8687
Z24 2-door notchback	11505	10274	10474
Destination charge	425	425	425

Standard equipment:

VL: 2.2-liter TBI 4-cylinder engine, 5-speed manual transmission, cloth front bucket seats, rear shoulder belts, remote tailgate lock release (wagon), 185/80R13 tires on styled steel wheels. **Base** adds: power steering, tinted glass, easy-entry passenger seat (2-door), AM/FM radio, wheel trim rings. **Z24** adds: 3.1-liter PFI V-6, front sport seats, center console, FE3 sport suspension, 215/60R14 Goodyear Eagle GT+4 tires on alloy wheels.

Optional equipment:

3.1-liter V-6	685	582	617
3-speed automatic transmission	465	395	419
Air conditioning	720	612	648
Preferred Group 1, VL	275	234	248
Power steering, bodyside moldings.			
Preferred Group 2, VL	443	377	399
Group 1 plus tinted glass, left remote and right manual mirrors, floormats.			

Prices are accurate at time of printing; subject to manufacturer's change.

	Retail Price	Dealer Invoice	Low Price
Preferred Group 1, base	318	270	286

Split folding rear seat, intermittent wipers, left remote and right manual mirrors, bodyside moldings, floormats.

	Retail Price	Dealer Invoice	Low Price
Preferred Group 2, base 2- & 4-door	1368	1163	1231
Base wagon	1483	1261	1335

Group 1 plus air conditioning, cruise control, tilt steering column, roof rack (wagon).

	Retail	Dealer	Low
Preferred Group 3, base 2-door	1913	1626	1722
Base 4-door	2018	1715	1816
Base wagon	2133	1813	1920

Group 2 plus AM/FM cassette, power windows and locks.

	Retail	Dealer	Low
Preferred Group 1, Z24	744	632	670

Air conditioning, dome reading lamp.

	Retail	Dealer	Low
Preferred Group 2, Z24	1302	1107	1172

Group 1 plus AM/FM cassette, cruise control, tilt steering column, intermittent wipers, floormats.

	Retail	Dealer	Low
Preferred Group 3, Z24	1907	1621	1716

Group 2 plus AM/FM cassette with EQ, power windows and locks, remote decklid release.

	Retail	Dealer	Low
AM/FM radio, VL	332	282	299
AM/FM cassette, VL	472	401	425
Base & Z24	140	119	126
AM/FM cassette w/EQ, Z24	290	247	261

Sound system prices are for base models; prices vary with option package content.

	Retail	Dealer	Low
Rear defogger	160	136	144
Power locks, 2-doors	175	149	158
4-doors & wagons	215	183	194
Tinted glass, VL	105	89	95
Bodyside moldings, VL & base	50	43	45
RS Pkg.	405	344	365

Black exterior accents, dual mirrors, FE2 sport suspension, tachometer and trip odometer, 195/70R14 tires on rally wheels.

	Retail	Dealer	Low
Removable sunroof	350	298	315
185/80R13 white-stripe tires	68	58	61
195/70R14 tires	156	133	140
215/60R14 OWL tires, Z24	102	87	92
Alloy wheels	265	225	239

Chevrolet Celebrity

1989 Chevrolet Celebrity Eurosport

What's New

Chevy continues to pare the Celebrity line as it grooms the Lumina to be its new bread-and-butter mid-size offering. Last year, the Celebrity 2-door coupe was dropped. This year, the 4-door sedan goes, leaving only the 5-door wagon. The front-drive wagon is offered in either a 2-seat, 6-passenger form or with a rear-facing third seat for 8-passenger capacity. Base and sporty Eurosport versions are offered. Changes for '90 center around more power under the hood. The standard 2.5-liter 4-cylinder engine now makes 110 horsepower, up from 98. Chevy attributes the increase to more precisely designed cylinder walls and a decrease in cylinder head weight. Optional on the base Celebrity and standard on the Eurosport is a 135-horsepower 3.1-liter V-6. It replaces last year's top engine, a 125-horsepower 2.8-liter V-6. The standard transmission is a 3-speed automatic; a 4-speed overdrive automatic is optional with the 3.1 and has been made standard for '90 on the Eurosport. Newly standard on both models are heavy-duty suspension components, intermittent wipers, a split, folding second seat, Scotchgard-brand fabric protection, and front-door map pockets. Celebritys also get passive front seat belts. Celebrity is built from the GM A-body design that includes the Buick Century, Oldsmobile Cutlass Ciera, and Pontiac 6000.

For

- Passenger and cargo room
- Quietness
- Handling (Eurosport)

Against

- Performance (4-cylinder)
- Handling (base suspension)

Summary

Even before Chevy dropped the sedan, Celebrity's age and sedate styling were no help against the arch-rival Ford Taurus, which is newer and fresher looking. That holds true when the Celebrity wagon is pitted against the Taurus wagon. Still, there's good value here, especially compared to more expensive imports such as the Toyota Camry wagon. With room for six adults (and two children in the 3-seat wagon), Celebrity is just as roomy inside as the Taurus, and offers more space than the Camry wagon. The standard 4-cylinder is hard pressed to handle a full load of people and/or cargo, but the V-6 furnishes enough power to accomplish most chores without strain. Taurus' standard suspension and tires offer better handling and a more controlled ride than Celebrity's, but the Eurosport package upgrades handling and cornering ability through firmer suspension pieces and larger tires, without a major penalty in ride comfort. With the V-6, 4-speed automatic, air conditioning, and a few amenities, the Celebrity wagon retails for less than $15,000; a loaded model with the Eurosport Group 3 package falls well short of $17,000. Substantial dealer and factory incentives are likely to drop these prices even further, making the Celebrity worth a look.

Specifications

	5-door wagon
Wheelbase, in.	104.9
Overall length, in.	190.8
Overall width, in.	69.3
Overall height, in.	54.3
Turn diameter, ft.	38.7
Curb weight, lbs.	2888
Cargo vol., cu. ft.	75.1
Fuel capacity, gals.	15.7
Seating capacity	8
Front headroom, in.	38.6
Front shoulder room, in.	56.2
Front legroom, max., in.	42.1
Rear headroom, in.	38.9
Rear shoulder room, in.	56.2
Rear legroom, min., in.	35.6

Powertrain layout: *transverse front engine/front-wheel drive.*

Engines

	ohv I-4	ohv V-6
Size, liters/cu. in.	2.5/151	3.1/191
Fuel delivery	TBI	PFI
Horsepower @ rpm	110 @	135 @
	5200	4400
Torque (lbs./ft.) @ rpm	135 @	180 @
	3200	3600
Availability	S	O[1]

EPA city/highway mpg

3-speed automatic	21/27	
4-speed OD automatic		19/30

1. Standard on Eurosport.

Prices

Chevrolet Celebrity	Retail Price	Dealer Invoice	Low Price
5-door 2-seat wagon	$12395	$10697	$10897
5-door 3-seat wagon	12645	10913	11113
Destination charge	450	450	450

Standard equipment:

2.5-liter TBI 4-cylinder engine, 3-speed automatic transmission, power steering, cloth front bench seat with center armrest, split folding second seat, rear shoulder belts, AM/FM radio, bodyside moldings, day/night mirror, left remote and right manual mirrors, intermittent wipers, tinted glass, 185/75R14 tires.

Optional equipment:

3.1-liter V-6	660	561	594
4-speed automatic transmission (V-6 req.) .	200	170	180
Air conditioning	805	684	725
55/45 front seat	133	113	120
Preferred Group 1	921	783	829
Air conditioning, Exterior Molding Pkg., auxiliary lighting, floormats.			
Preferred Group 2	1710	1454	1539
Group 1 plus power locks, cruise control, tilt steering column, roof rack, gauge package with trip odometer, remote liftgate release.			
Preferred Group 3	2259	1920	2033
Group 2 plus AM/FM cassette, power windows, Cargo Security Pkg., deluxe rear compartment decor, remote mirrors.			
Eurosport Base Group	1895	1611	1706
3.1-liter V-6, 4-speed automatic transmission, air conditioning.			
Eurosport Group 1	2011	1709	1810
Base Group plus Exterior Molding Pkg., auxiliary lighting, floormats.			
Eurosport Group 2	2800	2380	2520
Group 1 plus power locks, cruise control, tilt steering column, roof rack, gauge package with trip odometer, remote liftgate release.			
Eurosport Group 3	3349	2847	3014
Group 2 plus AM/FM cassette, power windows, Cargo Security Pkg., deluxe rear compartment decor, remote mirrors.			
Rear defogger	160	136	144
Power locks	215	183	194
Power driver's seat	270	230	243
Power seatback recliners	110	94	99
Inflatable rear shock absorbers	64	54	58
Alloy wheels	195	166	176
Rear wiper/washer	125	106	113
AM/FM cassette	140	119	126

Chevrolet Corsica

What's New

A higher level of standard equipment and larger engines highlight changes to this strong-selling front-drive compact. Corsica continues in 4-door notchback and 5-door hatchback bodystyles, but the base cars are now outfitted to last year's

1989 Chevrolet Corsica

mid-level LT grade. This includes gloss-black exterior trim and previously up-level interior door panels with new cloth inserts. The hatchback's rear seatback folds down for a 39-cubic foot cargo area. The sporty LTZ comes as a notchback only and for '90 gets standard reclining front bucket seats with 4-way headrests and adjustable lumbar supports and new cabin fabrics and colors. The LTZ upgrades the LT's road manners with gas-pressurized shock absorbers, front and rear stabilizer bars, quicker-ratio power steering, and 205/60R15 tires on alloy wheels in place of 185/75R14s on steel wheels. Supplanting a 2.0-liter 4-cylinder as the standard LT engine this year is a 2.5-liter four. Horsepower jumps from 90 to 98, torque is up from 108 pounds/feet to 120. The change brings tuned radiator mounts that Chevy says reduce engine vibration and noise. Standard in the LTZ and optional on the LT is a 3.1-liter V-6. It replaces a 2.8 and bumps horsepower from 130 to 135 and torque from 160 pounds/feet to 180. The 2.2 comes standard with an Isuzu-built 5-speed manual transmission, the 3.1 with a Muncie-Getrag 5-speed manual. A 3-speed automatic is optional with either engine. Scotchgard-brand fabric protection has been added as standard to all Corsicas, and a new molded, non-metallic tank increases fuel capacity from 13.6 gallons to 15.6. All models come with 3-point rear shoulder belts and front shoulder belts that can be left buckled for automatic deployment. Corsica and the Beretta coupes and convertibles are built on the same platform but differ in exterior styling, interior furnishings, and chassis components.

For

● Performance (V-6)   ● Handling/roadholding

Against

● Performance (4-cylinder)   ● Rear seat room

Summary

Corsica lacks any outstanding features, but is generally competent and offers enough value for the money to make it worth a look. At around $12,000 for an LT 4-door with Equipment Group 2 and automatic transmission, it stacks up well against the Ford Tempo and undercuts the price of such import rivals

> **KEY: ohv** = overhead valve; **ohc** = overhead cam; **dohc** = double overhead cam; **I** = inline cylinders; **V** = cylinders in V configuration; **flat** = horizontally opposed cylinders; **bbl.** = barrel (carburetor); **PFI** = port (multi-point) fuel injection; **TBI** = throttle-body (single-point) fuel injection; **rpm** = revolutions per minute; **OD** = overdrive transmission; **S** = standard; **O** = optional; **NA** = not available.

Prices are accurate at time of printing; subject to manufacturer's change.

as a comparably equipped Toyota Camry. Be forewarned that the 4-cylinder engine isn't likely to have a surplus of power and the base suspension will cower in the face of even moderately aggressive driving. The LTZ, with its standard V-6 and air conditioning, is a stylish and sporty domestic alternative to cars like the Acura Integra, especially for around $15,000 with an automatic transmission and Equipment Group 2. This is the optimal Corsica setup for power and handling, though the LTZ suffers a noticeable loss in ride comfort. Corsica was introduced in the spring of 1987 as a 1989 model and hasn't yet been able to match the refined driving feel and quality assembly of the Japanese competition, but plenty of buyers find this compact perfectly acceptable for a variety of tasks.

Specifications

	4-door notchback	5-door hatchback
Wheelbase, in.	103.4	103.4
Overall length, in.	183.4	183.4
Overall width, in.	68.2	68.2
Overall height, in.	56.2	56.2
Turn diameter, ft.	35.5	35.5
Curb weight, lbs.	2491	2609
Cargo vol., cu. ft.	13.5	39.1
Fuel capacity, gals.	15.6	15.6
Seating capacity	5	5
Front headroom, in.	38.1	38.1
Front shoulder room, in.	55.4	55.4
Front legroom, max., in.	43.4	43.4
Rear headroom, in.	37.4	37.4
Rear shoulder room, in.	55.6	55.6
Rear legroom, min., in.	35.0	35.0

Powertrain layout: transverse front engine/front-wheel drive.

Engines

	ohv I-4	ohv V-6
Size, liters/cu. in.	2.2/133	3.1/191
Fuel delivery	TBI	PFI
Horsepower @ rpm	95 @ 5200	135 @ 4200
Torque (lbs./ft.) @ rpm	120 @ 3200	180 @ 3600
Availability	S	O[1]

EPA city/highway mpg

5-speed OD manual	NA	19/30
3-speed automatic	NA	20/27

1. Standard on LTZ.

Prices

Chevrolet Corsica	Retail Price	Dealer Invoice	Low Price
LT 4-door notchback	$9495	$8479	$8679
LT 5-door hatchback	9895	8836	9036
LTZ 4-door notchback	12795	11426	11626
Destination charge	425	425	425

Standard equipment:

LT: 2.2-liter TBI 4-cylinder engine, 5-speed manual transmission, power steering, cloth reclining front bucket seats, 4-way driver's seat, door pockets,

rear shoulder belts, left remote and right manual mirrors, AM/FM radio, 185/75R14 tires; hatchback has folding rear seat, sliding package tray, cargo cover. **LTZ** adds: 3.1-liter PFI V-6, FE3 sport suspension, luggage rack, sport steering wheel, sport front seats, 60/40 split rear seatback with center armrest, gauge package with tachometer, overhead console, 205/60R15 tires on alloy wheels.

Optional equipment:	Retail Price	Dealer Invoice	Low Price
3.1-liter V-6, LT	685	582	617
3-speed automatic transmission	540	459	486
Air conditioning	780	663	702
Custom cloth CL bucket seats, LT 4-door	425	361	383
LT 5-door	275	234	248
Preferred Group 1, LT	232	197	209
Tinted glass, intermittent wipers, floormats, map lamps with consolette.			
Preferred Group 2, LT	1342	1141	1208
Group 1 plus air conditioning, cruise control, tilt steering column.			
Preferred Group 3, LT	2042	1736	1838
Group 2 plus AM/FM cassette, power windows and locks, remote decklid release.			
Preferred Group 1, LTZ	363	309	327
Cruise control, tilt steering column, floormats.			
Preferred Pkg. 2, LTZ	1063	904	957
Group 1 plus AM/FM cassette, power windows and locks, remote decklid release.			
AM/FM cassette	140	119	126
AM/FM cassette w/EQ	290	247	261
Sound system prices are for base models; prices vary with option package content.			
Floor console	60	51	54
Rear defogger	160	136	144
Power locks	215	183	194
Gauge pkg., LT	139	118	125
Tachometer, coolant temperature and oil pressure gauges, voltmeter, trip odometer.			
185/75R14 white-stripe tires, LT	68	58	61
Styled steel wheels, LT	56	48	50
Two-tone paint	123	105	111
Decklid luggage carrier, LT	115	98	104
California emissions pkg.	100	85	90

Chevrolet Corvette

Chevrolet Corvette ZR-1

What's New

The ultra-high-performance ZR-1 option and an all-new interior are the highlights. The long-awaited ZR-1 debuts with a Lotus-designed 32-valve, dual-overhead-cam, 5.7-liter V-8 rated at 380 horsepower. In addition to the LT5 engine, the ZR-1 option brings standard Corvette 275/40ZR17 tires in front and wider 315/35ZR17 tires in the rear. Available in the coupe body style only, the ZR-1 needs wider rear bodywork to accommodate its fatter back tires, but about the only other external mark of a ZR-1 is a convex tail with square taillamps in place of the standard car's concave panel and round lights. Also standard on the ZR-1 is the new FX3 adjustable suspension. FX3 also is optionally available on standard 'Vette coupes equipped with the manual transmission. The base 'Vette's 5.7-liter engine, known as the L98, gets a 5 horsepower boost, to 245, and 5 more pounds/feet of torque, to 340. The sport-muffler version goes to 250 horsepower and 345 pounds/feet of torque. Standard on all Corvettes is the new 6-speed manual transmission; a 4-speed overdrive automatic is optional on L98 cars only. The L98 also gets improved cooling, making a heavy-duty radiator unnecessary. Among new standard items are 17-inch alloy wheels, an engine oil cooler, and an improved anti-lock braking system called ABS II-S. The Corvette convertible gets a new flexible backlight made of "Ultrashield," a material with better ultraviolet filtration and scratch resistance than the previous plastic. All '90 'Vettes will get a new interior featuring a new steering wheel that incorporates an air bag. The new dashboard uses a combination of digital and analog gauges in place of the previous all-digital instrumentation. There are also new seats, new door panels, and a new center console. Power door lock and window switches have been relocated from the console to the door panel, and the wiper switch goes from the door panel to the turn-signal stalk. The power seat controls also are simplified. And there's a new optional Delco/Bose "Gold" sound system with 200 watts, twice that of the previous optional system, and with six speakers instead of four.

For

● Performance   ● Handling   ● Anti-lock brakes

Against

● Ride   ● Noise   ● Fuel economy   ● Insurance costs

Summary

While Corvette is one of the most impractical cars that more than $30,000 can buy, the even more outrageous $59,000 ZR-1 is actually a practical move by Chevrolet. It will generate tremendous attention for Chevy and GM as an example of what the No. 1 U.S. automaker can do. Aside from the ZR-1, Chevrolet still has to sell the "garden-variety" Corvette and convertible, which hasn't been easy the past couple of years. Production outpaced demand in '89, bloating dealer inventories and encouraging big discounts. As for the '90 model, the new cabin is much more appealing and functional than the old. Mixing an analog tachometer and a digital speedometer, however, forces the driver to process two different signals—a tall order during high-performance driving. The driving experience itself also is improved, thanks to the 6-speed manual. Its shifts are sure, but some low-speed maneuvers are hampered by a device designed to help fuel economy. In light throttle applications, the computer-assisted ZF 6-speed activates a pin in the shift linkage to block shifts from first to second gear; instead, the pin bumps the shift lever directly to fourth gear. With a heavier throttle foot, the transmission allows normal shifting through all the gears. As for the ZR-1, it genuinely is one of the world's fastest production cars, capable of speeds approaching 180 mph and 0-60-mph times of 4.5 seconds. Significantly, its wider rear rubber seems to reduce a serious Corvette flaw, that of juddering badly over rough pavement. Overall, the 'Vette remains a vehicle of limited dimension, an image car that delivers thrilling performance so long as the road is smooth and dry.

Specifications

	2-door notchback	2-door conv.
Wheelbase, in.	96.2	96.2
Overall length, in.	176.5	176.5
Overall width, in.	71.0[1]	71.0
Overall height, in.	46.7	46.4
Turn diameter, ft.	40.0	40.0
Curb weight, lbs.	3223[2]	3263
Cargo vol., cu. ft.	17.9	6.6
Fuel capacity, gals.	20	20
Seating capacity	2	2
Front headroom, in.	36.4	36.4
Front shoulder room, in.	54.1	54.1
Front legroom, max., in.	42.6	42.6
Rear headroom, in.	—	—
Rear shoulder room, in.	—	—
Rear legroom, min., in.	—	—

1. ZR-1, 74.0.   2. ZR-1, 3465.

Powertrain layout: longitudinal front engine/rear-wheel drive.

Engines

	ohv V-8	dohc V-8
Size, liters/cu. in.	5.7/350	5.7/350
Fuel delivery	PFI	PFI
Horsepower @ rpm	245 @ 4000	380 @ 6200
Torque (lbs./ft.) @ rpm	340 @ 3200	370 @ 4500
Availability	S	S[1]

EPA city/highway mpg

6-speed OD manual	16/25	17/26
4-speed OD automatic	16/24	

1. ZR-1.

Prices

Chevrolet Corvette	Retail Price	Dealer Invoice	Low Price
3-door hatchback	$31979	$26958	$27358
2-door convertible	37264	31414	31814
ZR-1 3-door hatchback	58995	NA	NA
Destination charge	500	500	500

Standard equipment:

5.7-liter PFI V-8, 6-speed manual or 4-speed automatic transmission, power steering, 4-wheel disc brakes, anti-lock braking system, driver's-side airbag, Pass Key theft deterrent system, air conditioning, AM/FM cassette, power antenna, cruise control, rear defogger, leather-wrapped steering wheel, tinted glass, heated power mirrors, fog lamps, power windows and locks, intermittent wipers, 275/40ZR17 Goodyear Eagle GT tires on alloy wheels. **ZR-1** adds: DOHC 32-valve engine, FX3 Selective Ride Control.

Optional equipment:

Leather seats	425	353	374
Leather sport seats	1050	872	924
Preferred Group 1	1273	1057	1120
Automatic climate control, Delco-Bose Gold audio system, power driver's seat.			
CD player	396	329	348
Automatic climate control	180	149	158
Performance axle ratio	22	18	19
Luggage rack, convertible	140	116	123
Engine oil cooler	110	91	97
Z51 Performance Handling Pkg.	460	382	405
Includes engine oil cooler and HD brakes.			
FX3 Selective Ride Pkg.	1695	1407	1492
Single removable roof panel	615	510	541
Dual removable roof panels	915	759	805
Removable hardtop, convertible	1995	1656	1756
Power seats, each	270	224	238
Engine block heater	20	17	18

Prices are accurate at time of printing; subject to manufacturer's change.

Chevrolet Lumina

Chevrolet Lumina Euro

What's New

The Lumina sedan is a new front-drive intermediate that arrived in the late spring of 1989 as an early 1990 model. A Lumina coupe came on line in the fall. The sedan is the first 4-door from the General Motors design that produced the 1988 Buick Regal, Oldsmobile Cutlass Supreme, and Pontiac Grand Prix 2-door coupes. Both Luminas are 6-passenger cars available in base guise and in a sportier Euro version. A 110-horsepower 2.5-liter 4-cylinder engine is standard in Lumina; a 135-horsepower 3.1-liter V-6 is optional and standard in the Euro. A 3-speed automatic transmission is standard; a 4-speed overdrive automatic is optional with the V-6. The coupe and sedan share the same 107.5-inch wheelbase, but the coupe's body is about one inch longer than the sedan's, at 198.4 inches. The wheelbase of the Lumina 4-door is three inches longer than that of the sedan it replaces, the Celebrity. The Lumina coupe is intended to replace the slightly larger rear-drive Monte Carlo, which was discontinued in 1988. The Euro has blackout exterior trim and a sport suspension not available on the base cars, plus 195/70R15 tires standard and 215/60R16 tires on alloy wheels optional; the base cars are available only with 195/75R14 tires. Lumina is designed to compete with the Ford Taurus and features among its standard equipment 4-wheel disc brakes, power steering, and an all-independent suspension. Euro models also feature standard air conditioning.

For

- Interior room
- Performance (Euro versions)
- Cargo space
- Climate system

Against

- Ride
- Steering
- Controls

Summary

The only Lumina we've subjected to our regular road testing is a Euro Sedan, so we'll confine our comments to it. The car

> KEY: **ohv** = overhead valve; **ohc** = overhead cam; **dohc** = double overhead cam; **I** = inline cylinders; **V** = cylinders in V configuration; **flat** = horizontally opposed cylinders; **bbl.** = barrel (carburetor); **PFI** = port (multi-point) fuel injection; **TBI** = throttle-body (single-point) fuel injection; **rpm** = revolutions per minute; **OD** = overdrive transmission; **S** = standard; **O** = optional; **NA** = not available.

moves GM intermediates up a notch in performance and handling, but overall, we're disappointed. Acceleration off the line is quick, but once underway, good performance with the 3.1 V-6 requires a heavy throttle foot to overcome the 4-speed automatic's reluctance to provide crisp downshifts. Still, highway cruising is quiet and relaxed. Body lean in turns is well controlled, and while the suspension absorbs most bumps without much disturbance, freeway dips set the body to jouncing. The steering feel is imprecise and very heavy and contributes to the car's ponderous feel around town. The standard 4-wheel disc brakes have good stopping power, but the pedal is too firm and not easy to modulate. The gauges are easy to read. The climate controls are large and simple, though their position in the center of the dash is a stretch for the driver. The power window switches are set on the steeply sloped forward edge of the armrest, where they're difficult to reach. The headlight switch is hidden near the base of the steering wheel column. Room and comfort in the front seat is good, though the lower cushion in Lumina's rear seat is too small to be comfortable. The trunk has a utility-enhancing flat floor and every door has a map pocket, though the tiny glovebox holds little more than the owner's manual. Judging Lumina's value means comparing it to the pacesetter in this class, the Ford Taurus, which was introduced in late 1985 as an '86 model. Lumina's cabin doesn't feel any larger than the Taurus's, though it is significantly airier, thanks to a larger greenhouse. The Taurus, however, has a superior over-the-road feel and its overall ergonomics are better. This is the root of our disappointment. The Lumina Euro is an advance over the Celebrity Eurosport it replaces. But despite having four model years to surpass, or even to match, the domestic leader, Taurus, Chevy has failed to produce a new mid-size standard-bearer.

Specifications

	2-door notchback	4-door notchback
Wheelbase, in.	107.5	107.5
Overall length, in.	198.4	197.6
Overall width, in.	71.1	71.0
Overall height, in.	53.3	53.6
Turn diameter, ft.	39.0	39.0
Curb weight, lbs.	3042	3122
Cargo vol., cu. ft.	15.5	15.7
Fuel capacity, gals.	17.1	17.1
Seating capacity	6	6
Front headroom, in.	37.6	38.8
Front shoulder room, in.	57.5	58.2
Front legroom, max., in.	42.4	42.4
Rear headroom, in.	37.2	38.1
Rear shoulder room, in.	56.9	56.2
Rear legroom, min., in.	34.8	36.9

Powertrain layout: transverse front engine/front-wheel drive.

Engines	ohv I-4	ohv V-67
Size, liters/cu. in.	2.5/151	3.1/191
Fuel delivery	TBI	PFI
Horsepower @ rpm	110 @ 5200	135 @ 4400
Torque (lbs./ft.) @ rpm	135 @ 3200	180 @ 3600
Availability	S	O[1]

EPA city/highway mpg

3-speed automatic	21/27	NA
4-speed OD automatic		19/30

1. Standard, Euro.

Prices

Chevrolet Lumina	Retail Price	Dealer Invoice	Low Price
2-door notchback	$12140	$10477	$10677
4-door notchback	12340	10649	10849
Euro 2-door notchback	14040	12117	12317
Euro 4-door notchback	14240	12289	12489
Destination charge	455	455	455

Standard equipment:

2.5-liter TBI 4-cylinder engine, 3-speed automatic transmission, 4-wheel disc brakes, power steering, front bench seat with reclining seatbacks, AM/FM radio, visor mirrors, tinted glass, left remote and right manual mirrors, intermittent wipers, 197/75R14 tires. **Euro** adds: 3.1-liter PFI V-6, air conditioning, decklid spoiler, 195/70R15 tires.

Optional equipment:

3.1-liter V-6, base	660	561	594
4-speed automatic transmission (V-6 req.) .	200	170	180
Air conditioning, base	805	684	725
Custom cloth bucket seats w/console . . .	299	254	269
Custom cloth 60/40 seat	199	169	179
Cloth 60/40 seat	159	135	143
Preferred Group 1, base	1180	1003	1062
Air conditioning, cruise control, tilt steering column, floormats.			
Preferred Group 2, base 2-door	1665	1415	1499
Base 4-door	1770	1505	1593
Group 1 plus power windows and locks, remote decklid release, remote mirrors.			
Preferred Group 1, Euro	475	404	428
Cruise control, tilt steering column, gauge package with tachometer, floormats.			
Preferred Group 2, Euro 2-door	1100	935	990
Euro 4-door	1205	1024	1085
Group 1 plus AM/FM cassette, power windows and locks, remote decklid release, remote mirrors.			
Rear defogger	160	136	144
Power locks, 2-doors	175	149	158
4-doors	215	183	194
AM/FM cassette	140	119	126
Power driver's seat	270	230	243
Rear spoiler delete (credit)	(128)	(109)	(109)
195/75R14 white-stripe tires, base	72	61	65
215/60R16 tires, Euro	76	65	68
Alloy wheels	250	213	225

Chevrolet Lumina APV

What's New

The APV, for "All Purpose Vehicle," is the Chevy version of the space-age-looking new front-wheel-drive minivan from General Motors. Pontiac and Oldsmobile get copies as well, but only Chevy offers a cargo version in addition to its passenger model. Available in base and CL trim levels, the APV offers five different seating configurations, accommodating between two and seven passengers. The only powertrain is a 120-horsepower 3.1-liter V-6 mounted transversely and accessible only through the front hood. A 3-speed automatic is the only transmission. In addition to two front doors, the APV has a sliding right-side door and a one-piece rear liftgate. Standard features include a 20-gallon fuel tank, a rear window wiper/washer, and depending on the seating configuration, up to 16 cup holders. The 3500-pound APV is built of fiberglass-like composite exterior panels bonded to a steel frame. An all-independent suspension, front-disc and rear-drum brakes, power rack-and-pinion steering, and 205/70R14 tires are on all APVs. The APV rides a 109.8-inch wheelbase,

Chevrolet Lumina APV

shorter than both the rear-drive Chevrolet Astro van and the short-wheelbase version of the front-drive Dodge Caravan/Plymouth Voyager. The APV's overall length of about 193 inches, however, is longer than any of these.

For

● Passenger room   ● Quietness   ● Entry/exit   ● Ride

Against

● Performance   ● Visibility

Summary

With a dramatically sloping nose, flush-mounted, wraparound tinted glass, and passenger-car-like interior accommodations, the Lumina APV is being marketed as a sporty alternative to its boxier minivan rivals. We believe a minivan's first mission is utility, not styling, however. The APV's snout works counter to this creed by putting nearly two feet of dash shelf between the driver and the base of the massive windshield. The front of the vehicle is invisible from the driver's vantage and the initial impression is that you're steering from one of the rear seats. The effect is less daunting the more time you spend behind the wheel, but it serves to overshadow some real APV attributes. This minivan does indeed drive much like a car, cornering with commendable control and absorbing most bumps without harshness or wallowing. The steering feels much too light, however. The APV's major shortfall is a lack of power. Movement off the line is acceptable, but the 3.1 V-6 quickly runs out of breath under the burden of 3500 pounds of minivan. Give yourself plenty of time and room to merge into traffic or overtake other vehicles, especially with the air conditioner on and passengers and luggage aboard. Once up to freeway speed, the APV settles into a quiet canter that's ideal for long trips. The dashboard's only serious flaw is under-sized climate controls. Storage bins abound and there's no engine hump to hinder passage to the rear. The modular seating allows for a variety of passenger and cargo configurations. The standard middle bench seat and the optional middle and rear buckets (which weigh just 34 pounds each) are designed for quick removal. The APV is indeed unique looking, its body is impervious to rust and resists dings, and it's priced to compete with the class leaders, the Mazda MPV and the Dodge Caravan/Plymouth Voyager. Its avant-garde nose and underpowered engine, however, are drawbacks in the utility sweepstakes.

Prices are accurate at time of printing; subject to manufacturer's change.

Specifications

	4-door van
Wheelbase, in.	109.8
Overall length, in.	193.9
Overall width, in.	74.2
Overall height, in.	65.5
Turn diameter, ft.	38.0
Curb weight, lbs.	3505
Cargo vol., cu. ft.	104.6
Fuel capacity, gals.	20.0
Seating capacity	7
Front headroom, in.	40.2
Front shoulder room, in.	53.5
Front legroom, max., in.	40.7
Rear headroom, in.	38.6
Rear shoulder room, in.	61.6
Rear legroom, min., in.	33.7

Powertrain layout: transverse front engine/front-wheel drive.

Engines

	ohv V-6
Size, liters/cu. in.	3.1/189
Fuel delivery	TBI
Horsepower @ rpm	120 @ 4200
Torque (lbs./ft.) @ rpm	170 @ 2200
Availability	S

EPA city/highway mpg

3-speed automatic	18/22

Prices

Chevrolet Lumina APV	Retail Price	Dealer Invoice	Low Price
Base van	$13995	$12498	—
CL van	15745	14060	—
Destination charge	500	500	500

Low price not available at time of publication.

Standard equipment:

3.1-liter TBI V-6, 3-speed automatic transmission, power steering, reclining front bucket seats, 3-passenger middle seat, tinted glass, left remote and right manual mirrors, rear wiper/washer, 205/70R14 tires. **CL** adds: air conditioning, tilt steering column, individual seats, misc. lights.

Optional equipment:

Air conditioning, base	805	684	—
6-passenger seating	510	434	—
Includes two front bucket seats and four modular rear seats.			
7-passenger seating, base	660	561	—
CL	425	361	—
Includes two front bucket seats and five modular rear seats.			
Load leveling suspension	170	145	—
Preferred Group 1, base	1000	850	—
Air conditioning, tilt steering column, auxiliary lighting.			
Preferred Group 2, base w/5-pass. seating	1895	1611	—
Base w/6- or 7-pass. seating	1910	1624	—
Group 1 plus AM/FM cassette, power windows and locks, cruise control, remote mirrors, floormats.			

> **KEY: ohv** = overhead valve; **ohc** = overhead cam; **dohc** = double overhead cam; **I** = inline cylinders; **V** = cylinders in V configuration; **flat** = horizontally opposed cylinders; **bbl.** = barrel (carburetor); **PFI** = port (multi-point) fuel injection; **TBI** = throttle-body (single-point) fuel injection; **rpm** = revolutions per minute; **OD** = overdrive transmission; **S** = standard; **O** = optional; **NA** = not available.

	Retail Price	Dealer Invoice	Low Price
Preferred Group 1, CL w/5-pass. seating	895	761	—
CL w/7-pass. seating	910	774	—
AM/FM cassette, power windows and locks, cruise control, remote mirrors, floormats.			
AM/FM cassette	140	119	—
AM/FM radio w/CD player	396	337	—
Sound system prices are for base models; prices vary with option package content.			
Rear defogger	160	136	—
Deep tinted glass	245	208	—
Power locks	255	217	—
Power driver's seat	270	230	—
195/70R15 tires	62	53	—
Alloy wheels	265	225	—

Chevrolet S10 Blazer/ GMC S15 Jimmy

Chevrolet S10 Blazer

What's New

The 4.3-liter V-6 has been made standard and equipment levels are upgraded on these best-selling compact sport-utility vehicles. The S10 Blazer/S15 Jimmy twins come only in a 3-door body style (a 5-door is planned for the future), but with a choice of 2- or 4-wheel drive. Last year's optional 4.3-liter six is now standard on all S10s and S15s. The 2.8-liter V-6 has been dropped. The 4.3's ratings of 160 horsepower and 230 pounds/feet of torque are unchanged from '89, though the engine is now optionally available with 5-speed manual transmission. The standard 4-speed overdrive automatic is carried over. S10s and S15s equipped with the 5-speed now have the option of ordering the trailering package, an item previously offered exclusively with the automatic. With the automatic and 2-wheel drive, maximum towing capacity increases from 5000 pounds to 6000 and from 4000 to 5500 for 4WD models. Three trim levels are again offered on the S10 and S15. All have a slightly redesigned instrument cluster that includes a voltmeter, coolant temperature, and oil pressure gages. The standard tire size also has been increased, from 195/75R15 to 205/75R15. Among the previously optional items added as standard equipment to the base models are a full-size spare tire, dual outside mirrors, halogen headlamps, fog lamps for 2WD models, and front tow hooks for 4 × 4s. Mid-level models add reclining front seatbacks and other convenience items, while previously optional alloy wheels are now part of the top-grade trim. Automatic locking front hubs are standard on 4 × 4s, which use GM's Insta-Trac, a part-time 4WD system not for use on dry pavement. It has full shift-on-the-fly capability.

For

- Performance
- 4WD traction
- Anti-lock rear brakes

Against

- Fuel economy
- Ride

Summary

GM's compact 4 × 4s lack some of the features of the Jeep Cherokee, such as a 5-door body style and a full-time 4WD system, plus Jeep offers a 4-wheel anti-lock brake system, while GM's anti-lock feature operates only on the rear wheels. However, the S10 Blazer and S15 Jimmy do boast an easy-to-use part-time 4WD system and a muscular V-6 engine. We applaud the availability of the 5-speed manual, but with either transmission, gas mileage will be nothing to rave about. The 4.3 develops considerable torque at low engine speeds for strong around-town acceleration and ample towing capacity. We recommend the optional heavy-duty shock absorbers for a more comfortable ride, and suggest you buy the off-road suspension only if you do a lot of off-road driving; the on-road ride can be punishing with that option. Until the 5-door body style arrives in 1991, the rear seat of the S10 and S15 will continue to be nearly inaccessible. And cargo space with the rear seatback up and inside spare tire in place isn't what we'd hope for. But while the Chevy/GMC twins get quite pricey as you add options, they're still not as expensive as a loaded Cherokee.

Specifications

	3-door wagon
Wheelbase, in.	100.5
Overall length, in.	170.3
Overall width, in.	65.7
Overall height, in.	64.0
Turn diameter, ft.	34.6
Curb weight, lbs.	NA
Cargo vol., cu. ft.	62.7
Fuel capacity, gals.	20.0
Seating capacity	4
Front headroom, in.	39.0
Front shoulder room, in.	53.9
Front legroom, max., in.	42.5
Rear headroom, in.	38.7
Rear shoulder room, in.	56.1
Rear legroom, min., in.	35.5

Powertrain layout: longitudinal front engine/rear-wheel drive or on-demand 4WD.

Engines

	ohv V-6
Size, liters/cu. in.	4.3/262
Fuel delivery	TBI
Horsepower @ rpm	160 @ 4000
Torque (lbs./ft.) @ rpm	230 @ 2800
Availability	S

EPA city/highway mpg

5-speed OD manual	16/20
4-speed OD automatic	17/21

Prices

Chevrolet S10 Blazer/ GMC S15 Jimmy

	Retail Price	Dealer Invoice	Low Price
S10 Blazer 2WD 3-door wagon	$12940	$11555	$11755
S10 Blazer 4WD 3-door wagon	14605	13042	13242
S15 Jimmy 2WD 3-door wagon	13133	11728	11928
S15 Jimmy 4WD 3-door wagon	14798	13215	13415
Destination charge	435	435	435

Standard equipment:

4.3-liter TBI V-6, 5-speed manual transmission, anti-lock rear brakes, power steering, front and rear chromed bumpers with black rub strips, tinted glass, bright metal hubcaps, coolant temperature and oil pressure gauges, voltmeter, AM radio, fog lamps (2WD), tow hooks (4WD), dual outside mirrors, front armrests, front and rear dome lamps, door sill plates, rubber floormat, headlamp warning buzzer, highback vinyl front bucket seats with easy-entry feature on passenger side, 205/75R15 tires with full-size spare, painted argent wheels.

Optional equipment:

4-speed automatic transmission	860	731	774
Optional axle ratio	38	32	34
Locking differential	252	214	227
Air conditioning	755	642	680
Tahoe/Sierra Classic (SC) Pkg., 2WD	841	715	757
4WD	809	688	728
Reclining seatbacks, bodyside and wheel opening moldings, special door trim (includes coin holder, armrest and pocket), console, floormats, visor mirror, reading lamp, added sound insulation, engine compartment lamp, rally wheels (2WD), trim rings (4WD).			
Sport/Gypsy Pkg.	1239	1053	1115
Tahoe/SC plus color-keyed bumpers, alloy wheels.			
Deluxe cloth trim, w/rear seat	26	22	23
Leather seat trim, Tahoe/SC w/o rear seat	386	328	347
Tahoe/SC w/rear seat	486	413	437
Sport/Gypsy w/o rear seat	312	265	281
Sport/Gypsy w/rear seat	412	350	371
Custom two-tone paint	324	275	292
w/Tahoe/SC	172	146	155
Special two-tone paint	218	185	196
w/Sunshine Striping	163	139	147
Deluxe two-tone paint	329	280	296
w/Tahoe/SC	177	150	159
HD battery	56	48	50
Outside spare tire carrier & cover	159	135	143
Cold Climate Pkg.	189	161	170
w/Tahoe/SC or Sport/Gypsy	146	124	131
HD battery, engine block heater, added insulation.			
Front floor console	135	115	122
HD radiator	56	48	50
HD radiator & trans oil cooler	118	100	106
w/A/C or Trailering Special	63	54	57
HD radiator & engine oil cooler	135	115	122
Driver Convenience Pkg. ZM7	180	153	162
Intermittent wipers, tilt steering column.			
Driver Convenience Pkg. ZM8	197	167	177
Rear defogger, remote tailgate release.			
Deep tinted glass	225	191	203
Electronic instruments	296	252	266
Lighted visor mirrors	75	64	68
w/Tahoe/SC or Sport/Gypsy	68	58	61
Bodyside & wheel opening moldings	152	129	137
Bright wheel opening moldings	31	26	28
Black wheel opening moldings	43	37	39
w/Tahoe/SC	13	11	12
Operating Convenience Pkg.	344	292	310
Power windows and locks.			
AM/FM radio	131	111	118
AM/FM cassette	253	215	228
AM/FM cassette w/EQ	403	343	363
AM radio delete (credit)	(95)	(81)	(81)
Folding rear bench seat	409	348	368

Prices are accurate at time of printing; subject to manufacturer's change.

	Retail Price	Dealer Invoice	Low Price
Shield Pkg., 4WD	75	64	68
Shields for transfer case, front differential, fuel tank and steering linkage.			
HD shock absorbers	40	34	36
Cruise control	225	191	203
Bodyside striping	55	47	50
Sunshine striping	125	106	113
w/Special two-tone paint	70	60	63
Non-removable glass sunroof	250	213	225
HD front suspension	63	54	57
Off-Road Suspension Pkg.	182	155	164
w/Tahoe/SC or Sport/Gypsy	122	104	110
HD Trailering Special	211	179	190
LD Trailering Special	165	140	149
Wheel trim rings	60	51	54
Rally wheels	92	78	83
Alloy wheels, 4WD	325	276	293
4WD w/Tahoe/SC or Off-Road Suspension	269	229	242
2WD	325	276	293
2WD w/Tahoe/SC	233	198	210
Sliding rear quarter window	257	218	231
Rear wiper/washer	125	106	113
Luggage carrier & air deflector	169	144	152
California emissions pkg.	100	85	90

Chrysler Imperial/ New Yorker Fifth Avenue

Chrysler Imperial

What's New

Chrysler returns full-bore to the domestic luxury market with a pair of new cars based on a stretched New Yorker platform. Resurrected for the occasion is the Imperial badge, last used in 1983. on a rear-drive "bustleback" luxury coupe. For '90, the Imperial becomes the corporation's flagship sedan, with the Fifth Avenue its slightly less plush sibling. The 1989 Fifth Avenue was a rear-drive sedan from a design that dated to 1982. Both new models are full-size front-drive, 6-passenger luxury 4-doors. They're based on the current New Yorker platform, but with a wheelbase stretched by five inches, to 109.3. The Imperial's body is 203-inches long overall, while the Fifth Avenue is more than 4 inches shorter, at 198.6. The difference in length is primarily in the body's front and rear overhang;

KEY: ohv = overhead valve; **ohc** = overhead cam; **dohc** = double overhead cam; **I** = inline cylinders; **V** = cylinders in V configuration; **flat** = horizontally opposed cylinders; **bbl.** = barrel (carburetor); **PFI** = port (multi-point) fuel injection; **TBI** = throttle-body (single-point) fuel injection; **rpm** = revolutions per minute; **OD** = overdrive transmission; **S** = standard; **O** = optional; **NA** = not available.

---

the cars share the same interior head- and leg-room dimensions. Both are powered by Chrysler's new 147-horsepower 3.3 V-6 mated to a 4-speed overdrive automatic transmission. A lengthy list of luxury equipment is standard on both the Imperial and Fifth Avenue, including highline trim inside and out, automatic rear load leveling, power windows and door locks, and an automatic climate control system. The Imperial offers as standard some features that are optional on the Fifth Avenue, including leather upholstery, power memory seatback recliners, a power deck-lid pulldown, and 4-wheel anti-lock disc brakes. Optional on the Imperial is an air suspension system that is unavailable on the Fifth Avenue, while the Fifth Avenue has exclusive rights to the optional power sun roof. The new cars will compete in the domestic luxury class against slightly larger front-drive models such as the V-6 Lincoln Continental and the V-8-powered Cadillac De Ville and Fleetwood sedans. The Imperial has a list price of $24,995, the Fifth Avenue lists for $21,395. By comparison, the Continental's base price of $23,699 includes anti-lock brakes, while the Sedan De Ville starts at $27,540 with a 180-horsepower V-8 engine, but with ABS as a $925 option. We have not yet driven either an Imperial or a Fifth Avenue.

Specifications

	Imperial 4-door notchback	Fifth Avenue 4-door notchback
Wheelbase, in.	109.3	109.3
Overall length, in.	203.0	198.6
Overall width, in.	68.9	68.9
Overall height, in.	56.3	55.9
Turn diameter, ft.	42.1	42.1
Curb weight, lbs.	3570	3452
Cargo vol., cu. ft.	16.7	16.5
Fuel capacity, gals.	16.0	16.0
Seating capacity	6	6
Front headroom, in.	38.4	38.4
Front shoulder room, in.	55.9	56.2
Front legroom, max., in.	43.0	43.0
Rear headroom, in.	55.7	55.7
Rear shoulder room, in.	37.9	37.9
Rear legroom, min., in.	41.7	41.7

Powertrain layout: transverse front engine/front-wheel drive.

Engines

	ohv V-6
Size, liters/cu. in.	3.3/201
Fuel delivery	PFI
Horsepower @ rpm	147 @ 4800
Torque (lbs./ft.) @ rpm	183 @ 3600
Availability	S

EPA city/highway mpg

4-speed OD automatic . . . . 17/25[1]

1. Fifth Avenue, 18/26.

Prices

Chrysler Imperial	Retail Price	Dealer Invoice	Low Price
4-door notchback	$24995	$21271	—
Destination charge	550	550	550

Low price not available at time of publication.

Standard equipment:

3.3-liter PFI V-6, 4-speed automatic transmission, anti-lock 4-wheel disc brakes, power steering, driver's-side airbag, rear shoulder belts, automatic temperature control air conditioning, leather/cloth 50/50 power bench seat with 2-position memory, power windows and locks, automatic load leveling suspension, cruise control, heated power mirrors with 2-position memory, Chrysler Infinity I AM/FM cassette with power antenna, rear defogger, tilt steering column, leather-wrapped steering wheel, headlamp delay, coolant temperature and oil pressure gauges, voltmeter, trip odometer, illuminated entry, remote fuel door and decklid releases, tinted glass, floormats, cornering lights, lighted visor mirrors, landau vinyl roof, wire wheel covers, 195/75R14 WSW tires.

Optional equipment:	Retail Price	Dealer Invoice	Low Price
Electronic Features Pkg.	1618	1375	
Overhead console with Vehicle Information Center, electronic instruments, automatic day/night mirror, Infinity II AM/FM cassette with EQ, security alarm.			
Security alarm	150	128	—
Electronically controlled air suspension . . .	628	534	—
Mark Cross leather	365	310	—
Pearl/clearcoat paint	75	64	—
Conventional spare tire	NC	NC	NC
California emissions pkg.	NC	NC	NC

Chrysler New Yorker Fifth Avenue

4-door notchback	$21395	$18461	—
Destination charge	550	550	550

Low price not available at time of publication.

Standard equipment:

3.3-liter PFI V-6, 4-speed automatic transmission, power steering, driver's-side airbag, rear shoulder belts, automatic temperature control air conditioning, 50/50 cloth bench seat with power driver's side and center armrest, power windows and locks, cruise control, AM/FM radio, heated power mirrors, rear defogger, coolant temperature and oil pressure gauges, voltmeter, trip odometer, remote fuel door and decklid releases, tilt steering column, leather-wrapped steering wheel, automatic rear load leveling, tinted glass, intermittent wipers, cornering lights, visor mirrors, landau vinyl roof, 195/75R14 WSW tires.

Optional equipment:

Anti-lock 4-wheel disc brakes	954	811	—
Luxury Equipment Pkg.	1550	1318	—
Bodyside molding, illuminated entry, floormats, headlamp delay, lighted visor mirrors, power antenna, power decklid pulldown, heated power mirrors with 2-position memory, power seats with 2-position memory, security alarm, undercoating, wire wheel covers.			
Mark Cross Edition	2133	1813	—
Luxury Pkg. plus leather interior.			
Interior Illumination Pkg.	197	167	—
Illuminated entry, lighted visor mirrors.			
Electronic Features Pkg.	1252	1064	—
Overhead console with Vehicle Information Center, electronic instrument cluster, automatic day/night mirror.			
Power decklid pulldown	82	70	—
AM/FM cassette w/Infinity speakers	497	422	—
AM/FM cassette w/Infinity speakers & EQ .	713	606	—
Requires Luxury or Mark Cross Pkg.			
Security alarm	150	128	—
Conventional spare tire	85	72	—
Alloy wheels	50	43	—
Requires Luxury or Mark Cross Pkg.			
Wire wheel covers	231	196	—
Pearl/clearcoat paint	75	64	—
California emissions pkg.	103	88	—

Chrysler LeBaron

What's New

The world's best-selling convertible and its coupe cousin are available for the first time with V-6 power and are treated to a new cabin design, while the LeBaron name has been ex-

Chrysler LeBaron GTC

tended to a 4-door sedan based on the Dodge Spirit/Plymouth Acclaim. First, the coupe and convertible. These front-drive cars have soldiered on since their 1987-model year debut with naturally aspirated and turbocharged 4-cylinder engines. For '90, a Mitsubishi-made 141-horsepower 3.0-liter V-6 is standard or optional on all LeBarons except the performance-oriented GTC coupe and convertible. Those models come standard with Chrysler's new 2.2-liter intercooled VNT (Variable Nozzle Turbo) Turbo IV engine. Also available for the first time is a 4-speed automatic transmission. It replaces a 3-speed automatic and is optional or standard on all but the VNT Turbo cars, which must use Chrysler's new 5-speed manual transmission. New on the GTC for '90 is an electronic variable damped suspension that allows the driver to alter shock absorber damping. Rear shoulder belts are now standard on the coupe and a security alarm is a new option on all LeBarons. The new interior replaces the severe angles of the previous dashboard with rounded forms that place controls closer to the driver. The seats and door trim also are new, and now optional on the LeBaron coupe is an overhead console that houses map lights and storage bins. The A-body LeBaron Sedan will reach showrooms in January 1990. It replaces the K-car-derived LeBaron sedan that was retired for the '89 model year. This front-wheel-drive 6-passenger sedan shares the Spirit/Acclaim 103.3-inch wheelbase. The Mitsubishi 3.0 V-6 mated to a 4-speed automatic is the only powertrain. Standard features include air conditioning, digital instrumentation, a landau roof, a cassette player, cruise control, a tilt steering column and driver's-side air bag and 195/70R14 tires.

For

- Performance (V-6 and VNT Turbo)
- Transmission (5-speed manual)
- Air bag (coupe and convertible)
- Comfort and quietness (sedan)

Against

- Engine noise (turbos)
- Rear seat and cargo room (coupe and convertible)

Summary

The LeBaron coupe and convertible have always had nice bodies, but never the kind of refined power that does justice to their looks. Now the Mitsubishi V-6 offers an alternative to the wheezing base 4-cylinder and the raucous turbo fours. The six has less power and torque than either of the turbocharged 2.2s, but it's much smoother and quieter and it

Prices are accurate at time of printing; subject to manufacturer's change.

delivers its power in a far more linear fashion. That last quality is vital. While a V-6 LeBaron coupe or convertible is plenty fast, these cars need slickness over outright quickness, and the 3.0 gives it to them at last. Complementing the newly available V-6 is a completely redesigned interior and a vastly improved 5-speed manual transmission. Both are steps toward the sophistication promised by LeBaron's exterior styling. The new dashboard is far more modern looking that the squared-off one it replaces. It's more user-friendly, as well. The gauges are easier to see, the controls easier to use. About its only failing is the chicken-wing-shaped turn signal lever. It feels flimsy and its position leaves it vulnerable to accidental activation. As for the new 5-speed, our limited test drives indicate the new transmission's shift action is a quantum leap ahead of the previous one's. The feel is meaty but smooth and direct, and a new gate pattern eliminates the need for the previous gear lever's reverse-lockout ring. No longer must manual-transmission fans shudder at the prospect of buying one in a Chrysler product. The LeBaron Sedan is also a pleasant surprise. A limited test drive of an early production model revealed a quiet and competent luxury compact that's a worthy first rung on the Chrysler-sedan ladder.

Specifications

	2-door notchback	2-door conv.	4-door notchback
Wheelbase, in.	100.3	100.3	103.3
Overall length, in.	184.9	184.9	182.7
Overall width, in.	68.5	68.5	68.1
Overall height, in.	51.0	52.3	53.7
Turn diameter, ft.	38.1	38.1	37.6
Curb weight, lbs.	2810	2929	2854
Cargo vol., cu. ft.	14.0	10.3	14.4
Fuel capacity, gals.	14.0	14.0	16.0
Seating capacity	5	4	6
Front headroom, in.	37.6	38.3	38.4
Front shoulder room, in.	55.9	55.9	53.9
Front legroom, max., in.	42.4	42.4	41.9
Rear headroom, in.	36.3	37.0	37.9
Rear shoulder room, in.	56.3	45.7	54.2
Rear legroom, min., in.	33.0	33.0	38.3

Powertrain layout: transverse front engine/front-wheel drive.

Engines

	ohc I-4	Turbo ohc I-4	Turbo ohc I-4	ohc V-6
Size, liters/cu. in.	2.5/153	2.5/153	2.2/135	3.0/181.4
Fuel delivery	TBI	PFI	PFI	PFI
Horsepower @ rpm	100 @ 4800	150 @ 4800	174 @ 5200	141 @ 5000
Torque (lbs./ft.) @ rpm	135 @ 2800	180 @ 2000	210 @ 2400	171 @ 2800
Availability	S	O	S[1]	S[2]

EPA city/highway mpg

5-speed OD manual	24/32	20/25	20/28	19/28
3-speed automatic	22/27	19/23		
4-speed OD automatic				20/26

1. GTC. 2. Premium and GT coupe and convertible; LeBaron Sedan.

KEY: ohv = overhead valve; **ohc** = overhead cam; **dohc** = double overhead cam; **I** = inline cylinders; **V** = cylinders in V configuration; **flat** = horizontally opposed cylinders; **bbl.** = barrel (carburetor); **PFI** = port (multi-point) fuel injection; **TBI** = throttle-body (single-point) fuel injection; **rpm** = revolutions per minute; **OD** = overdrive transmission; **S** = standard; **O** = optional; **NA** = not available.

Prices

Chrysler LeBaron Coupe/Convertible	Retail Price	Dealer Invoice	Low Price
Highline (HL) 2-door notchback	$12495	$11046	$11246
Premium (PR) 2-door notchback	16415	14456	14656
GT 2-door notchback	15725	13856	14056
GTC 2-door notchback	18238	16042	16242
Highline 2-door convertible	14995	13221	13421
Premium 2-door convertible	19595	17223	17423
GT 2-door convertible	17799	15660	15860
GTC 2-door convertible	20406	17928	18128
Destination charge	465	465	465

Standard equipment:

Highline: 2.5-liter TBI 4-cylinder engine, 3-speed automatic transmission, power steering, 4-wheel disc brakes, driver's-side airbag, rear shoulder belts, cloth reclining front bucket seats, coolant temperature and oil pressure gauges, voltmeter, trip odometer, mini trip computer, AM/FM radio, power windows, intermittent wipers, console with storage, remote fuel door and decklid releases, tinted glass, remote mirrors, visor mirrors, 195/70R14 tires; convertible has power top. **Premium** adds: 3.0-liter PFI V-6, 4-speed automatic transmission, power locks, 60/40 folding rear seat (coupe), leather-wrapped steering wheel, overhead console (coupe), floormats, electronic instruments, cornering lights, heated power mirrors, rear defogger, 205/60R15 touring tires; convertible has illuminated entry, lighted visor mirrors, cruise control, tilt steering column, AM/FM cassette with Infinity speakers and power antenna, undercoating. **GT** adds to Highline: 3.0-liter PFI V-6, 5-speed manual transmission, sport handling suspension, air conditioning, rear defogger, power locks, heated power mirrors, AM/FM cassette with Infinity speakers and power antenna, floormats, cruise control, tilt steering column, leather-wrapped steering wheel, undercoating, 205/60R15 performance tires on alloy wheels. **GTC** adds: 2.2-liter intercooled Turbo IV PFI 4-cylinder engine, HD transmission and brakes, performance suspension, overhead console, illuminated entry, decklid luggage rack, lighted visor mirrors, 205/55R16 tires.

Optional equipment:

2.5-liter turbo engine, HL	700	595	630
3.0-liter V-6, HL	700	595	630
2.5-liter turbo engine, GT & GTC	NC	NC	NC
5-speed manual transmission, HL w/3.0 (credit)	(552)	(469)	(469)
3-speed automatic transmission, GT	552	469	497
GTC	NC	NC	NC
GTC includes 2.5-liter turbo engine instead of Turbo IV.			
4-speed automatic transmission, GT w/3.0	646	549	581
HL w/3.0	94	80	85
Air conditioning, HL	819	696	737
Popular Equipment Pkg., HL cpe	1269	1079	1142
HL coupe w/Deluxe Convenience	914	777	823
HL convertible	1084	921	976

Air conditioning, rear defogger, floormats, cruise control, tilt steering column, undercoating.

Chrysler LeBaron GTC

	Retail Price	Dealer Invoice	Low Price
Luxury Equipment Pkg., HL coupe	2278	1936	2050
HL coupe w/Power Convenience	2008	1707	1807
PR coupe	815	693	734

Popular Pkg. plus illuminated entry, lighted visor mirrors, overhead console, power locks, heated power mirrors, power driver's seat, leather-wrapped steering wheel.

Deluxe Convenience Pkg., HL & PR	325	276	293

Cruise control, tilt steering column; standard on Premium convertible.

Light Pkg., HL & PR	197	167	177

Illuminated entry, lighted visor mirrors; standard on Premium convertible.

Power Convenience Pkg., HL	300	255	270

Power locks, heated power mirrors.

Overhead console, GT	268	228	241
Rear defogger, HL coupe	155	132	140
Electronic instruments, HL	308	262	277

Requires Popular Pkg.

Vehicle Info Center, PR convertible & GTC .	698	593	628
PR coupe	544	462	490
Leather power driver's seat, PR & GT coupes	970	825	873
PR & GT convertibles	1227	1043	1104
Leather power enthusiast seat, GTC coupe .	1227	1043	1104
Power driver's seat, convertibles exc. GTC .	258	219	232

HL requires Power Convenience Pkg.

8-way power driver's seat, PR & GT convertibles	324	275	292

Requires leather trim.

Vinyl seat trim, HL & GT convertibles . . .	103	88	93
AM/FM cassette, HL	157	133	141
AM/FM cassette, PR coupe	569	484	512
AM/FM cassette w/EQ, HL & PR coupes . .	785	667	707
PR & GTC convertibles, GTC coupe . . .	216	184	194

Convertibles require Popular Pkg.; coupes require Popular or Luxury Pkg.

Security alarm, PR & GTC	150	128	135
Removable sunroof, HL & GT coupes . . .	408	347	367
PR & GTC coupes	229	195	206
Sport handling suspension, HL	59	50	53
195/70R14 WSW touring tires, HL	74	63	67
205/60R15 WSW touring tires, PR	78	66	70
Alloy wheels & sport suspension, PR . . .	547	465	492
Alloy wheels, HL	332	282	299
Two-tone paint, HL coupe	233	198	210

Chrysler New Yorker

What's New

Chrysler reasserted itself in the full-size luxury market with the redesigned New Yorker in 1988. For '90, the Landau continues as the full-zoot companion to the base New Yorker, which is now called the Salon. The big mechanical change is the introduction of the Chrysler-made 3.3-liter V-6 as the standard engine in place of a Mitsubishi-made 3.0-liter V-6. To last year's long list of Landau standard equipment, which included a landau vinyl roof, automatic rear load leveling, and air conditioning, Chrysler adds a driver's-side air bag, a one-touch driver power window, and rear outboard shoulder belts, among other items. The Salon basically is a stripped Landau aimed at what Chrysler terms "value-oriented buyers seeking room, ride and comfort attributes at an affordable price." Its trim is akin to that of the similar front-drive Dodge Dynasty LE. This 6-passenger sedan relegates to the options list such traditional luxury items as power windows and air conditioning. Optional equipment common to both New Yorker models includes 4-wheel disc brakes with an anti-lock feature in place of the standard front disc/rear drum setup. A power memory driver's seat and a power sunroof are other mutual options. Exclusive to the Salon options list is a road-handling suspension. The cars share powertrains, linking a 4-speed overdrive automatic transmission to the new V-6. The 3.3-liter Chrysler

Chrysler New Yorker Salon

engine has 147 horsepower, six more than the Mitsubishi V-6, and 183 pounds/feet of torque, 12 more than the Mitsubishi.

For

● Ride   ● Anti-lock brakes   ● Interior room

Against

● Performance   ● Handling

Summary

A conservative sedan that evokes Chrysler's big-car luxury heritage, the New Yorker is smooth, quiet and unexciting. We haven't yet driven a New Yorker with the 3.3, but equipped with the Mitsubishi 3.0, the car had adequate power for most driving, but did not perform well on an upgrade with a full load and the air conditioner on. The New Yorker's front-drive manners feature good around-town handling, but succumb to tire-squealing body lean at the first hint of spirited cornering. The chassis filters out most bumps, yet the car doesn't float excessively at speed. The available anti-lock brakes are a big plus. The interior will seat five adults in true comfort, though three in front is a bit of a squeeze. Soft, flat seats coddle your body rather than support it. Dashboard controls are generally easy to reach and well labeled. Trunk space is good. Overall, Chrysler takes no chances with the New Yorker's styling or performance. Sales in 1989 were running well ahead of those in '88, so it appears the traditional-luxury audience is being well served by this car. As for the Salon, the Dynasty is Dodge's biggest-selling car, so there obviously is a market for such a package. Comparing a similarly equipped Salon to a Dynasty LE, however, buyers will find the one with the Chrysler label about $2000 more expensive.

Specifications

	4-door notchback
Wheelbase, in.	104.3
Overall length, in.	193.6
Overall width, in.	68.5
Overall height, in.	54.8
Turn diameter, ft.	40.4
Curb weight, lbs.	3066
Cargo vol., cu. ft.	16.5
Fuel capacity, gals.	16.0
Seating capacity	6
Front headroom, in.	38.3
Front shoulder room, in.	56.0
Front legroom, max., in.	41.9
Rear headroom, in.	37.8
Rear shoulder room, in.	55.7
Rear legroom, min., in.	38.9

Prices are accurate at time of printing; subject to manufacturer's change.

Chrysler

Powertrain layout: transverse front engine/front-wheel drive.

Engines

	ohv V-6
Size, liters/cu. in.	3.3/201
Fuel delivery	PFI
Horsepower @ rpm	147 @ 4800
Torque (lbs./ft.) @ rpm	183 @ 3600
Availability	S

EPA city/highway mpg

4-speed OD automatic	18/25

Prices

Chrysler New Yorker	Retail Price	Dealer Invoice	Low Price
Salon 4-door notchback	$16395	$14186	$14756
Landau 4-door notchback	18795	16226	16916
Destination charge	520	520	520

Low price not available at time of publication.

Standard equipment:

Salon: 3.3-liter PFI V-6, 4-speed automatic transmission, power steering, driver's-side airbag, rear shoulder belts, 50/50 cloth front bench seat with seatback pockets, AM/FM radio, intermittent wipers, rear defogger, remote fuel door and decklid releases, coolant temperature and oil pressure gauges, voltmeter, trip odometer, remote mirrors, tinted glass, visor mirrors, 195/75R14 WSW tires. **Landau** adds: air conditioning, power windows and mirrors, cornering lamps, landau vinyl roof, automatic rear load leveling.

Optional equipment:

	Retail	Dealer	Low
Anti-lock 4-wheel disc brakes	954	811	859
Air conditioning, Salon	819	696	737
Popular Equipment Pkg., Salon	1560	1326	1404

Air conditioning, power windows and locks, floormats, heated power mirrors, cruise control, tilt steering column, undercoating.

Luxury Equipment Pkg., Salon	2756	2343	2480

Popular Pkg. plus Interior Illumination Pkg., automatic day/night mirror, leather-wrapped steering wheel, power seats, security alarm, wire wheel covers.

Interior Illumination Pkg., Salon	197	167	177

Illuminated entry, lighted visor mirrors; requires Popular Pkg.

Deluxe Convenience Pkg.	325	276	293

Cruise control, tilt steering column.

Power Accessories Pkg.	154	131	139

Power decklid pulldown, power antenna; requires Luxury Pkg.

Luxury Equipment Pkg., Landau	1671	1420	1504

Power locks, floormats, headlamp delay system, illuminated entry, lighted visor mirrors, bodyside moldings, power seats, cruise control, tilt steering column, undercoating, wire wheel covers.

Mark Cross Edition, Landau	2315	1968	2084

Luxury Pkg. plus leather upholstery, leather-wrapped steering wheel.

Electronic Features Pkg., Landau	1252	1064	1127

Overhead console with Vehicle Information Center, automatic day/night mirror, electronic instruments.

Power locks	304	258	274
AM/FM cassette, Salon	157	133	—
w/seek/scan, Landau	262	223	—
Infinity I AM/FM cassette	497	422	—
Infinity II AM/FM cassette	713	606	—

Requires Luxury Pkg.

	Retail Price	Dealer Invoice	Low Price
Security alarm	150	128	—

Salon requires Popular Pkg.; Landau requires power locks.

Power driver's seat	258	219	—

Salon requires Popular Pkg.

Memory power seats	372	316	—

Requires Luxury Pkg.

Power sunroof	799	679	—

Salon requires Luxury Pkg.

Road handling suspension, Salon	59	50	—

Requires Popular Pkg.; not available with automatic rear load leveling.

Automatic rear load leveling, Salon	185	157	—

Requires Popular or Luxury Pkg.

Conventional spare tire	85	72	—
Wire wheel covers	231	196	—
Alloy wheels	281	239	—
w/Luxury Pkg. or Mark Cross	50	43	—

Salon without Luxury Pkg. requires Popular Pkg.

Pearl/clearcoat paint	75	64	—
California emissions pkg.	103	88	—

Chrysler's TC by Maserati

Chrysler's TC by Maserati

What's New

Introduced on the West Coast in January 1989, Chrysler's 2-seat luxury convertible is now available throughout the U.S. A driver's-side air bag in a new woodgrain steering wheel and the availability of a V-6 engine mark the changes for the '90 edition. The front-drive TC is assembled in Europe by the Italian automaker, Maserati, of which Chrylser owns a portion. There are no extra-cost options on this $33,000 car, but a pair of engine/transmission teams is available. The most sporting is a 200-horsepower turbocharged and intercooled 2.2-liter four. Its dual-overhead cam, 16-valve cylinder head was designed by Maserati and it's available only with a Getrag 5-speed manual transmission. When ordered with a Chrysler 4-speed automatic, the TC gets a 141-horsepower Mistubishi-made 3.0-liter V-6. This replaces a Chrysler-made 160-horsepower turbocharged 2.2-liter 4-cylinder as the engine furnished when a buyer specifies automatic. All TCs have a full leather interior, a Maserati-tuned suspension, and 4-wheel anti-lock disc brakes. The convertible top is manually operated, but an electric motor pulls the fabric taut when the top is up. When down, the top is stowed beneath a metal tonneau cover. TC's removable fiberglass hardtop is notable for the circular glass opera windows in its rear pillars. It also has a glass rear window with an electric defroster.

For

- Exclusivity ● Styling

CONSUMER GUIDE®

Against

● Price ● Performance ● Refinement

Summary

Chrysler describes the TC as a "beautiful little high-performance convertible with a designer label on it." After a test drive at Chrysler's Michigan proving grounds, we doubt whether the TC's performance or its label will score a hit in the demanding sports-luxury market. The car is attractive, but it looks very much like a Chrysler LeBaron convertible, which lists for about $8000 less, fully equipped. The pre-production 200-horsepower TC we drove was indeed quick, with an engine that pressed us back in the seat and sounded great above 3000 rpm. Precise steering, strong brakes, and good handling were evident, though the limp seats offered little support in hard cornering. The clutch was extremely heavy, and the shifter had to be forced through most gear changes. Mechanical flaws are common in pre-production examples, but other shortcomings soured the car's luxury-touring air. The cowl shook noticeably over bumps and the dashboard controls appeared borrowed from the Chrysler parts bin. Most TCs will be sold with automatic transmission, so Chrysler is wise to install Mitsubishi's smooth V-6 for that application. Despite an early flurry of sales on the West Coast, however, the TC will need more than a Japanese V-6 to earn its stripes in this class.

Specifications

	2-door conv.
Wheelbase, in.	93.0
Overall length, in.	175.8
Overall width, in.	68.5
Overall height, in.	51.9
Turn diameter, ft.	37.1
Curb weight, lbs.	3200
Cargo vol., cu. ft.	NA
Fuel capacity, gals.	14.0
Seating capacity	2
Front headroom, in.	37.4
Front shoulder room, in.	55.9
Front legroom, max., in.	42.4
Rear headroom, in.	—
Rear shoulder room, in.	—
Rear legroom, min., in.	—

Powertrain layout: transverse front engine/front-wheel drive.

Engines	Turbo dohc I-4	ohc V-6
Size, liters/cu. in.	2.2/135	3.0/181
Fuel delivery	PFI	PFI
Horsepower @ rpm	200 @ 5500	141 @ 5000
Torque (lbs./ft.) @ rpm	220 @ 3400	171 @ 2800
Availability	S	O
EPA city/highway mpg		
5-speed OD manual	20/32	
4-speed OD automatic		NA

Prices

Chrysler's TC by Maserati (1989 prices)	Retail Price	Dealer Invoice	Low Price
2-door convertible	$33000	NA	NA
Destination charge	550	550	550

Standard equipment:

2.2-liter SOHC 8-valve turbocharged, intercooled PFI 4-cylinder engine with 3-speed automatic transmission or 2.2-liter DOHC 16-valve turbocharged, intercooled engine with 5-speed manual, anti-lock braking system, 4-wheel disc brakes, power steering, manual folding convertible top with glass backlight, removable hardtop with rear defogger, air conditioning, leather upholstery, AM/FM ST ET cassette with CD player and graphic EQ, power windows and locks, power front seats, heated power mirrors, tinted glass, tilt steering column, cruise control, illuminated entry, intermittent wipers, remote fuel door and decklid releases, door pockets, console with storage, P205/60VR15 Michelin MXV SBR tires on alloy wheels.

Options prices are not available at time of publication.

Chrysler Town & Country

Chrysler Town & Country

What's New

Chrysler packs a long-wheelbase example of its hot-selling minivan with luxury features and a new V-6 engine to create the Town & Country. This version of the front-drive Dodge Grand Caravan/Plymouth Grand Voyager comes in a single trim level with two front buckets and middle and rear benches for 7-passenger seating. Whitewall tires, a California emissions package, and a front license-plate bracket are the only options on this $25,000 minivan. Targeted as an alternative to the upscale sedan or station wagon, the Town & Country comes standard with a leather interior and front and rear air conditioning. The mirrors, windows, locks, and driver's seat are power operated. Chrysler's 3.3-liter V-6 engine, rated here at 150 horsepower, and a 4-speed overdrive automatic transmission comprise the only powertrain. Exterior touches exclusive to the Town & Country include a vertical grille pattern, lower bodyside cladding, woodgrain appliques, and alloy wheels (painted body color with a white exterior).

For

● Passenger room ● Cargo room ● Ride/handling

Against

● Fuel economy

Summary

The Town & Country wraps all the Chrysler minivan virtues in an envelope of luxury. In a brief test drive of an early production model over public roads, the T&C felt little different

Prices are accurate at time of printing; subject to manufacturer's change.

from a Dodge Grand Caravan LE. Its ride was soft and well controlled, handling and roadholding was quite carlike, and there wasn't undue wind or road noise. The Chrysler 3.3-liter V-6 seemed to move the 3800-pound minivan adequately, though it sounded gruffer when pushed than does the slightly less powerful Mitsubishi V-6 that previously powered the extended versions of Chrysler's minivans. The Town & Country will help Chrysler answer Oldsmobile's Silhouette, the plushest version of the new General Motors minivans. With leather and a full complement of luxury equipment, the front-drive, 7-passenger Silhouette lists for less than $20,000, though it doesn't have as much cargo space as the Chrysler. A Dodge Grand Caravan LE equipped very similarly to the Town & Country lists for about $21,000. The question is whether the T&C's Chrysler badge makes it worth another $4000. The Town & Country is, however, the only vehicle we know of that takes such diverse styling influences as fake wood body panels, lower-body cladding, and body-colored alloy wheels and combines them in one package.

Specifications

	4-door van
Wheelbase, in.	119.1
Overall length, in.	190.5
Overall width, in.	72.0
Overall height, in.	64.8
Turn diameter, ft.	43.0
Curb weight, lbs.	3817
Cargo vol., cu. ft.	150.0
Fuel capacity, gals.	20.0
Seating capacity	7
Front headroom, in.	39.0
Front shoulder room, in.	58.4
Front legroom, max., in.	38.2
Rear headroom, in.	37.6
Rear shoulder room, in.	61.3
Rear legroom, min., in.	37.8

Powertrain layout: transverse front engine/front-wheel drive.

Engines	ohv V-6
Size, liters/cu. in.	3.3/201
Fuel delivery	PFI
Horsepower @ rpm	150 @ 4800
Torque (lbs./ft.) @ rpm	185 @ 3600
Availability	S

EPA city/highway mpg

4-speed OD automatic	18/24

Prices

Chrysler Town & Country	Retail Price	Dealer Invoice	Low Price
4-door van	$25000	$22200	NA
Destination charge	515	515	515

KEY: **ohv** = overhead valve; **ohc** = overhead cam; **dohc** = double overhead cam; **I** = inline cylinders; **V** = cylinders in V configuration; **flat** = horizontally opposed cylinders; **bbl.** = barrel (carburetor); **PFI** = port (multi-point) fuel injection; **TBI** = throttle-body (single-point) fuel injection; **rpm** = revolutions per minute; **OD** = overdrive transmission; **S** = standard; **O** = optional; **NA** = not available.

Standard equipment:

3.3-liter PFI V-6, 4-speed automatic transmission, power steering, front and rear air conditioning, 7-passenger seating with front bucket seats, power driver's seat, quick-release middle and rear bench seats, leather upholstery, power front windows and quarter vents, power locks, cruise control, overhead console, rear defogger, tilt steering column, leather-wrapped steering wheel, remote fuel door and liftgate releases, coolant temperature and oil pressure gauges, voltmeter, trip odometer, rear wiper/washer, intermittent wipers, AM/FM cassette with Infinity speakers, floormats, tinted windshield and front door glass (sunscreen glass on other windows), roof rack, storage drawer under passenger seat, forward storage console, simulated woodgrain exterior applique, 205/70R15 tires on alloy wheels.

Optional equipment:	Retail Price	Dealer Invoice	Low Price
195/75R15 WSW tires	NC	NC	NC
California emissions pkg.	100	85	90

Daihatsu Charade

Daihatsu Charade SX

What's New

Daihatsu was the last Japanese automaker to enter the U.S. market when it introduced the Charade minicompact for 1988. For 1990, Daihatsu issues a 4-door notchback version of the front-drive Charade, plus a restructured lineup for the returning 3-door hatchback. The new sedan is essentially the Charade hatchback with two extra doors and 13.3 inches tacked on at the rear to provide a 9.6-cubic-foot trunk. Daihatsu's dealer network is mainly in Western and Sunbelt states. Daihatsu's car allotment in the Japanese quota system grows from 17,000 to 20,000 this year and the company will be opening more dealerships in the Pacific Northwest and the northeastern U.S. This year's Charade roster includes SE and SX hatchbacks powered by a 53-horsepower 1.0-liter 3-cylinder engine and available only with a 5-speed manual transmission. An 80-horsepower 1.3-liter 4-cylinder introduced during 1989 is available on the hatchbacks and standard on the new sedan. The 5-speed manual is standard with the 1.3-liter, except on the SE hatchback, which comes only with a 3-speed automatic transmission. The automatic is optional on other Charades with the 1.3. Non-motorized automatic front shoulder belts are standard on the hatchback and motorized front shoulder belts are standard on the sedan to meet the federal requirement for passive restraints; both have separate manual lap belts.

For

● Fuel economy   ● Handling   ● Maneuverability

Against

- Noise • Ride • Passenger room • Trunk space

Summary

The small-car market is rougher than ever, but Daihatsu has it rougher than most. A little-known name and a late start are handicaps enough in the U.S. now, but Daihatsu further suffers by being one of Japan's smallest automakers and in having just a single car line to sell through a limited number of dealers in relatively few states. Worse, Daihatsu's pricing makes Charade rather expensive against most rivals. Daihatsu's prospects would be rosier if the Charade were head-and-shoulders above the competition, but it isn't. It offers the usual small-car virtues of high fuel economy (even the 1.3-liter with automatic returns 30-plus mpg), nimble handling, and easy maneuvering. It also has the typical small-car vices of a lively ride, too much noise, and limited interior space. Acceleration ranges from modest with the 4-cylinder engine (0-60 mph: nearly 13 seconds with automatic) to snail-like with the 3-cylinder (15.5 seconds). To its credit, the Charade offers solid construction and good-quality interior materials, but so do the Honda Civic, the new Mazda Protege/323, and the Toyota Corolla. We're not too excited about Charade, but you shouldn't discount it, mainly because dealers are offering big discounts—on the bottom line, where it counts.

Specifications

	3-door hatchback	4-door notchback
Wheelbase, in.	92.1	92.1
Overall length, in.	146.3	159.6
Overall width, in.	63.6	63.6
Overall height, in.	54.5	54.5
Turn diameter, ft.	1825[1]	2045
Curb weight, lbs.	31.5	31.5
Cargo vol., cu. ft.	33.0	9.6
Fuel capacity, gals.	10.6	10.6
Seating capacity	4	4
Front headroom, in.	37.5	37.5
Front shoulder room, in.	NA	NA
Front legroom, max., in.	41.1	41.1
Rear headroom, in.	35.7	35.7
Rear shoulder room, in.	NA	NA
Rear legroom, min., in.	31.8	31.8

1. 1945 lbs., w/1.3-liter engine.

Powertrain layout: transverse front engine/front-wheel drive.

Engines

	ohc I-3	ohc I-4
Size, liters/cu. in.	1.0/61	1.3/81
Fuel delivery	PFI	PFI
Horsepower @ rpm	53 @ 5200	80 @ 6000
Torque (lbs./ft.) @ rpm	58 @ 3600	74 @ 4400
Availability	S	S
EPA city/highway mpg		
5-speed OD manual	38/42	35/39
3-speed automatic		31/34

Prices

Daihatsu Charade (1989 prices)	Retail Price	Dealer Invoice	Low Price
CES 3-door hatchback, 3-cyl.	$6197	$5825	$5794
CLS 3-door hatchback, 3-cyl.	6697	6094	6164
CLX 3-door hatchback, 3-cyl.	7497	6598	6793

	Retail Price	Dealer Invoice	Low Price
CLS 3-door hatchback, 4-cyl., 5-speed	7097	6459	6533
CLS 3-door hatchback, 4-cyl., automatic	7497	6823	6901
CLX 3-door hatchback, 4-cyl., automatic	8657	7619	7844
Destination charge	259	259	259

Standard equipment:

CES: 1.0-liter PFI 3-cylinder engine, 5-speed manual transmission, cloth/vinyl reclining front bucket seats, partial folding rear seat, tinted glass, rear defogger, trip odometer, intermittent wipers, 145/80R13 tires. **CLS** adds: upgraded interior trim, full console, remote fuel door and hatch releases, visor mirrors, full-folding rear seat. **CLX** adds: center armrests, digital clock, door courtesy lights and map pockets, power mirrors, bodyside moldings, 155/80R13 tires, wheel covers. Four cylinder models have 1.3-liter PFI 4-cylinder engine, power steering (CLX).

Optional equipment:

Power steering, CLS 4-cyl.	241	220	222
Air conditioning	730	621	651
Plus Pkg. A, CLS	540	395	451
AM/FM ST ET cassette, premium wheel covers, bodyside moldings, right outside mirror, front mudguards, pinstriping.			
Plus Pkg. B, CLX	500	415	441
Premium AM/FM ST ET cassette, rear spoiler, pinstriping.			
Power Option Pkg.	320	266	282
Power windows and locks.			
Premium AM/FM ST ET cassette	415	323	356
AM/FM ST ET cassette	310	242	266
Above stereos include four speakers and clock.			
AM/FM ST ET cassette w/2 speakers	230	180	198
Rear spoiler	185	154	163
Alloy wheels, 4-cyl. models	490	407	432
Rear wiper/washer, CLS 4-cyl. automatic	150	132	136

Daihatsu Rocky

Daihatsu Rocky

What's New

Rocky is a new compact 4-wheel-drive sport-utility vehicle that is supposed to go on sale in November as a rival for the Suzuki Sidekick/Geo Tracker twins. Rocky was delayed from a planned early-fall U.S. debut by squabbles with MGM/UA, maker of the Sylvester Stallone "Rocky" movies. MGM/UA claimed copyright infringement and demanded a royalty from Daihatsu for using the name. The two parties reached an undisclosed agreement in September allowing use of the name. Features include on-demand 4WD and a 1.6-liter 4-cylinder engine with 94 horsepower. Only a 5-speed manual transmission is offered. Two-door soft top and hardtop body styles are available; both have a removable rear roof section.

Prices are accurate at time of printing; subject to manufacturer's change.

Daihatsu • Dodge

Wheelbase is 85.6 inches and overall length is 148.2, within a few inches of the Sidekick/Tracker dimensions. Daihatsu boasts that Rocky's 57.9-inch tracks (width between wheels on the same axle) are wider than any rivals in the low end of the 4WD market, and even exceed those of the Chevrolet S10 Blazer, Ford Bronco II, and Mitsubishi Montero. Though Rocky looks ready for off-road service, Daihatsu promises it doesn't "drive like a truck" and is engineered to be quieter than rivals. Seats for four are standard and there isn't any bare metal inside, as there is on some competitors. As a 2-door sport-utility vehicle, Rocky carries a 25-percent import tariff. Prices hadn't been announced; Daihatsu said it is still shooting for a base price of less than $10,000. We haven't driven the Rocky, so we cannot comment on its performance.

Specifications

	2-door wagon
Wheelbase, in.	85.6
Overall length, in.	148.2
Overall width, in.	62.2
Overall height, in.	67.7
Turn diameter, ft.	32.8
Curb weight, lbs.	2794
Cargo vol., cu. ft.	38.5
Fuel capacity, gals.	15.9
Seating capacity	4
Front headroom, in.	NA
Front shoulder room, in.	NA
Front legroom, max., in.	NA
Rear headroom, in.	NA
Rear shoulder room, in.	NA
Rear legroom, min., in.	NA

Powertrain layout: longitudinal front engine/rear-wheel drive or on-demand 4WD.

Engines

	ohc I-4
Size, liters/cu. in.	1.6/97
Fuel delivery	PFI
Horsepower @ rpm	94 @ 5700
Torque (lbs./ft.) @ rpm	94 @ 4200
Availability	S

EPA city/highway mpg

5-speed OD manual	23/23

Prices not available at time of publication.

Daihatsu Rocky

Dodge Caravan

Dodge Grand Caravan LE

What's New

America's best-selling minivan—and Chrysler's best-selling nameplate—gets a Chrysler-made V-6 for '90. Other changes are minimal as the front-drive Caravan sails into its sixth model year. Nearly identical to the Plymouth Voyager, Caravan is available in base, SE and LE trim in a 175.9-inch-long body on a 112-inch wheelbase, and as the Grand Caravan in SE and LE trim in a 190.5-inch body on a 119-inch wheelbase. Caravan's standard length provides 5-passenger seating and a convert-a-bed seat option. Seven-passenger seating, however, is standard for '90 on the regular-length LE; it had been a $389 option. Grand Caravan standard seating is for 7. Standard on Grand models is the new 3.3-liter V-6 manufactured by Chrysler. Still available as an option on the regular-length SE and LE models is a Mitsubishi-made 3.0-liter V-6. A 4-speed overdrive automatic transmission is standard with the 3.3 and optional with the 3.0, which comes standard with a 3-speed automatic. Carried over is the base 2.5-liter 4-cylinder and its turbocharged cousin. A reworked 5-speed manual is the standard transmission with the fours, a 3-speed automatic the optional choice with either 2.5. For '90, the parking brake system has improved holding power and the air conditioning systems have higher cooling capacity and provide a more rapid cool down. A 20-gallon fuel tank, up from 15, is now standard on all models. A towing package allows V-6 models to pull trailers weighing up to 3350 pounds.

For

● Passenger room ● Cargo room ● Ride/handling

Against

● Performance (4-cylinder) ● Fuel economy

Summary

We drove a 3.3 V-6-equipped Caravan at Chrysler's new-product preview and found that it is indeed faster to 60 mph than the Mitsubishi 3.0. Plus, at speeds between 30 and 50 mph, the 3.3 didn't force the 4-speed automatic into as many unwanted upshifts and downshifts. One drawback was that the 3.3 sounded gruffer than the smooth-running Japanese engine. Either of the sixes is still a better choice than either of the fours, however. The base 2.5 is underpowered, while the turbocharged 2.5's turbo lag and coarse nature is ill suited to the Caravan. Chrysler has wisely done little to alter the character of its minivans for '90. With superior outward visibility and a conventional box shape, we find them more user-friendly than the new-wave General Motors minivans, and slightly more car-like to drive, as well. The Mazda MPV feels more solidly built than the Chrysler minivans, but you have to order an MPV with 4-wheel drive before the rear-drive Mazda can match the front-drive Chryslers' poor-weather traction. Plus, the roominess of the stretch Caravan/Voyager exceeds nearly all competitors. The Chrysler products remain a bit plasticky inside, but the main drawback for these fine vehicles is that a continued high demand for them fosters a seller's market.

Specifications

	4-door van	4-door van
Wheelbase, in.	112.0	119.1
Overall length, in.	175.9	190.5
Overall width, in.	72.0	72.0
Overall height, in.	64.8	64.8
Turn diameter, ft.	41.0	43.0
Curb weight, lbs.	3100	3584
Cargo vol., cu. ft.	125.0	150.0
Fuel capacity, gals.	20.0	20.0
Seating capacity	7	7
Front headroom, in.	39.0	39.0
Front shoulder room, in.	58.4	58.4
Front legroom, max., in.	38.2	38.2
Rear headroom, in.	37.7	37.6
Rear shoulder room, in.	61.3	61.3
Rear legroom, min., in.	37.7	37.8

Powertrain layout: transverse front engine/front-wheel drive.

Engines

	ohv I-4	Turbo ohv I-4	ohc V-6	ohv V-6
Size, liters/cu. in.	2.5/153	2.5/153	3.0/181	3.3/201
Fuel delivery	TBI	PFI	PFI	PFI
Horsepower @ rpm	100 @ 4800	150 @ 4800	142 @ 5000	150 @ 4800
Torque (lbs./ft.) @ rpm	135 @ 2800	180 @ 2000	173 @ 2800	185 @ 3600
Availability	S	O	O	S[1]

EPA city/highway mpg

5-speed OD manual	22/28	18/26		
3-speed automatic	21/23	19/23	19/24	
4-speed OD automatic			19/24	18/24

1. Grand Caravan.

Prices

Dodge Caravan

	Retail Price	Dealer Invoice	Low Price
Base SWB 4-door van	$11995	$10756	$11376
SE SWB 4-door van	12675	11354	12015
LE SWB 4-door van	16125	14390	15258
SE Grand 4-door van	15395	13748	14572
LE Grand 4-door van	18325	16326	17326
Destination charge	515	515	515

SWB denotes short-wheelbase models.

Standard equipment:

2.5-liter TBI engine, 5-speed manual transmission, power steering, power brakes, liftgate wiper/washer, headlamps-on tone, 5-passenger seating, variable intermittent wipers, tinted glass, left remote mirror, AM/FM radio, P185/75R14 SBR tires. **SE** adds: highback reclining front seats, rear seat (Grand), front folding center armrests, upgraded door panels, power liftgate release. **LE** adds: front air conditioning, 7-passenger seating, added sound insulation, remote mirrors, bodyside moldings, woodgrain exterior applique, upgraded steering wheel. **Grand SE** and **LE** add 3.3-liter PFI V-6, 4-speed automatic transmission.

Optional equipment:

	Retail Price	Dealer Invoice	Low Price
2.5-liter turbo engine, SWB	700	595	644
3.0-liter V6, SE & LE SWB	700	595	644
3-speed automatic transmission, SWB	582	495	535
4-speed automatic transmission, SE & LE SWB	757	643	696
Requires 3.0-liter V-6.			
Front air conditioning (std. LE)	865	735	796
Rear air conditioning & heater, Grand	577	490	531
Requires front air conditioning.			
Converta-Bed seating, SE & LE SWB	558	474	513
7-passenger seating, base & SE SWB	401	341	369
Popular Equipment Pkg., SE SWB	1003	853	923
SE SWB w/Value Wagon Pkg.	752	639	692
SE Grand	883	751	812
Light Pkg., cruise control, tilt steering column, forward storage console, overhead console, floormats, tachometer, coolant temperature and oil pressure gauges, 125-mph speedometer, added sound insulation, power rear quarter vent windows, conventional spare tire.			
Luxury Equipment Discount Pkg., SE SWB	2115	1798	1946
SE SWB w/Value Wagon Pkg.	1765	1500	1624
SE Grand	1994	1695	1834
LE SWB	913	776	840
Popular Pkg. plus rear defogger, lighted visor mirror, power windows and locks, power mirrors, power driver's seat (LE), Infinity I AM/FM cassette, sport steering wheel.			
Value Wagon Pkg. w/5-speed, base & SE SWB	1265	1075	1164
w/3-speed automatic, base & SE SWB	1847	1570	1699
Front air conditioning, rear defogger, dual horns, added sound insulation, Light Pkg.			
ES Decor Pkg., LE SWB	1311	1114	1206
2.5-liter turbo engine, warm silver fascia and bodyside moldings, HD suspension, 205/70R15 tires on Eurocast alloy wheels.			
HD Trailer Tow Pkg., SE	689	586	634
SE w/Popular or Luxury Pkg.	582	495	535
Turbo Sport Pkg., SE SWB	1378	1171	1268
SE SWB w/Popular or Luxury Pkg.	1258	1069	1157
2.5-liter turbo engine, tachometer, coolant temperature and oil pressure gauges, 125-mph speedometer, HD suspension, 205/70R15 tires on Eurocast alloy wheels.			
Deluxe Convenience Pkg., base & SE	346	294	318
Cruise control, tilt steering column.			
Power Convenience Pkg., SE	438	372	403
Power windows and locks.			
AY4 Sport Roadwheel Pkg., SE	487	414	448
LE	462	393	425
205/70R15 tires on alloy wheels, conventional spare tire (LE).			
AYA Sport Roadwheel Pkg., base	456	388	420
AY4 Pkg. but with 14-inch tires.			
Luxury vinyl trim, base & SE	NC	NC	NC
Leather trim, LE	848	721	780
Woodgrain applique, LE	NC	NC	NC
Rear defogger	170	145	156
Power locks, base & SE	214	182	197
Requires Value Wagon or Popular Pkg.			
Sunscreen glass	418	355	385
Luggage rack, base & SE	144	122	132
AM/FM cassette	157	133	144
Infinity I AM/FM cassette	411	349	378
Infinity II AM/FM cassette w/EQ	220	187	202
Requires Luxury or ES Decor Pkg.			
Power sunroof, SE	809	688	744
LE	959	815	882
Requires Popular Pkg. on SE.			

> **KEY: ohv** = overhead valve; **ohc** = overhead cam; **dohc** = double overhead cam; **I** = inline cylinders; **V** = cylinders in V configuration; **flat** = horizontally opposed cylinders; **bbl.** = barrel (carburetor); **PFI** = port (multi-point) fuel injection; **TBI** = throttle-body (single-point) fuel injection; **rpm** = revolutions per minute; **OD** = overdrive transmission; **S** = standard; **O** = optional; **NA** = not available.

Prices are accurate at time of printing; subject to manufacturer's change.

	Retail Price	Dealer Invoice	Low Price
HD suspension	70	60	64
205/70R14 WSW tires	139	118	128
Requires Value Wagon, Popular, Luxury or Sport Roadwheel Pkg. on base and SE.			
195/75R15 tires (NA base)	70	60	64
w/rear A/C & heater	145	123	133
Requires sunroof or HD Trailer Tow Pkg.			
Conventional spare tire	107	91	98
Wire wheel covers, LE	246	209	226
Pearl coat paint	75	64	69
Two-tone paint	243	207	224
California emissions pkg.	103	88	95

Dodge/Plymouth Colt

Dodge Colt GT

What's New

Chrysler tones down the performance of its nimble captive import for '90 by deleting the 3-door's optional turbocharged engine. The 5-door Colt wagon continues with only minor trim changes. Sold in identical forms under the Dodge and Plymouth nameplates, these cars are made by Chrysler's Japanese partner, Mitsubishi. The current-generation 3-door front-drive Colt debuted last year. It returns in three trim levels: base; GL (which replaces last year's E as the mid-level Colt); and GT. Gone is last year's optional 135-horsepower double-overhead cam 1.6-liter turbo 4-cylinder. This year's top powerplant is essentially the same 1.6-liter dohc four, but without the turbocharger. It's available on the Colt GT and is rated at 113 horsepower. An 81-horsepower 1.5-liter four remains the standard engine on all Colt 3-door models. Transmission choices have broadened, however, and an automatic is now available on all except the base Colt. The automatic is a 3- or 4-speed, depending on engine choice; both get a shift lock that requires the driver to have a foot on the brake before shifting from "park." The wagon for '90 gets a slightly altered grille, dual manual remote outside mirrors, and a new steering wheel. The front-drive, 5-passenger, 5-door wagon gets the hatchback's 1.5-liter four. The 4-wheel-drive wagon features a permanently engaged 4WD system that uses a center differential with a viscous coupling to split power between front and rear axles as needed to maintain traction. Its only power-

train is an 87-horsepower 1.8-liter four mated to a 5-speed manual. The 4WD wagon's body is raised about two inches to provide additional ground clearance.

For

- Performance (dohc engine)
- Fuel economy
- Handling
- 4WD traction

Against

- Performance (automatic transmission)
- Cargo room (hatchbacks)

Summary

The 3-door Colt is vastly improved over the previous generation, which was introduced for 1985. Its trim, aero-shape, build quality, and over-the-road feel all recall the pace-setting Honda Civic hatchbacks. The base model with the 4-speed and manual steering has a pleasing, no-nonsense manner. The GT model with the dohc engine is slick and quick, with fluid clutch and gear-shift action, direct steering, a rev-happy engine and good handling. Four-wheel disc brakes are part of the optional GT performance package. The 3-door provides decent space for four adults, though rear headroom is at a premium. There's better room all around in the wagon, plus the 4WD version allows you to accelerate hard in loose gravel or on wet pavement without spinning a tire. Power is adequate on the wagon with liberal use of the 5-speed manual; the automatic saps too much power for our tastes. Both Colt body styles, and especially the 4WD wagon, are sleepers in their classes and well worth checking out.

Specifications

	3-door hatchback	5-door wagon
Wheelbase, in.	93.9	93.9
Overall length, in.	158.7	169.3
Overall width, in.	65.7	64.4
Overall height, in.	51.9	56.1
Turn diameter, ft.	30.2	32.5
Curb weight, lbs.	2194	2568
Cargo vol., cu. ft.	34.7	60.4
Fuel capacity, gals.	13.2	12.4
Seating capacity	5	5
Front headroom, in.	38.3	37.7
Front shoulder room, in.	53.5	52.8
Front legroom, max., in.	41.9	40.6
Rear headroom, in.	36.9	38.0
Rear shoulder room, in.	52.1	52.6
Rear legroom, min., in.	32.5	34.1

Powertrain layout: transverse front engine/front-wheel drive or permanent 4WD.

Engines

	ohc I-4	dohc I-4	ohc I-4
Size, liters/cu. in.	1.5/90	1.6/97	1.8/107
Fuel delivery	PFI	PFI	PFI
Horsepower @ rpm	81 @ 5500[1]	113 @ 6500	87 @ 5000
Torque (lbs./ft.) @ rpm	91 @ 3000	99 @ 5000	102 @ 3000
Availability	S	O[2]	S

EPA city/highway mpg

4-speed OD manual	32/38		
5-speed OD manual		23/28	23/28
3-speed automatic	27/29[3]		
4-speed OD automatic		23/28	

1. 75 @ 5500/87 lbs/ft @ 2500, DL Wagon FWD. 2. Colt GT. 3. 30/35 DL Wagon FWD.

KEY: **ohv** = overhead valve; **ohc** = overhead cam; **dohc** = double overhead cam; **I** = inline cylinders; **V** = cylinders in V configuration; **flat** = horizontally opposed cylinders; **bbl.** = barrel (carburetor); **PFI** = port (multi-point) fuel injection; **TBI** = throttle-body (single-point) fuel injection; **rpm** = revolutions per minute; **OD** = overdrive transmission; **S** = standard; **O** = optional; **NA** = not available.

Dodge Colt DL Wagon

Prices

Dodge/Plymouth Colt (1989 prices)	Retail Price	Dealer Invoice	Low Price
3-door hatchback	$6678	$6110	$6238
E 3-door hatchback	7505	6822	6989
GT 3-door hatchback	8863	7711	8085
Destination charge	255	217	235

Standard equipment:

1.5-liter PFI 4-cylinder engine, 4-speed manual transmission, power brakes, vinyl bucket seats, center console with storage, split folding rear seatback, coolant temperature gauge, trip odometer, motorized front shoulder belts and manual lap belts, outboard rear lap/shoulder belts, locking fuel-filler door, 145/80R13 SBR tires. **E** adds: 5-speed manual transmission, rear defogger, cloth seat inserts, bodyside moldings, 155/80R13 tires. **GT** adds: wide bodyside moldings, remote left mirror, assist grips, cloth upholstery, rear security panel.

Optional equipment:

	Retail	Dealer	Low
3-speed automatic transmission, GT	499	414	459
Power steering, E & GT	259	215	238
Air conditioning	739	613	680
Turbo Pkg., GT	2819	2340	2593

1.6-liter DOHC turbo engine, power steering, 4-wheel disc brakes, 195/60R14 tires, tachometer, low washer fluid light, sport steering wheel, sport suspension, upgraded seat trim, tilt/telescopic steering column, power mirrors, intermittent wipers, remote fuel door and hatch releases, foot rest, cargo lamp, digital clock, rear wiper/washer, front air dam, sill extensions, rear spoiler.

AM/FM ST ET, base & E	273	227	251
GT	298	247	274
AM/FM ST ET cassette, E & GT	465	386	428
AM/FM ST ET cassette w/EQ, GTw/Turbo Pkg	734	609	675
Carpet protectors, E & GT	28	23	26
Digital clock, GT	54	45	50
Cruise control & intermittent wipers, GT . .	208	173	191
Tinted glass	63	52	58
Power mirrors, GT	87	72	80
Power windows, GT	211	175	194
Rear shelf, base & E	51	42	47
Rear defogger, base	66	55	61
Rear wiper/washer, E & GT	133	110	122
Wheel trim rings, E	55	46	51
Intermittent wipers, GT	28	23	26
13"alloy wheels, GT	293	243	270
14"alloy wheels, GT w/Turbo Pkg	275	228	253
Two-tone paint	157	130	144

Colt DL Wagon (1989 prices)	Retail Price	Dealer Invoice	Low Price
5-door wagon, 2WD	$9316	$8105	$8498
5-door wagon, 4WD	11145	9696	10166
Destination charge	255	255	255

Standard equipment:

1.5-liter PFI 4-cylinder engine, 5-speed manual transmission, power brakes, cloth reclining front bucket seats, outboard rear lap/shoulder belts, trip odometer, coolant temperature gauge, rear defogger, locking fuel-filler door, rear wiper/washer, 175/70R13 SBR tires. **4WD** adds: 1.8-liter engine, permanent, full-time 4WD, power steering, 185/70R14 tires.

Optional equipment:

	Retail Price	Dealer Invoice	Low Price
3-speed automatic transmission, 2WD . . .	499	414	459
Power steering	259	215	238
Air conditioning	739	613	680
Tinted glass	63	52	58
AM/FM ST ET	273	227	251
AM/FM ST ET cassette	424	352	390
Digital clock	54	45	50
Power mirrors	81	67	75
Intermittent wipers	52	43	48
Alloy wheels	299	248	275
Custom Pkg	516	428	475

Velour sport seats, power mirrors, intermittent wipers, rear heat ducts, remote fuel and liftgate releases, tape stripes.

Limited-slip differential, 4WD	218	181	201
Driver's seat height control	19	16	17
Carpet protectors	28	23	26
Luggage rack	128	106	118

Dodge/Plymouth Colt Vista

Dodge Colt Vista

What's New

The 4-wheel drive version of the Vista gets a viscous coupling system that engages all four wheels when the driving conditions warrant. This replaces the previous part-time 4WD system, in which the driver had to press a dashboard button to activate all-wheel power. Otherwise, these 7-passenger front-drive and 4-wheel-drive wagons continue with only trim changes. New to the exterior are the grille, black bodyside moldings, optional wheels, and a new selection of colors. Vista is made by Chrysler's Japanese partner, Mitsubishi. Power is provided by a 96-horsepower 2.0-liter 4-cylinder engine. The front-drive version comes standard with a 5-speed manual transmission; a 3-speed automatic is optional. It also has 13-inch tires and independent rear suspension. The 4WD model comes with a 5-speed manual transmission only, 14-inch tires, and a torsion-bar rear suspension. Both have a standard adjustable roof rack, front bucket seats, and two sets of 50/50 split folding rear seats. With the 3-place middle-row and 2-position back-row seats folded forward, a carpeted cargo area of 78 cubic feet is formed. Fold them

Prices are accurate at time of printing; subject to manufacturer's change.

Dodge

backward and their cushions form a single or double bed. The 4WD model substitutes a lap belt for a shoulder belt in the third seat's right-side position; the front-drive model has shoulder belts at all outboard seating positions.

For

• Passenger room   • Cargo space   • 4WD traction

Against

• Performance   • Noise

Summary

Colt Vista is one of the most unusual and versatile wagons on the market. It can seat up to seven people, the seats can be folded for use as beds, or you can haul a good deal of luggage by folding the rear seat and expanding the rear cargo area. The 2-place rear seat is cramped, so it's better suited to children than adults, and there isn't much room for climbing in or out of the middle or rear seats. This year's improved 4WD system couldn't be more convenient and adds an important dimension in snow-belt states. Trailer towing is limited to 1500 pounds on the front-drive model and 2000 pounds on the 4×4. Vista's main drawback is a lack of engine power. With 96 horsepower for nearly 2700 pounds of curb weight on the front-drive model (and nearly 3000 on the 4WD model), you don't have much in reserve for climbing hills or accelerating briskly out of turns. Add four or five people and the engine is overmatched, especially with automatic transmission. Still, the utility of a 7-passenger cabin in a vehicle of such modest exterior dimensions is appealing, as is the availability of 4WD.

Specifications

	5-door wagon	5-door 4WD wagon
Wheelbase, in.	103.3	103.5
Overall length, in.	176.6	176.6
Overall width, in.	64.8	64.8
Overall height, in.	57.3	59.4
Turn diameter, ft.	34.8	34.8
Curb weight, lbs.	2667	2965
Cargo vol., cu. ft.	63.9	63.9
Fuel capacity, gals.	13.2	14.5
Seating capacity	7	7
Front headroom, in.	38.3	38.3
Front shoulder room, in.	53.1	53.1
Front legroom, max., in.	38.8	38.8
Rear headroom, in.	38.3	38.3
Rear shoulder room, in.	53.2	53.2
Rear legroom, min., in.	36.5	36.5

Powertrain layout: transverse front engine/front-wheel drive or permanent 4WD.

Engines

	ohc I-4
Size, liters/cu. in.	2.0/122
Fuel delivery	PFI
Horsepower @ rpm	96 @ 5000
Torque (lbs./ft.) @ rpm	113 @ 3500
Availability	S

EPA city/highway mpg

5-speed OD manual	22/28[1]
3-speed automatic	22/23

1. 19/25 Vista 4WD.

Prices

Dodge/Plymouth Colt Vista (1989 prices)	Retail Price	Dealer Invoice	Low Price
5-door wagon, 2WD	$11518	$9790	$10394
5-door wagon, 4WD	12828	10904	11577
Destination charge	255	255	255

Standard equipment:

2.0-liter PFI 4-cylinder engine, 5-speed manual transmission, power steering (4WD), power brakes, reclining front bucket seats, cloth and vinyl upholstery, trip odometer, coolant temperature gauge, left remote mirror, variable intermittent wipers, outboard rear lap/shoulder belts, rear defogger, remote fuel filler release, tinted glass, optical horn, rear seat heat ducts, wide bodyside moldings, 165/80R13 SBR tires (2WD), 185/70R14 SBR tires (4WD).

Optional equipment:

3-speed automatic transmission, 2WD	499	414	459
Air conditioning	739	613	680
Limited-slip differential, 4WD	218	181	201
Power steering, 2WD	259	215	238
AM/FM ST ET	273	227	251
AM/FM ST ET cassette	431	358	397
Cruise control	183	152	168
Rear wiper/washer	152	126	140
Power windows	260	216	239
Power door locks	173	144	159
Alloy wheels, 2WD w/o Custom Pkg	311	258	286
2WD w/Custom Pkg	269	223	247
4WD	299	248	275
Custom Pkg., 2WD	445	369	409
4WD	365	303	336

Power mirrors, velour upholstery, visor mirrors, digital clock, map lights, remote liftgate release, tachometer, courtesy lights, tape stripes, 185/70R13 SBR tires (2WD), wheel covers (2WD).

Luggage rack	128	106	118
Two-tone paint, w/o Custom Pkg	305	253	281
w/Custom Pkg	252	209	232

Dodge Daytona

What's New

Dodge's performance leader gets two new engines and a new interior for 1990. Available for the first time in the front-drive sports coupe is a V-6 engine, the 141-horsepower 3.0-liter made by Mitsubishi. It's optional on the base and ES models and is available with Chrysler's new 5-speed manual transmission or with either a 3- or 4-speed automatic. Standard in the Daytona Shelby model and optional in the C/S competition package for 1990 is Chrysler's 2.2-liter four with variable-nozzle turbocharging (VNT). VNT works by pivoting vanes inside the turbocharger to reduce turbo lag for improved throttle response. The 174-horsepower VNT Turbo IV is available only with a 5-speed manual transmission. A naturally aspirated 2.5-liter four remains standard on base and ES Daytonas, while its turbocharged cousin is standard on the ES Turbo and is the engine fitted to Shelbys when they're ordered with the 3-speed automatic. Shelbys, which get slight exterior trim changes for '90, also are available for the first time with Chrysler's electronic variable suspension, which allows the driver to manually select from firm, normal, or soft shock absorber damping via console switches. All Daytonas for 1990 get a new interior, highlighted by a new dashboard. A new steering wheel houses an air bag and there are now rear-seat shoulder belts. An overhead console with map lights and storage bins is available on the ES Turbo and Shelby models. The optional front sport bucket seats are also of a new design.

Dodge Daytona ES

For

● Performance (V-6, Turbo IV)   ● Handling/roadholding

Against

● Ride   ● Engine noise (turbos)   ● Rear seat room

Summary

Dodge's interpretation of the front-drive sport coupe has improved each year since its 1984 introduction. The styling has matured and the addition in '89 of standard 4-wheel disc brakes and the new C/S package show that performance is taken seriously. The news for '90 is even better. Chrysler says the VNT Turbo IV produces full boost as much as 50 percent faster than its previous hottest turbo engine. Test drives at the Chrysler proving grounds indicated that turbo lag is indeed reduced significantly. The other good news under the hood is the V-6. It's not as quick as the Turbo IV, but it makes its power with less work and in a smoother, more linear fashion. It's a welcome addition and should mate well with an automatic transmission for the most refined Daytona yet. Don't overlook Chrysler's new 5-speed manual, however. Test drives of early production versions showed its shift action and feel to be the equal of the best front-drive gearboxes. Inside, the squared-off look of previous Daytonas gives way to softer, rounded shapes. Housed in a new instrument pod, the analog gauges are now easier to see and the controls are closer to the driver and easier to reach. Dodge has always given the imports a big edge in refinement and assembly quality while making up for it with lower prices.

Specifications

	3-door hatchback
Wheelbase, in.	97.0
Overall length, in.	179.2
Overall width, in.	69.3
Overall height, in.	50.1
Turn diameter, ft.	34.3
Curb weight, lbs.	2751
Cargo vol., cu. ft.	33.0
Fuel capacity, gals.	14.0
Seating capacity	4
Front headroom, in.	37.1
Front shoulder room, in.	55.9
Front legroom, max., in.	42.4
Rear headroom, in.	34.3
Rear shoulder room, in.	53.6
Rear legroom, min., in.	30.0

Powertrain layout: transverse engine/front-wheel drive.

Engines

	ohc I-4	Turbo ohc I-4	Turbo ohc I-4	ohc V-6
Size, liters/cu. in.	2.5/153	2.5/153	2.2/135	3.0/181
Fuel delivery	TBI	PFI	PFI	PFI
Horsepower @ rpm	100 @ 4800	150 @ 4800	174 @ 5200	141 @ 5000
Torque (lbs./ft.) @ rpm	135 @ 2800	180 @ 2000	210 @ 2400	171 @ 2800
Availability	S	O	S[1]	O

EPA city/highway mpg

5-speed OD manual	24/32	20/29	20/28	19/27
3-speed automatic	22/27	19/23		
4-speed OD automatic				19/26

1. Daytona Shelby.

Prices

Dodge Daytona	Retail Price	Dealer Invoice	Low Price
3-door hatchback	$9795	$8893	$9116
ES 3-door hatchback	10995	9961	10222
ES Turbo 3-door hatchback	12895	11652	11974
Shelby 3-door hatchback	14295	12898	13265
Destination charge	454	454	454

Standard equipment:

2.5-liter TBI 4-cylinder engine, 5-speed manual transmission, power steering, driver's-side airbag, rear shoulder belts, reclining front bucket seats, split folding rear seat, tinted glass, intermittent wipers, console with armrest and storage, rear defogger, remote fuel door and hatch releases, tachometer, coolant temperature and oil pressure gauges, voltmeter, trip odometer, remote mirrors, visor mirrors, AM/FM radio, 185/70R14 all-season tires. **ES** adds: fog lights, sill extensions, rear spoiler, tonneau cover, 205/60R15 all-season tires on Eurocast alloy wheels. **ES Turbo** adds: 2.5-liter Turbo I PFI engine, misc. lights, AM/FM cassette with Infinity speakers, enthusiast seats, performance handling suspension, tilt steering column, leather-wrapped steering wheel. **Shelby** adds: 2.2-liter intercooled Turbo II engine, maximum performance suspension, 205/55VR16 unidirectional tires on "pumper" alloy wheels.

Optional equipment:

3.0-liter V-6, base & ES	700	595	630
3-speed automatic transmission	552	469	497
4-speed automatic transmission	646	549	581
Requires 3.0-liter V-6.			
4-wheel disc brakes, ES	184	156	166
Requires V-6 Pkg. or V-6 Performance Pkg.			
Popular Equipment Pkg., base & ES	1007	856	906
ES Turbo & Shelby	1317	1119	1185
Base & ES: air conditioning, front floormats, misc. lights, heated power mirrors. ES Turbo and Shelby add: power windows and locks, cruise control, tilt steering column.			
Popular Equipment Pkg. w/o A/C, base	338	287	304
Floormats, misc. lights, heated power mirrors, tilt steering column.			
Value Pkg., base	554	471	499
Base w/Power Convenience Pkg.	348	296	313
Power locks, cruise control, AM/FM cassette.			
C/S Performance Pkg., base	1550	1318	1395
2.5-liter turbo engine, 4-wheel disc brakes, rear spoiler, performance handling suspension, 205/60R15 all-season performance tires on Eurocast alloy wheels.			

KEY: ohv = overhead valve; **ohc** = overhead cam; **dohc** = double overhead cam; **I** = inline cylinders; **V** = cylinders in V configuration; **flat** = horizontally opposed cylinders; **bbl.** = barrel (carburetor); **PFI** = port (multi-point) fuel injection; **TBI** = throttle-body (single-point) fuel injection; **rpm** = revolutions per minute; **OD** = overdrive transmission; **S** = standard; **O** = optional; **NA** = not available.

Prices are accurate at time of printing; subject to manufacturer's change.

	Retail Price	Dealer Invoice	Low Price
C/S Competition Pkg., base	2778	2361	2500
2.2-liter intercooled Turbo IV engine, 4-wheel disc brakes, rear spoiler, tilt steering column, maximum-performance suspension, 225/50VR15 unidirectional tires on alloy wheels.			
V-6 Pkg., ES	884	751	796
3.0-liter V-6, 4-wheel disc brakes.			
V-6 Performance Pkg., ES	2415	2053	2174
ES w/Power Convenience Pkg.	1782	1515	1604
3.0-liter V-6 with tuned exhaust, 4-wheel disc brakes, performance handling suspension, wheelhouse carpet, power windows and locks, cloth enthusiast seats, door pockets, leather-wrapped steering wheel, AM/FM cassette with Infinity speakers.			
Premium Light Pkg., base & ES	197	167	177
Base & ES w/T-bar roof	78	66	70
Illuminated entry, lighted visor mirrors.			
T-Bar Roof Pkg., base & ES	1563	1329	1407
Base & ES w/Power Convenience Pkg. . .	1336	1136	1202
ES Turbo & Shelby	1336	1136	1202
T-bar roof, power windows, lighted visor mirrors.			
Overhead Convenience Pkg., ES Turbo & Shelby	387	329	348
Overhead console with compass and outside temperature readout, lighted visor mirrors.			
Security Pkg., ES Turbo & Shelby	228	194	205
Anti-theft security system, illuminated entry; requires Popular Pkg.			
Power Convenience Pkg., base & ES	433	368	390
Power windows and locks.			
Automatic Transmission Pkg., Shelby . . .	NC	NC	NC
Shelby w/Popular Equipment (credit) . .	(191)	(163)	(163)
2.5-liter Turbo I engine, 3-speed automatic transmission, cruise control.			
Overhead console, ES	268	228	241
AM/FM cassette, base & ES	157	133	141
AM/FM cassette w/Infinity speakers, base & ES	497	422	447
AM/FM cassette w/EQ & Infinity speakers, base & ES	713	606	642
ES Turbo & Shelby	216	184	194
Power driver's seat, base & ES	258	219	232
Power enthusiast seat, ES, ES Turbo & Shelby	324	275	292
w/leather, ES Turbo & Shelby	983	836	885
ES requires V-6 Performance Pkg.; ES Turbo and Shelby require Popular Pkg.			
Cruise control, base & ES	191	162	172
Rear window sun louver	216	184	194
Removable sunroof	409	348	368
Requires Popular Pkg.			
Conventional spare tire, base	85	72	77
ES & ES Turbo w/Eurocast wheels	244	207	220
Tonneau cover, base	75	64	68
Rear wiper/washer	130	111	117
Styled steel wheels, base	103	88	93
Alloy wheels, base	332	282	299
Pearl coat/clearcoat paint	75	64	68
California emissions pkg.	103	88	93

Dodge Dynasty

What's New

Dynasty is Chrysler Motors' best-selling car and it's back for a third model year with a larger available V-6 engine and a

> **KEY: ohv** = overhead valve; **ohc** = overhead cam; **dohc** = double overhead cam; **I** = inline cylinders; **V** = cylinders in V configuration; **flat** = horizontally opposed cylinders; **bbl.** = barrel (carburetor); **PFI** = port (multi-point) fuel injection; **TBI** = throttle-body (single-point) fuel injection; **rpm** = revolutions per minute; **OD** = overdrive transmission; **S** = standard; **O** = optional; **NA** = not available.

Dodge Dynasty LE

driver's-side air bag. Available in base and L trim, Dynasty is a front-drive, 6-passenger, 4-door notchback sedan. It's Dodge's version of the C-body car that Chrysler uses for its New Yorker. The new Chrysler-built 3.3-liter V-6 is now optional on the Dynasty L. The standard L engine remains the 3.0-liter V-6 manufactured by Chrysler's Japanese partner, Mitsubishi. The 3.0 is optional on the base Dynasty in place of its standard 2.5-liter four. A 4-speed overdrive automatic transmission is mandatory with the 3.3 and optional with the 3.0. A 3-speed automatic is standard with the 2.5 and the 3.0. A new two-spoke luxury steering wheel accommodates the new air bag system and the cruise control moves from the turn-signal stalk to the steering wheel. Among other changes for '90: a new battery that Chrysler says can tolerate inadvertent electrical drains and still be rechargeable; double-sided keys that can be inserted either side up; side marker lights that flash with the turn signals; and three new exterior colors. New L options include an automatic day/night mirror and leather upholstery. Four-wheel anti-lock disc brakes are optional again in place of the standard front disc/rear drum setup.

For

- Ride
- Anti-lock brakes option
- Passenger and cargo room

Against

- Performance
- Handling

Summary

Dynasty is a well-designed family sedan with plenty of room and tolerable engine performance. We haven't driven a Dynasty with the new 3.3 V-6, but we find the 3.0 V-6 a bit sluggish in these cars, especially from a standing start. Passing response is better, but it's still no ball of fire. The ride is soft and generally quite comfortable. Handling is a different story. The body leans heavily in turns and the soft all-season tires roll over onto their sidewalls, scrubbing off speed with noticeable squealing. Dynasty's best available feature is the anti-lock brake option, which helps control the car in panic stops on slippery pavement. We recommend you order ABS, even if it means sacrificing another expensive option, such as a power sunroof. Dynasty has ample interior room, so five adults ride in comfort, while fitting six isn't a major squeeze. The functional design provides plenty of leg room in the rear seat and adequate head room. Cargo space also is more than adequate. Other than the anti-lock brakes, there's nothing technically interesting, and the styling is purposely middle of the road, but evidently, right on target.

Specifications

	4-door notchback
Wheelbase, in.	104.3
Overall length, in.	192.0
Overall width, in.	68.5
Overall height, in.	54.8
Turn diameter, ft.	40.4
Curb weight, lbs.	2992
Cargo vol., cu. ft.	16.5
Fuel capacity, gals.	16.0
Seating capacity	6
Front headroom, in.	38.3
Front shoulder room, in.	56.4
Front legroom, max., in.	41.9
Rear headroom, in.	37.8
Rear shoulder room, in.	55.9
Rear legroom, min., in.	38.0

Powertrain layout: transverse front engine/front-wheel drive.

Engines

	ohc I-4	ohc V-6	ohv V-6
Size, liters/cu. in.	2.5/153	3.0/181	3.3/201
Fuel delivery	TBI	PFI	PFI
Horsepower @ rpm	100 @ 4800	141 @ 5000	147 @ 4800
Torque (lbs./ft.) @ rpm	135 @ 2800	171 @ 2800	183 @ 3600
Availability	S	O[1]	O

EPA city/highway mpg

3-speed automatic	22/27		
4-speed OD automatic		20/26	18/25

1. Standard on Dynasty LE.

Prices

Dodge Dynasty	Retail Price	Dealer Invoice	Low Price
4-door notchback	$12295	$11246	$12745
LE 4-door notchback	14395	12436	14845
Destination charge	520	520	520

Standard equipment:

2.5-liter TBI 4-cylinder engine, 3-speed automatic transmission, power steering, driver's-side airbag, rear shoulder belts, bench seat, cloth upholstery, headlamps-on tone, front cup holder, rear defogger, trip odometer, voltmeter, coolant temperature and oil pressure gauges, intermittent wipers, tinted glass, dual remote mirrors, visor mirrors, bodyside moldings, AM/FM ST ET, remote decklid and fuel filler releases, P195/75R14 SBR tires. **LE** adds: 3.0-liter PFI V-6, 4-speed automatic transmission, 50/50 bench seat, leather-wrapped steering wheel, upgraded wheel covers.

Optional equipment:

3.0-liter V-6, base	700	595	630
3.3-liter V-6, LE	103	88	93
4-speed automatic transmission, base	94	80	85
Requires 3.0-liter V-6.			
Anti-lock brakes	954	811	859
Not available with 4-cylinder engine.			
Air conditioning	819	696	737
Popular Equipment Pkg., base	1212	1030	1091
LE	1589	1351	1430
Base: air conditioning, power locks, floormats, cruise control, tilt steering column, undercoating. LE adds: 3.3-liter V-6, power windows, heated power mirrors.			
Luxury Equipment Pkg., LE	2785	2367	2507
Popular Pkg., Interior Illumination Pkg., Power Convenience Pkg., Deluxe Convenience Pkg., automatic day/night mirror, power front seats, security alarm, leather-wrapped steering wheel, wire wheel covers.			

	Retail Price	Dealer Invoice	Low Price
Deluxe Convenience Pkg., LE	325	276	293
Cruise control, tilt steering column.			
Power Convenience Pkg., base	360	306	324
Power windows and mirrors; requires Popular Pkg.			
Interior Illumination Pkg.	197	167	177
Illuminated entry, lighted visor mirrors; base requires Popular Pkg.			
Power Accessories Pkg., LE	154	131	139
Power decklid pulldown, power antenna; requires Luxury Pkg.			
Power locks	304	258	274
AM/FM cassette	157	133	141
Infinity I AM/FM cassette	497	422	447
Requires Popular Pkg.			
Infinity II AM/FM cassette w/EQ, LE	713	606	642
Requires Luxury Pkg.			
Memory power seats, LE	372	316	335
Requires Luxury Pkg.			
Power driver's seat, LE	258	219	232
Requires Popular Pkg.			
Security alarm	150	128	135
Requires Popular Pkg.			
Conventional spare tire	85	72	77
Power sunroof, LE	799	679	719
Requires Popular Pkg.			
Road handling suspension, LE	59	50	53
Requires Popular Pkg.			
Automatic rear load leveling	185	157	167
LE requires Popular or Luxury Pkg.			
Wire wheel covers	231	196	208
Requires Popular Pkg.			
Alloy wheels, LE	281	239	253
LE w/Luxury Pkg.	50	43	45
Requires Popular Pkg.			
Pearl coat/clearcoat paint	75	64	68
California emissions pkg.	103	88	93

Dodge Monaco

Dodge Monaco ES

What's New

Dodge has scheduled a January 1990 introduction for its new sedan based on the Eagle Premier. Dodge says the front-wheel-drive 4-door, 5-passenger sedan will differ only slightly from the Premier, with altered trim packages, new seats, and its own grille and taillamp treatments. It will use the Premier's Renault-built 150-horsepower 3.0-liter V-6 engine and a 4-speed overdrive automatic transmission. Chrysler inherited the design in its acquisition of American Motors. The car was designed jointly by American Motors and Renault; its styling is by Italian designer Giorgetto Giugiaro and it is built in Ontario, Canada. Dimensionally, it's a mid-size car, 192.8 inches

Prices are accurate at time of printing; subject to manufacturer's change.

Dodge

long overall on a 106-inch wheelbase. It weighs around 3000 pounds and uses 14- or 15-inch diameter wheels, depending on trim level. Premier comes standard for '90 with 4-wheel disc brakes. Dodge last used the Monaco name in 1978, on a mid-size rear-drive sedan. The automaker has not released further information on the car or its price. We have not yet driven a Monaco.

Dodge Shadow

Dodge Shadow ES

What's New

A new optional turbocharged engine and a standard driver's-side air bag are among the changes for Dodge's front-drive subcompact. Shadow shares the Plymouth Sundance's 3- and 5-door hatchback body styles and most of its mechanicals, but the Dodge is marketed as the sportier car. Chrysler's Shelby performance arm developed the 2.2-liter VNT Turbo IV 4-cylinder engine in 1989 for use in its modified Shadow, the Shelby CXS. VNT stands for variable nozzle turbocharger and is a technology designed to minimize turbo lag and increase throttle response. It's now available on regular-production Shadows in sporty ES trim or on those optionally equipped with the competition package. The VNT engine must be used with a 5-speed manual transmission. The 2.5-liter Turbo I engine continues as an option on all Shadows. As with Shadow's naturally aspirated 2.2- and 2.5-liter 4-cylinder engines, a 5-speed manual is standard and a 3-speed automatic is an option with the Turbo I. Shadow ES, which features 4-wheel disc brakes and performance tires on alloy wheels, also gets a minor facelift for '90. New front and rear fascias incorporate fog laps and body ground-effects panels and bodyside tape graphics are new. The competition package is available only on 3-door models and basically adds to a base Shadow the ES performance-oriented tires, suspension components and spoilers, and the Turbo I engine. Along with the air bag, all Shadows get a redesigned instrument cluster, improved sound insulation, an upgraded optional stereo system, a trio of new exterior colors, and new sport wheels.

> **KEY: ohv** = overhead valve; **ohc** = overhead cam; **dohc** = double overhead cam; **I** = inline cylinders; **V** = cylinders in V configuration; **flat** = horizontally opposed cylinders; **bbl.** = barrel (carburetor); **PFI** = port (multi-point) fuel injection; **TBI** = throttle-body (single-point) fuel injection; **rpm** = revolutions per minute; **OD** = overdrive transmission; **S** = standard; **O** = optional; **NA** = not available.

For

- Performance (turbo engines)   • Ride/handling
- Cargo room

Against

- Engine noise   • Rear seat room

Summary

Shadow shares its basic platform with the Dodge Daytona, but offers a more upright design for better passenger and cargo space. Overall, the interior is nicely packaged, with reclining front bucket seats, a tachometer, and other gauges among the amenities. Rear-seat room is slightly below par, though dropping the rear seatbacks creates a generous cargo hold. The standard suspension is firm for a domestic car and results in competent handling and a stable highway ride. (We haven't tested the ES suspension.) With base curb weights over 2600 pounds, Shadow is portly for its external dimensions, however, and performance is listless with the base 2.2-liter four. Acceleration is much stronger with either turbo engine, but so is the commotion from under the hood and from the exhaust system. A good compromise is the naturally aspirated 2.5, a smooth-running engine with reasonable performance. Chrysler's dramatically improved 5-speed manual is now a good alternative to the 3-speed automatic transmission, which lacks an overdrive fourth gear that would allow the engine to cruise at lower rpm for less noise and better fuel economy. The new 5-speed and the quick VNT Turbo IV make the Shadow worth a look to performance enthusiasts on a budget. A base Shadow with the 2.5 engine, automatic transmission, air conditioning, stereo, and other options goes for around $12,000.

Specifications

	3-door hatchback	5-door hatchback
Wheelbase, in.	97.0	97.0
Overall length, in.	171.7	171.7
Overall width, in.	67.3	67.3
Overall height, in.	52.6	52.6
Turn diameter, ft.	34.0	34.0
Curb weight, lbs.	2606	2642
Cargo vol., cu. ft.	33.3	33.3
Fuel capacity, gals.	14.0	14.0
Seating capacity	5	5
Front headroom, in.	38.3	38.3
Front shoulder room, in.	54.4	54.7
Front legroom, max., in.	41.5	41.5
Rear headroom, in.	37.4	37.4
Rear shoulder room, in.	52.5	54.5
Rear legroom, min., in.	34.0	34.0

Powertrain layout: transverse front engine/front-wheel drive.

Engines	ohc I-4	ohc I-4	Turbo ohc I-4	Turbo ohc I-4
Size, liters/cu. in.	2.2/135	2.5/153	2.5/153	2.2/135
Fuel delivery	TBI	TBI	PFI	PFI
Horsepower @ rpm	93 @ 4800	100 @ 4800	150 @ 4800	174 @ 5200
Torque (lbs./ft.) @ rpm	122 @ 3200	$35 @ 2800	180 @ 2000	210 @ 2400
Availability	S	O	O	O
EPA city/highway mpg				
5-speed OD manual	24/32	24/32	21/29	20/28
3-speed automatic	23/26	22/27	20/23	

CONSUMER GUIDE®

Prices

Dodge Shadow	Retail Price	Dealer Invoice	Low Price
3-door hatchback	$8735	$7987	$8157
5-door hatchback	8935	8167	8342
Destination charge	440	440	440

Standard equipment:

2.2-liter TBI 4-cylinder engine, 5-speed manual transmission, power steering and brakes, reclining front bucket seats, cloth upholstery, driver's-side airbag, rear shoulder belts, one-piece folding rear seatback, removable shelf panel, dual remote mirrors, intermittent wipers, trip odometer, tachometer, coolant temperature gauge, voltmeter, optical horn, mini console with storage bin, remote liftgate release, bodyside moldings, AM/FM radio, 185/70R14 SBR tires.

Optional equipment:

2.5-liter engine	288	245	259
3-speed automatic transmission	552	469	497
Competition Pkg.	2619	2226	2357

2.2-liter intercooled Turbo IV PFI engine, 4-wheel disc brakes, remote hatch release, message center, remote mirrors, performance front seats, 60/40 split rear seat, spoiler, sport suspension, 195/60HR15 all-season performance tires on alloy wheels.

Air conditioning	798	678	718
4-wheel disc brakes	184	156	166
Rear defogger	155	132	140
Power locks, 3-door	160	136	144
5-door	211	179	190
Power windows, 3-door	227	193	204
5-door	304	258	274
Power mirrors	58	49	52
AM/FM cassette	207	176	186
AM/FM cassette w/Infinity speakers	435	370	392
Cruise control	191	162	172
Tilt steering column	134	114	121
Removable sunroof	383	326	345
Tinted glass	108	92	97
Conventional spare tire, 14"	85	72	77
w/turbo engine	104	88	94
15", w/ES non-turbo	185	157	167
15", w/ES turbo	215	183	194
Alloy wheels	332	282	299
Floormats	46	39	41
Pearl/clearcoat paint	75	64	68
California emissions pkg.	103	88	93

Note: ES Pkg. and other equipment is available in Customer Preferred Packages. Space limitations prevent listing these packages.

Dodge Spirit

What's New

Dodge's version of Chrysler's new line of front-drive, 4-door notchback sedans went on sale in January 1989, and comes back this fall with a variety of improvements. Spirit is a near twin to the new Plymouth Acclaim. Both are known as A-cars under Chrysler's product code. Spirit is available in base, LE, and sporty ES trim. For '90, all Spirits get a driver's-side air bag and a new tilt steering column. And 4-wheel disc brakes have been added as standard equipment to the ES. Engine choices are unchanged, though significantly, the V-6 option is no longer an ES exclusive and has been extended to all Spirit models. The Mitsubishi-made 3.0-liter V-6 is mated only to a 4-speed automatic transmission. Standard on base and LE Spirits is a 2.5-liter 4-cylinder engine; a turbocharged version of the 2.5 is optional. The ES has the turbo engine as standard. A 5-speed manual is standard with either 2.5, and

Dodge Spirit LE

a 3-speed automatic is optional. Chrysler equips '90 Spirits with semi-flexible, self-restoring bumpers that can return to their original position after collisions at up to 5 mph. Base Spirits come with front bucket seats and 14-inch tires. A front bench seat and a folding split-back rear seat are optional. The LE gets the folding split rear seat as standard, plus an adjustable lumbar bolster in the driver's bucket seat, cruise control, tilt steering wheel, rear defroster, and a mini trip computer. Spirit ES builds on the LE with sport bucket seats, aero body panels, fog lamps, and a monochromatic paint scheme. On white models, Spirit's standard 15-inch alloy wheels are painted to match the body color.

For

- Interior room ● Cargo space ● Ride
- Performance (V-6 engine)

Against

- Rear seat comfort ● Noise (turbo engine)

Summary

While Plymouth tailors its A-car for family duty, Dodge tilts the Spirit toward the sporty. Spirits also have what Chrysler calls a "handling suspension" with shocks that are firmer than those on the base and mid-level Acclaim. Indeed, the Spirit rides much more firmly than the Acclaims we've tried. Its handling is sharper, too, with better response to the nicely weighted steering. Control is quite good and Spirit feels composed in tight corners and on high-speed straights. The 2.5 turbo in one of our test vehicles suffered from turbo lag that hampered acceleration below 3000 rpm, but power was delivered promptly above that. We've driven a V-6 Acclaim and found its power good, though the 4-speed automatic transmission hurt performance by shifting too quickly into higher gears and by delaying downshifts in passing situations. Chrysler's new 5-speed manual has a vastly improved shift action. Spirit avoids the obvious aerodynamics of the Ford Taurus or Chevrolet Lumina. It opts instead for a tall, square greenhouse that increases interior room, affords good outward visibility, and enhances entry and exit. The gauges are readable and the dashboard is well-laid out. Front-seat comfort is good, but the trade off for adequate rear head and knee room is a back-seat cushion that's too low and short. Cabin storage benefits from front-door map pockets, a center console, and cup holders for rear-seat passengers. The large trunk has a flat floor and a low liftover. Spirit breaks no new ground, but emerges as a domestic sedan that's solid, roomy, and competent.

Prices are accurate at time of printing; subject to manufacturer's change.

CONSUMER GUIDE®   95

Dodge • Eagle

Specifications

	4-door notchback
Wheelbase, in.	103.3
Overall length, in.	181.2
Overall width, in.	68.1
Overall height, in.	53.5
Turn diameter, ft.	37.6
Curb weight, lbs.	2854
Cargo vol., cu. ft.	14.4
Fuel capacity, gals.	16.0
Seating capacity	6
Front headroom, in.	38.4
Front shoulder room, in.	54.3
Front legroom, max., in.	41.9
Rear headroom, in.	37.9
Rear shoulder room, in.	55.0
Rear legroom, min., in.	38.3

Powertrain layout: transverse front engine/front-wheel drive.

Engines

	ohc I-4	Turbo ohc I-4	ohc V-6
Size, liters/cu. in.	2.5/153	2.5/153	3.0/181
Fuel delivery	TBI	PFI	PFI
Horsepower @ rpm	100 @ 4800	150 @ 4800	141 @ 5000
Torque (lbs./ft.) @ rpm	135 @ 2800	180 @ 2000	171 @ 2800
Availability	S	O[1]	O

EPA city/highway mpg

5-speed OD manual	24/32	21/29	
3-speed automatic	22/27	19/23	
4-speed OD automatic			20/26

1. Standard, Spirit ES

Prices

Dodge Spirit	Retail Price	Dealer Invoice	Low Price
4-door notchback	$10485	$9377	$9689
LE 4-door notchback	11845	10574	10936
ES 4-door notchback	13145	11718	12128
Destination charge	440	440	440

Standard equipment:

2.5-liter TBI 4-cylinder engine, 5-speed manual transmission, power steering, driver's-side airbag, rear shoulder belts, cloth reclining front bucket seats, visor mirrors, AM/FM radio, remote fuel filler and decklid releases, 195/70R14 all-season SBR tires. **LE** adds: fog lamps, tinted glass, driver's seat lumbar support adjustment, split folding rear seatback, dual remote mirrors, rear defogger, cruise control, tilt steering column, message center. **ES** adds: 2.5-liter turbo engine, 4-wheel disc brakes, AM/FM cassette, lighted visor mirrors, sill extensions, front air dam with fog lights, trip computer, 205/60R14 Goodyear Eagle GT all-season tires on alloy wheels.

Optional equipment:

2.5-liter turbo engine, base & LE	700	595	630
Base requires Popular Pkg.			
3.0-liter V-6, base & LE	700	595	630
ES	NC	NC	NC
3-speed automatic transmission	552	469	497
4-speed automatic transmission	646	549	581
Air conditioning, LE & ES	819	696	737
Super Discount Pkg. A, base	1110	944	999
Air conditioning, rear defogger, floormats, tinted glass, time-delay ignition switch light, cruise control, tilt steering column.			
Super Discount Pkg. B, base	1411	1199	1270
Pkg. A plus heated power windows and locks, heated power mirrors.			

	Retail Price	Dealer Invoice	Low Price
Super Discount Pkg. C, LE & ES	775	659	698
Air conditioning, power windows and locks, heated power mirrors.			
Popular Equipment Pkg., base	941	800	847
Air conditioning, rear defogger, tinted glass.			
Premium Equipment Pkg., base	301	256	271
Base w/Super Discount or Deluxe Convenience	293	249	264
Front bucket seats, split folding rear seat, front center armrest, premium sound insulation, misc. lights, message center.			
Deluxe Convenience Pkg., base	329	280	296
Floormats, time-delay ignition switch light, cruise control, tilt steering column.			
Power Equipment Pkg.	568	483	511
Power windows and locks, heated power mirrors.			
Rear defogger, base	155	132	140
Power locks	221	188	199
AM/FM cassette, base	207	176	186
Base w/Super Discount or Popular Pkg., LE	157	133	141
AM/FM cassette w/Infinity speakers, base & LE	435	370	392
ES	278	236	250
Base requires Popular Pkg.			
AM/FM cassette w/Infinity speakers & EQ, LE	651	553	586
ES	494	420	445
Power driver's seat	258	219	232
Base requires Popular Pkg.			
Bench seats, base	103	88	93
Not available with manual transmission.			
Front bench & 55/45 folding rear seat	62	53	56
Base requires Premium Pkg.			
Pop-up sunroof	409	348	368
Base requires Popular Pkg.			
195/70R14 all-season touring tires, base	74	63	67
205/60R15 all-season tires, base & LE	169	144	152
Requires alloy wheels.			
Conventional spare tire, 14", base & LE	95	81	86
Alloy wheels, base & LE	332	282	299
Requires 205/60R15 tires.			
Pearl coat/clearcoat paint	75	64	68
California emissions pkg.	103	88	93

Eagle Premier

What's New

Chrysler's international-flavored sedan enters its second full model year with some noteworthy refinements. Four-wheel power disc brakes are now standard on all models and a floor shift lever for the automatic transmission replaces the awkwardly shaped column shifter. Chrysler inherited this front-wheel-drive 4-door in its acquisition of American Motors. Premier was designed jointly by American Motors and Renault. Its styling is by Italian designer Giorgetto Giugiaro and it's built at a former AMC plant in Ontario, Canada. Premier comes in base LX, mid-line ES, and sporty ES Limited trim. All are powered by a Renault-built 150-horsepower 3.0-liter V-6; a 2.5-liter 4-cylinder offered previously has been dropped for '90. A 4-speed overdrive automatic is the only transmission. Among other changes this year, the touring suspensions that are standard on the ES and ES Limited have been upgraded, and a stainless steel exhaust system and rear shoulder belts are standard on all Premiers. The ES gets the ES Limited's 205/60R15 tires as standard, and a compact disc player is a new option. Dodge has set January for its release of a slightly retrimmed version of the Premier, which it will call the Monaco.

Eagle Premier ES Limited

For

- Performance - Handling/roadholding - Ride
- Passenger room - Cargo space

Against

- Instruments/controls

Summary

This may be the best driving, most efficiently designed sedan in the Chrysler stable. The smooth V-6 is teamed with a precise-shifting automatic transmission to deliver ample power. Premier's ride is firm, but pliant and well controlled. Inside, there are supportive seats and plenty of room for five in an airy cabin. The trunk is roomy. Some of Premier's controls are quirky, however. Controls for the headlamps, wipers, and climate system are on pods mounted adjacent to the steering wheel. The controls are easy to reach, but some are illogical in their operation: changing the heater fan speed, for instance, usually requires you to cycle through all the speeds to reach the one you want. And the tiny lights that indicate the climate system's mode are on the dashboard, not the pod. The turn signals, meanwhile, are activated not by a traditional stalk that clicks into place, but by a springy lever that sets off a soft electronic tone. Chrysler corrected a flaw for '90 by dumping the transmission's awkwardly shaped and hard-to-shift steering-column shaft for a floor-mounted gear-change lever. Overall, though, Premier is a sound car, but one nonetheless saddled with ancestral ties to Renault and AMC, companies with tarnished reputations for quality and resale value.

Specifications

	4-door notchback
Wheelbase, in.	106.0
Overall length, in.	192.8
Overall width, in.	70.0
Overall height, in.	54.7
Turn diameter, ft.	35.9
Curb weight, lbs.	3083
Cargo vol., cu. ft.	17.0
Fuel capacity, gals.	17.0
Seating capacity	5
Front headroom, in.	38.5
Front shoulder room, in.	57.8
Front legroom, max., in.	43.8
Rear headroom, in.	37.5
Rear shoulder room, in.	56.9
Rear legroom, min., in.	39.4

Powertrain layout: longitudinal front engine/front-wheel drive.

Engines

	ohc V-6
Size, liters/cu. in.	3.0/180
Fuel delivery	PFI
Horsepower @ rpm	150 @ 5000
Torque (lbs./ft.) @ rpm	171 @ 3600
Availability	S

EPA city/highway mpg

4-speed OD automatic	17/26

Prices

Eagle Premier	Retail Price	Dealer Invoice	Low Price
LX 4-door notchback	$15350	$13248	$13448
ES 4-door notchback	17845	15368	15568
ES Limited 4-door notchback	20272	17431	17631
Destination charge	465	465	465

Standard equipment:

3.0-liter PFI V-6, 4-speed automatic transmission, power steering, 4-wheel disc brakes, 45/45 front seat, tachometer, coolant temperature and oil pressure gauges, voltmeter, trip odometer, AM/FM radio, rear shoulder belts, leather-wrapped steering wheel, tinted glass, intermittent wipers, remote mirrors, center console with armrest, rear defogger, floormats, 195/70R14 tires. **ES** adds: air conditioning, AM/FM cassette with eight Jensen speakers, trip computer, vehicle maintenance monitor, lighted visor mirrors, 205/60R15 tires on alloy wheels. **ES Limited** adds: leather upholstery, monochrome exterior treatment, cruise control, tilt steering column, premium audio system with EQ, power antenna, power locks, remote keyless entry, illuminated entry, power windows, remote fuel door and decklid releases, power front seats, 205/60HR15 tires with full-size spare.

Optional equipment:

Air conditioning, LX	876	745	788
Popular Option Group, LX	1386	1178	1247
Air conditioning, cruise control, tilt steering column.			
Luxury Option Group, LX	2330	1981	2097
Popular Group plus power mirrors, lighted visor mirrors, premium audio system, power antenna, power windows.			
Popular Option Group, ES	635	540	572
Cruise control, tilt steering column, Power Lock Group.			
Luxury Option Group, ES	1071	910	964
Popular Group plus power windows, premium audio system, power antenna.			
45/45 leather & vinyl seats, ES	583	496	525
Requires power seats.			
Power seats	515	438	464
Convenience Group, LX & ES	325	276	293
Cruise control, tilt steering column.			
Electronic Information Pkg., LX			
Trip computer, vehicle maintenance monitor.			
Power Lock Group, LX & ES	425	361	383
Power locks with remote keyless entry, remote fuel door and decklid releases, illuminated entry.			
Power windows	304	258	274
Requires Power Lock Group.			
AM/FM cassette, LX	241	205	217

> **KEY: ohv** = overhead valve; **ohc** = overhead cam; **dohc** = double overhead cam; **I** = inline cylinders; **V** = cylinders in V configuration; **flat** = horizontally opposed cylinders; **bbl.** = barrel (carburetor); **PFI** = port (multi-point) fuel injection; **TBI** = throttle-body (single-point) fuel injection; **rpm** = revolutions per minute; **OD** = overdrive transmission; **S** = standard; **O** = optional; **NA** = not available.

Prices are accurate at time of printing; subject to manufacturer's change.

	Retail Price	Dealer Invoice	Low Price
Premium audio system, LX	548	466	493
ES	134	114	121
AM/FM cassette with EQ, power amp and eight Accusound by Jensen speakers.			
Premium audio system w/CD player, LX ..	830	706	747
ES	416	354	374
ES Limited	282	240	254
Power glass sunroof	799	679	719
Conventional spare tire, LX & ES	85	72	77
Lace-style alloy wheels, LX	480	408	432
ES	304	258	274
Decklid luggage rack	118	100	106
California emissions pkg.	103	88	93

Eagle Summit

Eagle Summit LX

What's New

This imported front-drive subcompact is the entry-level car in Chrysler's Eagle line. Designed by Mitsubishi Motors Corporation, Chrysler's Japanese partner, Summit is a 4-door version of a 3-door Mitsubishi hatchback that Dodge and Plymouth dealers sell as the Colt. Mitsubishi dealers market a similar 4-door sedan as the Mirage. Summit was introduced for 1989, and the lineup gets juggled for '90. Added is a base sedan that lists for $8895 and features manual steering and a budget-oriented interior with cloth low-back bucket seats. The base sedan, along with the carried over mid-level DL and luxury-oriented LX models, is powered by an 81-horse-power 1.5-liter 4-cylinder engine. A 5-speed manual transmission is standard and a 3-speed automatic is optional with the 1.5. Also new to the roster is the performance-oriented ES Sport. Its standard features include a sport suspension, 4-wheel disc brakes, sports bucket seats, monochromatic exterior trim, and 195/60R14 tires (175/70R13s are standard on other Summits). The ES is powered by a 113-horsepower double-overhead cam 16-valve 1.6-liter four. The dohc 1.6 is an option on the Summit LX. A 5-speed manual transmission is standard with the 1.6, a 4-speed overdrive automatic is optional.

> **KEY: ohv** = overhead valve; **ohc** = overhead cam; **dohc** = double overhead cam; **I** = inline cylinders; **V** = cylinders in V configuration; **flat** = horizontally opposed cylinders; **bbl.** = barrel (carburetor); **PFI** = port (multi-point) fuel injection; **TBI** = throttle-body (single-point) fuel injection; **rpm** = revolutions per minute; **OD** = overdrive transmission; **S** = standard; **O** = optional; **NA** = not available.

For

- Fuel economy   • Maneuverability
- Performance (dohc engine)

Against

- Interior room   • Noise
- Performance (automatic transmission)

Summary

The Summit is a pleasant example of the contemporary Japanese subcompact. The Summit LX 5-speed we tested had competent road manners, with an especially pleasing ride. Its handling and roadholding fell well short of sporty, however. The 1.5-liter four revved smoothly and delivered adequate power, though the shift action of the 5-speed manual felt loose and crude. The 5-speed won't sap as much engine power as the 3-speed automatic, though, and it'll make for quieter and more fuel-efficient highway cruising. With the 5-speed, the 1.5 turns 2900 rpm at 65 mph; it's running a buzzy 3400 rpm at 65 with the 3-speed automatic. Storage bins and pockets are placed thoughtfully throughout Summit's airy cabin. Front-seat room is fine for a subcompact, though rear-seat head room is scarce for those over 5-foot-10. Usable trunk space is above average for the class. Overall, the Summit is a well-rounded subcompact that hasn't yet reached the high level of refined design or assembly quality enjoyed by such rivals as the Honda Civic and Toyota Corolla. A well-equipped Summit LX, with automatic transmission and air conditioning, lists for about $12,600, some $400 more than a comparably outfitted Honda Civic LX. An Eagle dealer, however, is more likely than a Honda dealer to negotiate on price.

Specifications

	4-door notchback
Wheelbase, in.	96.7
Overall length, in.	170.1
Overall width, in.	65.7
Overall height, in.	52.8
Turn diameter, ft.	30.8
Curb weight, lbs.	2271
Cargo vol., cu. ft.	10.3
Fuel capacity, gals.	13.2
Seating capacity	4
Front headroom, in.	39.1
Front shoulder room, in.	53.5
Front legroom, max., in.	41.9
Rear headroom, in.	37.5
Rear shoulder room, in.	53.1
Rear legroom, min., in.	34.3

Powertrain layout: transverse front engine/front-wheel drive.

Engines

	ohc I-4	dohc I-4
Size, liters/cu. in.	1.5/90	1.6/97
Fuel delivery	PFI	PFI
Horsepower @ rpm	81 @ 5500	113 @ 6500
Torque (lbs./ft.) @ rpm	91 @ 3000	99 @ 5000
Availability	S	S[1]

EPA city/highway mpg

5-speed OD manual	28/34	23/28
3-speed automatic	27/29	
4-speed OD automatic		23/28

1. Summit ES.

CONSUMER GUIDE®

Prices

Eagle Summit

	Retail Price	Dealer Invoice	Low Price
4-door notchback	$8895	$8264	$8464
DL 4-door notchback	9456	8541	8741
LX 4-door notchback	10408	9388	9588
ES 4-door notchback	11257	10144	10344
Destination charge	295	295	295

Standard equipment:

1.5-liter PFI 4-cylinder engine, 5-speed manual transmission, cloth reclining front bucket seats, coolant temperature gauge, trip odometer, remote mirrors, rear shoulder belts, center console with storage, 155/80R13 tires on styled steel wheels. **DL** adds: intermittent wipers, upgraded carpet, remote fuel door and decklid releases, rear defogger, tinted glass. **LX** adds: power steering, tachometer, velour upholstery, driver's-seat height adjustment, split folding rear seat, tilt/telescopic steering column, visor mirrors, rear heat ducts, 175/70R13 tires. **ES** adds: 1.6-liter DOHC 16-valve engine, 4-wheel disc brakes, sport seats, sport suspension, 195/60R14 tires.

Optional equipment:

3-speed automatic transmission, w/1.5 . .	505	429	455
4-speed automatic transmission, w/1.6 . .	682	580	614
Air conditioning	748	636	673
Pkg. IFF, base	130	111	117
Rear defogger, tinted glass.			
Pkg. IFG, base	434	369	391
Pkg. IFF plus AM/FM radio.			
Pkg. IFH, base	696	592	626
Pkg. IFG plus power steering.			
Pkg. IFB, DL	621	528	559
Power steering, digital clock, AM/FM radio.			
Pkg. IFC, DL	839	713	755
Pkg. IFB plus AM/FM cassette, power mirrors.			
Pkg. IFD, DL	1135	965	1022
Pkg. IFC plus alloy wheels.			
Pkg. IFA, LX	353	300	318
Power mirrors, AM/FM radio.			
Pkg. IFB, LX	962	818	866
Pkg. IFA plus AM/FM cassette, power windows and locks.			
Pkg. IFC, LX	1234	1049	1111
Pkg. IFB plus alloy wheels.			
DOHC Pkg. IFD, LX	1319	1121	1187
1.6-liter DOHC 16-valve engine, power mirrors, AM/FM cassette, 195/60R14 tires.			
DOHC Pkg. IFE, LX	1970	1675	1773
Pkg. IFD plus power windows and locks, cruise control, variable intermittent wipers.			
DOHC Pkg. IFF, LX	2242	1906	2018
Pkg. IFE plus alloy wheels.			
Pkg. IFA, ES	365	310	329
Power mirrors, AM/FM radio.			
Pkg. IFB, ES	1017	864	915
Pkg. IFA plus AM/FM cassette, cruise control, variable intermittent wipers, alloy wheels.			
Pkg. IFC, ES	1729	1470	1556
Pkg. IFB plus premium audio system with cassette, power windows and locks.			
Decklid luggage rack	94	80	85
Floormats	50	43	45

Eagle Talon

What's New

Talon is the third badge to grace the new sports coupe built by Diamond-Star Motors, the Chrysler-Mitsubishi joint venture factory in Normal, Illinois. The others are the Mitsubishi Eclipse and the Plymouth Laser, though only the Talon and

Eagle Talon TSi AWD

the Eclipse are available with full-time 4-wheel-drive. Talon is a 2+2 hatchback marketed though Jeep-Eagle dealers in three levels of performance. The base car has a 135-horse-power 2.0-liter double-overhead-cam 4-cylinder engine. The mid-level Talon TSi has a turbocharged and intercooled version of that engine rated at 190 horsepower. Both of these cars are front-wheel drive. The TSi AWD has the turbo engine (rated at 195 horsepower) and a full-time 4WD system. A 50-50 split of engine power is normally maintained between the front and rear axles, though the system is capable of apportioning power to the wheels with the most traction up to a theoretical 100-0 or 0-100 split. Only the base Talon is available with anything other than a 5-speed manual transmission; it has a 4-speed automatic option. Equipment differences between the cars are otherwise slight. The turbo models come with aero exterior body panels, a leather-wrapped steering wheel, and performance-bolstered front bucket seats. They're the only Diamond-Star cars available with optional leather upholstery. The TSi AWD gets its own handling suspension and all Talons have 4-wheel disc brakes standard; an anti-lock system is not offered. All share the same-size 205/55 tires on 16-inch alloy wheels, though the tires on the TSi models are V-rated for higher speeds.

For

● Performance   ● Handling/roadholding   ● 4WD traction

Against

● Rear seat room   ● Cargo space

Summary

The 2+2 coupes jointly designed and built by Chrysler and Mitsubishi are stellar performers, offering fine handling, smooth engines, and an outstanding sports-car driving environment enveloped by a modern body. The rear seat is fit only for packages, and the skimpy cargo hold—even with the rear seatbacks folded—is small even by sports-coupe standards. The front bucket seats are comfortable and supportive, though no height adjustment is offered. With Talon's high beltline, tall cowling, and steep dashboard, shorter drivers might feel as if they're sitting in a bathtub. After that, there's little negative to say. Talon's clear analog instrumentation, simple and conveniently arranged controls, and the silken shift action of its 5-speed manual are all models of design. On the road, the most accessible Talon is the base dohc 2.0 liter. It has plenty of power and brings it on smoothly, so there are few surprises when accelerating briskly. The turbo front-drive version is clearly much faster, but its engine delivers

Prices are accurate at time of printing; subject to manufacturer's change.

power in massive bursts that can wrench the front tires off course, especially in turns. We've saved the best for last. The Talon TSi AWD tames the turbo's power with 4-wheel-drive to create one of the most appealing performance cars on the road. The 4WD system goes largely unnoticed, leaving the driver to savor acceleration, roadholding, and handling exceeding that of many hard-core sports cars. At around $19,000 fully equipped, the TSi AWD is a high-performance bargain.

Specifications

	3-door hatchback
Wheelbase, in.	97.2
Overall length, in.	172.4
Overall width, in.	66.9
Overall height, in.	52.0
Turn diameter, ft.	34.0
Curb weight, lbs.	2651
Cargo vol., cu. ft.	10.2
Fuel capacity, gals.	15.9
Seating capacity	4
Front headroom, in.	37.9
Front shoulder room, in.	53.9
Front legroom, max., in.	42.5
Rear headroom, in.	34.1
Rear shoulder room, in.	53.1
Rear legroom, min., in.	28.5

Powertrain layout: transverse front engine/front-wheel drive or permanent all-wheel drive.

Engines

	dohc I-4	Turbo dohc I-4
Size, liters/cu. in.	2.0/122	2.0/122
Fuel delivery	PFI	PFI
Horsepower @ rpm	135 @ 6000	190 @ 6000
Torque (lbs./ft.) @ rpm	125 @ 5000	203 @ 5000
Availability	S	S[1]
EPA city/highway mpg		
5-speed OD manual	22/29	20/25
4-speed OD automatic	24/34	

1. Standard on TSi.

Prices

Eagle Talon	Retail Price	Dealer Invoice	Low Price
3-door hatchback	$12995	$11807	$12401
TSi 3-door hatchback	14753	13305	14029
TSi AWD 3-door hatchback	16437	14804	15621
Destination charge	454	454	454

Standard equipment:

2.0-liter DOHC 16-valve PFI 4-cylinder engine, 5-speed manual transmission, 4-wheel disc brakes, reclining front bucket seats, driver's seat adjustable lumbar support, one-piece folding rear seat, center console with storage, rear defogger, tilt steering column, intermittent wipers, tinted glass, tachometer, coolant temperature and oil pressure gauges, voltmeter, power

KEY: **ohv** = overhead valve; **ohc** = overhead cam; **dohc** = double overhead cam; **I** = inline cylinders; **V** = cylinders in V configuration; **flat** = horizontally opposed cylinders; **bbl.** = barrel (carburetor); **PFI** = port (multi-point) fuel injection; **TBI** = throttle-body (single-point) fuel injection; **rpm** = revolutions per minute; **OD** = overdrive transmission; **S** = standard; **O** = optional; **NA** = not available.

mirrors, AM/FM radio, remote fuel door and hatch releases, rear shoulder belts, front floormats, map lights, visor mirrors, cargo cover, 205/55R16 tires on alloy wheels. **TSi** adds: intercooled turbocharged engine, driving lamps, turbo boost gauge, leather-wrapped steering wheel and shift knob, performance seats with adjustable thigh and lateral support, 205/55VR16 tires. **TSi AWD** adds: permanent 4-wheel drive, split folding rear seat, sport suspension.

Optional equipment:	Retail Price	Dealer Invoice	Low Price
4-speed automatic transmission, base	682	580	614
Air conditioning	802	682	722
Popular Equipment Group	1495	1271	1346
Air conditioning, cruise control, power windows and locks, rear wiper/washer.			
Luxury Equipment Group, base & TSi	2021	1718	1819
TSi AWD	2186	1858	1967
Popular Group plus premium audio system and alloy wheels, security alarm (TSi AWD).			
Leather seat facings, TSi & TSi AWD	430	366	387
Premium audio system, base & TSi	242	206	218
w/security alarm, TSi AWD	407	346	366
All models w/Luxury Group	414	352	373
AM/FM cassette with EQ and six speakers.			
Premium audio system w/CD player, base & TSi	656	558	590
TSi AWD (includes security alarm)	821	698	739
Alloy wheels	284	241	256

Ford Aerostar

Ford Aerostar

What's New

Optional full-time 4-wheel drive, a larger available engine, and standard anti-lock rear brakes highlight changes to Ford's rear-drive minivan. Aerostar is available as a 2-seat cargo hauler, called the Aerostar Van, or as the Wagon, a passenger model with standard seating for five and optional seating for seven. Six trim levels are offered. An extended-length model joined the line in '89. It retains the 118.9-inch wheelbase of the regular models, but has 15.4 inches added to the rear cargo area for a 28-cubic-foot boost in cargo volume. It also gains one inch of leg room for the second-row seats and two inches for the third-row seats. For '90, both standard and extended-length models will be available with the new 4WD system, which is permanently engaged. Under normal conditions, one-third of the engine's torque is sent to the front wheels and two-thirds to the rear, but a center differential locks in a 50-50 split if wheelspin is detected. The new 4.0-liter

V-6 is optional on 2-wheel-drive extended-length Aerostars and standard on the 4WD version. The 4.0 will be teamed only with a new heavy-duty 4-speed automatic transmission. Remaining Aerostars come standard with a 3.0-liter V-6; a 5-speed manual is standard with this engine and a 4-speed overdrive automatic is optional. Ford has not yet released horsepower and torque ratings for the 4.0, but expect it to concentrate on low-rpm pulling power instead of boasting significantly higher horsepower than the 3.0. Other changes for '90 include a lockable storage compartment under the passenger seat when captain's chairs are fitted, and five new two-tone paint combinations.

For

- Passenger room • Cargo space • 4WD availability
- Trailer towing ability

Against

- Fuel economy • Entry/exit • Ride

Summary

Aerostar is the first of the domestic minivans available with both 4WD and an extended-length body. A 4WD version of the rival Chevrolet Astro/GMC Safari debuts in the fall of '89, but buyers will have to wait for its stretched body until January 1990. The lighter-duty Dodge Caravan/Plymouth Voyager, meanwhile, are not yet offered with 4WD, though they've had extended-length models since 1987. None of this changes the fact that both the Aerostar and Astro remain better suited to heavy-duty work like hauling hefty payloads or towing trailers than the front-drive Chrysler minivans. We haven't yet road tested the new 4.0-liter Aerostar six, though we've found its 3.0 V-6 to have more than adequate muscle. We suspect the extra grunt of the 4.0 will be needed to offset the added weight of the 4WD hardware, but don't expect fuel mileage to be very good with either. Ride quality also is an Aerostar sore spot, even with the long wheelbase. Cabins are roomy, however, and the XLT and Eddie Bauer models' interior furnishings are plush and comfortable. Getting into the front seats requires a high step up compared to Caravan/Voyager. On the standard-size model, cargo space is unimpressive with all seats in place. The rear seat is quite heavy, so removing it is a chore, but once accomplished there's room aplenty. On balance, we like Aerostar a little better than the Astro/Safari. Caravan and Voyager are still tops for passenger use, with the Mazda MPV most certainly worth a look, but Aerostar has the edge in brawn.

Specifications

	4-door van	4-door van
Wheelbase, in.	118.9	118.9
Overall length, in.	174.9	190.3
Overall width, in.	61.5	61.5
Overall height, in.	71.7	72.0
Turn diameter, ft.	39.8	39.8
Curb weight, lbs.	3359	3502
Cargo vol., cu. ft.	139.3	167.7
Fuel capacity, gals.	21.0	21.0
Seating capacity	7	7
Front headroom, in.	39.5	39.5
Front shoulder room, in.	60.0	60.0
Front legroom, max., in.	41.4	41.4
Rear headroom, in.	38.1	38.3
Rear shoulder room, in.	NA	NA
Rear legroom, min., in.	37.9	38.8

Powertrain layout: longitudinal front engine/rear-wheel drive or permanent 4-wheel drive.

Engines	ohv V-6	ohv V-6
Size, liters/cu. in.	3.0/182	4.0/245
Fuel delivery	PFI	PFI
Horsepower @ rpm	145 @ 4800	NA
Torque (lbs./ft.) @ rpm	165 @ 3600	NA
Availability	S	S[1]

EPA city/highway mpg

5-speed OD manual	16/23	
4-speed OD automatic	17/22	NA

1. Standard Aerostar 4WD; optional, Aerostar Extended Length 2WD.

Prices

Ford Aerostar	Retail Price	Dealer Invoice	Low Price
RL van	$12469	$11212	$11552
EL van	13216	11869	12237
4WD RL van	14669	13148	13569
4WD EL van	15416	13805	14254
Destination charge	475	475	475

RL and EL denote regular-length and extended-length models.

Standard equipment:

XL: 3.0-liter PFI V-6, 5-speed manual transmission, power steering, anti-lock rear brakes, front bucket seats, 3-passenger middle seat, remote fuel door release, tinted glass, dual outside mirrors, visor mirrors, AM radio, 215/70R14SL tires.

Optional equipment:

4.0-liter V-6, 2WD EL	316	268	284
4-speed automatic transmission, RL	623	530	561
Limited-slip axle	248	210	223
Air conditioning	846	719	761
High-capacity A/C w/auxiliary heater, base	1422	1209	1280
w/any Preferred Pkg.	576	489	518
XL Plus Pkg. 401A	2080	1768	1872

Air conditioning, 7-passenger seating with two captain's chairs, privacy glass, cruise control, tilt steering column, rear wiper/washer.

XL Plus 4WD Special Value Pkg. 402A	3405	2894	3065

Pkg. 401A plus rear defogger, Exterior Appearance Group, AM/FM cassette.

XLT Pkg. 403A	3100	2635	2790

Pkg. 401A plus premium wheel covers, door pockets, rear grab handle, Light Group, upgraded interior trim, dual-note horn, leather-wrapped steering wheel, AM/FM cassette.

XLT Plus Pkg. 404A	4476	3804	4028

Pkg. 403A plus Electronics Group, luggage rack, Power Convenience Group.

Eddie Bauer Pkg. 405A	6697	5692	6027

Pkg. 404A plus high-capacity air conditioning with auxiliary heater, two rear seats fold into a bed, floor console, forged alloy wheels, two-tone paint, floormats.

7-pass. seating w/front bucket seats	296	252	266
Captain's chairs	517	440	465
7-pass. seating w/captain's chairs & seat/bed	1405	1194	1265
w/Pkg. 401 or 402	539	458	485
7-passenger seating w/2 captain's chairs	866	736	779
w/4 captain's chairs, XLT	585	498	527
w/4 captain's chairs, Eddie Bauer	NC	NC	NC
Floor console	174	148	157
Rear defogger, base	224	191	202
XL Plus	166	141	149
Electronics Group, base or w/Pkg. 401	1027	873	924
w/Pkg. 402 or 403	745	633	671

Overhead console (includes trip computer, automatic day/night mirror, map lights), electronic instruments, Super Sound System with EQ.

Prices are accurate at time of printing; subject to manufacturer's change.

Ford

	Retail Price	Dealer Invoice	Low Price
Exterior Appearance Group, base	857	729	771
w/Pkg. 401	268	228	241
w/Pkg. 403 or 404	189	161	170
Privacy glass, two-tone paint, rear wiper/washer, swing-lock A-pillar mirrors, styled wheel covers.			
Light Group	159	135	143
Luggage rack	141	120	127
Swing-lock A-pillar mirrors	52	45	47
Bodyside molding, base	63	54	57
XLT or Eddie Bauer	35	30	32
Power Convenience Group	501	426	451
Power windows, locks and mirrors.			
Cruise control & tilt steering column	296	252	266
Trailer Towing Pkg.	282	239	254
Rear wiper/washer, w/rear defogger	139	118	125
w/o rear defogger	198	168	178
Forged alloy wheels, base	326	277	293
w/XLT or Exterior Appearance Group . .	287	244	258
AM/FM radio	211	179	190
AM/FM cassette	313	266	282
Engine block heater	33	28	30
California emissions pkg.	99	84	89

Ford Bronco II

Ford Bronco II

What's New

This compact sport-utility is carried over largely unaltered as Ford readies a replacement for '91. Bronco II is available in a 3-door configuration only in either 2- or 4-wheel drive. A 2.9-liter V-6 is the only engine. A 5-speed manual transmission is standard, while a 4-speed automatic is optional. Bronco II was given new front-end styling and a new dashboard in '89, both patterned after those of its big-brother Bronco 4 × 4 and the F-Series pickup trucks. For 1990, changes are minor. Ford says the new air-conditioning compressor is more reliable, the Eddie Bauer model now has floormats as standard items, and XLT and Eddie Bauer models get color-keyed instrument panel appliques. Manual locking front hubs continue as standard on the 4WD model. The optional Touch Drive system

---

KEY: ohv = overhead valve; **ohc** = overhead cam; **dohc** = double overhead cam; **I** = inline cylinders; **V** = cylinders in V configuration; **flat** = horizontally opposed cylinders; **bbl.** = barrel (carburetor); **PFI** = port (multi-point) fuel injection; **TBI** = throttle-body (single-point) fuel injection; **rpm** = revolutions per minute; **OD** = overdrive transmission; **S** = standard; **O** = optional; **NA** = not available.

---

includes automatic locking front hubs and allows changing into or out of 4WD on the fly. Bronco II's replacement, the Explorer, is expected to debut for 1991 in both 3- and 5-door configurations. Wheelbase on the 3-door version will grow to 102.1 inches from the current 94.0; on the 5-door, wheelbase will measure 111.9 inches. A 4.0-liter V-6 engine will be available for '91.

For

● 4WD traction ● Performance ● Anti-lock rear brakes

Against

● Ride ● Fuel economy ● Rear seat room

Summary

Bronco II's 2.9-liter V-6 has enough power to merge safely with expressway traffic, pass quickly on the highway, or tow a trailer weighing up to 5200 pounds. It also works well with the optional automatic transmission, which shifts crisply and doesn't hurry into overdrive or balk at changing down a gear or two for passing. The 4WD model is saddled with standard manual locking front hubs, so you have to get out and lock them by hand, then engage 4WD by shifting a transfer case lever. The optional Touch Drive system, which includes automatic locking front hubs, is far more convenient since it allows changing into or out of 4WD on the fly by simply pushing a button from the driver's seat. Bronco II's short 94-inch wheelbase aids maneuverability, but makes for a bouncy ride and pronounced body lean in turns. Its short body limits rear-seat leg room and cargo space. And its elevated ride height makes for a tall step up into the interior. Still, Bronco II is a quiet riding and generally polished package. We like the interior, the engine, the Touch Drive 4WD system and the standard anti-lock rear brakes. When it comes to 4WD convenience and cabin space, Bronco II compromises more than do such rivals as the Chevy S10 Blazer and Jeep Cherokee.

Specifications

	3-door wagon
Wheelbase, in.	94.0
Overall length, in.	161.9
Overall width, in.	68.0
Overall height, in.	69.9
Turn diameter, ft.	32.4
Curb weight, lbs.	3371
Cargo vol., cu. ft.	56.9
Fuel capacity, gals.	23.0
Seating capacity	4
Front headroom, in.	39.5
Front shoulder room, in.	54.6
Front legroom, max., in.	43.9
Rear headroom, in.	39.0
Rear shoulder room, in.	55.9
Rear legroom, min., in.	35.0

Powertrain layout: longitudinal front engine/rear-wheel drive or on-demand 4WD.

Engines

	ohv V-6
Size, liters/cu. in.	2.9/179
Fuel delivery	PFI
Horsepower @ rpm	140 @ 4600
Torque (lbs./ft.) @ rpm	170 @ 2600
Availability	S

EPA city/highway mpg	ohv V-6
5-speed OD manual	18/22
4-speed OD automatic	17/21

Prices

Ford Bronco II	Retail Price	Dealer Invoice	Low Price
2WD 3-door wagon	$13001	$11676	$11876
4WD 3-door wagon	14704	13174	13374
Destination charge	425	425	425

Standard equipment:

2.9-liter PFI V-6, 5-speed manual transmission, power steering, anti-lock rear brakes, vinyl front bucket seats, split folding rear seat, intermittent wipers, tinted glass, dual outside mirrors, coolant temperature and oil pressure gauges, voltmeter, right visor mirror, AM/FM radio, 205/75R15SL all-season SBR tires.

Optional equipment:

4-speed automatic transmission	957	814	861
Limited-slip rear axle	267	227	240
Air conditioning	750	638	675
XL Sport Pkg. 922A	1188	1010	1069
Light Group, Sport Trim Pkg. (black front bumper, black tubular rear bumper, spats), sport two-tone paint, alloy wheels.			
XLT Free A/C Pkg. 923A	622	529	560
Air conditioning, aero headlights with bright doors, bodyside moldings, deluxe wheel trim, cloth and vinyl door panels with pockets, flocked glovebox with courtesy light, cloth captain's chairs, leather-wrapped steering wheel.			
XLT Free A/C Plus Pkg. 931A	931	790	838
Pkg. 923A plus privacy glass on quarter windows, Power Window/Lock Group, cruise control, tilt steering column, deluxe two-tone paint.			
Eddie Bauer Pkg. 932A	2939	2498	2645
Pkg. 931A plus premium AM/FM cassette, outside swingaway spare tire carrier, cargo cover, rear defogger and wiper/washer, bright low-mount swingaway mirrors, alloy wheels, floormats, premium captain's chairs with matching rear seat.			
Manual Transmission Special Value Pkg. 922A	1188	1009	1069
923A	622	528	560
931A	930	791	837
OWL all-season tires	96	82	86
OWL all-terrain tires	199	169	179
w/Special Value or Pkg. 932	128	109	115
Captain's chairs w/console, XL	274	233	247
Sport bucket seats w/power lumbar &			
console, XL	702	597	632
XLT	450	383	405
60/40 split bench seat, XL	232	197	209
XLT	NC	NC	NC
Super engine cooling	57	49	51
Privacy glass	144	122	130
Manual locking hubs, 4WD (credit)	(104)	(88)	(88)
Light Group	29	25	26
Bright low-mount western swingaway mirrors	87	74	78
Power Window/Lock Group, XL	485	413	437
XLT	344	292	310
Luggage rack	126	107	113
Outside spare tire carrier, w/BSW tires . . .	328	279	295
w/OWL all-season tires	348	295	313
w/OWL all-terrain tires	365	310	329
Includes cargo cover and full-size spare.			
Cruise control & tilt steering column	294	250	265
Deluxe two-tone paint, XL	241	205	217
XLT	130	111	117
Alloy wheels	326	277	293
w/Special Value Pkg. or XLT	224	191	202
Deluxe wheel trim	110	93	99
Rear defogger & wiper/washer	226	192	203
AM/FM cassette	100	85	90

	Retail Price	Dealer Invoice	Low Price
Premium AM/FM cassette	221	188	199
w/Special Value Pkg.	121	103	109
Engine block heater	33	28	30
Sport tape stripe, XL	159	135	143
XLT	48	40	43
California emissions pkg.	100	85	90

Ford Escort

Ford Escort

What's New

America's best-selling car in 1989 heads into '90 with few changes as Ford gears up to introduce an all-new model for '91. For '90, rear shoulder belts become standard; as before, motorized front shoulder belts with manual lap belts help meet federal passive restraint requirements. The optional polycast wheels have a slightly different appearance, and the premium sound system and heavy duty alternator are now available only as part of the LX and GT Special Value Packages. Escort is a front-drive subcompact available as a 3- and 5-door hatchback and as a 5-door wagon. Pony and LX models are powered by a 90-horsepower 1.9-liter 4-cylinder engine, while the GT's 1.9 produces 110 horsepower. Escort is expected to be new from the ground up for 1991. Based on Mazda 323 chassis and running gear, the '91 Escort probably will be available as a 3- and a 5-door hatchback, as well as a 5-door wagon.

For

● Fuel economy   ● Maneuverability

Against

● Driveability (automatic transmission)   ● Passenger room

Summary

Escort is average in most ways, but still ranks as a pretty good value by virtue of its fairly low price and good warranties. Most optional equipment is available in money-saving option packages, which also simplifies ordering. However, Escort is still priced quite a bit higher than the equally archaic Dodge Omni/Plymouth Horizon subcompacts. You can probably pick up an Escort for less than suggested retail, though, either through direct dealer discounts or factory incentives. Like the Omni/Horizon, Escort shows its age in some key areas. The interior is cramped compared to newer Japanese designs

Prices are accurate at time of printing; subject to manufacturer's change.

and the control layout isn't as convenient. The 1.9-liter engine has adequate power and is economical, but it's not nearly as strong as Chrysler's 2.2 or the smaller, multi-valve engines offered in the Toyota and Honda subcompacts. The optional 3-speed automatic transmission doesn't work well with this engine. It rushes into top gear too soon for good around-town performance, and then balks at downshifting for passing power when you need it. You'll pay less for an Escort with manual shift, and get better performance and mileage in the bargain. As for the Escort GT, it is stylish, but promises more performance than it delivers. There are several newer Japanese small cars with more to offer than Escort, but they're also more expensive, so don't cross this Ford off your list.

Specifications

	3-door hatchback	5-door hatchback	5-door wagon
Wheelbase, in.	94.2	94.2	94.2
Overall length, in.	169.4	169.4	169.4
Overall width, in.	65.9	65.9	65.9
Overall height, in.	53.7	53.7	53.4
Turn diameter, ft.	35.7	35.7	35.7
Curb weight, lbs.	2242	2310	2313
Cargo vol., cu. ft.	38.8	38.8	58.8
Fuel capacity, gals.	13.0	13.0	13.0
Seating capacity	4	4	4
Front headroom, in.	38.1	38.1	38.1
Front shoulder room, in.	51.3	51.3	51.3
Front legroom, max., in.	41.5	41.5	41.5
Rear headroom, in.	37.1	37.1	38.2
Rear shoulder room, in.	51.5	51.4	51.4
Rear legroom, min., in.	35.1	35.1	35.1

Powertrain layout: transverse front engine/front-wheel drive.

Engines

	ohc I-4	ohc I-4
Size, liters/cu. in.	1.9/114	1.9/114
Fuel delivery	TBI	PFI
Horsepower @ rpm	90 @ 4600	110 @ 5400
Torque (lbs./ft.) @ rpm	106 @ 3400	115 @ 4200
Availability	S	S[1]

EPA city/highway mpg

4-speed OD manual	32/42	
5-speed OD manual	27/36	25/32
3-speed automatic	26/31	

1. GT.

Prices

Ford Escort	Retail Price	Dealer Invoice	Low Price
Pony 3-door hatchback	$7402	$6879	$7079
LX 3-door hatchback	7806	7090	7290
LX 5-door hatchback	8136	7391	7591
LX 5-door wagon	8737	7919	8119
GT 3-door hatchback	9804	8904	9104
Destination charge	335	335	335

KEY: ohv = overhead valve; **ohc** = overhead cam; **dohc** = double overhead cam; **I** = inline cylinders; **V** = cylinders in V configuration; **flat** = horizontally opposed cylinders; **bbl.** = barrel (carburetor); **PFI** = port (multi-point) fuel injection; **TBI** = throttle-body (single-point) fuel injection; **rpm** = revolutions per minute; **OD** = overdrive transmission; **S** = standard; **O** = optional; **NA** = not available.

Standard equipment:

Pony: 1.9-liter TBI 4-cylinder engine, 4-speed manual transmission, cloth and vinyl reclining front bucket seats, folding rear seat, rear lap/shoulder belts, removable cargo cover, 175/70R14 tires. **LX** adds: AM radio, full cloth upholstery, door pockets; wagon has 5-speed manual transmission and retractable cargo cover. **GT** adds: PFI engine, 5-speed manual transmission, handling suspension, sport seats, remote fuel door and liftgate releases, power mirrors, tachometer, coolant temperature gauge, trip odometer, visor mirrors, overhead console with digital clock and stopwatch, map lights, center console with graphic monitor and folding armrest, AM/FM radio, split folding rear seatback, 195/60HR15 tires on alloy wheels.

Optional equipment:	Retail Price	Dealer Invoice	Low Price
5-speed manual transmission, LX hatchbacks	76	64	68
3-speed automatic transmission,			
LX hatchbacks & Pony	515	437	464
LX wagon	439	373	395
Power steering, Pony & LX	235	200	212
Air conditioning	720	612	648
Special Value Pkg. 320A, LX hatchbacks	562	478	506
LX wagon	486	414	437
5-speed manual transmission, power steering, overhead console with clock, rear defogger, tinted glass, Instrumentation Group, Light/Security Group, power mirrors, wide bodyside moldings, AM/FM radio, power steering, luxury wheel covers, intermittent wipers.			
Special Value Pkg. 321A, LX hatchbacks	965	820	869
LX wagon	889	756	800
Pkg. 320A but with 3-speed automatic transmission.			
Special Value Pkg. 330A, GT	829	706	746
Air conditioning, rear defogger, tinted glass, Light/Security Group, AM/FM cassette, cruise control, tilt steering column, intermittent wipers.			
Overhead console w/clock	82	69	74
Rear defogger	150	128	135
Tinted glass	105	89	95
Instrumentation Group	87	74	78
Light/Security Group, LX	78	66	70
GT	67	57	60
Luggage rack	115	98	104
Power mirrors	98	83	88
Wide bodyside moldings	50	43	45
AM radio, Pony	54	46	49
AM/FM radio, Pony	206	175	185
LX	152	130	137
AM/FM cassette, Pony	343	291	309
LX	289	246	260
GT	137	116	123
Premium sound system	138	117	124
Cruise control	191	162	172
Split folding rear seat	50	43	45
Tilt steering column	124	106	112
Luxury wheel covers	71	60	64
Vinyl trim	37	31	33
Polycast wheels	193	164	174
Intermittent wipers	55	47	50
Rear wiper/washer	126	107	113
WSW tires, LX	73	62	66
HD battery	27	23	24
Clearcoat paint, LX	91	78	82
Clearcoat two-tone paint, GT	183	155	165
Two-tone paint	91	78	82

Ford Festiva

What's New

This diminutive front-driver now comes standard with a 5-speed manual transmission and a fuel-injected engine and it offers power steering for the first time. Festiva is a 3-door hatchback based on a design by Mazda, which is owned partly by Ford Motor Co. It's built for Ford in South Korea by Kia Motors and comes in L, L Plus, and LX trim. Standard

Ford Festiva

LX there's plenty of wind, road, and engine noise. Outward visibility is great, though Festiva's cabin is Spartan. There's little cargo room behind the back seat; even with the rear seatback folded, it's only mediocre.

on all for '90 is a fuel-injected 1.3-liter 4-cylinder engine and a 5-speed manual transmission. Previously, a carbureted 1.3 was standard and the 5-speed was exclusive to the LX (the others used a 4-speed manual). The only way to get the slightly more powerful fuel-injected engine had been to order the optional 3-speed automatic, which was offered only on the L Plus and LX. This year, the automatic is offered on all three trim levels. Power steering, previously unavailable, can now be ordered on L Plus and LX models. The rear wiper/washer remains standard on LX, but is newly optional on L and L Plus. All-season tires are now standard on all models. Cosmetic changes include a new grille and taillamps. Inside, motorized front shoulder belts replace manual belts, while rear shoulder belts are now standard. Front seat cushions are larger and the upholstery is new. The AM radio has been dropped; an AM/FM stereo is standard on L Plus and LX, optional on L. Among cars sold in the U.S., only the Suzuki-built Geo Metro and the Subaru Justy have base curb weights lower than Festiva's 1713 pounds.

For

● Fuel economy ● Maneuverability

Against

● Performance ● Handling/roadholding ● Noise
● Passenger room

Summary

In most respects, Festiva is competent and efficient, though a little harsh mechanically and no trend setter. Low base prices make it a decent entry-level buy. Acceleration is no more than adequate. Light, precise manual shift linkage gets the most from the little 1.3-liter, which doesn't produce much of its power at low engine speeds, yet thrashes above 4000 rpm or so. High gas mileage compensates some for the mediocre performance and lack of refinement. We haven't tested the automatic transmission model, but expect performance and economy to suffer with it. The manual steering is heavy at parking speeds and you have to fight the wheel in bumpy corners to keep the little car on course. A tall body, forward weight bias, and skinny 12-inch tires encourage the body to roll and the nose to plow in corners. Head room is adequate all around, but most adults will consent to the back seat only for short trips. Ride comfort is good, all things considered. The suspension feels a little stiff and hoppy over freeway expansion joints, but it's reasonably absorbent on rough patches. Even with the added sound insulation on the

Specifications

	3-door hatchback
Wheelbase, in.	90.2
Overall length, in.	140.5
Overall width, in.	63.2
Overall height, in.	55.3
Turn diameter, ft.	28.9
Curb weight, lbs.	1713
Cargo vol., cu. ft.	26.5
Fuel capacity, gals.	10.0
Seating capacity	4
Front headroom, in.	38.8
Front shoulder room, in.	51.9
Front legroom, max., in.	40.6
Rear headroom, in.	37.7
Rear shoulder room, in.	50.9
Rear legroom, min., in.	35.7

Powertrain layout: transverse front engine/front-wheel drive.

Engines

	ohc I-4
Size, liters/cu. in.	1.3/81
Fuel delivery	PFI
Horsepower @ rpm	63 @ 5000
Torque (lbs./ft.) @ rpm	73 @ 3000
Availability	S

EPA city/highway mpg

5-speed OD manual	35/41
3-speed automatic	31/33

Prices

Ford Festiva	Retail Price	Dealer Invoice	Low Price
L 3-door hatchback	$6319	$5877	$6077
L Plus 3-door hatchback	7111	6613	6813
LX 3-door hatchback	7750	7208	7408
Destination charge	255	255	255

Standard equipment:

L: 1.3-liter PFI 4-cylinder engine, 5-speed manual transmission, cloth and vinyl reclining bucket seats, one-piece folding rear seat, coolant temperature gauge, locking fuel door, rear shoulder belts, 145SR12 tires. **L Plus** adds: wide bodyside moldings, door pockets, tachometer and trip odometer, rear defogger, AM/FM radio, 165/70R12 tires. **LX** adds: power mirrors, intermittent wipers, rear wiper/washer, cargo cover, tilt steering column, soft-feel steering wheel, upgraded seats with see-through head restraints, split folding rear seat, upgraded sound insulation.

Optional equipment:

3-speed automatic transmission	515	437	464
Power steering	235	200	212
Air conditioning, L Plus	824	701	742
LX	720	612	648
Rear defogger	267	227	240
Rear wiper/washer	126	107	113
AM/FM radio	245	208	221
AM/FM cassette, L	382	324	344
L Plus & LX	137	116	123
Alloy wheels, L Plus	421	358	379
LX	396	337	356

Prices are accurate at time of printing; subject to manufacturer's change.

Ford LTD Crown Victoria

Ford LTD Crown Victoria

What's New

A standard driver's-side airbag highlights a number of changes to the Crown Vic, Ford's rear-drive full-size car. A new instrument panel features revised graphics and, for the first time, a coolant temperature gauge. The glovebox is larger, but the door map pockets have been deleted. Rear shoulder belts are now standard, and the full bench seat retires in favor of a split bench with folding armrests and reclining backrests. Power windows and mirrors and a tilt steering column are standard instead of optional. Pivoting front vent windows and the Tripminder computer, previously optional, are no longer available. On the outside, five new paint colors supplement seven that are carried over. The lineup continues with the Crown Victoria 4-door sedan and the Crown Vic and Country Squire 5-door wagons. A 5.0-liter V-8 with multi-point fuel injection and a 4-speed overdrive automatic transmission is the sole powertrain. The LTD is among the few cars still using a body-on-frame construction. The Crown Vic appeared on its current platform in 1978, underwent a facelift in '88, and will get a major restyling in 1991. The revamp will incorporate a Taurus-like sloping hood with composite headlamps. Functional revisions are expected to parallel those made to the 1990 Lincoln Town Car, and a new 4.6-liter V-8 may debut.

For

• Performance   • Driveability   • Passenger room
• Trunk space   • Quietness   • Trailer towing ability

Against

• Fuel economy   • Size and weight   • Maneuverability

Summary

A single direct rival remains for Ford's line of rear-drive, V-8 big cars: the Chevrolet Caprice. Caprice is comparable in most ways, but we prefer the Crown Vic. Ford's 5.0-liter V-8 is slightly smoother and has more torque for better acceleration than either of the V-8s available in Caprice. Ford's automa-

tic transmission doesn't rush into overdrive as fast as GM's, and it downshifts more readily for prompter passing. Fuel economy is similar: a lackluster 15 mpg or less in the city and into the low 20s on the highway. The Crown Vic's ample proportions give it true 6-passenger capacity and good cargo room, plus insurance-industry statistics show it has an impressive record for occupant protection in crashes. And its body-on-frame construction often means lower repair costs from collision damage. Size and weight also work against the Crown Vic, however. It's cumbersome in tight spots. Body lean is excessive in turns, there's lots of bouncing and swaying at highway speeds, and the nose dips sharply in hard stops. Caprice has similar road manners; that's the way American sedans of this size and vintage behave. But if you want a full-size car with a V-8, there's probably no better choice than the Crown Vic. Mercury's Grand Marquis is a little plusher inside and a little more expensive than the Crown Vic, but is otherwise the same.

Specifications

	4-door notchback	5-door wagon
Wheelbase, in.	114.3	114.3
Overall length, in.	211.0	215.7
Overall width, in.	77.5	79.3
Overall height, in.	55.6	56.5
Turn diameter, ft.	39.1	39.1
Curb weight, lbs.	3821	3978
Cargo vol., cu. ft.	21.0	90.4
Fuel capacity, gals.	18.0	18.0
Seating capacity	6	8
Front headroom, in.	38.3	39.2
Front shoulder room, in.	61.6	61.6
Front legroom, max., in.	42.5	42.5
Rear headroom, in.	37.2	39.1
Rear shoulder room, in.	61.6	61.6
Rear legroom, min., in.	39.7	38.5

Powertrain layout: longitudinal front engine/rear-wheel drive.

Engines

	ohv V-8
Size, liters/cu. in.	5.0/302
Fuel delivery	PFI
Horsepower @ rpm	150 @ 3200
Torque (lbs./ft.) @ rpm	270 @ 2000
Availability	S

EPA city/highway mpg

4-speed OD automatic	17/24

Prices

Ford LTD Crown Victoria	Retail Price	Dealer Invoice	Low Price
4-door notchback	$17257	$14924	$15124
LX 4-door notchback	17894	15465	15665
5-door wagon	17668	15273	15473
Country Squire 5-door wagon	17921	15488	15688
LX 5-door wagon	18418	15911	16111
LX Country Squire 5-door wagon	18671	16125	16325
Destination charge	505	505	505

Standard equipment:

5.0-liter PFI V-8, 4-speed automatic transmission, power steering, driver's-side airbag, reclining cloth and vinyl split bench seat with center armrests, air conditioning, power windows, power mirrors, AM/FM radio, coolant temperature gauge, trip odometer, Autolamp system, automatic parking

---

KEY: **ohv** = overhead valve; **ohc** = overhead cam; **dohc** = double overhead cam; **I** = inline cylinders; **V** = cylinders in V configuration; **flat** = horizontally opposed cylinders; **bbl.** = barrel (carburetor); **PFI** = port (multi-point) fuel injection; **TBI** = throttle-body (single-point) fuel injection; **rpm** = revolutions per minute; **OD** = overdrive transmission; **S** = standard; **O** = optional; **NA** = not available.

---

brake release, tinted glass, intermittent wipers, tilt steering column, right visor mirror, 215/70R15 tires; wagon has luggage rack, 3-way tailgate with power window, simulated woodgrain (Country Squire). **LX** adds: Light Group, lighted visor mirrors, upgraded upholstery, rear armrest (except wagon), seatback pockets, dual facing rear seats (wagon).

Optional equipment:	Retail Price	Dealer Invoice	Low Price
Traction-Lok axle	100	85	90
Automatic temperature control A/C	216	183	194
w/Pkg., 112A, 113A, 131A or 133A . . .	66	56	59
Preferred Pkg. 112A, LX 4-door	420	358	378
Bumper guards, rear defogger, cruise control, Power Lock Group, AM/FM cassette.			
Preferred Pkg. 113A, LX 4-door	859	731	773
Pkg. 112A plus power driver's seat, alloy wheels, cornering lamps, illuminated entry, leather-wrapped steering wheel.			
Preferred Pkg. 114A, LX 4-door	1490	1266	1341
Pkg. 113A plus floormats, automatic temperature control, high-level audio system, power antenna, power front seats.			
Preferred Pkg. 131A, wagons exc. LX . . .	938	798	844
Bumper guards, rear defogger, cruise control, Power Lock Group, AM/FM cassette, power driver's seat, dual facing rear seats.			
Preferred Pkg. 133A, LX wagons	779	663	701
Pkg. 131A plus alloy wheels, HD battery, cornering lamps, floormats, illuminated entry, leather-wrapped steering wheel.			
Preferred Pkg. 134A, LX wagons	1117	949	1005
Pkg. 133A plus automatic temperature control, high-level audio system, power antenna, power front seats.			
Front cornering lamps	68	58	61
Rear defogger	150	128	135
Illuminated entry	82	69	74
Light Group	59	50	53
Power Lock Group	255	217	230
Bodyside moldings	66	56	59
High-level audio system	472	401	425
w/Pkg. 112A, 113A, 131A or 133A . . .	335	285	302
AM/FM cassette	137	116	123
AM/FM delete (credit)	(206)	(175)	(175)
Premium sound system	168	143	151
Power antenna	76	64	68
Power seats, each	261	222	235
Dual facing rear seats, wagons	173	147	156
Cruise control	191	163	172
Leather-wrapped steering wheel	63	54	57
Automatic load-leveling suspension	195	166	176
HD/handling suspension	26	22	23
HD Trailer Towing Pkg.	405	344	365
w/Pkg. 133A or 134A	378	321	340
Delete vinyl roof (credit)	(200)	(170)	(170)
Wire wheel covers	228	194	205
Alloy wheels	440	374	396
Insta-Clear heated windshield	250	213	225
Brougham half vinyl roof treatment	665	565	599
All-vinyl seat trim	37	31	33
Duraweave vinyl seat trim	96	82	86
Leather seat trim	489	416	440
HD battery	27	23	24
Bumper guards	62	53	56
Floormats	43	36	39
Engine block heater	20	17	18
Clearcoat paint	230	196	207
Two-tone paint/tape treatment	159	135	143
California emissions pkg.	100	85	90

Ford Mustang

What's New

Mustang gallops into 1990 with a driver's-side airbag and rear shoulder belts, but without a tilt steering column and console armrest. The same basic front-engine, rear-drive platform introduced in the fall of 1978 continues in two basic trim levels,

Ford Mustang LX 5.0L Sport

LX and GT. The LX comes standard with a 2.3-liter 4-cylinder engine and is available as a 2-door coupe, 3-door hatchback or 2-door convertible. The GT has a 5.0-liter V-8 in either the hatchback or convertible body style. The GT's V-8, beefed-up suspension, and wider tires—but not its body spoilers and air dams—are standard on the LX 5.0L. All models are available with a 5-speed manual transmission or a 4-speed over-drive automatic. For '90, map pockets have been added to the door panels, and LX models feature a driver's "dead pedal" foot rest previously restricted to the GT. New options include a Power Equipment Group, leather interior trim for GT and LX 5.0L hatchbacks, and clearcoat paint.

For

● Performance (V-8) ● Handling/roadholding ● Price

Against

● Performance (4-cylinder) ● Fuel economy (V-8)
● Passenger room

Summary

The 2.3-liter four is too weak for this 2800-pound car, so if you want a Mustang, get the V-8. There are plenty of reasons to recommend a Mustang GT or an LX 5.0L. You get blistering acceleration and capable handling. The manual shifts like a champ and the automatic isn't much of a performance penalty because the engine has a surplus of torque. All this comes at a reasonable price. We realize an aging high-powered, rear-drive car with a small interior, a rough ride, and a formidable thirst for fuel isn't everyone's cup of tea. But for performance-minded buyers on a budget, few other mounts deliver this kind of bang for the buck. An LX 5.0L is less gaudy than the GT, but both are easier to live with than the arch-rival Camaro IROC-Z, which has a less accommodating cabin and a harsher ride. There's not much rear passenger room in the Ford, but plenty of space in front for two. The hatchback has adequate cargo capacity with the rear seatback folded. A V-8 convertible is loads of fun and, like the Mustang GT, will no doubt be a collectible car years from now. With this level of performance, we'd prefer a suspension that didn't jiggle and jounce over rough pavement. And shame on Ford for saddling a 135-mph car with mediocre front-disc/rear-drum brakes instead of genuine high-performance stoppers. Nonetheless, a V-8 Mustang is still the best of a vanishing breed. Check with your insurance agent before you buy, however. Depending on your age, driving record and where you live, a V-8 Mustang could be costly to insure.

Prices are accurate at time of printing; subject to manufacturer's change.

Specifications

	2-door notchback	3-door hatchback	2-door conv.
Wheelbase, in.	100.5	100.5	100.5
Overall length, in.	179.6	179.6	179.6
Overall width, in.	68.3	68.3	68.3
Overall height, in.	52.1	52.1	52.1
Turn diameter, ft.	37.4	37.4	37.4
Curb weight, lbs.	2759	2824	2960
Cargo vol., cu. ft.	10.0	30.0	6.4
Fuel capacity, gals.	15.4	15.4	15.4
Seating capacity	4	4	4
Front headroom, in.	37.0	37.0	37.6
Front shoulder room, in.	55.5	55.5	55.5
Front legroom, max., in.	41.7	41.7	41.7
Rear headroom, in.	35.9	35.7	37.0
Rear shoulder room, in.	54.3	54.3	48.9
Rear legroom, min., in.	30.7	30.7	30.7

Powertrain layout: longitudinal front engine/rear-wheel drive.

Engines

	ohc I-4	ohv V-8
Size, liters/cu. in.	2.3/140	5.0/302
Fuel delivery	PFI	PFI
Horsepower @ rpm	88 @ 4000	225 @ 4200
Torque (lbs./ft.) @ rpm	132 @ 2600	300 @ 3200
Availability	S[1]	S[2]

EPA city/highway mpg

5-speed OD manual	23/29	17/24
4-speed OD automatic	NA	17/25

1. LX 2. GT, LX 5.0L.

Prices

Ford Mustang	Retail Price	Dealer Invoice	Low Price
LX 2-door notchback	$9456	$8618	$8818
LX 3-door hatchback	9962	9068	9268
LX 2-door convertible	15141	13677	13877
LX 5.0L Sport 2-door notchback	12164	11023	11233
LX 5.0L Sport 3-door hatchback	13007	11778	11978
LX 5.0L Sport 2-door convertible	18183	16384	16584
GT 3-door hatchback	13986	12650	12850
GT 2-door convertible	18805	16938	17138
Destination charge	400	400	400

Standard equipment:

LX: 2.3-liter PFI 4-cylinder engine, 5-speed manual transmission, power steering, driver's-side airbag, rear shoulder belts, cloth reclining bucket seats, tinted glass, tachometer, trip odometer, coolant temperature and oil pressure gauges, voltmeter, intermittent wipers, remote mirrors, door pockets, cargo area cover (3-door), AM/FM radio, 195/70R14 tires. **LX 5.0L Sport** adds: 5.0-liter PFI V-8, Traction-Lok axle, articulated sport seats (hatchback and convertible), 215/65R15 Goodyear Eagle GT + 4 tires on alloy wheels. **GT** adds: power windows and locks, remote hatch release, tilt steering column, fog lights, driver's foot rest, pivoting map light. **Convertibles** have power top, power windows and locks, remote decklid release, luggage rack, footwell lights, 225/60VR15 unidirectional tires.

> **KEY: ohv** = overhead valve; **ohc** = overhead cam; **dohc** = double overhead cam; **I** = inline cylinders; **V** = cylinders in V configuration; **flat** = horizontally opposed cylinders; **bbl.** = barrel (carburetor); **PFI** = port (multi-point) fuel injection; **TBI** = throttle-body (single-point) fuel injection; **rpm** = revolutions per minute; **OD** = overdrive transmission; **S** = standard; **O** = optional; **NA** = not available.

Optional equipment:	Retail Price	Dealer Invoice	Low Price
4-speed automatic transmission	539	458	485
Air conditioning	807	686	726
Lighted visor mirrors	100	85	90
Custom Equipment Group 60B, LX 2.3 exc. conv.	807	686	726
Air conditioning, lighted visor mirrors.			
Preferred Pkg. 240B, LX 2.3	NC	NC	NC
Power Equipment Group (power windows and locks, power mirrors), AM/FM cassette, cruise control.			
Preferred Pkg. 245B/249B, LX 5.0/GT exc. conv.	1003	852	903
Power Equipment Group (power windows and locks, power mirrors), AM/FM cassette, cruise control, air conditioning, lighted visor mirrors, premium sound system.			
Rear defogger	150	128	135
Flip-up sunroof	355	302	320
Wire wheel covers	193	164	174
Premium sound system	168	143	151
Leather articulated sport seats	489	416	440
Vinyl seat trim	37	31	33
Clearcoat paint	91	78	82
WSW tires, LX 2.3	82	69	74
California emissions pkg.	100	85	90

Ford Probe

Ford Probe GL

What's New

This new-wave front-drive sporty coupe enters 1990 with a number of important changes. On LX models, a V-6 engine and 4-wheel disc brakes are now standard, while anti-lock brakes are a new option. The GT keeps its turbocharged 4-cylinder engine, but an automatic transmission is now optional. And all models get subtle exterior alterations. Originally intended to replace the rear-drive Mustang, Probe was introduced in May 1988 as an '89 model. It shares its chassis and many mechanical components with Mazda's new MX-6 coupe; both are built at Mazda's plant in Flat Rock, Michigan. Ford styled the Probe's hatchback exterior and interior, however. Base GL models use a Mazda-built 2.2-liter 12-valve 4-cylinder engine. Probe GT comes with a turbocharged and intercooled version of the 2.2. The LX's Ford-made 3.0-liter V-6— the same engine used in the Taurus—is unavailable on the other Probes. All models have a 5-speed manual transmission as standard and a 4-speed automatic as optional; the GT was previously offered only with the manual. For '90, all Probes sport new front and rear fascias and taillamps, while the GT is fitted with new bodyside moldings and cladding and restyled alloy wheels. Rear shoulder belts are standard, and the front shoulder belts are now motorized. Seats wear new upholstery, the GL gets a soft-feel steering wheel, and leather adorns the steering wheel and shift knob on the others. LX and GT also ride on wider tires, and the options list now includes leather upholstery.

For

- Performance (GT and LX) • Handling/roadholding
- Cargo space • Anti-lock brakes option

Against

- Performance (LX) • Rear seat room
- Torque steer (GT) • Noise

Summary

Probe is a sales hit, outselling such established rivals as the Toyota Celica, Honda Prelude, and Dodge Daytona. And no Ford has ever scored higher on independent surveys of customer satisfaction. The Probe gets even more satisfying for '90, primarily through the availability of V-6 power. The 3.0 blesses the LX with far more power than the moribund 4-cylinder GL and gives it a sense of refinement absent from the turbocharged GT. Hooked to automatic transmission, the engine's low-speed oomph and mid-range response grants the 2800-pound Probe outstanding flexibility. Mated to a 5-speed manual, the V-6 adapts well to sporting, high-rpm driving, but also pulls cleanly from as low as 2000 rpm in second gear. The added weight of the V-6 doesn't seem to hurt the LX's handling. The V-6 keeps the Probe abreast of the Daytona, which also gets a V-6 option for '90. Equipped with such extra-cost items as analog instrumentation, 205/60HR15 tires, and ABS, the LX is the most appealing Probe of all. The GL rides well for a small coupe, but handling, braking and roadholding are nothing more than average for the class. By contrast, the GT is quite fast, and its wide tires and sports-oriented suspension offer fine handling. But the GT can be an unpredictable handful under hard throttle. At low speeds, turbo boost comes on abruptly with a rush of power that wrenches the front wheels off course, even in second gear. All Probes share a Ford-designed interior that borrows liberally from the Mazda, including most controls and a main instrument binnacle that tilts along with the steering wheel. There's ample cargo space, even with the rear seatback up, though the liftover is high. The tiny back seat is suitable only for children.

Specifications

	3-door hatchback
Wheelbase, in.	99.0
Overall length, in.	177.0
Overall width, in.	57.3
Overall height, in.	51.8
Turn diameter, ft.	34.8
Curb weight, lbs.	2731
Cargo vol., cu. ft.	41.9
Fuel capacity, gals.	15.1
Seating capacity	4
Front headroom, in.	37.3
Front shoulder room, in.	54.7
Front legroom, max., in.	42.5
Rear headroom, in.	35.0
Rear shoulder room, in.	53.7
Rear legroom, min., in.	29.9

Powertrain layout: transverse front engine/front-wheel drive.

Engines

	ohc I-4	Turbo ohc I-4	ohv V-6
Size, liters/cu. in.	2.2/133	2.2/133	3.0/182
Fuel delivery	PFI	PFI	PFI
Horsepower @ rpm	110 @ 4700	145 @ 4300	140 @ 4800
Torque (lbs./ft.) @ rpm	130 @ 3000	190 @ 3500	160 @ 3000
Availability	S	S[1]	S[2]
EPA city/highway mpg			
5-speed OD manual	24/31	21/27	19/26
4-speed OD automatic	22/29	19/25	19/26

1. Probe GT   2. Probe LX.

Prices

Ford Probe	Retail Price	Dealer Invoice	Low Price
GL 3-door hatchback	$11470	$10420	$10620
LX 3-door hatchback	13006	11789	11989
GT 3-door hatchback	14726	13318	13518
Destination charge	290	290	290

Standard equipment:

GL: 2.2-liter PFI 4-cylinder engine, 5-speed manual transmission, power steering, cloth reclining front bucket seats with driver's seat height adjustment, rear shoulder belts, tachometer, coolant temperature and oil pressure gauges, ammeter, AM/FM radio, tinted backlight and quarter windows, cargo cover, full console with storage, split folding rear seatbacks, right visor mirror, digital clock, 185/70R14 tires. **LX** adds: 3.0-liter PFI V-6, 4-wheel disc brakes, remote fuel door and liftgate releases, intermittent wipers, rear defogger, full tinted glass, tilt steering column and instrument cluster, power mirrors, overhead console with map light, leather-wrapped steering wheel and shift knob, upgraded carpet and upholstery, door pockets, left visor mirror, folding armrest, driver's seat lumbar and side bolster adjustments, 195/70R14 tires. **GT** adds: 2.2-liter turbocharged engine, performance suspension with automatic adjustment, passenger lumbar support adjustment, fog lights, 205/60VR15 tires on alloy wheels.

Optional equipment:

4-speed automatic transmission	617	525	555
Air conditioning, GL	927	788	834
GL w/Pkg. 251A, LX & GT	807	686	726
Electronic air conditioning, LX & GT	990	842	891
Anti-lock brakes, LX & GT	924	786	832
Preferred Pkg. 251A, GL	158	135	142
Tinted glass, tilt steering column and instrument cluster, rear defogger, Convenience Group.			
Preferred Pkg. 253A, LX	2088	1775	1879
Electronic instruments with vehicle maintenance monitor, electronically controlled air conditioning, illuminated entry, power driver's seat, trip computer, rear wiper/washer, walk-in passenger seat, power windows and locks, cruise control, AM/FM cassette with premium sound and power antenna, cargo tiedown net.			
Preferred Pkg. 261A, GT	2795	2376	2516
Anti-lock brakes, electronically controlled air conditioning, illuminated entry, power driver's seat, trip computer, vehicle maintenance monitor, rear wiper/washer, walk-in passenger seat, power windows and locks, cruise control, AM/FM cassette with premium sound and power antenna, lighted visor mirrors, cargo tiedown net.			
Cruise control, LX & GT	191	163	172
Power locks, LX & GT	155	132	140
Requires power windows.			
Power windows, LX & GT	241	205	217
Requires power locks.			
AM/FM cassette	344	292	310
Includes premium sound and power antenna.			
Premium sound	168	143	151
AM/FM cassette w/CD player	1052	895	947
LX w/Pkg. 253A, GT w/Pkg. 261A	709	602	638
Rear defogger, GL	150	128	135

Prices are accurate at time of printing; subject to manufacturer's change.

	Retail Price	Dealer Invoice	Low Price
Leather seating surface trim	489	416	440
Flip-up sunroof, LX & GT	355	302	320
Alloy wheels, GL	313	266	282
LX	252	215	227
Engine block heater	20	17	18

Ford Taurus

Ford Taurus LX

What's New

This popular front-drive intermediate gains a driver's-side airbag and a new instrument panel, while sedans can now be fitted with optional anti-lock brakes. Taurus continues in 4-door sedan and 5-door station wagon body styles. The base L sedan has a 2.5-liter 4-cylinder and a 3-speed automatic. L and GL wagons and the LX sedan have a 3.0-liter V-6. Optional on all but the L sedan is a 3.8-liter V-6. Both these V-6s come only with a 4-speed overdrive automatic transmission. The high-performance SHO sedan continues with its Yamaha-designed double overhead-cam, 24-valve 3.0-liter V-6 and Mazda 5-speed manual transmission. In place of the front-disc/rear drum brakes on other Taurus, the SHO has standard 4-wheel discs. The optional ABS system adds rear disc brakes to all models, though Ford doesn't offer the system on the wagon. A tilt steering wheel with an airbag in its hub has been made standard for '90. The new dashboard retains the old one's same basic layout, but adds slightly reworked controls, a cup holder, and a coin holder. A tachometer is optional with the standard instrumentation; digital gauges remain an extra-cost choice. The headlamp switch is now illuminated, and the dome lamp incorporates a time delay. Speed-sensitive power steering is available on LX models and a compact-disc player is a new option.

For

- Performance (SHO and 3.8 V-6)
- Handling/roadholding   • Ride   • Passenger room
- Cargo space

KEY: **ohv** = overhead valve; **ohc** = overhead cam; **dohc** = double overhead cam; **I** = inline cylinders; **V** = cylinders in V configuration; **flat** = horizontally opposed cylinders; **bbl.** = barrel (carburetor); **PFI** = port (multi-point) fuel injection; **TBI** = throttle-body (single-point) fuel injection; **rpm** = revolutions per minute; **OD** = overdrive transmission; **S** = standard; **O** = optional; **NA** = not available.

Against

- Performance (4-cylinder)   • Fuel economy (V-6s)

Summary

When Taurus debuted in 1985 as an '86 model, it brought aerodynamic styling to mainstream America and introduced domestic family car buyers to a new standard of handling that emphasized a taut ride, responsive steering, and composed cornering. General Motors originally scoffed at Taurus's "jellybean" shape and European countenance, but soon GM, too, was streamlining its bread-and-butter cars. Now, a battle of the domestic titans is shaping up between the Taurus and arch-rival Chevrolet's new Lumina sedan. Comparing a V-6 Lumina Euro Sedan to a comparably equipped Taurus LX, we prefer the Ford. Both cars are roomy enough for five adults, six in a pinch, though Lumina's interior is airier by virtue of its glassier greenhouse. And both have trunks that will swallow a family's vacation luggage. Ford's road manners give it an edge, however. The Taurus feels more composed over bumps and in corners, with more precise steering and better control of its suspension movements. Absent in the Taurus is the Lumina's cumbersome feel in city driving. The Chevy's cabin seems more isolated from wind and road noise on the highway, but its V-6 is gruffer than the Ford's under acceleration and its 4-speed overdrive automatic transmission suffers a glut of unwanted upshifts and downshifts. Taurus shoppers should avoid the weak and noisy 2.5-liter four and bear in mind that compared to the 3.0 six, the torquier 3.8 delivers noticeably stronger acceleration from a standstill and better mid-range response. The SHO's acceleration rivals that of the world's leading sports sedans, though all that power can force its front tires to stray from their intended course if you use hard throttle with the steering wheel cocked. We've found that the SHO's mandatory 5-speed manual occasionally balks going into gear, though overall, this is a very good value in a performance sedan.

Specifications

	4-door notchback	5-door wagon
Wheelbase, in.	106.0	106.0
Overall length, in.	188.4	191.9
Overall width, in.	70.8	70.8
Overall height, in.	54.6	55.4
Turn diameter, ft.	38.1	38.1
Curb weight, lbs.	2956	3244
Cargo vol., cu. ft.	21.0	90.4
Fuel capacity, gals.	16.0	16.0
Seating capacity	6	8
Front headroom, in.	38.3	38.6
Front shoulder room, in.	57.7	57.5
Front legroom, max., in.	41.7	41.7
Rear headroom, in.	37.6	38.4
Rear shoulder room, in.	57.5	57.5
Rear legroom, min., in.	37.5	36.6

Powertrain layout: transverse front engine/front-wheel drive.

Engines

	ohv I-4	ohv V-6	ohv V-6	dohc V-6
Size, liters/cu. in.	2.5/153	3.0/182	3.8/232	3.0/182
Fuel delivery	TBI	PFI	PFI	PFI
Horsepower @ rpm	90 @ 4400	140 @ 4800	140 @ 3800	220 @ 6200
Torque (lbs./ft.) @ rpm . . .	130 @ 2600	160 @ 3000	215 @ 2200	200 @ 4800
Availability	S	S[1]	O	S[2]

EPA city/highway mpg	ohv I-4	ohv V-6	ohv V-6	dohc V-6
5-speed OD manual				18/27
3-speed automatic	21/27			
4-speed OD automatic . . .		21/29	19/28	

1. LX, wagons   2. SHO.

Prices

Ford Taurus

	Retail Price	Dealer Invoice	Low Price
L 4-door notchback	$12640	$10970	$11170
L 5-door wagon	14272	12357	12557
GL 4-door notchback	13113	11372	11572
GL 5-door wagon	14722	12740	12940
SHO 4-door notchback	21633	18614	18814
LX 4-door notchback	16180	13979	14179
LX 5-door wagon	17771	15331	15531
Destination charge	450	450	450

Standard equipment:

L: 2.5-liter TBI 4-cylinder engine, 3-speed automatic transmission (wagon has 3.0-liter PFI V-6 and 4-speed automatic), power steering, driver's-side airbag, tilt steering column, power mirrors, cloth reclining split bench seat, rear shoulder belts, 60/40 folding rear seatbacks (wagon), cargo tiedowns (wagon), intermittent wipers, trip odometer, coolant temperature gauge, AM/FM radio, tinted glass, luggage rack (wagon), 195/70R14 SBR tires. **GL** adds: split bench or bucket seats with console and recliners, seatback pockets, rear armrest, rear head restraints (4-door), cargo net (4-door). **LX** adds: 3.0-liter V-6 (4-door; wagon has 3.8-liter V-6), air conditioning, power windows and locks, power lumbar support, diagnostic alert lights, remote fuel door and decklid/liftgate releases, Light Group, automatic parking brake release, lower bodyside cladding, cornering lights, upgraded door panels, lighted visor mirrors, 205/70R14 SBR tires. **SHO** adds: 3.0-liter DOHC 24-valve PFI V-6, 5-speed manual transmission, 4-wheel disc brakes, handling suspension, dual exhausts, sport seats with power lumbar, 8000-rpm tachometer, 140-mph speedometer, fog lamps, special bodyside cladding, wheel spats, rear defogger, cruise control, leather-wrapped steering wheel, 215/65R15 performance tires on alloy wheels.

Optional equipment:

3.0L V-6 & 4-speed auto trans, L &			
GL 4-doors	696	592	626
3.8L V-6, GL wagon & LX 4-door . .	400	340	360
GL 4-door	1096	932	986
Anti-lock braking system	985	838	887
Preferred Pkg. 204A, GL	1688	1436	1519

Air conditioning, cruise control, remote fuel door and decklid/liftgate release, Light Group, rear defogger, rocker panel moldings, paint stripe, power windows and locks, AM/FM cassette, power driver's seat, finned wheel covers.

Preferred Pkg. 207A, LX	748	635	673

Cruise control, rear defogger, paint stripe, AM/FM cassette with premium sound system, alloy wheels, Autolamp system, floormats, illuminated entry, leather-wrapped steering wheel.

Preferred Pkg. 208A, LX 4-door	3099	2634	2789
LX wagon	1714	1456	1543

Pkg. 207A plus 3.8-liter V-6, anti-lock braking system, speed-sensitive power steering, high-level audio system, electronic instruments, keyless entry, power antenna, power front seats.

Preferred Pkg. 211A, SHO	533	452	480

Autolamp system, floormats, illuminated entry, high-level audio system.

Preferred Pkg. 212A, SHO	2724	2316	2452

Pkg. 211A plus automatic air conditioning, keyless entry, power antenna, Ford JBL Audio System, power front seats, leather seat trim, power moonroof.

Automatic air conditioning	990	842	891
SHO, LX or GL w/204A	183	155	165
Manual air conditioning	807	686	726
Autolamp system	73	62	66
Cargo area cover, wagons	66	56	59
Cornering lamps	68	58	61
Rear defogger	150	128	135

	Retail Price	Dealer Invoice	Low Price
Remote fuel door and decklid releases . . .	91	78	82
Remote fuel door release, wagons	41	35	37
Extended range fuel tank	46	39	41
Illuminated entry	82	69	74
Diagnostic instrument cluster	89	76	80
Electronic instruments, LX	239	203	215
GL	351	299	316
Keyless entry	218	186	196
w/Pkg. 207A or 211A	137	116	123
Light Group	59	50	53
Picnic table load floor extension, wagons .	66	56	59
Power locks	205	174	185
Lighted visor mirrors	100	85	90
Rocker panel moldings	55	47	50
Power moonroof	741	630	667
Automatic parking brake release	12	10	11
CD player	491	418	442
High-level audio system	472	401	425
GL w/Pkg. 204A	335	285	302
LX w/Pkg. 207A . . .	167	142	150
AM/FM cassette	137	116	123
Premium sound system	168	143	151
Power antenna	76	64	68
Ford JBL Audio System	488	415	439
Rear facing third seat	155	132	140
Power seats, each	261	222	235
Cruise control	191	163	172
Leather-wrapped steering wheel	63	54	57
HD suspension	26	22	23
Speed-sensitive steering	104	88	94
Rear wiper/washer	126	107	113
Finned wheel covers	65	55	59
Alloy wheels, GL	279	237	251
LX or GL w/Pkg. 204A	215	182	194
Styled road wheels, GL	193	164	174
LX or GL w/Pkg. 204A	128	109	115
Power windows	306	260	275
Insta-Clear heated windshield	250	213	225
Bucket seats	NC	NC	NC
Leather seat trim, LX & SHO	489	416	440
GL	593	504	534
Vinyl seat trim, L	51	44	46
GL	37	31	33
205/70R14 WSW tires	82	69	74
205/65R15 tires	65	55	59
205/65R15 WSW tires	146	124	131
Conventional spare tire	73	62	66
HD battery	27	23	24
Engine block heater	20	17	18
Floormats	43	36	39
Clearcoat paint	188	160	169
Paint stripe	61	52	55
California emissions pkg.	100	85	90

Ford Tempo

What's New

This strong-selling compact is little changed for 1990, but Ford is readying a completely restyled version that is expected to debut for '92. For this year, footwell and trunk lights are standard, and all models come with floormats. The polycast wheels are restyled, and rear shoulder belts are scheduled to be added during the year. A front center armrest has joined the GL options list, and the sport instrument cluster is now available only as part of GL Special Value packages. For '90, front-wheel drive Tempos continue in GL and GLS trim as 2- and 4-door sedans; the top-of-the line LX is a 4-door sedan only. The All-Wheel Drive model features a part-time 4-wheel drive system (for use on slippery pavement only) and is avail-

Prices are accurate at time of printing; subject to manufacturer's change.

Ford Tempo

able only as a 4-door. A 98-horsepower 2.3-liter 4-cylinder is standard on the GL and LX; a 100-horsepower version is standard on the GLS and All-Wheel Drive. A 5-speed manual transmission is standard and a 3-speed automatic is optional in all models except the All-Wheel Drive, which has the automatic standard. Tempo in 1988 received the first major facelift since its 1983 introduction. The revamp made it more closely resemble the aerodynamic Ford Taurus, and it also received a stylish new dashboard. The '92 recast will replace the imitation-Taurus look with a pronounced wedge shape. A steeply sloping new hoodline will be made possible by a new compact quad headlamp design in which each lamp is less that two inches in height and width.

For

- 4WD traction (All-Wheel Drive sedan)   - Airbag option

Against

- Engine noise   - Driveability

Summary

We're not going to recommend Tempo for its power or performance, which are barely adequate with either engine. Worse, the automatic transmission hurries into top gear and then balks at changing back down for passing. Nor do its passenger room, trunk space, ride, or handling rise above average in the compact field. Still, this car is a strong seller and there are solid reasons for that. Prices are attractive and the '88 restyle brought a smartly updated exterior and one of the most ergonomically sound dashboards in an American-built car. The All-Wheel Drive sedan is better than run-of-the-mill by virtue of its easy-to-use 4WD system. Engaged or disengaged on the fly at the flip of a switch, the convenient system provides impressive traction in slippery conditions. Another nice feature is the available driver's-side airbag. It became a regular production option on Tempo and similar Topaz for 1987, though fleet buyers for government agencies and insurance companies have made up the bulk of the sales. Except for its 4WD system, Tempo can't compete with Japanese rivals in sophistication, but it beats most of them on sticker price.

KEY: **ohv** = overhead valve; **ohc** = overhead cam; **dohc** = double overhead cam; **I** = inline cylinders; **V** = cylinders in V configuration; **flat** = horizontally opposed cylinders; **bbl.** = barrel (carburetor); **PFI** = port (multi-point) fuel injection; **TBI** = throttle-body (single-point) fuel injection; **rpm** = revolutions per minute; **OD** = overdrive transmission; **S** = standard; **O** = optional; **NA** = not available.

Specifications

	2-door notchback	4-door notchback
Wheelbase, in.	99.9	99.9
Overall length, in.	176.7	177.0
Overall width, in.	68.3	68.3
Overall height, in.	52.8	52.9
Turn diameter, ft.	38.7	38.7
Curb weight, lbs.	2462[1]	2515[2]
Cargo vol., cu. ft.	13.2	13.2
Fuel capacity, gals.	15.9	15.9[3]
Seating capacity	5	5
Front headroom, in.	37.5	37.5
Front shoulder room, in.	53.9	53.9
Front legroom, max., in.	41.5	41.5
Rear headroom, in.	36.8	36.9
Rear shoulder room, in.	54.0	53.3
Rear legroom, min., in.	36.0	36.0

1. 2667 with 4WD   2. 2720 with 4WD   3. 14.2 with 4WD.

Powertrain layout: transverse front engine/front-wheel drive or on-demand 4WD.

Engines

	ohv I-4	ohv I-4
Size, liters/cu. in.	2.3/141	2.3/141
Fuel delivery	PFI	PFI
Horsepower @ rpm	98 @ 4400	100 @ 4400
Torque (lbs./ft.) @ rpm	124 @ 2200	130 @ 2600
Availability	S	S[1]

EPA city/highway mpg

5-speed OD manual	23/32	21/28
3-speed automatic	22/26	22/27

1. GLS and 4WD.

Prices

Ford Tempo	Retail Price	Dealer Invoice	Low Price
GL 2-door notchback	$9483	$8605	$8805
GL 4-door notchback	9633	8739	8939
GLS 2-door notchback	10300	9333	9533
GLS 4-door notchback	10448	9464	9664
LX 4-door notchback	10605	9604	9804
All Wheel Drive 4-door notchback	11331	10251	10451
Destination charge	425	425	425

Standard equipment:

GL: 2.3-liter PFI 4-cylinder engine, 5-speed manual transmission, power steering, cloth reclining front bucket seats, rear shoulder belts, AM/FM radio, coolant temperature gauge, tinted glass, intermittent wipers, door pockets, 185/70R14 tires. **GLS** adds: high-output engine, Light Group, tachometer and trip odometer, leather-wrapped steering wheel, AM/FM cassette, power mirrors, sport seats, luggage tiedown, front center armrest, performance tires on alloy wheels. **LX** adds to GL: illuminated entry, power locks, remote fuel door and decklid releases, Light Group, power mirrors, tachometer and trip odometer, tilt steering column, front center armrest, upgraded upholstery, seatback pockets, polycast wheels. **All Wheel Drive** adds to GL: high-output engine, 3-speed automatic transmission, part-time 4-wheel drive, tachometer and trip odometer, Light Group, power mirrors, polycast wheels.

Optional equipment:

3-speed automatic transmission	539	458	485
Air conditioning	807	686	726
Supplemental airbag restraint system,			
GL 4-door	815	692	734
GL 4-door w/226A, LX	690	587	621
Requires automatic transmission.			

	Retail Price	Dealer Invoice	Low Price
Preferred Pkg. 226A, GL 2-door	486	414	437
GL 4-door	538	458	484

Air conditioning, rear defogger, Light Group, Power Lock Group, power mirrors, tilt steering column.

Preferred Pkg. 229A, GLS 2-door	1267	1078	1140
GLS 4-door	1319	1122	1187

Air conditioning, Power Lock Group, tilt steering column, power driver's seat, premium sound system, cruise control.

Preferred Pkg. 233A, LX	911	774	820

3-speed automatic transmission, air conditioning, rear defogger, decklid luggage rack.

Preferred Pkg. 232A, AWD	378	322	340

Rear defogger, Power Lock Group, tilt steering column, power windows.

Front center armrest, GL	55	47	50
Rear defogger	150	128	135
Sport instrument cluster, GL	87	74	78
Light Group, GL	38	32	34
Decklid luggage rack	115	97	104
Power Lock Group (std. LX), 2-doors . . .	246	209	221
4-doors	298	253	268

Power locks, remote decklid and fuel door releases.

Power mirrors, GL	121	103	109
AM/FM cassette (std. LX)	137	116	123
Premium sound system	138	117	124
Power driver's seat	261	222	235
Cruise control	191	163	172
Sports Appearance Group, GLS	1178	1001	1060
Tilt steering column (std. LX)	124	106	112
Polycast wheels, GL	193	164	174
Power windows, 4-doors	306	260	275
All vinyl seat trim	37	31	33
WSW tires (NA GLS)	82	69	74
Clearcoat metallic paint	91	78	82
Lower accent paint treatment	159	135	143
California emissions pkg.	100	85	90

Ford Thunderbird

Ford Thunderbird

What's New

All new last year, the mid-size, rear-drive Thunderbird wings into 1990 with few changes while looking forward to the return of V-8 power for '91. Thunderbird's '89 redesign brought the car's first all-independent suspension and a new body that's shorter, wider, and lower than its predecessor, yet rides on a wheelbase that's nine inches longer. Every cabin measurement was increased versus the '88 model. Base and LX Thunderbirds continue with a 3.8-liter V-6 and a 4-speed overdrive automatic transmission. The Super Coupe runs with a supercharged and intercooled version of the 3.8. This engine is exclusive to the SC and can be mated to either the automatic or a 5-speed manual transmission. Next year, V-8 power is to reappear as Ford installs its familiar 5.0-liter engine as an option on base and LX models. The SC will keep its supercharged V-6. This year, two new option packages are available: a Power Equipment Group (power locks, remote fuel door and decklid releases, power driver's seat); and a Luxury Group (cruise control, tilt steering column, power mirrors, light group, etc.). This 5-seat coupe is otherwise unchanged. The SC comes standard with aero body flares and 4-wheel anti-lock disc brakes; these brakes are optional on base and LX models in place of their standard front disc/rear drum setup. Standard on the supercharged model are 16-inch tires on alloy wheels and an Automatic Adjustable Suspension that allows the driver to change shock absorber damping for a soft or a firm ride. Thunderbird is similar to the likewise redesigned Mercury Cougar.

For

- Performance (Super Coupe) ● Handling/roadholding
- Anti-lock brakes

Against

- Performance (Base and LX)

Summary

Thunderbird's previous revamp, in 1983, introduced aero styling to domestic-car buyers and strongly influenced U.S. car design in the '80s. The '89 version builds on that without rejecting the long-hood, short-deck look T-Bird loyalists love. And significantly, it retains rear-wheel drive, something General Motors shelved in its 1988 redo of the Grand Prix, Oldsmobile Cutlass Supreme, and Buick Regal. Unfortunately, the '89 T-Bird gained about 300 pounds over comparable 1988 models. It is indeed roomier inside, though, and while the rear seat is wide enough for three adults, the middle rider will be unhappy straddling the wide driveline tunnel. Controls on the cockpit-style dashboard are clear and easy to reach. The flagship Super Coupe is like a swift battle cruiser; its weight slows its reflexes, but once underway, it picks up speed with alacrity and changes direction credibly. Pass on the manual transmission with its balky shift linkage, however. The base and LX T-Birds don't suffer the SC's overly firm ride, but they're far less fleet than the supercharged car. The 3600-pound bulk really takes its toll with the naturally aspirated 3.8, and progress in the base and LX versions can be positively sedate. Overall, though, Thunderbird is a solid-feeling, quiet-riding, and modern-looking personal coupe. We like it better than the competition from GM, but yearn for a lighter, more efficiently sized bird.

Specifications

	2-door notchback
Wheelbase, in.	113.0
Overall length, in.	198.7
Overall width, in.	72.7
Overall height, in.	52.7
Turn diameter, ft.	34.9
Curb weight, lbs.	3581
Cargo vol., cu. ft.	14.7
Fuel capacity, gals.	19.0
Seating capacity	5
Front headroom, in.	38.1
Front shoulder room, in.	59.1
Front legroom, max., in.	42.5
Rear headroom, in.	37.5
Rear shoulder room, in.	59.1
Rear legroom, min., in.	35.8

Prices are accurate at time of printing; subject to manufacturer's change.

Ford • Geo

Powertrain layout: longitudinal front engine/rear-wheel drive.

Engines	ohv V-6	Supercharged ohv V-6
Size, liters/cu. in.	3.8/232	3.8/232
Fuel delivery	PFI	PFI
Horsepower @ rpm	140 @ 3800	210 @ 4000
Torque (lbs./ft.) @ rpm	215 @ 2400	315 @ 2600
Availability	S	S[1]

EPA city/highway mpg

5-speed OD manual		17/24
4-speed OD automatic	19/27	17/23

1. Super Coupe.

Prices

Ford Thunderbird	Retail Price	Dealer Invoice	Low Price
2-door notchback	$14980	$12997	$13197
LX 2-door notchback	17283	14938	15138
Super Coupe 2-door notchback	20390	17596	17796
Destination charge	455	455	455

Standard equipment:

3.8-liter PFI V-6, 4-speed automatic transmission, power steering, air conditioning, cloth reclining front bucket seats, rear shoulder belts, tinted glass, power windows, intermittent wipers, left remote mirror, full-length console with armrest and storage bin, coolant temperature gauge, trip odometer, visor mirrors, AM/FM radio, 205/70R15 all-season tires. **LX** adds: power driver's seat, illuminated entry, remote fuel door and decklid releases, power locks, cruise control, maintenance monitor, power mirrors, folding rear armrest, electronic instruments, Light Group, lighted visor mirrors, AM/FM cassette, leather-wrapped steering wheel, tilt steering column, instrument panel storage compartment. **Super Coupe** adds to base: supercharged engine with dual exhaust, 5-speed manual transmission, 4-wheel disc brakes, anti-lock braking system, handling suspension, articulated sport seats, lower bodyside cladding, fog lights, analog instruments with tachometer, soft-feel steering wheel, remote fuel door release, maintenance monitor, power mirrors, folding rear armrest, Light Group, instrument panel storage compartment, 225/60VR16 tires on alloy wheels.

Optional equipment:

4-speed automatic transmission, SC	539	458	485
Anti-lock brakes, base & LX	1085	923	977
Traction-Lok axle, base & LX	100	85	90
Preferred Pkg. 151A, base	1288	1096	1159
AM/FM cassette, rear defogger, power passenger seat, Power Equipment Group, Luxury Group.			
Preferred Pkg. 155A, LX	819	695	737
Rear defogger, power passenger seat, keyless entry, AM/FM cassette with premium sound, power antenna, front floormats, Luxury Group.			
Preferred Group 157A, SC	NC	NC	NC
AM/FM cassette, rear defogger, power passenger seat, Power Equipment Group, Luxury Group.			
Anti-theft system	183	155	165
Keyless entry, base & SC	219	185	197
Base w/Luxury Group, SC w/Luxury Light/Convenience Group, LX	137	116	123
Front floormats	33	28	30

KEY: ohv = overhead valve; **ohc** = overhead cam; **dohc** = double overhead cam; **I** = inline cylinders; **V** = cylinders in V configuration; **flat** = horizontally opposed cylinders; **bbl.** = barrel (carburetor); **PFI** = port (multi-point) fuel injection; **TBI** = throttle-body (single-point) fuel injection; **rpm** = revolutions per minute; **OD** = overdrive transmission; **S** = standard; **O** = optional; **NA** = not available.

	Retail Price	Dealer Invoice	Low Price
Luxury Light/Convenience Group, SC	426	361	383
Cornering lamps, lighted visor mirrors, illuminated entry, Autolamp system, automatic day/night mirror, vehicle maintenance monitor.			
Power moonroof, SC	841	715	757
Base, LX or SC with Luxury Light/Convenience Group	741	630	667
AM/FM cassette, base & SC	137	116	123
AM/FM cassette w/premium sound, base & SC	442	375	398
Base w/151A, SC w/157A	305	259	275
Ford JBL audio system	488	415	439
CD player	491	418	442
Power antenna	76	64	68
Wire wheel covers, base	228	194	205
Base w/151A	143	121	129
LX w/155A & 205/70R15 WSW tires . .	NC	NC	NC
215/70R15 tires on alloy wheels, base . . .	298	254	268
Base w/151A	213	181	192
Leather seating surfaces, LX	489	416	440
SC	622	529	560
Rear defogger	150	128	135
Power passenger seat	261	222	235
Power Equipment Group, base & SC	507	431	456
Power Lock Group, power driver's seat.			
Luxury Group, base	1158	986	1042
LX	457	388	411
SC	315	269	284
Cruise control, tilt steering column, power mirrors, wheel covers, Luxury Light/Convenience Group, 215/70R15 tires on alloy wheels.			
205/70R15 tires, base & LX	73	62	66
225/60R16 Eagle GT + 4 tires, SC	73	62	66
Conventional spare tire, base & LX	73	62	66
Clearcoat paint	188	160	169
California emissions pkg.	100	85	90

Geo Metro

Geo Metro LSi

What's New

Changes in trim and standard equipment mark this front-drive minicompact, which retains the title of U.S. fuel economy leader. Metro is built for General Motors by Suzuki in Japan. GM sells it under its new Geo-brand collection of "captive imports" built by several manufacturers in Japan and in North America. Geo franchises are held by Chevrolet dealers. Metro is offered in 3- and 5-door hatchback body styles. The economy-leader gets the XFi designation for '90 and is the only version that's not also available as a 5-door. Preliminary estimates place the XFi's mileage at 53 mph city/58 mpg highway. One step up from the stripper XFi is the base Metro, followed by the higher content LSi. All are powered by a 1.0-liter 3-cylinder engine. A 5-speed manual transmission—with overdrive fourth and fifth gears—is standard; a 3-speed automatic is offered on base and LSi models. New for '90 on base and LSi Metros are full wheel covers, black body-side moldings, and intermittent wipers. The LSi tag brings a remote trunk release and new interior fabrics.

For

- Fuel economy
- Maneuverability

Against

- Interior room
- Noise
- Size/weight

Summary

Metro's main virtue is high fuel economy. We averaged a commendable 42.3 mpg in a 1988 model with the 5-speed manual and economy gear ratio. Oddly, there was little difference in economy among our drivers, even though some do mostly city driving while others do mostly suburban expressway driving. You'll lose some mileage and acceleration with the automatic transmission, but not enough to cross the automatic off your shopping list. With the 5-speed, Metro feels lively in the lower gears and can easily keep pace with traffic. Trouble is, excessive engine noise and the unfiltered sounds of tires and surrounding traffic turn the tiny cabin into an audio penalty box. Metro's short wheelbases and light curb weight put it at the mercy of bumpy pavement and make the ride bouncy and jarring. We're also leery of the crash protection cars this small provide. However, if low prices and high fuel economy are important to you, this is a good place to look. You should also look at the similarly sized Ford Festiva and Subaru Justy.

Specifications

	3-door hatchback	5-door hatchback
Wheelbase, in.	89.2	93.2
Overall length, in.	146.3	150.4
Overall width, in.	62.0	62.7
Overall height, in.	53.4	53.5
Turn diameter, ft.	30.2	31.5
Curb weight, lbs.	1591	1640
Cargo vol., cu. ft.	29.1	31.4
Fuel capacity, gals.	10.6	10.6
Seating capacity	4	4
Front headroom, in.	37.8	38.8
Front shoulder room, in.	51.6	51.6
Front legroom, max., in.	42.5	42.5
Rear headroom, in.	36.6	38.0
Rear shoulder room, in.	50.5	50.6
Rear legroom, min., in.	29.8	32.6

Powertrain layout: transverse front engine/front-wheel drive.

Engines

	ohc I-3
Size, liters/cu. in.	1.0/61
Fuel delivery	TBI
Horsepower @ rpm	55 @ 5700
Torque (lbs./ft.) @ rpm	58 @ 3300
Availability	S

EPA city/highway mpg

5-speed OD manual	53/58
3-speed automatic	38/40

Prices

Geo Metro	Retail Price	Dealer Invoice	Low Price
XFi 3-door hatchback	$5995	$5755	$5855
3-door hatchback	6695	6159	6359
5-door hatchback	6995	6435	6635
LSi 3-door hatchback	7495	6895	7095
LSi 5-door hatchback	7795	7171	7371
Destination charge	255	255	255

Standard equipment:

XFi & base: 1.0-liter TBI 3-cylinder engine, 5-speed manual transmission, cloth and vinyl reclining front bucket seats, one-piece folding rear seatback, rear shoulder belts, intermittent wipers, left door pocket, 145/80R13 tires. **LSi** adds: composite headlamps, full cloth upholstery, trip odometer, door pockets, split folding rear seatback, wheel covers, remote hatch release, rear defogger.

Optional equipment:

Air conditioning	670	590	603
XFi Preferred Group 2	150	132	135
Rear defogger.			
Base Preferred Group 2	576	507	518
AM/FM radio, rear defogger, rear wiper/washer.			
Base Preferred Group 3	465	409	419
3-speed automatic transmission.			
Base Preferred Group 4	1041	916	937
3-speed automatic transmission, AM/FM radio, rear defogger, rear wiper/washer.			
LSi Preferred Group 2	451	397	406
AM/FM radio, rear defogger, rear wiper/washer, console.			
LSi Preferred Group 3	465	409	419
3-speed automatic transmission, rear defogger.			
LSi Preferred Group 4	916	806	824
3-speed automatic transmission, AM/FM radio, rear defogger, rear wiper/washer, console.			
Left remote & right manual mirrors	20	18	18
AM/FM radio	301	265	271
AM/FM cassette	441	388	397
Sound system prices are for base models; prices vary with option package content.			
Console	25	22	23
Floormats	25	22	23
Bodyside moldings	50	44	45
Mud guards	30	26	27
Sport stripe, base	50	44	45
XFi	100	88	90

Geo Prizm

What's New

The flagship of the Geo line is the Prizm, which went on sale in February 1989 as an early '90 model. The front-drive subcompact is available as a 4-door notchback or a 5-door hatchback. It's based on the Toyota Corolla and replaces the Nova in the Chevy/Geo showroom. Both the Prizm and the 4-door version of the Corolla are built by New United Motor Manufacturing, Inc., the General Motors/Toyota joint-venture in Fremont, California. Standard on the base and LSi Prizm is a 102-horsepower 1.6-liter 4-cylinder engine. New this fall is a GSi sport model in either notchback or hatchback body style. Its exterior is identified by a rear spoiler and by its body-color grille and bumpers. GSi models use a 130-horsepower version of the 1.6. They have 185/60HR14 tires on alloy wheels, compared to the 175/70SR13 tires on base and LSi models, and feature sport-fabric inserts on doors and seats and 4-wheel

Prices are accurate at time of printing; subject to manufacturer's change.

Geo Prizm GSi

disc brakes. A 5-speed manual transmission is standard on all Prizms. A 3-speed automatic is optional on the base and LSi; a 4-speed automatic is optional on the GSi.

For

- Performance (LSi) • Ride

Against

- Interior room • Cargo space

Summary

The only Prizm we've road tested is an LSi 5-speed notchback. We found it an extremely easy-to-drive, high-comfort subcompact that ranks just below the Honda Civic for all-around small-sedan goodness. It's not fast, but the 16-valve 1.6-liter is smooth and refined. Take advantage of the 5-speed's slick shift action, and the Prizm can surprise with its quickness. We suspect the automatic-equipped version would be far less spry. The cabin, while not generously sized for those over 6 feet, is airy and contemporary, and the controls are sensibly laid out, though the unavailability of a tachometer on the LSi is a painful omission. The quality of materials and assembly also is just a half-step shy of Honda's. On the road, straight-line stability can be compromised by strong cross winds. Handling prowess is sacrificed to a soft suspension—a trade-off most Prizm buyers will accept in exchange for the car's outstanding ability to smooth out bumps in the road. Prizm's ride quality is far above average for the subcompact class, and is in fact a good ride by any measure. The suspension is absorbent and composed, with little bounding on the highway and almost no harshness. Only on particularly sharp ridges, which tax the car's moderate wheel travel and 13-inch tires, does a jolt go unbuffered. At around $13,000, an LSi equipped as ours is slightly more expensive than a similarly outfitted Toyota Corolla LE or a Civic EX sedan. Of the three, however, your Geo-dealing Chevy seller is likely to offer the best price in the end.

Specifications

	4-door notchback	5-door hatchback
Wheelbase, in.	95.7	95.7
Overall length, in.	170.7	170.7
Overall width, in.	65.2	65.2

KEY: **ohv** = overhead valve; **ohc** = overhead cam; **dohc** = double overhead cam; **I** = inline cylinders; **V** = cylinders in V configuration; **flat** = horizontally opposed cylinders; **bbl.** = barrel (carburetor); **PFI** = port (multi-point) fuel injection; **TBI** = throttle-body (single-point) fuel injection; **rpm** = revolutions per minute; **OD** = overdrive transmission; **S** = standard; **O** = optional; **NA** = not available.

	4-door notchback	5-door hatchback
Overall height, in.	52.4	52.3
Turn diameter, ft.	31.5	31.5
Curb weight, lbs.	2321	2376
Cargo vol., cu. ft.	11.2	32.2
Fuel capacity, gals.	13.2	13.2
Seating capacity	5	5
Front headroom, in.	38.3	38.3
Front shoulder room, in.	53.2	53.2
Front legroom, max., in.	40.9	40.9
Rear headroom, in.	36.1	35.5
Rear shoulder room, in.	52.7	52.7
Rear legroom, min., in.	31.6	31.6

Powertrain layout: transverse front engine/front-wheel drive.

Engines

	dohc I-4	dohc I-4
Size, liters/cu. in.	1.6/98	1.6/98
Fuel delivery	PFI	PFI
Horsepower @ rpm	102 @ 5800	130 @ 6800
Torque (lbs./ft.) @ rpm	101 @ 4800	105 @ 6000
Availability	S	S[1]

EPA city/highway mpg

5-speed OD manual	28/34	25/31
3-speed automatic	25/29	
4-speed OD automatic		23/30

1. GSi.

Prices

Geo Prizm	Retail Price	Dealer Invoice	Low Price
4-door notchback	$10125	$9315	$9515
5-door hatchback	10425	9591	9791
GSi 4-door notchback	11900	10948	11148
GSi 5-door hatchback	12285	11302	11502
Destination charge	335	335	335

Standard equipment:

1.6-liter DOHC PFI 4-cylinder engine, 5-speed manual transmission, velour reclining front bucket seats, tinted glass, door pockets, cup holders, left remote mirror, folding rear seat (hatchbacks), remote fuel door release, bodyside molding, 175/70SR13 SBR tires. **GSi** adds: higher-output engine, power steering, uprated suspension, sport seats, tachometer and oil pressure gauge, rear spoiler, rear wiper/washer (hatchback), left remote and right manual mirrors, AM/FM radio, 185/60HR14 Goodyear Eagle tires on alloy wheels.

Optional equipment:

Air conditioning	690	587	621
Power sunroof	530	451	477
Preferred Group 1, base	609	518	548
Power steering, AM/FM radio, left remote and right manual mirrors, full wheel covers.			
Preferred Group 2, base	1074	913	967
Group 1 plus 3-speed automatic transmission.			
Preferred Group 3, base	1554	1321	1399
Group 2 plus air conditioning, 5-speed manual transmission, power locks, remote decklid/hatch release.			
Preferred Group 4, base	2019	1716	1817
Group 3 plus 3-speed automatic transmission.			

	Retail Price	Dealer Invoice	Low Price
LSi Preferred Group 5, base 4-door	2084	1771	1876
Base 5-door	2019	1716	1817

Group 4 plus 5-speed manual transmission, console with storage box, soft-feel steering wheel, visor mirrors, assist grips, split folding rear seat, rear wiper/washer (5-door), tilt steering column.

LSi Preferred Group 6, base 4-door	2549	2167	2294
Base 5-door	2484	2111	2236

Group 5 plus 3-speed automatic transmission.

LSi Preferred Group 7, base 4-door	3049	2592	2744
Base 5-door	2984	2536	2686

Group 6 plus power windows, cruise control, intermittent wipers.

GSi Preferred Group 2	775	659	698

4-speed automatic transmission.

GSi Preferred Group 3, 4-door	1059	900	953
5-door	909	773	818

Group 2 plus 5-speed manual transmission, air conditioning, split folding rear seat, tilt steering column, remote decklid/hatch release, floormats, visor mirrors.

GSi Preferred Group 4, 4-door	1834	1559	1651
5-door	1684	1431	1516

Group 3 plus 4-speed automatic transmission.

GSi Preferred Group 5, 4-door	1904	1618	1714
5-door	1754	1491	1579

Group 4 plus 5-speed manual transmission, AM/FM cassette, power windows and locks, cruise control, intermittent wipers.

GSi Preferred Group 6, 4-door	2679	2277	2411
5-door	2529	2150	2276

Group 5 plus 4-speed automatic transmission.

AM/FM cassette	140	119	126
Floormats	40	34	36
California emissions pkg.	100	85	90

Geo Storm

Geo Storm GSi

What's New

Chevrolet's import outlet, Geo, gets a subcompact performance coupe for '90, the Storm. The front-drive, 2300-pound 2 + 2 hatchback is made by Isuzu in Japan. Storm's 96.5-inch wheelbase and 163.4-inch overall length slot it in size between the 2-seat Honda CRX and the new Plymouth Laser/Mitsubishi Eclipse 2 + 2s. Two Storm models are available. The base coupe is aimed at style-conscious shoppers on a budget. It has a 1.6-liter, 12-valve 4-cylinder engine rated at 95 horsepower. Targeting the junior sports-car crowd is the GSi, with its 130-horsepower 16-valve, double-overhead cam, 1.6-liter four. Both Storms have 4-wheel independent suspension, power steering, 185/60R14 tires, front-disc and rear-drum brakes, and a driver's-side air bag. The GSi gets aero body add-ons, alloy wheels, road-tuned suspension, sports seats, and upgraded gauges. A 5-speed manual transmission is standard; a 3-speed automatic is optional on the base car, a 4-speed automatic is optional on the GSi.

For

- Performance (GSi)   ● Handling   ● Air bag

Against

- Rear seat room   ● Cargo room

Summary

Blowing into a crowded sporty subcompact scene, the new Storm shapes up as a formidable force. An important consideration in this market is styling. Storm scores here. Its combination of planes and curves are not obviously derivative of its competitors, yet the car looks cute enough in base form and aggressive enough in bespoiled GSi trim to interest a wide range of buyers. Inside, you'll find some nice touches and a sporty feel. The supportive front bucket seats are quite low to the floor and don't adjust for height. This helps head room, but combined with a steep wraparound dashboard and a rather high beltline, the cabin can be a tad claustrophobic. The analog instrumentation is clear and unobstructed, the controls are simple but feel plasticy. An air bag is in the hub of a steering wheel that's unadjustable for height or reach, but the driving position is good overall. There are plenty of storage bins, but the rear seat is so small as to be virtually useless for anything but inanimate objects. Underway, the dohc 1.6-liter four in the GSi is quite willing, but must be revved above 4000 rpm to produce any snap. Highway cruising can be somewhat buzzy, as the GSi engine turns 3300 rpm in fifth gear at 65 mph. Both Storms boast sharp steering and a light clutch, though their shift action is a little rubbery. Both are nimble in corners and the GSi in particular has the kind of friendly nature that encourages you to drive it with brio right out of the box.

Specifications

	3-door hatchback
Wheelbase, in.	96.5
Overall length, in.	163.4
Overall width, in.	66.7
Overall height, in.	51.1
Turn diameter, ft.	32.2
Curb weight, lbs.	2282
Cargo vol., cu. ft.	10.9
Fuel capacity, gals.	12.4
Seating capacity	4
Front headroom, in.	37.5
Front shoulder room, in.	53.3
Front legroom, max., in.	43.8
Rear headroom, in.	31.9
Rear shoulder room, in.	51.2
Rear legroom, min., in.	30.4

Powertrain layout: transverse front engine/front-wheel drive.

Engines	ohc I-4	dohc I-4
Size, liters/cu. in.	1.6/98	1.6/98
Fuel delivery	PFI	PFI
Horsepower @ rpm	95 @ 5800	130 @ 7000
Torque (lbs./ft.) @ rpm	97 @ 4800	102 @ 5800
Availability	S	S[1]

Prices are accurate at time of printing; subject to manufacturer's change.

EPA city/highway mpg	ohc I-4	dohc I-4
5-speed OD manual	31/36	26/34
3-speed automatic	24/32	24/32

1. GSi.

Prices

Geo Storm	Retail Price	Dealer Invoice	Low Price
3-door hatchback	$10390	$9351	—
GSi 3-door hatchback	11650	10485	—
Destination charge	315	315	315

Standard equipment:

1.6-liter 12-valve PFI 4-cylinder engine, 5-speed manual transmission, power steering, driver's-side airbag, cloth and vinyl reclining front bucket seats, one-piece folding rear seatback, AM/FM radio, rear defogger, remote mirrors, tachometer, tinted glass, door pockets, visor mirror, remote hatch release. **GSi** adds: DOHC 16-valve engine, sport suspension, faster steering ratio, contoured front seats with bolsters, rocker extensions, rear spoiler, oil pressure gauge, V-rated tires.

Optional equipment:

Air conditioning	690	587	621
Preferred Group 2, base	545	463	491
3-speed automatic transmission.			
Preferred Group 2, GSi	745	633	671
4-speed automatic transmission.			
AM/FM cassette	140	119	126
California emissions pkg.	70	60	63
Floormats	30	26	27

Geo Tracker

Geo Tracker

What's New

Geo's version of this Suzuki-designed 4-wheel-drive compact sport utility gets an uplevel convertible model for '90. Called the LSi Convertible, the new drop top shares its appointments with the top-of-the-line LSi hardtop. The base and LSi hardtop and the base convertible are carried over with few changes. Tracker is a larger and more modern big brother to the much-maligned Suzuki Samurai, which started the mini-4×4 revolution in 1986. Some Trackers are built in Japan by Suzuki, others are manufactured in Ontario, Canada, by CAMI, a Suzuki/General Motors of Canada joint venture. Suzuki sells the Tracker under the Sidekick name, though it offers the vehicle with 2WD as well as 4WD. All Trackers use a fuel-injected 1.6-liter 4-cylinder engine. A 5-speed manual transmission is standard and a 3-speed automatic is optional. Standard is an on-demand, part-time 4WD system (not for use on dry pavement) with a floor-mounted transfer case. The manual locking front hubs have to be engaged by hand from outside the vehicle before 4WD can be employed. Power steering is unavailable. Rear shoulder belts and 5-mph bumpers are standard. All Trackers sport two new exterior colors and new standard interior trim for '90. Convertibles have a removable canvas top that can be folded part-way back for a sunroof-like effect. LSi versions add to the base models such standard features as tinted glass, upgraded seats, intermittent wipers, and larger tires on 15-inch chrome rally wheels. The LSi hardtop gets a rear wiper/washer.

For

- 4WD traction   • Driveability

Against

- Inconvenient 4WD system   • Ride   • Rear seat room

Summary

The Tracker/Sidekick is a vast improvement over the smaller, cruder, and slower Samurai. Tracker's engine has adequate power for everyday use and with the easy-shifting 5-speed gives the 4×4 a sporty flair. Though its large tires take the jarring edge off rough pavement, Tracker's ride is still quite choppy. The Tracker is tall and narrow and its high center of gravity must be treated with respect when changing direction; the copious body lean should scare you into low cornering speeds. The driver's bucket seat doesn't have much rearward travel or shoulder room on the left, while the 2-place rear seat is best suited for children. Cargo space behind the rear seat is minuscule, though it's ample with the seat folded forward. If you want a small 4WD sport-utility with a "cute" body and a reasonable price, Tracker is a place to start. It's less expensive than any of the larger 4×4s, which don't offer convertible versions. It also undercuts most Jeep Wranglers while feeling more modern and refined than the Jeep stalwart. Though their appeal is clear, none of these vehicles really makes a good daily driver. Safety considerations aside, their ride is too rough, their noise levels too high.

Specifications

	2-door wagon
Wheelbase, in.	86.6
Overall length, in.	142.5
Overall width, in.	64.2
Overall height, in.	65.0
Turn diameter, ft.	32.2
Curb weight, lbs.	2238
Cargo vol., cu. ft.	31.9
Fuel capacity, gals.	11.1
Seating capacity	4
Front headroom, in.	39.5
Front shoulder room, in.	52.1
Front legroom, max., in.	42.1
Rear headroom, in.	38.3
Rear shoulder room, in.	50.2
Rear legroom, min., in.	31.7

Powertrain layout: *longitudinal front engine/rear-wheel drive or on-demand 4WD.*

Engines

	ohc I-4
Size, liters/cu. in.	1.6/97
Fuel delivery	TBI
Horsepower @ rpm	80 @ 5500
Torque (lbs./ft.) @ rpm	94 @ 3000
Availability	S
EPA city/highway mpg	
5-speed OD manual	28/29
3-speed automatic	25/26

Prices

Geo Tracker	Retail Price	Dealer Invoice	Low Price
3-door wagon	$11035	$10373	$10473
LSi 3-door wagon	12245	11510	11610
2-door convertible	10725	10082	10182
LSi 2-door convertible	11795	11087	11187
Destination charge	270	270	270

Standard equipment:

1.6-liter TBI 4-cylinder engine, 5-speed manual transmission, part-time 4-wheel drive, cloth reclining front bucket seats, folding rear bench seat, rear shoulder belts, tachometer, coolant temperature gauge, trip odometer, door pockets, assist straps, dual outside mirrors, tow hooks, rear defogger (except convertible), 205/75R15 all-terrain tires with full-size spare. **LSi** adds: tinted glass, upgraded upholstery, spare tire cover, rear bucket seats, intermittent wipers, rear wiper/washer, RWL tires on chrome wheels.

Optional equipment:

Air conditioning	695	612	626
Power steering	275	242	248
Preferred Group 2, base & LSi	565	497	509
3-speed automatic transmission.			
Spare tire cover, base	33	29	30
Floormats	28	25	25
AM/FM radio	302	266	272
AM/FM cassette	441	388	397
Transfer case shield	75	66	68
Trailering special equipment	109	96	98
Wiring harness and trailer hitch.			

Honda Accord

What's New

The new Accord that went on sale in October rides a 4.7-inch longer wheelbase and is 5.1 inches longer overall, making it nearly mid-sized. While primary targets remain Japanese compacts such as the Toyota Camry, Honda also mentions the mid-size Ford Taurus as one of the new Accord's rivals. Styling on the new Accord evolves from the 1986-89 generation's; the most apparent change is at the front, where flush-mounted, exposed headlamps replace the hidden headlamps of the previous model. Two body styles are offered, a 4-door notchback sedan and a 2-door notchback coupe. The 3-door hatchback, part of the roster since Accord debuted for 1976, has been discontinued. Hatchback sales in general, and Accord hatchback sales in particular, have been declining. Next year, a 5-door station wagon conceived, designed, and built in the U.S. will join the lineup. The new Accord still has front-wheel drive and a transverse-mounted 4-cylinder engine. However, the engine is a new 2.2-liter aluminum design that replaces a pair of 2.0-liter fours, one carbureted and one fuel

Honda Accord EX

injected. The new 2.2 comes two ways: 125 horsepower in the base DX and mid-level LX models and 130 horsepower in the top-shelf EX (which replaces last year's LXi), both with multi-point fuel injection. A dual exhaust manifold on the EX boosts horsepower by five. Two new transmissions are available, a standard 5-speed manual and a 4-speed automatic with Normal and Sport shift modes. All models have motorized front shoulder belts with manual lap belts. Most 4-door Accords sold in the U.S. and all 2-door Accords are built in Ohio. In addition, engines and other components are now built at Honda's Ohio facilities and the company says U.S. Accords have more than 70 percent domestic content, including labor.

For

- Ride • Handling/roadholding • Passenger room
- Cargo space • Driveability • Visibility

Against

- Road noise • Rear seat comfort

Summary

On the outside, the new Accord looks like a conservative update of the previous generation, with few substantive changes. On the inside, though, the new Accord is much roomier. The extra 4.7 inches in the wheelbase provides generous rear-seat leg room, while a 1.4-inch increase in body height improves head room. Cargo room has also increased; the trunk on both body styles is deep, wide at the rear, and easy to load, thanks to a bumper-height opening. The rear seatback on all models flops down for extra cargo space. Honda's advertising slogan for the new Accord is, "You have to drive it to believe it;" We drove it and we believe it boasts several performance improvements. The new engines are quieter and smoother; the new automatic transmission has smoother shift quality; wind noise has been reduced; and a new variable-assist power steering system changes the amount of assist gradually, rather than abruptly, as on the old model. The new Accord corners with less body lean and better road grip, thanks partly to larger standard tires (14-inch instead of 13-inch on the DX and LX, and 15-inch on the EX). The ride is absorbent, yet stable and well-controlled at high

> **KEY: ohv** = overhead valve; **ohc** = overhead cam; **dohc** = double overhead cam; **I** = inline cylinders; **V** = cylinders in V configuration; **flat** = horizontally opposed cylinders; **bbl.** = barrel (carburetor); **PFI** = port (multi-point) fuel injection; **TBI** = throttle-body (single-point) fuel injection; **rpm** = revolutions per minute; **OD** = overdrive transmission; **S** = standard; **O** = optional; **NA** = not available.

Prices are accurate at time of printing; subject to manufacturer's change.

speeds. A comfortable position behind the wheel and an attractive, convenient dashboard design help drivers feel at home in the new Accord, while tall windows and slim roof pillars aid visibility. There are a few disappointments. The new Accord has more power, but also more weight (275 pounds more on the 4-door), so there isn't much improvement in acceleration. Accord still delivers more than adequate pickup and brisk passing response, but since Honda intends to compete with Taurus and other mid-size cars, a V-6 engine would help. The arch-rival Camry already has one, but Honda has been mum about whether it will offer a V-6. Also missing are anti-lock brakes, which are available on Taurus, Camry, and several other competitors. Honda indicates anti-lock brakes will be available for 1991. While the new Accord has little engine or wind noise on the highway, road noise intrudes as an unwelcome interior guest, spoiling an otherwise quiet ambience. Finally, the rear seat is much roomier, but the seatback is so reclined that it forces passengers to practically lie down to enjoy any shoulder support; a more upright seating position would be more comfortable. However, the new Accord's spacious interior, greater refinement, solid construction, improved dynamic qualities, and impressive overall quality make it a fine choice, whether you consider it a large compact car or a small mid-size. Prices are $700 to $800 higher this year, not a huge jump considering the larger dimensions. As with the previous generation, the mid-level LX models, at about $15,000 to $16,000, offer the most value.

Specifications

	2-door notchback	4-door notchback
Wheelbase, in.	107.1	107.1
Overall length, in.	184.8	184.8
Overall width, in.	67.9	67.9
Overall height, in.	53.9	54.7
Turn diameter, ft.	36.1	36.1
Curb weight, lbs.	2738	2773
Cargo vol., cu. ft.	14.4	14.4
Fuel capacity, gals.	17.0	17.0
Seating capacity	5	5
Front headroom, in.	38.8	38.9
Front shoulder room, in.	54.9	54.8
Front legroom, max., in.	42.9	42.6
Rear headroom, in.	36.5	37.5
Rear shoulder room, in.	54.3	54.8
Rear legroom, min., in.	32.3	34.3

Powertrain layout: transverse front engine/front-wheel drive.

Engines

	ohc I-4	ohc I-4
Size, liters/cu. in.	2.2/132	2.2/132
Fuel delivery	PFI	PFI
Horsepower @ rpm	125 @ 5200	130 @ 5200
Torque (lbs./ft.) @ rpm	137 @ 4000	142 @ 4000
Availability	S[1]	S[2]

EPA city/highway mpg

5-speed OD manual	24/30	24/30
4-speed OD automatic	22/28	22/28

1. DX, LX   2. EX.

KEY: ohv = overhead valve; **ohc** = overhead cam; **dohc** = double overhead cam; **I** = inline cylinders; **V** = cylinders in V configuration; **flat** = horizontally opposed cylinders; **bbl.** = barrel (carburetor); **PFI** = port (multi-point) fuel injection; **TBI** = throttle-body (single-point) fuel injection; **rpm** = revolutions per minute; **OD** = overdrive transmission; **S** = standard; **O** = optional; **NA** = not available.

Prices

Honda Accord	Retail Price	Dealer Invoice	Low Price
DX 2-door notchback, 5-speed	$12145	$10201	$10900
DX 2-door notchback, automatic	12895	10831	10574
LX 2-door notchback, 5-speed	14695	12343	13189
LX 2-door notchback, automatic	15445	12973	13862
EX 2-door notchback, 5-speed	16395	13771	14715
EX 2-door notchback, automatic	17145	14401	15388
DX 4-door notchback, 5-speed	12345	10369	11080
DX 4-door notchback, automatic	13095	10999	11753
LX 4-door notchback, 5-speed	14895	12511	13369
LX 4-door notchback, automatic	15645	13141	14042
EX 4-door notchback, 5-speed	16595	13939	14895
EX 4-door notchback, automatic	17345	14569	15568
Destination charge	245	245	245

Standard equipment:

DX: 2.2-liter SOHC 16-valve PFI 4-cylinder engine, 5-speed manual or 4-speed automatic transmission, power steering, cloth reclining front bucket seats, folding rear seatback, tachometer, coolant temperature gauge, trip odometer, tinted glass, tilt steering column, intermittent wipers, rear defogger, remote fuel door and decklid releases, door pockets, rear shoulder belts, 185/70R14 tires. **LX** adds: air conditioning, cruise control, power windows and locks, power mirrors, AM/FM cassette, rear armrest, beverage holder. **EX** adds: driver's seat lumbar support adjuster, front spoiler, power sunroof, sport suspension, 195/60R15 Michelin MXV3 tires on alloy wheels.

OPTIONS are available as dealer-installed accessories.

Honda Civic

Honda Civic EX

What's New

A new EX 4-door with a 108-horsepower engine has been added, while all versions of the subcompact Civic have new instrument panels with larger gauges. The EX 4-door, which supplants the LX as the top-of-the-line model, uses the same 1.6-liter 4-cylinder engine as the sporty Civic Si hatchback. The EX also has 14-inch tires instead of the LX's 13-inchers, and larger front disc brakes. All hatchbacks and 4-door models have new front and rear bumpers for 1990, and new taillamp designs. The DX 4-door also gains a fold-down rear seatback. This year's lineup includes the base Civic Hatchback, with a 70-horsepower 1.5-liter engine; DX hatchback and 4-door sedan, and the LX 4-door, with a 92-horsepower 1.5-liter engine; and the EX 4-door and Si hatchback with the 108-horsepower 1.6-liter engine. All have front-wheel drive. The 5-door wagon again comes two ways: front-wheel drive with the 92-

horsepower engine and 4-wheel drive with the 108-horse-power engine. The 4WD system engages automatically, distributing power to the rear wheels as needed to maintain traction. The base Hatchback and Si come only with manual transmissions; a 4-speed automatic is available on all other Civics. Hatchbacks have 3-point front seat belts that can be left buckled all the time, while the 4-doors and wagons have motorized front shoulder belts with separate manual lap belts. All 1990 Civic 4-door models sold in the U.S. will be built in Ohio and all hatchbacks will be built in Canada; only wagons will be imported from Japan.

For

- Fuel economy
- Acceleration (Si, EX)
- Visibility
- 4WD traction (Wagon)
- Resale value

Against

- Cargo space (hatchbacks)
- Noise
- Driveability (auto transmission)

Summary

Civic ranks at the top of the subcompact class because of its overall quality, high refinement, and good resale value. The fact that it's also enjoyable to drive puts it a couple of more notches higher above most rivals. A Civic Si or EX with the 5-speed manual transmission displays the frisky eagerness of a sports car. An LX or DX with the 5-speed is no slouch either (11.5 seconds to 60 mph in our test). With automatic transmission you'll lose a little acceleration, but not so much that we would advise you to stick with manual shift. The automatic shifts roughly at times and hunts annoyingly between gears in the 40-55 mph range, but returns impressive fuel economy. We averaged 26.7 mpg in urban driving with an LX/automatic. By comparison, we averaged 28.7 with a DX hatchback/5-speed and 28.6 with an Si from similar driving. Road noise can be intrusive on all models at highway speeds, and especially on the hatchbacks because of the open cargo area. All versions have adequate space for four people (five in a pinch) and simple, functional dashboards with clearly marked gauges and handy controls. The hatchbacks suffer from having too little cargo room behind the rear seat; you'll have to fold the rear seatback to carry more than a few grocery bags. Dependability and the promise of high resale value compensate for Civic's prices, which are higher than most competitors'. You'll pay more for a Civic, but you'll get your money's worth.

Specifications

	3-door hatchback	4-door notchback	5-door wagon
Wheelbase, in.	98.4	98.4	98.4
Overall length, in.	157.1	168.8	161.7
Overall width, in.	66.3	66.7	66.1
Overall height, in.	52.5	53.5	56.1
Turn diameter, ft.	32.4	32.4	32.2
Curb weight, lbs.	2127	2262	2335[1]
Cargo vol., cu. ft.	25.0	12.0	60.3
Fuel capacity, gals.	11.9	11.9	11.9
Seating capacity	5	5	5
Front headroom, in.	38.2	38.5	39.4
Front shoulder room, in.	53.5	53.5	53.5
Front legroom, max., in.	43.3	43.1	41.2
Rear headroom, in.	36.6	37.4	38.0
Rear shoulder room, in.	53.2	53.0	53.5
Rear legroom, min., in.	30.4	32.0	33.2

1. 2628 lbs., 4WD Wagon.

Powertrain layout: transverse front engine/front-wheel drive or automatic 4WD (Wagon).

Engines

	ohc I-4	ohc I-4	ohc I-4
Size, liters/cu. in.	1.5/91	1.5/91	1.6/97
Fuel delivery	TBI	TBI	PFI
Horsepower @ rpm	70 @ 5500	92 @ 6000	108 @ 6000
Torque (lbs./ft.) @ rpm	83 @ 3000	89 @ 4500	100 @ 5000
Availability	S[1]	S[2]	S[3]

EPA city/highway mpg

4-speed OD manual	33/37		
5-speed OD manual		31/34	28/32
6-speed OD manual			24/26
4-speed OD automatic		28/33	25/29

1. Hatchback   2. DX, LX, 2WD Wagon   3. Si, EX, 4WD Wagon.

Prices

Honda Civic	Retail Price	Dealer Invoice	Low Price
3-door hatchback, 4-speed	$6635	$5971	$6271
DX 3-door hatchback, 5-speed	8695	7390	7640
DX 3-door hatchback, automatic	9575	8138	8388
Si 3-door hatchback, 5-speed	10245	8708	8958
DX 4-door notchback, 5-speed	9440	8024	8324
DX 4-door notchback, automatic	10370	8814	9114
LX 4-door notchback, 5-speed	10450	8882	9182
LX 4-door notchback, automatic	11150	9477	9777
EX 4-door notchback, 5-speed	11145	9473	9773
EX 4-door notchback, automatic	11845	10068	10368
2WD 5-door wagon, 5-speed	10325	8776	9076
2WD 5-door wagon, automatic	11370	9664	9964
4WD 5-door wagon, 6-speed	12410	10548	10848
4WD 5-door wagon, automatic	13140	11169	11469
Destination charge	245	245	245

Standard equipment:

1.5-liter TBI 16-valve 70-bhp 4-cylinder engine, 4-speed manual transmission, reclining front bucket seats, 50/50 split folding rear seatback, rear shoulder belts, remote fuel door and hatch releases, tinted glass, rear defogger, 165/70R13 tires. **DX** adds: 92-bhp engine, 5-speed manual or 4-speed automatic transmission, power steering (with automatic transmission), rear wiper/washer (hatchback), tilt steering column, cargo cover (hatchback), intermittent wipers, 175/70R14 tires. **Si** adds: 108-bhp PFI engine, dual manual mirrors, power moonroof, digital clock, tachometer, sport seats, 185/60R14 tires. **LX** adds to DX 4-door: power mirrors, power windows and locks, cruise control, digital clock, tachometer. **EX** adds: 108-bhp PFI engine, upgraded interior trim, 175/65HR14 tires. **2WD wagon** has DX equipment plus digital clock, tachometer; **4WD wagon** has 108-bhp PFI engine, 6-speed manual or 4-speed automatic transmission, permanent 4WD.

OPTIONS are available as dealer-installed accessories.

Honda CRX

What's New

New bumpers and a new instrument panel are the major changes for 1990 on the CRX, Honda's front-drive, 2-seat hatchback. The new bumpers are complemented by new front turn signals and taillamps. Inside, the instrument panel retains the basic layout of the previous design, but has larger gauges. The CRX Si gains rear disc brakes this year (in place of drum brakes) and new-design alloy wheels. The Si is powered by

Prices are accurate at time of printing; subject to manufacturer's change.

Honda CRX HF

a 108-horsepower 1.6-liter 4-cylinder engine and comes only with a 5-speed manual transmission. The base CRX HF has a 62-horsepower 1.5-liter and also comes only with a 5-speed manual, but it's geared for fuel economy, not acceleration; the HF earns EPA estimates of 49 mpg city and 52 highway. The mid-level CRX comes with a 92-horsepower 1.5-liter engine and a choice of 5-speed manual or 4-speed automatic transmissions. CRX meets the federal passive-restraint requirement with 3-point front seat belts that can be left buckled all the time for automatic deployment.

For

- Acceleration (CRX, Si) • Fuel economy
- Handling/maneuverability

Against

- Driveability (automatic transmission) • Ride • Noise

Summary

Two-seaters are supposed to be fun to drive, and the CRX certainly is, but they aren't supposed to be practical, and the CRX is that, too. It's practical because the seats have enough rearward travel to allow tall people to stretch their legs, partly compensating for a lack of headroom. The cargo area is big enough for most routine chores or a twosome's luggage, and the interior has several storage bins and pockets for small items. Where the CRX is really practical is in fuel economy; we averaged 29 mpg with a hot-shot Si last year from urban commuting. We would expect well into the 30s on the highway, and into the 40s with the miserly HF model. A mid-level CRX with the 5-speed manual or an Si are the logical choices if brisk acceleration is your priority. You'll lose some zip with automatic transmission on the CRX; the automatic requires a heavy throttle foot to induce downshifts for passing power and shifts abruptly at times. By contrast, the slick-shifting 5-speed manual and smooth clutch have light, precise action. CRX's petite size and low center of gravity help it take corners with remarkable agility and minimal body lean. Power steering isn't offered, so you supply all the turning muscle. The ride can be quite harsh on rough surfaces, especially in the Si model, and the interior is constantly bombarded by engine,

wind, and road noise, so living with a CRX isn't always a bowl of cherries. However, if you're after high times at low cost, this is one little car that should keep you smiling most of the time, even if the price of gasoline goes way up.

Specifications

	3-door hatchback
Wheelbase, in.	90.6
Overall length, in.	148.5
Overall width, in.	65.9
Overall height, in.	50.1
Turn diameter, ft.	30.4
Curb weight, lbs.	1967
Cargo vol., cu. ft.	23.2
Fuel capacity, gals.	11.9[1]
Seating capacity	2
Front headroom, in.	37.0
Front shoulder room, in.	53.5
Front legroom, max., in.	40.8
Rear headroom, in.	—
Rear shoulder room, in.	—
Rear legroom, min., in.	—

1. 10.6 gals., HF.

Powertrain layout: transverse front engine/front-wheel drive.

Engines	ohc I-4	ohc I-4	ohc I-4
Size, liters/cu. in.	1.5/91	1.5/91	1.6/97
Fuel delivery	PFI	TBI	PFI
Horsepower @ rpm	62 @ 4500	92 @ 6000	108 @ 6000
Torque (lbs./ft.) @ rpm	90 @ 2000	89 @ 4500	100 @ 5000
Availability	S[1]	S[2]	S[3]
EPA city/highway mpg			
5-speed OD manual	49/52	32/35	28/33
4-speed OD automatic		29/35	

1. HF   2. CRX   3. Si.

Prices

Honda CRX	Retail Price	Dealer Invoice	Low Price
HF 3-door hatchback, 5-speed	$9145	$7773	$8073
3-door hatchback, 5-speed	9410	7999	8296
3-door hatchback, automatic	10010	8509	8808
Si 3-door hatchback, 5-speed	11130	9461	9760
Destination charge	245	245	245

Honda CRX Si

KEY: **ohv** = overhead valve; **ohc** = overhead cam; **dohc** = double overhead cam; **I** = inline cylinders; **V** = cylinders in V configuration; **flat** = horizontally opposed cylinders; **bbl.** = barrel (carburetor); **PFI** = port (multi-point) fuel injection; **TBI** = throttle-body (single-point) fuel injection; **rpm** = revolutions per minute; **OD** = overdrive transmission; **S** = standard; **O** = optional; **NA** = not available.

Standard equipment:

HF: 1.5-liter 8-valve PFI 4-cylinder engine, 5-speed manual transmission, reclining front bucket seats, left remote mirror, tinted glass, tachometer, coolant temperature gauge, trip odometer, intermittent wipers, rear defogger, remote fuel door and hatch releases, bodyside moldings, 165/70R13 tires. **CRX** adds: 1.5-liter SOHC 16-valve PFI engine, tilt steering column, dual remote mirrors, rear wiper/washer, cargo cover. **Si** adds: 1.6-liter engine, 4-wheel disc brakes, sport suspension, power sunroof, front spoiler, 185/60HR14 tires on alloy wheels.

OPTIONS are available as dealer-installed accessories.

Honda Prelude

1989 Honda Prelude

What's New

Nothing is new on the front-drive Prelude sports coupe until early in 1990, when a slightly larger engine and minor cosmetic changes will be introduced. Until then, Honda dealers will be selling 1989 models. Details on the 1990 models weren't available, but the slight increase in engine displacement will be slight indeed—about three cubic inches. Horsepower and torque will grow a little as well. Here's how the carryover 1989 models line up: The base S is powered by a 104-horsepower 2.0-liter 4-cylinder with two single-barrel carburetors. The Si uses a 135-horsepower 2.0-liter engine with dual-overhead cams and multi-point fuel injection. The Si 4WS has the 135-horsepower engine and Honda's mechanical 4-wheel-steering system. With 4WS, the rear wheels steer a few degrees right or left, depending on steering-wheel angle, to improve handling and maneuverability. With 4WS, Prelude's turning diameter is 31.5 feet; without 4WS, it's 34.8. All models have 3-point front seat belts that can be left permanently buckled, thus satisfying the federal mandate for passive restraints. Prelude, available only as a 2-door coupe, was redesigned for 1988.

For
● Acceleration ● Handling/roadholding ● Braking

Against
● Passenger room ● Driveability (automatic transmission)

Summary

The current Prelude has been a sales disappointment, so if a local Honda dealer has several in stock that are collecting dust, you should be able to negotiate a good deal. Prelude is a good car that has suffered partly because of its conserva-

tive styling compared to rivals such as the Nissan 240SX, Mitsubishi Eclipse, and Toyota Celica. Underneath the skin, though, Prelude has a well-designed front-drive chassis that provides competent handling without a punishing ride, strong brakes, and high-revving engines that deliver brisk acceleration. The fuel-injected Si engine is the better of the two, not just because it has more power, but because it's easier to start than the carbureted engine and more responsive. The automatic transmission is slow to react to the throttle unless you tromp on the gas pedal and it shifts abruptly in hard acceleration. The 5-speed manual is precise and easy to manage in traffic, and helps get the most out of Prelude's engines. While 4WS improves Prelude's maneuverability, it doesn't do enough in routine driving to justify a $1485 price premium above the Si model. You can save even more on a base S model, though you'll lose some acceleration and standard features. Prelude isn't the most exciting sports coupe around, but it should be one of the most reliable and have good resale value.

Specifications

	2-door notchback
Wheelbase, in.	101.0
Overall length, in.	175.6
Overall width, in.	67.3
Overall height, in.	49.2
Turn diameter, ft.	34.8[1]
Curb weight, lbs.	2571
Cargo vol., cu. ft.	11.0
Fuel capacity, gals.	15.9
Seating capacity	4
Front headroom, in.	36.9
Front shoulder room, in.	53.1
Front legroom, max., in.	43.1
Rear headroom, in.	34.1
Rear shoulder room, in.	51.1
Rear legroom, min., in.	27.1

1. 31.5 ft., Si 4WS.

Powertrain layout: transverse front engine/front-wheel drive.

Engines	ohc I-4	dohc I-4
Size, liters/cu. in.	2.0/119	2.0/119
Fuel delivery	2 × 1 bbl.	PFI
Horsepower @ rpm	104 @ 5800	135 @ 6200
Torque (lbs./ft.) @ rpm	111 @ 4000	127 @ 4500
Availability	S[1]	S[2]

EPA city/highway mpg

5-speed OD manual	23/38	23/26
4-speed OD automatic	20/26	21/26

1. S 2. Si.

Prices

Honda Prelude (1989 prices)	Retail Price	Dealer Invoice	Low Price
S 2-door notchback, 5-speed	$13945	$11713	$12213
S 2-door notchback, automatic	14670	12322	12822
Si 2-door notchback, 5-speed	16965	14250	14750
Si 2-door notchback, automatic	17690	14859	15359
Si 4WS 2-door notchback, 5-speed	18450	15498	15998
Si 4WS 2-door notchback, automatic	19175	16107	16607
Destination charge	245	245	245

Prices are accurate at time of printing; subject to manufacturer's change.

Standard equipment:

S: 2.0-liter 12-valve carbureted 4-cylinder engine, 5-speed manual or 4-speed automatic transmission, power steering, 4-wheel disc brakes, cloth reclining front bucket seats, tilt steering column, console, AM/FM cassette, power antenna, tachometer, coolant temperature gauge, trip odometer, intermittent wipers, 185/70HR13 tires. **Si** adds: DOHC 16-valve PFI engine, air conditioning, cruise control, adjustable lumbar support and side bolsters, diversity antenna, 195/60HR14 tires. **Si 4WS** adds: 4-wheel steering, power door locks, bronze tinted glass, alloy wheels.

OPTIONS are available as dealer-installed accessories.

Hyundai Excel

Hyundai Excel

What's New

Hyundai came to the U.S four years ago with the subcompact Excel as its only model, but quickly claimed fourth place in import car sales, largely on the strength of bargain prices and liberal dealer financing. Hyundai has since slipped to fifth, but hopes this year's redesigned Excel will help it regain lost ground. Like the old Excel, the new one is built in Korea from a front-drive design derived from the Mitsubishi Mirage (a.k.a. Dodge/Plymouth Colt). Styling is wholly Hyundai's work and deliberately resembles that of the larger Sonata. Hyundai also builds more of the new Excel, relying less on its Japanese partner for major components and technical assistance (Mitsubishi owns part of Hyundai Motor Corporation). Models dwindle from eight to six: base and sporty GS 3-door hatchbacks, GL 5-door hatchback, and a notchback 4-door in base, GL, and top-shelf GLS trim. Interior volume gains three cubic feet, but other dimensions are little changed. Excel still uses a 1.5-liter 4-cylinder Mitsubishi-designed engine, but it now has 81-horsepower (instead of 68) and sequential multi-point fuel injection (instead of a carburetor). Base models come with a 4-speed overdrive manual transmission, others with a 5-speed manual or new 4-speed overdrive automatic. The overdrive automatic replaces a 3-speed automatic with direct-drive top gear. Like the previous Excel, Hyundai supplies the new one to U.S. Mitsubishi dealers for sale as the nearly-identical Precis, but only in the 3-door body style.

For

● Fuel economy ● Maneuverability ● Ride ● Price

Against

● Acceleration ● Handling ● Interior room ● Noise

Summary

It's hardly grown at all, but the new Excel is a more mature small car: quieter, smoother-riding, and happier with automatic transmission than the first-generation model. Economy is still a plus, but performance remains only adequate with either transmission (0-60 mph: nearly 15 seconds with automatic, about 12 with manual). The 5-speed isn't as slick as the best Japanese gearboxes but is good enough. The new automatic shifts with a jolt at full throttle, a common problem in small-engine cars, but is otherwise smooth. The overdrive top gear provides reasonably relaxed cruising (2700 rpm at 60 mph). Hyundai has much to learn about taming road noise, which borders on excessive even for a low-end car. Soft springing means a compliant ride but also sloppy cornering, aggravated by skinny tires that howl at the mere hint of a change in direction. Interior room remains adequate for four, five if you must. The main deficits are limited rear leg room and little head clearance for 6-footers beneath the optional power moonroof. Interior materials, if still far from opulent, look a step up from those of past Excels. However, one brand-new test car we drove had excessive orange-peel texture in the paint, a bird-like chirp from the moonroof over bumps, loose carpet around the console, and front headrest inserts that wouldn't stay in. If Hyundai would sweat such details, the Excel would be a serious competitor for subcompact stars like the Honda Civic and Toyota Corolla. For now, it's still mainly for those who value a rock-bottom price over first-rate fit and finish. Be advised that availability may be limited until dealers clear bulging stocks of the old model, which hasn't been selling well lately.

Specifications

	3-door hatchback	5-door hatchback	4-door notchback
Wheelbase, in.	93.9	93.9	93.9
Overall length, in.	161.4	161.4	163.3
Overall width, in.	63.2	63.2	63.2
Overall height, in.	54.5	54.5	54.5
Turn diameter, ft.	30.2	30.2	30.2
Curb weight, lbs.	2040	NA	2185
Cargo vol., cu. ft.	14.2	14.2	11.4
Fuel capacity, gals.	11.9	11.9	11.9
Seating capacity	5	5	5
Front headroom, in.	37.8	37.8	37.8
Front shoulder room, in.	52.2	52.2	52.2
Front legroom, max., in.	41.7	41.7	41.7
Rear headroom, in.	37.6	37.6	37.6
Rear shoulder room, in.	52.2	52.2	52.2
Rear legroom, min., in.	33.1	33.1	33.1

Powertrain layout: transverse front engine/front-wheel drive.

Engines

	ohc I-4
Size, liters/cu. in.	1.5/90
Fuel delivery	PFI
Horsepower @ rpm	81 @ 5500
Torque (lbs./ft.) @ rpm	91 @ 3000
Availability	S

EPA city/highway mpg

4-speed OD manual	29/33
5-speed OD manual	29/36
4-speed OD automatic	28/32

Prices

Hyundai Excel	Retail Price	Dealer Invoice	Low Price
3-door hatchback, 4-speed	$5899	—	—
3-door hatchback, automatic	6474	—	—
GS 3-door hatchback, 5-speed	6999	—	—
GS 3-door hatchback, automatic	7499	—	—
GL 5-door hatchback, 5-speed	7599	—	—
GL 5-door hatchback, automatic	8099	—	—
4-door notchback, 4-speed	6999	—	—
4-door notchback, automatic	7574	—	—
GL 4-door notchback, 5-speed	7879	—	—
GL 4-door notchback, automatic	8379	—	—
GLS 4-door notchback, 5-speed	8479	—	—
GLS 4-door notchback, automatic	8979	—	—

Dealer invoice, low price and destination charge not available at time of publication.

Standard equipment:

1.5-liter PFI 4-cylinder engine, 4-speed manual transmission, cloth-insert reclining front bucket seats, 60/40 split rear seat (hatchbacks), rear defogger, trip odometer, center console, locking fuel door, variable intermittent wipers, cargo cover, rear shoulder belts, 155/80R13 tires. **GS** adds: 5-speed manual or 4-speed automatic transmission, sport seats with driver's-side lumbar support and cushion height adjustments, upgraded upholstery, wheel covers, 175/70R13 tires. **GL** adds to base: digital clock, remote OS mirrors, tinted glass, rear wiper/washer (5-door), door pockets, remote fuel door and decklid/hatch releases, wheel covers, upgraded upholstery, right visor mirror, console with cassette storage, 60/40 split rear seat, rear heat ducts. **GLS** adds: AM/FM cassette, upgraded carpet, windshield sunshade band, 6-way driver's seat, tilt steering column, storage tray under passenger seat.

Optional equipment:

Air conditioning	755	—	—
Power steering, GS & GLS	260	—	—
Power Steering/Tilt Wheel Pkg., GL	335	—	—
Alloy wheels, GS & GLS	250	—	—
Alloy Wheel Pkg., GS & GLS	325	—	—
Includes 175/70R13 tires.			
Console armrest, GL, GS & GLS	99	—	—
Excel Option Pkg.(NA base)	180	—	—
Right OS mirror, tinted glass, bodyside moldings.			
AM/FM cassette, GL & GS	295	—	—
Hi-Power AM/FM cassette, GL & GS	440	—	—
GLS	145	—	—
Power sunroof (NA base)	415	—	—
Wind deflector for sunroof	49	—	—
Rear spoiler, GS	50	—	—
Security system (NA base)	185	—	—
Trim rings, base	59	—	—
Two-tone paint, GLS	130	—	—
Floormats	54	—	—

Hyundai Sonata

What's New

The Korean-built Sonata arrived last February as Hyundai's compact entry and has been a slow seller so far. For 1990, Hyundai banks on several new options to bolster Sonata's appeal. Heading the list is a Hyundai-built 3.0-liter V-6 engine, copied from Japanese partner Mitsubishi. The 142-horsepower V-6 is identical to the one used in the Mitsubishi Sigma. It teams only with a 4-speed overdrive automatic transmission with Normal and Power shift ranges. A 116-horsepower 2.4-liter 4-cylinder remains standard. Included with the V-6 option are a heavy-duty battery, larger fuel tank (17.2 vs. 15.8 gallons), and 195/70R14 tires. The front-drive Sonata comes as a 4-door sedan with choice of standard and plusher GLS trim.

Hyundai Sonata GLS

The V-6 is optional for both, as is a new 15-inch wheel/tire package with cast aluminum rims wearing H-rated 205/60 all-season rubber. Also new are a leather interior option for the GLS and two acoustically tuned Polk Audio sound systems (manufactured by Alpine), including a premium setup for the GLS with "directional" rear speakers, 12 speakers in all, and a compact disc player. Motorized front shoulder belts are standard this year to meet the federal passive-restraint requirement.

For

- Acceleration
- Room
- Standard equipment
- Price

Against

- Fuel economy (V-6)
- High-speed braking

Summary

We might have expected too much, but the V-6 option doesn't drastically change Sonata. Against a 4-cylinder/automatic GLS, the V-6 version is only 0.7-second faster 0-60 mph (10.1 seconds vs. 10.8 in our tests), but much thirstier, averaging just 16.6 mpg vs. 20.5 in similar city/highway driving mixes. We also tested a 4-cylinder/5-speed model that averaged 25.7 mpg in mostly city driving. In our tests of V-6 and 4-cylinder models, simulated panic stops from 60 mph were marred by sudden, early rear-wheel locking and longer-than-average stopping distances (up to 175 feet in our latest test), though the brakes worked well in routine stops. In its favor, the V-6 provides somewhat quieter cruising and swifter passing than the 4-cylinder. Regardless of engine, Sonata appeals for its roomy interior, attractively low prices, and lots of standard goodies. Sonata is mechanically quiet, but there's noticeable wind noise on the highway and too much road noise, especially with the new 15-inch wheel/tire option. The 15-inch tires also spoil Sonata's comfortable ride, creating a jittery feel. Beware the costly new premium audio system (a whopping $1450 with the CD). It sounds great, but its bulky rear speaker enclosures eat up 1.4 cubic feet of trunk space and preclude carrying anything taller than a hero sandwich. The lower-cost Polk system with six speakers is a far better value and sounds almost as good. Though Sonata isn't perfect, we recommend it as a competent compact sedan that undercuts Japanese rivals such as the Honda Accord and Toyota Camry in price. Slow sales might make it easier to get one at a discount.

> **KEY: ohv** = overhead valve; **ohc** = overhead cam; **dohc** = double overhead cam; **l** = inline cylinders; **V** = cylinders in V configuration; **flat** = horizontally opposed cylinders; **bbl.** = barrel (carburetor); **PFI** = port (multi-point) fuel injection; **TBI** = throttle-body (single-point) fuel injection; **rpm** = revolutions per minute; **OD** = overdrive transmission; **S** = standard; **O** = optional; **NA** = not available.

Prices are accurate at time of printing; subject to manufacturer's change.

Specifications

	4-door notchback
Wheelbase, in.	104.3
Overall length, in.	184.3
Overall width, in.	68.9
Overall height, in.	55.4
Turn diameter, ft.	NA
Curb weight, lbs.	2717[1]
Cargo vol., cu. ft.	14.0
Fuel capacity, gals.	15.8[2]
Seating capacity	5
Front headroom, in.	38.5
Front shoulder room, in.	57.0
Front legroom, max., in.	42.4
Rear headroom, in.	37.4
Rear shoulder room, in.	56.5
Rear legroom, min., in.	37.5

1. Base model; 2926 lbs., GLS V6   2. 17.2 gals. with V-6.

Powertrain layout: transverse front engine/front-wheel drive.

Engines

	ohc I-4	ohc V-6
Size, liters/cu. in.	2.4/143	3.0/181
Fuel delivery	PFI	PFI
Horsepower @ rpm	116 @ 4500	162 @ 5200
Torque (lbs./ft.) @ rpm	142 @ 3500	180 @ 3600
Availability	S	O

EPA city/highway mpg

5-speed OD manual	21/28	
4-speed OD automatic	21/26	18/24

Prices

Hyundai Sonata	Retail Price	Dealer Invoice	Low Price
4-door notchback, 5-speed	$9999	—	—
4-door notchback, automatic	10694	—	—
GLS 4-door notchback, 5-speed	12349	—	—
GLS 4-door notchback, automatic	13044	—	—
4-door notchback w/V-6, automatic	11389	—	—
GLS 4-door notchback w/V-6, automatic	13739	—	—

Dealer invoice, low price and destination charge not available at time of publication.

Standard equipment:

2.4-liter PFI 4-cylinder engine, 5-speed manual or 4-speed automatic transmission, power steering, tachometer, trip odometer, tilt steering column, rear shoulder belts, reclining front bucket seats, remote fuel door and decklid releases, rear defogger, door pockets, remote OS mirrors, tinted glass, variable intermittent wipers, visor mirror, 185/70R14 Michelin EP-X tires. **GLS** adds: power windows and locks, cruise control, power mirrors, AM/FM cassette with power antenna, 6-way driver's seat, 60/40 split rear seat with storage armrest, upgraded upholstery and carpet, voltmeter, oil pressure gauge, windshield sunshade band, underseat storage tray, lighted visor mirror, seatback pockets, full wheel covers. **V-6** models add: 3.0-liter PFI V-6, 4-speed automatic transmission, larger fuel tank, 195/70R14 tires.

Optional equipment:

	Retail Price	Dealer Invoice	Low Price
Air conditioning	780	—	—
Alloy Wheel Pkg., 4-cyl.	390	—	—
Includes 195/70R14 tires.			
High Performance Alloy Wheel Pkg., V-6	450	—	—
Includes 205/60R15 tires.			
Leather Pkg., GLS	575	—	—
Power Pkg., base	795	—	—
Power windows and locks, power mirrors, power antenna, cruise control.			
AM/FM cassette, base	335	—	—
Deluxe AM/FM cassette, base	450	—	—
GLS	115	—	—
Hyundai/Polk Audio sound system, base	795	—	—
GLS	460	—	—
Premium Hyundai/Polk system, GLS V-6	390	—	—
CD player, GLS	600	—	—
Remote keyless entry	125	—	—
Power glass sunroof	475	—	—
Wind deflector for sunroof	49	—	—
Security system	185	—	—
Two-tone paint, GLS	150	—	—
Floormats	60	—	—
Door edge guards	37	—	—

Infiniti M30

Infiniti M30

What's New

The entry-level model from Nissan's new Infiniti Division, the $23,500 M30 coupe is essentially an Americanized version of the Japanese-market Nissan Leopard, which dates from early 1986. A full convertible goes on sale around the first of the year (price to be announced). It's an open secret that the M30 is an interim offering. Nissan admits that a new-design replacement will bow in about two years, following release of a mid-size V-6 sports sedan for 1991 to round out the Infiniti line. Sizewise, the M30 is close to Nissan's front-drive Maxima sedan but some 300 pounds heavier. Seating is strictly for four. The rear-drive M30 comes with anti-lock brakes (ABS) and a driver's-side airbag standard. Power comes from Nissan's 3.0-liter V-6, also used in the Maxima, but mounted "north-south" rather than "east-west." It teams exclusively with a 4-speed overdrive automatic transmission. A standard feature inherited from the Maxima is "Sonar Suspension II," which uses an ultrasonic sensor mounted beneath the radiator to "read" road surfaces and adjust shock absorber damping to suit. A cockpit switch allows choosing soft, medium, or firm damping modes. Like its big brother, the Q45 sedan, the M30 is marketed as a fully equipped "one-price" car. Standard equipment includes limited-slip differential, automatic climate control, leather upholstery, power windows and door locks, 2-way power driver's seat, 4-speaker Nissan/Bose audio system, and anti-theft alarm. Options are limited to a cellular telephone and a compact disc player/changer, both dealer installed.

For

● Acceleration ● Anti-lock brakes ● Airbag ● Quietness

Against

● Rear seat room ● Cargo room

Summary

Brief acquaintances can be misleading, but after a brief drive in a pre-production prototype, the M30 strikes us as a pleasant but unexceptional mid-size luxury coupe. From its dated, angular styling to the tight cockpit and trunk space, this is a car of Nissan's past, and not state-of-the-art. There are attractions, though. The 3.0-liter V-6 provides brisk acceleration (Nissan claims 9.7 seconds 0-60 mph) and quiet, relaxed cruising. The 4-speed automatic suits it well, being just as responsive and almost as smooth. Ample insulation keeps noise from all sources quite low. Ride comfort was good on the mostly benign surfaces we encountered, but the M30 gets a little floppy on sharp bumps and dips. This, together with rather numb power steering, also compromises handling, which is not very direct or agile. Inside, the M30 offers typical 2+2 accommodations, which means decent adult-size room fore and little space aft. Head room is at a premium all around, but at least the front bucket seats are supportive and the driving position is comfortable. The instruments are easy to read and the controls are obvious in operation, but the low-mounted radio has a bank of duplicate controls to the right of the wheel; those duplicate controls would be unnecessary if the radio were higher. We're also put off by the fixed rear side windows. Why can't they throw in windows that open? Infiniti isn't saying much about the M30 convertible right now, but we've seen it and it has even less back seat and trunk room. Still, it looks like an interesting alternative to the BMW 325i and Saab 900 Turbo convertibles. As for the coupe, it's a decent alternative to the 2-door Acura Legend on a price/equipment basis but not as much fun to drive. The Buick Riviera and Olds Toronado/Trofeo offer similar packages for around the same money, but lack Japanese workmanship and reliability. At first blush, then, the M30 is a nice but unexciting car that doesn't strike us as a great buy among premium coupes.

Specifications

	2-door notchback
Wheelbase, in.	103.0
Overall length, in.	188.8
Overall width, in.	66.5
Overall height, in.	54.3
Turn diameter, ft.	32.2
Curb weight, lbs.	3333
Cargo vol., cu. ft.	11.6
Fuel capacity, gals.	17.2
Seating capacity	4
Front headroom, in.	36.8
Front shoulder room, in.	53.6
Front legroom, max., in.	42.2
Rear headroom, in.	35.7
Rear shoulder room, in.	50.3
Rear legroom, min., in.	30.2

Powertrain layout: longitudinal front engine/rear-wheel drive.

Engines

	ohc V-6
Size, liters/cu. in.	3.0/181
Fuel delivery	PFI
Horsepower @ rpm	162 @ 5200
Torque (lbs./ft.) @ rpm	180 @ 3600
Availability	S

EPA city/highway mpg

4-speed OD automatic	19/25

Prices

Infiniti M30	Retail Price	Dealer Invoice	Low Price
2-door notchback	$23500	—	—
2-door convertible	NA	—	—
Destination charge	—	—	—

Standard equipment:

3.0-liter PFI V-6, 4-speed automatic transmission, 4-wheel disc brakes, anti-lock braking system, power steering, limited-slip differential, driver's-side airbag, cruise control, automatic climate control, Nissan/Bose AM/FM cassette with power antenna, leather upholstery, power sunroof, tinted glass, power windows and locks, power driver's seat, tilt steering column, power mirrors, remote fuel door and decklid releases, intermittent wipers, front and rear folding armrests, theft deterrent system, 215/60HR15 tires on alloy wheels.

Infiniti Q45

Infiniti Q45

What's New

Infiniti, Nissan's new luxury division, opened for business November 8 with about 50 dealers selling two models. There should be 90 dealers by next November. As with Toyota's upscale Lexus operation, which got underway about two months earlier, most attention focuses on the flagship 4-door. Infiniti's is the Q45. Like the Lexus LS 400, the Q45 is a large notchback sedan that aims to beat premium Europeans like the Mercedes-Benz S-Class, Jaguar XJ6, and BMW 7-Series. Other rivals include the popular Legend from Honda's Acura Division (whose success largely prompted the Nissan and Toyota luxury channels), the Lincoln Continental, Cadillac De Ville/Fleetwood and Seville, and Chrysler Imperial. Against its import competition, the Q45 is second only to the big Mercedes in size and weight. Excepting the M-B 560SEL, it packs the largest engine, 4.5 liters, and has the most horsepower, 278. Like the Lexus, the Q45 is powered by an aluminum, dual-cam V-8 with four valves per cylinder; a high compression ratio (10.2:1) necessitates premium fuel. Like most every other rival, it comes with a 4-speed automatic transmission (your only choice) and an anti-lock braking system (ABS). The one major option is "Super HICAS," Nissan's 4-wheel-steering system that's been offered for several years on various Japanese-market models. It's part of an optional Touring Package that also gives you a rear stabilizer bar,

> **KEY: ohv** = overhead valve; **ohc** = overhead cam; **dohc** = double overhead cam; **I** = inline cylinders; **V** = cylinders in V configuration; **flat** = horizontally opposed cylinders; **bbl.** = barrel (carburetor); **PFI** = port (multi-point) fuel injection; **TBI** = throttle-body (single-point) fuel injection; **rpm** = revolutions per minute; **OD** = overdrive transmission; **S** = standard; **O** = optional; **NA** = not available.

Prices are accurate at time of printing; subject to manufacturer's change.

lighter forged alloy wheels (versus cast alloy), and integrated decklid spoiler. Otherwise, the Q45 is a "one-price" car with most everything standard, including automatic climate control, power sunroof, 6-way power driver's seat with 2-position memory linked to a power tilt/telescope steering wheel, 4-speaker Nissan/Bose AM/FM/cassette stereo, anti-theft system with "pick-resistant" locks, power windows and door mirrors, electric trunk and fuel filler releases, and a driver's-side airbag. Dealer-installed options number only two: cellular telephone and a trunk-mounted compact disc player/changer. At $38,000, the Q45 comes in quite a bit less than its European competitors but $3000 above the LS 400, though some of its standard features are optional on the Lexus.

For

- Acceleration ● Ride ● Anti-lock brakes ● Airbag
- Quietness

Against

- Rear seat room ● Cargo space

Summary

A quiet, silky, and responsive powertrain gives the Q45 high refinement and good off-the-line pickup—provided you put your foot down. Like Mercedes' automatic, the Q45's starts in second gear at anything less than ¾ throttle; only tromping on the pedal persuades the transmission's electronic control to give you first. Do that and the car comes alive. Nissan claims 7.5 seconds for the 0-60-mph dash, which seems optimistic. Midrange response is strong despite a high 4000-rpm torque peak; evidently, most of the maximum 292 lbs/ft torque is available way below that. The automatic transmission selector encourages manual operation for best performance, its Mercedes-type gate providing logical, positive operation. In ride, the big Infiniti isn't quite as smooth as the LS 400 or Jaguar XJ6, but easily equals the big BMW and the aging Mercedes. You notice broken pavement and such, but not much. Handling and braking are good from what we've been able to tell in restricted driving. Mild understeer (resistance to turning) predominates and body lean is noticeable, but you have to be reckless to induce a tail slide. The steering helps no matter what you do. It's fast (2.6 turns lock-to-lock), informative, and properly assisted. Big 11-inch-diameter disc brakes with ABS work well in routine use. Moving inside the Q45, rear leg and shoulder room are unexceptional for a car this large. Putting the front seats fully aft forces adults in back to sit knees-up, and rear-seat width is just sufficient for three medium-size grownups. Fortunately, generous seat travel allows those in front to move up some without cramping, and six-footers enjoy about 1.5 inches of ceiling clearance despite the space-robbing power sunroof. Cargo room is unexceptional. The 14.8-cubic-foot trunk is only 31 inches long and 21.5 inches high, though it has a flat floor and a large aperture that extends nearly to bumper level. The Q45 shapes up as a good BMW and Mercedes alternative, especially at its price, though we think Nissan hasn't reached quite as far as Toyota has with the Lexus LS 400. A full road test may change our minds. We encourage you to try both new Japanese luxury sedans.

KEY: ohv = overhead valve; **ohc** = overhead cam; **dohc** = double overhead cam; **I** = inline cylinders; **V** = cylinders in V configuration; **flat** = horizontally opposed cylinders; **bbl.** = barrel (carburetor); **PFI** = port (multi-point) fuel injection; **TBI** = throttle-body (single-point) fuel injection; **rpm** = revolutions per minute; **OD** = overdrive transmission; **S** = standard; **O** = optional; **NA** = not available.

Specifications

	4-door notchback
Wheelbase, in.	113.2
Overall length, in.	199.8
Overall width, in.	71.9
Overall height, in.	56.3
Turn diameter, ft.	37.3
Curb weight, lbs.	3950
Cargo vol., cu. ft.	14.8
Fuel capacity, gals.	22.5
Seating capacity	5
Front headroom, in.	38.2
Front shoulder room, in.	58.3
Front legroom, max., in.	43.9
Rear headroom, in.	36.3
Rear shoulder room, in.	57.5
Rear legroom, min., in.	32.0

Powertrain layout: longitudinal front engine/rear-wheel drive.

Engines

	dohc V-8
Size, liters/cu. in.	4.5/274
Fuel delivery	PFI
Horsepower @ rpm	278 @ 6000
Torque (lbs./ft.) @ rpm	292 @ 4000
Availability	S

EPA city/highway mpg

4-speed OD automatic	16/22

Prices

Infiniti Q45	Retail Price	Dealer Invoice	Low Price
4-door notchback	$38000	—	—
Destination charge	—	—	—

Dealer invoice, low price and destination charge not available at time of publication.

Standard equipment:

4.5-liter DOHC 32-valve V-8, 4-speed automatic transmission, 4-wheel disc brakes, anti-lock braking system, power steering, limited-slip differential, driver's-side airbag, cruise control, automatic climate control, leather reclining front bucket seats (wool is available at no charge), Nissan/Bose AM/FM cassette, power antenna, power sunroof, tinted glass, power windows and locks, power driver's seat with 2-position memory (memory includes tilt/telescopic steering column), power passenger seat, heated power mirrors, remote fuel door and decklid releases, intermittent wipers, front and rear folding armrests, theft deterrent system, 215/65R15 tires on alloy wheels.

Optional equipment:

Touring Pkg.	2500	—	—

Super HICAS 4-wheel steering, rear spoiler, forged alloy wheels.

Note: Cellular telephone and CD changer are available as dealer-installed accessories; prices may vary.

Isuzu Amigo

What's New

Amigo is a compact sport-utility vehicle that Isuzu introduced last spring, emphasizing the sport attributes more than the utility. Amigo is aimed at the same young buyers as the Suzuki Sidekick/Geo Tracker, Jeep Wrangler, and new Daihatsu Rocky. Amigo offers buyers several choices: 2-wheel drive or

1989 Isuzu Amigo

EPA city/highway mpg	ohc I-4	ohc I-4
5-speed OD manual	19/22	17/21

Prices

Isuzu Amigo (1989 prices)	Retail Price	Dealer Invoice	Low Price
S 2WD, 2.3	$8999	$8100	—
S 2WD, 2.6	9569	8421	—
XS 2WD	10269	9037	—
S 4WD	11769	10357	—
XS 4WD	12969	11413	—
Destination charge	259	259	259

Low price not available at time of publication.

Standard equipment:

S: 2.3-liter 2bbl. 4-cylinder engine, 5-speed manual transmission, vinyl reclining bucket seats, dual outside mirrors, 225/75R15 M + S tires with full-size spare; 4WD has 2.6-liter PFI engine, part-time 4WD with manual locking front hubs, power steering, 4-wheel disc brakes, triple skid plates. **XS** adds: 2.6-liter PFI engine, power steering, intermittent wipers, tachometer, floor console, tilt steering column, carpet, 31.0 × 10.5R15 tires on alloy wheels, spare tire cover.

Optional equipment:

Power steering, S 2WD	325	275	—
Air conditioning	750	638	—
Sunroof	250	213	—
10.5R Tire/Aluminum Wheel Pkg.,			
S 2WD 2.6 & S 4WD	900	765	—
California emissions controls	50	43	—
AM/FM ST ET	185	130	—
AM/FM ST ET cassette	385	270	—
Floormats, XS	40	28	—
Spare tire cover, S	50	30	—
S w/10.5R tires	55	33	—
Trim rings	60	42	—

on-demand 4-wheel drive; two seats or four; open or enclosed cargo area; two 4-cylinder engines; and two trim levels. All versions come with two side doors and a side-opening tailgate, and a full-size spare tire mounted on the tailgate. Styling resembles that of a pickup truck without a glass rear window; the cab opens at the rear to the cargo bed. An optional vinyl/canvas top that attaches with snaps is available to enclose the cargo area. Power steering is standard with 4WD, optional on 2WD models. A 96-horsepower 2.3-liter 4-cylinder engine is standard on the base 2WD S model; other Amigos use a 120-horsepower 2.6-liter four. Both engines are used in Isuzu's pickups, while the 2.6 also is standard on the Trooper II 4WD vehicle. Buyers have no transmission choices on Amigo; a 5-speed manual comes with either engine. The 4WD system is an on-demand, part-time system (not for use on dry pavement) that requires stopping the vehicle to engage or disengage 4WD. A pair of vinyl front bucket seats are standard and a 2-place rear bench seat is optional. A new option this fall is a removable stereo radio/cassette player. Air conditioning and a pop-up/removable glass sunroof also are optional for all models. We have not driven the Amigo so we cannot comment on its performance.

Specifications

	2-door wagon
Wheelbase, in.	91.7
Overall length, in.	164.2
Overall width, in.	70.1
Overall height, in.	65.2
Turn diameter, ft.	33.5
Curb weight, lbs.	2890[1]
Cargo vol., cu. ft.	NA
Fuel capacity, gals.	21.9
Seating capacity	4
Front headroom, in.	38.2
Front shoulder room, in.	55.5
Front legroom, max., in.	44.1
Rear headroom, in.	NA
Rear shoulder room, in.	NA
Rear legroom, min., in.	NA

1. 3265 lbs., 4WD.

Powertrain layout: longitudinal front engine/rear-wheel drive or on-demand 4WD.

Engines

	ohc I-4	ohc I-4
Size, liters/cu. in.	2.3/138	2.6/156
Fuel delivery	2 bbl.	PFI
Horsepower @ rpm	96 @ 4600	120 @ 5000
Torque (lbs./ft.) @ rpm	123 @ 2600	146 @ 2600
Availability	S	O

Isuzu Impulse/Stylus

Isuzu Stylus

What's New

Isuzu will introduce a pair of new passenger cars in the spring of 1990 as replacements for the rear-drive Impulse and the front-drive I-Mark. The new models are a sporty, 2 + 2 hatchback called Impulse and a subcompact 4-door sedan called Stylus. They will share a front-drive chassis and two engines, but Impulse also will be available as a high-performance coupe with a 160-horsepower turbocharged engine and permanently engaged 4-wheel-drive system. Isuzu, which is partly owned by General Motors, supplies a similar version of the Impulse to GM for sale through Chevrolet dealers as

Prices are accurate at time of printing; subject to manufacturer's change.

the Geo Storm. Chevrolet has not announced plans to sell either the turbo/4WD coupe or the 4-door sedan. All Impulse and Stylus models will have a driver's-side airbag as standard equipment. Standard equipment on the base Impulse XS will include a sport suspension tuned by Lotus, the British car company now owned by GM; 4-wheel disc brakes; power steering; and 185/60HR14 tires. The XS will use a 125-horsepower 1.6-liter engine, with either a 5-speed manual or 4-speed automatic transmission. The 4WD Impulse RS will have the 160-horsepower turbo version of the 1.6 and will come only with a 5-speed manual. The base 4-door sedan, the Stylus S, will have a 95-horsepower engine and a choice of 5-speed manual or 3-speed automatic transmissions. The Stylus XS will use the 125-horsepower engine and same transmissions as the Impulse XS. The Stylus S will have 13-inch tires, manual steering, and front disc/rear drum brakes, while the higher-priced XS will include 14-inch tires, power steering, 4-wheel disc brakes, and a firmer, Lotus-tuned suspension. We have not driven the new Impulse or Stylus, nor were prices available at time of publication. See the Geo Storm report for driving impressions that will apply to the Impulse.

Specifications

	Impulse 3-door hatchback	Stylus 4-door notchback
Wheelbase, in.	96.5	96.5
Overall length, in.	166.0	165.1
Overall width, in.	66.7	66.1
Overall height, in.	51.1	54.0
Turn diameter, ft.	32.2	32.2
Curb weight, lbs.	2411[1]	2261
Cargo vol., cu. ft.	21.8	11.4
Fuel capacity, gals.	12.4	12.4
Seating capacity	4	5
Front headroom, in.	37.5	39.0
Front shoulder room, in.	53.3	53.6
Front legroom, max., in.	43.8	43.3
Rear headroom, in.	31.9	37.9
Rear shoulder room, in.	51.2	52.8
Rear legroom, min., in.	30.4	31.9

1. 2714 lbs., 4WD.

Powertrain layout: transverse front engine/front-wheel drive or permanent 4WD (Impulse RS).

Isuzu Impulse RS

KEY: ohv = overhead valve; **ohc** = overhead cam; **dohc** = double overhead cam; **I** = inline cylinders; **V** = cylinders in V configuration; **flat** = horizontally opposed cylinders; **bbl.** = barrel (carburetor); **PFI** = port (multi-point) fuel injection; **TBI** = throttle-body (single-point) fuel injection; **rpm** = revolutions per minute; **OD** = overdrive transmission; **S** = standard; **O** = optional; **NA** = not available.

Engines

	ohc I-4	dohc I-4	Turbo dohc I-4
Size, liters/cu. in.	1.6/98	1.6/98	1.6/98
Fuel delivery	PFI	PFI	PFI
Horsepower @ rpm	95 @ 5800	125 @ 6800	160 @ 6600
Torque (lbs./ft.) @ rpm	97 @ 3400	102 @ 4600	150 @ 4800
Availability	S[1]	S[2]	S[3]

EPA city/highway mpg

5-speed OD manual	32/37	26/34	22/28
3-speed automatic	27/32		
4-speed OD automatic		24/32	

1. Stylus S   2. XS models   3. Impulse RS

Isuzu Trooper

1989 Isuzu Trooper

What's New

A new 4-speed overdrive automatic transmission is available with the optional 2.8-liter V-6 engine this year on Trooper, Isuzu's compact 4-wheel-drive vehicle. Last year, the General Motors V-6 was available only with a 5-speed manual transmission. Trooper comes in 2- and 4-door body styles (we list the number of side doors only; dual swing-out rear doors are standard on all models). The 2-door version (called Trooper II) was redesigned for 1989 and rides a wheelbase that's nearly 14 inches shorter than the 4-door (called Trooper). The 2-door also is nearly 14 inches shorter overall than the 4-door, but the two are identical in width. All models come with 4-wheel disc brakes standard, a departure from the customary front discs/rear drums found on most compact 4WD vehicles. The 120-horsepower GM V-6 is available only on the 4-door model. The standard engine for all models remains a 120-horsepower 2.6-liter 4-cylinder, also available with either a 5-speed manual or 4-speed automatic. An on-demand, part-time 4WD system (not for use on dry pavement) is standard across the board. Models with manual transmission also have automatic locking front hubs; those with the automatic transmission come with manual front hubs that have to be locked or unlocked by hand. Neither version has shift-on-the-fly, so you have to stop the vehicle to engage or disengage 4WD, and back up a few feet to unlock the automatic front hubs.

For

● 4WD traction   ● Passenger room (4-door)   ● Cargo space

Against

● Ride   ● Noise   ● Rear seat room (2-door)

Summary

We haven't tested the 2-door Trooper, but we are familiar with the 4-door model, whose tall, boxy design gives this 4×4 ample passenger room and cargo space. In fact, the 4-door version is roomier than every rival, save the 5-door Mitsubishi Montero. Head room is generous all around, leg room is adequate, and three can fit in the back seat without too much squeezing. While the cargo area isn't as long as a van's, it's tall and wide, plus the rear doors open at bumper level for easier loading and unloading. The spare tire is conveniently mounted outside, so it doesn't rob any cargo space. With four side doors, everyone enjoys easy entry/exit. What this vehicle has always lacked is snappy, quiet performance. The base 4-cylinder engine is adequate, but lacks the low-end torque that 3800-pound vehicles of this type need. The V-6 makes little difference in acceleration or fuel economy, but at least it's quieter than the raucous 4-cylinder. With either engine there's way too much wind and road noise for peaceful long-distance cruising. The absence of shift-on-the-fly for the 4WD system can be awfully inconvenient, especially if you need to frequently change in or out of 4WD. Trooper is a rugged, reasonably priced 4×4 for off-road work, but if you want a more luxurious, refined vehicle mainly for on-road use, then the Montero, Jeep Cherokee, and Toyota 4Runner are better choices.

Specifications

	Trooper II 2-door wagon	Trooper 4-door wagon
Wheelbase, in.	90.6	104.3
Overall length, in.	162.3	176.0
Overall width, in.	65.0	65.0
Overall height, in.	72.6	71.7
Turn diameter, ft.	34.1	38.7
Curb weight, lbs.	3500	3755
Cargo vol., cu. ft.	62.1	71.3
Fuel capacity, gals.	21.9	21.9
Seating capacity	5	5
Front headroom, in.	40.2	40.2
Front shoulder room, in.	53.7	53.7
Front legroom, max., in.	39.9	39.9
Rear headroom, in.	39.3	39.4
Rear shoulder room, in.	53.3	53.3
Rear legroom, min., in.	33.1	36.1

Powertrain layout: longitudinal front engine/rear-wheel drive or on-demand 4WD.

Engines

	ohc I-4	ohv V-6
Size, liters/cu. in.	2.6/156	2.8/173
Fuel delivery	PFI	TBI
Horsepower @ rpm	120 @ 5000	120 @ 4800
Torque (lbs./ft.) @ rpm	146 @ 2600	150 @ 3600
Availability	S	O[1]

EPA city/highway mpg

5-speed OD manual	16/18	15/18
4-speed OD automatic	15/18	15/18

1. NA 2-door.

Prices

Isuzu Trooper II (1989 prices)	Retail Price	Dealer Invoice	Low Price
S 4-door wagon, 5-speed	$13149	$11703	$12103
S 4-door wagon, automatic	14149	12593	12993

	Retail Price	Dealer Invoice	Low Price
S V6 4-door wagon, 5-speed	14249	12649	13049
XS 4-door wagon, 5-speed	14149	12593	12993
XS 4-door wagon, automatic	15149	13483	13883
RS 2-door wagon, 5-speed	14899	13261	13661
RS 2-door wagon, automatic	15899	14151	14551
LS 4-door wagon, 5-speed	15839	14097	14497
LS 4-door wagon, automatic	16839	14987	15387
LS V6 4-door wagon, 5-speed	17409	15447	15847
Destination charge	259	259	259

Standard equipment:

S: 2.6-liter PFI 4-cylinder engine, 5-speed manual or 4-speed automatic transmission, automatic locking front hubs (with 5-speed), manual locking front hubs (with automatic), power steering, power 4-wheel disc brakes, cloth reclining front bucket seats, driver's seat height adjustment, tachometer, trip odometer, passenger assist grips, carpet, center console, door pockets; V6 has 2.8-liter TBI V-6, air conditioning. **XS** adds: digital clock, rear defogger, AM/FM ST ET cassette, rear wiper. **RS** adds: cruise control, adjustable front armrest, dual horns, right visor mirror, leather-wrapped steering wheel, intermittent wipers. **LS** adds: retractable cargo cover, cloth door panels with carpeted lower section, spare tire cover; V6 has power windows and locks.

Optional equipment:

Air conditioning, 4-cyl.	850	723	787
Power Windows & Door Locks Pkg., LS 4-cyl.	475	404	440
Tire/Wheel Pkg., S 4-cyl.	900	765	833
XS, LS 4-cyl.	450	383	417
10.5R tires on alloy wheels.			
Air deflector, S	50	35	43
Rear defogger & wiper/washer, S	200	170	185
Grille/brush guard	195	137	166
Carpet floormats	50	35	43
AM/FM ST, S	185	130	158
AM/FM ST cassette & 2 speakers, S	385	270	328
w/4 speakers, S	475	335	405
Black roof rack, S	142	100	121
Chrome roof rack, XS & LS	142	100	121
Rear seat, S & XS	420	363	392
RS & LS	520	448	484
Spare tire cover, S & XS	50	30	40
10.5R tires, S & XS	55	33	44
Trim rings, S	60	42	51

Jaguar XJ-S and XJ6

What's New

Jaguar's XJ6 sedan has a larger, more powerful engine, a new automatic transmission and anti-lock braking system, and more models for 1990. Besides the returning XJ6 and Vanden Plas, this year's sedan lineup includes the new Sovereign and Vanden Plas Majestic (available only in red). The XJ6's dual-overhead cam 6-cylinder engine grows from 3.6 liters to 4.0 and horsepower from 195 to 223. Torque increases from 232 pounds/feet to 278. Jaguar claims the 0-60 mph time has been cut nearly one second, to 8.6 seconds. The EPA highway fuel-economy estimate has dropped by one mpg, to 22, but the city estimate is unchanged at 17, so the XJ6 avoids the federal gas-guzzler tax. The new automatic transmission has sport and normal shift modes. New electronic engine controls interface with the transmission and momentarily retard the ignition during acceleration to improve shift quality. Also new is a Teves anti-lock brake system, which replaces a Girling/Bosch system. The new anti-lock system uses a power brake booster run by an electric pump instead of being driven by the engine. Inside, all gauges are now

Prices are accurate at time of printing; subject to manufacturer's change.

Jaguar

Jaguar XJ6 Sovereign

analog; previously only the speedometer and tachometer were analog. In addition, conventional warning lights replace the Vehicle Condition Monitor system. The sedans have motorized front shoulder belts and manual lap belts. Outside, the base XJ6 retains four round headlamps, but the other sedans have new dual, rectangular headlamps. The XJ-S lineup has a new member, the limited-production Collection Rouge (also available only in red). The Rouge and the car-ryover XJ-S coupe and convertible this year have a standard driver's-side airbag. With the airbag, the XJ-S models lose their telescoping steering column, but gain a tilt feature. All XJ-S models are powered by a 262-horsepower V-12 engine.

For

- Acceleration   • Anti-lock brakes   • Ride   • Quietness
- Airbag (XJ-S)

Against

- Fuel economy   • Interior room (XJ-S)

Summary

We haven't driven the 1990 XJ6, but the new engine addresses one of our prime complaints about last year's: not enough power for the weight or the price. Even better news is that the base price on the XJ6 has dropped from $44,000 to $39,700, though a couple of standard features (self-leveling suspension and power sunroof among them) are gone. Even so, the XJ6 is a better car for 1990, and better value. Prices are unchanged from 1989 on the XJ-S despite the new airbag. Why is Jaguar being so generous? Lower sales volume in the U.S. and new competition from Lexus and Infiniti, plus new features on BMW and Mercedes-Benz models. The luxury-car market is fiercely competitive these days and Jaguar is fighting for its share. That means the company is bending over backwards to sell cars, and dealers should be doing the same. Ford Motor Company is buying an equity interest in Jaguar and after 1990 may acquire a controlling interest. That could be a plus for Jaguar, giving this small British company needed financial and technological assistance.

Specifications

	XJ-S 2-door notchback	XJ-S 2-door conv.	XJ6 4-door notchback
Wheelbase, in.	102.0	102.0	113.0
Overall length, in.	191.7	191.7	196.4
Overall width, in.	70.6	70.6	78.9
Overall height, in.	47.8	47.8	54.3
Turn diameter, ft.	39.4	39.4	40.8
Curb weight, lbs.	4015	4190	3903
Cargo vol., cu. ft.	10.6	NA	12.7

	XJ-S 2-door notchback	XJ-S 2-door conv.	XJ6 4-door notchback
Fuel capacity, gals.	24.0	21.6	23.2
Seating capacity	4	2	5
Front headroom, in.	36.1	36.1	36.6
Front shoulder room, in.	55.5	NA	57.5
Front legroom, max., in.	41.3	41.3	41.7
Rear headroom, in.	33.4	—	36.5
Rear shoulder room, in.	52.0	—	57.6
Rear legroom, min., in.	23.4	—	33.1

Powertrain layout: longitudinal front engine/rear-wheel drive.

Engines

	dohc I-6	ohc V-12
Size, liters/cu. in.	4.0/243	5.3/326
Fuel delivery	PFI	PFI
Horsepower @ rpm	223 @ 4750	262 @ 5000
Torque (lbs./ft.) @ rpm	278 @ 3650	290 @ 3000
Availability	S[1]	S[2]

EPA city/highway mpg

3-speed automatic		13/17
4-speed OD automatic	17/22	

1. Sedans   2. XJ-S.

Prices

Jaguar XJ6

	Retail Price	Dealer Invoice	Low Price
XJ6 4-door notchback	$39700	—	—
XJ6 Sovereign 4-door notchback	43000	—	—
XJ6 Vanden Plas 4-door notchback	48000	—	—
XJ6 Majestic 4-door notchback	53000	—	—
Destination charge	500	500	500

Dealer invoice and low price not available at time of publication.

Standard equipment:

4.0-liter DOHC 24-valve PFI 6-cylinder engine, 4-speed automatic transmission, anti-lock 4-wheel disc brakes, power steering, power front bucket seats, leather seat facings, automatic climate control, power windows and locks, cruise control, heated power mirrors, heated door locks and windshield washer nozzles, trip computer, adjustable steering wheel, remote fuel door and decklid releases, rear defogger, AM/FM cassette with CB channel 19 monitor, folding rear armrest, lighted visor mirrors, seatback pockets, console with storage, map light, 205/70VR15 tires on alloy wheels. **Sovereign** adds: hydraulic ride leveling, power sunroof, burl walnut inlays, rear head restraints. **Vanden Plas** adds: limited-slip differential, headlight washers with heated nozzles, footwell rugs, heated front seats, folding burl walnut picnic tables on front seatbacks, leather on seatbacks and borders, storage in rear armrest, rear reading lights, fog lights. **Majestic** adds: Regency Red mica-tone paint, Magnolia leather interior, alarm system, diamond-polished alloy wheels.

Jaguar XJ-S

	Retail Price	Dealer Invoice	Low Price
XJ-S 2-door notchback	$48000	—	—
XJ-S convertible	56000	—	—
Collection Rouge 2-door notchback	51000	—	—
Destination charge	450	450	450

Dealer invoice and low price not available at time of publication.

Standard equipment:

5.3-liter PFI V-12, 3-speed automatic transmission, 4-wheel anti-lock disc brakes, automatic climate control, full leather interior, heated reclining front bucket seats with power lumbar, rear shoulder belts, power windows and locks, heated power mirrors, cruise control, trip computer, tinted glass, intermittent wipers, tachometer, coolant temperature and oil pressure gauges, AM/FM cassette with power antenna, rear defogger, leather-wrapped steering wheel, front fog lights, Pirelli P600 235/60VR15 tires on alloy wheels. **Collection Rouge** adds: Signal Red paint, Magnolia leather interior, elm burl veneer, diamond-polished alloy wheels.

Jeep Cherokee/Wagoneer

Jeep Cherokee Limited

What's New

Jeep's restyled Cherokee 4 × 4 has been a hit since its 1984-model-year introduction and continues for '90 with few changes. A redesigned model is due for 1991, however. This year, an AM/FM stereo radio and rear shoulder belts have been made standard. A new overhead console is newly optional on Cherokee Laredo and is standard on Cherokee Limited and Wagoneer Limited. The console features a compass, outside temperature reading, map lights, and compartments for a garage-door opener and sunglasses. Cherokee and Wagoneer are basically trim and equipment variations on the same 3- and 5-door bodies. The base Cherokee has a 2.5-liter 4-cylinder engine and 2WD. Standard on the Cherokee 4 × 4 is Command-Trac, a part-time 4WD system (for use on wet or slippery surfaces only) with shift-on-the-fly capability. A Cherokee Sport 3-door is available in 2WD or Command-Trac 4WD and only with the 4.0-liter inline 6-cylinder engine and 5-speed manual transmission. The plush Limited models come standard with the 4.0-liter six, a 4-speed automatic transmission, and Selec-Trac 4WD, which can be used on smooth, dry pavement. Optional anti-lock brakes are available on models with the 6-cylinder engine, automatic transmission, and Selec-Trac. Jeep's Bendix-designed ABS works on all four wheels; most other light-truck anti-lock systems work only on the rear wheels. Another distinction is that the Jeep system works in both 2WD and 4WD; most anti-lock systems on 4 × 4s work in 2WD only. The Cherokee/Wagoneer replacement due for '91 is slightly bigger than the present vehicle and has more rounded styling. The new sporty utility also will show up at Dodge dealerships now that Chrysler Motors owns Jeep. The Dodge version will look slightly different, with larger aerodynamic headlamps and a bold chrome grille.

For

● 4WD traction ● Performance (6-cylinder)
● Passenger room ● Cargo space ● Anti-lock brakes

Against

● Fuel economy ● Performance (4-cylinder) ● Price

Summary

We rate these the best compact 4 × 4s because of their convenient 4WD systems, abundant passenger and cargo room, good towing ability, off-road capabilities, and civilized on-road manners. Though it uses quite a lot of fuel, the 4.0 six puts the Cherokee and Wagoneer among the most powerful vehicles in this class. And 4-wheel ABS makes them the only ones with that added measure of control under 4WD braking. We prefer the 6-cylinder. The base 4-cylinder is weak under a heavy load and downright feeble with automatic transmission. Cherokee and Wagoneer are spacious inside for their modest exterior dimensions. Head room is adequate all around and the back seat accommodates three adults. Folding the rear seatback gives you great luggage space for the modest overall length. Plus, their reasonable ride height doesn't hinder entry and exit from the cabin. Limited versions are the Cadillacs of compact 4 × 4s, with prices to match. An alternative is a more modestly equipped Cherokee. It'll have fewer comfort and convenience features, but still be a well-rounded vehicle.

Specifications

	3-door wagon	5-door wagon
Wheelbase, in.	101.4	101.4
Overall length, in.	165.3	165.3
Overall width, in.	70.5	70.5
Overall height, in.	64.1	64.1
Turn diameter, ft.	35.7	35.7
Curb weight, lbs.	3033	3076[1]
Cargo vol., cu. ft.	71.2	71.2
Fuel capacity, gals.	20.2	20.2
Seating capacity	5	5
Front headroom, in.	38.3	38.3
Front shoulder room, in.	55.3	55.3
Front legroom, max., in.	39.9	39.9
Rear headroom, in.	38.0	38.0
Rear shoulder room, in.	55.3	55.3
Rear legroom, min., in.	35.3	35.3

1. Wagoneer Limited, 3453.

Powertrain layout: longitudinal front engine/rear-wheel drive or on-demand 4-wheel drive.

Engines

	ohv I-4	ohv I-6
Size, liters/cu. in.	2.5/150	4.0/242
Fuel delivery	TBI	PFI
Horsepower @ rpm	121 @ 5250	177 @ 4500
Torque (lbs./ft.) @ rpm	141 @ 3250	224 @ 2500
Availability	S	O

EPA city/highway mpg

5-speed OD manual 2WD	21/24	17/23
4-speed OD automatic 2WD	18/24	16/21
4-speed OD automatic 4WD	18/23	16/20
5-speed OD manual 4WD	19/24	17/22

Prices

Jeep Cherokee	Retail Price	Dealer Invoice	Low Price
3-door wagon, 2WD	$13220	$11904	$12104
5-door wagon, 2WD	14095	12674	13074
3-door wagon, 4WD	14495	13026	13226

KEY: ohv = overhead valve; **ohc** = overhead cam; **dohc** = double overhead cam; **I** = inline cylinders; **V** = cylinders in V configuration; **flat** = horizontally opposed cylinders; **bbl.** = barrel (carburetor); **PFI** = port (multi-point) fuel injection; **TBI** = throttle-body (single-point) fuel injection; **rpm** = revolutions per minute; **OD** = overdrive transmission; **S** = standard; **O** = optional; **NA** = not available.

Prices are accurate at time of printing; subject to manufacturer's change

	Retail Price	Dealer Invoice	Low Price
Limited 3-door wagon, 4WD	24550	21874	22074
5-door wagon, 4WD	15370	13796	14196
Limited 5-door wagon, 4WD	25675	22864	23264
Destination charge	450	450	450

Standard equipment:

2.5-liter TBI 4-cylinder engine, 5-speed manual transmission, Command-Trac part-time 4WD (4WD models) power steering, vinyl front bucket seats, AM/FM radio, tinted glass, 195/75R15 all-season SBR tires. **Limited** adds: 4.0-liter PFI 6-cylinder engine, Selec-Trac full-time 4WD, air conditioning, retractable cargo area cover, cruise control, deep-tinted glass, upgraded sound insulation, floormats, fog lights, Gauge Group with tachometer, Light Group, power mirrors, power windows and locks, keyless entry system, AM/FM ST ET cassette with six Jensen speakers, front vent windows, rear quarter vent windows (3-door), roof rack, tilt steering column, intermittent wipers, rear defogger and wiper/washer, carpet, cargo tiedowns, console with armrest, rear heat ducts, upgraded interior and exterior trim, spare tire cover, leather-wrapped steering wheel, front bumper guards, 225/70R15 Goodyear Eagle GT + 4 tires on alloy wheels.

Optional equipment:

	Retail Price	Dealer Invoice	Low Price
4.0-liter 6-cylinder engine, base	613	521	552
4-speed automatic transmission, exc. Ltd .	819	696	737
Selec-Trac, 4WD (auto trans req.)	398	338	358
Anti-lock brakes	998	848	898
Requires 4.0-liter engine and Selec-Trac; available on 4WD only.			
Rear Trac-Loc differential	287	244	258
Air conditioning	845	718	761
Sport Decor Group	973	827	876
4.0-liter engine, carpet, black exterior trim, 225/75R15 OWL tires on 10-hole alloy wheels.			
Pioneer Decor Group	1740	1479	1566
4.0-liter engine, rear ashtrays, front hockey-stick-style armrests, carpet, cargo tiedown hooks, dome/map light, coolant temperature and oil pressure gauges, voltmeter, trim odometer, canyon fabric reclining bucket seats, spare tire cover, air dam and fender flares, bright bumpers with black end caps, pinstripes, dual horns, Light Group, rear quarter vent windows (3-door), soft-feel steering wheel, rear wiper/washer, 205/75R15 tires, wheel trim rings, hub covers.			
Laredo Decor Group	3492	2968	3143
Pioneer Group plus luggage fabric wingback seats with see-through head restraints, dark argent bumper end caps, bumper guards, remote mirrors, cargo cover, center console with armrest, cargo skid strips and tiedowns, door edge guards, upgraded sound insulation, floormats, deep-tinted glass (3-door), rear quarter vent windows (3-door), roof rack, leather-wrapped steering wheel, tachometer, front door vent windows, intermittent wipers, rear defogger, 215/75R15 OWL tires on 10-spoke alloy wheels.			
Quick-Order Group ALK, base 3-door . . .	269	229	242
Base 5-door	369	314	332
Carpet, spare tire cover, wheel trim rings, 205/75R15 tires.			
Quick-Order Group ALL, base 3-door	1345	1143	1211
Base 5-door	1645	1398	1481
Group ALK plus air conditioning, console with armrest, roof rack, rear wiper/washer.			
Sport Quick-Order Group ALM	1525	1296	1373
Sport Decor Group plus console with armrest, gauge group with tachometer, AM/FM cassette, spare tire cover.			
Pioneer Quick-Order Group ALN, 3-door . .	3032	2577	2729
5-door	3632	3087	3269
Pioneer Decor Group plus air conditioning, console with armrest, rear defogger, upgraded sound insulation, Protection Group, roof rack, tilt steering column, remote mirrors, intermittent wipers.			

	Retail Price	Dealer Invoice	Low Price
Pioneer Quick-Order Group ALP, 3-door . .	3705	3149	3335
5-door	4652	3954	4187
Group ALN plus cruise control, Power Window and Lock Group, AM/FM cassette.			
Laredo Quick-Order Group ALR, 3-door . .	4735	4025	4262
5-door	5982	5085	5384
Laredo Decor Group plus air conditioning, overhead console, cruise control, fog lamps, Power Window and Lock Group, AM/FM cassette with six premium speakers, tilt steering column.			
Canyon fabric seats, base & Sport	138	117	124
Carpet, base	211	179	190
Console with armrest, base, Sport & Pioneer	143	122	129
Cruise control	229	195	206
Rear defogger	163	139	147
HD Alternator/HD Battery Group	136	116	122
w/A/C	73	62	66
Extra-Quiet Insulation Pkg., Pioneer	128	109	115
Halogen fog lamps, Laredo	111	94	100
Gauge Group, Sport	160	136	144
Tachometer, trip odometer, coolant temperature and oil pressure gauges, voltmeter.			
Tachometer, Pioneer	64	54	58
Remote mirrors, base, Sport & Pioneer . .	77	65	69
Power mirrors, Laredo	101	86	91
Power Window & Lock Group, Pioneer &			
Laredo 3-door	441	375	397
Pioneer & Laredo 5-door	588	500	529
Power windows and locks, keyless entry.			
Power seats, Laredo	420	357	378
Protection Group, base, Sport & Pioneer . .	201	171	181
AM/FM cassette (std. Ltd)	203	173	183
Six Jensen speakers, Pioneer & Laredo . .	176	150	158
Roof rack	140	119	126
Skid Plate Group, 4WD	145	123	131
OS spare tire carrier, base, Pioneer & Sport .	175	149	158
Laredo	102	87	92
Spare tire cover, base & Sport	46	39	41
Leather-wrapped steering wheel, Sport . . .	48	41	43
Manual sunroof, Pioneer & Laredo	361	307	325
Limited	156	133	140
Off-Road Suspension Pkg., base 4WD . . .	992	843	893
Sport 4WD	557	473	501
Pioneer	881	749	793
Laredo	585	497	527
Tilt steering column, exc. Ltd	133	113	120
Trailer Tow Pkg. B	362	308	326
w/Off-Road Suspension Pkg.	244	207	220
Visibility Group, base, Sport & Pioneer . .	139	118	125
Remote mirrors, intermittent wipers.			
Wheel trim rings, base	66	56	59
Deep-tinted glass, base & Sport 3-door . .	310	264	279
Pioneer 3-door	147	125	132
Includes rear quarter vent windows.			
Rear quarter vent windows, base &			
Sport 3-door	163	139	147
Front door vent windows, base, Sport &			
Pioneer	92	78	83
Rear wiper/washer, base & Sport	148	126	133
Metallic paint	175	149	158
California emissions pkg.	126	107	113

Jeep Wagoneer

	Retail Price	Dealer Invoice	Low Price
5-door wagon	$24695	$22052	$22252
Destination charge	450	450	450

Standard equipment:

4.0-liter PFI 6-cylinder engine, 4-speed automatic transmission, Selec-Trac full-time 4WD, power steering, air conditioning, leather and fabric wing-back reclining front bucket seats, rear shoulder belts, power windows and locks, keyless entry, power front seats, overhead console (with compass, outside temperature readout, map lights and storage bins), AM/FM radio, retractable

---

> **KEY: ohv** = overhead valve; **ohc** = overhead cam; **dohc** = double overhead cam; **I** = inline cylinders; **V** = cylinders in V configuration; **flat** = horizontally opposed cylinders; **bbl.** = barrel (carburetor); **PFI** = port (multi-point) fuel injection; **TBI** = throttle-body (single-point) fuel injection; **rpm** = revolutions per minute; **OD** = overdrive transmission; **S** = standard; **O** = optional; **NA** = not available.

cargo cover, roof rack, cruise control, tilt steering column, tinted glass, rear defogger and wiper/washer, intermittent wipers, cargo tiedowns, coolant temperature and oil pressure gauges, voltmeter, trip odometer, leather-wrapped steering wheel, 205/75R15 self-sealing tires on alloy wheels.

Optional equipment:	Retail Price	Dealer Invoice	Low Price
4-wheel anti-lock brakes	998	848	898
Rear Trac-Lok differential	287	244	258
Metallic paint	175	149	158
AM/FM cassette	203	173	183
Six Jensen speakers & power antenna	176	150	158
Skid Plate Group	145	123	131
Manual sunroof	156	133	140
Conventional spare tire	203	173	183
Trailer Towing Pkg. B	362	308	326
California emissions pkg.	126	107	113

Jeep Wrangler

Jeep Wrangler Laredo

What's New

Jeep's popular 4×4 gets a host of minor changes for '90, and foremost among them is a lock system for soft-top models with half steel doors. The doors can be locked from the outside with a key and from the inside with a sliding lever located on the door panel. Also for '90, a rear wiper/washer has been added to the hard top. The top, along with locking full metal doors, is standard on the top-of-the-line Laredo and optional on the base, Wrangler S, Islander, and Sahara models. A 20-gallon fuel tank, previously an option in place of a 15-gallon unit, is now standard on Sahara and Laredo. The off-road package now includes 225/75R15 tires, up from 215s. All models have new high-back front bucket seats that feature revised backrest wings designed to improve lateral support. A removable folding rear seat is now available on the S and continues as standard on all other Wranglers. The only engine available with the entry-level Wrangler S is a fuel-injected 2.5-liter 4-cylinder engine. That engine also is standard on the base Wrangler, and on the Islander and the Sahara, two "theme" trim and color models. A carbureted 4.2-liter 6-cylinder is standard on the top-line Laredo and optional on all but the Wrangler S. A 3-speed automatic transmission is optional in place of the standard 5-speed manual on all but the S. All models come with an on-demand, part-time 4WD system (not for use on dry pavement) with full shift-on-the-fly capability.

For

• 4WD traction • Maneuverability

Against

• Ride and handling • Fuel economy • Cargo room

Summary

The all-new Wrangler debuted in 1987, but Jeep's marketing strategy dictated that it retain the personality and appeal of its CJ predecessor. Thus, you get a rugged, military-style vehicle with a stiff, jarring suspension and a high center of gravity that makes it feel tipsy in corners. You get mediocre acceleration from the 2.5 four, and only adequate power and driveability from the 4.2 six. It's a tall step up over the door sills into the interior, which has a cramped rear seat and tiny cargo area; with the rear seat tilted out of the way cargo room is adequate. While its overall behavior and performance is about equal to that of the Geo Tracker/Suzuki Sidekick, we'd buy one of these vehicles only if we frequently went off road or slogged through deep snow. There, a Wrangler is in its element, with fine maneuverability and reassuring traction from the convenient 4WD system. We recognize that these sporty-looking vehicles are jam packed with "character," and so emotion often prevails over matters of practicality at buying time. Still, consider seriously how you'd use a Wrangler and if the compromises in on-road ride, handling, and fuel economy are worth it.

Specifications

	2-door w/hardtop	2-door w/soft top
Wheelbase, in.	93.4	93.4
Overall length, in.	152.0	152.0
Overall width, in.	66.0	66.0
Overall height, in.	69.3	72.0
Turn diameter, ft.	32.9	32.9
Curb weight, lbs.	2936[1]	NA
Cargo vol., cu. ft.	43.2	43.2
Fuel capacity, gals.	15.0[2]	15.0[2]
Seating capacity	4	4
Front headroom, in.	40.2	41.4
Front shoulder room, in.	53.1	53.1
Front legroom, max., in.	39.5	39.5
Rear headroom, in.	40.5	40.3
Rear shoulder room, in.	56.3	56.3
Rear legroom, min., in.	35.0	35.0

1. 3062 with 6-cylinder engine   2. 20.0 on Sahara and Laredo.

Powertrain layout: longitudinal front engine/rear-wheel drive or on-demand 4-wheel drive.

Engines

	ohv I-4	ohv I-6
Size, liters/cu. in.	2.5/150	4.2/258
Fuel delivery	TBI	2 bbl.
Horsepower @ rpm	117 @ 5250	112 @ 3000
Torque (lbs./ft.) @ rpm	138 @ 3500	210 @ 2000
Availability	S	O

EPA city/highway mpg
5-speed OD manual	18/20	16/20
3-speed automatic	—	15/16

Prices

Jeep Wrangler	Retail Price	Dealer Invoice	Low Price
Wrangler S	$9393	$8930	$9130
Wrangler Base	11599	10402	10602
Destination charge	450	450	450

Prices are accurate at time of printing; subject to manufacturer's change

Standard equipment:

S: 2.5-liter TBI 4-cylinder engine, 5-speed manual transmission, denim vinyl front bucket seats, soft top with half metal doors, tachometer, coolant temperature and oil pressure gauges, voltmeter, trip odometer, tinted windshield, fuel-tank skid plate, 205/75R15 OWL tires. **Base** adds: right outside mirror, fold and tumble rear seat, AM/FM radio, spare tire cover, 215/75R15 all-terrain tires.

Optional equipment:

	Retail	Dealer	Low
4.2-liter engine, base, Islander & Sahara . .	430	366	387
3-speed automatic transmission (NA S)	512	435	461
Requires 4.2-liter engine and tilt steering column.			
Rear Trac-Lok differential (NA S)	281	239	253
Power steering, S, base & Islander	303	258	273
Air conditioning (NA S)	887	754	798
Requires 4.2-liter engine, power steering and carpeting.			
Islander Decor Group	746	634	671
Carpeting, door pocket, color-keyed fender flares, full mud guards with integrated bodyside step, spare tire cover, 215/75R15 OWL all-terrain tires on six-spoke styled wheels.			
Sahara Decor Group	1878	1596	1690
Power steering, khaki carpeting, door pocket, khaki trailcloth fabric seats, leather-wrapped steering wheel, khaki soft top, spare tire cover, color-keyed fender flares, full mud guards with integrated bodyside steps, front tow hooks, Convenience Group, fog lamps, 20-gallon fuel tank, floormats, off-road gas shock absorbers, 215/75R15 all-terrain tires on six-spoke styled wheels.			
Laredo Decor Group	4144	3522	3730
4.2-liter engine, power steering, hardtop with full metal doors and rear wiper/washer, trailcloth fabric seats, carpeting, extra-quiet insulation, floormats, leather-wrapped steering wheel, carpeted door panels with pockets, black bumper extensions, front tow hooks, color-keyed fender flares, full mud guards with integrated bodyside steps, chrome front bumper and rear bumperettes, deep-tinted glass, right outside mirror, Convenience Group, 20-gallon fuel tank, fog lamps, off-road gas shock absorbers, 215/75R15 OWL tires on 5-spoke alloy wheels.			
Quick-Order Group ALP, S	900	765	810
Power steering, carpeting, fold and tumble rear seat.			
Quick-Order Group ALK, base	1013	861	912
Power steering, carpeting, Convenience Group, tilt steering column, 215/75R15 OWL tires.			
Quick-Order Group ALL, Islander	1390	1182	1251
Islander Decor Group, power steering, tilt steering column, Convenience Group.			
Quick-Order Group ALM, Sahara	2706	2300	2435
4.2-liter engine, Sahara Decor Group, tilt steering column, AM/FM cassette.			
Quick-Order Group ALN, Laredo	4708	4002	4237
Laredo Decor Group, rear defogger, AM/FM cassette, tilt steering column.			
Hardtop w/full metal doors, S & base . . .	762	648	686
Islander & Sahara	918	780	826
Islander and Sahara include deep-tinted glass.			
Trailcloth fabric seats, Islander	108	92	97
Carpeting, S & base	138	117	124
Convenience Group, S, base & Islander . .	209	178	188
w/tilt steering column	146	124	131
Courtesy light with door switches, engine compartment light, intermittent wipers, glovebox lock, center console.			
Cruise control, Sahara & Laredo	230	196	207
Requires 4.2-liter engine, automatic transmission and tilt steering column.			
Rear defogger	166	141	149
Requires hardtop.			
HD Alternator/HD Battery Group	136	116	122
Off-Road Pkg., base	554	471	499
Islander	453	385	408
HD gas shock absorbers, draw bar, tow hooks, 225/75R15 OWL tires.			

KEY: ohv = overhead valve; **ohc** = overhead cam; **dohc** = double overhead cam; **I** = inline cylinders; **V** = cylinders in V configuration; **flat** = horizontally opposed cylinders; **bbl.** = barrel (carburetor); **PFI** = port (multi-point) fuel injection; **TBI** = throttle-body (single-point) fuel injection; **rpm** = revolutions per minute; **OD** = overdrive transmission; **S** = standard; **O** = optional; **NA** = not available.

	Retail Price	Dealer Invoice	Low Price
AM/FM radio, S	273	232	246
AM/FM cassette, S	540	459	486
Others	267	227	240
Fold & tumble rear seat, S	459	390	413
Tilt steering column, S, base & Islander . .	195	166	176
Sahara & Laredo	131	111	118

Lexus ES 250

Lexus ES 250

What's New

The entry-level Lexus is the ES 250, a 4-door sedan based on the Toyota Camry's front-drive platform and powered by the 2.5-liter V-6 that's optional in Camry. This year the dual-cam V-6 gains a knock-control system and three horsepower, to 156. Premium unleaded is recommended for maximum performance; regular unleaded can be used with a slight loss of performance. The ES 250 is available with either a 5-speed manual or a 4-speed automatic transmission with electronic shift controls. While the ES 250's chassis has the same 102.4-inch wheelbase as Camry, the ES 250 has firmer springs and shock absorbers, a rear stabilizer bar and thicker front stabilizer, and 4-wheel disc brakes with anti-lock control standard. The standard tires are a new design, Goodyear Eagle GA; all-season tires are optional. Exterior styling is different than Camry's and body panels are made of corrosion-resistant Excelite steel. Inside, standard features include a driver's-side airbag, air conditioning, power windows and locks, and maple wood trim. A 6-speaker stereo system with cassette player is standard and a compact disc player is optional. Lexus predicts the ES 250 will account for 40 percent of sales this fall, and perhaps 50 percent during calendar 1990.

For

● Acceleration ● Anti-lock brakes ● Airbag
● Handling/roadholding

Against

● Tire noise ● Driveability (automatic transmission)

Summary

Against nearly all "sport sedans" under $30,000 the ES 250 scores well in the performance areas, but whenever the ES 250 is compared to the Lexus LS 400, it always comes out second best, except in price. Base price is $21,050, which is the low end of the Acura Legend line and about $2000 more than a Nissan Maxima SE, but a few grand below a BMW

3-Series. Tire noise is much more prominent in the ES 250 than the LS 400, so at 65 mph tire whine can be intrusive, and you feel the road more in the smaller Lexus. Not that ES 250 is a noisy or harsh-riding car; it's actually quieter and smoother than most. The ES 250 has a sporty, European feel, with a stable, well-controlled high-speed ride and moderate body lean in fast turns. The steering is light at all speeds, despite a variable-assist feature that is supposed to make it firmer on the highway, and the light steering is in marked contrast to the firm suspension. The standard anti-lock brakes provide strong, safe stops with good control. With automatic transmission, the V-6 works harder to get the ES 250 up to highway speed. The automatic also more clearly shows the engine's lack of low-end torque; you have to coax engine speed above 3000 rpm before much happens and at times you have to floor the throttle to get the automatic transmission to downshift. With the 5-speed manual, the ES 250 displays more spirit, revealing an eager, sporting character that's missing from the LS 400. The ES 250 has a bright, airy interior with tall windows, giving the driver excellent visibility. Head and leg room are generous in front; rear leg room is adequate, but there's not much head room for someone over 5-foot-10. The dashboard has large, clear analog gauges and an attractive, well-planned layout, except the stereo is low, in the center of the dashboard, where it's hard to reach. You can buy a Camry LE with the V-6, ABS, leather seats, and fancy stereo for less than $20,000, but you don't get the ES 250's airbag, superior ride and handling ability, and longer, more complete warranty coverage. For those who can't justify spending $35,000 or more on an LS 400, the ES 250 is a good consolation prize. However, between $21,000 and $35,000, there are several other good cars to consider, such as the Legend, the Infiniti M30, the BMW 3-Series, the Mazda 929, even the Mercedes-Benz 190E.

Specifications

	4-door notchback
Wheelbase, in.	102.4
Overall length, in.	183.0
Overall width, in.	66.9
Overall height, in.	53.1
Turn diameter, ft.	36.0
Curb weight, lbs.	3163
Cargo vol., cu. ft.	13.1
Fuel capacity, gals.	15.9
Seating capacity	5
Front headroom, in.	37.8
Front shoulder room, in.	53.9
Front legroom, max., in.	42.9
Rear headroom, in.	36.6
Rear shoulder room, in.	53.3
Rear legroom, min., in.	32.2

Powertrain layout: transverse front engine/front-wheel drive.

Engines

	dohc V-6
Size, liters/cu. in.	2.5/153
Fuel delivery	PFI
Horsepower @ rpm	156 @ 5600
Torque (lbs./ft.) @ rpm	160 @ 4400
Availability	S

EPA city/highway mpg

5-speed OD manual	19/26
4-speed OD automatic	19/25

Prices

Lexus ES 250	Retail Price	Dealer Invoice	Low Price
4-door notchback, 5-speed	$21050	—	—
4-door notchback, automatic	21800	—	—
Destination charge	350	350	350

Dealer invoice and low price not available at time of publication.

Standard equipment:

2.5-liter PFI V-6, 5-speed manual or 4-speed automatic transmission, anti-lock 4-wheel disc brakes, power steering, driver's-side airbag, air conditioning, cruise control, power windows and locks, AM/FM cassette, cloth reclining front bucket seats, folding rear seatback, bird's-eye maple trim, theft deterrent system, 195/60R15 tires on alloy wheels.

Optional equipment:

Leather Pkg.	950	—	—
Requires power driver's seat.			
Power driver's seat	250	—	—
Moonroof	700	—	—
CD player	700	—	—
Floormats	105	—	—
Trunk mat	62	—	—
Car cover	185	—	—
Wheel locks	45	—	—

Lexus LS 400

Lexus LS 400

What's New

Toyota moves into the luxury-car league for 1990, challenging Mercedes-Benz, BMW, Jaguar, Acura, and others with its new Lexus Division. Among the others is Nissan's new Infiniti Division. Lexus offers two cars initially: the $35,000 LS 400 flagship and the $21,050 ES 250, both of which are 4-door notchback sedans. A sports coupe will be added for 1991. About 70 dealers in major markets were in operation for the September 1 launch date; 85 are supposed to be in business by January 1990. As with Honda's Acura Division, Toyota requires dealers to provide separate facilities for Lexus franchises. The LS 400 is a rear-drive sedan powered by a 250-horsepower 4.0-liter V-8, the first Japanese car sold in the U.S. with an 8-cylinder engine. Lexus claims a top speed of 150 mph. The V-8 mates with a 4-speed automatic transmission with electronic shift controls. With EPA fuel economy estimates of 18 mpg city and 23 mpg highway, the LS 400 avoids the federal gas-guzzler tax. Body features include corrosion-resistant Excelite II exterior panels, a 5-coat paint finish, and plastic-lined inner panels for better sound insula-

---

Prices are accurate at time of printing; subject to manufacturer's change

tion. Standard equipment includes anti-lock disc brakes, a driver's-side airbag, tilt/telescope steering wheel, automatic climate control system, power windows and locks, and walnut interior trim. An optional traction-control system uses the anti-lock brake sensors to detect wheel slip. If one or both of the rear wheels slip, power is momentarily retarded until traction is restored. Two suspensions are offered: a standard coil-spring system and an optional air suspension. The air suspension automatically adjusts spring and damping rates, and the ride height. Or, the driver can choose a Sport setting for a firmer ride all the time. Among other options are leather upholstery, 2-position memory system for the driver's seat, power moonroof, remote entry system, heated front seats, and all-season tires.

For

- Quietness • Acceleration • Ride
- Anti-lock brakes • Airbag

Against

- Rear seat room/comfort

Summary

The LS 400 is one of the quietest cars available, perhaps *the* quietest. The engine is nearly silent at idle and not much louder underway; road noise is minimal; and wind noise is low even at 80 mph. It's easy to exceed the speed limit in the LS 400 without noticing because the car is so quiet; 60 mph sounds and feels like 40, while 80 mph sounds and feels like 60. Riding in the LS 400 is like riding in a cocoon, isolated from the outside world. The 4.0-liter V-8 is also incredibly smooth, from idle up to more than 6000 rpm. You never feel vibration or harshness, just more power building as you press on the accelerator. The transmission shifts unobtrusively, even in full-throttle acceleration. The LS 400 rides with reassuring stability at high speed and has an amazing ability to absorb tar strips and other bumps. The optional traction-control system works nearly instantly on gravel and other slippery surfaces to get the LS 400 going in situations where other rear-drive cars would literally be spinning their wheels. It will be most useful on snow and ice. Standard anti-lock brakes stop the LS 400 in a straight line with excellent control and little nosedive. Inside the LS 400, an electronic gauge cluster literally pops out at you with a 3-D effect when you turn on the ignition, providing bright analog gauges and warning lights that are easy to read, even in bright sunlight. The driver's seat has generous rearward travel that easily exceeds the reach of most drivers. There's ample leg room in back, but little room under the front seats for feet. Though the interior is wide enough to hold three people, the center rear passenger has to straddle the driveline hump. Worse, the center of the seat cushion is higher and harder, plus the folding rear armrest creates a huge bulge that hits a passenger's lower back. That effectively makes this a 4-passenger sedan. Trunk space isn't great; the load floor is flat and wide, but not very long, though the lid opens 90 degrees from bumper level for easier loading. While the base price for the LS 400 is $35,000, with all the extras the price can get over $42,000. That puts the LS 400

considerably higher than a Legend LS, but cheaper than any mid-size or larger BMW or Mercedes. Where the LS 400 exceeds all those rivals is in mechanical refinement and noise suppression. The LS 400 is an extremely rewarding car that provides hushed, relaxed, efficient, virtually vice-free motoring. We also encourage you to try the Infiniti Q45 for comparison.

Specifications

	4-door notchback
Wheelbase, in.	110.8
Overall length, in.	196.7
Overall width, in.	71.7
Overall height, in.	55.3
Turn diameter, ft.	36.1
Curb weight, lbs.	3755
Cargo vol., cu. ft.	14.2
Fuel capacity, gals.	22.5
Seating capacity	5
Front headroom, in.	38.6
Front shoulder room, in.	57.1
Front legroom, max., in.	43.8
Rear headroom, in.	36.8
Rear shoulder room, in.	56.3
Rear legroom, min., in.	34.3

Powertrain layout: longitudinal front engine/rear-wheel drive.

Engines

	dohc V-8
Size, liters/cu. in.	4.0/242
Fuel delivery	PFI
Horsepower @ rpm	250 @ 5600
Torque (lbs./ft.) @ rpm	260 @ 4400
Availability	S

EPA city/highway mpg

4-speed OD automatic	18/23

Prices

Lexus LS 400	Retail Price	Dealer Invoice	Low Price
4-door notchback	$35000	—	—
w/Luxury Features Group	39400	—	—
Destination charge	350	350	350

Dealer invoice and low price not available at time of publication.

Standard equipment:

4.0-liter DOHC 32-valve PFI V-8, 4-speed automatic transmission, anti-lock braking system, 4-wheel disc brakes, power steering, driver's-side airbag, automatic climate control, cloth reclining front bucket seats, power windows and locks, cruise control, power mirrors, tachometer, trip odometer, coolant temperature gauge, tilt/telescopic steering column, AM/FM cassette, intermittent wipers, toolkit, first aid kit, 205/65R15 tires on alloy wheels. **Luxury Features Group Pkg.** adds: remote entry, Leather Pkg., moonroof, Lexus/Nakamichi audio system with CD changer.

Optional equipment:

Remote entry	200	—	—
Leather Pkg.	1400	—	—
Moonroof	900	—	—
Traction control & heated front seats	1600	—	—
Electronic air suspension	1500	—	—
Requires Leather Pkg., moonroof and memory system.			
Memory system	800	—	—
Lexus/Nakamichi audio system	1000	—	—
Requires CD changer.			

KEY: ohv = overhead valve; **ohc** = overhead cam; **dohc** = double overhead cam; **I** = inline cylinders; **V** = cylinders in V configuration; **flat** = horizontally opposed cylinders; **bbl.** = barrel (carburetor); **PFI** = port (multi-point) fuel injection; **TBI** = throttle-body (single-point) fuel injection; **rpm** = revolutions per minute; **OD** = overdrive transmission; **S** = standard; **O** = optional; **NA** = not available.

	Retail Price	Dealer Invoice	Low Price
Remote 6-CD auto-changer	900	—	—
Floormats	113	—	—
Trunk mat	62	—	—
Rear window sunshade	140	—	—
Car cover	198	—	—
Wheel locks	45	—	—

Lincoln Continental

Lincoln Continental Signature

What's New

The luxury sedan that introduced Lincoln buyers to front-wheel drive and V-6 power coasts into 1990 with minor trim and equipment changes. The grille features bolder vertical bars, the hood wears a new ornament, and the taillamps are slightly revised. An automatic power antenna also has been adopted, eliminating the dashboard-mounted rocker switch. "Highly styled" aluminum wheels are a new option and the fake wire wheel covers have been dropped. As before, Continental is available in base and Signature Series versions, both powered by a 3.8-liter V-6 coupled to a 4-speed automatic transmission. Airbags are standard for both the driver and front-seat passenger. The driver's-side airbag is contained in the steering wheel hub; the passenger's is loaded above the glove compartment. Available only as a 4-door, 6-passenger notchback, Continental is 4.4 inches longer but 170 pounds lighter and has more interior room than the rear-drive car it replaced. Continental's chassis has a computer-controlled damping system designed to maintain a smooth ride by adjusting in fractions of a second to changes in the road surface. Its power steering has speed-sensitive and variable-effort assist. Standard are 4-wheel anti-lock disc brakes.

For

- Airbags
- Anti-lock brakes
- Ride
- Interior room
- Quietness

Against

- Performance
- Instrumentation

Summary

Continental's styling is contemporary and aerodynamic, yet it's still a large car that's unmistakably American. Judging from its healthy sales, Continental's front-wheel drive doesn't seem to put off an audience used to traditional rear-drive premium sedans. Neither does the V-6, though we consider it Continental's Achilles' heel. Performance is adequate, but a car in this class needs more power. Ford evidently agrees, and is reportedly working on a 4.6-liter V-8 for use in the 1991 Continental. Another of our complaints is that the digital instrumentation washes out in sunlight. Still, with its fake wood accents and cushy seats, the roomy interior has all the amenities buyers of domestic luxury cars expect. Rear leg room is ample and three adults can sit in back without undue crowding. Leather upholstery is standard, but cloth is available as a no-cost option. The airbags are unobtrusively mounted so they look like extra padding on the steering wheel hub and dashboard. In addition, the trunk is spacious. Lincoln makes good use of high technology, including anti-lock brakes and the dual air bags. The car cruises quietly and its sophisticated suspension provides a comfortable ride. Two suspension-related flaws have gone uncorrected, however: the car grows a touch floaty over high-speed dips, and the nose dives when the brakes are applied with anything more than the gentlest press of the pedal. Overall, the Acura Legend offers more spirited performance at a similar price, but we still find the Continental a worthy luxury car.

Specifications

	4-door notchback
Wheelbase, in.	109.0
Overall length, in.	205.1
Overall width, in.	72.7
Overall height, in.	55.6
Turn diameter, ft.	38.0
Curb weight, lbs.	3663
Cargo vol., cu. ft.	19.0
Fuel capacity, gals.	18.6
Seating capacity	6
Front headroom, in.	38.7
Front shoulder room, in.	57.5
Front legroom, max., in.	41.7
Rear headroom, in.	38.4
Rear shoulder room, in.	57.4
Rear legroom, min., in.	39.2

Powertrain layout: transverse front engine/front-wheel drive.

Engines

	ohv V-6
Size, liters/cu. in.	3.8/232
Fuel delivery	PFI
Horsepower @ rpm	140 @ 3800
Torque (lbs./ft.) @ rpm	215 @ 2200
Availability	S

EPA city/highway mpg

4-speed OD automatic	19/28

Prices

Lincoln Continental	Retail Price	Dealer Invoice	Low Price
4-door notchback	$29258	$25008	$25208
Signature Series 4-door notchback	31181	26623	26823
Destination charge	550	550	550

Standard equipment:

3.8-liter PFI V-6 engine, 4-speed automatic transmission, power steering, 4-wheel anti-lock disc brakes, dual front airbags, automatic climate control, 50/50 front seats with recliners, leather upholstery (cloth is available at no cost), folding front and rear armrests, rear shoulder belts, cruise control, automatic parking brake release, AM/FM cassette, tinted glass, heated power mirrors, rear defogger, remote fuel door and decklid releases, power windows and locks, intermittent wipers, tilt steering column, right visor mirror, electronic instruments with coolant temperature, oil pressure and voltage

Prices are accurate at time of printing; subject to manufacturer's change

Lincoln

gauges, trip computer, service interval reminder, digital clock, vinyl bodyside moldings, bright rocker panel moldings, cornering lamps, 205/70R15 tires. **Signature** adds: power recliners, power passenger seat, power decklid pulldown, Autolamp system, automatic headlamp dimmer, upgraded upholstery, lighted visor mirrors, alloy wheels.

Optional equipment:

Keyless illuminated entry, base	225	189	200
Anti-theft alarm system	225	189	200
Power moonroof	1420	1193	1264
Memory seat with power lumbar	301	253	268
Cellular phone	926	778	824
Leather-wrapped steering wheel, base	120	101	107
Ford JBL audio system	525	441	467
CD player	617	519	549
Insta-Clear windshield	253	213	225
Comfort/Convenience Group, base	819	688	729

Power decklid pulldown, power passenger seat, lighted visor mirrors, Headlamp Convenience Group (automatic dimmer, Autolamp system), rear floormats, power passenger recliner.

Overhead console group	236	198	210

Digital compass, electrochromic day/night mirror.

Styled alloy wheels, base	556	467	495
Geometric alloy wheels, base	556	467	495
Signature	NC	NC	NC
California emissions pkg.	100	84	89

Lincoln Mark VII

Lincoln Mark VII LSC

What's New

Lincoln's slow-selling luxury coupe enters 1990 with a revised grille, a new dashboard, and a driver's-side airbag. The sporty LSC version gets standard BBS alloy wheels and revised seats. Rear shoulder belts have been added on both models, and the front head restraints are smaller to improve visibility. The new dash places the audio controls higher for easy use, but the optional compact-disc player replaces rather than supplements the cassette deck. Puncture-sealant tires have been dropped from the options list. As before, anti-lock brakes are standard. Two Mark VII models are offered: the LSC and the luxury Bill Blass Designer Series. Both are rear-drive, 5-seat, 2-door coupes. They use a 5.0-liter V-8 coupled to a 4-speed overdrive automatic transmission. The LSC has 225/60R16 black-sidewall high-performance tires on alloy wheels, quick-ratio power steering, a handling suspension and leather upholstery. The Designer Series gets 215/70R15 whitewalls, regular power steering, added chrome exterior trim, and a choice of leather or cloth seating. Standard equipment on both includes automatic climate control, a self-leveling suspension, remote decklid release and power decklid pulldown and 6-way

power front seats. A power glass moonroof is among the options.

For

- Performance
- Anti-lock brakes
- Handling/roadholding (LSC)
- Luxury appointments
- Quietness

Against

- Fuel economy
- Rear seat room
- Trunk space

Summary

Mark VII's V-8 packs enough power to squeal the tires in hard takeoffs, though you have to wait out the transmission's troublesome tendency toward tardy downshifts before the engine's fine passing power can be tapped. In normal braking the pedal is spongy and the front end dips noticeably, but in emergencies the anti-lock system stops this heavy coupe short and with fine control. The LSC corners flatly and has a stable highway ride, but it also transmits to the cabin some impact harshness over bumps. Since the Bill Blass model has a softer suspension and smaller tires, test drive both to see which one suits your desires. Inside, there's spacious seating for two in front on bucket seats that use Mercedes-style power controls—separate buttons shaped like the seat cushion and backrest. There's ample rear-seat leg room for adults, but not much head room, and the driveline hump discourages squeezing three people into the back. The trunk's center well is shallow and narrow, and the spare tire eats up luggage space. On balance, the Mark VII has much to offer, including a reasonable price for the luxury-coupe class. Still, don't decide without first trying the Acura Legend Coupe and the Cadillac Eldorado, both of which have front-wheel drive.

Specifications

	2-door notchback
Wheelbase, in.	108.5
Overall length, in.	202.8
Overall width, in.	70.9
Overall height, in.	54.2
Turn diameter, ft.	40.1
Curb weight, lbs.	3779
Cargo vol., cu. ft.	14.2
Fuel capacity, gals.	22.1
Seating capacity	5
Front headroom, in.	37.8
Front shoulder room, in.	56.0
Front legroom, max., in.	42.0
Rear headroom, in.	37.1
Rear shoulder room, in.	57.8
Rear legroom, min., in.	36.9

Powertrain layout: longitudinal front engine/rear-wheel drive.

Engines

	ohv V-8
Size, liters/cu. in.	5.0/302
Fuel delivery	PFI
Horsepower @ rpm	225 @ 4200
Torque (lbs./ft.) @ rpm	300 @ 3200
Availability	S

EPA city/highway mpg

4-speed OD automatic	17/24

Prices

Lincoln Mark VII

	Retail Price	Dealer Invoice	Low Price
Bill Blass 2-door notchback	$29215	$24945	$25145
LSC 2-door notchback	29437	25132	25332
Destination charge	550	550	550

Standard equipment:

LSC: 5.0-liter PFI V-8, 4-speed automatic transmission, power steering, 4-wheel disc brakes, anti-lock braking system, driver's-side airbag, rear shoulder belts, electronic air suspension with automatic level control, automatic climate control, overhead console with warning lights and reading lamps, power decklid release, rear defogger, power windows and locks, remote fuel door release, tinted glass, automatic headlamp dimmer, Autolamp system, illuminated entry, analog instruments including tachometer and coolant temperature gauge, heated power mirrors, AM/FM cassette, power seats, cruise control, tilt steering column, intermittent wipers, full-length console with lockable compartment, leather interior trim including steering wheel, shift knob, and console, handling suspension, P225/60R16 tires on aluminum wheels. **Bill Blass** has electronic instrument cluster, prairie mist metallic clearcoat paint, bodyside and decklid paint stripes, choice of leather, UltraSuede or cloth/leather seat trim, P215/70R15 tires on wire-spoke aluminum wheels.

Optional equipment:

Traction-Lok axle	101	86	90
Anti-theft alarm system	225	189	200
Power moonroof	1420	1193	1264
Cellular phone	926	778	824
AM/FM radio w/CD player	299	251	266
Automatic day/night mirror	89	75	79
Ford JBL audio system	525	441	467
Engine block heater	26	22	23
California emissions pkg.	100	84	89

Lincoln Town Car

Lincoln Town Car

What's New

Lincoln's largest-selling model receives its first major redesign since it was introduced under the Town Car label for 1980. The V-8 engine and rear-drive platform of the previous Town Car are retained, but the previous car's sharply squared off body work gives way to rounded corners patterned after those on the smaller Continental. The 117.3-inch wheelbase, 220.2-inch overall length, and 4025-pound curb weight are virtually identical to the original Town Car's, but the '90 model's aerodynamic coefficient of drag is a commendable 0.36, compared to the '89's block-like 0.45. Such traditional styling touches as opera windows are retained, but progress is made with aircraft-type doors that extend their openings into the roof. The brakes are brought up to date with an anti-lock option, while the revamped interior incorporates driver and passenger airbags. There's also a new instrument panel, seat design, rear shoulder belts, automatic power antenna, and a remote fuel-door release. Base, mid-level Signature Series, and top-shelf Cartier Designer Series are offered. The power steering is now speed sensitive, and the rear suspension is self-leveling via air springs. The 5.0-liter V-8 carries over as before, except that on Cartier models it exhales through dual exhausts for slightly higher power output.

For

- Airbags
- Luxury appointments
- Passenger room
- Trunk space
- Driveability
- Quietness

Against

- Fuel economy
- Handling/roadholding

Summary

The new Town Car is as long, as tall, and just as wide as the previous version, but it looks nowhere near as ungainly. The cabin is airy and far more contemporary as well. The driver sits on a redesigned and firmer seat. The new dashboard is easier to use and nicer to look at. It's still quite Detroit-traditional in its shiny surfaces and imitation wood, but we laud the driver's-side and passenger airbags. The rear seat is cavernous and comfortable. Lincoln engineers paid much attention to the car's "rolling feel," and indeed, there isn't much of it. Isolation from the road is nearly complete, yet firmer steering and a recalibrated suspension provide just enough feedback to avoid the numb, floaty feel of the previous Town Car and the current Cadillac Brougham. Power is adequate, though a 0-60-mph time of about 11.7 seconds and sedate midrange response make it clear that the 140-horsepower V-8 is close to being overmatched by the 4100-pound curb weight. The '91 Town Car will be one of the first Ford products with the new 4.6-liter V-8, which should produce about 180 horsepower and 10-second 0-60 times, according to Lincoln engineers. Also expect a traction-control system for '91.

Specifications

	4-door notchback
Wheelbase, in.	117.4
Overall length, in.	220.2
Overall width, in.	78.1
Overall height, in.	56.7
Turn diameter, ft.	40.0
Curb weight, lbs.	4025
Cargo vol., cu. ft.	22.0
Fuel capacity, gals.	18.0
Seating capacity	6
Front headroom, in.	39.0
Front shoulder room, in.	62.0
Front legroom, max., in.	42.5
Rear headroom, in.	38.1
Rear shoulder room, in.	62.0
Rear legroom, min., in.	42.8

KEY: ohv = overhead valve; **ohc** = overhead cam; **dohc** = double overhead cam; **I** = inline cylinders; **V** = cylinders in V configuration; **flat** = horizontally opposed cylinders; **bbl.** = barrel (carburetor); **PFI** = port (multi-point) fuel injection; **TBI** = throttle-body (single-point) fuel injection; **rpm** = revolutions per minute; **OD** = overdrive transmission; **S** = standard; **O** = optional; **NA** = not available.

Prices are accurate at time of printing; subject to manufacturer's change.

Lincoln • Mazda

Powertrain layout: longitudinal front engine/rear-wheel drive.

Engines

	ohv V-8
Size, liters/cu. in.	5.0/302
Fuel delivery	PFI
Horsepower @ rpm	150 @ 3200
Torque (lbs./ft.) @ rpm	160 @ 3400
Availability	S

EPA city/highway mpg

4-speed OD automatic	17/24

Prices

Lincoln Town Car	Retail Price	Dealer Invoice	Low Price
4-door notchback	$27315	$23343	$23543
Signature 4-door notchback	30043	25635	25835
Cartier 4-door notchback	32137	27394	27594
Destination charge	550	550	550

Standard equipment:

5.0-liter PFI V-8, 4-speed automatic transmission, speed-sensitive power steering, driver's side airbag, automatic climate control, cloth reclining front split bench seat with folding center armrests, power driver's seat, folding rear armrest, power windows and locks, heated power mirrors, tinted glass, intermittent wipers, cruise control, tilt steering column, AM/FM cassette with power antenna, electronic instruments with coolant temperature gauge, front and rear reading lights, lighted right visor mirror, rear shoulder belts, remote fuel door and decklid releases, rear defogger, cornering lights, automatic parking brake release, 215/70R15 tires. **Signature** adds: power passenger seat, lighted visor mirrors, leather-wrapped steering wheel, power decklid pulldown, automatic headlamp dimmer, Autolamp system, door pockets, keyless illuminated entry, floormats. **Cartier** adds: dual exhaust, Ford JBL audio system, cloth and supple leather upholstery (supple leather is available at no extra cost), memory power seats with power recliners and lumbar support.

Optional equipment:

Anti-lock braking system	936	786	833
Traction-Lok axle	101	85	90
Keyless illuminated entry, base	225	189	200
Anti-theft alarm system	225	189	200
Power moonroof	1420	1193	1264
Programmable memory seat, base & Signature	502	422	447
Cellular phone	926	778	824
Leather-wrapped steering wheel, base ...	120	101	107
AM/FM radio w/CD player	299	251	266
Ford JBL audio system, base & Signature .	525	441	467
Passenger-side airbag	494	415	440
Electrochromic day/night mirror	99	83	88
Insta-Clear windshield	253	213	225
Base requires Comfort/Convenience Group.			
Leather seat trim, Signature	509	427	453
Base	570	479	507
Comfort/Convenience Group, base	694	583	618
Power decklid pulldown, lighted left visor mirror, Headlamp Convenience Group (automatic dimmer, Autolamp system), power passenger seat, floormats.			
Dual exhaust	83	70	74

KEY: ohv = overhead valve; ohc = overhead cam; dohc = double overhead cam; I = inline cylinders; V = cylinders in V configuration; flat = horizontally opposed cylinders; bbl. = barrel (carburetor); PFI = port (multi-point) fuel injection; TBI = throttle-body (single-point) fuel injection; rpm = revolutions per minute; OD = overdrive transmission; S = standard; O = optional; NA = not available.

	Retail Price	Dealer Invoice	Low Price
Class III Trailer Tow Pkg.	417	351	371
High altitude	335	281	298
Geometric spoke alloy wheels, base	556	467	495
Signature	NC	NC	NC
Turbine spoke alloy wheels, base	556	467	495
California emissions pkg.	100	84	89

Mazda Miata

Mazda Miata

What's New

Built in Japan but conceived at Mazda's U.S. headquarters in California, Miata is the 2-seat roadster that instantly became the star of the automotive world when it debuted in July as an early 1990 model. Mazda dealers were reportedly demanding—and getting—as much as $5000 over Miata's suggested retail price of $13,800 because so many eager buyers were waiting in line for this new sports car. And, some of those who bought Miatas turned around and sold them at an even greater profit. Only 20,000 Miatas are scheduled to be sent to the U.S. during calendar 1989 and 40,000 during all of 1990, though if high demand continues then Mazda might increase the allotment. However, Miata also is a big hit in Japan, so there may not be any extra cars available. The rear-drive Miata comes with a 116-horsepower, dual-cam 1.6-liter engine and a 5-speed manual transmission. An automatic transmission is planned for the future and a 1.8-liter engine is possible. Standard features include 4-wheel disc brakes, a driver's-side airbag, and a manual folding top that can be raised or lowered by one person from inside the car. Power steering and a removable hardtop that weighs about 40 pounds are optional.

For

- Acceleration   • Handling/roadholding   • Fuel economy

Against

- Dealer price gouging   • Cargo room

Summary

Miata is loads of fun to drive. If only you could buy it for suggested retail price. Our biggest complaint about Miata so far is that high demand and dealer greed have driven selling prices sky high. When it comes to driving the Miata, we have lots of good things to say. We timed a Miata at 8.6 seconds 0-60 mph, which is quick enough, while with one test car we averaged 29 mpg in an even city/highway driving mix, and in another we averaged nearly 27 mpg in city/suburban commuting. The engine has little low-end power, so you have to shift gears frequently for best go, which is a joy because the shifter has super-short throws and light, switch-like action. Handling, roadholding, and maneuverability are great, too, with good grip in fast corners and fine overall balance, and Miata won't jar your gums on poor surfaces the way a lot of sports cars will. The cockpit is low and not that wide, but never feels cramped. Ample rearward seat travel will give most people at least adequate room. The clean, simple dashboard has easy-to-read analog gauges and handy controls. Cargo space is meager, but this is a sports car, not a family wagon. Miata has perhaps the best manual soft top around. It's simple and fast to raise or lower, and you can do it from the driver's seat. Miata is a sensational entry-level sports car—everything you ever liked about British roadsters, with none of the hassle.

Specifications

	2-door conv.
Wheelbase, in.	89.2
Overall length, in.	155.4
Overall width, in.	65.9
Overall height, in.	48.2
Turn diameter, ft.	30.6
Curb weight, lbs.	2182
Cargo vol., cu. ft.	3.6
Fuel capacity, gals.	11.9
Seating capacity	2
Front headroom, in.	37.1
Front shoulder room, in.	50.4
Front legroom, max., in.	42.7
Rear headroom, in.	—
Rear shoulder room, in.	—
Rear legroom, min., in.	—

Powertrain layout: longitudinal front engine/rear-wheel drive.

Engines	dohc I-4
Size, liters/cu. in.	1.6/97
Fuel delivery	PFI
Horsepower @ rpm	116 @ 6500
Torque (lbs./ft.) @ rpm	100 @ 5500
Availability	S

EPA city/highway mpg	
5-speed OD manual	25/30

Prices

Mazda Miata	Retail Price	Dealer Invoice	Low Price
2-door convertible	$13800	$11963	$13800
Destination charge	269	269	269

Standard equipment:

1.6-liter DOHC 16-valve PFI 4-cylinder engine, 5-speed manual transmission, 4-wheel disc brakes, driver's-side airbag, cloth reclining front bucket seats, tachometer, coolant temperature gauge, trip odometer, intermittent wipers, 185/60R14 tires.

Optional equipment:

Air Conditioning	795	635	795
Detachable hardtop	1100	891	1100
Requires Option Pkg. A or B.			
Option Pkg. A	1145	962	1145
Power steering, alloy wheels, leather-wrapped steering wheel, AM/FM cassette.			

	Retail Price	Dealer Invoice	Low Price
Option Pkg. B	1730	1453	1730
Pkg. A plus power windows, cruise control, headrest speakers.			
Limited-slip differential	250	200	250
CD player	600	480	600
Requires Option Pkg. A or B.			
Floormats	59	41	59

Mazda MPV

Mazda MPV 4WD

What's New

Rear anti-lock brakes are standard on all MPV models and the 4-wheel-drive version is available with a new 5-speed manual transmission as the major changes this year on Mazda's minivan. The rear-drive MPV ("Multi-Purpose Vehicle") was introduced in fall 1988 and was followed in the spring by the 4WD model, which for 1989 came only with a 150-horsepower 3.0-liter V-6 engine and 4-speed automatic transmission. This year, a 5-speed manual is standard on the 4WD MPV and the automatic is optional. The 4WD system is the on-demand type that can be engaged by an interior switch. A 121-horsepower 2.6-liter 4-cylinder is standard on the rear-drive MPV and the V-6 is optional. MPV is unique among minivans for its swing-out rear side door; other compact vans have a sliding side door. The MPV's rear door is a one-piece liftgate. Seats for five are standard (two front buckets and a removable 3-place bench) and seats for seven are optional (two front buckets, a removable 2-place middle bench, and a folding 3-place rear bench). As a multi-purpose vehicle, the MPV is not required to have passive restraints; it has manual seat belts, including shoulder belts for outboard middle- and rear-seat passengers.

For

- Acceleration (V-6) • Anti-lock rear brakes
- 4WD traction • Passenger and cargo room
- Ride and handling

Against

- Acceleration (4-cylinder) • Fuel economy (V-6)

Summary

The MPV differs from other Japanese-made minivans in that it was designed primarily as a passenger vehicle for the U.S. market, not as a cargo vehicle for the Japanese market. It shows; the MPV is the most car-like minivan since the front-drive Dodge Caravan/Plymouth Voyager, and the best-selling Japanese minivan in the U.S. after one year. The MPV is

Prices are accurate at time of printing; subject to manufacturer's change.

Mazda

slightly shorter than the standard-size Caravan/Voyager and has a similar low profile. The compact dimensions aid parking and maneuvering through urban traffic, and the MPV matches the Chrysler minivans in overall driving ease. The suspension is neither too firm nor too soft and it soaks up most bumps with little reaction. We were impressed by the V-6 engine's acceleration, averaging 12.4 seconds in our 0-60 runs. The 4-cylinder engine will be some two seconds slower to 60 mph and have less snap for highway passing. We averaged an unimpressive 17.2 mpg with the V-6/automatic, though most of that was urban commuting. Behind the wheel, the driver feels like he's in a car, not a van. The dashboard and control layout look like they were lifted from one of Mazda's passenger cars. Unusual for a Japanese vehicle, the shift lever is mounted on the steering column with automatic transmission, not on the floor. This allows more walk-through space to the middle and rear seats. On 7-passenger models, the 3-place rear bench is bolted to the floor (requiring hand tools for removal), an inconvenience. The rear bench can be folded forward against the middle seat for more cargo space, or the seatback can be folded backwards for use as a bed. The side-opening right-rear door is easier to open and close than the sliding doors on most minivans, but it opens nearly 90 degrees, which requires a lot of space, and its window doesn't roll down or flip open for ventilation. The MPV lives up to its name by combining station-wagon comfort and driving ease with minivan versatility in a compact package.

Specifications

	4-door van
Wheelbase, in.	110.4
Overall length, in.	175.8
Overall width, in.	71.9
Overall height, in.	68.1
Turn diameter, ft.	36.1[1]
Curb weight, lbs.	3459[2]
Cargo vol., cu. ft.	37.5
Fuel capacity, gals.	15.9[3]
Seating capacity	7
Front headroom, in.	40.0
Front shoulder room, in.	57.5
Front legroom, max., in.	40.6
Rear headroom, in.	39.0
Rear shoulder room, in.	57.5
Rear legroom, min., in.	34.8

1. 39.6, 4WD   2. 3920 lbs., 4WD   3. 19.6 gals., V-6; 19.8 gals., 4WD.

Powertrain layout: longitudinal front engine/rear-wheel drive or on-demand 4WD.

Engines

	ohc I-4	ohc V-6
Size, liters/cu. in.	2.6/159	3.0/180
Fuel delivery	PFI	PFI
Horsepower @ rpm	121 @ 4600	150 @ 5000
Torque (lbs./ft.) @ rpm	149 @ 3500	165 @ 4000
Availability	S	O

> **KEY: ohv** = overhead valve; **ohc** = overhead cam; **dohc** = double overhead cam; **I** = inline cylinders; **V** = cylinders in V configuration; **flat** = horizontally opposed cylinders; **bbl.** = barrel (carburetor); **PFI** = port (multi-point) fuel injection; **TBI** = throttle-body (single-point) fuel injection; **rpm** = revolutions per minute; **OD** = overdrive transmission; **S** = standard; **O** = optional; **NA** = not available.

EPA city/highway mpg	ohc I-4	ohc V-6
5-speed OD manual	20/24	18/22
4-speed OD automatic	19/24	17/22

Prices

Mazda MPV	Retail Price	Dealer Invoice	Low Price
Wagon, 2-row seating, 2.6, 5-speed	$13699	$11876	$12376
Wagon, 2-row seating, 2.6, automatic	14399	12478	12978
Wagon, 3-row seating, 2.6, 5-speed	14944	12947	13447
Wagon, 3-row seating, 2.6, automatic	15644	13549	14049
Wagon, 3-row seating, 3.0, automatic	16394	14194	14694
4WD wagon, 3-row seating, 3.0, 5-speed	18894	16344	16844
4WD wagon, 3-row seating, 3.0, automatic	19394	16774	17274
Destination charge	319	319	319

Standard equipment:

2.6-liter PFI 4-cylinder or 3.0-liter PFI 6-cylinder engine, 5-speed manual or 4-speed automatic transmission, anti-lock rear brakes, power steering, cloth reclining front bucket seats, 3-passenger middle seat (with 2-row seating), 2-passenger middle and 3-passenger rear seats (with 3-row seating), power mirrors, tachometer, coolant temperature gauge, trip odometer, tilt steering column, intermittent wipers, illuminated entry, rear wiper/washer, tinted glass, AM/FM cassette, lighted visor mirrors, floormats, remote fuel door release, 205/70R14 all-season SBR tires. **4WD** adds: selectable full-time 4WD.

Optional equipment:

Single air conditioning	849	696	773
Dual air conditioning (3.0 req.)	1497	1228	1363
Cold Pkg.	298	256	277
HD battery, larger windshield washer solvent reservoir, rear heater.			
Option Pkg. A	995	826	911
Power windows and locks, cruise control, privacy glass; not available with 2-row seating or 4WD.			
Option Pkg. B, 2WD	1635	1465	1550
Pkg. A plus alloy wheels, color-keyed trim, electronic heater mode control.			
Option Pkg. C, 4WD	1185	984	1085
Color-keyed trim, electronic heater mode control.			
CD player (3.0/auto req.)	699	559	629
Two-tone paint	251	206	229
Towing Pkg., 2WD w/3.0	498	428	463
4WD automatic	398	342	370
Transmission oil cooler, HD radiator and fan, conventional spare, automatic load leveling (2WD).			
Floormats, w/2-row seating	59	42	51
w/3.0	84	59	72

Mazda RX-7

What's New

Mazda's rotary-powered sports car was mechanically and cosmetically revised last March, when it arrived as a late 1989 model, so for 1990 there is only one change of note: A driver's-side airbag is standard on the convertible. Other models continue with motorized front shoulder belts to satisfy the federal passive-restraint requirement. Last spring's revisions included 14 more horsepower for the naturally aspirated twin-rotor engine and 18 more for the turbocharged version. At the same time, the 4-speed automatic transmission gained electronic shift controls and a gear hold feature, plus it became available on the convertible. The 1990 RX-7 lineup includes GTU, GXL, Turbo, and convertible models, all with rear-wheel drive. All but the Turbo use the 160-horsepower naturally aspirated rotary engine. The Turbo is rated at 200 horsepower; it is the only RX-7 that isn't available with automatic transmission.

144

CONSUMER GUIDE®

	3-door hatchback	2+2 3-door hatchback	2-door conv.
Cargo vol., cu. ft.	6.5	6.5	4.1
Fuel capacity, gals.	18.5	18.5	18.5
Seating capacity	2	4	2
Front headroom, in.	37.2	37.2	36.3
Front shoulder room, in.	52.8	52.8	52.8
Front legroom, max., in.	43.7	43.7	43.7
Rear headroom, in.	—	33.0	—
Rear shoulder room, in.	—	NA	—
Rear legroom, min., in.	—	NA	—

Powertrain layout: longitudinal front engine/rear-wheel drive.

Engines	2-rotor Wankel	Turbo 2-rotor Wankel
Size, liters/cu. in.	1.3/80	1.3/80
Fuel delivery	PFI	PFI
Horsepower @ rpm	160 @ 7000	200 @ 6500
Torque (lbs./ft.) @ rpm	140 @ 4000	196 @ 3500
Availability	S	S

EPA city/highway mpg

5-speed OD manual	17/25	16/24
4-speed OD automatic	17/23	

Mazda RX-7 Turbo

The GXL is available in 2-seat and 2+2 configurations; the others are 2-seaters. All models have 4-wheel disc brakes, while the Turbo also has a standard anti-lock system.

For

- Acceleration   • Handling/roadholding
- Anti-lock brakes (Turbo)   • Airbag (convertible)

Against

- Ride   • Interior room   • Fuel economy

Summary

Mazda's rotary engines provide thrilling acceleration, especially in turbocharged form, despite having little low-end torque. That's no real handicap with manual transmission, but it is with automatic. We tested a GXL with automatic that needed 10.4 seconds to reach 60 mph—mediocre when cars that cost half as much can be quicker. Fuel economy has never been an RX-7 strong point, but we averaged a disheartening 15.4 mpg from an equal city/highway driving mix. You'll get much more enjoyment out of an RX-7 with the 5-speed manual transmission, which makes better use of the rotary's high-revving character. As with most other sports cars, the RX-7 has firm tires that combine with a stiff suspension to make the ride jiggly even on smooth pavement and downright rough on pockmarked surfaces. There's compensation in sharp, responsive, agile handling, which remains one of RX-7's main virtues. The small cockpit affords adequate leg room but inadequate head room for occupants over about 5-foot-10, who will need to recline their backrest to avoid the ceiling. Sports cars generally don't offer great value for the money and the RX-7 has climbed in price considerably the past few years. Since there's so much interest in the Mazda Miata roadster, you might be able to talk a dealer into a big price cut on an RX-7. In today's market, you might even be able to buy an RX-7 for less than a Miata. If you're interested in a convertible, the RX-7 is one of the nicest.

Prices

Mazda RX-7	Retail Price	Dealer Invoice	Low Price
GTU 3-door hatchback	$17880	$15512	$16262
GTU S 3-door hatchback	20180	17295	18045
2-door convertible	26530	22427	23177
GXL 3-door hatchback	22330	18899	19649
GXL 2+2 3-door hatchback	22830	19319	20069
Turbo 3-door hatchback	26530	22427	23177
Destination charge	269	269	269

Standard equipment:

GTU: 1.3-liter PFI rotary engine, 5-speed manual transmission, 4-wheel disc brakes, power steering, cloth reclining front bucket seats, theft deterrent system, AM/FM cassette with power diversity antenna, full console with storage, rear defogger, remote fuel door and hatch releases, tinted glass, power mirrors, intermittent wipers, 205/60VR15 SBR tires on alloy wheels. **GTU S** adds: limited-slip differential, front air dam with fog lights, sill extensions, 205/55VR16 tires. **GXL** adds to GTU: air conditioning, fog lights, cargo cover, cruise control, power windows and locks, graphic equalizer, door pockets, tilt steering column, driver's seat cushion angle and lumbar support adjustments, leather-wrapped steering wheel and shift knob, rear wiper/washer. **Turbo** deletes tilt steering column and adds: turbocharged, intercooled engine, anti-lock braking system, air dam with fog lights, sill extensions, 205/55VR16 tires, auto adjusting suspension. **Convertible** adds to GTU: power top, driver's-side airbag, CD player, leather upholstery, cruise control, power windows and locks, fog lights, door pockets, leather-wrapped steering wheel and shift knob, tilt steering column.

Optional equipment:

4-speed automatic transmission	750	638	661
Available on GTU, convertible and GXL 2-seater.			
Air conditioning, GTU, GTU S & conv. . . .	859	688	737
Graphic equalizer, GTU	219	175	188
CD player, GXL & Turbo	875	705	752
Power sunroof, GTU	650	553	573
Leather seats, GXL 2-seater	850	680	729
Turbo	1000	800	857
Armrest lid, conv.	55	42	46
Floormats	59	41	48

Specifications	3-door hatchback	2+2 3-door hatchback	2-door conv.
Wheelbase, in.	95.7	95.7	95.7
Overall length, in.	169.9	169.9	169.9
Overall width, in.	66.5	66.5	66.5
Overall height, in.	49.8	49.8	49.8
Turn diameter, ft.	32.2	32.2	32.2
Curb weight, lbs.	2800	2888	3045

Prices are accurate at time of printing; subject to manufacturer's change.

Mazda 323/Protege

Mazda 323 SE

What's New

The subcompact 323 has been redesigned, offering a choice of two body styles, three engines, and two distinct model series. The 3-door hatchback is still called 323, while the 4-door sedan comes calling as the 323 Protege. Most of the marketing emphasis will be on the Protege, which Mazda touts as roomier than competitors such as the Honda Civic, Nissan Sentra, and Toyota Corolla. Though they have similar front styling, Protege and the hatchback share none of their sheetmetal. Protege has a 98.4-inch wheelbase, nearly four inches longer than last year's 323 sedan and nearly two inches longer than the new hatchback's. Mazda lists passenger space at 92 cubic feet for Protege, four more cubic feet than last year. Trunk space, however, drops from 14.7 cubic feet to 12.8 on the 4-door. The base Protege SE is powered by a 103-horsepower 1.8-liter 4-cylinder with four valves per cylinder. The LX uses a 125-horsepower 1.8 with dual camshafts and four valves per cylinder. Hatchbacks come in base and SE trim, both with an 82-horsepower 1.6-liter 4-cylinder carried over from the previous 323. All models have front-wheel drive; a 4-wheel-drive sedan, with a permanently engaged 4WD system and the 103-horsepower engine, is scheduled to be available at mid-year in all states but California. Not returning from last year's roster are the sporty GTX 4WD hatchback and the 132-horsepower turbocharged 1.6-liter that came with it. All models have motorized front shoulder belts and manual lap belts. Those with the optional automatic transmission have a shift lock that requires the brake pedal be applied to shift out of Park. The basic design for the 323 and Protege will be used for the 1991 Ford Escort and Mercury Tracer, which will go on sale next spring. Mazda will supply most mechanical components, while Ford will do its own styling. Ford owns an equity interest in Mazda.

For

- Acceleration (Protege LX) • Fuel economy
- Passenger room

Against

- Engine noise

Summary

The new 323 and Protege have spacious interiors with ample front head room and generous leg room. In the back seat, there's plenty of leg room, thanks to this year's longer wheelbase. The only place where the 4-door seems to have lost room is in the trunk. Whereas the previous 323's trunk was

a deep, dark hole that swallowed suitcases, the Protege's trunk is shallower and is wide only at the rear. However, the trunk lid opens 90 degrees and the load level is at bumper height, plus all models have split, folding rear seatbacks. In our limited exposure to the new models we didn't notice a huge difference between the two Protege engines in routine driving. The LX's engine has an edge in throttle response, which is a little more prompt, and at high speeds, when the SE's engine runs out of breath sooner. There's an apparent loss in performance with automatic transmission compared to the 5-speed manual, yet acceleration is still adequate and the automatic downshifts quickly for brisk passing. Unfortunately, engine noise is prominent, even when cruising. Our early impressions of the Protege 4-door and the 323 hatchback are that they're well-designed, roomy small cars with above-average performance. Put them on your shopping list.

Specifications

	323 3-door hatchback	Protege 4-door notchback
Wheelbase, in.	96.5	98.4
Overall length, in.	163.6	171.5
Overall width, in.	65.7	65.9
Overall height, in.	54.3	54.1
Turn diameter, ft.	31.5	32.2
Curb weight, lbs.	2238	2359[1]
Cargo vol., cu. ft.	15.8	12.8
Fuel capacity, gals.	13.2	14.5[2]
Seating capacity	5	5
Front headroom, in.	38.6	38.4
Front shoulder room, in.	53.6	53.4
Front legroom, max., in.	42.2	42.2
Rear headroom, in.	37.6	37.1
Rear shoulder room, in.	53.4	53.7
Rear legroom, min., in.	34.2	34.6

1. 2634 lbs., 4WD   2. 15.9 gals., 4WD.

Powertrain layout: transverse front engine/front-wheel drive or permanent 4WD.

Engines	ohc I-4	ohc I-4	dohc I-4
Size, liters/cu. in.	1.6/97	1.8/112	1.8/112
Fuel delivery	PFI	PFI	PFI
Horsepower @ rpm	82 @ 5000	103 @ 5500	125 @ 6500
Torque (lbs./ft.) @ rpm	92 @ 5000	111 @ 4000	114 @ 4500
Availability	S[1]	S[2]	S[3]

EPA city/highway mpg

5-speed OD manual	29/37	28/36	25/30
4-speed OD automatic	26/33	24/31	23/29

1. 323   2. Protege SE and 4WD   3. Protege LX.

Mazda Protege LX

Prices

Mazda 323/Protege

	Retail Price	Dealer Invoice	Low Price
323 3-door hatchback	$6599	$6121	$6321
323 SE 3-door hatchback	8329	7498	7698
Protege SE 4-door notchback	9339	8313	8613
Protege LX 4-door notchback	10349	9099	9399
Protege 4WD 4-door notchback	NA	NA	NA
Destination charge	269	269	269

Standard equipment:

323: 1.6-liter PFI 4-cylinder engine, 5-speed manual transmission, rear defogger, center console, coolant temperature gauge, trip odometer, 155SR13 tires. **323 SE** adds: tinted glass, cloth upholstery, upgraded interior trim, 175/70SR13 tires. **Protege SE** has: 1.8-liter SOHC 16-valve 4-cylinder engine, 5-speed manual transmission, cloth reclining front bucket seats, coolant temperature gauge, trip odometer, tinted glass, dual outside mirrors, 175/70SR13 tires. **4WD** adds: power steering, intermittent wipers, 185/65R14 tires. **LX** adds: DOHC 16-valve engine, 4-wheel disc brakes, tachometer, power mirrors, tilt steering column, upgraded upholstery, 185/60R14 tires.

Optional equipment:

4-speed automatic transmission	700	630	633
Air conditioning	785	630	674
Power steering, 323, Protege SE	250	213	220
AM/FM cassette, Protege	450	342	377
Power sunroof, Protege LX	555	444	476
Alloy wheels, Protege LX	400	320	343
Cruise control, Protege LX	220	176	189
Power windows & locks, Protege LX	300	240	257
Floormats	59	42	48

Mazda 626/MX-6

Mazda 626 LX

What's New

Anti-lock brakes (ABS) are a new option for the LX models of the 626 sedans and the MX-6 sports coupe, which are derived from the same front-drive platform. The optional anti-lock feature includes rear disc brakes in place of the standard drum brakes. Previously, ABS was available only on GT models. Along with the ABS option, the 626 also gains U.S. citizenship. The 626 4-door sedan is being built at Mazda's Flat Rock, Michigan, plant, where the MX-6 and similar Ford Probe are built. All 626 Touring Sedan 5-door hatchbacks, and some of the 626 4-doors and MX-6 models are still imported from Japan. All models wear new styling touches for 1990. The 626 has a new grille and taillamps, while the MX-6 has new bumpers, wider body-side moldings, a body-color grille, and new taillamps. DX models gain a stereo radio with cassette player as standard equipment this year. Model and engine

choices are similar for the 626 and MX-6 lines. DX and LX models are powered by a 110-horsepower 2.2-liter 4-cylinder. GT models use a 145-horsepower turbocharged 2.2. In addition, the MX-6 GT 4WS has Mazda's 4-wheel-steering system.

For

● Acceleration (GT)   ● Anti-lock brakes   ● Fuel economy

Against

● Driveability (automatic transmission)   ● Torque steer (GT)

Summary

Since we highly recommend anti-lock brakes because they provide greater stopping ability in emergencies, we're happy to see they're now optional on the higher-volume LX versions of the 626 and MX-6, not just the high-performance, higher-priced GT models. The optional ABS is a good reason to consider the 626 if you're in the market for a family compact. We tested a 626 LX for more than 12,000 miles, averaging nearly 25 mpg overall while regularly getting more than 30 mpg in highway driving. Our test car suffered no mechanical problems, though the driver's front shoulder belt had to be replaced after the motor quit. The 110-horsepower engine provides fairly brisk acceleration and lively passing power, but the automatic transmission shifts harshly in hard acceleration and balks at downshifting to furnish more power. The 145-horsepower turbocharged engine delivers ferocious acceleration, but excessive torque steer as well; the front end pulls markedly to one side under hard acceleration, a common problem among high-powered front-drive cars. The 626's wheelbase is shorter than either the Honda Accord's or Toyota Camry's, so it has less leg room, and the optional sunroof eats up some front head room, leaving too little for tall people. It still holds four adults without serious cramping. All 626 and MX-6 models have split rear seatbacks that fold down for more cargo space. These cars are more appealing to us with the wider availability of anti-lock brakes, but if you're interested in the MX-6, also check out the similar Ford Probe.

Specifications

	MX-6 2-door notchback	626 4-door notchback	626 5-door hatchback
Wheelbase, in.	99.0	101.4	101.4
Overall length, in.	177.0	179.3	179.3
Overall width, in.	66.5	66.5	66.5
Overall height, in.	53.5	55.5	54.1
Turn diameter, ft.	35.3[1]	36.0	36.0
Curb weight, lbs.	2560[2]	2610	2710
Cargo vol., cu. ft.	15.4	15.9	22.4
Fuel capacity, gals.	15.9	15.9	15.9
Seating capacity	4	5	5
Front headroom, in.	38.4	39.0	38.7
Front shoulder room, in.	54.9	54.9	54.9
Front legroom, max., in.	43.6	43.7	43.6
Rear headroom, in.	37.8	37.8	37.2
Rear shoulder room, in.	53.3	54.9	54.9
Rear legroom, min., in.	31.8	36.6	32.9

1. 33.5 ft. GT 4WS.   2. 2920 lbs., GT 4WS.

> **KEY: ohv** = overhead valve; **ohc** = overhead cam; **dohc** = double overhead cam; **I** = inline cylinders; **V** = cylinders in V configuration; **flat** = horizontally opposed cylinders; **bbl.** = barrel (carburetor); **PFI** = port (multi-point) fuel injection; **TBI** = throttle-body (single-point) fuel injection; **rpm** = revolutions per minute; **OD** = overdrive transmission; **S** = standard; **O** = optional; **NA** = not available.

Prices are accurate at time of printing; subject to manufacturer's change.

Mazda

Powertrain layout: transverse front engine/front-wheel drive.

Engines	ohc I-4	Turbo ohc I-4
Size, liters/cu. in.	2.2/133	2.2/133
Fuel delivery	PFI	PFI
Horsepower @ rpm	110 @ 4700	145 @ 4300
Torque (lbs./ft.) @ rpm	130 @ 3000	190 @ 3500
Availability	S	S
EPA city/highway mpg		
5-speed OD manual	24/31	21/28
4-speed OD automatic	22/28	19/25

Prices

Mazda 626/MX-6	Retail Price	Dealer Invoice	Low Price
626 DX 4-door notchback	$12459	$10872	$11172
626 LX 4-door notchback	13929	12004	12304
626 LX Touring Sedan 5-door hatchback	14129	12175	12475
626 GT Touring Sedan 5-door hatchback	15699	13518	13818
MX-6 DX 2-door notchback	12279	10594	10794
MX-6 LX 2-door notchback	13769	11730	11930
MX-6 GT 2-door notchback	16029	13640	13840
MX-6 GT 4WS 2-door notchback	17229	14654	14854
Destination charge	269	269	269

Standard equipment:

DX: 2.2-liter PFI 4-cylinder engine, 5-speed manual transmission, power steering, cloth reclining front bucket seats, AM/FM cassette, tachometer, coolant temperature gauge, tip odometer, tilt steering column, tinted glass, intermittent wipers, center console, rear defogger, remote fuel door and trunk/hatch releases, remote mirrors, 185/70R14 tires. **LX** adds: power windows and locks, cruise control, upgraded audio system with subwoofer, power antenna, map lights, variable intermittent wipers; **Touring Sedan** has removable shelf panel and rear wiper/washer. **GT** adds: turbocharged, intercooled engine, 4-wheel disc brakes, auto adjusting suspension (except MX-6 4WS), graphic equalizer (MX-6), 195/60HR15 tires on alloy wheels.

Optional equipment:

4-speed automatic transmission	720	634	645
Not available on MX-6 4WS.			
Anti-lock brakes, GT	1000	850	881
w/rear disc brakes, LX	1150	977	1013
Air conditioning	810	649	695
Rear spoiler, MX-6 LX	375	300	321
Alloy wheels, LX	400	320	343
Power moonroof, LX & GT	700	560	600
Standard on MX-6 4WS.			
Cruise control, DX	220	176	189
Theft alarm, LX & GT	100	80	86

Mazda MX-6 GT

	Retail Price	Dealer Invoice	Low Price
CD player, 626 LX & GT, MX-6 GT	700	560	600
205/60 tires, MX-6 GT	30	24	26
Armrest, 626 LX & GT	57	44	48
Floormats	59	41	48

Mazda 929

Mazda 929 S

What's New

The rear-drive 929, Mazda's flagship sedan, rolls into its third model year in the U.S. with a mild facelift and a sportier model powered by a stronger engine. The new 929 S has a 190-horse-power version of Mazda's 3.0-liter V-6 with dual camshafts and four valves per cylinder, and it exhales into a dual exhaust system with two catalytic converters. The base 929 returns with last year's 158-horsepower 3.0, with a single camshaft and three valves per cylinder. Both models are available only with a 4-speed automatic transmission with electronic shift controls. The 929 S also has firmer springs and shock absorbers than the base model and standard anti-lock brakes (ABS remains optional on the base). Other differences are that the variable-assist power steering on the 929 S varies with vehicle speed instead of engine speed and the tires are 205/60HR15 (instead of 195/65HR15) on wire alloy wheels. Styling changes are a new grille and bumpers, lower body cladding, and contrasting lower-body paint. Inside, a new steering wheel houses the cruise-control switches and the seats have been redesigned for more lateral support. Both models have motorized front shoulder belts to meet the federal passive-restraint rule. Gone from last year's options list are the Automatic Adjusting Suspension and the electronic instrument cluster. Mazda says there wasn't enough buyer interest to justify continuing the adjustable suspension, which was available only with anti-lock brakes last year in a $1355 package. Slow sales also caused the demise of the electronic instruments, a $530 extra last year.

For

- Acceleration ● Anti-lock brakes ● Ride
- Passenger room

Against

- Engine and road noise ● Fuel economy

Summary

The 929 S feels livelier starting off and in highway passing than the base engine, which delivers enough power to keep pace with traffic, but feels lethargic rather than eager. The 929 S engine is more energetic, responding quicker to the throttle and running smoothly to higher speeds. Unfortunately, both 929 engines become quite loud under a heavy throttle foot, plus highway cruising is marred by prominent road noise that is annoying on long drives. The 929 S has more cornering power thanks to its firmer suspension and wider tires, without a big penalty in ride quality. The base 929 copes well with sharp bumps and handily smothers rough patches. A spacious interior provides ample room for up to five adults, though the person in the middle of the rear has to straddle the drive shaft tunnel. Getting in and out of the roomy cabin is easy, thanks to tall wide doorways and trunk space is more than adequate. The 929 is a functional, comfortable car that looks and feels bland compared to rivals such as the Acura Legend and Nissan Maxima SE.

Specifications

	4-door notchback
Wheelbase, in.	106.7
Overall length, in.	193.9
Overall width, in.	67.9
Overall height, in.	54.5
Turn diameter, ft.	35.4
Curb weight, lbs.	3477
Cargo vol., cu. ft.	15.1
Fuel capacity, gals.	18.5
Seating capacity	5
Front headroom, in.	37.8
Front shoulder room, in.	55.2
Front legroom, max., in.	43.3
Rear headroom, in.	37.4
Rear shoulder room, in.	55.2
Rear legroom, min., in.	37.0

Powertrain layout: longitudinal front engine/rear-wheel drive.

Engines

	ohc V-6	dohc V-6
Size, liters/cu. in.	3.0/180	3.0/180
Fuel delivery	PFI	PFI
Horsepower @ rpm	158 @ 5500	190 @ 5600
Torque (lbs./ft.) @ rpm	170 @ 4000	191 @ 4500
Availability	S	S
EPA city/highway mpg		
4-speed OD automatic	19/23	18/22

Prices

Mazda 929	Retail Price	Dealer Invoice	Low Price
4-door notchback	$23300	$19474	$19974
S 4-door notchback	24800	20719	21219
Destination charge	269	269	269

Standard equipment:

3.0-liter PFI V-6 engine, 4-speed automatic transmission, power steering, 4-wheel disc brakes, automatic climate control, cloth reclining front bucket seats, power driver's seat, power windows and locks, cruise control, leather-wrapped steering wheel, power mirrors, power moonroof, rear armrest, tachometer, coolant temperature gauge, voltmeter, trip odometer, intermittent wipers, AM/FM cassette with EQ, 195/65R15 tires on alloy wheels. **S** adds: DOHC 24-valve engine, anti-lock brakes, uprated suspension, 205/60R15 tires.

Mazda ● Mercedes-Benz

Optional equipment:	Retail Price	Dealer Invoice	Low Price
Anti-lock brakes, base	1000	850	881
CD player	700	560	600
Leather power seats	880	730	767
Cold Pkg.	250	208	218

All-weather tires, HD battery, semi-concealed wipers, heated driver's seat, larger washer fluid reservoir.

Armrest lid	79	55	64

Mercedes-Benz S-Class

Mercedes-Benz 500SL

What's New

A new SL roadster is set to arrive by January as the featured attraction in the S-Class. The new 2-seat SL succeeds a design that endured 18 years and comes two ways for 1990: The 300SL has a 228-horsepower 3.0-liter inline 6-cylinder engine and the 500SL a 322-horsepower 5.0-liter V-8. Both engines have dual overhead cams and four valves per cylinder. Both models come with a removable aluminum hardtop and a power soft top; they are visually the same except for trunk-lid badging. They are built on a new rear-drive platform with a 99-inch wheelbase, two inches longer than the 1989 560SL's, but the body is 4.3 inches shorter at 176.0. At 4163 pounds, the 500SL is 458 pounds heavier than the 560SL; the 3970-pound 300SL is 265 pounds heavier. Both the 6- and 8-cylinder SLs are likely to be socked with gas guzzler taxes. Prices haven't been announced, but Mercedes has hinted the 500SL will be around $80,000 and the 300SL about $10,000 cheaper. The 300SL comes standard with a 5-speed manual transmission; fifth gear has direct drive, not overdrive. A 5-speed automatic transmission is optional in the 300SL, essentially the 4-speed automatic used in the 300E with an overdrive fifth gear. The V-8-powered 500SL comes only with a 4-speed automatic transmission with a direct-drive top gear. A driver's-side and a passenger-side airbag are standard. The most innovative safety feature is a roll-over bar designed to flip into place behind the seats when needed. The roll bar is made of foam-covered steel tubing that lays flush with the

> **KEY: ohv** = overhead valve; **ohc** = overhead cam; **dohc** = double overhead cam; **I** = inline cylinders; **V** = cylinders in V configuration; **flat** = horizontally opposed cylinders; **bbl.** = barrel (carburetor); **PFI** = port (multi-point) fuel injection; **TBI** = throttle-body (single-point) fuel injection; **rpm** = revolutions per minute; **OD** = overdrive transmission; **S** = standard; **O** = optional; **NA** = not available.

Prices are accurate at time of printing; subject to manufacturer's change.

Mercedes-Benz

rear tonneau cover, ready to deploy in 0.3 seconds if sensors detect signs of an impending roll over. The roll bar works with either top in place and can be raised and lowered by a dashboard button. Anti-lock brakes are standard on both models, and a traction-control system is scheduled to be offered in 1991. Elsewhere in the S-Class lineup, all models have a new fuel injection system borrowed from the SL engines and a revised stereo system. The V-8 models (420SEL, 560SEL, and 560SEC) have dual front airbags as standard; the 6-cylinder models (300SE and 300SEL) have a driver's side airbag standard and a passenger-side airbag optional. Anti-lock brakes are standard on all. Next spring, the SEL body will be fitted with a 3.5-liter 6-cylinder turbocharged diesel engine to create the 350SDL, the first Mercedes turbodiesel in the U.S. since 1987. New S-Class sedans are planned for 1992. Mercedes is expected to offer a V-12 engine to rival the 12-cylinder BMW 750iL.

For

- Anti-lock brakes • Airbags • Acceleration (V-8s)
- Resale value

Against

- Fuel economy • Price

Summary

The new Mercedes-Benz SL is much more athletic than its predecessor and, in V-8 form, has a top speed of 155 mph. Once the V-8 gets above about 3000 rpm, it feels like a runaway freight train; a light press of the gas pedal is answered by a gush of power. The 300SL is no slouch, but passing on 2-lane roads that is effortless in the 500SL can be dicey in the 300SL. Both SLs are impressively stable at speed, with a rock-solid bearing that inspires confidence. These are also comfortable, luxurious cars, as well as sporting roadsters, with sound ergonomics and attention to detail. When the new SL arrives, the very rich will have a good excuse to spend lots of money. Among the S-Class sedans, there are some relative bargains available these days, but you have to settle for one of the slow-selling 6-cylinder models—and rather slow acceleration as well. Our advice is to spend more for a V-8 model to get stronger acceleration and better resale value. However, before you fork over $60,000 or more for a Mercedes SEL, check out the BMW 750iL and its V-12 engine. The 750iL is newer and more enjoyable to drive. We also suggest you try the Infiniti Q45 and Lexus LS 400 luxury sedans, two impressive newcomers from Japan. You'll lose some snob appeal, but save $20,000-$30,000 that can be invested or spent on something else.

Specifications

	SL 2-door conv.	560SEC 2-door notchback	300SE 4-door notchback	SEL 4-door notchback
Wheelbase, in.	99.0	112.2	115.6	121.1
Overall length, in.	176.0	199.2	202.6	208.1
Overall width, in.	71.3	72.0	71.7	71.7
Overall height, in.	50.7	55.0	56.6	56.7
Turn diameter, ft.	35.2	38.1	39.0	40.6
Curb weight, lbs.	3970	3915	3730	3770
Cargo vol., cu. ft.	7.9	14.9	15.2	15.2
Fuel capacity, gals.	21.1	27.1	27.1	27.1
Seating capacity	2	4	5	5
Front headroom, in.	37.1	36.8	37.2	37.3
Front shoulder room, in.	55.4	57.2	56.2	56.2
Front legroom, max., in.	42.4	41.9	41.9	41.9

	SL 2-door conv.	560SEC 2-door notchback	300SE 4-door notchback	SEL 4-door notchback
Rear headroom, in.	—	36.0	36.5	36.6
Rear shoulder room, in.	—	54.2	55.7	55.7
Rear legroom, min., in.	—	30.6	33.4	39.6

Powertrain layout: longitudinal front engine/rear-wheel drive.

Engines

	dohc I-6	ohc V-8	dohc V-8	ohc V-8
Size, liters/cu. in.	3.0/181	4.2/256	5.0/303	5.6/338
Fuel delivery	PFI	PFI	PFI	PFI
Horsepower @ rpm	228 @ 6300	201 @ 5200	322 @ 5500	238 @ 4800
Torque (lbs./ft.) @ rpm	201 @ 4600	228 @ 3600	332 @ 4000	278 @ 3500
Availability	S[1]	S[2]	S[3]	S[4]

EPA city/highway mpg

5-speed manual	15/21			
4-speed automatic		15/18	14/18	14/16
5-speed OD automatic	16/22			

1. 300SL; 300SE and 300 SEL have 177 horsepower and 188 lbs/ft torque. 2. 420 SEL 3. 500SL. 4. 560SEC and 560SEL.

Prices

Mercedes-Benz S-Class (1989 prices)

	Retail Price	Dealer Invoice	Low Price
300SE 4-door notchback	$51400	$41120	$44620
300SEL 4-door notchback	55100	44080	47580
420SEL 4-door notchback	61210	48968	52468
560SEL 4-door notchback	72280	57824	61324
560SEC 2-door notchback	79840	63872	67372
560SL 2-door convertible	64230	51384	54884
Destination charge	250	250	250
Gas Guzzler Tax, 300SE, SEL	650	650	650
420SEL	1050	1050	1050
560SL	1300	1300	1300
560SEL, SEC	1500	1500	1500

Standard equipment:

300SE, 300SEL, 420SEL: 3.0-liter PFI 6-cylinder or 4.2-liter PFI V-8 engine, 4-speed automatic transmission, power steering, anti-lock braking system, 4-wheel disc brakes, Supplemental Restraint System, outboard rear lap/shoulder belts, anti-theft alarm, central locking, power windows, air conditioning, automatic climate control, AM/FM ST ET cassette, leather power front seats with 2-position memory, power telescopic steering column, leather-wrapped steering wheel and shift handle, rear defogger, cruise control, headlight wipers and washers, heated power mirrors, outside temperature indicator, tachometer, coolant temperature and oil pressure gauges, lighted visor mirrors, 205/65VR15 SBR tires on alloy wheels. **560SEL and 560SEC** add: 5.6-liter PFI V-8, automatic rear level control, limited-slip differential. **560SL** has removable hardtop and folding convertible top.

Optional equipment:

Passenger-side airbag, 300s	600	480	540
Includes knee bolster and lockable center console.			
Power rear-window sunshade, exc. 560SL	355	284	320
Orthopedic front backrests (each), exc. 560SL	315	252	284
560SL	110	88	99
Power rear seat, 300SEL & 420SEL	665	532	599
Four-place seating pkg., 300 & 420SEL	2835	2268	2552
560SL	2175	1740	1958
Heated front seat, 300SE, 300SEL, 420SEL, 560SL	495	396	446
Heated rear seat, 300SE, 300SEL, 420SEL	495	396	446

Mercedes-Benz 190E 2.6

1989 Mercedes-Benz 190E 2.6

What's New

The 190D 2.5, Mercedes' only diesel model last year, has been dropped, so the "Baby Benz" line consists of a single model this year, the 190E 2.6 4-door sedan. Mercedes will add two new turbocharged diesel models next spring, the mid-size 250D and the larger 350SDL. The compact 190E uses a 158-horsepower 2.6-liter 6-cylinder engine that's also found in the mid-size 260E. The 190E comes with either a 5-speed manual or 4-speed automatic transmission, the only Mercedes sedan that offers that choice. Changes for 1990 are that power front seats are standard instead of optional, the fuel injection system is a new design borrowed from the SL roadster, and the new stereo radio/cassette player has anti-theft coding and a new location—lower in the center of the dashboard so a cassette holder could be built into the area above. The base of the center console has been trimmed to allow more knee room, while the top portion has more wood trim. A driver's-side airbag and anti-lock brakes are standard.

For

- Acceleration • Anti-lock brakes • Airbag
- Ride • Handling

Against

- Rear seat room • Trunk space • Price

Summary

Prices on the 190E soared from $23,000 in 1984 to nearly $34,000 in 1988, but they have actually dropped since then even though more features have been made standard. No wonder: $34,000 for a compact sedan with a cramped rear seat and small trunk is hard to swallow, even if it is a Mercedes. For less money, you could buy a roomier Acura Legend with similar features—and a lot of people did just that. The 190E has the same high-quality materials, sound engineering, and impeccable fit and finish as other Mercedes; all it lacks is the size to justify its price. Two people are comfortable, but carrying more than that requires using the back seat, which can hold two adults maximum, and probably not in comfort. If you always wanted a Benz, but just can't afford $40,000 or more for one of the larger models, then the 190 is your ticket to heaven. If you want more space than the 190 provides, then the Legend is a much better value. So are other luxury sedans for less than $30,000, such as the Nissan Maxima and Cadillac De Ville. They don't match Mercedes' quality, but they won't cramp your style the way the 190 does.

Specifications

	4-door notchback
Wheelbase, in.	104.9
Overall length, in.	175.1
Overall width, in.	66.5
Overall height, in.	54.7
Turn diameter, ft.	34.8
Curb weight, lbs.	2955
Cargo vol., cu. ft.	11.7
Fuel capacity, gals.	16.7
Seating capacity	5
Front headroom, in.	36.9
Front shoulder room, in.	53.5
Front legroom, max., in.	41.9
Rear headroom, in.	36.3
Rear shoulder room, in.	53.2
Rear legroom, min., in.	31.1

Powertrain layout: longitudinal front engine/rear-wheel drive.

Engines

	ohc I-6
Size, liters/cu. in.	2.6/159
Fuel delivery	PFI
Horsepower @ rpm	158 @ 5800
Torque (lbs./ft.) @ rpm	162 @ 4600
Availability	S

EPA city/highway mpg

5-speed OD manual	19/27
4-speed automatic	20/23

Prices

Mercedes-Benz 190 (1989 prices)	Retail Price	Dealer Invoice	Low Price
190D 2.5 4-door notchback, automatic	$30980	$24784	$26784
190E 2.6 4-door notchback, 5-speed	31590	25272	27272
190E 2.6 4-door notchback, automatic	32500	26000	28000
Destination charge	250	250	250

Standard equipment:

2.6-liter PFI 6-cylinder engine (2.5-liter diesel on 190D 2.5), 5-speed manual or 4-speed automatic transmission, power steering, anti-lock braking system, 4-wheel disc brakes, Supplemental Restraint System, outboard rear lap/shoulder belts, automatic climate control, power windows and locks, cruise control, intermittent wipers, rear defogger, vinyl reclining front bucket seats, heated power mirrors, AM/FM ST ET cassette, tachometer, coolant temperature and oil pressure gauges, trip odometer, lighted visor mirrors, wide bodyside moldings, 185/65R15 (V-rated on 190E 2.6) SBR tires on alloy wheels.

Optional equipment:

Anti-theft alarm system	515	412	464
Rear head restraints	295	236	266
Headlamp wipers and washers	280	224	252
Metallic paint	390	312	351
Power front seats	950	760	855
Orthopedic front backrests, each	315	252	284
Heated front seats	495	396	446
Leather upholstered seats	1425	1140	1283
Velour upholstered seats	1405	1124	1265

> **KEY: ohv** = overhead valve; **ohc** = overhead cam; **dohc** = double overhead cam; **I** = inline cylinders; **V** = cylinders in V configuration; **flat** = horizontally opposed cylinders; **bbl.** = barrel (carburetor); **PFI** = port (multi-point) fuel injection; **TBI** = throttle-body (single-point) fuel injection; **rpm** = revolutions per minute; **OD** = overdrive transmission; **S** = standard; **O** = optional; **NA** = not available.

Prices are accurate at time of printing; subject to manufacturer's change.

Mercedes-Benz 260/300

1989 Mercedes-Benz 300CE

What's New

Mercedes' automatic 4-wheel-drive system, available in Europe since 1987, appears this fall on the 300E sedan and the 300TE station wagon. Called 4Matic, the system automatically engages 4WD for more traction on slippery surfaces or when taking off from a standstill. When cruising on smooth, dry surfaces, all the power normally goes to the rear wheels. On slippery surfaces, 4Matic uses the same sensors as the anti-lock brakes to detect wheel slip and determine when to transfer some of the engine torque to the front wheels. An indicator light on the dashboard signals when 4Matic is engaged. The standard anti-lock brake system remains fully operational when 4Matic is engaged. Rear-drive versions of the 300E and 300TE also return this fall. Elsewhere in the mid-size 260/300 series, the 300CE 2-door coupe gets 40 more horsepower thanks to a new engine: the dual-camshaft, 24-valve 3.0-liter 6-cylinder also used in the 300SL roadster. Horsepower is rated at 217 in the 300CE, 11 fewer than in the SL because of a more restrictive catalytic converter. Other 300 models use a 177-horsepower 3.0-liter six with a single camshaft and 12 valves. The 260E sedan uses a 158-horse-power 2.6-liter six. Next spring, a 2.5-liter 5-cylinder turbocharged diesel engine will be added in a sedan called the 250D. Other changes this fall are that all models have a new fuel-injection system and a revised Becker stereo system; leather upholstery is standard on the 300E; and the 300CE gains burl walnut trim throughout the interior and a wood-trimmed storage bin between the rear seats. Other models have new seats with map pockets rather than nets, and wood trim across the dashboard and doors. Outside, lower-body panels have new protective panels and the mirrors are painted body color. A driver's-side airbag is standard on all models and a passenger-side airbag is optional. Anti-lock brakes are standard across the board.

For

- Acceleration • Anti-lock brakes • Airbags
- Handling • Ride • 4WD traction (4Matic)
- Passenger and cargo room

KEY: ohv = overhead valve; **ohc** = overhead cam; **dohc** = double overhead cam; **I** = inline cylinders; **V** = cylinders in V configuration; **flat** = horizontally opposed cylinders; **bbl.** = barrel (carburetor); **PFI** = port (multi-point) fuel injection; **TBI** = throttle-body (single-point) fuel injection; **rpm** = revolutions per minute; **OD** = overdrive transmission; **S** = standard; **O** = optional; **NA** = not available.

Against

- Fuel economy • Price

Summary

Mercedes is calling in fresh troops for its mid-size line to combat the BMW 5-Series sedan and new competitors from Japan, the Infiniti Q45 and Lexus LS 400, which are less expensive than the 260/300 models yet offer V-8 engines. Mercedes' prices jumped substantially during most of the 1980s, but have only crept up the past couple of years because fewer buyers were willing to pay so much money—even for the vaunted 3-pointed star. We're highly impressed by the Infiniti and Lexus luxury sedans, but we still find much to like about the Mercedes 260/300 line. These cars have the high-quality finish and purposeful engineering you expect from this brand, plus responsive performance, ample room inside, and the extra safety of anti-lock brakes and airbags. Service and maintenance can be expensive on a Mercedes, but the assurances of longevity and good resale value compensate in the long run. We wonder, though, will Infiniti and Lexus be just as reliable, and will they be less expensive to maintain? If so, what will that do to Mercedes' resale value? Don't expect Mercedes to stand still in the face of this new competition. The 4Matic models are only the first wave of changes we expect from Mercedes in an effort to stay on top.

Specifications

	300CE 2-door notchback	260E/300E 4-door notchback	300TE 5-door wagon
Wheelbase, in.	106.9	110.2	110.2
Overall length, in.	183.9	187.2	188.2
Overall width, in.	68.5	68.5	68.5
Overall height, in.	55.5	56.9	59.8
Turn diameter, ft.	35.8	36.7	36.7
Curb weight, lbs.	3310	3210	3530
Cargo vol., cu. ft.	14.4	14.6	76.8
Fuel capacity, gals.	20.9	20.9	21.4
Seating capacity	4	5	5
Front headroom, in.	36.0	36.9	37.4
Front shoulder room, in.	55.7	55.9	55.9
Front legroom, max., in.	41.9	41.7	41.7
Rear headroom, in.	35.5	36.9	36.8
Rear shoulder room, in.	50.2	55.7	55.6
Rear legroom, min., in.	29.6	33.5	33.9

Powertrain layout: longitudinal front engine/rear-wheel drive or automatic 4-wheel drive.

Engines

	ohc I-6	ohc I-6	dohc I-6
Size, liters/cu. in.	2.6/159	3.0/181	3.0/181
Fuel delivery	PFI	PFI	PFI
Horsepower @ rpm	158 @ 5800	177 @ 5700	217 @ 6300
Torque (lbs./ft.) @ rpm	162 @ 4600	188 @ 4400	201 @ 4600
Availability	S[1]	S[2]	S[3]

EPA city/highway mpg

4-speed automatic	20/24	18/22	NA

1. 260E. 2. 300E and 300TE. 3. 300CE.

Prices

Mercedes-Benz 260/300 (1989 prices)	Retail Price	Dealer Invoice	Low Price
260E 4-door notchback	$39200	$31360	$33860
300E 4-door notchback	44850	35880	38380

	Retail Price	Dealer Invoice	Low Price
300CE 2-door notchback	53880	43104	45604
300TE 5-door wagon	48210	38568	41068
Destination charge	250	250	250
Gas Guzzler Tax, 300TE	650	650	650

Standard equipment:

260E: 2.6-liter PFI 6-cylinder engine, 4-speed automatic transmission, power steering, anti-lock braking system, 4-wheel disc brakes, Supplemental Restraint System, cruise control, rear headrests, outboard rear lap/shoulder belts, heated power mirrors, automatic climate control, power windows and locks, rear defogger, tachometer, coolant temperature and oil pressure gauges, trip odometer, intermittent wipers, heated windshield washer fluid reservoir and nozzles, 195/65VR15 SBR tires; power sunroof is available at no charge. **300E** adds: 3.0-liter engine, headlamp wipers and washers, anti-theft alarm system, power telescopic steering column, power front seat, outside temperature indicator (300CE has leather upholstery; velour is available at no charge). **300TE wagon** adds: automatic level control, roof rack, rear wiper/washer.

Optional equipment:

Anti-theft alarm system, 260E	580	464	522
Metallic paint, 260E	425	340	383
Others	NC	NC	NC
Partition net & luggage cover, 300TE . . .	425	340	383
Passenger-side airbag	600	480	540
Includes knee bolster and lockable center console.			
Rear reading lamps, 260E & 300E	80	64	72
Power rear-window sunshade, exc. 300TE .	355	284	320
Power front seats, 260E	950	760	855
Orthopedic front backrests, each	315	252	284
Heated front seats	495	396	446
Rear-facing third seat, 300TE	1070	856	963
Leather upholstered seats, exc. 300CE . . .	1425	1140	1283
Velour upholstered seats, exc. 300CE . . .	1405	1124	1265
300CE	NC	NC	NC

Mercury Capri

Mercury Capri (prototype)

What's New

Mercury dealers are scheduled to get a Mazda Miata-fighter in the spring of 1990. The Capri, a front-drive 2 + 2 convertible, is set to be introduced then as a 1991 model. Capri is based on a Mazda 323 chassis and will be built by Ford in Australia. Its body is designed by Italian stylist Giorgetto Giugiaro. Ford hopes Capri will sell for several thousand dollars less than the hot-selling rear-drive Miata sports car. It also portrays the Capri's front-drive traction and rear-seat space as advantages over Miata. Two series are planned: a base model powered by a 1.6-liter single-cam four with a choice of manual or au-

Mercury Capri (prototype)

tomatic transmissions, and a high-performance XR2 with a twincam, turbocharged 1.6 available only with a 5-speed manual. Both versions are to be available with an optional removable hard top. Capri is derived from a Ghia show car called the Barchetta. Specifications and prices were unavailable at publication time.

Mercury Cougar

Mercury Cougar

What's New

After a clean-sheet redesign for 1989, this mid-size coupe slips into 1990 with only minor changes. The head restraints are now contoured, and items included in the Luxury Lamp Group are now available individually. The Luxury Light Group has been dropped, but its components return as separate options. Cougar shares with the Ford Thunderbird coupe an all-new design that's bigger on the inside and smaller on the outside than the 6-year-old model it replaced. The '89 remake brought an all-independent suspension but retained the rear-drive layout. The base Cougar LS comes only with a 3.8-liter V-6 and a 4-speed overdrive automatic transmission. The XR7 has a supercharged and intercooled version of the 3.8. XR7s come standard with 4-wheel anti-lock disc brakes, a setup that's optional on the LS in place of its disc/drum brakes. Standard on the supercharged car is variable shock-absorber damping that adjusts automatically or lets the driver dial in a soft or a firm ride. XR7 has power front seats with adjustable backrest wings and inflatable lumbar bolsters. All models get automatic front shoulder belts, with manual-locking lap belts, and shoulder belts for outboard rear-seat passengers. XR7s also get split, folding rear seatbacks that open to the trunk for added cargo capacity.

Prices are accurate at time of printing; subject to manufacturer's change.

Mercury

For

- Performance (XR7)   • Handling/roadholding
- Anti-lock brakes   • Transmission (5-speed manual)

Against

- Performance (LS)   • Fuel economy (XR7)

Summary

Cougar's squared-off roofline gives its rear seat passengers a hair more head room and nearly one inch more rear-seat leg room than the Thunderbird. And Cougar is slightly less aerodynamic than its Ford sibling. Otherwise, the two are functionally identical. Cougar's best attributes are ride and handling. The LS suspension remains absorbent at all speeds, and while the XR7 is more capable than the LS in hard driving, its harsher ride is a stiff price to pay. Stopping power is outstanding and noise is well muffled except for engine harshness under hard throttle. The cabin offers good room for four adults; a middle-rear-seat passenger must straddle a wide driveline tunnel. Alas, the base LS is downright sluggish when called upon for more than gentle acceleration. Even the supercharged engine occasionally struggles against the 3500-pound curb weight. Automatic transmission is the sensible XR7 choice; performance suffers little and you avoid the recalcitrant shift action and heavy clutch of the 5-speed manual. Fortunately, Ford is working on a 4.6-liter V-8 for the '91 Cougar, but will offer it only on the LS. Our road tests yielded an unremarkable 19.7 mph with an LS and only 17.4 mpg with an XR7 automatic, and that on the supercharged engine's required—and expensive—premium unleaded fuel. Overall, though Cougar has the style, size, and comfort that should justify its price to mid-size specialty-car buyers. A similarly equipped front-wheel drive Oldsmobile Cutlass Supreme with anti-lock brakes costs about the same. The Cougar rides and handles at least as well and is more spacious inside.

Specifications

	2-door notchback
Wheelbase, in.	113.0
Overall length, in.	198.7
Overall width, in.	72.7
Overall height, in.	52.7
Turn diameter, ft.	34.9
Curb weight, lbs.	3608
Cargo vol., cu. ft.	14.7
Fuel capacity, gals.	19.0
Seating capacity	5
Front headroom, in.	38.1
Front shoulder room, in.	59.1
Front legroom, max., in.	42.5
Rear headroom, in.	37.6
Rear shoulder room, in.	59.1
Rear legroom, min., in.	36.6

Powertrain layout: longitudinal front engine/rear-wheel drive.

Engines

	ohv V-6	Supercharged ohv V-6
Size, liters/cu. in.	3.8/232	3.8/232
Fuel delivery	PFI	PFI
Horsepower @ rpm	140 @ 3800	210 @ 4000
Torque (lbs./ft.) @ rpm	215 @ 2400	315 @ 2600
Availability	S	S[1]

EPA city/highway mpg	ohv V-6	Supercharged ohv V-6
5-speed OD manual		17/24
4-speed OD automatic	19/27	17/23

1. XR7.

Prices

Mercury Cougar	Retail Price	Dealer Invoice	Low Price
LS 2-door notchback	$15911	$13780	$14483
XR7 2-door notchback	20217	17441	18370
Destination charge	455	455	455

Standard equipment:

LS: 3.8-liter PFI V-6, 4-speed automatic transmission, power steering and brakes, air conditioning, cloth reclining front bucket seats, tinted glass, intermittent wipers, electronic instruments (tachometer, coolant temperature, oil pressure, voltmeter, trip computer, service interval reminder), power windows and mirrors, visor mirrors, AM/FM radio, motorized front shoulder belts with manual lap belts, rear lap/shoulder belts, 205/70R15 tires. **XR7** adds: supercharged engine with dual exhaust, 5-speed manual transmission, handling suspension, Traction-Lok axle, sport seats with power lumbar and side bolsters, analog instruments (tachometer, coolant temperature, oil pressure, boost/vacuum), Diagnostic Maintenance Monitor, 225/60VR16 tires on alloy wheels.

Optional equipment:

4-speed automatic transmission, XR7	539	458	485
Performance Traction-Lok axle, LS	100	85	90
Required with anti-lock brakes.			
Anti-lock braking system, LS	985	838	887
Preferred Pkg. 261B	262	226	236
Preferred Pkg. 262B	1164	990	1048
Preferred Pkg. 263A	1965	1671	1769
Preferred Pkg. 265B	NC	NC	NC
Preferred Pkg. 266B	1013	861	912
WSW tires, LS	73	62	66
225/60VR16 Eagle GT+4 tires, XR7	73	62	66
Conventional spare tire, LS	73	62	66
Radial spoke wheels covers, LS	228	194	205
w/Pkg. 261	143	121	129
Alloy wheels, LS	298	254	268
LS w/Pkg. 261	213	181	192
Styled sport wheel covers, LS	85	73	77
Power Lock Group	246	209	221
Diagnostic maintenance monitor, LS	89	76	80
Power moonroof	741	630	667
Power seats, each	261	222	235
AM/FM cassette	137	116	123
AM/FM cassette w/High Level Audio	441	375	397
w/Pkg. 262 or 265	304	259	274
JBL sound system	488	415	439
CD player	491	418	442
Power antenna	76	64	68
AM/FM delete (credit)	(245)	(208)	(208)
Clearcoat metallic paint	188	160	169
Leather trim	489	416	440
Split fold-down rear seat	133	113	120
Cold Weather Group, LS, XR7 5-speed	195	167	176
XR7 automatic	168	145	151
w/Pkg. 261, 262 or 263	45	38	41
XR7 5-speed w/Pkg. 265 or 266	45	38	41
XR7 automatic w/Pkg. 265 or 266	18	16	16
Rear defogger	150	128	135
Light Group	46	39	41
Lighted visor mirrors	100	85	90
Illuminated entry	82	69	74
Luxury Lamp Group	244	207	220
Headlamp Convenience Group	176	149	158
Cornering lamps	68	58	61
Keyless entry	219	185	197
w/Pkg. 262, 263 or 266	137	226	123

	Retail Price	Dealer Invoice	Low Price
Cruise control	191	163	172
Tilt steering column	124	106	112
Leather-wrapped steering wheel	63	54	57
Front floormats	33	28	30
Anti-theft alarm system	183	155	165
California emissions pkg.	100	85	90

Mercury Grand Marquis

Mercury Grand Marquis Colony Park LS

What's New

These traditional full-size, rear-drive sedans and wagons weigh in with a new dashboard and instrument panel, a driver's-side air bag, rear shoulder belts, standard tilt steering column, and other revisions. Grand Marquis is a slightly plusher version of the Ford LTD Crown Victoria. It uses the same 5.0-liter fuel-injected V-8 and 4-speed overdrive automatic transmission as its sole powertrain. The carried-over sedan seats six. The wagon, which is called the Colony Park, has 8-passenger capacity with the optional dual rear-facing seats. Both are available in base GS and upscale LS trim. For '90, the all-new instrument panel features a new backlit gauge cluster, modified climate controls, side-window demisters, and a larger-capacity glove box. Front speakers have been moved from the dashboard to the door panels, eliminating the map pockets; top-level audio systems drive four instead of six speakers. The previously optional pivoting vent windows and Tripminder computer have been dropped, while bumper guards, formerly standard on sedans, have moved to the options list. A new rear axle increases the rear track from 62 inches to 63.3 and there's now a single key for doors and ignition. Ordering the optional power antenna requires that you also purchase a rear-window defroster.

For

- Performance • Driveability • Passenger room
- Cargo space • Quietness • Trailer towing ability

Against

- Fuel economy • Size and weight • Maneuverability

Summary

Among the dwindling number of full-size, rear drive sedans and wagons, the Grand Marquis and LTD Crown Victoria are our favorites. Their direct competitors are the Chevrolet Caprice sedan and wagon, and the Buick Estate and Oldsmobile Custom Cruiser wagons. We prefer the Fords mainly for their driveability and better engine performance. The Grand Mar-

quis/LTD V-8 has slightly more torque than GM's, plus Ford's automatic transmission is better behaved. It stays out of overdrive until 40-45 mph, which reduces the amount of gear shifting and improves engine response in urban traffic. In most other areas, the GM cars are comparable to the Ford and Mercury. You get true 6-passenger seating, ample cargo room, and the ability to tow hefty trailers (up to 5000 pounds on a properly equipped Grand Marquis). What you also get are abysmal fuel economy, a cumbersome feel around town, and loose handling and a floaty ride on the open road. In their favor, these heavy cars get high insurance-industry ratings for occupant crash protection. Many more modern midsize cars cost nearly as much, yet don't have as much room or brawn. Mercury doesn't offer anything of substance over the Ford versions of this car, so shop both for the best deal.

Specifications

	4-door notchback	5-door wagon
Wheelbase, in.	114.3	114.3
Overall length, in.	213.6	218.0
Overall width, in.	77.5	79.3
Overall height, in.	55.6	56.5
Turn diameter, ft.	39.1	39.1
Curb weight, lbs.	3832	4006
Cargo vol., cu. ft.	21.0	90.4
Fuel capacity, gals.	18.0	18.0
Seating capacity	6	8
Front headroom, in.	38.3	39.2
Front shoulder room, in.	61.6	61.6
Front legroom, max., in.	42.5	42.5
Rear headroom, in.	37.2	39.1
Rear shoulder room, in.	61.5	61.5
Rear legroom, min., in.	39.7	38.5

Powertrain layout: longitudinal front engine/rear-wheel drive.

Engines

	ohv V-8
Size, liters/cu. in.	5.0/302
Fuel delivery	PFI
Horsepower @ rpm	150 @ 3200
Torque (lbs./ft.) @ rpm	270 @ 2000
Availability	S

EPA city/highway mpg

4-speed OD automatic	17/24

Prices

Mercury Grand Marquis	Retail Price	Dealer Invoice	Low Price
GS 4-door notchback	$17633	$15262	$16046
LS 4-door notchback	18133	15687	16498
Colony Park GS 5-door wagon	18348	15869	16691
Colony Park LS 5-door wagon	18920	16356	17208
Destination charge	505	505	505

Standard equipment:

GS: 5.0-liter PFI V-8 engine, 4-speed automatic transmission, power steering, driver's-side airbag, rear shoulder belts, air conditioning, tinted glass,

> **KEY: ohv** = overhead valve; **ohc** = overhead cam; **dohc** = double overhead cam; **I** = inline cylinders; **V** = cylinders in V configuration; **flat** = horizontally opposed cylinders; **bbl.** = barrel (carburetor); **PFI** = port (multi-point) fuel injection; **TBI** = throttle-body (single-point) fuel injection; **rpm** = revolutions per minute; **OD** = overdrive transmission; **S** = standard; **O** = optional; **NA** = not available.

Prices are accurate at time of printing; subject to manufacturer's change.

reclining front seats, cloth trim (vinyl on wagon), power windows, intermittent wipers, tilt steering column, digital clock, coolant temperature gauge, trip odometer, Autolamp system, padded half vinyl roof, right visor mirror, AM/FM radio, power 3-way tailgate (wagon), lockable storage compartments (wagon), simulated woodgrain exterior applique (wagon), 215/70R15 WSW SBR tires. **LS** adds: rear armrest (4- door), front seatback map pockets, Light Group.

Optional equipment:

Traction-Lok axle	100	85	90
Preferred Pkg. 156A, GS 4-door	975	830	878
Pkg. 157A w/alloy wheels, GS 4-door	1233	1048	1110
w/wire wheel covers	1021	868	919
Pkg. 172A, LS 4-door	1253	1064	1128
Pkg. 192A, GS wagon	1132	963	1019
LS wagon	1086	924	977
Pkg. 193A, GS wagon	1385	1177	1247
LS wagon	1339	1138	1205
Conventional spare tire	85	73	77
Automatic climate control	216	183	194
w/rear defogger	66	56	59
Rear defogger	150	128	135
Insta-Clear heated windshield	250	213	225
HD battery	27	23	24
Power Lock Group	255	217	230
Power decklid release	50	43	45
Power seats, each	261	222	235
AM/FM cassette	137	112	123
High Level Audio System	472	401	425
w/Pkg. 157 or 172	335	285	302
w/Pkg. 193	167	142	150
Premium sound system	168	143	151
Power antenna	76	64	68
AM/FM delete (credit)	(206)	(175)	(175)
Cornering lamps	68	58	61
Bodyside moldings, wagons	66	56	59
Two-tone paint	159	135	143
Formal coach vinyl roof	665	565	599
Clearcoat paint	230	196	207
Leather-wrapped steering wheel	63	54	57
Floormats	43	46	39
Cruise control	191	163	172
Illuminated entry	82	69	74
Light Group	46	39	41
Lighted visor mirrors	109	92	98
Automatic load leveling	195	166	176
Handling/HD suspension	26	22	23
Trailer Tow III Pkg.	405	332	365
Inboard-facing rear seats, wagons	173	147	156
Leather seat trim, LS	489	416	440
Wire wheel covers	228	194	205
Turbine-spoke alloy wheels	228	194	205
w/Pkg. having wire wheel covers	212	180	191

Mercury Sable

What's New

Sable, Mercury's line of mid-size front-drive sedans and wagons, returns with a standard driver's-side air bag and newly optional anti-lock brakes. ABS is available only on sedans, and replaces the rear drums with discs. The dashboard and instrument cluster are new, and slide-out coin and cup holder trays have been added. A tilt steering column is now standard, and a compact-disc player is a new option. Sable is a slightly plusher version of the Ford Taurus and comes in GS and LS grades. As before, power is supplied by a standard 3.0-liter V-6 or an optional 3.8-liter V-6. Ordering the 3.8 this year brings variable assist power steering. The only transmission is a 4-speed overdrive automatic. Among other changes for '90, the automatic parking brake release remains standard

Mercury Sable LS

on LS models, but is no longer available on others. And front and rear headrests on the sedans get a trimmer profile intended to improve rearward visibility.

For

- Performance (3.8 V-6) • Handling/roadholding • Ride
- Passenger room • Cargo space

Against

- Fuel economy • Electronic instruments

Summary

The standard 3.0-liter V-6 is adequate for Sable, but since these cars debuted for 1986 we've felt that more power was desirable. The 3.8 provides it, with greater torque for brisker acceleration from a standing start and stronger passing response. Neither engine is particularly fuel efficient, however. Expect under 20 mpg in city driving and around 23-25 mpg on the highway. Like the similar Ford Taurus, Sable has uncommonly good handling for a domestic family car. The well-designed suspension promotes spirited cornering with minimal body lean, while the responsive power steering is firm and accurate. Even the standard tires combine good grip in turns with reassuring wet-road traction. Sable's suspension is a little softer than Taurus's, so the Mercury rides a little better over rough pavement, though it's still firmer than many American-car buyers are accustomed to. Interior space and furnishings are nearly identical to those found in Taurus. Among our few complaints: the optional electronic instrument cluster is hard to read in sunlight and offers few advantages over the standard analog cluster.

Specifications

	4-door notchback	5-door wagon
Wheelbase, in.	106.0	106.0
Overall length, in.	192.2	193.2
Overall width, in.	70.8	70.8
Overall height, in.	54.3	55.1
Turn diameter, ft.	38.1	38.1
Curb weight, lbs.	3131	3260
Cargo vol., cu. ft.	18.5	90.4
Fuel capacity, gals.	16.0	16.0
Seating capacity	6	8
Front headroom, in.	38.3	38.6
Front shoulder room, in.	57.5	57.5
Front legroom, max., in.	41.7	41.7
Rear headroom, in.	37.6	38.4
Rear shoulder room, in.	57.5	57.5
Rear legroom, min., in.	37.1	36.6

Powertrain layout: transverse front engine/front-wheel drive.

Engines

	ohv V-6	ohv V-6
Size, liters/cu. in.	3.0/182	3.8/232
Fuel delivery	PFI	PFI
Horsepower @ rpm	140 @ 4800	140 @ 3800
Torque (lbs./ft.) @ rpm	160 @ 3000	215 @ 2200
Availability	S	O

EPA city/highway mpg

4-speed OD automatic	21/29	19/28

Prices

Mercury Sable	Retail Price	Dealer Invoice	Low Price
GS 4-door notchback	$15009	$12995	$13660
LS 4-door notchback	16011	13847	14565
GS 5-door wagon	15711	13592	14294
LS 5-door wagon	16789	14509	15267
Destination charge	450	450	450

Standard equipment:

GS: 3.0-liter PFI V-6 engine, 4-speed automatic transmission, power steering, driver's-side airbag, air conditioning, 50/50 cloth reclining front seats with armrests, 60/40 split rear seatback (wagons), rear shoulder belts, tinted glass, digital clock, intermittent wipers, tilt steering column, tachometer, coolant temperature gauge, trip odometer, coin and cup holders, tiedown hooks (wagon), front cornering lamps, power mirrors, luggage rack (wagon), AM/FM radio, front door pockets, rear armrest (except wagons), covered package tray storage bin (4- doors), visor mirrors, 205/70R14 all-season SBR tires. **LS** adds: power windows, automatic parking brake release, warning lights, Light Group, bodyside cladding, remote fuel door and liftgate releases, upgraded upholstery, power front lumbar support adjustments, front seatback map pockets, lighted visor mirrors.

Optional equipment:

Anti-lock brakes, 4-doors	985	838	887
3.8-liter V-6	400	340	360
Preferred Pkg. 450A	743	633	669
Preferred Pkg. 451A	1032	878	929
Preferred Pkg. 461A	1244	1058	1120
Preferred Pkg. 462A	2036	1732	1832
Variable-assist power steering	104	88	94
Automatic air conditioning	183	155	165
Autolamp system	73	62	66
Lighted visor mirrors, GS	100	85	90
Electronic instrument cluster	351	299	316
Insta-Clear heated windshield	250	213	225
Keyless entry	218	186	196
Power moonroof	741	630	667
Rear defogger	150	128	135
Cruise control	191	163	172
Luxury Touring Pkg., LS 4-door	2015	1653	1814
Anti-lock brakes, moonroof, leather bucket seats.			
Light Group, GS	59	50	53
HD battery	27	23	24
HD suspension	26	22	23
Extended-range fuel tank	46	39	41
Power Lock Group, GS 4-door	296	252	266
GS wagon	244	207	220
LS 4-door	205	174	185
Power seats, each	261	222	235
Power windows	306	260	275
AM/FM cassette	137	116	123
AM/FM radio delete (credit)	(206)	(175)	(175)
Premium sound system	168	143	151
High Level Audio System	472	401	425
w/Pkg. 451	335	285	302
w/Pkg. 461	167	142	150
JBL sound system	488	415	439

	Retail Price	Dealer Invoice	Low Price
CD player	491	418	442
Power antenna	76	64	68
Clearcoat paint	188	160	169
Bodyside accent stripes	61	52	55
Floormats	43	36	39
Leather-wrapped steering wheel	63	54	57
Leather seat trim	489	416	440
All-vinyl trim	37	31	33
Picnic tray, wagons	66	56	59
Rear-facing third seat, wagons	155	132	140
Rear wiper/washer, wagons	126	107	113
Cargo area cover, wagons	66	56	59
205/70R14 WSW tires	82	69	74
205/65R15 tires	65	55	59
205/65R15 WSW tires	146	124	131
Conventional spare tire	73	62	66
Alloy wheels	224	191	202
Polycast wheels	138	117	124
California emissions pkg	100	85	90

Mercury Topaz

Mercury Topaz

What's New

Mercury's front-drive compact receives only minor changes this year. Rear shoulder belts are now standard, and sound insulation has been upgraded. Footwell and trunk lights are newly standard on all models, as are floormats. Two-way head restraints replace the 4-way design used previously on some models, and wire wheel covers have been dropped from the options list. Topaz is a corporate clone of the Ford Tempo. The 2-door Topaz comes in GS and sporty XR5 trim, while the 4-door is available in GS, LS and sporty LTS guise. GS and LS models are available with an All Wheel Drive option, a part-time 4-wheel-drive system not for use on dry pavement. The base 2.3-liter 4-cylinder engine, standard in Topaz GS and LS, has 98 horsepower. The high-output 2.3-liter four, standard in the XR5, LTS, and All Wheel Drive models, is rated at 100 horsepower. Front-drive Topazes have a 5-speed manual transmission standard with both engines and a 3-speed automatic optional. Automatic transmission is mandatory with All Wheel Drive models. A driver's-side air bag is an $815 stand-alone option on GS models (it's $690 on the GS

> **KEY: ohv** = overhead valve; **ohc** = overhead cam; **dohc** = double overhead cam; **I** = inline cylinders; **V** = cylinders in V configuration; **flat** = horizontally opposed cylinders; **bbl.** = barrel (carburetor); **PFI** = port (multi-point) fuel injection; **TBI** = throttle-body (single-point) fuel injection; **rpm** = revolutions per minute; **OD** = overdrive transmission; **S** = standard; **O** = optional; **NA** = not available.

Prices are accurate at time of printing; subject to manufacturer's change.

Mercury

as part of an extra-equipment package) and a $622 stand-alone option on LS and LTS models. Motorized automatic front shoulder belts are standard on all Topazes.

For

- 4WD traction (All Wheel Drive option)   - Air bag option

Against

- Engine noise   - Driveability

Summary

Since Topaz is nearly identical to the Ford Tempo except for styling, see our comments under that entry as well. Freshened styling in '88 improved Topaz's exterior appearance, and a redesign inside gave it a more functional dashboard. But on-the-road performance remains only adequate. Part of the problem is that either 2.3 continues to generate more noise than useful power. Also, the 3-speed automatic transmission changes up to high gear too quickly to maintain good acceleration, and then it balks at downshifting for prompt passing response. Topaz can be nicely equipped for a reasonable price. But there are other compact sedans with more interior room, plus more overall refinement (the Accord and Toyota Camry to name two), though at higher cost. Topaz's All Wheel Drive option is reasonably priced and gives these compacts great traction in rain and snow. The added weight of 4WD, however, slows acceleration and raises fuel consumption.

Specifications

	2-door notchback	4-door notchback
Wheelbase, in.	99.9	99.9
Overall length, in.	176.7	177.0
Overall width, in.	68.3	68.3
Overall height, in.	52.8	52.9
Turn diameter, ft.	36.5	36.5
Curb weight, lbs.	2546	2602
Cargo vol., cu. ft.	13.2	13.2
Fuel capacity, gals.	15.9[1]	15.9[1]
Seating capacity	5	5
Front headroom, in.	37.5	37.5
Front shoulder room, in.	53.9	53.9
Front legroom, max., in.	41.5	41.5
Rear headroom, in.	36.8	37.0
Rear shoulder room, in.	54.0	53.3
Rear legroom, min., in.	36.0	36.0

1. 14.2 with 4WD.

Powertrain layout: transverse front engine/front-wheel drive or on-demand 4WD.

Engines

	ohv I-4	ohv I-4
Size, liters/cu. in.	2.3/141	2.3/141
Fuel delivery	PFI	PFI
Horsepower @ rpm	98 @ 4400	100 @ 4400
Torque (lbs./ft.) @ rpm	124 @ 2200	130 @ 2600
Availability	S	S[1]

```
KEY: ohv = overhead valve; ohc = overhead cam; dohc =
double overhead cam; I = inline cylinders; V = cylinders in
V configuration; flat = horizontally opposed cylinders;
bbl. = barrel (carburetor); PFI = port (multi-point) fuel
injection; TBI = throttle-body (single-point) fuel injection;
rpm = revolutions per minute; OD = overdrive transmission;
S = standard; O = optional; NA = not available.
```

EPA city/highway mpg	ohv I-4	ohv I-4
5-speed OD manual	23/31	23/31
3-speed automatic	22/26	22/26

1. XR5, LTS, 4WD.

Prices

Mercury Topaz	Retail Price	Dealer Invoice	Low Price
GS 2-door notchback	$10027	$9098	$9329
GS 4-door notchback	10184	9238	9474
XR5 2-door notchback	10988	9954	10216
LS 4-door notchback	11507	10415	10694
LTS 4-door notchback	12514	11311	11622
Destination charge	425	425	425

Standard equipment:

GS: 2.3-liter PFI 4-cylinder engine, 5-speed manual transmission, power steering, reclining cloth and vinyl front bucket seats, motorized front shoulder belts, manual lap belts, rear shoulder belts, tachometer, coolant temperature gauge, trip odometer, tinted glass, intermittent wipers, AM/FM radio, diagnostic alert module, door pockets, map lights, floormats, 185/70R14 tires. **LS** adds: tilt steering column, power windows and locks, cruise control, all-cloth upholstery, rear defogger, remote decklid and fuel door releases, Light Group, cargo net, headlamps-on tone, front armrest, console cassette storage, touring suspension, performance tires. **XR5** adds to GS: high-output engine, 3.73 final drive ratio, performance suspension, leather-wrapped steering wheel, tilt steering column, sport seats with power lumbar, Light Group, cargo net, front armrest, remote decklid and fuel door releases, performance tires on alloy wheels. **LTS** adds to LS: high-output engine, 3.73 final drive ratio, performance suspension, air conditioning, cruise control, sport seats with power lumbar, cargo net, performance tires on alloy wheels.

Optional equipment:

3-speed automatic transmission	539	458	485
Driver's side airbag, GS	815	692	734
GS w/Pkg. 361 or 363	690	587	621
LS, LTS	622	529	560
Air conditioning	807	686	726
All Wheel Drive, GS	1466	1246	1319
GS w/Pkg. 363	927	788	834
LTS	1356	1153	1220
LS	1454	1236	1309
LS w/Pkg. 365	915	777	824
Special Value Pkg. 361A, GS	454	387	409
Special Value Pkg. 363A, GS	793	675	714
Special Value Pkg. 371A, XR5	456	388	410
Special Value Pkg. 365A, LS	NC	NC	NC
Comfort/Convenience Group, GS	173	147	156
Folding armrest, Light Group, remote fuel door and decklid releases.			
Rear defogger	150	128	135
Power Lock Group, GS 2-door	246	209	221
XR5	166	141	149
GS 4-door	298	253	268
GS 2-door w/Comfort/Convenience	166	141	149
GS 4-door w/Comfort/Convenience	217	185	195
Clearcoat paint	91	78	82
Cruise control	191	163	172
Tilt steering column	124	106	112
Polycast wheels	193	164	174
Decklid luggage rack	115	97	104
Power windows, 4-doors	306	260	275
Power driver's seat	261	222	235
AM/FM cassette, GS	137	116	123
AM/FM delete (credit), GS	(245)	(208)	(208)
AM/FM cassette delete (credit), XR5, LS & GTS	(382)	(324)	(324)
Premium sound system	138	117	124
Lower accent paint	159	135	143
Vinyl seat trim	37	31	33
California emissions pkg.	100	85	90

Mercury Tracer

Mercury Tracer

addition, Tracer is solidly built, reasonably priced and comes with Ford's competitive warranties. Overall, not a bad little car, and sure to be discounted heavily.

What's New

The front-drive subcompact Tracer will not be offered as a 1990 model. High inventories and the need to include passive restraints prompted Ford to stop production with a 1989½ model, examples of which should be available well into the 1990 model year. Only a red instead of chrome stripe on the bodyside molding and bumpers distinguishes the '89½ Tracer from the '89. Next spring, an all-new 1991 model is expected, sharing platform and powertrains with the '91 Ford Escort (see Escort report). Introduced in March 1987 as an '88 model, Tracer is built in Mexico and uses running gear from the previous-generation Mazda 323. Tracer was marketed as an upscale replacement for the Lynx, which has been Mercury's version of the Ford Escort. It comes in 3-and 5-door hatchback and 5-door wagon body styles. All models have folding rear seatbacks that enlarge the cargo hold. Mercury revised Mazda's transmission gearing and replaced some suspension pieces for its versions, but it neglected to pick up the 323's 4-speed overdrive automatic transmission, opting instead for an optional 3-speed automatic. A 5-speed manual is standard. Mercury markets Tracer as a fully-equipped subcompact, listing only a handful of individual options and option groups.

For

- Fuel economy   ● Handling/roadholding   ● Cargo room

Against

- Noise   ● Driveability (automatic transmission)

Summary

Mercury should have picked up the 323's 4-speed automatic transmission for the Tracer. The 3-speed automatic has the engine running at a frantic 3300 rpm at 60 mph. With the 5-speed manual, it runs a more relaxed and hushed 2600 rpm at 60. An overdrive top gear added to the automatic would cut engine speed, reduce noise and improve fuel economy. As it is, Tracer is still pretty economical with automatic (a 27-mpg average in our last test). However, you'll get better fuel economy and improved driveability with the 5-speed. Tracer is a generally enjoyable subcompact that handles competently, feels surefooted and rides fairly well for a small car. The rear seat is a little cramped, but all models have folding rear seatbacks that create a generous-sized cargo area. In

Specifications

	3-door hatchback	5-door hatchback	5-door wagon
Wheelbase, in.	94.7	94.7	94.7
Overall length, in.	162.0	162.0	169.7
Overall width, in.	65.2	65.2	65.2
Overall height, in.	53.0	53.0	53.7
Turn diameter, ft.	30.8	30.8	30.8
Curb weight, lbs.	2158	2185	2233
Cargo vol., cu. ft.	28.9	28.9	57.6
Fuel capacity, gals.	11.9	11.9	11.9
Seating capacity	5	5	5
Front headroom, in.	38.3	38.3	38.2
Front shoulder room, in.	51.9	51.9	51.9
Front legroom, max., in.	41.5	41.5	41.5
Rear headroom, in.	37.0	37.0	37.0
Rear shoulder room, in.	51.9	51.9	51.9
Rear legroom, min., in.	34.7	34.7	34.7

Powertrain layout: transverse front engine/front-wheel drive.

Engines

	ohc I-4
Size, liters/cu. in.	1.6/97
Fuel delivery	PFI
Horsepower @ rpm	82 @ 5000
Torque (lbs./ft.) @ rpm	92 @ 2500
Availability	S

EPA city/highway mpg

5-speed OD manual	26/29
3-speed automatic	26/29

Prices

Mercury Tracer (1989 prices)	Retail Price	Dealer Invoice	Low Price
3-door hatchback	$8556	$7718	$8137
5-door hatchback	9242	8328	8785
5-door wagon	9726	8759	9243
Destination charge	335	335	335

Standard equipment:

1.6-liter PFI 4-cylinder engine, 5-speed manual transmission, tachometer, trip odometer, coolant temperature gauge, digital clock, tinted glass, cloth reclining front bucket seats, driver's seat height and lumbar support adjustments. split folding rear seatback with headrests and recliners, AM/FM ST ET, rear defogger, power mirrors, map lights, center console with storage, remote fuel door and liftgate releases, right visor mirror, cargo area cover, P175/70R13 tires on steel wheels (hatchbacks; alloy on wagon), full wheel covers.

Optional equipment:

3-speed automatic transmission	415	352	384
Air conditioning	688	585	637
AM/FM ST ET cassette	137	116	127
AM/FM ST ET delete (credit)	(206)	(175)	(175)
Preferred Pkg. 551A	235	200	218
Power steering.			
Sport Pkg., exc. wagon	268	228	248
Two-tone paint, alloy wheels, tape stripe.			
Cruise control	182	154	168
Alloy wheels (std. wagon)	183	155	169
Delete alloy wheels, wagon (credit)	(183)	(155)	(155)

Prices are accurate at time of printing; subject to manufacturer's change.

Merkur Scorpio

Merkur Scorpio

What's New

Driver and passenger air bags and a new instrument panel highlight changes to this rear-drive luxury/sports sedan for 1990. Scorpio is imported from Ford of Germany and sold through Lincoln-Mercury dealers with Merkur franchises. Merkur (pronounced mare-COOR) is the German word for Mercury. Scorpio comes only as a 5-door hatchback with a 2.9-liter V-6 engine and standard anti-lock disc brakes. It was brought to the U.S. in May 1987 as an '88 model after being named Europe's 1986 "Car of the Year." The XR4Ti, a smaller 3-door sport sedan with a turbocharged 4-cylinder engine, kicked off the Merkur program in 1985, but Ford is not importing it for 1990. Scorpio's engine for '90 gets a higher compression ratio, 9.5:1, up from 9.0:1, for a slight power boost. Horsepower goes from 144 to 145, while torque increases from 162 pounds/feet to 170; peak rpm ratings are unchanged. Premium fuel is now required. The 4-speed automatic transmission features electronic instead of hydraulic lockup in third and fourth gears, and a new 5-speed with lower shift effort is now available. Ford says a modified climate control system with new controls is more effective, and the standard AM/FM/cassette audio system is upgraded. Outside, the bumpers, grille, and body-side cladding are now color-keyed, and the standard alloy wheels change to a 7-spoke design.

For

- Anti-lock brakes
- Handling/roadholding
- Ride
- Passenger room
- Cargo space

Against

- Fuel economy

Summary

Ford has been advertising the Scorpio without using the Merkur name, though it continues to appear on the cars and on dealers' signs. That's an indication of the muddled marketing that has contributed to lackluster sales for this credible "captive import." Sales of the Scorpio have suffered in part because Lincoln-Mercury dealers, accustomed to conservative, domestic-car customers, seem ill at ease with the European hatchback and its mysterious Merkur tag. Scorpio sales in the first half of 1989 totaled just 1811, down from 3837 for the first half of '87. To shore up customer confidence, Ford indexes Scorpio's resale value to that of the Mercedes-Benz 190E 2.6 and pays any difference in cash to Scorpio owners who trade for a new Lincoln, Mercury, or another Scorpio. Our major complaint with the Scorpio is under the hood, where its V-6 provides only adequate performance for this price class. Scorpio is otherwise a fine luxury tourer, with an absorbent and well-controlled ride and confidence-inspiring road manners. Its cabin is cavernous and well appointed, its seats supportive and comfortable. Overall, it's a worthwhile European-flavored alternative to the Lincoln Continental.

Specifications

	5-door hatchback
Wheelbase, in.	108.7
Overall length, in.	186.4
Overall width, in.	69.5
Overall height, in.	54.6
Turn diameter, ft.	34.1
Curb weight, lbs.	3304
Cargo vol., cu. ft.	37.2
Fuel capacity, gals.	16.9
Seating capacity	5
Front headroom, in.	37.0
Front shoulder room, in.	56.4
Front legroom, max., in.	41.3
Rear headroom, in.	37.3
Rear shoulder room, in.	56.4
Rear legroom, min., in.	38.6

Powertrain layout: longitudinal front engine/front-wheel drive.

Engines

	ohv V-6
Size, liters/cu. in.	2.9/177
Fuel delivery	PFI
Horsepower @ rpm	145 @ 5500
Torque (lbs./ft.) @ rpm	170 @ 3000
Availability	S

EPA city/highway mpg

5-speed OD manual	17/23
4-speed OD automatic	17/23

Prices

Merkur Scorpio (1989 prices)	Retail Price	Dealer Invoice	Low Price
5-door hatchback	$25052	$20543	$22500
Destination charge	170	170	170

Standard equipment:

2.9-liter PFI V-6 engine, 5-speed manual transmission, power steering, 4-wheel disc brakes, anti-lock braking system, power windows and locks, automatic climate control, front bucket seats with 16-way adjustments, 60/40 split folding rear seatback with electric recliners, cruise control, tilt/telescopic steering column, heated power mirrors, remote fuel door release, intermittent wipers, rear wiper/washer, AM/FM ST ET cassette, overhead console with digital clock, calendar, stopwatch and outside thermometer, P205/60HR15 Pirelli P6 tires on cast aluminum wheels.

KEY: ohv = overhead valve; **ohc** = overhead cam; **dohc** = double overhead cam; **I** = inline cylinders; **V** = cylinders in V configuration; **flat** = horizontally opposed cylinders; **bbl.** = barrel (carburetor); **PFI** = port (multi-point) fuel injection; **TBI** = throttle-body (single-point) fuel injection; **rpm** = revolutions per minute; **OD** = overdrive transmission; **S** = standard; **O** = optional; **NA** = not available.

Optional equipment:	Retail Price	Dealer Invoice	Low Price
4-speed automatic transmission	550	468	510
Power moonroof	1125	957	1041
Touring Pkg.	2635	2240	2438
Power moonroof with shade, leather seats, trip computer.			
Heated front seats	225	192	209

Mitsubishi Eclipse

Mitsubishi Eclipse GSX

What's New

The front-drive Eclipse arrived last January as an early 1990 model and an all-wheel-drive version was added last summer. Changes this fall are nil. All Eclipses are built at the Normal, Illinois, Diamond-Star Motors plant that Mitsubishi operates with Chrysler, which offers a similar mix of front-drive Plymouth Lasers and front- and all-drive Eagle Talons. The mechanical design is basically Mitsubishi's, with styling input from Chrysler. The five Eclipse models comprise base and GS models powered by a 1.8-liter single-overhead-cam engine with 92 horsepower; midrange GS DOHC-16 with a dual-cam 2.0-liter engine and 135 horsepower; and the top-rung GS DOHC Turbo and AWD GSX, which use an intercooled, turbocharged 2.0-liter with 190 horsepower. The GSX 4-wheel-drive system (shared by the Talon TSi AWD) is a permanently engaged setup with a viscous-coupling center differential to apportion power between front and rear wheels as needed for optimum traction. A 5-speed manual transmission is standard across the board and a 4-speed automatic transmission with Power and Economy shift programs is optional for all but turbo Eclipses. All models have motorized front shoulder belts and manual lap belts.

For

- Acceleration (DOHC, Turbo, GSX)
- 4WD traction (GSX) • Handling/roadholding
- Instruments/controls

Against

- Acceleration (1.8-liter) • Visibility • Interior room
- Noise

Summary

We really like this line of sports coupes, especially the GS DOHC-16 and the 4WD GSX. None of these cars cost a bundle, and all but the 1.8-liter models are a ball to drive. The 1.8-liter base and GS editions don't have enough low-speed power to pull the automatic transmission with any gusto; even the manual versions need more gear-rowing than some buyers may like. At the other end of the line, the turbocharged models deliver ferocious acceleration. Torque steer (sudden pulling to one side in hard acceleration) is a problem in the Turbo but not the all-wheel drive GSX, which spreads the abundant power among all four wheels, not just the front two. Even better, the GSX grips the road like a leech. The 135-horsepower engine is smooth, responsive, and has more low-end power than the 1.8. Ride varies with model, ranging from compliant but occasionally choppy on the base and GS models to abrupt and thumpy on the others, which have firmer suspensions and larger tires. Low-slung fastback styling and compact dimensions make for mediocre outward vision and a tight cockpit with a closed-in feel even up front. Back seat space? It's more for pets than people. The command post is comfortable and convenient, with handy controls close at hand. Noise levels are reasonable except that tire noise can be excessive on coarse pavement. On balance, though, Eclipse has much to offer, including reasonable prices that run from about $11,000 for the base car to under $18,000 for a loaded GSX.

Specifications

	3-door hatchback
Wheelbase, in.	97.2
Overall length, in.	170.5
Overall width, in.	66.5
Overall height, in.	51.4
Turn diameter, ft.	34.1
Curb weight, lbs.	2524[1]
Cargo vol., cu. ft.	10.2
Fuel capacity, gals.	15.9
Seating capacity	4
Front headroom, in.	37.9
Front shoulder room, in.	53.9
Front legroom, max., in.	43.9
Rear headroom, in.	34.1
Rear shoulder room, in.	NA
Rear legroom, min., in.	28.5
1. 3095 lbs., GSX	

Powertrain layout: transverse front engine/front-wheel drive or permanent 4WD (GSX).

Engines	ohc I-4	dohc I-4	Turbo dohc I-4
Size, liters/cu. in.	1.8/107	2.0/122	2.0/122
Fuel delivery	PFI	PFI	PFI
Horsepower @ rpm	92 @ 5000	135 @ 6000	190 @ 6000[1]
Torque (lbs./ft.) @ rpm	105 @ 3500	125 @ 3000	203 @ 3000
Availability	S[2]	S[3]	S[4]

EPA city/highway mpg			
5-speed OD manual	23/32	22/29	22/29
4-speed OD automatic	23/30	22/27	
1. GSX: 195 horsepower 2. Base, GS 1.8 3. GS DOHC 16 4. GS Turbo, GSX.			

Prices

Mitsubishi Eclipse	Retail Price	Dealer Invoice	Low Price
3-door hatchback, 5-speed	$10819	—	—
3-door hatchback, automatic	11469	—	—
GS 1.8 3-door hatchback, 5-speed	11839	—	—
GS 1.8 3-door hatchback, automatic	12489	—	—
GS DOHC 3-door hatchback, 5-speed . . .	12679		

Prices are accurate at time of printing; subject to manufacturer's change.

Mitsubishi

	Retail Price	Dealer Invoice	Low Price
GS DOHC 3-door hatchback, automatic . .	13329	—	—
GS Turbo 3-door hatchback, 5-speed . . .	14639	—	—
GSX 3-door hatchback, 5-speed	16449	—	—
Destination charge	285	285	285

Dealer invoice and low price not available at time of publication.

Standard equipment:

1.8-liter PFI 4-cylinder engine, 5-speed manual or 4-speed automatic transmission, 4-wheel disc brakes, cloth reclining front bucket seats, folding rear seatback, tilt steering column, map lights, remote fuel door and hatch releases, visor mirrors, rear shoulder belts, tachometer, coolant temperature gauge, dual trip odometers, intermittent wipers, automatic-off headlamp feature, AM/FM radio, tinted glass, remote mirrors, 185/70R14 tires. **GS** adds: power steering, 3-way driver's seat, upgraded door panels, power mirrors, rear defogger, cargo cover, center console with coin and cup holders, AM/FM cassette, full wheel covers. **GS DOHC** adds: 2.0-liter DOHC 16-valve engine, sport suspension, 205/55R16 tires. **GS DOHC Turbo** adds: turbocharged engine, rear wiper/washer, air dam and rear spoiler, sill extensions, alloy wheels. **GSX** adds: permanent 4-wheel drive, cruise control, 6-way driver's seat, driving lamps.

Optional equipment:

Power steering, base	241	—	—
Air conditioning	811	—	—
AM/FM cassette, base	170	—	—
AM/FM cassette w/EQ, exc. base	241	—	—
AM/FM cassette w/CD player, 16V models .	628	—	—
Power Pkg., exc. base	366	—	—
Power windows and locks.			
Leather front seating surfaces, GSX	427	—	—
Security alarm, GSX	163	—	—
Alloy wheels, GS DOHC	315	—	—
Rear wiper/washer, base, GS & GS DOHC .	129	—	—
Cruise control, exc. GSX	187	—	—
Sunroof	366	—	—
Limited-slip differential, GSX	477	—	—
Rear defogger, base	119	—	—
Wheel covers, base	100	—	—
Floormats	27	—	—

Mitsubishi Galant

Mitsubishi Galant GS

What's New

Mitsubishi's front-drive compact sedan returns from its 1989 redesign with no major change save the addition of a fourth model with all-wheel drive. Called GSX, the newcomer uses the 135-horsepower 2.0-liter 4-cylinder engine of the sporty front-drive GS model and is likewise available only with a 5-speed manual transmission. Its permanently engaged all-wheel drive system comes from the domestically built Mitsubishi Eclipse GSX and Eagle Talon TSi AWD coupes, which use a shortened version of the Galant platform. Base and

upscale LS Galants continue with a 102-horsepower 2.0-liter. The LS comes only with a 4-speed automatic transmission; a 5-speed manual is standard on the base and the automatic is optional. Automatic will become available on the GS in January. GS and GSX get rear disc brakes instead of drums, as well as speed-sensitive, variable-assist power steering with Normal and Sport modes. The GS also has an electronically controlled suspension with variable-rate air springs and shock absorbers controlled by three driver-selected programs—Soft, Auto, and Sport. An anti-lock braking system (ABS) is optional for GS and GSX. Motorized front shoulder belts are standard on all models; separate lap belts have to be buckled manually.

For

- Acceleration (GS, GSX) • Anti-lock brakes (GS, GSX)
- Ride • Handling/roadholding • Passenger room

Against

- Acceleration (base, LS) • Ride

Summary

All Galant models have the robust solidity and precise, "well-oiled" feel associated with the premium German brands. And, all models but the GS have a supple, well-damped suspension that smothers bumps with a soft thump rather than a jolting thud. The GS is annoyingly jittery on anything other than ice-smooth surfaces yet handles little better than the more softly sprung LS, which corners with lots of understeer (resistance to turning) but only mild body lean for a family compact. All-wheel drive makes the new GSX an enthusiast's delight. It leans less through tight turns and hangs on tenaciously. Alas, Galant's all-of-a-piece feel has been achieved partly through added weight and the engines have relatively weak low-end torque; this makes for less-than-sparkling performance. With the automatic transmission, the base and LS amble from 0 to 60 mph in 12.5 seconds. The GS and GSX are quicker, but require frequent gear changes to keep pace with give-and-take traffic. Fortunately, both Galant engines are smooth runners and quiet cruisers. Wind and road noise are low, too. The interior offers ample room for four adults, a comfortable driving stance, good outward vision, and a pleasingly modern ambience matched by quality materials. Pricewise, Galant is in line with Japanese rivals but upstream of comparable domestics and the Korean-built Hyundai Sonata. Nevertheless, it's a strong, capable compact with some obvious virtues and no real vices.

Specifications

	4-door notchback
Wheelbase, in.	102.4
Overall length, in.	183.9
Overall width, in.	66.7
Overall height, in.	53.5
Turn diameter, ft.	34.8
Curb weight, lbs.	2601[1]
Cargo vol., cu. ft.	12.3
Fuel capacity, gals.	15.9
Seating capacity	5
Front headroom, in.	38.6
Front shoulder room, in.	54.7
Front legroom, max., in.	41.9
Rear headroom, in.	37.4
Rear shoulder room, in.	54.4
Rear legroom, min., in.	36.0

1. 2799 lbs., GS.

Powertrain layout: transverse front engine/front-wheel drive or permanent 4WD (GSX).

Engines

	ohc I-4	dohc I-4
Size, liters/cu. in.	2.0/122	2.0/122
Fuel delivery	PFI	PFI
Horsepower @ rpm	102 @ 5000	135 @ 6000
Torque (lbs./ft.) @ rpm	116 @ 2500	125 @ 3000
Availability	S	S

EPA city/highway mpg

5-speed OD manual	23/29	21/27
4-speed OD automatic	22/27	

Prices

Mitsubishi Galant	Retail Price	Dealer Invoice	Low Price
4-door notchback, 5-speed	$10989	—	—
4-door notchback, automatic	12389	—	—
LS 4-door notchback, automatic	13969	—	—
GS 4-door notchback, 5-speed	15669	—	—
GSX 4-door notchback, 5-speed	16369	—	—
Destination charge	285	285	285

Dealer invoice and low price not available at time of publication.

Standard equipment:

2.0-liter PFI 4-cylinder engine, 5-speed manual or 4-speed automatic transmission, power steering, tinted glass, remote mirrors, intermittent wipers, tachometer, dual trip odometers, tilt steering column, cloth reclining front bucket seats, center console, rear defogger, remote fuel door and decklid releases, right visor mirror, 185/70SR14 tires. **LS** adds: 4-speed automatic transmission, power windows and locks, power mirrors, variable intermittent wipers, front map lights, driver's seat height and lumbar support adjustments, velour upholstery, seatback pockets, storage tray beneath right front seat, bilevel center console with armrest, rear center armrest w/trunk pass-through, AM/FM cassette with power antenna, full wheel covers. **GS** adds to base: DOHC 16-valve engine, 4-wheel disc brakes, speed-sensitive power steering, electronically controlled suspension, dark upper windshield band, upgraded upholstery, speed-sensitive intermittent wipers, leather-wrapped steering wheel and shift knob, switchable green/orange instrument illumination, cruise controlo, power windows and locks, power mirrors, front and rear map lights, driver's-seat height adjustment, AM/FM cassette with power antenna, front mud guards, 195/60HR15 tires on alloy wheels. **GSX** adds permanent 4-wheel drive.

Optional equipment:

Anti-lock brakes, GS & GSX	1495	—	—
Air conditioning	802	—	—
AM/FM cassette, base	552	—	—
AM/FM cassette w/EQ, LS, GS & GSX	316	—	—
Power sunroof, LS, GS & GSX	685	—	—
Wheel covers, base	78	—	—

Mitsubishi Mirage

What's New

A redesigned Mirage went on sale in June 1988 as a more upscale subcompact than Mitsubishi's Korean-built Precis. The front-drive Mirage sees no major design changes for 1990, but models and equipment are revised to make the line more price-competitive. Last year's Turbo 3-door hatchback is gone because demand for "pocket rockets" has shifted to small turbocharged coupes like Mitsu's own Eclipse. The new order begins with a VL ("Value Leader") 3-door hatchback, followed by a standard 3-door and 4-door notchback sedan.

Mitsubishi Mirage

Topping the line are "exe Special Edition" versions of both body styles (basically the previous LS model with a different name) and a sporty RS 3-door. The VL is available only with a 4-speed manual transmission, the RS with a 5-speed manual. Other models have the 5-speed standard and a 3-speed automatic optional. The automatic has a new shift-lock that requires the brake pedal be applied before the transmission can be shifted out of Park. Standard Mirages can effectively become "exe" models with the addition of the optional air conditioning, power steering, and AM/FM stereo/cassette player. Just to confuse things, there's an "exe" package option with these same items for the RS 3-door. For now, Mitsubishi's 1.5-liter 4-cylinder engine with 81 horsepower is standard across the board. Come January, Diamond-Star Motors, the Chrysler-Mitsubishi plant in Illinois that builds the Eclipse, Plymouth Laser and Eagle Talon coupes, begins turning out 4-door Mirages to give Mitsubishi extra potential sales volume. At that point, the LS 4-door will return, the "exe" version may be dropped, and a new GS 4-door, a twin to the Mirage-based Eagle Summit LX and powered by the same 113-horsepower 1.6-liter engine, will be added to the line. The GS will be the only Mirage available with a 4-speed automatic transmission, now used in the Summit as well as the latest Hyundai Excel/Mitsubishi Precis.

For

● Fuel economy ● Maneuverability ● Handling ● Ride

Against

● Acceleration (automatic transmission)
● Rear seat room (3-door)

Summary

Though it breaks no new ground, Mirage is a competent, well-rounded small car with some surprising pluses and fewer of the usual small-car minuses. Handling is nimble, though cornering grip runs out early on the standard-equipment tires. Fuel economy is great; we averaged 37 mpg last year with a manual-transmission 4-door. What you don't expect are a comfortable ride (less so in the 3-door, though still acceptable)

KEY: ohv = overhead valve; **ohc** = overhead cam; **dohc** = double overhead cam; **I** = inline cylinders; **V** = cylinders in V configuration; **flat** = horizontally opposed cylinders; **bbl.** = barrel (carburetor); **PFI** = port (multi-point) fuel injection; **TBI** = throttle-body (single-point) fuel injection; **rpm** = revolutions per minute; **OD** = overdrive transmission; **S** = standard; **O** = optional; **NA** = not available.

Prices are accurate at time of printing; subject to manufacturer's change.

Mitsubishi

and really usable, adult-size back-seat space in the 4-door. The engine growls when worked hard, but wind noise is low and cruising quite relaxed with the overdrive manual transmissions. Other credits include a sensible dashboard design and a solid, substantial feel. The main debit involves performance: There isn't much. Automatic models take some 13 seconds to do 0-60 mph; manual versions are just a little quicker. Choose the hatchback and you'll also lose a lot in both cargo room and rear-seat space. Still, this year's new price structure makes any Mirage a better buy. The price spread has moved down from a range of about $9150-$12,000 to the $7000-$10,000 neighborhood, and there aren't as many options to run up the total. That *does* break new ground—reason enough for Mirage to be on your small-car shopping list.

Specifications

	3-door hatchback	4-door notchback
Wheelbase, in.	93.9	96.7
Overall length, in.	158.7	170.1
Overall width, in.	65.7	65.7
Overall height, in.	52.0	52.8
Turn diameter, ft.	30.2	30.8
Curb weight, lbs.	2238	2271
Cargo vol., cu. ft.	34.7	10.3
Fuel capacity, gals.	13.2	13.2
Seating capacity	5	5
Front headroom, in.	38.3	39.1
Front shoulder room, in.	53.5	53.5
Front legroom, max., in.	41.9	41.9
Rear headroom, in.	36.9	37.5
Rear shoulder room, in.	52.1	53.1
Rear legroom, min., in.	32.5	34.4

Powertrain layout: transverse front engine/front-wheel drive.

Engines

	ohc I-4
Size, liters/cu. in.	1.5/90
Fuel delivery	PFI
Horsepower @ rpm	81 @ 5500
Torque (lbs./ft.) @ rpm	91 @ 3000
Availability	S
EPA city/highway mpg	
4-speed OD manual	31/36
5-speed OD manual	28/34
3-speed automatic	27/29

Prices

Mitsubishi Mirage	Retail Price	Dealer Invoice	Low Price
VL 3-door hatchback, 4-speed	$6929	—	—
3-door hatchback, 5-speed	7839	—	—
3-door hatchback, automatic	8299	—	—
RS 3-door hatchback, 5-speed	8759	—	—
EXE 3-door hatchback, 5-speed	8339	—	—
EXE 3-door hatchback, automatic	8799	—	—

KEY: ohv = overhead valve; **ohc** = overhead cam; **dohc** = double overhead cam; **I** = inline cylinders; **V** = cylinders in V configuration; **flat** = horizontally opposed cylinders; **bbl.** = barrel (carburetor); **PFI** = port (multi-point) fuel injection; **TBI** = throttle-body (single-point) fuel injection; **rpm** = revolutions per minute; **OD** = overdrive transmission; **S** = standard; **O** = optional; **NA** = not available.

	Retail Price	Dealer Invoice	Low Price
4-door notchback, 5-speed	8559	—	—
4-door notchback, automatic	9019	—	—
EXE 4-door notchback, 5-speed	9509	—	—
EXE 4-door notchback, automatic	9979	—	—
Destination charge	285	285	285

Dealer invoice and low price not available at time of publication.

Standard equipment:

VL: 1.5-liter PFI 4-cylinder engine, 4-speed manual transmission, reclining front bucket seats, split folding rear seat, center console with storage, rear shoulder belts, coolant temperature gauge, trip odometer, locking fuel door. **Base** adds: 5-speed manual or 3-speed automatic transmission, cloth upholstery, wide bodyside molding, rear defogger, dual outside mirrors (4-door). **RS** adds: carpet, cloth door panels with pockets, driver's foot rest, rear parcel shelf, storage tray under passenger seat, remote fuel door and hatch releases, tinted glass, dual outside mirrors. **EXE** adds: air conditioning, power steering, AM/FM cassette, remote decklid release, full wheel covers, 175/70R13 tires.

Optional equipment:

Air conditioning (std. EXE)	756	—	—
Power steering, base & RS	262	—	—
AM/FM radio w/4 speakers, base	280	—	—
VL	327	—	—
AM/FM cassette w/6 speakers, RS	507	—	—
Dual remote mirrors, base 3-door	32	—	—
Rear defogger, VL & base 4-door	62	—	—
Digital clock, RS	56	—	—
Radio accommodation pkg., VL	47	—	—
Floormats, VL, base & RS	63	—	—
Mud guards, VL, base & RS	74	—	—
Trim rings, VL, base 4-door, EXE 3-door	66	—	—

Mitsubishi Montero

Mitsubishi Montero

What's New

Last year Mitsubishi bolstered its Montero sport-utility line with longer-wheelbase 5-door models and new V-6 power. For 1990 the 3.0-liter V-6 becomes standard on all models; the 2.6-liter 4-cylinder is gone. The base 5-door is retitled RS, a lower-priced 5-door with fewer standard features joins the line, and the 3-door Sport model joins the LS 5-door in being available only with a 4-speed overdrive automatic transmission. All other Monteros carry a standard 5-speed manual and offer the automatic as an option. The 143-horsepower

V-6 is the same engine that powers Mitsubishi's Sigma luxury sedan, the 1990 Hyundai Sonata, and several Chrysler products, including the Dodge Caravan/Plymouth Voyager minivans. Montero 5-doors are 13.6 inches longer in wheelbase and 28 inches longer overall than the 3-door SP and Sport. Standard on all versions is an on-demand 4-wheel drive system with automatic-locking front hubs. The vehicle has to be stopped to lock the hubs, and driven in reverse briefly to unlock them. Once the hubs are locked, 4WD can be engaged or disengaged without stopping. Dodge dealers sold a copy of the 3-door Montero as the Raider from 1987 through 1989, but that clone has been dropped for 1990.

For

- 4WD traction
- Passenger room
- Cargo space
- Ride (5-door)

Against

- Fuel economy
- Noise

Summary

Buyers are flocking to sport-utility vehicles with four side doors now that imports with only two side doors are classified by the Customs Service as trucks subject to a 25 percent tariff (versus 2.5 percent on cars). That means the 3-door models cost a lot more than they used to, so importers like Mitsubishi are putting more emphasis on their 5-door models. There's a lot to like about the big Mitsubishi. The longest wheelbase among compact 4 × 4s gives it ample passenger and cargo room, while the V-6 delivers easy cruising and decent around-town pickup. The 5-door Montero nearly matches the Toyota 4Runner in all-out acceleration and hillclimbing, but isn't as strong as a 6-cylinder Jeep Cherokee. At around 17.5 mpg average, fuel economy is good for a 4 × 4 but not great. Like others of its ilk, the tall, boxy Montero feels tippy in spirited cornering, notices gusts on the highway, and suffers a lot of wind and road noise. However, the 5-door rides comfortably and entry/exit isn't difficult despite the high build. The 4WD system lacks full shift-on-the-fly capability between 2- and 4-wheel drive, while all Jeeps and some 4Runners have full shift-on-the-fly. Though prices are up by as much as $1100 on some models, you can still get a well-equipped Montero for under $20,000, which undercuts the Cherokee and the 4Runner.

Specifications

	3-door wagon	5-door wagon
Wheelbase, in.	92.5	106.1
Overall length, in.	155.1	183.1
Overall width, in.	66.1	66.1
Overall height, in.	72.8	74.4
Turn diameter, ft.	34.1	38.7
Curb weight, lbs.	3528	3924
Cargo vol., cu. ft.	62.3	94.9
Fuel capacity, gals.	19.8	24.3
Seating capacity	5	5
Front headroom, in.	40.7	40.7
Front shoulder room, in.	55.1	55.1
Front legroom, max., in.	39.6	39.6
Rear headroom, in.	39.8	40.5
Rear shoulder room, in.	57.1	57.1
Rear legroom, min., in.	34.4	34.6

Powertrain layout: longitudinal front engine/rear-wheel drive or on-demand 4WD.

Mitsubishi

Engines

	ohc V-6
Size, liters/cu. in.	3.0/181
Fuel delivery	PFI
Horsepower @ rpm	143 @ 5000
Torque (lbs./ft.) @ rpm	168 @ 2500
Availability	S

EPA city/highway mpg

5-speed OD manual	16/19
4-speed OD automatic	16/18

Prices

Mitsubishi Montero	Retail Price	Dealer Invoice	Low Price
SP 3-door wagon, 5-speed	$13949	—	—
SP 3-door wagon, automatic	14719	—	—
Sport 3-door wagon, automatic	15409	—	—
5-door wagon, 5-speed	15519	—	—
5-door wagon, automatic	16389	—	—
RS 5-door wagon, 5-speed	18139	—	—
RS 5-door wagon, automatic	18959	—	—
LS 5-door wagon, automatic	19499	—	—
Destination charge	285	285	285

Dealer invoice and low price not available at time of publication.

Standard equipment:

SP: 3.0-liter PFI V-6, 5-speed manual or 4-speed automatic transmission, part-time 4WD with automatic locking front hubs and 2-speed transfer case, power steering, reclining front bucket seats, tilt steering column, center console with storage, remote fuel door release, cargo tiedown hooks, remote rear door lock switch, map lights, right visor mirror, intermittent wipers, rear defogger, tachometer, coolant temperature and oil pressure gauges, voltmeter, inclinometer, trip odometer, skid plates, front and rear tow hooks, tinted glass, opening front vent windows, dual outside mirrors, 235/75R15 tires with full-size spare. **Sport** adds: 4-speed automatic transmission, limited-slip differential, digital clock, AM/FM cassette, two-tone paint, halogen headlights, headlight washers, rear wiper/washer. **4-door** deletes remote fuel door release, tachometer, oil pressure gauge, and voltmeter from base and adds: 5-speed manual transmission, limited-slip differential, reclining rear seats, 24.3-gallon fuel tank. **RS** deletes reclining rear seat and adds: suspension driver's seat, folding rear seat, rear heat outlets, remote fuel door release, inclinometer, tachometer, oil pressure gauge, voltmeter, digital clock, AM/FM cassette, bodyside molding, raccoon paint treatment. **LS** adds: 4-speed automatic transmission, reclining rear seat, power windows and locks, cruise control.

Optional equipment:

Air conditioning	810	—	—
AM/FM radio, SP	327	—	—
AM/FM cassette, SP & base 5-door	506	—	—
AM/FM cassette w/EQ, Sport & LS	824	—	—
Digital clock, SP & base 5-door	56	—	—
Rear wiper/washer, SP & base 5-door	166	—	—
Alloy wheels & spare tire cover	428	—	—
Power Pkg., Sport, base 5-door & RS	644	—	—
Power sunroof, 5-doors	685	—	—
Bodyside molding, SP & Sport	89	—	—
5-doors	99	—	—
Cargo Pkg., 5-doors	161	—	—
Cover, net and mat.			
Floormats, SP & Sport	73	—	—
5-doors	79	—	—

Prices are accurate at time of printing; subject to manufacturer's change.

Mitsubishi Precis

Mitsubishi Precis

What's New

What goes for Hyundai's redesigned 1990 Excel mostly goes for this nearly-identical cousin. Hyundai builds Precis in Korea for Mitsubishi to sell in the U.S. The big difference is in models and equipment, as the Precis line shrinks from six models and two body styles to just a pair of 3-door hatchbacks, base and RS. Why the cutback? The start of 4-door Mitsubishi Mirage production at Diamond-Star Motors in Illinois, set for January 1990. This allows Mitsubishi to bring in more Japanese-built Mirages under the voluntary import quotas, thus reducing its need for the Korean-built Precis. There are no import limits on Korean cars. Precis' main role now is not necessarily to generate significant sales volume but to be Mitsubishi's price leader, a car to lure buyers who, dealers hope, might drive away in something more expensive—such as a Mirage. While the Mirage and the new Precis differ in styling, they're quite close in dimensions and mechanical specifications. That's because the Precis/Excel is derived from an earlier Mirage design and uses a similar front-drive chassis and mechanical components. Precis has the 81-horsepower 1.5-liter 4-cylinder engine found in Mirage, and the same 4- and 5-speed manual transmissions. The automatic transmission optional for Precis is a 4-speed overdrive unit, while currently Mirage's automatic is a 3-speed, direct-drive transmission. Mirage will gain a 4-speed automatic and a larger engine next spring.

For

● Fuel economy ● Maneuverability ● Ride ● Price

Against

● Acceleration ● Handling ● Interior room ● Noise

Summary

See the Hyundai Excel for our evaluation of this new model. Except for a few variations in standard features, options, and prices, the 1990 Precis is a clone of the new Excel.

KEY: ohv = overhead valve; **ohc** = overhead cam; **dohc** = double overhead cam; **I** = inline cylinders; **V** = cylinders in V configuration; **flat** = horizontally opposed cylinders; **bbl.** = barrel (carburetor); **PFI** = port (multi-point) fuel injection; **TBI** = throttle-body (single-point) fuel injection; **rpm** = revolutions per minute; **OD** = overdrive transmission; **S** = standard; **O** = optional; **NA** = not available.

Specifications

	3-door hatchback
Wheelbase, in.	93.8
Overall length, in.	161.4
Overall width, in.	63.3
Overall height, in.	51.6
Turn diameter, ft.	31.8
Curb weight, lbs.	2040
Cargo vol., cu. ft.	37.9
Fuel capacity, gals.	11.9
Seating capacity	5
Front headroom, in.	37.8
Front shoulder room, in.	52.3
Front legroom, max., in.	41.9
Rear headroom, in.	37.5
Rear shoulder room, in.	52.3
Rear legroom, min., in.	32.9

Powertrain layout: transverse front engine/front-wheel drive.

Engines

	ohc I-4
Size, liters/cu. in.	1.5/90
Fuel delivery	PFI
Horsepower @ rpm	81 @ 5500
Torque (lbs./ft.) @ rpm	91 @ 3000
Availability	S

EPA city/highway mpg

4-speed OD manual	29/33
5-speed OD manual	29/36
4-speed OD automatic	28/32

Prices

Mitsubishi Precis (1989 prices)	Retail Price	Dealer Invoice	Low Price
3-door hatchback, 4-speed	$5499	$5004	$5123
RS 3-door hatchback, 5-speed	6699	5895	6143
LS 3-door hatchback, 5-speed	7349	6246	6632
LS 3-door hatchback, automatic	7839	6668	7077
LS 5-door hatchback, 5-speed	7599	6459	6858
LS 5-door hatchback, automatic	8089	6881	7302
Destination charge	265	265	265

Standard equipment:

1.5-liter 2bbl. 4-cylinder engine, 4-speed manual transmission, power brakes, vinyl reclining front bucket seats, folding rear seatbacks, cargo cover, variable intermittent wipers, rear defogger, rear heat ducts, trip odometer, coolant temperature gauge, low fuel and door/hatch ajar warning lights, locking fuel door, 155/80R13 all-season tires with full-size spare. **RS** adds: 5-speed manual transmission, cloth trim, upgraded door panels with map pockets, console, analog clock, wide bodyside moldings, remote fuel door and hatch releases, rear wiper/washer, dual remote mirrors, tinted glass. **LS** adds: 5-speed manual or 3-speed automatic transmission, tachometer, digital clock, upgraded steering wheel, storage tray under front passenger seat (5-door), right visor mirror, AM/FM ST ET cassette, dark upper windshield band, roll-down rear windows (5-door), wheel covers, 175/70R13 all-season tires.

Optional equipment:

Air conditioning (NA base)	735	588	662
AM/FM ST ET cassette, base & RS	295	206	251
High Power, LS	135	88	112
High Power, RS	430	280	355
Passive restraint, LS 5-door	75	64	70
Alloy Wheel Pkg., LS	295	221	258
Power steering, LS	260	221	241
Power sunroof, LS	395	316	356

Mitsubishi Sigma

Mitsubishi Sigma

What's New

This slow-selling compact luxury sedan says *sayonara* after 1990, so noteworthy changes for this final edition are limited to a standard driver's-side airbag, new 4-spoke steering wheel with duplicate audio controls, and modestly revised dashboard. Sigma originated as the 2.6-liter 4-cylinder Galant of 1985. It then became Galant Sigma in a 1988 makeover that brought V-6 power and available anti-lock braking system (ABS). Last year the name was changed to simply Sigma to avoid confusion with the new Galant. Mitsubishi's 3.0-liter V-6 (also offered in a variety of Chrysler products and the Hyundai Sonata) drives the front wheels through a 4-speed automatic transmission with Power and Economy electronic shift programs. Electronics also vary assist in the standard power steering. ABS remains a separate option and is also combined with electronic auto-leveling air shocks in the extra-cost "Eurotech" package. Leather interior and a power sliding moonroof are the only other factory extras. Not much is known about Sigma's 1991 successor, but Mitsubishi hints it will be an all-wheel-drive sedan that's larger and much costlier than the current model—between the $30,000 Acura Legend and the $35,000 Lexus LS 400.

For

● Acceleration ● Airbag ● Anti-lock brakes ● Quietness

Against

● Fuel economy ● Electronic suspension option
● Interior room

Summary

With 142 horsepower, the 3100-pound Sigma accelerates on par with rivals such as the Acura Legend, Mazda 929, Nissan Maxima, and Toyota Cressida. Mileage is below par—in our experience closer to the EPA's 18-mpg city rating than the 22-mpg highway estimate as an overall average. The V-6 is smooth, quiet, and well matched to the 4-speed automatic. The anti-lock brake system is a costly option, but more worthwhile than the electronically controlled suspension (ECS) it teams with in the even costlier Eurotech Package. We find the ECS more high-tech frill than helpful function, while the ABS pays for itself even if it only helps you avoid one major crunch. Sigma's main shortcoming is literally that: an interior that's tight for four adults, let alone five. All-around head room is barely adequate—really inadequate beneath the optional moonroof—while seat travel isn't sufficient to give tall drivers

a comfortable reach to the wheel. Rear leg space is limited. Trunk space isn't great, either. Balancing the ledger is a full helping of standard luxuries at a starting price below $18,000. Your bucks may go even further, as continuing slow sales should make dealers quite willing to discount. Sigma isn't our first choice in this league, but it might be yours if you fancy a smooth, well-equipped luxury sedan at a reasonable price, and don't mind if it's a little cozy.

Specifications

	4-door notchback
Wheelbase, in.	102.4
Overall length, in.	185.8
Overall width, in.	66.7
Overall height, in.	51.6
Turn diameter, ft.	34.8
Curb weight, lbs.	3108
Cargo vol., cu. ft.	12.4
Fuel capacity, gals.	15.9
Seating capacity	5
Front headroom, in.	37.5
Front shoulder room, in.	53.5
Front legroom, max., in.	40.3
Rear headroom, in.	36.7
Rear shoulder room, in.	53.2
Rear legroom, min., in.	36.4

Powertrain layout: transverse front engine/front-wheel drive.

Engines

	ohc V-6
Size, liters/cu. in.	3.0/181
Fuel delivery	PFI
Horsepower @ rpm	142 @ 5000
Torque (lbs./ft.) @ rpm	168 @ 2500
Availability	S

EPA city/highway mpg

4-speed OD automatic	18/22

Prices

Mitsubishi Sigma	Retail Price	Dealer Invoice	Low Price
4-door notchback	$17879	—	—
Destination charge	285	285	285

Dealer invoice and low price not available at time of publication.

Standard equipment:

3.0-liter PFI V-6 engine, 4-speed automatic transmission, power steering, driver's-side airbag, automatic climate control, velour reclining front bucket seats, 8-way adjustable driver's seat, underseat tray, seatback pockets, folding rear seatbacks, rear armrest, door pockets, rear heat ducts, power windows and locks, heated power mirrors, tinted glass with dark upper band, tilt steering column, rear defogger, speed-sensitive intermittent wipers, digital clock, trip odometer, tachometer, coolant temperature gauge, voltmeter, cruise control, AM/FM cassette with EQ, additional audio system switches in steering wheel hub, power antenna, leather-wrapped steering wheel, theft deterrent system, remote fuel door and decklid releases, 195/60HR15 tires on alloy wheels.

Optional equipment:

Anti-lock braking system	1495	—	—
Eurotech Pkg.	2042	—	—
Anti-lock brakes, electronically controlled suspension.			
Power glass sunroof	685	—	—
Leather seats	816	—	—

Prices are accurate at time of printing; subject to manufacturer's change.

Mitsubishi Wagon

Mitsubishi Wagon

What's New

Mitsubishi's compact van gets minor standard-equipment revisions for 1990, but is otherwise unchanged from last year. The Wagon comes in base and LS price levels, both with seats for seven standard: two reclining front bucket seats; two middle captain's chairs that recline, swivel 360 degrees, and move 20 inches fore/aft; and a removable 3-place rear bench seat with reclining seatback. Mitsubishi's minivan has a rear-drive, mid-engine design that's similar to the Toyota Van's. A 107-horsepower 2.4-liter 4-cylinder engine is mounted behind the front axle and between the front seats. The engine teams with a 4-speed overdrive automatic transmission.

For

● Passenger room   ● Cargo space   ● Maneuverability

Against

● Ride   ● Driver seating   ● Entry/exit

Summary

Since Mitsubishi and Toyota use similar mid-engine layouts on rear-drive chassis (Toyota also offers 4-wheel-drive), their vans have similar dynamic qualities. The short wheelbase and considerable body overhang results in a bouncy, uncomfortable ride under most conditions. Mitsubishi's firm suspension has stiff reactions to bumps, yet still suffers from excessive bouncing, though the Wagon feels more stable and has less body lean in turns than the Toyota Van. The short wheelbase and tiny 29.5-foot turn circle aid maneuverability, a plus for parking and city driving. Acceleration at low speeds is adequate, but you have to keep the throttle wide open to climb hills and pass other vehicles on the highway. The front doors are located directly over the front wheels, making it hard to step up into the interior without getting your clothes dirty. The driving position is cramped and bus-like, and with the engine between the front seats, the driver and front passenger can't move to the rear of the Wagon from the inside, and there's little shoulder room to the driver's left. On the plus side, interior space is competitive with most other compact vans and Mitsubishi offers one of the most flexible seating arrangements on wheels. There's little cargo space behind the rear bench seat, but you can pivot the whole seat forward for plenty of room, or remove it. Despite the Wagon's roomy interior and flexible seating, the front-drive Dodge Caravan/Plymouth Voyager and the Mazda MPV (available with rear- or 4-wheel drive) are better choices because of their superior ride, handling, and ergonomics.

Specifications

	4-door van
Wheelbase, in.	88.0
Overall length, in.	175.2
Overall width, in.	66.5
Overall height, in.	71.3
Turn diameter, ft.	29.5
Curb weight, lbs.	3285
Cargo vol., cu. ft.	161.6
Fuel capacity, gals.	14.2
Seating capacity	7
Front headroom, in.	38.6
Front shoulder room, in.	57.3
Front legroom, max., in.	40.4
Rear headroom, in.	39.0
Rear shoulder room, in.	60.6
Rear legroom, min., in.	41.1

Powertrain layout: longitudinal mid engine/rear-wheel drive.

Engines	ohc I-4
Size, liters/cu. in.	2.4/143
Fuel delivery	PFI
Horsepower @ rpm	107 @ 5000
Torque (lbs./ft.) @ rpm	132 @ 3500
Availability	S

EPA city/highway mpg

4-speed OD automatic	18/21

Prices

Mitsubishi Wagon	Retail Price	Dealer Invoice	Low Price
4-door van	$14929	—	—
4-door van w/LS Pkg.	16579	—	—
Destination charge	285	285	285

Dealer invoice and low price not available at time of publication.

Standard equipment:

2.4-liter PFI 4-cylinder engine, 4-speed automatic transmission, console with storage, rear defogger and wiper/washer, power locks, remote fuel door release, tinted glass, rear heater, dual outside mirrors, velour upholstery, two recline/swivel/slide middle seats, third fold-down, removable bench seat, tilt steering column, rear side storage bins, variable intermittent wipers, P205/75R14 tires. **LS Pkg.** adds: power steering, power mirrors, digital clock, cruise control, power windows, bronze tinted glass, bodyside molding, AM/FM cassette.

Optional equipment:

Power steering, base	268	—	—
Dual air conditioning	1426	—	—

KEY: **ohv** = overhead valve; **ohc** = overhead cam; **dohc** = double overhead cam; **I** = inline cylinders; **V** = cylinders in V configuration; **flat** = horizontally opposed cylinders; **bbl.** = barrel (carburetor); **PFI** = port (multi-point) fuel injection; **TBI** = throttle-body (single-point) fuel injection; **rpm** = revolutions per minute; **OD** = overdrive transmission; **S** = standard; **O** = optional; **NA** = not available.

CONSUMER GUIDE®

	Retail Price	Dealer Invoice	Low Price
AM/FM cassette, base	511	—	—
Power glass sunroof	685	—	—
Alloy wheels, w/LS Pkg.	335	—	—
Power mirrors, base	65	—	—
Digital clock, base	56	—	—
Protection Pkg.	162	—	—
Floormats, cargo net.			

Nissan Axxess

Nissan Axxess XE All-Wheel Drive

What's New

Axxess arrived last spring as an early 1990 model to replace the Stanza station wagon. Like its predecessor, Axxess is a tall, compact wagon with two sliding rear side doors and a choice of front- or 4-wheel drive, which Nissan calls all-wheel drive (AWD). Both versions offer a standard 5-speed manual or optional 4-speed automatic transmission linked to a 138-horsepower 2.4-liter 4-cylinder engine. It's the same engine used in the new Nissan Stanza and the 240SX sports coupe. Axxess is longer, lower, wider, and heavier than the Stanza wagon and nearly four inches longer in wheelbase. AWD models have a permanently engaged 4WD system. Torque is normally split 50/50 front/rear, but in slippery conditions a center viscous coupling delivers more power to the wheels with the most traction—either fore/aft or side-to-side as conditions demand. Seats for five are standard and an optional 2-place rear seat is available, bringing with it a 70/30 split middle bench with fore/aft adjustment. Base models are called XE and top-line models are called SE; the SE comes only with automatic transmission.

For

- 4WD traction   • Passenger room   • Cargo space
- Entry/exit

Against

- Noise   • Fuel economy (AWD model)

Summary

Dual sliding side doors and a tall liftgate make the Axxess easy to get in or out of and/or load cargo, so Nissan's claim that this is more than just a wagon is apt. Unfortunately, it's not quite a minivan. The optional 5+2 seating package is accurately named: The third seat is too narrow and cramped to take anyone larger than small children. The split middle seat folds out of the way only on its narrower right side, thus leaving a slim crawl-space to the rear. Cargo room is ample with the standard 5-passenger seating, while a bumper-height opening helps prevent backache. The third seat double-folds for extra hauling space, but neither the third nor the second seat can be removed. With automatic transmission, the front-drive Axxess is no slingshot, but it provides respectable acceleration for a family vehicle: 11.5 seconds to 60 mph. A full load of people or cargo (up to 800 pounds) makes Axxess struggle to crest hills or merge onto fast-moving freeways. The AWD model is nearly 300 pounds heavier, and it shows in slower acceleration. We tested an AWD with the 5-speed manual and averaged just 17.6 mpg from mainly city driving. However, the AWD instantly delivers impressive traction on slippery roads, with no input from the driver required. The engine becomes vocal above 3000 rpm and there's a lot of road noise on coarse pavement. Axxess runs from under $15,000 for a base front-drive model to $19,000 for an SE AWD version. That's pretty high for a compact wagon, but a lot cheaper than most minivans. Axxess is competent, pleasant to drive, and practical. It's a good choice for those who have outgrown a small sedan or wagon, but don't need or want a 7-passenger minivan.

Specifications

	5-door wagon	AWD 5-door wagon
Wheelbase, in.	102.8	102.4
Overall length, in.	171.9	171.9
Overall width, in.	66.5	66.5
Overall height, in.	64.6	64.6
Turn diameter, ft.	34.8	35.4
Curb weight, lbs.	2877	3146
Cargo vol., cu. ft.	35.5	35.5
Fuel capacity, gals.	17.2	15.9
Seating capacity	7	7
Front headroom, in.	39.7	39.7
Front shoulder room, in.	55.4	55.4
Front legroom, max., in.	38.6	38.6
Rear headroom, in.	39.4	39.4
Rear shoulder room, in.	56.6	56.6
Rear legroom, min., in.	36.0	36.0

Powertrain layout: transverse front engine/front-wheel drive or permanently engaged 4WD.

Engines

	ohc I-4
Size, liters/cu. in.	2.4/146
Fuel delivery	PFI
Horsepower @ rpm	138 @ 5600
Torque (lbs./ft.) @ rpm	148 @ 4400
Availability	S

EPA city/highway mpg

5-speed OD manual	21/27
4-speed OD automatic	20/24

Prices

Nissan Axxess	Retail Price	Dealer Invoice	Low Price
XE 2WD 5-door wagon, 5-speed	$13949	$12205	—
XE 2WD wagon, automatic	14699	12862	—
SE 2WD wagon, automatic	16749	14655	—
XE All Wheel Drive wagon, 5-speed	15749	13780	—

Prices are accurate at time of printing; subject to manufacturer's change.

	Retail Price	Dealer Invoice	Low Price
XE All Wheel Drive wagon, automatic . . .	16499	14437	—
SE All Wheel Drive wagon, automatic . . .	18749	16405	—
Destination charge	260	260	260

Low price not available at time of publication.

Standard equipment:

XE: 2.4-liter PFI 12-valve 4-cylinder engine, 5-speed manual or 4-speed automatic transmission, power steering, cloth reclining front bucket seats, 3-passenger middle bench seat, motorized front shoulder belts with manual lap belts, outboard lap/shoulder belts for middle seat, power locks, tonneau cover, storage bin under driver's seat, AM/FM ST ET cassette with diversity antenna, intermittent wipers, rear defogger and wiper/washer, remote fuel door and liftgate releases, 195/70R14 all-season M + S tires; All Wheel Drive has permanent 4-wheel drive, viscous limited-slip rear differential. **SE adds:** 4-speed automatic transmission, air conditioning, 7-passenger seating (2WD), sunroof, power windows and mirrors, cruise control, leather-wrapped steering wheel, tinted glass, upgraded upholstery, alloy wheels.

Optional equipment:

5 + 2 Seating Pkg., XE	400	332	—
Third seat with lap/shoulder belts and head restraints, 70/30 split middle seat, fore/aft middle seat adjustments.			
Power Value Option Pkg., XE	900	788	—
Air conditioning, power windows and mirrors, cruise control.			
Power/Sunroof Value Option Pkg., XE . . .	1385	1212	—
Two-tone paint, XE	300	249	—
Luggage rack	140	116	—

Nissan Maxima

Nissan Maxima GXE

What's New

Maxima was redesigned last year, so this year's changes are minor. On the sporty SE, anti-lock brakes and a sport suspension are now in a $995 SE Sport Package; last year, a similar package with window graphics cost $1500. SE models also have new cloth upholstery standard. Leather upholstery has been optional on the SE since last spring, and on the luxury GXE model since last fall. Both the SE and GXE are front-drive 4-door sedans with a 160-horsepower 3.0-liter V-6 engine. The SE comes with either a 5-speed manual or 4-speed

> **KEY: ohv** = overhead valve; **ohc** = overhead cam; **dohc** = double overhead cam; **I** = inline cylinders; **V** = cylinders in V configuration; **flat** = horizontally opposed cylinders; **bbl.** = barrel (carburetor); **PFI** = port (multi-point) fuel injection; **TBI** = throttle-body (single-point) fuel injection; **rpm** = revolutions per minute; **OD** = overdrive transmission; **S** = standard; **O** = optional; **NA** = not available.

automatic transmission, the GXE only with the automatic. While the anti-lock brakes are available only on the SE, the GXE has two exclusive option groups. The Luxury Package has power front seats, a power sunroof, and a Nissan-Bose sound system. The Electronic Equipment Package adds a digital instrument cluster with a head-up display that displays the speedometer reading in the lower left corner of the windshield, plus automatic temperature control and "Sonar Suspension II," which uses a sonar sensor to "read" the road surface and automatically adjust shock-absorber firmness to maintain ride comfort. The electronic suspension also has firm and soft settings. Motorized front shoulder belts and separate manual lap belts are standard on Maxima.

For

- Acceleration - Anti-lock brakes (SE) - Handling
- Passenger room

Against

- Ride (Sonar Suspension)
- Digital instrument cluster (GXE)

Summary

Maxima is a capable all-around performer, and in SE trim a close overall match for the Acura Legend—at a much lower price. Nissan has boosted base prices this fall by only $200, so Maxima still starts out on the right side of $20,000. We tested an SE with the 5-speed manual that ran 0-60 mph in a brisk 8.9 seconds, slightly slower than a Legend with automatic. A Maxima GXE did the sprint to 60 mph in 9.3 seconds. We prefer the Maxima SE because it comes with rear disc brakes (instead of drums) standard and anti-lock brakes optional. Braking performance is good on the GXE, but it's better on the SE, especially with the anti-lock feature. Cornering is stable, body lean minimal, and the ride is firm but supple. We had different conclusions about the GXE with the Sonar Suspension, which banged crudely over sharp bumps. In its soft mode, the Sonar Suspension allowed a floaty ride, while in the firm mode the ride was more stable. Our advice: Just say no to Sonar Suspension. GXE buyers should forget the optional Electronic Equipment Package with its digital and graphic-display instruments, which are far less comprehensible that the standard analog gauges. The head-up speedometer display is of little help. With its spirited performance, comfortable interior, and modest price, Maxima is a bargain among luxury sedans.

Specifications

	4-door notchback
Wheelbase, in.	104.3
Overall length, in.	187.6
Overall width, in.	69.3
Overall height, in.	55.1
Turn diameter, ft.	36.7
Curb weight, lbs.	3193
Cargo vol., cu. ft.	14.5
Fuel capacity, gals.	18.5
Seating capacity	5
Front headroom, in.	39.5
Front shoulder room, in.	NA
Front legroom, max., in.	43.7
Rear headroom, in.	36.9
Rear shoulder room, in.	NA
Rear legroom, min., in.	33.2

Powertrain layout: transverse front engine/front-wheel drive.

Engines

	ohc V-6
Size, liters/cu. in.	3.0/181
Fuel delivery	PFI
Horsepower @ rpm	160 @
	5200
Torque (lbs./ft.) @ rpm	182 @
	2800
Availability	S

EPA city/highway mpg
5-speed OD manual	20/26
4-speed OD automatic	19/26

Prices

Nissan Maxima	Retail Price	Dealer Invoice	Low Price
GXE 4-door notchback, automatic	$17699	—	—
SE 4-door notchback, 5-speed	18749	—	—
SE 4-door notchback, automatic	19679	—	—
Destination charge	260	260	260

Dealer invoice and low price not available at time of publication.

Standard equipment:

3.0-liter PFI V-6, 4-speed automatic transmission, power steering, air conditioning, power windows and locks with keyless entry, velour reclining front bucket seats, driver's seat height and lumbar adjustments, split folding rear seat, power mirrors, cruise control, tinted glass, AM/FM cassette with diversity antenna, motorized front shoulder belts with manual lap belts, theft deterrent system, tilt steering column, variable intermittent wipers, rear defogger, remote fuel door and decklid releases, illuminated entry, tachometer, dual trip odometers, coolant temperature gauge, digital clock, 195/60R16 tires on alloy wheels. **SE** adds: 5-speed manual or 4-speed automatic transmission, 4-wheel disc brakes, Nissan-Bose audio system, leather-wrapped steering wheel and shift knob, power glass sunroof, fog lights.

Optional equipment:

Luxury Pkg., GXE	1900	—	—
Power seats, power sunroof, Nissan-Bose audio system.			
Electonic Equipment Pkg., GXE	1550	—	—
Digital instruments, head-up display, automatic temperature control, Nissan Sonar Suspension II, speed-sensitive power steering; requires Luxury Pkg.			
Leather trim	950	—	—
Sport Pkg., SE	995	—	—
Anti-lock brakes, sport suspension.			
Pearlglow paint	350	—	—

Nissan Pathfinder

What's New

A 5-door Pathfinder is scheduled to go on sale by early 1990 as the biggest change for Nissan's sport-utility vehicle. Pathfinder has been available only in a 3-door body style, which will still be offered. Last spring a 25 percent import tariff was levied on sport-utility vehicles with two side doors, causing a $1500 price hike on Pathfinder at that time. Models with four side doors carry a 2.5-percent tariff. The other big change for 1990 is that the standard 3.0-liter V-6 engine gains multi-point fuel injection (one injector for each cylinder) instead of single-point injection (one injector on top of the engine). Horsepower grows by 10 to 155 and torque by 14 pounds/feet to 180. The 3-door Pathfinder will continue for 1990 only in SE trim and

Nissan Pathfinder SE

last year's Sport Package standard. The Sport Package includes 4-wheel disc brakes, larger tires, a limited-slip differential, adjustable suspension, and other amenities. The 5-door model will be offered in base XE and costlier SE trim levels. All models will be offered with on-demand 4WD, plus a base XE 5-door will be sold with rear-wheel drive. Other changes for 1990 will include rear headrests and shoulder belts for the outboard rear seats. Since the 1990 models aren't scheduled to arrive until December or January, prices and specifications weren't available at publication time.

For

• 4WD traction • Passenger room • Cargo space

Against

• Fuel economy • Noise

Summary

Since we haven't driven the 1990 versions, we can't say how much this year's additional power improves performance. At more than 3700 pounds, Pathfinder won't be overpowered, even with the 155-horsepower engine. The 4×4s have an on-demand, part-time 4-wheel-drive system with automatic locking front hubs and limited shift-on-the-fly. You can shift from 2WD to 4WD High below 25 mph, but have to stop and then back up slightly to disengage 4WD, which is inconvenient. However, once you've engaged 4WD, you can intermittently shift between 2WD and 4WD High. Pathfinder's suspension absorbs small bumps fairly well, though the ride can be bouncy and jittery on pockmarked pavement. Off-road, it handles the rough stuff with aplomb. There's a high step up into the cabin and getting into the rear seat on the 3-door model requires some contortions, but Pathfinder's long wheelbase means there's plenty of leg room in the rear. Cargo volume is impressive; the load floor is wide and long, and the folding rear seatbacks lie flat if you tilt the cushions forward. We're anxious to try this year's stronger engine and the more convenient 5-door model, which should make Pathfinder more of a family vehicle and be cheaper than the 3-door because of the lower tariff. If you can't wait for the 1990 Pathfinder, look at the Jeep Cherokee and Toyota 4Runner instead.

1989 Specifications	3-door wagon
Wheelbase, in.	104.3
Overall length, in.	171.9
Overall width, in.	66.5
Overall height, in.	65.7

Prices are accurate at time of printing; subject to manufacturer's change

	3-door wagon
Turn diameter, ft.	35.5
Curb weight, lbs.	3735
Cargo vol., cu. ft.	71.3
Fuel capacity, gals.	21.1
Seating capacity	5
Front headroom, in.	39.3
Front shoulder room, in.	54.4
Front legroom, max., in.	42.6
Rear headroom, in.	36.8
Rear shoulder room, in.	55.1
Rear legroom, min., in.	33.1

Powertrain layout: longitudinal front engine/rear-wheel drive or on-demand 4WD.

Engines

	ohc V-6
Size, liters/cu. in.	3.0/181
Fuel delivery	TBI
Horsepower @ rpm	145 @ 4800
Torque (lbs./ft.) @ rpm	166 @ 2800
Availability	S

EPA city/highway mpg
5-speed OD manual	15/18
4-speed OD automatic	14/16

Prices

Nissan Pathfinder (1989 prices)	Retail Price	Dealer Invoice	Low Price
XE 2WD 3-door wagon, 5-speed	$15399	$13859	$14272
XE 2WD 3-door wagon, automatic	16554	14899	15343
XE 4WD 3-door wagon, 5-speed	17399	15659	16126
XE 4WD 3-door automatic	18554	16699	17197
SE 4WD 3-door wagon, 5-speed	20499	18449	18999
SE 4WD 3-door wagon, automatic	21429	19286	19861
Destination charge	260	260	260

Standard equipment:

XE: 3.0-liter TBI V-6, 5-speed manual or 4-speed automatic transmission, part-time 4-wheel drive with automatic locking front hubs (4WD), power steering, cloth reclining front bucket seats, split folding rear seat, tinted glass, dual outside mirrors, skid plates, AM/FM ST ET cassette with diversity antenna, tilt steering column, rear defogger, remote fuel door release, tachometer, coolant temperature gauge, trip odometer, digital clock, 215/75R15 all-season SBR tires. **SE** adds: air conditioning, power windows and locks, vehicle security system, upgraded audio system, variable intermittent wipers, rear wiper/washer, right visor mirror, voltmeter, dual trip odometers, power mirrors, rear side and quarter window privacy glass, 235/75R15 tires on chrome wheels with locks.

Optional equipment:

Air conditioning	825	701	754
Power Plus Pkg., XE 2WD	1700	1445	1553
XE 4WD	1900	1615	1736

Limited-slip differential (4WD), power windows and locks, power mirrors, upgraded audio system, fog lamps, fender flares, outside spare tire carrier, spare tire cover, wheel locks, 235/75R15 tires on chrome wheels.

KEY: ohv = overhead valve; **ohc** = overhead cam; **dohc** = double overhead cam; **I** = inline cylinders; **V** = cylinders in V configuration; **flat** = horizontally opposed cylinders; **bbl.** = barrel (carburetor); **PFI** = port (multi-point) fuel injection; **TBI** = throttle-body (single-point) fuel injection; **rpm** = revolutions per minute; **OD** = overdrive transmission; **S** = standard; **O** = optional; **NA** = not available.

	Retail Price	Dealer Invoice	Low Price
Sport Pkg., SE	2000	1700	1827

Limited-slip differential, 4-wheel disc brakes, driver adjustable suspension, fender flares, wheel locks, flip-up glass sunroof, outside spare tire carrier, spare tire cover, fog lamps, 31X10.5R15 tires on alloy wheels.

Two-tone paint	300	255	274
Graphics	105	89	96
Luggage rack/air deflector	175	149	160

Nissan Pulsar NX

Nissan Pulsar NX XE

What's New

The SE model and its dual-camshaft, 125-horsepower 1.8-liter 4-cylinder engine have been dropped from the Pulsar NX lineup. That leaves the XE model with its single-cam, 90-horsepower 1.6-liter 4-cylinder. The 1989 Pulsar SE model was $13,000 with manual transmission and $13,800 with automatic, the same price range as the larger Nissan 240SX sports coupe. Nissan decided there was room for only one sports coupe at that price, so the Pulsar SE is history. The front-drive Pulsar is a 3-door hatchback with a removable hatch lid and removable roof panels, making it nearly topless when all three pieces are off the car. Two front buckets and a folding 2-place rear seat are standard, giving Pulsar nominal seating for four. A driver's-side airbag, optional last year, is standard this year.

For

● Fuel economy ● Handling/roadholding ● Versatility ● Airbag

Against

● Driveability (automatic transmission) ● Visibility ● Noise

Summary

Pulsar created a bit of a stir when it debuted for 1987 in its present form, offering nearly open-air motoring in a low-cost, sporty package. However, success is fleeting in the sports coupe market and Pulsar sales have tumbled. That means you should be able to get a good deal on one these days, especially if you find a leftover 1989 model. Grab an '89 SE model if you can, since its 125-horsepower engine provides brisker acceleration. The 90-horsepower XE engine delivers unspectacular performance, especially with automatic transmission, but returns pleasing fuel economy. The automatic is slow to downshift for passing and shifts harshly under hard throttle. Handling is above average, and the ride is compliant for a sporty small car. Inside, the control layout is excellent, but visibility is hampered by the low seating position and too many roof pillars to the rear and over the shoulders. The 2-place rear seat is fine for children and acceptable for adults only on short trips. Although interior and exterior assembly are tight, there's lots of wind and road noise even before you start removing roof panels. Popping the T-tops is simple; taking off the rear hatch is more of a chore, requiring removal of four screws, four bolts, and the struts that hold up the hatchlid. Nissan provides a wrench and screwdriver, but you'll need two people to lift off the hatch, plus a place to store it, since it doesn't fit in the car (leaving you vulnerable to unexpected rain showers). While this isn't as convenient as a convertible, it's still quite versatile. Can't afford a 240SX or a Mazda Miata, but want something sporty? The versatile Pulsar has a unique body design and is economical to operate.

Specifications

	3-door hatchback
Wheelbase, in.	95.7
Overall length, in.	166.5
Overall width, in.	66.1
Overall height, in.	51.0
Turn diameter, ft.	33.5
Curb weight, lbs.	2388
Cargo vol., cu. ft.	17.0
Fuel capacity, gals.	13.2
Seating capacity	4
Front headroom, in.	38.0
Front shoulder room, in.	NA
Front legroom, max., in.	42.0
Rear headroom, in.	33.9
Rear shoulder room, in.	NA
Rear legroom, min., in.	24.5

Powertrain layout: transverse front engine/front-wheel drive.

Engines

	ohc I-4
Size, liters/cu. in.	1.6/97
Fuel delivery	TBI
Horsepower @ rpm	90 @ 6000
Torque (lbs./ft.) @ rpm	96 @ 3200
Availability	S

EPA city/highway mpg

5-speed OD manual	26/34
3-speed automatic	25/31

Prices

Nissan Pulsar NX (1989 prices)	Retail Price	Dealer Invoice	Low Price
XE 3-door hatchback, 5-speed	$11999	$10499	$10713
XE 3-door hatchback, automatic	12539	10972	11196
SE 3-door hatchback, 5-speed	12999	11374	11606
SE 3-door hatchback, automatic	13799	12057	12312
Destination charge	260	260	260

Standard equipment:

XE: 1.6-liter TBI 4-cylinder engine, 5-speed manual or 3-speed automatic transmission, power steering and brakes, T-bar roof, removable hatchback lid, variable intermittent wipers, tachometer, coolant temperature gauge, trip odometer, AM/FM ST ET with diversity antenna, power mirrors, tilt steering column, center console, remote fuel door and hatch releases, reclining front cloth bucket seats, 185/70R13 tires. **SE** adds: 1.8-liter DOHC 16-valve PFI engine, 5-speed manual or 4-speed automatic transmission, tweed-type upholstery, 195/60R14 tires on alloy wheels.

Optional equipment:	Retail Price	Dealer Invoice	Low Price
Air conditioning	825	685	755
Driver's side airbag, SE	850	NA	NA
Security system/alloy wheel locks, SE	199	165	182
Fog lights, SE	145	120	133
Sport graphics	105	87	96

Nissan Sentra

Nissan Sentra XE

What's New

The 4-wheel-drive station wagon has been dropped and the E price series has disappeared, so the subcompact Sentra line has been trimmed from 19 models to 11. All 1990 Sentras have non-motorized automatic front shoulder belts to satisfy the federal passive-restraint rule; separate lap belts have to be buckled manually. The 4WD wagon was dropped after two seasons and its role is filled elsewhere in Nissan's lineup by the All-Wheel Drive Axxess wagon, introduced last spring. With the E price series gone, Sentra now comes in Standard trim as a 2-door sedan; XE trim as a 2- and 4-door sedan, 5-door wagon, and 3-door Sport Coupe hatchback. The hatchback also comes in higher-priced SE trim. All 1990 models have front-wheel drive. There was an XE trim level last year, but the 1989 models had more standard equipment and were priced about $1400 higher than the 1990 versions. The Standard 2-door comes with a 4-speed manual transmission; all other Sentras come with a 5-speed manual or extra-cost 3-speed automatic. All models use a 90-horsepower 1.6-liter 4-cylinder engine with single-point fuel injection. Some Sentras are built at Nissan's Tennessee assembly plant and some are imported from Japan. Sentra is scheduled to be redesigned for the 1991 model year.

For

● Fuel economy   ● Visibility   ● Maneuverability

Against

● Acceleration (automatic transmission)
● Rear seat room   ● Noise

Summary

With this year's streamlining of the Sentra roster, it's much easier to pick the model that suits your needs and budget. Trouble is, Sentra is no longer priced as an entry level model. The cheapest 4-door sedan is nearly $10,000 with automatic transmission, and over $11,000 with air conditioning and the XE Value Option Package. If you can live without the option

Prices are accurate at time of printing; subject to manufacturer's change

package, air conditioning, or automatic transmission, a Sentra is a pretty good deal as basic, low-cost transportation. Acceleration and fuel economy will be better on Sentras with one of the manual transmission. Once you add automatic and a few other features, you're getting close to Honda Civic, Toyota Corolla, and Geo Prizm territory, and those three subcompacts offer stronger acceleration and more refinement. The Civic and Corolla also offer 4-speed automatic transmissions with an overdrive top gear that provides quieter, more economical highway cruising than the Sentra's 3-speed automatic. Inside Sentra, there isn't any rear leg room to speak of unless front-seaters are willing to scrunch up some. A relatively high driving position combines with a tall glass area and boxy body contours for fine outward vision. You can see the right-rear corner without neck strain, a boon for parking.

Specifications

	2-door notchback	3-door hatchback	4-door notchback	5-door wagon
Wheelbase, in.	95.7	95.7	95.7	95.7
Overall length, in.	168.7	166.5	168.7	172.7
Overall width, in.	64.6	65.6	64.6	64.6
Overall height, in.	54.3	52.2	54.3	54.3
Turn diameter, ft.	30.2	30.2	30.2	30.2
Curb weight, lbs.	2156	2304	2208	2301
Cargo vol., cu. ft.	12.0	16.0	12.0	24.0
Fuel capacity, gals.	13.2	13.2	13.2	13.2
Seating capacity	5	4	5	5
Front headroom, in.	38.2	37.0	38.2	38.2
Front shoulder room, in.	52.1	52.1	52.3	52.1
Front legroom, max., in.	41.8	41.6	41.8	41.8
Rear headroom, in.	36.8	29.2	36.8	39.3
Rear shoulder room, in.	51.3	52.1	50.3	52.1
Rear legroom, min., in.	31.4	31.4	31.4	31.4

Powertrain layout: transverse front engine/front-wheel drive.

Engines

	ohc I-4
Size, liters/cu. in.	1.6/97
Fuel delivery	TBI
Horsepower @ rpm	90 @ 6000
Torque (lbs./ft.) @ rpm	96 @ 3200
Availability	S

EPA city/highway mpg

4-speed manual	29/36
5-speed OD manual	28/36
3-speed automatic	26/31

Nissan Sentra SE

Prices

Nissan Sentra	Retail Price	Dealer Invoice	Low Price
Standard 2-door notchback, 4-speed	$7299	—	—
XE 2-door notchback, 5-speed	8549	—	—
XE 2-door notchback, automatic	9149	—	—
XE 4-door notchback, 5-speed	9149	—	—
XE 4-door notchback, automatic	9749	—	—
XE 5-door wagon, 5-speed	9899	—	—
XE 5-door wagon, automatic	10499	—	—
XE 3-door hatchback, 5-speed	10999	—	—
XE 3-door hatchback, automatic	11924	—	—
SE 3-door hatchback, 5-speed	12299	—	—
SE 3-door hatchback, automatic	12839	—	—
Destination charge	260	260	260

Dealer invoice and low price not available at time of publication.

Standard equipment:

Standard: 1.6-liter TBI 4-cylinder engine, 4-speed manual transmission, coolant temperature gauge, rear defogger, reclining front bucket seats, center console, 155/80R13 tires. **XE** adds: 5-speed manual or 3-speed automatic transmission, cloth seats, split folding rear seat (wagon and hatchback), upgraded interior trim, intermittent wipers, left door pocket, trip odometer, tachometer (hatchback), AM/FM radio (hatchback with automatic transmission). **SE** adds: flip-up sunroof, rear wiper/washer, upgraded upholstery, multi-adjustable driver's seat, AM/FM radio with diversity antenna, 185/60R14 tires on alloy wheels.

Optional equipment:

Air conditioning	825	—	—
Two-tone paint, SE	300	—	—
Metallic paint, Standard	100	—	—
XE Value Option Pkg.	600	—	—

AM/FM radio, power steering, wheel covers, remote mirrors, remote fuel door and decklid/hatch release, visor mirrors, 175/70R13 tires.

Power steering & tilt steering column, XE	300	—	—

Nissan Stanza

What's New

After introducing four new models during the past year—Maxima, 240SX, 300ZX, and Axxess—Nissan brings one new model out this fall, the Stanza, a front-drive compact 4-door sedan that competes against the Honda Accord, Toyota Camry, Mazda 626, Mitsubishi Galant, and others. Nissan's front-drive family compact is based on the latest version of the Japanese-market Bluebird, now two years old. The 1990 Stanza is thus an interim offering. Nissan unofficially admits that another new Stanza will arrive for 1992, with styling created at the firm's California design center. The model arriving this fall sports a more rounded look on the same 100.4-inch wheelbase as the square-rigged 1987-89 Stanza, but is 2.1 inches longer overall at 179.9. Model choices comprise a base XE and upscale GXE. The big news involves engine and brakes. The previous 94-horsepower 2.0-liter 4-cylinder gives way to the 138-horsepower 2.4-liter four introduced in the 240SX sport coupe and Axxess wagon. It teams with a standard 5-speed manual or optional 4-speed automatic transmission. Front disc/rear drum brakes are standard, but the GXE can be ordered with an optional all-disc package that includes an anti-locking braking system (ABS)—both firsts for Stanza. A claimed world first for front-drive sedans is the GXE's standard viscous-coupling limited-slip differential. It is designed to increase traction in slippery conditions and in hard cornering. All 1990 Stanzas have motorized front shoulder belts.

Nissan Stanza GXE

For

- Acceleration • Anti-lock brakes • Ride • Quietness

Against

- Rear seat room • Cargo space

Summary

The new Stanza feels more solid than the old one and delivers much spunkier performance. It weighs about the same, yet its engine is 20 percent larger, packs 42 percent more horsepower, and 30 percent more torque. We timed a 1990 GXE with automatic in the 0-60 mph run in 10.5 seconds—much livelier than the old Stanza and competitive with other compacts. We'd estimate the manual version to be a second quicker. Forget the drag strip stats, though, because the bigger engine's real payoff is swifter, safer passing in the 30-50 mph range, aided by a responsive automatic transmission that's almost always in the right gear. We were also impressed with the stopping distances on our ABS-equipped Stanza: less than 120 feet in 60-mph panic stops. It's great to see ABS ($995 extra) available on a car in this price league. With virtually the same cabin proportions, the new Stanza has no more usable passenger space than its predecessor, so it remains a 4-seater that can be stretched to hold five adults. The new Stanza has 14 cubic feet of cargo space, two feet more than the old one, but utility is spoiled by a narrow floor between the wheels and a high load sill. Also, the previous Stanza's fold-down back seat is no longer offered. However, there's good news on the price front. The 1990 Stanza XE is $749 cheaper than the 1989 equivalent. The GXE is $526 more than last year, but air conditioning is now standard instead of optional.

Specifications

	4-door notchback
Wheelbase, in.	100.4
Overall length, in.	179.9
Overall width, in.	66.8
Overall height, in.	54.1
Turn diameter, ft.	35.4
Curb weight, lbs.	2788
Cargo vol., cu. ft.	14.0
Fuel capacity, gals.	16.4
Seating capacity	5
Front headroom, in.	38.6
Front shoulder room, in.	54.7
Front legroom, max., in.	42.6
Rear headroom, in.	36.8
Rear shoulder room, in.	53.9
Rear legroom, min., in.	33.6

Powertrain layout: transverse front engine/front-wheel drive.

Engines

	ohc I-4
Size, liters/cu. in.	2.4/146
Fuel delivery	PFI
Horsepower @ rpm	138 @ 5600
Torque (lbs./ft.) @ rpm	148 @ 4400
Availability	S

EPA city/highway mpg

5-speed OD manual	22/29
4-speed OD automatic	21/27

Prices

Nissan Stanza	Retail Price	Dealer Invoice	Low Price
XE 4-door notchback, 5-speed	$11450	—	—
XE 4-door notchback, automatic	12250	—	—
GXE 4-door notchback, 5-speed	14775	—	—
GXE 4-door notchback, automatic	15575	—	—
Destination charge	260	260	260

Dealer invoice and low price not available at time of publication.

Standard equipment:

XE: 2.4-liter 12-valve PFI 4-cylinder engine, 5-speed manual or 4-speed automatic transmission, power steering, cloth reclining front bucket seats, tinted glass, rear shoulder belts, dual OS mirrors, tilt steering column, rear defogger, coolant temperature gauge, remote fuel door and decklid releases, right visor mirror, console with beverage holders, 195/65R14 tires. **GXE** adds: air conditioning, limited-slip differential, driver's seat lumbar and height adjustments, tachometer, dark upper windshield band, power windows and locks, power mirrors, AM/FM cassette, cruise control, velour upholstery, upgraded interior trim, left visor mirror, map lights, rear center armrest, alloy wheels.

Optional equipment:

Air conditioning, XE	825	—	—
Anti-lock brakes, GXE	995	—	—
AM/FM cassette, XE	400	—	—
Power Convenience Group, XE	1240	—	—
Power windows and locks, power mirrors, velour upholstery, upgraded interior trim, driver's-seat lumbar and height adjustments, tachometer, rear center armrest.			
Two-tone paint, GXE	300	—	—
Power glass sunroof, GXE	800	—	—
Alloy wheels, XE	435	—	—
Requires Power Convenience Group.			
Cruise control, XE	175	—	—
Not available with 5-speed.			

Nissan 240SX

What's New

Nissan's rear-drive sports coupe was redesigned last year, when it acquired new styling, larger dimensions, and a new engine. For 1990, there's one major change: The Sport Package that was available only on the SE hatchback last year is

> **KEY: ohv** = overhead valve; **ohc** = overhead cam; **dohc** = double overhead cam; **I** = inline cylinders; **V** = cylinders in V configuration; **flat** = horizontally opposed cylinders; **bbl.** = barrel (carburetor); **PFI** = port (multi-point) fuel injection; **TBI** = throttle-body (single-point) fuel injection; **rpm** = revolutions per minute; **OD** = overdrive transmission; **S** = standard; **O** = optional; **NA** = not available.

Prices are accurate at time of printing; subject to manufacturer's change

Nissan 240SX SE

now available on the XE notchback coupe as well. The package includes a sport suspension, alloy wheels, wider tires, front and rear spoilers, and cruise control. A power antenna is a new standard feature on both the SE and XE. Both are powered by a 140-horsepower 2.4-liter 4-cylinder engine and are available with either a 5-speed manual or 4-speed automatic transmission. Four-wheel disc brakes are standard and anti-lock control is optional on the SE. A head-up instrument display is available only on the XE as part of the Power Convenience Group. It projects a digital speedometer reading onto the lower left-hand corner of the windshield. The 240SX meets the federal passive-restraint requirement with motorized front shoulder belts; separate lap belts have to be buckled manually.

For

● Handling ● Anti-lock brakes ● Instruments/controls

Against

● Ride (Sport Package) ● Noise ● Entry/exit
● Rear seat room

Summary

Poised, spirited handling is the 240SX's strong suit, especially with the optional Sport package. Those who favor rear-wheel drive over front-wheel drive will find the 240SX a rewarding yet undemanding car on twisting roads. Unfortunately, the engine doesn't match the capabilities of the suspension. We averaged 10.5 seconds to 60 mph with the 5-speed manual, which is more than adequate but disappointing for a car that looks so sporting. We matched that 0-60 mph time with a 4-cylinder Hyundai Sonata, a family sedan with an automatic transmission. The 240SX engine becomes hoarse and vibratory above 4000 rpm and tire noise invades the interior through the open rear cargo area in the SE hatchback. The optional anti-lock brakes are considerably cheaper this year ($995 instead of $1450), but you still have to buy the Sport Package and air conditioning to get them. That means spending at least $16,500 to get anti-lock brakes on a 240SX. On the other hand, you can't get anti-lock brakes on most other sports coupes, no matter how much you spend; they're not offered

KEY: **ohv** = overhead valve; **ohc** = overhead cam; **dohc** = double overhead cam; **I** = inline cylinders; **V** = cylinders in V configuration; **flat** = horizontally opposed cylinders; **bbl.** = barrel (carburetor); **PFI** = port (multi-point) fuel injection; **TBI** = throttle-body (single-point) fuel injection; **rpm** = revolutions per minute; **OD** = overdrive transmission; **S** = standard; **O** = optional; **NA** = not available.

on most rivals. The firmer suspension in the Sports Package causes a harsher, choppier ride than the base suspension, so you should try both before you buy. As with most sports coupes, there's virtually no rear leg room, but the front is adequately roomy. The dashboard has clear, well-marked analog gauges and most controls are convenient to use. Against the 240SX, we like the Mitsubishi Eclipse and its Eagle Talon/Plymouth Laser clones for their livelier performance, and the Acura Integra for its more refined character.

Specifications

	2-door notchback	3-door hatchback
Wheelbase, in.	97.4	97.4
Overall length, in.	178.0	178.0
Overall width, in.	66.5	66.5
Overall height, in.	50.8	50.8
Turn diameter, ft.	30.8	30.8
Curb weight, lbs.	2657	2684
Cargo vol., cu. ft.	8.6	14.2
Fuel capacity, gals.	15.9	15.9
Seating capacity	4	4
Front headroom, in.	37.8	37.8
Front shoulder room, in.	52.0	52.0
Front legroom, max., in.	42.0	42.0
Rear headroom, in.	34.5	33.3
Rear shoulder room, in.	52.0	51.8
Rear legroom, min., in.	23.8	23.8

Powertrain layout: longitudinal front engine/rear-wheel drive.

Engines

	ohc I-4
Size, liters/cu. in.	2.4/146
Fuel delivery	PFI
Horsepower @ rpm	140 @ 5600
Torque (lbs./ft.) @ rpm	152 @ 4400
Availability	S

EPA city/highway mpg

5-speed OD manual	20/27
4-speed OD automatic	20/25

Prices

Nissan 240SX	Retail Price	Dealer Invoice	Low Price
XE 2-door notchback, 5-speed	$13249	—	—
XE 2-door notchback, automatic	14079	—	—
SE 3-door hatchback, 5-speed	13499	—	—
SE 3-door hatchback, automatic	14329	—	—
Destination charge	260	260	260

Dealer invoice and low price not available at time of publication.

Standard equipment:

XE & SE: 2.4-liter PFI 4-cylinder engine, 5-speed manual or 4-speed automatic transmission, power steering, 4-wheel disc brakes, reclining front bucket seats with driver's side lumbar support adjustment, center console with storage, rear shoulder belts, tilt steering column, tachometer, coolant temperature gauge, trip odometer, variable intermittent wipers, tinted glass, dual remote mirrors, AM/FM radio with power diversity antenna, rear defogger, door pockets, remote fuel door and decklid releases, visor mirrors, cargo cover (SE), 195/60R15 tires.

Optional equipment:

Anti-lock brakes, SE	995	—	—
Requires Sport Pkg. and air conditioning.			
Air conditioning	825	—	—

	Retail Price	Dealer Invoice	Low Price
XE Power Convenience Group	1350	—	—

Upgraded audio system with cassette and active speakers, head-up display, cruise control, power windows and locks, power mirrors, map lights.

SE Power Convenience Group	1150	—	—

Upgraded audio system with cassette, cruise control, power windows and locks, power mirrors, rear wiper/washer.

Sport Pkg.	1150	—	—

XE: cruise control, sport suspension, front air dam, rear spoiler, leather-wrapped steering wheel and shift knob, 205/60R15 tires on alloy wheels. SE adds seamless-style front seat cloth.

Power Convenience Group & Sport Pkg., XE	2300	—	—
SE	2100	—	—
Two-tone paint, XE	300	—	—
Power sunroof, XE	800	—	—

Requires Power Convenience Group or Sport Pkg.

Flip-up sunroof, SE	450	—	—

Requires Power Convenience Group or Sport Pkg.

Nissan 300ZX

Nissan 300ZX GS

What's New

The 1990 300ZX 2-seat sports car went on sale last spring with a 222-horsepower 3.0-liter V-6, and a 2+2 coupe with the same engine joined the lineup during the summer. The main attraction this fall is the 300ZX Turbo, with two turbochargers helping its 3.0-liter V-6 pump 300 horsepower with the standard 5-speed manual transmission (280 with automatic). The turbocharged engine has two intercoolers, four camshafts, and 24 valves. A different turbocharger and intercooler serves each bank of cylinders. The turbochargers are cooled by both water and oil. Other features unique to the Turbo are intercooler inlets in the front air dam, a rear spoiler, Z-rated tires (for speeds over 149 mph), and Super HICAS, Nissan's 4-wheel steering system. HICAS stands for High Capacity Actively Controlled Steering; the rear wheels first turn slightly in the opposite direction as the fronts, and then in the same direction. Nissan says this improves stability in fast lane changes and provides crisper steering response. The maximum steering range at the rear wheels is one degree, but Nissan says in "normal driving situations" the rear wheels will seldom steer more than 0.4 degree. To discourage thieves, the vehicle-identification number will be etched into the windows and T-tops of 300ZX Turbos. Anti-lock brakes and motorized front shoulder belts are standard on all models.

For

- Acceleration   • Anti-lock brakes   • Handling
- Instruments/controls

Against

- Ride   • Tire noise   • Fuel economy

Summary

First, the good news, because there's lots of it. The new 300ZX is more of a sports car than a luxury car, yet it doesn't cheat its occupants out of comfort or convenience. We've driven only the naturally aspirated 2-seater and were highly impressed with its strong low-end acceleration and prompt, spirited passing response. When it comes time to stop, the standard anti-lock brakes do a commendable job. The new Z-car also feels more nimble and zips around tight corners with admirable agility. Inside, the seats are comfortable and supportive, there's adequate room for tall people to stretch out, and the attractive dashboard has large, easy-to-read gauges and handy controls. Now the bad news: Base prices range from $27,300 for the GS 2-seater to $33,800 for the Turbo with automatic. A year ago the comparable 1989 models were $5000 to $8000 cheaper. If you can afford this much for a sports car, you'll be rewarded with top-notch performance, good assembly quality, and an ergonomically correct interior. As impressive as the 300ZX Turbo sounds on paper, we think most drivers will manage nicely with one of the naturally aspirated, less-expensive models.

Specifications

	3-door hatchback	2+2 3-door hatchback
Wheelbase, in.	96.5	101.2
Overall length, in.	169.5	178.0
Overall width, in.	70.5	70.9
Overall height, in.	49.2	49.4
Turn diameter, ft.	34.1	35.4
Curb weight, lbs.	3219[1]	3313
Cargo vol., cu. ft.	23.7	NA
Fuel capacity, gals.	18.7	18.7
Seating capacity	2	4
Front headroom, in.	NA	NA
Front shoulder room, in.	NA	NA
Front legroom, max., in.	NA	NA
Rear headroom, in.	NA	NA
Rear shoulder room, in.	NA	NA
Rear legroom, min., in.	NA	NA

1. 3474 lbs., Turbo.

Powertrain layout: longitudinal front engine/rear-wheel drive.

Engines	dohc V-6	Turbo dohc V-6
Size, liters/cu. in.	3.0/181	3.0/181
Fuel delivery	PFI	PFI
Horsepower @ rpm	222 @ 6400	300 @[1] 6400
Torque (lbs./ft.) @ rpm	198 @ 4800	283 @ 3600
Availability	S	S
EPA city/highway mpg		
5-speed OD manual	18/24	18/24
4-speed OD automatic	19/24	18/24

1. 280 horsepower with automatic transmission.

Prices

Nissan 300ZX	Retail Price	Dealer Invoice	Low Price
GS 3-door hatchback, 5-speed	$27300	—	—
GS 3-door hatchback, automatic	28100	—	—

Prices are accurate at time of printing; subject to manufacturer's change.

	Retail Price	Dealer Invoice	Low Price
Turbo 3-door hatchback, 5-speed	33000	—	—
Turbo 3-door hatchback, automatic	33800	—	—
GS 2 + 2 3-door hatchback, 5-speed	28500	—	—
GS 2 + 2 3-door hatchback, automatic . . .	29300	—	—
Destination charge	260	260	260

Dealer invoice and low price not available at time of publication.

Standard equipment:

3.0-liter DOHC 24-valve PFI V-6, 5-speed manual or 4-speed automatic transmission, 4-wheel anti-lock disc brakes, power steering, air conditioning, power windows and locks, power mirrors, cloth reclining front bucket seats, driver's seat height, lumbar and lateral support adjustments, cruise control, tinted glass, T-bar roof, theft-deterrent system, AM/FM cassette with power diversity antenna, variable intermittent wipers, rear defogger and wiper/washer, remote fuel door and hatch releases, tachometer, coolant temperature and oil pressure gauges, leather-wrapped steering wheel and manual shift knob, fog lamps, 225/60R16 tires on alloy wheels. **Turbo** adds: turbocharged, intercooled engine, 4-wheel steering, limited-slip differential, front air dam and rear spoiler, Nissan-Bose audio system, 245/45ZR16 rear tires.

Optional equipment:

Electronic Equipment Pkg., GS	1600	—	—
Turbo	900	—	—

Nissan-Bose audio system, automatic temperature control, power driver's seat, heated OS mirrors, illuminated entry.

Leather Trim Pkg., 2-seater	1000	—	—
2 + 2	1200	—	—

Leather seating surfaces, cargo cover, bronze-tinted glass; requires Electronic Equipment Pkg.

Nissan-Bose audio system, GS	700	—	—
Pearlglow paint	350	—	—

Oldsmobile Custom Cruiser

Oldsmobile Custom Cruiser

What's New

The full-size, rear-drive Custom Cruiser wagon gains door-mounted passive seat belts for outboard front-seat passengers, some new interior and exterior colors, and an aluminum wheel option. Otherwise, this traditional alternative to the mini-van is carried over unaltered. Custom Cruiser is built from the same design as the Buick Estate, Chevrolet Caprice, and Pontiac Safari wagons. All use a 140-horsepower, carbureted 5.0-liter V-8 engine and 4-speed overdrive automatic transmission. With a folding, rear-facing third seat standard, there's seating for eight. A 5000-pound towing package is optional on Custom Cruiser, whose design dates to the 1977 model year.

For

● Room/comfort ● Cargo room ● Trailer towing capacity

Against

● Fuel economy ● Size and weight
● Handling/maneuverability

Summary

Full-size rear-drive wagons such as the Custom Cruiser have become scarce, yet they still have enough of a following to justify continuing their production. It's easy to see why when you look at the plus points: Room for eight people, generous cargo capacity (enough to swallow a four-by-eight-foot sheet of plywood), plus the ability to tow a 5000-pound trailer. You'll have to look to a van to beat those figures, and a van just isn't everyone's cup of tea. Nor can a van match the smoothness and quietness delivered by the Olds wagon's full-length perimeter frame, slow-revving 5.7-liter V-8, and 4-speed automatic transmission. But while the Cruiser's pluses come from its size and brawn, so do its minuses. The V-8 works up a heavy thirst hauling around two tons of curb weight, a thirst that's likely to doom these vehicles if the price of gasoline soars again. Ponderous handling makes the big wagons cumbersome to drive in urban areas, so they're at home on the open road. We prefer something smaller and more agile. Still, cars like the Custom Cruiser aren't much more expensive than most front-drive, mid-size wagons.

Specifications

	5-door wagon
Wheelbase, in.	115.9
Overall length, in.	220.3
Overall width, in.	79.8
Overall height, in.	58.5
Turn diameter, ft.	39.2
Curb weight, lbs.	4221
Cargo vol., cu. ft.	87.2
Fuel capacity, gals.	22.0
Seating capacity	8
Front headroom, in.	39.6
Front shoulder room, in.	60.6
Front legroom, max., in.	42.2
Rear headroom, in.	39.3
Rear shoulder room, in.	60.5
Rear legroom, min., in.	37.2

Powertrain layout: longitudinal front engine/rear-wheel drive.

Engines

	ohv V-8
Size, liters/cu. in.	5.0/307
Fuel delivery	4 bbl.
Horsepower @ rpm	140 @ 3200
Torque (lbs./ft.) @ rpm	255 @ 2000
Availability	S

EPA city/highway mpg

4-speed OD automatic	17/24

Prices

Oldsmobile Custom Cruiser	Retail Price	Dealer Invoice	Low Price
5-door wagon	$17595	$15185	$15385
Destination charge	505	505	505

Standard equipment:

5.0-liter 4bbl. V-8, 4-speed automatic transmission, power steering, power tailgate window, air conditioning, tinted glass, left remote and right manual mirrors, trip odometer, AM/FM radio, right visor mirror, locking rear storage compartment, 55/45 bench seat, rear shoulder belts, rear-facing third seat, P225/75R15 tires.

Optional equipment:	Retail Price	Dealer Invoice	Low Price
Option Pkg. 1SB	1078	916	970
Driver Convenience Pkg., power mirrors, passenger seatback recliner, power antenna, Reminder Pkg., rear defogger, luggage rack, accent stripe, door edge guards, floormats.			
Option Pkg. 1SC	2237	1901	2013
Pkg. 1SB plus power windows and locks, lower bodyside moldings, lighted visor mirrors, power driver's seat, AM/FM cassette.			
Option Pkg. 1SD	3084	2621	2776
Pkg. 1SC plus automatic climate control, reading lamps, Illumination Pkg., cornering lamps, exterior lamp monitor, automatic day/night mirror, power passenger seat, wire wheel covers.			
Bodyside & tailgate paneling	255	217	230
Rear defogger	160	136	144
Automatic leveling system	175	149	158
Limited-slip differential	100	85	90
Alloy wheels	320	272	288
Instrument panel cluster	66	56	59
Trailering Pkg.	96	82	86
Engine block heater	18	15	16
California emissions pkg.	100	85	90

Oldsmobile Cutlass Calais

Oldsmobile Cutlass Calais I Series

What's New

Oldsmobile has revived the revered 442 name for 1990, but this incarnation is quite different from the rear-drive, mid-size muscle car that made the badge famous. Back in 1964, 442 was a Cutlass option package offering a 330-cubic-inch V-8 engine with a 4-barrel carburetor, a 4-speed manual transmission, and dual exhausts. This year, 442 is an option package on the front-drive compact Cutlass Calais S 2-door coupe. Now, it stands for a Quad 4 engine, 4-valves per cylinder, and two camshafts. The 2.3-liter 16-valve 4-cylinder is rated at 180 horsepower and is available with a 5-speed manual transmission only. Standard equipment includes the FE3 sport suspension, 215/60R14 tires on alloy wheels, full instrumentation, a rear-deck spoiler, and Quad 442 exterior graphics. Elsewhere in the Cutlass Calais lineup of coupes and 4-door sedans, the S model gets a new instrument cluster and the SL's standard 14-inch alloy wheels replace 13 inchers. A remote keyless entry system is a new option on all models, while the SL can now be ordered with an optional compact disc player. A 110-horsepower 2.5-liter four is standard on the base and S model. Standard on the SL and optional on the S and International Series is a 160-horsepower version of the Quad 4. The Quad 442's 180-horsepower HO Quad 4 is standard on the I-Series. A 160-horsepower 3.3-liter V-6 is optional only on the SL. Calais is built from the same design as the Buick Skylark and Pontiac Grand Am.

For

● Performance (V-6, Quad 4)

Against

● Noise (Quad 4)   ● Rear seat room   ● Trunk space

Summary

Along with its Buick and Pontiac cousins the Cutlass Calais suffers as a family car compared to such Japanese compacts as the Honda Accord and Toyota Camry. Too little interior and cargo space are its main drawbacks, though the imports also enjoy an edge in refinement, ride, and ergonomics. While we can't get too excited about Calais, it does offer more powertrain choices than most compacts, plus its price is right. Slapping the hallowed 442 badge on a front-drive, 4-cylinder compact is sure to sour some muscle-car purists. The Quad 442 does at least fulfill its mission. At around $13,000, its 7.5-second 0-60-mph time and credible road manners are a match for such competitors as the turbocharged Plymouth Sundance and the Mazda MX-6 GT. Typical of 16-valvers, the Quad 4 must be revved above about 4000 rpm to deliver a kick, though the Olds engine is quite adequate at lower rpm around town. Either Calais Quad 4 works better with a manual gearbox, however, which should nudge many buyers toward the 3.3 V-6. The quietest and most refined of Calais engines, the 3.3 also has the most low-end torque, making it the best with automatic transmission. Calais' base 2.5-liter four delivers adequate acceleration and decent fuel economy, but insufficient amounts of either to be the best choice.

Specifications	2-door notchback	4-door notchback
Wheelbase, in.	103.4	103.4
Overall length, in.	178.8	178.8
Overall width, in.	66.6	66.6
Overall height, in.	52.4	52.4
Turn diameter, ft.	35.4	35.4
Curb weight, lbs.	2518	2585
Cargo vol., cu. ft.	13.2	13.2
Fuel capacity, gals.	13.6	13.6
Seating capacity	5	5
Front headroom, in.	37.8	37.8
Front shoulder room, in.	53.9	53.9
Front legroom, max., in.	42.9	42.9
Rear headroom, in.	37.1	37.1
Rear shoulder room, in.	55.1	53.5
Rear legroom, min., in.	34.3	34.3

> **KEY: ohv** = overhead valve; **ohc** = overhead cam; **dohc** = double overhead cam; **I** = inline cylinders; **V** = cylinders in V configuration; **flat** = horizontally opposed cylinders; **bbl.** = barrel (carburetor); **PFI** = port (multi-point) fuel injection; **TBI** = throttle-body (single-point) fuel injection; **rpm** = revolutions per minute; **OD** = overdrive transmission; **S** = standard; **O** = optional; **NA** = not available.

Prices are accurate at time of printing; subject to manufacturer's change

Oldsmobile

Powertrain layout: transverse front engine/front-wheel drive.

Engines

	ohv I-4	dohc I-4	dohc I-4	ohv V-6
Size, liters/cu. in.	2.5/151	2.3/138	2.3/138	3.3/204
Fuel delivery	TBI	PFI	PFI	PFI
Horsepower @ rpm	110 @ 5200	160 @ 6200	180 @ 6200	160 @ 5200
Torque (lbs./ft.) @ rpm ...	135 @ 3200	155 @ 5200	150 @ 5200	185 @ 2000
Availability	S	O[1]	S[2]	O

EPA city/highway mpg

5-speed OD manual	23/33		22/27	
3-speed automatic	23/30	23/32		20/27

1. Standard on SL   2. Quad 4 and International Series.

Prices

Oldsmobile Cutlass Calais

	Retail Price	Dealer Invoice	Low Price
2-door notchback	$9995	$9225	$9425
4-door notchback	9995	9225	9425
S 2-door notchback	10895	9729	9929
S 4-door notchback	10995	9819	10019
SL 2-door notchback	13195	11783	11983
LS 4-door notchback	13295	11872	12072
I Series 2-door notchback ..	14895	13301	13501
I Series 4-door notchback ..	14995	13391	13591
Destination charge	425	425	425

Standard equipment:

2.5-liter TBI 4-cylinder engine, 5-speed manual transmission, power steering, cloth front bucket seats (reclining on 2-door), AM/FM radio, trip odometer, dual outside mirrors, tinted glass, rear shoulder belts, 185/80R13 all-season SBR tires. **S** adds: full-length console with armrest and storage bin, left remote mirror, reclining front seatbacks. **SL** adds: 3-speed automatic transmission, Convenience Group (reading lights, lighted right visor mirror, misc. lights), 4-way driver's seat, split folding rear seat, upgraded steering wheel, two-tone paint, alloy wheels. **International Series** adds: 2.3-liter DOHC PFI HO Quad 4 engine, FE3 suspension, air conditioning, door pockets, floormats, fog lamps, rocker panel extensions and wheel flares, Driver Information System (trip computer, service reminder), rallye instruments (tachometer, coolant temperature, oil pressure, voltmeter), AM/FM cassette, tilt steering column, leather-wrapped steering wheel and shift handle, power decklid release, intermittent wipers, 205/55R16 tires on alloy wheels.

Optional equipment:

3.3-liter V-6, SL	50	43	45
2.3-liter Quad 4, S	660	561	594
I Series	400	340	360
I Series includes 3-speed automatic transmission.			
3-speed automatic transmission, base & S .	540	459	486
Column shift, base (credit)	(110)	(94)	(94)
Air conditioning, base, S & SL	720	612	648
Quad 442 Sport Performance Pkg., S 2-door	1667	1417	1500
HO Quad 4 engine, 5-speed manual transmission, FE3 suspension, rallye instruments, rear spoiler, leather-wrapped steering wheel, 215/60R14 Goodyear Eagle GT tires on alloy wheels.			
Value Option Pkg. I, S	166	141	149
Rallye instruments, decklid luggage rack.			
Value Option Pkg. II, S	391	332	352
Pkg. I plus rallye instruments.			

KEY: **ohv** = overhead valve; **ohc** = overhead cam; **dohc** = double overhead cam; **I** = inline cylinders; **V** = cylinders in V configuration; **flat** = horizontally opposed cylinders; **bbl.** = barrel (carburetor); **PFI** = port (multi-point) fuel injection; **TBI** = throttle-body (single-point) fuel injection; **rpm** = revolutions per minute; **OD** = overdrive transmission; **S** = standard; **O** = optional; **NA** = not available.

	Retail Price	Dealer Invoice	Low Price
Value Option Pkg., SL	315	268	284
Removable glass sunroof, decklid luggage rack.			
Option Pkg. 1SB, base	460	391	414
Tilt steering column, bodyside moldings, 4-way manual driver's seat, cruise control, floormats.			
Option Pkg. 1SC, base 2-door	1410	1199	1269
Base 4-door	1450	1233	1305
Pkg. 1SB plus air conditioning, power locks, intermittent wipers.			
Option Pkg. 1SB, S	965	820	869
Tilt steering column, air conditioning, remote mirrors, 4-way manual driver's seat, floormats.			
Option Pkg. 1SC, S	1402	1192	1262
Pkg. 1SB plus intermittent wipers, visor mirrors, underhood lamp, cruise control, rear defogger.			
Option Pkg. 1SD, S 2-door	2067	1757	1860
S 4-door	2172	1846	1955
Pkg. 1SC plus power windows, power antenna, remote lock control pkg.			
Option Pkg. 1SB, SL 2-door	1590	1352	1431
SL 4-door	1630	1386	1467
Air conditioning, power locks, tilt steering column, intermittent wipers, cruise control, power antenna, rear defogger, remote mirrors, floormats.			
Option Pkg. 1SC, SL 2-door	2460	2091	2214
SL 4-door	2565	2180	2309
Pkg. 1SB plus power windows, power driver's seat, Driver Information System, lighted visor mirrors, remote lock control pkg.			
Option Pkg. 1SB. I Series 2-door	1235	1050	1112
I Series 4-door	1340	1139	1206
Power driver's seat, power windows, remote mirrors, cruise control, power antenna, rear defogger, remote lock control pkg.			
Removable glass sunroof (NA base)	350	298	315
Power locks, base & S 2-doors	175	149	158
Base & S 4-doors	215	183	194
Rear defogger	160	136	144
FE3 suspension pkg., S	526	447	473
SL	182	155	164
Alloy wheels, S	354	301	319
185/75R14 WSW tires, base & S	68	58	61
Rallye instruments, S	126	107	113
AM/FM cassette, base, S & SL	165	140	149
AM/FM radio w/CD player, S & SL	421	358	379
I Series	274	233	247
AM/FM cassette w/EQ, I Series	150	128	135
Custom leather trim, I Series	400	340	360

Oldsmobile Cutlass Ciera

What's New

Juggled trim levels and a simplified engine lineup mark Ciera, Oldsmobile's front-drive intermediate. Ciera continues in 2-door coupe and 4-door sedan body styles, and as a 5-door wagon under the Cutlass Cruiser Wagon badge. For '90, the base coupe has been dropped and a mid-level S model has been created in coupe and sedan configuration. The plush SL coupe is gone, but the SL sedan remains. The sporty International Series continues as a coupe or a sedan while the wagons carry on in S and SL trim. Standard on base and S models is a 2.5-liter 4-cylinder engine, which this year goes from 98 to 110 horsepower thanks to revised intake and exhaust ports and to more aggressive valve timing. Gone is the optional 125-horsepower 2.8-liter V-6. The 160-horsepower 3.3-liter V-6 introduced last year is carried over. It's standard on the SL and I-Series, and optional on other Cieras and the S wagon. A 3-speed automatic is standard with both engines; a 4-speed overdrive automatic is optional with the V-6. Ciera's exterior got freshened styling for '89. Olds focuses on the interior this year, adding door-mounted passive seat belts for outboard front-seat passengers, new door trim panels with lighted switch controls, and slight changes to the instrument panel. The center armrest has more storage space and

Oldsmobile Cutlass Ciera SL

Olds says SL bucket seats have more contour and better lumbar support. Ciera, which debuted for 1982, is similar to the Buick Century, Chevrolet Celebrity, and Pontiac 6000.

For

- Performance (3.3-liter V-6) ● Passenger room
- Trunk space

Against

- Performance (4-cylinder) ● Handling (base suspension)

Summary

Ciera is similar to the Buick Century in packaging and price, and has only one mechanical advantage over the Chevy and Pontiac versions of this design, the 3.3-liter V-6, which isn't offered on the Celebrity or 6000. The 3.3 replaced a 3.8-liter V-6 in '89 and nearly matches the larger engine in acceleration while being stingier with fuel. Where the discontinued 2.8 V-6 was adequate for this car, the 3.3 gives it more pep for brisk takeoffs from low speeds and prompt passing response on the highway. Most Cieras are sold with the soft base suspension, which provides a cushy ride but lacks good cornering grip and high-speed stability. The I-Series improves handling with its firmer suspension and wider tires, yet Olds has managed to retain more ride comfort than some of its corporate cousins have in their sporty versions of this body. The I-Series also has a tastefully done, functional interior. Ciera and the other A-bodies aren't as modern as the Ford Taurus and Mercury Sable, yet they offer comparable passenger and cargo room at competitive prices.

Specifications

	2-door notchback	4-door notchback	5-door wagon
Wheelbase, in.	104.9	104.9	104.9
Overall length, in.	190.3	190.3	194.4
Overall width, in.	69.5	69.5	69.5
Overall height, in.	54.1	54.1	54.5
Turn diameter, ft.	38.1	38.1	38.1
Curb weight, lbs.	2736	2764	2913
Cargo vol., cu. ft.	15.8	15.8	74.4
Fuel capacity, gals.	15.7	15.7	15.7
Seating capacity	6	6	8
Front headroom, in.	38.6	38.6	38.6
Front shoulder room, in.	55.9	56.2	56.2
Front legroom, max., in.	42.1	42.1	42.1
Rear headroom, in.	37.6	38.0	38.9
Rear shoulder room, in.	56.9	56.2	56.2
Rear legroom, min., in.	35.8	35.8	34.7

Powertrain layout: transverse front engine/front-wheel drive.

Engines

	ohv I-4	ohv V-6
Size, liters/cu. in.	2.5/151	3.3/204
Fuel delivery	TBI	PFI
Horsepower @ rpm	110 @ 5200	160 @ 5200
Torque (lbs./ft.) @ rpm	135 @ 3200	185 @ 2000
Availability	S	O[1]

EPA city/highway mpg

3-speed automatic	23/30	20/27
4-speed OD automatic		20/29

1. Standard SL and I-Series.

Prices

Oldsmobile Cutlass Ciera	Retail Price	Dealer Invoice	Low Price
4-door notchback	$11995	$10592	$10792
S 2-door notchback	12395	10945	11145
S 4-door notchback	12995	11215	11415
Cruiser S 5-door wagon	13395	11560	11760
SL 4-door notchback	14695	12612	12812
Cruiser SL 5-door wagon	15295	13200	13400
I Series 2-door notchback	15995	14124	14324
I Series 4-door notchback	16795	14494	14694
Destination charge	450	450	450

Standard equipment:

Base & S: 2.5-liter TBI 4-cylinder engine, 3-speed automatic transmission, power steering, front bench seat with folding armrest, rear shoulder belts, tinted glass, door pockets, left remote and right manual mirrors, AM/FM radio, 185/75R14 tires. **SL** adds: 3.3-liter PFI V-6, air conditioning, 55/45 front seat with storage armrest, power driver's seatback recliner, reading lamps, lighted right visor mirror, AM/FM cassette, white-stripe tires. **International Series** adds: 4-speed automatic transmission with floorshift, front bucket seats, front air dam with fog lamps, sill extensions, Driver Information System (trip and service reminders), tachometer, coolant temperature and oil pressure gauges, voltmeter, trip odometer, floormats, tilt steering column, intermittent wipers, remote decklid release, 215/60R14 tires on alloy wheels.

Optional equipment:

3.3-liter V-6, base & S	710	604	639
4-speed automatic transmission, S & SL	200	170	180
Air conditioning, S	805	684	725
Option Pkg. 1SB, base	805	684	725
Air conditioning.			
Option Pkg. 1SC, base	995	846	896
Pkg. 1SB plus tilt steering column, intermittent wipers.			
Option Pkg. 1SD, base	1210	1029	1089
Pkg. 1SC plus power locks.			
Option Pkg. 1SE, base	1505	1279	1355
Pkg. 1SD plus power windows.			
Option Pkg. 1SB, S 2- & 4-door	1040	884	936
S wagon	1124	955	1012
Air conditioning, tilt steering column, intermittent wipers, floormats; wagon includes air deflector and Convenience Group.			
Option Pkg. 1SC, S 2-door	1525	1296	1373
S 4-door	1305	1109	1175
S wagon	1374	1168	1237
Pkg. 1SB plus cruise control, accent stripe (exc. wagon), power windows (2-door), door edge guards, remote mirrors (wagon).			
Option Pkg. 1SD, S 2-door	1801	1531	1621
S 4-door	1916	1629	1724
S wagon	2009	1708	1808
Pkg. 1SC plus Convenience Group, power windows and locks, remote decklid release, power antenna (wagon).			

Prices are accurate at time of printing; subject to manufacturer's change.

Oldsmobile

	Retail Price	Dealer Invoice	Low Price
Option Pkg. 1SE, S 2-door	2372	2016	2135
S 4-door	2487	2114	2238
Pkg. 1SD plus power antenna, molding pkg., power passenger seatback recliner, remote mirrors, power driver's seat.			
Value Option Pkg., S	440	374	396
Rallye instruments, luggage rack, alloy wheels.			
Option Pkg. 1SB, SL 4-door	570	485	513
SL wagon	475	404	428
Tilt steering column, intermittent wipers, cruise control, power passenger seatback recliner (4-door), floormats, accent stripe, door edge guards (4-door).			
Option Pkg. 1SC, SL 4-door	1155	982	1040
SL wagon	770	655	693
Wagon: Pkg. 1SB plus power windows. 4-door adds: power locks, power antenna.			
Option Pkg. 1SD, SL 4-door	1455	1237	1310
SL wagon	1480	1258	1332
4-door: Pkg. 1SC plus power driver's seat, remote mirrors. Wagon adds: power windows and locks, power antenna, power passenger seatback recliner.			
Value Option Pkg., SL 4-door	382	325	344
SL wagon	267	227	240
Rallye instruments, luggage rack (4-door), alloy wheels.			
Option Pkg. 1SB, I Series 2-door	975	829	878
I Series 4-door	1080	918	972
Power windows and locks, cruise control, power antenna, power driver's seat, remote mirrors.			
Divided bench seat, S 2- & 4-door	253	215	228
S wagon	323	275	291
SL 4-door	275	234	248
Power locks, S 2-door	175	149	158
S 4-door	215	183	194
S wagon	265	225	239
Power windows, S 2-door	230	196	207
S 4-door & wagon	295	251	266
XC Special Edition Pkg., S 2- & 4-door	489	416	440
S wagon	604	513	544
Power sunroof, SL 4-door, I Series	775	659	698
Rear defogger	160	136	144
FE3 suspension pkg. (NA wagons), S	505	429	455
SL	447	380	402
Super Stock wheels, S 2- & 4-door	115	98	104
Wire wheel covers, S	283	241	255
SL	215	183	194
Alloy wheels, S	333	283	300
SL	275	234	248
185/75R14 WSW tires, base & S	68	58	61
Rallye instruments, S & SL	142	121	128
AM/FM cassette, base & S	165	140	149
AM/FM cassette w/EQ, SL & I Series	150	128	135
High-capacity cooling, S & SL	40	34	36
Luggage rack, S & SL	115	98	104
Custom leather trim, I Series	400	340	360
Accent stripe, S	45	38	41
Engine block heater	18	15	16
Front floormats, base	25	21	23
Rear floormats, base	20	17	18
California emissions pkg.	100	85	90

Oldsmobile Cutlass Supreme

What's New

The introduction of a 4-door sedan body style and a new convertible make news for Oldsmobile's front-drive mid-size offering. Like the Cutlass Supreme coupe, the new sedan is available in base, SL, and International Series trim. Styling follows the coupe's aerodynamic theme, though the sedan has a unique wraparound rear window. Five- or 6-passenger

Oldsmobile Cutlass Supreme I Series

seating is available on all but the I-Series, which has bucket seating for four. A fold-down rear seatback is standard in SL and I-Series sedans. Sedans and coupes share the same engine lineup: the 180-horsepower High Output Quad 4 engine is standard with a 5-speed manual transmission in the base and I-Series; a 160-horsepower Quad 4 with a 3-speed automatic is optional in the base car. Standard in the SL and optional on the base and I-Series is a 3.1-liter V-6 coupled to a 4-speed automatic. All Cutlass Supremes come standard with air conditioning and 4-wheel disc brakes; an anti-lock brake system is optional. A head-up instrument display, which projects the digital speedometer reading and turn signal arrows onto the windshield, is now a regular option on the I-Series coupe. The convertible is the first to wear the Cutlass badge since 1975. It features seating for five, a power top with a glass backlight, and the 3.1 V-6 with automatic transmission. The convertible shares its interior trim with the Cutlass Supreme SL while exterior appointments are those of the I-Series.

For

- Anti-lock brakes • Ride • Passenger room
- Trunk space

Against

- Performance • Engine noise

Summary

The front-drive Cutlass Supreme was introduced for 1988 as a replacement for a successful rear-drive model. It debuted along with the similarly reconfigured Pontiac Grand Prix and Buick Regal as a 2-door coupe and suffered tepid sales. Buyers may have been holding out for the sedan versions of those cars. Indeed, a car of the Cutlass Supreme's size works best as a 4-door because it's more appealing to families. It also gives Olds an aero-styled rival to the Mercury Sable. While adding two doors makes the Cutlass Supreme's roomy rear passenger area far more accessible, the back seat's lower cushion remains too low to the floor, too short, and too shapeless for adult comfort. There's an odd fit under the hood as well, where the standard engine is a high-revving high-performance HO Quad 4 that's available only with a 5-speed manual gearbox. If you want a 4-cylinder engine with automatic in your Cutlass Supreme, you must order a slightly less powerful but just as rev-hungry version of the Quad 4. Either engine is ill-suited to this car; even with the I-Series sports suspension and wide tires, the Cutlass Supreme does a poor impersonation of a sports sedan. Opt for the 3.1-liter six (standard on the SL and convertible) with its 4-speed automatic transmission. It's the most sensible choice, especially with the family oriented 4-door. We haven't yet tested the convertible. It features a structural top bar that allows Olds to retain the coupe's door handle and shoulder belt anchor positions. While the top bar is not designed to act as a protective roll bar, Olds says it does help stiffen the car's body and cut down on wind buffeting with the top down.

Specifications

	2-door notchback	2-door conv.	4-door notchback
Wheelbase, in.	107.5	107.5	107.5
Overall length, in.	192.3	192.3	192.2
Overall width, in.	71.0	71.0	70.9
Overall height, in.	53.3	54.3	54.8
Turn diameter, ft.	37.5	40.3	37.5
Curb weight, lbs.	3133	3501	3221
Cargo vol., cu. ft.	15.5	12.1	15.5
Fuel capacity, gals.	16.5	16.5	16.5
Seating capacity	6	5	6
Front headroom, in.	37.8	38.5	38.8
Front shoulder room, in.	57.6	57.6	57.4
Front legroom, max., in.	42.3	42.3	42.4
Rear headroom, in.	37.1	38.4	38.4
Rear shoulder room, in.	57.2	56.3	56.6
Rear legroom, min., in.	34.8	34.8	36.2

Powertrain layout: transverse front engine/front-wheel drive.

Engines

	dohc I-4	dohc I-4	ohv V-6
Size, liters/cu. in.	2.3/138	2.3/138	3.1/189
Fuel delivery	PFI	PFI	PFI
Horsepower @ rpm	180 @ 6200	160 @ 6200	135 @ 4400
Torque (lbs./ft.) @ rpm	160 @ 5200	155 @ 5200	180 @ 3600
Availability	S	O	O[1]

EPA city/highway mpg

5-speed OD manual	22/27		
3-speed automatic		23/32	
4-speed OD automatic			19/30

1. Standard, SL and convertible.

Prices

Oldsmobile Cutlass Supreme	Retail Price	Dealer Invoice	Low Price
2-door notchback	$14495	$12509	$12709
4-door notchback	14595	12595	12795
SL 2-door notchback	16095	13890	14090
SL 4-door notchback	16195	13976	14176
I Series 2-door notchback	17995	13976	14176
I Series 4-door notchback	17995	15530	15730
Destination charge	455	455	455

Standard equipment:

2.3-liter DOHC 16-valve HO Quad 4 engine, 5-speed manual transmission, power steering, 4-wheel disc brakes, air conditioning, front bucket seats, trip odometer, left remote and right manual mirrors, AM/FM radio, rear shoulder belts, tinted glass, 195/75R14 all-season SBR tires. **SL** adds: 3.1-liter PFI V-6, 4-speed automatic transmission, Convenience Group (reading lamps, right visor mirror, misc. lights), AM/FM cassette, remote decklid release, alloy wheels. **International Series** adds: 2.3-liter DOHC 16-valve HO Quad 4, 5-speed manual transmission, FE3 suspension, fast-ratio steering, Driver Information System (trip computer and service reminder), electronic instruments (tachometer, coolant temperature, oil pressure, voltmeter), power locks with remote control, rocker panel extensions, power front bucket seats, rear bucket seats, tilt steering column, intermittent wipers, 215/60R16 tires on alloy wheels.

Optional equipment:

	Retail Price	Dealer Invoice	Low Price
2.3-liter non-HO Quad 4, base	325	276	293
Includes 3-speed automatic transmission.			
3.1-liter V-6, base & I Series	500	425	450
Includes 4-speed automatic transmission.			
Anti-lock brakes	925	786	833
Option Pkg. 1SB, base	627	533	564
Tilt steering column, intermittent wipers, power mirrors, cruise control, Convenience Group, floormats.			
Option Pkg. 1SC, base 2-door	862	733	776
Base 4-door	872	741	785
Pkg. 1SB plus Appearance & Molding Pkg., rear defogger.			
Option Pkg. 1SD, base 2-door	1527	1298	1374
Base 4-door	1642	1396	1478
Pkg. 1SC plus power antenna, Remote Lock Control Pkg., power windows.			
Option Pkg. 1SE, base 2-door	1797	1527	1617
Base 4-door	1912	1625	1721
Pkg. 1SD plus power driver's seat.			
Value Option Pkg., base	320	272	288
Rallye interior, luggage rack.			
Option Pkg. 1SB, SL 2-door	712	605	641
SL 4-door	722	614	650
Cruise control, tilt steering column, floormats, intermittent wipers, Appearance & Molding Pkg., rear defogger, power mirrors.			
Option Pkg. 1SC, SL 2-door	1597	1357	1437
SL 4-door	1712	1455	1541
Pkg. 1SB plus power antenna, Remote Lock Control Pkg., power windows, power driver's seat.			
Option Pkg. 1SD, SL 2-door	2142	1821	1928
SL 4-door	2257	1918	2031
Pkg. 1SC plus automatic climate control, steering wheel touch control, Driver Information System.			
Option Pkg. 1SB, I Series 2-door	670	570	603
I Series 4-door	745	633	671
Cruise control, power windows, rear defogger, Appearance & Molding Pkg.			
Option Pkg. 1SC, I Series 2-door	980	833	882
I Series 4-door	1055	897	950
Pkg. 1SB plus power driver's seat, power antenna.			
Option Pkg. 1SD, I Series 2-door	2200	1870	1980
Pkg. 1SC plus anti-lock brakes, head-up instrument display.			
Easy-entry passenger seat, 2-doors	16	14	14
55/45 front seat, base	NC	NC	NC
Front bucket seats, SL	339	288	305
Power locks, base 2-door	175	149	158
Base 4-door	215	183	194
Power windows, base 2-door	240	204	216
Base 4-door	305	259	275
Power glass sunroof, SL & I Series	650	553	585
Rear defogger	160	136	144
FE3 suspension pkg., base	549	467	494
Alloy wheels, base	343	292	309
AM/FM cassette, base	165	140	149
AM/FM cassette w/EQ, SL	255	217	230
I Series	225	191	203
AM/FM radio w/CD player, SL	399	339	359
I Series	369	314	332
High-capacity cooling equipment	125	106	113
Luggage rack, base & SL	115	98	104
Rallye interior, base	355	302	320
Custom leather trim, SL	490	417	441
I Series	400	340	360
Engine block heater	18	15	16
California emissions pkg.	100	85	90

KEY: ohv = overhead valve; **ohc** = overhead cam; **dohc** = double overhead cam; **I** = inline cylinders; **V** = cylinders in V configuration; **flat** = horizontally opposed cylinders; **bbl.** = barrel (carburetor); **PFI** = port (multi-point) fuel injection; **TBI** = throttle-body (single-point) fuel injection; **rpm** = revolutions per minute; **OD** = overdrive transmission; **S** = standard; **O** = optional; **NA** = not available.

Prices are accurate at time of printing; subject to manufacturer's change.

Oldsmobile Eighty Eight Royale

Oldsmobile Eighty Eight Royale Brougham

What's New

Changes to Oldsmobile's full-size front drive car come under the heading of refinements for '90. The grille, headlamps, taillamps, and front and rear fascias all get a subtle restyle. Inside, there's more center armrest storage on the standard 55/45 split front bench seat. Remote-control door locks are a new option. Beneath the skin, the body structure has been stiffened for what Olds says is a better, quieter ride. Improving the ride also was behind a reduction in recommended tire inflation, from 35 to 30 psi. Revised front brake linings are supposed to reduce noise, while a larger-volume brake booster and slight changes to front brake calipers are intended to improve pedal feel. Anti-lock brakes and a driver's-side airbag remain options. The Eighty Eight is available in 2- and 4-door body styles and in base or Brougham trim. No changes have been made to the powertrain, which remains a 165-horsepower 3.8-liter V-6 coupled to a 4-speed automatic transmission. The Eighty Eight is similar to the Buick LeSabre and Pontiac Bonneville, which were derived from the design for the Buick Electra/Park Avenue and Olds Ninety-Eight.

For

- Performance • Room/comfort • Airbag
- Anti-lock brakes

Against

- Fuel economy

Summary

Adding to the Eighty Eight Royale's strong appeal in the American big-car sweepstakes is the availability of both anti-lock brakes and a driver's-side air bag. Both of these highly desirable safety features are expensive: ABS costs $925 and the airbag, available only on the 4-door, is $850. However, they will more than pay for themselves if just once they prevent a serious

KEY: **ohv** = overhead valve; **ohc** = overhead cam; **dohc** = double overhead cam; **I** = inline cylinders; **V** = cylinders in V configuration; **flat** = horizontally opposed cylinders; **bbl.** = barrel (carburetor); **PFI** = port (multi-point) fuel injection; **TBI** = throttle-body (single-point) fuel injection; **rpm** = revolutions per minute; **OD** = overdrive transmission; **S** = standard; **O** = optional; **NA** = not available.

accident or injury. A fully equipped Eighty Eight with those two options probably will list for $18,000-$20,000, but the Royale has other attributes that help justify the price. It enjoys a quiet and roomy interior, a large trunk with a flat floor, and a responsive powertrain that delivers satisfying acceleration. Plus, its front-wheel drive provides better traction in rain and snow than such rear-drive rivals as the Ford LTD Crown Victoria. Eighty Eight's corporate cousins, the LeSabre and Bonneville, offer all the same features, except the optional air bag. These three cars are lower-priced versions of the same design used for the more luxurious Oldsmobile Ninety-Eight and Buick Electra.

Specifications

	2-door notchback	4-door notchback
Wheelbase, in.	110.8	110.8
Overall length, in.	196.3	196.3
Overall width, in.	72.6	72.6
Overall height, in.	53.9	54.6
Turn diameter, ft.	39.4	39.4
Curb weight, lbs.	3248	3293
Cargo vol., cu. ft.	16.2	16.4
Fuel capacity, gals.	18.0	18.0
Seating capacity	6	6
Front headroom, in.	38.1	38.9
Front shoulder room, in.	59.3	59.3
Front legroom, max., in.	42.4	42.4
Rear headroom, in.	37.6	38.3
Rear shoulder room, in.	57.8	59.5
Rear legroom, min., in.	37.4	39.1

Powertrain layout: transverse front engine/front-wheel drive.

Engines

	ohv V-6
Size, liters/cu. in.	3.8/231
Fuel delivery	PFI
Horsepower @ rpm	165 @ 5200
Torque (lbs./ft.) @ rpm	210 @ 2000
Availability	S

EPA city/highway mpg

4-speed OD automatic	19/28

Prices

Oldsmobile Eighty Eight	Retail Price	Dealer Invoice	Low Price
Royale 2-door notchback	$15895	$13717	$13917
Royale 4-door notchback	15995	13804	14004
Brougham 2-door notchback	17295	14926	15126
Brougham 4-door notchback	17395	15012	15212
Destination charge	505	505	505

Standard equipment:

Royale: 3.8-liter PFI V-6, 4-speed automatic transmission, power steering, air conditioning, tinted glass, left remote mirror, AM/FM radio, bench seat with center armrests, rear shoulder belts, 205/75R14 tires. **Brougham** adds: Convenience Group (lamps, right visor mirror, chime tones), 55/45 front seat with storage armrest, remote decklid release.

Optional equipment:

Anti-lock brakes	925	786	833
Inflatable Restraint System, 4-doors	850	723	765
Option Pkg. 1SB, Royale	839	713	755
Divided bench seat with dual controls, intermittent wipers, cruise control, tilt steering column, Convenience Group, rear defogger, floormats.			
Option Pkg. 1SC, Royale 2-door	1389	1181	1250
Royale 4-door	1504	1278	1354

	Retail Price	Dealer Invoice	Low Price
Pkg. 1SB plus power windows and locks, door edge guards, power antenna, driver's seatback recliner.			
Option Pkg. 1SD, Royale 2-door	1905	1619	1715
Royale 4-door	2020	1717	1818
Pkg. 1SC plus Remote Control Lock Pkg., power driver's seat, Reminder Pkg.			
Value Option Pkg., Royale	349	297	314
Alloy wheels, instrument panel cluster, decklid luggage rack.			
Option Pkg. 1SB, Brougham 2-door . . .	1290	1097	1161
Brougham 4-door	1405	1194	1265
Intermittent wipers, cruise control, tilt steering column, power windows and locks, floormats, door edge guards, power driver's seat, rear defogger.			
Option Pkg. 1SC, Brougham 2-door . . .	1661	1412	1495
Brougham 4-door	1776	1510	1598
Pkg. 1SB plus power antenna, Reminder Pkg., driver's seatback recliner, electronic air conditioning.			
Option Pkg. 1SD, Brougham 2-door	1936	1646	1742
Brougham 4-door	2051	1743	1846
Pkg. 1SC plus Driver Information System, Remote Control Lock Pkg.			
Value Option Pkg., Brougham	712	605	641
Convenience Value Group, AM/FM cassette with EQ, custom leather trim.			
Power passenger seat, Brougham	270	230	243
Power locks, Royale 2-door	175	149	158
Royale 4-door	215	183	194
Power windows, Royale 2-door	240	204	216
Royale 4-door	305	259	275
Rear defogger	160	136	144
FE3 Touring Car Ride & Handling Pkg. . . .	779	662	701
Wire wheel covers, Royale	291	247	262
Brougham	215	183	194
Alloy wheels, Regency	368	313	331
Brougham	302	257	272
205/75R14 WSW tires, Royale	76	65	68
Convenience Value Group, Royale	317	269	285
Brougham	287	244	258
AM/FM cassette, Royale	140	119	126
w/EQ, Brougham	235	200	212
AM/FM radio w/CD player, Brougham . . .	359	305	323
Instrument panel cluster	66	56	59
Driver Information System, Brougham . . .	150	128	135
Towing Pkg.	271	230	244
Custom leather trim	490	417	441

Oldsmobile Ninety-Eight/ Touring Sedan

What's New

Minor changes designed to improve the ride of Oldsmobile's front-drive luxury sedan and to enhance its convenience quotient are on tap for 1990. Both the Ninety-Eight and its European-sedan-inspired sibling, the Touring Sedan, continue as full-size 4-door cars that use only a 3.8-liter V-6 mated to a 4-speed overdrive automatic transmission. Olds says increased body-structure stiffness and reinforced joints make the cars quieter and more creak-free over pavement irregularities. The steering gear also has been revised to improve on-center feel. Inside, a remote control power door lock system is a new option, the driver's window has a standard auto-down feature, and the optional sunroof has an express-open switch position. The center armrest has more storage space and now will hold compact discs. In addition to these changes, the Touring Sedan gets additional sound insulation and smaller front and rear headrests. It also switches from Goodyear Eagle GT tires to Eagle GA touring tires in an effort to improve the ride quality, fuel economy, and snow traction. Anti-lock brakes remain standard on Touring Sedan, optional on Ninety-Eights. Steering-wheel controls covering most cli-

Oldsmobile Ninety-Eight Regency

mate and stereo-system functions are optional on Ninety-Eight and standard on the Touring Sedan. But since the airbag cannot be ordered with the steering-wheel controls, this supplemental restraint is not available on the Touring Sedan. Ninety-Eight and Touring Sedan are built front the same design as the Buick Electra/Park Avenue and Cadillac De Ville/Fleetwood.

For

- Performance
- Room/comfort
- Airbag (Ninety-Eight)
- Anti-lock brakes

Against

- Fuel economy
- Ride (Touring Sedan)

Summary

Oldsmobile has given its full-size luxury sedan a dual personality: The Ninety-Eight serves the traditional Olds buyer, while the Touring Sedan is aimed at a younger buyer who might look first at an import. We think the regular Ninety-Eight is more on target than the Touring Sedan, which doesn't quite make the transition from American luxury car to European sports sedan. While the Touring Sedan handles better than a Ninety-Eight, it lacks the polished moves of a BMW or an Audi and suffers from a stiff ride that sacrifices a noticeable degree of comfort. Inside, leather upholstery and analog gauges give the Touring Sedan the right cues, but the seats are flat and unsupportive—far more American than European. We like the Touring Sedan's standard anti-lock brakes and brisk performance, but you can get both on any Ninety-Eight. In addition, you can order an air bag on Ninety-Eights.

Specifications

	4-door notchback
Wheelbase, in.	110.8
Overall length, in.	196.3
Overall width, in.	72.6
Overall height, in.	54.8
Turn diameter, ft.	39.4
Curb weight, lbs.	3325
Cargo vol., cu. ft.	16.4
Fuel capacity, gals.	18.0
Seating capacity	6
Front headroom, in.	39.3
Front shoulder room, in.	58.9
Front legroom, max., in.	42.4
Rear headroom, in.	38.1
Rear shoulder room, in.	58.8
Rear legroom, min., in.	41.5

Prices are accurate at time of printing; subject to manufacturer's change.

Oldsmobile

Powertrain layout: transverse front engine/front-wheel drive.

Engines

	ohv V-6
Size, liters/cu. in.	3.8/231
Fuel delivery	PFI
Horsepower @ rpm	165 @ 5200
Torque (lbs./ft.) @ rpm	210 @ 2000
Availability	S

EPA city/highway mpg

4-speed OD automatic	18/27

Prices

Oldsmobile Ninety-Eight	Retail Price	Dealer Invoice	Low Price
Regency 4-door notchback	$19995	$17256	$17456
Brougham 4-door notchback	21595	23124	23324
Touring Sedan 4-door notchback	26795	23124	23324
Destination charge	550	550	550

Standard equipment:

3.8-liter PFI V-6, 4-speed automatic transmission, power steering, air conditioning, tinted glass, power windows and locks, 55/45 seat with power driver's side and storage armrest, rear shoulder belts, remote mirrors, opera lamps, front and rear armrests, right visor mirrors, trip odometer, reading lamp, AM/FM cassette, automatic load leveling, 205/75R14 all-season SBR tires, wire wheel covers. **Brougham** adds: automatic climate control, cruise control, tilt steering column, cornering lamps, sail panel reading lamps, intermittent wipers, opera lamps, alloy wheels. **Touring Sedan** adds: anti-lock braking system, FE3 suspension, 215/65R15 Goodyear Eagle GT+4 tires on alloy wheels, front console with storage, Driver Information System (trip computer, service reminder), gauge cluster including tachometer, fog lamps, illumination package, power mirrors with heated left, AM/FM cassette w/EQ, Twilight Sentinel, steering wheel touch controls, remote decklid and fuel door releases.

Optional equipment:

Anti-lock brakes, base & Brougham	925	786	833
Inflatable Restraint System, base & Brougham	850	723	765
Option Pkg. 1SB, base	949	807	854
Intermittent wipers, cruise control, rear defogger, tilt steering column, power antenna, lighted visor mirrors, Remote Lock Control Pkg., floormats.			
Option Pkg. 1SC, base	2068	1758	1861
Pkg. 1SC plus manual driver's seatback recliner, automatic climate control, power passenger seat, cornering lamps, steering wheel touch controls.			
Value Option Pkg., base & Brougham	801	681	721
Convenience Value Group, custom leather trim, AM/FM cassette w/EQ.			
Padded vinyl roof, base & Brougham	260	221	234
Power glass sunroof	1230	1046	1107
Rear defogger, base & Brougham	160	136	144
Accent stripe, base	45	38	41
FE3 suspension pkg., base	339	288	305
Brougham	246	209	221
Alloy wheels, base	103	88	93
Wire wheel covers, Brougham	NC	NC	NC
Convenience Value Group, base & Brougham	376	320	338
AM/FM cassette w/EQ, base & Brougham	235	200	212
AM/FM radio w/CD player, base & Brougham	359	305	323
Touring Sedan	124	105	112
Delco/Bose music system, Touring Sedan	523	445	471
Instrument panel cluster, base & Brougham	66	56	59
Driver Information System, base & Brougham	150	128	135
High-capacity cooling, base & Brougham	66	56	59
Glamour metallic paint, base & Brougham	210	179	189
Luggage rack, base & Brougham	115	98	104
Custom leather trim, base & Brougham	490	417	441
Engine block heater	18	15	16

Oldsmobile Silhouette

Oldsmobile Silhouette

What's New

Oldsmobile ventures for the first time into the people-mover class for 1990, but its Silhouette minivan is anything but another boxy family hauler. It's of the new-age General Motors design that also spawned the '90 Pontiac Trans Sport and Chevrolet Lumina APV. It shares with those minivans a slope-snout 194.2-inch body stretched over a 109.8-inch wheelbase. Drive is to the front wheels via a 3-speed automatic transmission and a 120-horsepower 3.1-liter V-6 mounted transversely in the nose. Silhouette's body is made of fiberglass and filler material bonded and bolted to a metal frame. Olds uses the grille, the design of the wheels, and some exterior graphics to differentiate the Silhouette from its Pontiac and Chevy stablemates. Inside, seven-passenger seating—optional on the base models of the other GM vans—is standard on the base Silhouette in a 2-3-2 layout. A three-place middle bench seat is available in place of the middle buckets. In keeping with its upmarket image, Silhouette is alone among the GM minivans in offering leather upholstery as an option. Electronic ride-level control is part of the FE3 touring suspension option, which also includes 15-inch wheels in place of the standard 14s.

For

● Passenger room ● Quietness ● Entry/exit ● Ride

Against

● Performance ● Visibility

Summary

Since the Silhouette is essentially the same vehicle as the Lumina APV and the Trans Sport, what we say for those new products holds here, as well. Suffice it to say, however, that this is not your father's minivan. Even Oldsmobile's staid image can do nothing to water down the Silhouette's 21st-Century shape. The shape is bait for shoppers who might otherwise eschew minivans as too utilitarian. But the risk is that it will also repel those for whom a minivan must first and foremost be utilitarian. The problem is one of acclimation to the severely angled nose. The windshield—a massive 17.25-square feet of glass—is sloped at a severe 66-degree angle. The driver must peer out over more than two feet of dashboard shelf, beyond which the sheetmetal is invisible, and then ponder where the front bumper might be. This does not make a good first impression. Nor do qualms about cleaning and defrosting the windshield, which is about a third larger than a full-size sedan's. Olds hopes to meet those challenges with a special fluidic air-motion defroster nozzle and a pair of two-foot long wiper blades incorporating "wet arm" washers. Some potential buyers are sure to conclude it's not worth the bother and go on to more traditional minivans like the Dodge Caravan or Mazda MPV. Others, however, are certain to see beyond the nose to the Silhouette's airy and versatile passenger compartment with its removable lightweight bucket seats. Once underway, they'll notice that the Silhouette indeed rides, steers, maneuvers, and tracks down the highway much like a mid-size front-drive GM car. There's little excuse for saddling the 3650-pound van with only 120 horsepower, however. A Silhouette loaded with passengers and vacation luggage, and with its air conditioner running, will challenge your patience when attempting to pass or to traverse a mountain. On balance, we suspect Olds will have little difficulty selling its modest allotment of GM minivans on their novelty value alone.

Specifications

	4-door van
Wheelbase, in.	109.8
Overall length, in.	194.2
Overall width, in.	73.9
Overall height, in.	65.2
Turn diameter, ft.	42.5
Curb weight, lbs.	3648
Cargo vol., cu. ft.	111.2
Fuel capacity, gals.	20.0
Seating capacity	7
Front headroom, in.	40.2
Front shoulder room, in.	53.5
Front legroom, max., in.	40.7
Rear headroom, in.	38.6
Rear shoulder room, in.	61.6
Rear legroom, min., in.	33.7

Powertrain layout: transverse front engine/front-wheel drive.

Engines

	ohv V-6
Size, liters/cu. in.	3.1/191
Fuel delivery	TBI
Horsepower @ rpm	120 @ 4200
Torque (lbs./ft.) @ rpm	175 @ 2200
Availability	S

EPA city/highway mpg
3-speed automatic	18/23

Prices

Oldsmobile Silhouette	Retail Price	Dealer Invoice	Low Price
4-door van	$17195	$15355	—
Destination charge	500	500	500

Low price not available at time of publication.

Standard equipment:

3.1-liter TBI V-6, 3-speed automatic transmission, power steering, air conditioning, seven bucket seats, tilt steering column, AM/FM radio, tachometer, coolant temperature and oil pressure gauges, voltmeter, trip odometer, map lights, rear defogger, dual remote mirrors, intermittent wipers, rear wiper/washer, floormats, 205/70R14 tires on alloy wheels.

Optional equipment:

	Retail Price	Dealer Invoice	Low Price
Option Pkg. 1SB	450	383	—
Power locks, cruise control.			
Option Pkg. 1SC	960	816	—
Pkg. 1SB plus power windows, power driver's seat.			
Value Option Pkg.	540	459	—
Custom leather trim, AM/FM cassette.			
6-passenger modular seating (credit)	(110)	(94)	(94)
Rear defogger	160	136	—
FE3 touring suspension	232	197	—
AM/FM cassette	140	119	—
AM/FM radio w/CD player	396	337	—
Custom leather trim	650	553	—
Includes 6-passenger seating.			
Engine block heater	18	15	—
California emissions pkg.	100	85	—

Oldsmobile Toronado/Trofeo

Oldsmobile Trofeo

What's New

Every body panel except the hood is new for '90 on Oldsmobile's front-drive personal luxury coupe. The changes add 12.4 inches to the Toronado's overall length, a stretch designed to recapture some of the big-car brashness lost in the Toro's 1986 downsizing. Olds has managed to expand the exterior without increasing interior space, though the trunk does gain 2.5 cubic feet, to a creditable 16.6. The controversial video Visual Information Center, added as an option last year, has been dropped from the Toronado's options list, but remains available on the sportier Trofeo. For '90, Toronados with bucket seats get analog gauges; digital instrumentation is fitted to those equipped with the optional 55/45 front bench seat and accompanying column gear shift. Also standard this year on both Toronado and Trofeo are a driver's-side airbag, a larger glovebox, illuminated power window switches, and an auto-down driver's window. A compact-disc player has been added to the options list. Suspension calibrations—spring rates, roll-bar sizes, bushing rates and shock damping—have been retuned to improve ride and handling. Oldsmobile's 2-door image leader, the Trofeo, is treated to the same exterior restyle as the Toronado. Trofeo buyers who order the Visual Informa-

> **KEY: ohv** = overhead valve; **ohc** = overhead cam; **dohc** = double overhead cam; **I** = inline cylinders; **V** = cylinders in V configuration; **flat** = horizontally opposed cylinders; **bbl.** = barrel (carburetor); **PFI** = port (multi-point) fuel injection; **TBI** = throttle-body (single-point) fuel injection; **rpm** = revolutions per minute; **OD** = overdrive transmission; **S** = standard; **O** = optional; **NA** = not available.

Prices are accurate at time of printing; subject to manufacturer's change.

tion Center will get a cathode ray tube with a screen roughly 4 X 2.4 inches mounted in the center of the dashboard. Break the appropriate color-coordinated light beam with a finger and the screen will allow you to manage the stereo and climate systems, as well as operate the onboard computer. Traditional switches and a new trip computer are used in the standard dash. The Trofeo shares its 165-horsepower 3.8-liter V-6 with the Toronado, but adds as standard such Toro options as anti-lock brakes, an FE3 sport suspension, and leather up- holstery. Last year's standard 215/60R15 tires are replaced by 215/60R16s.

For

- Performance
- Anti-lock brakes
- Quietness

Against

- Fuel economy
- Rear seat space

Summary

Critics attributed slow sales of the 1986-'89 Toronado to the fact that its styling could be mistaken for that of an Olds Cutlass Calais coupe. Olds hopes this year's revamp will duplicate the sales surge Buick enjoyed when it enlarged the Riviera last year. The importance of new sheetmetal to sales emphasizes how much cars like this value image over hard- core driving satisfaction. On the road, however, Toronado de- livers all that most of its owners will ask of it. The new body adds only about 100 pounds to the base curb weight, so the 3.8 V-6 is able to continue supplying sufficient acceleration. Toronado's front-drive chassis provides competent handling and a liveable ride. The Trofeo's firmer suspension improves cornering ability at the expense of ride comfort, so we recom- mend you try both to see which serves you better. Inside, gadgets galore provide the comfort and convenience you ex- pect in this price range, though rear-seat room is modest. Credit Oldsmobile for offering buyers an ergonomically sound alternative to the Visual Information Center, which complicates rather than simplifies stereo and climate system controls.

Specifications

	2-door notchback
Wheelbase, in.	108.0
Overall length, in.	200.3
Overall width, in.	72.8
Overall height, in.	53.0
Turn diameter, ft.	39.4
Curb weight, lbs.	3462
Cargo vol., cu. ft.	15.8
Fuel capacity, gals.	18.0
Seating capacity	6
Front headroom, in.	37.8
Front shoulder room, in.	58.3
Front legroom, max., in.	43.0
Rear headroom, in.	37.8
Rear shoulder room, in.	57.5
Rear legroom, min., in.	35.7

KEY: **ohv** = overhead valve; **ohc** = overhead cam; **dohc** = double overhead cam; **I** = inline cylinders; **V** = cylinders in V configuration; **flat** = horizontally opposed cylinders; **bbl.** = barrel (carburetor); **PFI** = port (multi-point) fuel injection; **TBI** = throttle-body (single-point) fuel injection; **rpm** = revolutions per minute; **OD** = overdrive transmission; **S** = standard; **O** = optional; **NA** = not available.

Powertrain layout: transverse front engine/front-wheel drive.

Engines

	ohv V-6
Size, liters/cu. in.	3.8/231
Fuel delivery	PFI
Horsepower @ rpm	165 @ 5200
Torque (lbs./ft.) @ rpm	210 @ 2000
Availability	S

EPA city/highway mpg
4-speed OD automatic	17/26

Prices

Oldsmobile Toronado/Trofeo	Retail Price	Dealer Invoice	Low Price
Toronado 2-door notchback	$21995	$18982	$19182
Trofeo 2-door notchback	24995	21571	21771
Destination charge	550	550	550

Standard equipment:

3.8-liter PFI V-6, 4-speed automatic transmission, power steering, 4-wheel disc brakes, driver's-side airbag, reclining front bucket seats, power driver's seat, automatic climate control, power windows and locks, power mirrors (heated left), cruise control, rear defogger, tachometer, AM/FM cassette, leather-wrapped steering wheel, tilt steering column, tinted glass, floormats, remote decklid release, Twilight Sentinel, anti-theft security system, intermit- tent wipers, 205/75R15 tires on alloy wheels. **Trofeo** adds: anti-lock brakes, FE3 suspension, automatic power locks, fog lights, cornering lamps, remote fuel door release, lighted visor mirrors, power decklid pulldown, 215/60R16 tires.

Optional equipment:

Anti-lock brakes, Toronado	925	786	833
Option Pkg. 1SB, Toronado	739	628	665
Power passenger seat, Illumination Pkg., lighted visor mirrors, power decklid pulldown, automatic day/night mirror, Remote Lock Control Pkg.			
Value Option Pkg., Toronado	460	391	414
Glamour metallic paint, custom leather trim.			
Divided bench seat, Toronado	NC	NC	NC
Power sunroof	1230	1046	1107
Two-tone paint, Toronado	101	86	91
FE3 suspension pkg., Toronado	126	107	113
205/75R15 tires, Toronado	76	65	68
Delco/Bose music system	703	598	633
AM/FM cassette w/EQ	120	102	108
AM/FM radio w/CD player	516	439	464
Mobile telephone	995	846	896
Visual Information Center	1295	1101	1166
Glamour metallic paint, Toronado	210	179	189
Custom leather trim, Toronado	400	340	360
Engine block heater	18	15	16
California emissions pkg.	100	85	90

Peugeot 405 and 505

What's New

A Pininfarina-designed 5-door station wagon went on sale in August as a companion to the compact 405 sedan, which debuted last year. Called the 405 Sportwagon, the new model has front-wheel drive, like the sedan. The Sportwagon comes in DL and S trim levels, both with a 110-horsepower 1.9-liter 4-cylinder engine. The 405 sedan also comes in DL and S trim with the 110-horsepower engine, and as the Mi 16 with a 150-horsepower, dual-cam 1.9 with four valves per cylinder instead of two. For 1990, the Mi 16 gains anti-lock brakes as standard equipment and new 15-inch tires and alloy wheels.

Peugeot 405 S Sportwagon

Pegeot might introduce a 4-wheel-drive version of the 405 sedan next spring or summer as a 1991 model. The 1990 405 and 505 models won't arrive until January, but when they do all will have automatic front shoulder belts to meet the federal passive-restraint requirement (motorized on 405s and non-motorized on 505s), with separate manual lap belts. Other changes for the 405 line are that the DL and S sedans gain a reflective red strip on the rear, while the DL also gets as standard a stereo radio with cassette player and a folding rear armrest with a pass-through opening to the trunk. For the larger, rear-drive 505 models, there are few changes and fewer choices this year. The STX V-6 and Turbo 4-door sedans have been dropped, leaving a 505S 4-door with a 120-horsepower 2.2-liter 4-cylinder and a 505S V-6 with a 145-horsepower 2.8-liter V-6. A 4-speed automatic transmission is standard on both. Four 505 wagons return from last year. The DL 5-passenger and SW8 8-passenger wagons have the 120-horsepower 2.2-liter 4-cylinder. Turbo versions of the 5-passenger and SW8 have a 180-horsepower turbocharged 4-cylinder and 4-speed automatic transmission.

For

- Acceleration (Mi 16, 505 Turbo wagons)
- Anti-lock brakes (Mi 16) • Ride • Passenger room
- Cargo room (wagons)

Against

- Driving position (405) • Fuel economy (505 wagon)
- Acceleration (505 DL, SW8 wagons)

Summary

Peugeot had high hopes for the 405 sedan when it was launched in the U.S. last year since it had been previously named European Car of the Year. However, Peugeot's sales fell about eight percent during the first eight months of 1989, including both the 405 and the 505. Peugeot apparently is going to concentrate on trying to sell the 405 in the U.S. Now that the 505 STX sedan is gone, none of the 505 models have anti-lock brakes, which are standard or optional on nearly all European rivals. With its 150-horsepower, dual-cam engine, the Mi 16 is the liveliest 405 model, but the others have decent getaway with manual transmission. We averaged 10.9 seconds in our 0-60-mph runs with a 405 S sedan. We haven't driven a 405 with automatic, but we suspect acceleration will be noticeably slower. The 405 DL and S models ride comfortably, thanks to a long wheelbase and supple suspension that combine to absorb ruts and tar strips rather than merely rolling over them. Handling is competent and the power steering is smooth, direct. The Mi 16 has a firmer ride, but also provides more tenacious handling. The long wheelbase also pays di-

vidends in generous leg room front and rear. However, the pedals are too close to the seat and the steering wheel too far away, so tall drivers are forced to scrunch up behind the wheel. In their favor, even DL and S models have lots of standard equipment and Peugeot has priced the 405 below most competitors in the low-end of the premium-sedan market. In addition, slow sales mean that Peugeot dealers should be offering big discounts. However, some 405s we've tested have been poorly assembled and suffered electrical problems that make us wary. Since Peugeot is having such a hard time selling cars in the U.S., that doesn't bode well for resale value either. Low demand for these cars when they're new means there will be even less demand when they're used.

Specifications	405 4-door notchback	405 5-door wagon	505 4-door notchback	505 5-door wagon
Wheelbase, in.	105.1	105.1	108.0	114.2
Overall length, in.	177.7	175.1	181.4	194.5
Overall width, in.	67.6	67.5	67.7	67.7
Overall height, in.	55.4	56.0	57.0	60.1
Turn diameter, ft.	34.6	34.6	35.1	36.7
Curb weight, lbs.	2460	2635	2998	3230
Cargo vol., cu. ft.	13.7	66.5	13.8	92.5
Fuel capacity, gals.	17.2	17.2	18.0	18.0
Seating capacity	5	5	5	8
Front headroom, in.	36.5	38.4	37.5	38.1
Front shoulder room, in.	NA	NA	NA	NA
Front legroom, max., in.	41.4	41.5	40.0	40.0
Rear headroom, in.	36.9	39.0	36.3	36.3
Rear shoulder room, in.	NA	NA	NA	NA
Rear legroom, min., in.	34.4	35.4	39.5	37.6

Powertrain layout 405: transverse front engine/front-wheel drive; **505:** longitudinal front engine/rear-wheel drive.

Engines	ohc I-4	dohc I-4	ohc I-4	Turbo ohc I-4
Size, liters/cu. in.	1.9/116	1.9/116	2.2/133	2.2/132
Fuel delivery	PFI	PFI	PFI	PFI
Horsepower @ rpm	110 @ 5200	150 @ 6400	120 @ 5200	180 @ 5200
Torque (lbs./ft.) @ rpm	120 @ 4250	128 @ 5000	131 @ 3500	205 @ 2500
Availability	S[1]	S[2]	S[3]	S[4]

EPA city/highway mpg

5-speed OD manual	20/27	20/28	18/22	
4-speed OD automatic	20/25		19/21	18/21

1. 405 DL, S   2. 405 Mi 16   3. 505 S sedan, DL and SW 8 wagons   4. Turbo wagons.

Prices

Peugeot 405/505	Retail Price	Dealer Invoice	Low Price
405 DL 4-door notchback	$15390	—	—
405 DL 5-door wagon	15990	—	—
405 S 4-door notchback	17700	—	—
405 S 5-door wagon	18495	—	—
405 Mi 16 4-door notchback	21990	—	—
505 DL 5-door wagon	18590	—	—
505 SW8 5-door wagon	20400	—	—
505 Turbo 5-door wagon	25940	—	—
505 Turbo SW8 5-door wagon	26100	—	—
505 S 4-door notchback	19945	—	—
505 S V6 4-door notchback	22485	—	—
Destination charge	400	—	—

Dealer invoice and low price not available at time of publication.

Prices are accurate at time of printing; subject to manufacturer's change.

Standard equipment:

405 DL: 1.9-liter PFI 4-cylinder engine, 5-speed manual transmission, power steering, 4-wheel disc brakes, automatic climate control, power locks, velour reclining front bucket seats, 60/40 split folding rear seat (wagon), AM/FM cassette, roof rails (wagon), tilt steering column, dual remote mirrors, tachometer, coolant temperature and oil level gauges, trip odometer, tinted glass, intermittent wipers, rear defogger, lighted visor mirrors, digital clock, Michelin MXV 185/65R14 tires with full-size spare. **405 S** adds: power windows, remote power locks, leather upholstery (wagon), cruise control, heated front seats, center armrest, rear armrest with trunk-through, power sunroof, heated power mirrors, Clarion AM/FM cassette, alloy wheels. **405 Mi 16** adds: DOHC 16-valve engine, anti-lock brakes, leather upholstery, leather-wrapped steering wheel, power driver's seat, driver's lumbar and side bolster adjustments, oil temperature gauge, Alpine AM/FM cassette, 195/65R14 tires on alloy wheels. **505 S 4-door** and **DL wagon:** 2.2-liter PFI 4-cylinder engine, 4-speed automatic transmission, limited-slip differential, power steering, 4-wheel disc brakes, automatic climate control, power windows, power locks (remote on 4-door), cruise control, Clarion AM/FM cassette, lighted visor mirrors, heated velour reclining front bucket seats, power sunroof (4-door), power mirrors (heated on 4-door), tinted glass, intermittent wipers, rear defogger, Michelin MXV 185/65HR15 tires; wagon has 5-speed manual transmission, rear wiper/washer; SW8 wagon has 8-passenger seating; turbo wagons have 2.2-liter turbocharged engine, 4-speed automatic transmission. **S V-6** adds: 2.8-liter PFI V-6, 4-speed automatic transmission, alloy wheels, oil level and temperature gauges.

Optional equipment:

4-speed automatic transmission, 405,			
505 wagons	650	—	—
Not available on 405 Mi 16.			
Leather upholstery, 405 S 4-door	990	—	—
Includes leather-wrapped steering wheel, seats with adjustable side			
bolsters and lumbar support.			
Metallic/black laquered paint, 405	375	—	—
505	395	—	—

Plymouth Acclaim

Plymouth Acclaim LX

What's New

A Mitsubishi-made 141-horsepower 3.0-liter V-6 mated to Chrysler's new 4-speed automatic transmission is optional on all models of the Acclaim for '90. The powertrain had been exclusive to the LX version. A standard driver's-side airbag and an optional Rallye Sport package are among other additions, while the tachometer and oil-pressure gauge have been subtracted from the base model's standard equipment. Acclaim and the similar Dodge Spirit are Chrysler's bread-and-butter cars for the 1990s. Introduced for the '89 model year, they are 4-door sedans that retain the front-drive layout and conservative, upright design of the Dodge Aires and Plymouth Reliant, the K-cars they replace. Their wheelbase and bodies

are about three inches longer than the K-cars and they have 2.6 inches of additional rear legroom. The Plymouth is tailored for family transportation, while the Spirit tilts toward the sporty. Base and LE Acclaims have a 100-horsepower 2.5-liter 4-cylinder engine standard and a 150-horsepower turbocharged version optional. A 5-speed manual transmission is standard with the fours, a 3-speed automatic is optional with the naturally aspirated 2.5. Mechanical problems with the new 4-speed automatic transmission had delayed introduced of the 1989 LX model—and thus the V-6 engine—until the spring of '89.

For

- Interior room • Cargo space • Ride
- Performance (V-6)

Against

- Rear seat comfort • Noise (turbo engine)

Summary

Chrysler officials acknowledge that their A-cars evolved from the K-car platform, but they bristle at any suggestion that the Acclaim and Spirit are simply more variations on a tired theme. We agree. The A-cars soundly beat the K-cars in terms of ride, handling, power, and quality feel. Neither the Acclaim nor the Spirit achieve the Honda Accord-like polish that Chrysler officials say was their goal, but they are comfortable, competent, and competitive with foreign and domestic rivals. Acclaim stresses value and equipment, so it targets a slightly younger family buyer than Spirit. Its personality is softer, but it has the same airy cabin and generously sized trunk. The optional front bench seat isn't uncomfortable, but it lacks the lateral and lower-back support of the available bucket seats. The dashboard has easy-to-read instruments and is flawed only by undersized climate-system buttons. Rear head and knee room are adequate, but the seat cushion is too low and too soft. Performance is best with the V-6, though the 4-speed automatic is slow to downshift for passing. The turbo 2.5 feels marginally quicker than the V-6, but the engine is much louder and coarser when pushed and it's available only with manual transmission. The base engine provides mediocre pickup. Control in turns is best with the LX's wider tires, though the suspension is still too flaccid over freeway dips. Nosedive in harder stops mars otherwise competent braking. Overall, Acclaim is a fine domestic compact with an appealing manner and an attractive price.

Specifications

	4-door notchback
Wheelbase, in.	103.3
Overall length, in.	181.2
Overall width, in.	68.1
Overall height, in.	53.5
Turn diameter, ft.	37.6
Curb weight, lbs.	2854
Cargo vol., cu. ft.	14.4
Fuel capacity, gals.	16.0
Seating capacity	6
Front headroom, in.	38.4
Front shoulder room, in.	54.3
Front legroom, max., in.	41.9
Rear headroom, in.	37.9
Rear shoulder room, in.	55.0
Rear legroom, min., in.	38.3

Powertrain layout: transverse front engine/front-wheel drive.

Engines

	ohc I-4	Turbo ohc I-4	ohc V-6
Size, liters/cu. in.	2.5/153	2.5/153	3.0/181
Fuel delivery	TBI	PFI	PFI
Horsepower @ rpm	100 @ 4800	150 @ 4800	141 @ 5000
Torque (lbs./ft.) @ rpm	135 @ 2800	180 @ 2000	171 @ 2800
Availability	S	O	S[1]
EPA city/highway mpg			
5-speed OD manual	24/32	21/29	
3-speed automatic	22/27		
4-speed OD automatic			NA

1. LX.

Prices

Plymouth Acclaim	Retail Price	Dealer Invoice	Low Price
4-door notchback	$10385	$9288	$9488
LE 4-door notchback	11815	10547	10747
LX 4-door notchback	13805	12298	12498
Destination charge	440	440	440

Standard equipment:

2.5-liter TBI 4-cylinder engine, 5-speed manual transmission, power steering, driver's-side airbag, cloth reclining front bucket seats, coolant temperature gauge, voltmeter, trip odometer, intermittent wipers, AM/FM radio, remote fuel door and decklid releases, 185/70R14 tires. **LE** adds: cruise control, tilt steering column, driver's seat lumbar support adjustment, lighted visor mirrors, rear defogger, message center, 55/45 folding rear seat, armrest with dual cupholders, 195/70R14 tires. **LX** adds: 3.0-liter PFI V-6, 4-speed automatic transmission, sport suspension, decklid luggage rack, trip computer, AM/FM cassette, leather-wrapped steering wheel, 205/60R15 tires on alloy wheels.

Optional equipment:

2.5-liter turbo engine, base & LE	700	595	630
3.0-liter V-6, base & LE	700	595	630
3-speed automatic transmission, base & LE	552	469	497
4-speed automatic transmission, base & LE	646	549	581
Air conditioning, LE & LX	819	696	737
Super Discount Pkg. A, base	1110	944	999
Air conditioning, rear defogger, floormats, tinted glass, time-delay ignition switch light, four speakers, cruise control, tilt steering column.			
Super Discount Pkg. B, base	1411	1199	1270
Pkg. A plus power windows and locks, heated power mirrors.			
Super Discount Pkg. C, LE & LX	775	659	698
Air conditioning, power windows and locks, heated power mirrors.			
Popular Equipment Discount Pkg., base	941	800	847
Air conditioning, rear defogger, tinted glass, four speakers.			
Premium Equipment Discount Pkg., base	301	256	271
Base w/Super Discount or Deluxe Convenience	293	249	264
Front bucket seats, 55/45 folding rear seat, console armrest, premium body sound insulation, misc. lights, message center.			
Deluxe Convenience Pkg., base	329	280	296
Floormats, time-delay ignition switch light, cruise control, tilt steering column.			
Power Equipment Discount Pkg.	568	483	511
Power windows and locks, heated power mirrors.			
Rallye Sport Pkg., base	163	139	147
Base w/Premium Pkg. & bench seat	93	79	84
Console armrest (with bucket seats), tachometer, oil pressure gauge.			
Rear defogger, base	155	132	140
Power locks	221	188	199
AM/FM cassette, base	207	176	186
Base w/Super Discount or Popular Pkg., LE	157	133	141
AM/FM cassette w/Infinity speakers, base & LE	435	370	392
LX	278	236	250
Base requires Popular Pkg.			

	Retail Price	Dealer Invoice	Low Price
AM/FM cassette w/Infinity speakers & EQ, LE	651	553	586
LX	494	420	445
Power driver's seat	258	219	232
Base requires Popular Pkg.			
Front bench seat, base	103	88	93
w/55/45 folding rear seat	62	53	56
Premium front bench seat w/55/45 folding rear, LE & LX	62	53	56
Pop-up glass sunroof	409	348	368
Base requires Popular Pkg.			
195/70R14 touring tires, base	31	26	28
195/75R14 WSW touring tires, base	105	89	95
Conventional spare tire	85	72	77
195/70R14, base & LE	95	81	86
Alloy wheels, base & LE	332	282	299
Pearl/clearcoat paint	75	64	68

Plymouth Horizon/ Dodge Omni

Plymouth Horizon

What's New

America's first domestically produced front-wheel-drive subcompacts enter their 13th model year with a slight name change, a driver's-side airbag, and some new interior touches. The Horizon is identical in price, specification, and equipment to the Dodge Omni. Chrysler had added the "America" suffix to their names in 1987 when a cost-cutting program consolidated the lines into a single trim level with limited options. The tag has been dropped for '90, but the aim of a basic package with few options remains. A new instrument panel with revised climate-control ducts, a new steering wheel incorporating the airbag, rear-seat shoulder belts, and a new outside mirror are the changes. A 93-horsepower 2.2-liter 4-cylinder engine mated to a standard 5-speed manual or an optional 3-speed automatic remains the only available engine.

For

● Air bag ● Value ● Fuel economy ● Performance

> **KEY: ohv** = overhead valve; **ohc** = overhead cam; **dohc** = double overhead cam; **I** = inline cylinders; **V** = cylinders in V configuration; **flat** = horizontally opposed cylinders; **bbl.** = barrel (carburetor); **PFI** = port (multi-point) fuel injection; **TBI** = throttle-body (single-point) fuel injection; **rpm** = revolutions per minute; **OD** = overdrive transmission; **S** = standard; **O** = optional; **NA** = not available.

Prices are accurate at time of printing; subject to manufacturer's change.

Plymouth

Against

● Rear seat room   ● Driving position

Summary

Horizon and Omni are aged subcompacts with a cramped interior and an ungainly driving position, but still stand as a value worth considering. Reinforcing their appeal for '90 is the driver's-side air bag, which makes them among the least expensive cars to offer this important safety feature as standard equipment. The 2.2-liter engine delivers good performance with the standard 5-speed manual transmission and, unlike most rivals, isn't underpowered with the optional automatic. Neither does this engine turn anemic when the air conditioner is on—which is the rule with smaller-displacement 4-cylinder engines. Fuel economy isn't bad either. There are many newer subcompacts with more interior room and better ride and handling, but none can match Horizon/Omni performance and standard equipment at such a low price. Chrysler's long warranties covering the powertrain and body rust are an added bonus. The airbag has helped push up the Horizon/Omni base price by $400 for 1990, to $6995. But even with automatic transmission, air conditioning, power steering, and a stereo radio, the total will still be less than $9500, not including the destination charge.

Specifications

	5-door hatchback
Wheelbase, in.	99.1
Overall length, in.	163.2
Overall width, in.	66.8
Overall height, in.	53.0
Turn diameter, ft.	35.5
Curb weight, lbs.	2296
Cargo vol., cu. ft.	33.0
Fuel capacity, gals.	13.0
Seating capacity	5
Front headroom, in.	38.1
Front shoulder room, in.	51.7
Front legroom, max., in.	42.1
Rear headroom, in.	36.9
Rear shoulder room, in.	51.5
Rear legroom, min., in.	33.3

Powertrain layout: transverse front engine/front-wheel drive.

Engines

	ohc I-4
Size, liters/cu. in.	2.2/135
Fuel delivery	TBI
Horsepower @ rpm	93 @ 4800
Torque (lbs./ft.) @ rpm	122 @ 3200
Availability	S

EPA city/highway mpg

5-speed OD manual	26/35
3-speed automatic	24/30

KEY: ohv = overhead valve; **ohc** = overhead cam; **dohc** = double overhead cam; **I** = inline cylinders; **V** = cylinders in V configuration; **flat** = horizontally opposed cylinders; **bbl.** = barrel (carburetor); **PFI** = port (multi-point) fuel injection; **TBI** = throttle-body (single-point) fuel injection; **rpm** = revolutions per minute; **OD** = overdrive transmission; **S** = standard; **O** = optional; **NA** = not available.

Prices

Plymouth Horizon/Dodge Omni	Retail Price	Dealer Invoice	Low Price
5-door hatchback	$6995	$6465	$6685
Destination charge	363	363	363

Standard equipment:

2.2-liter 4-cylinder TBI engine, 5-speed manual transmission, driver's-side airbag, rear shoulder belts, rear defogger, rear wiper/washer, trip odometer, tachometer, coolant temperature, oil pressure and voltage gauges, luggage compartment light, black bodyside moldings, left remote mirror, right visor mirror, folding shelf panel, intermittent wipers, cloth and vinyl upholstery, P165/80R13 tires on styled steel wheels.

Optional equipment:

Air conditioning	798	678	718
Requires Transmission Discount Pkg.			
Basic Equipment Automatic Transmission Pkg.	799	679	719
3-speed automatic transmission, power steering.			
Manual Transmission Discount Pkg.	868	738	781
Power steering, AM/FM radio, highback reclining front seats, trunk dress-up, floormats, remote mirrors, rallye wheels.			
Automatic Transmission Discount Pkg.	1290	1097	1161
Manual Transmission Discount Pkg. plus 3-speed automatic transmission.			
Rear defogger	155	132	140
Tinted glass	108	92	97
AM/FM cassette	157	133	141
Requires Transmission Discount Pkg.			
Conventional spare tire	75	64	68
165/80R13 WSW tires	65	55	59
California emissions pkg.	103	88	93

Plymouth Laser

Plymouth Laser RS

What's New

The front-drive Laser 2+2 went on sale in January 1989 as an early 1990 model. It's built in Normal, Illinois, by Diamond-Star Motors, a new joint venture between Chrysler and its Japanese partner, Mitsubishi. Diamond-Star also builds the same car for sale as the Mitsubishi Eclipse and Eagle Talon, though the Laser is the only one that doesn't offer a 4-wheel drive model. These cars are based on a Mitsubishi Galant chassis and use Mitsubishi engines and transmissions. A 92-horsepower 1.8-liter 4-cylinder is standard on the base Laser and the slightly better-equipped RS. A 135-horsepower, 16-valve double overhead-cam 2.0-liter is optional on the RS. A turbocharged version of the DOHC 2.0 pumping out 190 horsepower is standard on the RS Turbo. A 5-speed manual

192

CONSUMER GUIDE®

transmission is standard, a 4-speed automatic is optional (except with the turbo). All models have 4-wheel disc brakes as standard equipment; an anti-lock system is not offered. The RS and RS Turbo models add such amenities as power outside mirrors, a cassette player, power steering, adjustable driver's-seat lumbar support, and a rear tonneau cover to hide luggage. They also come standard with 205/55R16 tires in place of the base Laser's 185/70R14.

For

- Performance (2.0 and 2.0 turbo)
- Handling/roadholding • Braking

Against

- Performance (automatic transmission) • Rear-seat room

Summary

Our praise of the Eclipse and Talon holds for the Laser, so consult those reports as well. Like its Diamond-Star siblings, Laser packs a lot of driving enjoyment in a reasonably priced package, though high demand has made dealers largely unwilling to negotiate price. The base 1.8-liter engine runs smoothly, though it doesn't deliver the kind of response with automatic transmission that does justice to the Laser's sporty looks. The more powerful 2.0-liter engine suffers less with automatic transmission. Because it doesn't have any low-end torque to spare, however, you'll enjoy peppier around-town driving with the 5-speed manual. Laser's 5-speed gearbox is one of the cleanest-shifting units around and, in tandem with the 2.0, creates the best-balanced Laser. A basic RS is plenty fast and doesn't suffer the turbocharged version's bad manners on quick getaways. Under hard throttle at low speeds, the turbo's power comes on abruptly and can wrench the front tires off course in an effect called torque steer. A turbo Laser is a seriously fast car, but we think its torque steer makes it a coupe with which only hard-core hot rodders will feel comfortable. All Lasers enjoy decent ride quality and good roadability, though the ride suffers some and the handling improves with the high-performance tires on the RS models. Minuscule rear seats and cargo space that's subpar even for the 2+2 class are negatives. A major positive is the outstanding dashboard, with its easy-to-read analog instruments and the simple, stylish arrangement of its smooth-working controls. Shorter drivers might feel a big closed in because Laser's dashboard and beltline are rather high compared to the low seat, but there's plenty to recommend here if you're shopping for a sporty coupe.

Specifications

	3-door hatchback
Wheelbase, in.	97.2
Overall length, in.	170.5
Overall width, in.	66.5
Overall height, in.	51.4
Turn diameter, ft.	34.0
Curb weight, lbs.	2524
Cargo vol., cu. ft.	10.2
Fuel capacity, gals.	15.9
Seating capacity	4
Front headroom, in.	37.9
Front shoulder room, in.	53.9
Front legroom, max., in.	42.5
Rear headroom, in.	34.1
Rear shoulder room, in.	53.1
Rear legroom, min., in.	28.5

Powertrain layout: transverse front engine/front-wheel drive.

Engines

	ohc I-4	dohc I-4	Turbo dohc I-4
Size, liters/cu. in.	1.8/107	2.0/122	2.0/122
Fuel delivery	PFI	PFI	PFI
Horsepower @ rpm	92 @ 5000	135 @ 6000	190 @ 6000
Torque (lbs./ft.) @ rpm	107 @ 3500	125 @ 5000	203 @ 5000
Availability	S	O[1]	O[1]

EPA city/highway mpg

	ohc I-4	dohc I-4	Turbo dohc I-4
5-speed OD manual	26/37	24/36	24/36
4-speed OD automatic	26/37	24/34	

1. RS.

Prices

Plymouth Laser	Retail Price	Dealer Invoice	Low Price
3-door hatchback	$10855	$9975	$10375
RS 3-door hatchback	11900	10885	11285
RS Turbo 3-door hatchback	13905	12691	13091
Destination charge	454	454	454

Standard equipment:

1.8-liter PFI 4-cylinder engine, 5-speed manual transmission, cloth and vinyl reclining front bucket seats, one-piece folding rear seat, tachometer, coolant temperature and oil pressure gauges, trip odometer, rear shoulder belts, tinted glass, variable intermittent wipers, remote fuel door and hatch releases, visor mirrors, remote mirrors, AM/FM radio, tilt steering column, 185/70R14 all-season tires. **RS** adds: power steering, power mirrors, AM/FM cassette, full cloth upholstery, driver's seat lumbar support adjustment, cargo cover, wheelcovers. **RS Turbo** adds: 2.0-liter DOHC 16-valve turbocharged engine, performance suspension, 205/55VR16 all-season performance tires.

Optional equipment:

2.0-liter DOHC engine, RS	873	742	786
4-speed automatic transmission, base & RS	682	580	614
Air conditioning	802	682	722
Base requires Popular Pkg.			
Basic Equipment Pkg., RS	732	622	659
Air conditioning, console cupholder, floormats, AM/FM radio with EQ and six speakers, cruise control power windows and locks, rear wiper/washer.			
Popular Equipment Pkg., base	609	518	548
Base: power steering, console cupholder, rear defogger, floormats, cargo cover, wheelcovers.			
Popular Equipment Pkg., RS & RS Turbo	1398	1188	1258
Air conditioning, console cupholder, floormats, AM/FM cassette with EQ, cruise control, rear wiper/washer.			
Deluxe Equipment Pkg., base	1767	1502	1590
Air conditioning, power steering, console cupholder, rear defogger, floormats, AM/FM cassette, cruise control, cargo cover, wheelcovers.			
Deluxe Equipment Pkg., RS & RS Turbo	1776	1510	1598
Air conditioning, console cupholder, floormats, AM/FM cassette with EQ, cruise control, power windows and locks, rear wiper/washer.			
Deluxe Pkg. w/CD player, RS & RS Turbo	2190	1862	1971
Rear defogger, base	150	128	135
AM/FM cassette, base	170	145	153
Requires Popular Pkg.			
AM/FM cassette w/EQ, RS & RS Turbo	242	206	218
RS requires Basic Pkg.			
Removable glass sunroof	378	321	340
Alloy wheels, RS & RS Turbo	321	273	289
California emissions pkg.	103	88	93

Prices are accurate at time of printing; subject to manufacturer's change.

Plymouth Sundance

Plymouth Sundance RS

What's New

Plymouth's front-drive subcompact gets a driver's-side airbag and a redesigned instrument cluster for '90. Sundance, a twin of the Dodge Shadow, comes in 3- and 5-door hatchback body styles with a range of 4-cylinder engines. The addition of the airbag brings a new steering wheel that now incorporates the optional cruise control buttons. The revamped instrument cluster complements the newly available Infinity I audio system. Sundance's base engine is a 2.2-liter 4-cylinder. A 2.5-liter four is optional on the base model. The 2.5 is standard with the Rallye Sport (RS) package, which includes a unique front fascia with fog lamps, two-tone exterior paint, and sporty interior touches. Optional with either base or RS trim is a turbo package that includes a turbocharged version of the 2.5 four. The turbo package retains the base car's 185/70R14 tire size, but adds equal-length drive shafts to help distribute the engine's power more evenly between the front tires. Optional with all engines is a 3-speed automatic transmission. Standard is Chrysler's redesigned 5-speed manual. Besides internal modifications designed to improve the shifting action, the 5-speed's shift pattern has been revised and the reverse lock-out ring eliminated. Three-point shoulder belts for outboard rear-seat passengers also are standard.

For

● Performance (turbo)   ● Ride/handling   ● Cargo room

Against

● Engine noise   ● Rear seat room

Summary

Sundance is second only to the Acclaim as Plymouth's most popular car, proof that a marketing strategy aimed at young buyers and women has paid off. Plymouth calls Sundance a compact based on interior volume, but we list it as a subcompact based on wheelbase, overall length, and its limited rear-seat leg room. There's plenty of head room all around and luggage space is adequate with the rear seatback up and

generous with the seatback folded down. The moderately firm suspension feels a little harsh on bumpy roads, but it's not punishing. There are no suspension or tire options, but Sundance enjoys capable cornering, good road grip, and a stable highway ride. Of the three available engines, the one we recommend is the naturally aspirated 2.5-liter. It's smoother and quieter than the 2.2 or the turbo 2.5, and it blends adequate performance with reasonable economy. Good news: No longer must you avoid Chrysler's 5-speed manual transmission if you're looking to maximize performance or fuel economy. The smooth, positive shift action of 1990's redesigned 5-speed is a quantum leap over the previous version's balky movement. Note that the optional automatic does not have an overdrive fourth gear, so highway cruising isn't as quiet or as economical as it might be. Sundance isn't the most polished small hatchback, but it does offer decent performance at an attractively low price.

Specifications

	3-door hatchback	5-door hatchback
Wheelbase, in.	97.0	97.0
Overall length, in.	171.7	171.7
Overall width, in.	67.3	67.3
Overall height, in.	52.6	52.6
Turn diameter, ft.	34.0	34.0
Curb weight, lbs.	2513	2544
Cargo vol., cu. ft.	33.3	33.0
Fuel capacity, gals.	14.0	14.0
Seating capacity	5	5
Front headroom, in.	38.3	38.3
Front shoulder room, in.	54.4	54.7
Front legroom, max., in.	41.5	41.5
Rear headroom, in.	37.4	37.4
Rear shoulder room, in.	52.5	54.5
Rear legroom, min., in.	34.0	34.0

Powertrain layout: transverse front engine/front-wheel drive.

Engines

	ohc I-4	ohc I-4	Turbo ohc I-4
Size, liters/cu. in.	2.2/135	2.5/153	2.5/153
Fuel delivery	TBI	TBI	PFI
Horsepower @ rpm	93 @ 4800	100 @ 4800	150 @ 4800
Torque (lbs./ft.) @ rpm	122 @ 3200	135 @ 2800	180 @ 2000
Availability	S	O	O

EPA city/highway mpg

5-speed OD manual	24/34	24/34	20/29
3-speed automatic	24/28	23/29	19/24

Prices

Plymouth Sundance	Retail Price	Dealer Invoice	Low Price
3-door hatchback	$8795	$8041	$8241
5-door hatchback	8995	8221	8421
Destination charge	440	440	440

Standard equipment:

2.2-liter TBI 4-cylinder engine, 5-speed manual transmission, power steering, driver's-side airbag, cloth reclining front bucket seats, split folding rear seatback, tachometer, coolant temperature gauge, voltmeter, trip odometer, intermittent wipers, remote liftgate release, remote mirrors, visor mirrors, bodyside moldings, AM/FM radio, removable shelf panel, 185/70R14 SBR tires.

KEY: ohv = overhead valve; **ohc** = overhead cam; **dohc** = double overhead cam; **I** = inline cylinders; **V** = cylinders in V configuration; **flat** = horizontally opposed cylinders; **bbl.** = barrel (carburetor); **PFI** = port (multi-point) fuel injection; **TBI** = throttle-body (single-point) fuel injection; **rpm** = revolutions per minute; **OD** = overdrive transmission; **S** = standard; **O** = optional; **NA** = not available.

CONSUMER GUIDE®

Optional equipment:	Retail Price	Dealer Invoice	Low Price
2.5-liter engine	288	245	259
3-speed automatic transmission	552	469	497
Air conditioning	798	678	718
Requires tinted glass.			
4-wheel disc brakes	184	156	166
Rear defogger	155	132	140
Power locks, 3-door	160	136	144
5-door	211	179	190
Power windows, 3-door	227	193	204
5-door	304	258	274
Requires power locks and mirrors.			
Power mirrors	58	49	52
AM/FM cassette	207	176	186
w/seek/scan & Infinity speakers	228	194	205
Cruise control	191	162	172
Requires tilt steering column.			
Tilt steering column	134	114	121
Sunroof	383	326	345
Tinted glass	108	92	97
Requires air conditioning.			
Conventional spare tire	85	72	77
w/turbo	104	88	94
w/RS	185	157	167
Alloy wheels	332	282	299
Floormats	46	39	41
Pearl coat/clearcoat paint	75	64	68
California emissions pkg.	103	88	93

Note: RS Pkg. and other equipment is available in Customer Preferred Packages. Space limitations prevent listing these packages.

Plymouth Voyager

Plymouth Grand Voyager LE

What's New

Voyager accounts for an astonishing 40 percent of Plymouth sales and gets some powertrain changes for 1990 that only enhance its appeal. Chrysler's new 3.3-liter V-6 is standard on the Grand Voyager version of Plymouth's front-drive mini-van. Exclusive to the Grand models, the 3.3 is rated at 150 horsepower and is available only with a 4-speed overdrive automatic transmission. Also new for '90 is a standard 20-gallon fuel tank on all models, replacing a 15-gallon unit. Plus, now optional in place of Voyager's standard 195/75R14 tires is a 15-inch sport road wheel package with 205/70R15 tires. Dodge sells identical vans as the Caravan, while a luxury Chrysler version, called the Town & Country, debuts for '90. Standard-size Voyagers come in base, SE, and LE trim in a 176-inch-long body on a 112-inch wheelbase. Grand Voyagers come in SE and LE trim in a 190-inch body on a 119-inch

wheelbase. Grand Voyagers come with 7-passenger seating. Regular-length models have seating for five standard and for seven as an option, though 7-passenger seating is standard for '90 on the regular-length LE. Regular-length Voyagers come with a 100-horsepower 2.5-liter 4-cylinder engine. Two engines are optional: a 142-horsepower 3.0-liter V-6 made by Mitsubishi; or Chrysler's 150-horsepower 2.5-liter turbocharged four. A 3-speed automatic transmission is standard with the 3.0 V-6; a 4-speed overdrive automatic is standard with the 3.3 and optional with the 3.0. The standard gearbox on the regular-length Voyagers is Chrysler's revamped 5-speed manual.

For

● Passenger room   ● Cargo space   ● Ride/handling

Against

● Fuel economy   ● Performance (4-cylinder)

Summary

Chrysler's front-drive minivans continue to sell briskly, even though price discounts are hard to come by. You're looking at more than $20,000 for a lavishly equipped Grand LE and $17,000-$20,000 for a well-furnished standard-size Voyager or Grand SE. We prefer a V-6 engine in the Voyager for its clearly superior performance. In a brief test-track drive, the 3.3 was quicker than the 3.0, but somewhat louder and cruder sounding under throttle. The 2.5 is barely adequate for a lightly loaded Voyager; it's inadequate for a fully loaded one. The turbo engine treats the Voyager to quick acceleration, but delivers its power mostly in bursts accompanied by an ugly roar. Most families will be happier with automatic transmission in their Voyager, though the manual shift linkage has been greatly improved. We find Voyager and the identical Dodge Caravan the easiest of the compact vans to drive. They have better traction than their rear-drive rivals, better stability on the open road, and more car-like handling and ride. Standard-length Voyagers match the new General Motors rivals in usable passenger room and cargo space, while the stretched versions improve luggage room dramatically. Despite the high prices, the Caravan/Voyager remain our favorites among compact vans for passenger use, though the Mazda MPV merits serious consideration.

Specifications	4-door van	4-door van
Wheelbase, in.	112.0	119.1
Overall length, in.	175.9	190.5
Overall width, in.	72.0	72.0
Overall height, in.	64.8	64.8
Turn diameter, ft.	41.0	43.0
Curb weight, lbs.	3100	3255
Cargo vol., cu. ft.	125.0	150.0
Fuel capacity, gals.	20.0	20.0
Seating capacity	7	7
Front headroom, in.	39.9	39.9
Front shoulder room, in.	58.4	58.4
Front legroom, max., in.	38.2	38.2
Rear headroom, in.	38.5	38.3
Rear shoulder room, in.	61.3	61.3
Rear legroom, min., in.	37.6	37.8

Powertrain layout: transverse front engine/front-wheel drive.

Prices are accurate at time of printing; subject to manufacturer's change.

Plymouth • Pontiac

Engines

Engines	ohc I-4	Turbo ohc I-4	ohc V-6	ohv V-6
Size, liters/cu. in.	2.5/153	2.5/153	3.0/181	3.3/201
Fuel delivery	TBI	PFI	PFI	PFI
Horsepower @ rpm	100 @ 4800	150 @ 4800	142 @ 5000	150 @ 4800
Torque (lbs./ft.) @ rpm	135 @ 2800	180 @ 2000	173 @ 2800	185 @ 3600
Availability	S	O	O	S[1]

EPA city/highway mpg

5-speed OD manual	22/28	18/26		
3-speed automatic	21/23	19/23	19/24	
4-speed OD automatic			19/24	18/24

1. Grand Voyager.

Prices

Plymouth Voyager

	Retail Price	Dealer Invoice	Low Price
Base SWB 4-door van	$11995	$10756	$11376
SE SWB 4-door van	12675	11354	12015
LE SWB 4-door van	16125	14390	15258
SE Grand 4-door van	15395	13748	14572
LE Grand 4-door van	18325	16326	17326
Destination charge	515	515	515

SWB denotes short-wheelbase models.

Standard equipment:

2.5-liter TBI engine, 5-speed manual transmission, power steering, liftgate wiper/washer, 5-passenger seating, variable intermittent wipers, tinted glass, left remote mirror, AM/FM radio, P185/75R14 SBR tires. **SE** adds: highback reclining front seats, rear seat (Grand), front folding center armrests, upgraded door panels, power liftgate release. **LE** adds: front air conditioning, 7-passenger seating, added sound insulation, remote mirrors, bodyside moldings, woodgrain exterior applique, upgraded steering wheel. **Grand SE** and **LE** add 3.3-liter PFI V-6, 4-speed automatic transmission.

Optional equipment:

2.5-liter turbo engine, SWB	700	595	644
3.0-liter V6, SE & LE SWB	700	595	644
3-speed automatic transmission, SWB	582	495	535
4-speed automatic transmission, SE & LE SWB	757	643	696
Requires 3.0-liter V-6.			
Front air conditioning (std. LE)	865	735	796
Rear air conditioning & heater, Grand	577	490	531
Requires front air conditioning.			
Converta-Bed seating, SE & LE SWB	558	474	513
7-passenger seating, base & SE SWB	401	341	369
Popular Equipment Pkg., SE SWB	1003	853	923
SE SWB w/Value Wagon Pkg.	752	639	692
SE Grand	883	751	812
Light Pkg., cruise control, tilt steering column, forward storage console, overhead console, floormats, tachometer, coolant temperature and oil pressure gauges, 125-mph speedometer, added sound insulation, power rear quarter vent windows, conventional spare tire.			
Luxury Equipment Discount Pkg., SE SWB	2115	1798	1946
SE SWB w/Value Wagon Pkg.	1765	1500	1624
SE Grand	1994	1695	1834
LE SWB	913	776	840
Popular Pkg. plus rear defogger, lighted visor mirror, power windows and locks, power mirrors, power driver's seat (LE), Infinity I AM/FM cassette, sport steering wheel.			
Value Wagon Pkg. w/5-speed, base & SE SWB	1265	1075	1164
w/3-speed automatic, base & SE SWB	1847	1570	1699
Front air conditionioning, rear defogger, dual horns, added sound insulation, Light Pkg.			

	Retail Price	Dealer Invoice	Low Price
LX Decor Pkg., LE SWB	1191	1012	1096
2.5-liter turbo engine, warm silver fascia and bodyside moldings, HD suspension, 205/70R15 tires on lace-style alloy wheels.			
HD Trailer Tow Pkg., SE	689	586	634
SE w/Popular or Luxury Pkg.	582	495	535
Deluxe Convenience Pkg., base & SE	346	294	318
Cruise control, tilt steering column.			
Power Convenience Pkg., SE	438	372	403
Power windows and locks.			
AY4 Sport Roadwheel Pkg., SE	487	414	448
LE	462	393	425
205/70R15 tires on alloy wheels, conventional spare tire (LE).			
AYA Sport Roadwheel Pkg., base	456	388	420
AY4 Pkg. but with 14-inch tires.			
Luxury vinyl trim, base & SE	NC	NC	NC
Leather trim, LE	848	721	780
Woodgrain applique, LE	NC	NC	NC
Rear defogger	170	145	156
Power locks, base & SE	214	182	197
Requires Value Wagon or Popular Pkg.			
Sunscreen glass	418	355	385
Luggage rack, base & SE	144	122	132
AM/FM cassette	157	133	144
Inifinity I AM/FM cassette	411	349	378
Infinity II AM/FM cassette w/EQ	220	187	202
Requires Luxury or ES Decor Pkg.			
Power sunroof, SE	809	688	744
LE	959	815	882
Requires Popular Pkg. on SE.			
HD suspension	70	60	64
205/70R14 WSW tires	139	118	128
Requires Value Wagon, Popular, Luxury or Sport Roadwheel Pkg. on base and SE.			
195/75R15 tires (NA base)	70	60	64
w/rear A/C & heater	145	123	133
Requires sunroof or HD Trailer Tow Pkg.			
Conventional spare tire	107	91	98
Wire wheel covers, LE	246	209	226
Pearl coat paint	75	64	69
Two-tone paint	243	207	224
California emissions pkg.	103	88	95

Pontiac Bonneville

What's New

Pontiac's full-size front-drive sedans have some new touches inside and out, but return mechanically unaltered for '90. These 4-door sedans continue in base LE, mid-line SE, and sporty SSE trim. All have had their front substructure redesigned in an effort to improve over-the-road behavior and for better noise isolation. SE and LE versions get an SSE-style grille and taillamps while the SE gets a rear spoiler in place of its previous rear-deck luggage rack. To improve comfort inside, lap belts are now mounted to the seats rather than to the inside of the roof pillar. Remote control door locks have been made optional on LE and SE and standard on the sporty SSE. On the LE, a 55/45 split front bench seat replaces last year's full bench as standard. New SE standard features include a power driver's seat, rear defogger, cassette deck, fog lamps, interior lamp group, and rear-deck release. Standard SE tires are now size 215/60R16, replacing 215/65R15s. Bonneville continues only with a 3.8-liter V-6 and a 4-speed automatic transmission. Anti-lock brakes remain standard on the SSE and optional on the others. Bonneville debuted for the 1987 model year with the same basic design as the Buick LeSabre and Oldsmobile Eighty Eight Royale, though Buick and Olds also offer 2-door versions, while the Eighty Eight is the only one available with a driver's-side air bag.

Pontiac Bonneville SSE

For

- Performance
- Room/comfort
- Anti-lock brakes
- Handling

Against

- Fuel economy
- Ride (SSE)

Summary

With any Bonneville you get a spacious interior, decent cargo volume, and an ample selection of convenience equipment. This is the sportiest of the three GM H-body full-size cars, a theme Pontiac carries over into a cabin that looks and feels more contemporary than the others. Of the individual models, the flagship SSE is a little too aggressively styled for us. There's nothing subtle about its rear spoiler, body-sill extensions, body-colored wheels, and deep exhaust note. We'd be more comfortable with the boy-racer looks if the performance were anything special. The ride is a little stiff, but the handling and roadholding are very good. The problem is that the 3.8 V-6 and automatic transmission betray the aggressive looks with only average acceleration. With anti-lock brakes optionally available on the LE and SE, we're more interested in those models. The SE has a less flamboyant exterior than the SSE and for less money delivers virtually all of the SSE's good pieces, including a sport suspension and the same high-performance and all-season tires. The LE has a softer suspension and smaller tires, and an even lower price. Since all three models use the same engine, the only performance difference comes from different final-drive ratios. The SSE has the shortest (highest numerical) ratio for slightly quicker acceleration.

Specifications

	4-door notchback
Wheelbase, in.	110.8
Overall length, in.	198.7
Overall width, in.	72.1
Overall height, in.	55.5
Turn diameter, ft.	38.4
Curb weight, lbs.	3325
Cargo vol., cu. ft.	15.2
Fuel capacity, gals.	18.0
Seating capacity	6
Front headroom, in.	38.9
Front shoulder room, in.	58.9
Front legroom, max., in.	42.4
Rear headroom, in.	38.2
Rear shoulder room, in.	59.1
Rear legroom, min., in.	38.4

Powertrain layout: transverse front engine/front-wheel drive.

Engines

	ohv V-6
Size, liters/cu. in.	3.8/231
Fuel delivery	PFI
Horsepower @ rpm	165 @ 5200
Torque (lbs./ft.) @ rpm	210 @ 2000
Availability	S

EPA city/highway mpg

4-speed OD automatic	18/27

Prices

Pontiac Bonneville	Retail Price	Dealer Invoice	Low Price
LE 4-door notchback	$15774	$13613	$13813
SE 4-door notchback	19144	16521	16721
SSE 4-door notchback	23994	20707	20907
Destination charge	505	505	505

Standard equipment:

LE: 3.8-liter PFI V-6, 4-speed automatic transmission, power steering and brakes, air conditioning, tinted glass, cloth 45/55 seat with recliners, rear shoulder belts, left remote and right manual mirrors, wide bodyside moldings, AM/FM radio, coolant temperature gauge, 205/75R14 tires. **SE adds:** 2.97 axle ratio, storage armrest, cargo security net, intermittent wipers, cruise control, tilt steering column, tachometer and trip odometer, power windows, AM/FM cassette with EQ, Rally Tuned Suspension, 215/60R16 Eagle GT + 4 tires on alloy wheels. **SSE adds:** 3.33 axle ratio, anti-lock braking system, Electronic Ride Control, automatic air conditioning with steering wheel controls, electronic compass, Driver Information System, heated power mirrors, headlamp sentinel, headlamp washers, power seat adjustments (including lumbar support, recliners and head restraints), fog lamps, aero bodyside extensions, eight-speaker audio system with Touch Control, power antenna, rear storage armrest, rear defogger, lighted visor mirrors, leather-wrapped steering wheel, illuminated entry, remote decklid release, power locks, first aid and accessory kits, uprated suspension, 215/60R16 Eagle GT + 4 tires.

Optional equipment:

Anti-lock brakes, LE & SE	925	786	833
LE requires Pkg. 1SD or 1SE.			
Option Pkg. 1SB, LE	269	229	242
Tilt steering column, intermittent wipers, Lamp Group.			
Option Pkg. 1SC, LE	464	394	418
Pkg. 1SB plus cruise control.			
Option Pkg. 1SD, LE	1716	1459	1544
Pkg. 1SC plus power windows and locks, power driver's seat, remote decklid release, lighted visor mirrors, rally gauges with tachometer, AM/FM cassette.			
Option Pkg. 1SE, LE	2414	2052	2173
Pkg. 1SD plus illuminated entry, power mirrors, leather-wrapped steering wheel, power antenna, remote fuel door release, remote keyless entry, power passenger seat.			
Value Option Pkg. R6A, LE	940	799	846
w/Pkg. 1SD or 1SE	465	395	419
Custom interior trim, 215/65R15 tires on alloy wheels.			
Option Pkg. 1SB, SE	330	281	297
Lighted visor mirrors, illuminated entry, power mirrors, power antenna.			

> **KEY: ohv** = overhead valve; **ohc** = overhead cam; **dohc** = double overhead cam; **I** = inline cylinders; **V** = cylinders in V configuration; **flat** = horizontally opposed cylinders; **bbl.** = barrel (carburetor); **PFI** = port (multi-point) fuel injection; **TBI** = throttle-body (single-point) fuel injection; **rpm** = revolutions per minute; **OD** = overdrive transmission; **S** = standard; **O** = optional; **NA** = not available.

Prices are accurate at time of printing; subject to manufacturer's change.

	Retail Price	Dealer Invoice	Low Price
Option Pkg. 1SC, SE	810	689	729

Pkg. 1SB plus remote fuel door release, remote keyless entry, power passenger seat, Twilight Sentinel.

Value Option Pkg. R6A, LE	610	519	549
SE w/Pkg. 1SB or 1SC	535	455	482

Custom two-tone paint, AM/FM cassette with EQ.

Value Option Pkg. R6A, SSE	1080	918	972

Power glass sunroof, theft deterrent system.

Rear defogger, LE	160	136	144
Custom two-tone paint, LE & SE	105	89	95
Power locks, LE	215	183	194
Power windows, LE	375	319	338
Power antenna, LE	75	64	68
AM/FM cassette, LE	140	119	126
AM/FM cassette w/EQ, SE	655	557	590
SE w/Pkg. 1SB or 1SC	580	493	522

Includes electronic air conditioning, power antenna, anti-theft feature, Touch Control.

AM/FM radio w/CD player & EQ, LE	1031	876	928
LE w/custom interior trim	931	791	838
LE w/Pkg. 1SD	891	757	802
LE w/Pkg. 1SD & custom interior trim .	791	672	712
LE w/Pkg. 1SE	766	651	689
LE w/Pkg. 1SE & custom interior trim .	666	566	599
SE	841	715	757
SE w/Pkg. 1SB or 1SC	766	651	689
SSE	186	158	167

Includes electronic air conditioning, leather-wrapped steering wheel, anti-theft feature, power antenna, Touch Control.

Metrix 45/45 seat w/console, SE	235	200	212
Ventura leather trim, SSE	779	662	701
Custom interior trim, LE	705	599	635
LE w/Pkg. 1SD or 1SE	230	196	207

Metrix 45/45 seat, six-speaker performance sound system, gauges, power windows, trunk security net; requires Pkg. 1SC, 1SD or 1SE.

Power driver's seat, LE	270	230	243
Power glass sunroof, SE & SSE	1230	1046	1107
WSW tires, LE	76	65	68
215/65R15 tires, LE	114	97	103
215/65R15 WSW tires, LE	184	156	166
LE w/Pkg. R6A	70	60	63
Diamond-spoke alloy wheels, LE	296	252	266

Requires 215/65R15 tires.

Theft deterrent system, SSE	150	128	135
Warranty enhancements for NY	65	55	59
California emissions pkg.	100	85	90

Pontiac Firebird

What's New

Additional power and some new interior appointments make news as Pontiac's ponycar perennial heads for a mid-year facelift. The rear-drive coupe continues in base, Formula, Trans Am, and GTA trim. For '90, all get a driver's-side airbag, installation of which eliminates the previously available steering-wheel-mounted radio controls. Door map pockets with integral cupholders have been added to cars equipped with power windows. Split folding rear seatbacks are no longer offered, though the one-piece fold-down seatback is retained. Under the hood, port fuel injection replaces throttle-body injec-

---

KEY: ohv = overhead valve; **ohc** = overhead cam; **dohc** = double overhead cam; **I** = inline cylinders; **V** = cylinders in V configuration; **flat** = horizontally opposed cylinders; **bbl.** = barrel (carburetor); **PFI** = port (multi-point) fuel injection; **TBI** = throttle-body (single-point) fuel injection; **rpm** = revolutions per minute; **OD** = overdrive transmission; **S** = standard; **O** = optional; **NA** = not available.

Pontiac Firebird GTA

tion on some versions of the 5.0-liter V-8. The change adds 5 or 10 horsepower, depending on the model and whether a manual or an automatic transmission is ordered. The 5.7-liter V-8, meanwhile, increases from 225 horsepower to 235. The base Firebird's new standard engine is a 140-horsepower 3.1-liter V-6. It replaces a 135-horsepower 2.8-liter V-6. Around January 1991, the Firebird will get new front and rear styling. The nose will be reshaped in the mold of the aggressive aero snout seen on the Pontiac Banshee show car and the tail will have an integrated spoiler. Pontiac also is considering the introduction of a turbocharged GTA to coincide with the facelift. The car would have the 250-horsepower 3.8-liter turbo V-6 used in the 1989 20th Anniversary Trans Am.

For

● Performance (V-8s)   ● Handling   ● Resale value

Against

● Fuel economy   ● Ride   ● Interior room

Summary

Firebird celebrates without apology an era when American performance meant V-8 power in rear-drive cars bigger and heavier than they needed to be. Check with your insurance agent before buying one, however. Even with the standard anti-theft system, Firebird ranks as one of America's most frequently stolen cars. That, plus its popularity with younger, more aggressive drivers, can make for stratospheric insurance rates. As with any car of its ilk, performance and styling reign over comfort and convenience. The Firebird's stiff suspension isn't sophisticated, but teamed with large tires, it helps the big coupe stick to the road—as long as the road is smooth and dry. Bumps set the rear axle to juddering and the body panels to shuddering. Wet pavement calls for the gentlest of throttle applications, lest the tail slip and slide. As for acceleration, the more you pay, the faster you go, from the sheep-in-wolf's-clothing base model to the howling-wolf GTA. Manual transmission fans will enjoy the way the 5-speed snicks into gear; plenty of torque with the V-8s means little sacrifice of power with automatic transmission. The airbag and other interior changes help update Firebird's cabin, but it's still a claustrophobic 2 + 2. Firebird's rounded exterior lines date to 1982, but they've held up better than sister-ship Camaro's angular ones in light of today's organic styling.

Specifications

	3-door hatchback
Wheelbase, in.	101.0
Overall length, in.	188.1

	3-door hatchback
Overall width, in.	72.4
Overall height, in.	50.0
Turn diameter, ft.	32.6
Curb weight, lbs.	3210
Cargo vol., cu. ft.	31.0
Fuel capacity, gals.	15.5
Seating capacity	4
Front headroom, in.	37.0
Front shoulder room, in.	57.7
Front legroom, max., in.	43.0
Rear headroom, in.	35.6
Rear shoulder room, in.	56.3
Rear legroom, min., in.	29.8

Powertrain layout: longitudinal front engine/rear-wheel drive.

Engines

	ohv V-6	ohv V-8	ohv V-8	ohv V-8
Size, liters/cu. in.	3.1/191	5.0/305	5.0/305	5.7/350
Fuel delivery	PFI	TBI	PFI	PFI
Horsepower @ rpm	140 @	170 @	225 @	235 @
	4400	4000	4400	4400
Torque (lbs./ft.) @ rpm . . .	180 @	255 @	300 @	340 @
	3600	2400	3200	3200
Availability	S[1]	S[2]	S[3]	S[4]

EPA city/highway mpg

5-speed OD manual	19/27	16/25	16/26	
4-speed OD automatic . . .	17/27	16/24	16/23	16/25

1. Base Firebird 2. Formula 3. Trans Am 4. GTA.

Prices

Pontiac Firebird	Retail Price	Dealer Invoice	Low Price
3-door hatchback	$11320	$10109	$10309
Formula 3-door hatchback	14610	13047	13247
Trans Am 3-door hatchback	16510	14743	14943
GTA 3-door hatchback	23320	20825	21025
Destination charge	439	439	439

Standard equipment:

3.1-liter PFI V-6, 5-speed manual transmisson, power steering, driver's-side airbag, cloth reclining front bucket seats, rear shoulder belts, power hatch pulldown, AM/FM radio, gauge cluster including tachometer, Pass Key theft-deterrent system, left visor mirror, 215/65R15 tires on alloy wheels. **Trans Am** adds: 5.0-liter PFI V-8, F41 suspension. **Formula** adds: 5.0-liter TBI V-8, dual exhaust, air conditioning, WS6 performance suspension, 245/50ZR16 tires on alloy wheels. **GTA** adds: 5.7-liter PFI V-8, 4-speed automatic transmission, 4-wheel disc brakes, limited-slip differential, rear defogger, power windows and locks, tinted glass, cruise control, tilt steering column, articulated bucket seats with inflatable lumbar support and thigh bolsters, floormats, upgraded upholstery, cargo cover, AM/FM cassette with EQ and Touch Control.

Optional equipment:

5.0-liter TBI V-8, base	350	298	315
Requires air conditioning.			
5.0-liter PFI V-8, Formula	745	633	671
GTA (credit)	(300)	(255)	(255)
5.7-liter PFI V-8, Formula	1045	888	941
T/A	300	255	270
Requires 4-speed automatic transmission, engine oil cooler, 4-wheel disc brakes, limited-slip axle and 245/50ZR16 tires.			
5-speed manual transmission, GTA w/5.0			
(credit)	(515)	(438)	(438)
4-speed automatic transmission, exc. GTA .	515	438	464
Air conditioning, base	805	684	725

	Retail Price	Dealer Invoice	Low Price
Limited-slip differential, base & Formula . .	100	85	90
4-wheel disc brakes, Formula & T/A	179	152	161
Option Pkg. 1SB, base w/V-6	865	735	779
Air conditioning, bodyside moldings.			
Option Pkg. 1SC, base w/V-6	1603	1363	1443
Pkg. 1SB plus power windows and locks, 4-way manual driver's seat, door pockets, cruise control, remote hatch release, reading lamps.			
Option Pkg. 1SB, base w/V-8, Formula &			
T/A	495	421	446
Bodyside moldings, power windows and locks, door pockets.			
Option Pkg. 1SC, base w/V-8, Formula . .	889	756	800
T/A	854	726	769
Pkg. 1SB plus 4-way manual driver's seat, cruise control, remote hatch release, power mirrors, reading lamps.			
Value Option Pkg. (VOP), base & Formula .	820	697	738
T-top roof, AM/FM cassette.			
Value Option Pkg., T/A	889	756	800
T-top roof, AM/FM cassette, cargo screen.			
Value Option Pkg., GTA	1020	867	918
T-top roof, leather interior.			
Rear defogger, exc. GTA	160	136	144
Dual converter exhaust	155	132	140
Engine oil cooler, Formula & T/A	110	94	99
Hatch roof (T-tops)	920	782	828
Two-tone paint, base	150	128	135
Delete lower accent paint, Formula (credit) .	(150)	(128)	(128)
Power locks, exc. GTA	175	149	158
Power windows, exc. GTA	260	221	234
Power antenna, exc. GTA	75	64	68
AM/FM cassette, exc. GTA	150	128	135
AM/FM cassette w/EQ, exc. GTA	300	255	270
w/VOP	150	128	135
AM/FM radio w/CD player, exc. GTA	526	447	473
w/VOP	376	320	338
GTA	226	192	203
Cargo security screen, exc. GTA	69	59	62
Ventura leather trim, GTA	450	383	405
Sport Appearance Pkg., base	450	383	405
Trans Am fascias, fog lamps, sill moldings; available only with V-6.			
245/50ZR16 tires, T/A	385	327	347
Includes WS6 performance suspension.			
Warranty enhancements for New York . . .	65	55	59
California emissions pkg.	100	85	90

Pontiac Grand Am

What's New

More power and bigger wheels and tires highlight changes to Pontiac's best-selling car. The front-drive Grand Am continues in 2-door coupe and 4-door sedan body styles, each available in base LE and upgraded SE trim. Last year's turbocharged 2.0-liter four has been dropped, to be replaced as the standard SE engine by the High Output Quad 4 engine, a 16-valve, double-overhead-cam 2.3-liter 4-cylinder rated at 180 horsepower. Ordering the optional 3-speed automatic transmission mandates a base Quad 4 rated at 160 horsepower, 10 more than last year. Replacing 215/60R14 tires on all SEs for '90 are 205/55R16 Goodyear Eagle GT+4 tires. LE retains as standard a 110-horsepower 2.5-liter 4-cylinder engine. The optional LE engine is now the base Quad 4. Last year's 185/80R13 standard LE tires give way to 185/75R14s. And the LE gets a new Sport Option package for '90. It includes monochrome exterior paint, fog lamps, and alloy wheels. Every Grand Am gets a new drive axle design that Pontiac says eliminates shudder and reduces torque steer plus all engines are treated to noise-reduction measures. Among the changes inside, a cassette radio is now an SE standard and power windows get an express-down feature.

Prices are accurate at time of printing; subject to manufacturer's change.

Pontiac

Pontiac Grand Am SE

Outside, bright red paint is available for all models and slate gray metallic replaces gunmetal. Grand Am is similar to the Buick Skylark and Oldsmobile Calais, which comprise GM's N-body family of cars. All offer a similar selection of 4-cylinder engines, but Buick and Olds also make available a 3.3-liter V-6.

For

● Performance (Quad 4)

Against

● Noise (Quad 4) ● Rear seat room ● Trunk space

Summary

Grand Am is by far the most successful of the three N-body compacts, easy outselling the Skylark and Calais combined. Credit Pontiac's focused marketing, which aims Grand Am at younger buyers who want performance, or at least the performance look. With the base 2.5-liter engine, Grand Am is quite unexceptional. Either Quad 4 is a huge leap forward. Like any dohc 16-valve four, they must be revved a bit to uncork their power. That means a delay in throttle response if the automatic transmission has the engine trundling along at low rpm. On the other hand, the HO Quad 4 and the good-shifting 5-speed manual are a genuine performance team. But while Grand Am steals its styling cues from a European sports sedan, it neglected to borrow the genuine article's buttoned-down road manners and no-nonsense seats and ergonomics. As for the Grand Am's utility, we applaud the availability of a 4-door body style with the full complement of SE performance pieces. Pontiac's compact still can't match the interior or trunk space of similarly sized imports, however.

Specifications

	2-door notchback	4-door notchback
Wheelbase, in.	103.4	103.4
Overall length, in.	180.1	180.1
Overall width, in.	66.5	66.5
Overall height, in.	52.5	52.5
Turn diameter, ft.	35.4	35.4
Curb weight, lbs.	2508	2592
Cargo vol., cu. ft.	13.1	13.1
Fuel capacity, gals.	13.6	13.6
Seating capacity	5	5
Front headroom, in.	37.7	37.7
Front shoulder room, in.	52.6	54.7
Front legroom, max., in.	42.9	42.9
Rear headroom, in.	37.1	37.1
Rear shoulder room, in.	55.2	54.1
Rear legroom, min., in.	34.3	34.3

Powertrain layout: transverse front engine/front-wheel drive.

Engines

	ohv I-4	dohc I-4	dohc I-4
Size, liters/cu. in.	2.5/151	2.3/138	2.3/138
Fuel delivery	TBI	PFI	PFI
Horsepower @ rpm	110 @ 5200	160 @ 6200	180 @ 6200
Torque (lbs./ft.) @ rpm	135 @ 3200	155 @ 5200	160 @ 5200
Availability	S[1]	O	S[2]
EPA city/highway mpg			
5-speed OD manual	23/31	25/36	24/37
3-speed automatic	23/33	24/27	

1. LE 2. SE.

Prices

Pontiac Grand Am	Retail Price	Dealer Invoice	Low Price
LE 2-door notchback	$10544	$9416	$9616
LE 4-door notchback	10744	9594	9794
SE 2-door notchback	14894	13300	13500
SE 4-door notchback	15194	13568	13768
Destination charge	425	425	425

Standard equipment:

LE: 2.5-liter TBI 4-cylinder engine, 5-speed manual transmission, power steering, rear shoulder belts, tinted glass, dual outside mirrors, AM/FM radio, cloth reclining front bucket seats, remote fuel door release, left visor mirror, 185/75R14 tires. **SE** adds: 2.3-liter DOHC 16-valve PFI HO Quad 4, WS6 sport suspension, monotone exterior treatment, sill moldings, air conditioning, remote decklid release, fog lamps, power windows and locks, split folding rear seat, tachometer, trip odometer, coolant temperature and oil pressure gauges, voltmeter, leather-wrapped steering wheel, shift knob and brake handle, 205/55R16 Goodyear Eagle GT + 4 tires on alloy wheels.

Optional equipment:

2.3-liter Quad 4, LE	660	561	594
SE (credit)	(140)	(119)	(119)
Available only with automatic transmission.			
3-speed automatic transmission	540	459	486
Air conditioning, base	720	612	648
Option Pkg. 1SB, LE	910	774	819
Air conditioning, tilt steering column, intermittent wipers.			
Option Pkg. 1SC, LE	1105	939	995
Pkg. 1SA plus cruise control.			
Option Pkg. 1SD, LE 2-door	1817	1544	1635
LE 4-door	1922	1634	1730
Pkg. 1SC plus remote decklid release, split folding rear seat, fog lamps, power windows and locks.			
Option Pkg. 1SB, SE	321	273	289
Power driver's seat, power mirrors.			
Value Option Pkg. (VOP) R6A, LE	394	335	355
AM/FM cassette, 195/70R14 tires on alloy wheels.			
Value Option Pkg. R6B, LE	455	387	410
LE 2-door w/Pkg. 1SD	40	34	36
LE 4-door	520	442	468
LE 4-door w/Pkg. 1SD	NC	NC	NC
Power windows and locks, AM/FM cassette.			
Rear defogger	160	136	144
Rally cluster gauges, LE	127	108	114
Decklid luggage rack	115	98	104
Two-tone paint, LE	101	86	91
Power locks, LE 2-door	175	149	158
LE 4-door	215	183	194
Power windows, LE 2-door	240	204	216
LE 4-door	305	259	275
Sport Option Pkg., LE	476	405	428
LE w/VOP R6A	97	82	87
LE w/Pkg. 1SD	379	322	341
Monotone paint treatment, fog lamps, 195/70R14 tires on alloy wheels.			

	Retail Price	Dealer Invoice	Low Price
AM/FM cassette, LE	140	119	126
AM/FM radio w/CD & EQ, LE	545	463	491
LE w/VOP, SE	405	344	365
Removable glass sunroof, SE	350	298	315
195/70R14 tires, LE	114	97	103
Alloy wheels, LE	265	225	239
Warranty enhancements for New York . . .	65	55	59
California emissions pkg.	100	85	90

Pontiac Grand Prix

Pontiac Grand Prix LE

What's New

The first 4-door to wear the Grand Prix name debuts as Pontiac's version of the front-drive General Motors W-body cars, which also appear in sedan form for '90 as the Chevrolet Lumina, Buick Regal, and Oldsmobile Cutlass Supreme. The Grand Prix sedan shares with the Grand Prix coupe its 107.5-inch wheelbase, but the sedan is about one inch longer overall and has slightly more head and rear leg room. Available initially only in LE trim, an STE (Special Touring Edition) version of the sedan is due about half-way through the model year. It'll give the 4-door Grand Prix a dose of horsepower unavailable on the other W-body sedans with its optional turbocharged 3.1-liter V-6, the same engine that's standard on the Turbo Grand Prix Coupe. The Turbo is a limited-production model, and pricing information wasn't available. The turbo engine is available only with a 4-speed automatic transmission. The STE's standard powertrain is a naturally aspirated 3.1-liter V-6 mated to a 5-speed manual transmission; a 4-speed automatic is optional. Compared to the LE, the STE gets a slightly altered grille and taillights, and its standard features include high-performance tires, alloy wheels, the Y99 sport suspension, anti-lock brakes, analog instrumentation, and an upgraded interior. The LE's standard powertrain is the 16-valve Quad 4 4-cylinder; its optional engine is the 3.1 V-6. A 40/60 split front bench seat is standard on the LE, anti-lock brakes are optional. In Grand Prix coupe news, the base coupe has been discontinued, leaving LE, SE, and Turbo trim levels. The Quad 4 is standard on the LE; the 3.1 V-6 is optional on the LE and standard on SE. The 2.8-liter V-6 has been dropped. The limited edition Turbo Grand Prix coupe, introduced during the '89 model year, returns unchanged for '90 with a planned production of 5000. It supplants analog instrumentation with a head-up display that projects a digital speedometer and turn-signal readouts onto the windshield in front of the driver.

For

- Anti-lock brakes
- Ride
- Handling (SE, STE)
- Passenger room
- Trunk space

Against

- Engine noise
- Instruments/controls

Summary

GM's sportiest W-body finally gets up some gumption with the high-performance turbocharged models, but the big news is that the Grand Prix name, long associated with personal-luxury coupes, has gone 4-door. Sedans accounted for 38 percent of all cars sold in 1980, but grew to 56 percent in '89. Pontiac hopes the upscale Grand Prix image will attract some of those new buyers to its 4-door. Image will be important, because in reality, the Grand Prix sedan differs little from its Buick, Olds, and Chevy cousins. Its cabin has more of a continental flair, but still doesn't capture the Europeans' maturity and purposefulness. Pontiac's suspension tuning gives the Grand Prix somewhat more composed road manners than the other W-body cars, especially over bumps and dips, though the differences are subtle. And just like the other W-body sedans, the Grand Prix works best not with a manual transmission or the Quad 4, but with an automatic and the V-6. The ace up the Grand Prix's sleeve is the turbocharged STE sedan. It gives committed domestic buyers a high-performance alternative to the Ford Taurus SHO. The Pontiac will probably cost several thousand more than the less luxurious and somewhat faster $21,500 SHO. But ABS is standard on the STE, optional on the SHO, and the STE has an automatic transmission, which is unavailable on the Ford.

Specifications	2-door notchback	4-door notchback
Wheelbase, in.	107.5	107.5
Overall length, in.	193.9	194.8
Overall width, in.	70.9	70.9
Overall height, in.	52.8	54.3
Turn diameter, ft.	37.4	37.4
Curb weight, lbs.	3186	3250
Cargo vol., cu. ft.	15.0	15.5
Fuel capacity, gals.	16.0	16.0
Seating capacity	6	6
Front headroom, in.	37.8	38.8
Front shoulder room, in.	57.3	57.2
Front legroom, max., in.	42.3	42.4
Rear headroom, in.	36.6	37.6
Rear shoulder room, in.	57.3	57.4
Rear legroom, min., in.	34.8	36.2

Powertrain layout: transverse front engine/front-wheel drive.

Engines	dohc I-4	ohv V-6	Turbo ohv V-6
Size, liters/cu. in.	2.3/138	3.1/191	3.1/191
Fuel delivery	PFI	PFI	PFI
Horsepower @ rpm	160 @ 6200	140 @ 4800	205 @ 4800
Torque (lbs./ft.) @ rpm	155 @ 5200	180 @ 3600	220 @ 3200
Availability	S	S[1]	S[2]

> **KEY: ohv** = overhead valve; **ohc** = overhead cam; **dohc** = double overhead cam; **I** = inline cylinders; **V** = cylinders in V configuration; **flat** = horizontally opposed cylinders; **bbl.** = barrel (carburetor); **PFI** = port (multi-point) fuel injection; **TBI** = throttle-body (single-point) fuel injection; **rpm** = revolutions per minute; **OD** = overdrive transmission; **S** = standard; **O** = optional; **NA** = not available.

Prices are accurate at time of printing; subject to manufacturer's change.

EPA city/highway mpg	Retail Price	Dealer Invoice	Low Price
5-speed OD manual		19/28	
3-speed automatic	22/29		
4-speed OD automatic		19/30	16/25

1. SE, STE 2. Grand Prix Turbo.

Prices

Pontiac Grand Prix	Retail Price	Dealer Invoice	Low Price
LE 2-door notchback	$14564	$12569	$12769
LE 4-door notchback	14564	12569	12769
SE 2-door notchback	17684	15261	15461
Destination charge	455	455	455

Standard equipment:

LE: 2.3-liter DOHC 16-valve PFI Quad 4, 3-speed automatic transmission, cloth 40/60 split bench seat with folding armrest and recliners, AM/FM radio, remote fuel door release, tinted glass, left remote and right manual mirrors, coolant temperature gauge, trip odometer, visor mirrors, door pockets, 195/75R14 tires (4-door), 205/65R15 tires (2-door). **SE** adds: 3.1-liter PFI V-6, 4-speed automatic transmission, power windows and locks, AM/FM cassette, articulating bucket seats, power driver's seat, rear bucket seats with pass-through, tachometer, oil pressure gauge, voltmeter, leather-wrapped steering wheel, tilt steering column, seatback pockets, 215/60R16 Goodyear Eagle GT+4 tires on alloy wheels.

Optional equipment:

	Retail	Dealer	Low
3.1-liter V-6, LE	NC	NC	NC
Requires 4-speed automatic transmission.			
4-speed automatic transmission, LE w/V-6 .	200	170	180
SE	640	544	576
5-speed manual transmission, LE 2-door w/V-6 (credit)	(440)	(374)	(374)
Anti-lock brakes	925	786	833
LE requires Pkg. 1SE.			
Option Pkg. 1SB, LE	190	162	171
Tilt steering column, intermittent wipers.			
Option Pkg. 1SC, LE 2-door	470	400	423
Pkg. 1SB plus cruise control, tachometer, oil pressure gauge, voltmeter.			
Option Pkg. 1SD, LE 2-door	1603	1363	1443
Pkg. 1SC plus power windows and locks, remote decklid release, custom trim, alloy wheels, AM/FM cassette, power antenna.			
Option Pkg. 1SE, LE 2-door	2162	1838	1946
Pkg. 1SD plus power driver's seat, lighted visor mirrors, power mirrors, remote keyless entry.			
Option Pkg. 1SC, LE 4-door	385	327	347
Pkg. 1SB plus cruise control.			
Option Pkg. 1SD, LE 4-door	1808	1537	1627
Pkg. 1SC plus tachometer, oil pressure gauge, voltmeter, security lighting, power windows and locks, remote decklid release, custom trim, styled steel wheels, AM/FM cassette, power antenna.			
Option Pkg. 1SE, LE 4-door	2487	2114	2238
Pkg. 1SD plus power driver's seat, lighted right visor mirror, power mirrors, remote keyless entry.			
Option Pkg. 1SB, SE	561	477	505
Power antenna, lighted visor mirrors, remote keyless entry, electronic compass with trip computer and service reminder.			
Value Option Pkg. (VOP), LE 2-door	865	735	779
Custom sport bucket seats, AM/FM cassette with EQ, sunroof.			
Value Option Pkg. R6A, LE 4-door	409	348	368
AM/FM cassette, 205/65R15 tires on alloy wheels.			

	Retail Price	Dealer Invoice	Low Price
Value Option Pkg. R6B, LE 4-door	464	394	418
Pkg. R6A plus two-tone paint.			
Value Option Pkg., SE	975	829	878
Articulating seats with leather trim, sunroof.			
Rear defogger	160	136	144
Two-tone paint, LE	105	89	95
Power locks, LE 2-door	175	149	158
LE 4-door	215	183	194
Power sunroof	650	553	585
Power windows, LE 2-door	240	204	216
LE 4-door	305	259	275
AM/FM cassette, LE	140	119	126
AM/FM cassette w/EQ, LE	400	340	360
Requires Pkg. 1SD or 1SE.			
AM/FM radio w/CD player & EQ, LE . . .	626	532	563
LE 2-door w/VOP, SE	226	192	203
Not available with Quad 4.			
Bucket seats & console, LE	110	94	99
Requires Pkg. 1SC.			
Custom sport bucket seats, LE	140	119	126
Ventura leather articulating seats, SE . . .	450	383	405
Requires Pkg. 1SB.			
Power driver's seat, LE	270	230	243
Requires Pkg. 1SC, 1SD or 1SE.			
Sport Appearance Pkg.			
LE 2-door w/Pkg. 1SB or 1SC	285	242	257
LE 2-door w/Pkg. 1SD or 1SE	160	136	144
LE 4-door w/Pkg. 1SB or 1SC	480	408	432
LE 4-door w/Pkg. 1SD	280	238	252
LE 4-door w/Pkg. 1SE or VOP	160	136	144
SE front fascia with fog lamps, specific moldings, 205/65R15 tires on alloy wheels.			
195/75R14 WSW tires, LE 4-door	72	61	65
205/65R15 tires, LE 4-door	54	46	49
15" styled wheels, LE 4-door	145	123	131
15" alloy wheels, LE 2-door	125	106	113
LE 4-door	265	225	239
LE 4-door w/Pkg. 1SD	120	102	108
Warranty enhancements for New York . . .	65	55	59
California emissions pkg.	100	85	90

KEY: ohv = overhead valve; **ohc** = overhead cam; **dohc** = double overhead cam; **I** = inline cylinders; **V** = cylinders in V configuration; **flat** = horizontally opposed cylinders; **bbl.** = barrel (carburetor); **PFI** = port (multi-point) fuel injection; **TBI** = throttle-body (single-point) fuel injection; **rpm** = revolutions per minute; **OD** = overdrive transmission; **S** = standard; **O** = optional; **NA** = not available.

Pontiac LeMans

Pontiac LeMans GSE

What's New

Introduction of the '90 version of Pontiac's Korean-built front-drive subcompact has been delayed until December '89 or January 1990. Pontiac blames the postponement on holdups in the installation of motorized front shoulder belts. When

LeMans does return, the uplevel SE sedan will have been dropped, leaving only the base LE sedan and a 3-door hatchback in stripper Value Leader trim, mid-line LE guise, and sporty GSE equipment. Built in Korea by Daewoo Motor Company (partly owned by General Motors), LeMans was designed by GM's Opel division in West Germany. All but the GSE use a 1.6-liter 4-cylinder engine. The GSE comes with a 2.0-liter four. GSE and LE models have a 5-speed manual transmission standard and are optional with a 3-speed automatic. The Value Leader is available only with a 4-speed manual transmission. For '90, the 1.6-liter cars get a brake-feel improvement package with a larger master cylinder and power brake booster. They also get a ride and handling improvement package with new spring and shock isolators, and a retuned suspension with a larger stabilizer bar. The GSE gets quicker-ratio steering this year. All models receive revised door trim panels and all except the Value Leader get a revised radio with knob controls instead of levers.

For

- Fuel economy   • Cargo space

Against

- Performance and driveability   • Noise

Summary

LeMans doesn't show much of its German heritage on the road, or much of a cost benefit from being built in Korea. The LE is reasonably surefooted on the road, but inordinately slow with automatic transmission. While the better-handling GSE's 2.0-liter and 5-speed make for acceptable power, the engine is coarse and noisy and the shift action is rubbery. Fuel economy is a high point, but LeMans in any guise suffers a stiff, jiggly ride on bumpy pavement. The car's 99.2-inch wheelbase is long for a subcompact, so there's more leg room and cargo space than in some rivals. The sedan's rear doors are too small for good access to the back seat and its trunk opening is undersized, though cargo volume can be increased by folding the rear seatback. The base LeMans is attractively priced, but not as well furnished or even as well built as a base Hyundai Excel, which also is made in Korea. The GSE can't hold a performance candle to such rivals as the Honda Civic Si, while an LE with automatic transmission, power steering and air conditioning runs well over $10,000, which isn't a bargain in this class. We can't recommend a LeMans.

Specifications

	3-door hatchback	4-door notchback
Wheelbase, in.	99.2	99.2
Overall length, in.	163.7	172.4
Overall width, in.	65.5	65.7
Overall height, in.	53.5	53.7
Turn diameter, ft.	32.8	32.8
Curb weight, lbs.	2136	2235
Cargo vol., cu. ft.	18.8	18.4
Fuel capacity, gals.	13.2	13.2
Seating capacity	5	5
Front headroom, in.	38.8	38.8
Front shoulder room, in.	53.5	53.5
Front legroom, max., in.	42.0	42.0
Rear headroom, in.	38.0	38.0
Rear shoulder room, in.	53.4	53.4
Rear legroom, min., in.	32.8	32.8

Powertrain layout: transverse front engine/front-wheel drive.

Engines

	ohc I-4	ohc I-4
Size, liters/cu. in.	1.6/98	2.0/121
Fuel delivery	TBI	TBI
Horsepower @ rpm	74 @	96 @
	5600	4800
Torque (lbs./ft.) @ rpm	90 @	118 @
	2800	3600
Availability	S	S[1]

EPA city/highway mpg

4-speed OD manual	30/39	
5-speed OD manual	31/40	24/30
3-speed automatic	27/32	22/28

1. GSE.

Prices

Pontiac LeMans (1989 prices)	Retail Price	Dealer Invoice	Low Price
Aerocoupe Value Leader 3-door hatchback	$6599	$6104	$6200
Aerocoupe LE 3-door hatchback	7999	7359	7492
LE 4-door notchback	8349	7681	7820
SE 4-door notchback	9749	8774	9036
Aerocoupe GSE 3-door hatchback	9499	8549	8804
Destination charge	315	315	315

Standard equipment:

Value Leader: 1.6-liter TBI 4-cylinder engine, 4-speed manual transmission, power brakes, reclining front bucket seats, rear defogger, tachometer, trip odometer, outboard rear lap/shoulder belts, cargo area cover, 175/70SR13 tires with full-size spare. **LE** adds: 5-speed manual transmission, tinted glass, dual remote mirrors, right visor mirror, AM/FM ST ET with clock, swing-out rear side windows (Aerocoupe; roll-down on 4-door). **SE** adds: 2.0-liter engine, sport suspension, sport seats with height adjusters, 60/40 folding rear seat, tilt steering column, fog lamps, 185/60HR14 tires. **GSE** adds: front air dam with fog lamps, sill extensions, rear spoiler, alloy wheels.

Optional equipment:

3-speed automatic transmission (NA VL)	445	378	409
Air conditioning	680	578	626
Requires power steering; not available on VL).			
Power steering, LE & SE	214	182	197
Cruise control	185	157	170
AM/FM ST ET, VL	307	261	282
AM/FM ST ET cassette, VL	429	365	395
Others	122	104	112
Luggage carrier	95	81	87
Removable sunroof	350	298	322

Pontiac Sunbird

What's New

Once, all General Motors divisions had a version of the front-drive J-car, but only the Sunbird and Chevrolet Cavalier survive into 1990. Sunbird wings its way into its ninth model year on a slightly revised exterior and some under-the-skin refinement. This subcompact is available as a 2-door coupe in LE, SE, and GT trim; as an LE 4-door sedan; and as an LE convertible. The SE and GT models get a new hood, front fenders, front fascia, and hidden headlamps for '90; the GT also gets new rear-fender and side-rocker extensions. The SE's standard tire size goes up from 185/80R13 to 185/75R14. All '90 Sunbirds get passive front restraints in the form of lap and shoulder belts that can remain buckled while the door opens, and Pontiac says new drive-axle machining means less shudder on acceleration. Most Sunbirds use a 96-horse-

Prices are accurate at time of printing; subject to manufacturer's change.

Pontiac Sunbird GT

power 2.0-liter 4-cylinder engine. A 165-horsepower turbocharged version of the 2.0 is standard on the GT coupe and optional on the convertible. With the Cavalier Z24 convertible replaced by the Beretta ragtop in the Chevy line for '90, the Sunbird LE becomes the sole J-car convertible. Pontiac had previously offered the Sunbird soft top in GT trim, but the car drops a notch to the LE level for 1990. Pontiac says it's a price-reducing move that will triple Sunbird convertible sales. The convertible features a power top and for 1990 has a new snap-on boot to cover the lowered roof.

For

- Performance (Turbo) • Fuel economy
- Handling/roadholding (SE, GT) • Convertible availability

Against

- Performance (base engine/automatic) • Rear seat room

Summary

Sunbird differs from its Cavalier and Skyhawk cousins by virtue of its overhead-cam engines (Chevy and Buick use overhead-valve engines) and a marketing approach that leans more toward sportiness and performance than value or luxury. The 96-horsepower base engine provides decent acceleration and good fuel economy with the 5-speed manual transmission, but loses some of its zest and economy with the optional 3-speed automatic. The 165-horsepower turbocharged four will snap your head back in hard acceleration. Keep both hands on the wheel, however, because the abrupt rush of power can wrench the front tires off course. And be prepared to endure a loud, raspy exhaust. Handling and roadholding are best on the GT, but its wide performance tires contribute to a stiff ride. The SE coupe's narrower, all-season tires improve the ride, but lack the cornering grip of the GT's rubber. The convertible is an attractively priced way to go topless, especially with the optional turbo package, which includes the turbo engine, 215/60R14 tires in place of 185/75R14s, a sport suspension, and rally instruments.

KEY: **ohv** = overhead valve; **ohc** = overhead cam; **dohc** = double overhead cam; **I** = inline cylinders; **V** = cylinders in V configuration; **flat** = horizontally opposed cylinders; **bbl.** = barrel (carburetor); **PFI** = port (multi-point) fuel injection; **TBI** = throttle-body (single-point) fuel injection; **rpm** = revolutions per minute; **OD** = overdrive transmission; **S** = standard; **O** = optional; **NA** = not available.

Specifications

	2-door notchback	4-door notchback	2-door conv.
Wheelbase, in.	101.2	101.2	101.2
Overall length, in.	178.2	181.7	178.2
Overall width, in.	65.0	65.0	65.0
Overall height, in.	50.4	53.8	51.9
Turn diameter, ft.	34.3	34.3	34.3
Curb weight, lbs.	2420	2487	2662
Cargo vol., cu. ft.	14.0	15.2	10.4
Fuel capacity, gals.	13.6	13.6	13.6
Seating capacity	5	5	4
Front headroom, in.	37.7	38.6	38.5
Front shoulder room, in.	53.7	48.8	53.7
Front legroom, max., in.	42.2	42.2	42.2
Rear headroom, in.	36.1	37.9	37.4
Rear shoulder room, in.	52.6	53.7	38.0
Rear legroom, min., in.	31.8	34.3	31.8

Powertrain layout: transverse front engine/front-wheel drive.

Engines

	ohc I-4	Turbo ohc I-4
Size, liters/cu. in.	2.0/121	2.0/121
Fuel delivery	TBI	PFI
Horsepower @ rpm	96 @ 4800	165 @ 5500
Torque (lbs./ft.) @ rpm	118 @ 3600	175 @ 4000
Availability	S	S[1]

EPA city/highway mpg

5-speed OD manual	27/36	21/31
3-speed automatic	23/31	20/27

1. GT Coupe.

Prices

Pontiac Sunbird	Retail Price	Dealer Invoice	Low Price
LE 2-door notchback	$8799	$7858	$8058
LE 4-door notchback	8899	7947	8147
LE 2-door convertible	13934	12434	12634
SE 2-door notchback	9204	8219	8419
GT 2-door notchback	11724	10470	10670
Destination charge	425	425	425

Standard equipment:

LE: 2.0-liter TBI 4-cylinder engine, 5-speed manual transmission, power brakes, rear deflector (wagon), reclining front bucket seats, outboard rear lap/shoulder belts, AM/FM radio, 185/75R14 tires; convertible has power top, power windows and locks. **SE** adds: moldings, rally gauges with tachometer, 195/70R14 tires. **GT** adds: turbo engine, rally suspension, console, engine block heater, rally gauges with tachometer and trip odometer, tinted glass, AM/FM cassette, left remote and right manual mirrors, 215/60R14 Goodyear Eagle GT tires on alloy wheels.

Optional equipment:

2.0-liter non-turbo engine, GT (credit)	(768)	(653)	(653)
2.0-liter turbo engine pkg., LE conv.	1402	1192	1262
LE conv. w/VOP	1023	870	921
Includes rally gauge cluster, engine block heater, FE3 suspension, 215/60R14 tires on alloy wheels.			
3-speed automatic transmission	465	395	419
Air conditioning	720	612	648
Option Pkg. 1SB, LE	416	354	374
Tinted glass, power steering, left remote and right manual mirrors, floormats.			
Option Pkg. 1SC, LE 2-door	1462	1243	1316
LE 4-door	1468	1248	1321
Pkg. 1SB plus air conditioning, tilt steering column, intermittent wipers, lamp group, front seat armrest, rally gauges.			

CONSUMER GUIDE®

	Retail Price	Dealer Invoice	Low Price
Option Pkg. 1SD, LE 2-door	1857	1578	1671
LE 4-door	1863	1584	1677

Pkg. 1SC plus cruise control, remote decklid release, split folding rear seat.

Option Pkg. 1SB, LE conv.	1046	889	941

Air conditioning, tilt steering column, intermittent wipers, lamp group, front seat armrest, rally gauges.

Option Pkg. 1SC, LE conv.	1369	1164	1232

Pkg. 1SB plus cruise control, remote decklid release, tachometer.

Option Pkg. 1SB, SE	416	354	374

Power steering, tinted glass, left remote and right manual mirrors, floormats.

Option Pkg. 1SC, SE	1413	1201	1272

Pkg. 1SB plus air conditioning, tilt steering column, intermittent wipers, lamp group, front seat armrest.

Option Pkg. 1SD, SE	1886	1603	1697

Pkg. 1SC plus cruise control, remote decklid release, rally gauges with tachometer, split folding rear seat.

Option Pkg. 1SB, GT	1122	954	1010

Air conditioning, tilt steering column, floormats, lamp group, intermittent wipers, split folding rear seat.

Option Pkg. 1SC, GT	1367	1162	1230

Pkg. 1SB plus cruise control and remote decklid release.

Value Option Pkg. (VOP), LE	374	318	337
SE	469	399	422

AM/FM cassette, 195/70R14 tires on alloy wheels.

Cruise control, LE	195	166	176
Rear defogger	160	136	144
Power locks, 2-door	175	149	158
4-door	215	183	194
Power windows, 2-door	230	196	207
4-door	295	251	266
AM/FM cassette, LE & SE	170	145	153
AM/FM radio w/CD player, SE & LE	396	337	356
SE & LE w/VOP, GT	192	163	173
Decklid spoiler, LE conv.	70	60	63
Removable sunroof, SE & GT	350	298	315
195/70R14 tires, LE & SE	114	97	103
14" alloy wheels, LE	265	225	239
SE (includes rear spoiler)	335	285	302
Two-tone paint, LE	101	86	91
Warranty enhancements for New York	65	55	59
California emissions pkg.	100	85	90

Pontiac Trans Sport

What's New

Pontiac's version of the new General Motors minivan is called the Trans Sport. It shares with the Chevrolet Lumina APV and the Oldsmobile Silhouette a front-drive layout and a mandatory 120-horsepower 3.1-liter V-6 hooked to a 3-speed automatic transmission. The Lumina APV is slanted toward family duty and will account for about 69 percent of the 140,000 GM minivans to be built during the 1990 production year. The Silhouette is geared toward a more upscale audience and will be about four percent of production. Pontiac, meanwhile hopes the Trans Sport can translate the division's performance image into the minivan arena. Trans Sport is available in base and SE versions. Both come with reclining front bucket seats. The base model has a 3-place middle bench with a pair of rear buckets optionally available. Optional on the base model and standard on SE is a 2+2+2 configuration. The second- and third-row seatbacks can be folded to form a flat load area of roughly 4-by-6 feet. The SE comes standard with alloy wheels and 195/70R15 tires in place of 205/70R14s on the base model. The SE also has a monochrome exterior treatment with polyurethane lower-body aero moldings and a gloss-black roof treatment and a load-leveling suspension. Because the full-size Safari station wagon has

Pontiac Trans Sport

been discontinued, the Trans Sport is now Pontiac's premier people mover.

For

- Passenger room • Quietness • Entry/exit • Ride

Against

- Performance • Visibility

Summary

Trans Sport's positive and negative features mirror those of the Lumina APV and the Silhouette, so see our reviews of those vehicles for an idea of what we like and don't like. In general, GM has achieved a car-like driving feel for its new minivans, though they seem underpowered when called upon for anything more than gentle acceleration. Trans Sport is easy to climb into and out of and its seatbacks fold down individually to make convenient tables with cup holders. The second- and third-row seats also can be tilted forward to increase floor space. Finally, the bucket seats weigh only 34 pounds each and have quick-release mounts that make their removal easier. The body panels are made of a plastic-like material designed to take minor impacts and spring back without damage. The Trans Sport's 17.25-square-foot windshield is sloped at a 66-degree angle. A special layer of metallic film, nearly invisible to the eye, is embedded in the windshield glass to reduce the solar load. The windshield wipers are 24 inches long and contain washer nozzles to clean the glass. Pontiac modeled the Trans Sport's dashboard on that of the Grand Prix. The instrument cluster is flanked by pods containing controls for the washer/wiper system and the headlamps. Storage includes front-door map pockets, a pullout ashtray and cup holder below the radio, an upper instrument-panel storage bin, and a traditional glovebox. Overriding all other impressions of the Trans Sport and its sister GM minivans is the snout-nosed styling. It does indeed set them apart visually from box-like rivals, but it also creates a daunting view from the driver's seat. You feel far removed from the road ahead, a problem that's more pronounced in city driving, where maneuvering room may be at a premium.

Specifications

	4-door van
Wheelbase, in.	109.9
Overall length, in.	194.5
Overall width, in.	74.2
Overall height, in.	65.5
Turn diameter, ft.	42.5

Prices are accurate at time of printing; subject to manufacturer's change.

	4-door van
Curb weight, lbs.	3500
Cargo vol., cu. ft.	104.6
Fuel capacity, gals.	20.0
Seating capacity	7
Front headroom, in.	40.2
Front shoulder room, in.	53.5
Front legroom, max., in.	40.7
Rear headroom, in.	38.6
Rear shoulder room, in.	61.6
Rear legroom, min., in.	33.7

Powertrain layout: transverse front engine/front-wheel drive.

Engines

	ohv V-6
Size, liters/cu. in.	3.1/191
Fuel delivery	TBI
Horsepower @ rpm	120 @ 4200
Torque (lbs./ft.) @ rpm	175 @ 2200
Availability	S

EPA city/highway mpg

3-speed automatic	18/23

Prices

Pontiac Trans Sport	Retail Price	Dealer Invoice	Low Price
4-door van	$14995	$13391	—
SE 4-door van	18125	16186	—
Destination charge	500	500	500

Low price not available at time of publication.

Standard equipment:

3.1-liter TBI V-6, 3-speed automatic transmission, power steering, 5-passenger seating (reclining front bucket seats, middle bench seat), tinted glass, tachometer, coolant temperature and oil pressure gauges, voltmeter, trip odometer, AM/FM radio, door pockets, beverage holders, 205/70R14 tires. **SE** adds: 6-passenger seating (three second row and two third row modular seats), air conditioning, pneumatic load leveling, deep-tint glass, AM/FM cassette, leather-wrapped steering wheel, Lamp Group, tilt steering column, cruise control, built-in inflator, 195/70R15 Goodyear Eagle GT + 4 tires on alloy wheels.

Optional equipment:

Air conditioning, base	805	684	—
6-passenger seating, base	525	446	—
Reclining front bucket seats, 2 second row and 2 third row modular seats.			
7-passenger seating, base	675	574	—
Reclining front bucket seats, 3 second row and 2 third row modular seats.			
Option Pkg. 1SB, base	1195	1016	—
Air conditioning, Lamp Group, cruise control, tilt steering column.			
Option Pkg. 1SC, base	1960	1666	—
Pkg. 1SB plus power windows and locks, power driver's seat.			
Option Pkg. 1SB, SE	765	650	—
Power windows and locks, power driver's seat.			
Rear defogger	160	136	—
Deep-tint glass, base	245	208	—

KEY: ohv = overhead valve; **ohc** = overhead cam; **dohc** = double overhead cam; **I** = inline cylinders; **V** = cylinders in V configuration; **flat** = horizontally opposed cylinders; **bbl.** = barrel (carburetor); **PFI** = port (multi-point) fuel injection; **TBI** = throttle-body (single-point) fuel injection; **rpm** = revolutions per minute; **OD** = overdrive transmission; **S** = standard; **O** = optional; **NA** = not available.

	Retail Price	Dealer Invoice	Low Price
Power locks	255	217	—
Power windows	240	204	—
Requires power locks.			
AM/FM cassette, base	140	119	—
AM/FM radio w/CD player & EQ, base	516	439	—
SE	376	320	—
Alloy wheels, base	265	225	—
Warranty enhancements for New York	65	55	—
California emissions pkg.	100	85	—

Pontiac 6000

Pontiac 6000 S/E AWD

What's New

Some label changes and a more powerful standard V-6 mark the 6000 for '90. This is Pontiac's version of the cars General Motors also markets as Buick Century and Oldsmobile Cutlass Ciera sedans and wagons and as the Chevrolet Celebrity wagon. Only Pontiac, however, offers a 4-wheel drive model. All-Wheel Drive has been made an option this year and is available only on the S/E sedan. Last year, the top-of-the-line 6000 STE came standard with 4WD. Pontiac this year has transferred the STE label to the new Grand Prix sedan, however. The 6000's 4WD hardware itself is unchanged, remaining a permanently engaged system that splits engine torque 60 percent front/40 percent rear. The S/E AWD gets most of the '89 STE's standard equipment, including a 3.1-liter V-6, 3-speed automatic transmission, and 4-wheel anti-lock disc brakes. The 3.1 six replaces a 2.8-liter V-6 as the standard engine on the front-wheel-drive S/E and LE wagon, and as the optional V-6 on the LE sedan. The 3.1 is rated at 140 horsepower, 10 more than the 2.8, and has 185 pounds/feet of torque, against 170 for the 2.8. A 110-horsepower 2.5-liter 4-cylinder engine remains standard on the LE sedan. Among other changes, the front shoulder/seat belts can be left buckled as a passive restraint system, air conditioning is now standard on all models except the LE sedan, and the LE gets new front seats with added contour.

For

- Passenger and cargo room   • Quietness
- Handling (S/E)   • 4WD traction (S/E)
- Anti-lock brakes (S/E AWD)

Against

- Performance (4-cylinder)   • Handling (LE)

Summary

Though they were introduced for the '82 model year, the 6000 and the similar Celebrity wagon remain mid-size cars that offer good value for the money. Passenger and cargo room are comparable to the Ford Taurus and Mercury Sable, and the 3.1-liter V-6 engine furnishes the power for adequate performance with a full load. In addition, the 6000 S/E models have firmer suspensions and wider tires that combine to improve handling and roadholding over the base LE versions. Buick and Oldsmobile offer similar versions of this same design at slightly higher prices, but their only real advantage is a 3.3-liter V-6 that produces 160 horsepower, 20 more than the 3.1 V-6 used by Pontiac and Chevy. The 4WD S/E costs a lot more than the other 6000s, but has the equipment to justify its higher price.

Specifications

	4-door notchback	5-door wagon
Wheelbase, in.	104.9	104.9
Overall length, in.	188.8	193.2
Overall width, in.	72.0	72.0
Overall height, in.	53.7	54.1
Turn diameter, ft.	37.0	37.0
Curb weight, lbs.	2843	3162
Cargo vol., cu. ft.	15.2	74.4
Fuel capacity, gals.	15.7	15.7
Seating capacity	6	8
Front headroom, in.	38.5	38.6
Front shoulder room, in.	56.3	56.2
Front legroom, max., in.	42.2	42.1
Rear headroom, in.	37.8	38.9
Rear shoulder room, in.	56.5	56.2
Rear legroom, min., in.	36.5	34.7

Powertrain layout: transverse front engine/front-wheel drive.

Engines

	ohv I-4	ohv V-6
Size, liters/cu. in.	2.5/151	3.1/191
Fuel delivery	TBI	PFI
Horsepower @ rpm	110 @ 5200	140 @ 4800
Torque (lbs./ft.) @ rpm	135 @ 3200	180 @ 3200
Availability	S[1]	S

EPA city/highway mpg

3-speed automatic	24/31	20/29

1. LE sedan.

Prices

Pontiac 6000

	Retail Price	Dealer Invoice	Low Price
LE 4-door notchback	$12149	$10485	$10685
LE 5-door wagon	15309	13212	13412
S/E 4-door notchback	16909	14592	14792
S/E 5-door wagon	18509	15973	16173
Destination charge	450	450	450

Standard equipment:

LE: 2.5-liter TBI 4-cylinder engine, 3-speed automatic transmission (4-door; wagon has 3.1-liter PFI V-6 and 4-speed automatic transmission), power steering, air conditioning (wagon), AM/FM radio, tinted glass, cloth front bench seat with armrest, split folding second seat (wagon), rear defogger (wagon), rear shoulder belts, 185/75R14 SBR tires. **S/E** adds: 3.1-liter PFI V-6, 4-speed automatic transmission, air conditioning, tachometer, trip odometer, voltmeter, coolant temperature and oil pressure gauges, intermittent wipers, power windows and locks, AM/FM cassette, rear defogger, luggage rack (wagon), cloth reclining bucket seats, leather-wrapped steering wheel, sport suspension, Electronic Ride Control (wagon), 195/70R15 Goodyear Eagle GT + 4 tires on alloy wheels.

Optional equipment:	Retail Price	Dealer Invoice	Low Price
3.1-liter V-6, LE 4-door	660	561	594
4-speed automatic transmission, LE 4-door	200	170	180
Requires V-6 and Pkg. 1SC or 1SD.			
All Wheel Drive Pkg., SE 4-door	3635	3090	3272
Includes anti-lock brakes, 3-speed automatic transmission, automatic level control, specific fog lamps, rear spoiler.			
Air conditioning, LE 4-door	805	684	725
Option Pkg. 1SB, LE 4-door	995	846	896
LE wagon	190	162	171
Air conditioning (std. wagon), tilt steering column, intermittent wipers.			
Option Pkg. 1SC, LE 4-door	1190	1012	1071
LE wagon	385	327	347
Pkg. 1SB plus cruise control.			
Option Pkg. 1SD, LE 4-door	2058	1749	1852
LE wagon	1243	1057	1119
Pkg. 1SC plus power windows and locks, remote tailgate release (wagon), power driver's seat, reading lamps.			
Option Pkg. 1SB, S/E 4-door	343	292	309
S/E wagon	293	249	264
Remote decklid release (4-door), power driver's seat, reading lamps.			
Value Option Pkg. (VOP) R6A, LE	412	350	371
45/55 split seat, AM/FM cassette, alloy wheels.			
Value Option Pkg. R6B, LE 4-door	413	351	372
LE wagon	528	449	475
LE w/Pkg. 1SD	198	168	178
AM/FM cassette, 45/55 split seat, power locks.			
Rear defogger, LE 4-door	160	136	144
Power locks, LE 4-door	215	183	194
LE wagon	255	217	230
Power windows, LE	310	264	279
AM/FM cassette, LE	140	119	126
AM/FM cassette w/EQ, S/E 4-door	350	298	315
S/E wagon	315	268	284
Includes steering wheel controls.			
AM/FM radio w/CD player & EQ, S/E 4-door	536	456	482
S/E wagon	501	426	451
45/55 seat, LE	133	113	120
Custom interior trim, LE	483	411	435
LE w/VOP	350	298	315
45/55 seat, power recliners, gauges.			
185/75R14 WSW tires, LE	68	58	61
14" alloy wheels, LE	265	225	239
Simulated woodgrain siding, LE wagon	295	251	266
Two-tone paint	115	98	104
Warranty enhancements for New York	65	55	59
California emissions pkg.	100	85	90

Porsche 911

What's New

The 911 Turbo is gone until 1991, when a turbocharged version of the all-wheel-drive 911 Carrera 4 is planned. For 1990, there are naturally aspirated 911 Carrera 4 and rear-drive Carrera 2 models, and they are more alike this year. Both are powered by a 247-horsepower 3.6-liter flat 6-cylinder engine. The 214-horsepower 3.2-liter engine used in last year's rear-drive 911 models has been dropped. Early in 1990, a 4-speed automatic transmission is scheduled to be offered on the Carrera 2, a first in the 911's illustrious history. The automatic, called the Porsche Double Function program and developed jointly with the German company, ZF, will have fully automatic and manual shift modes. Until the automatic arrives, all 911 models will have a 5-speed manual transmission. The Carrera 4 is initially available only as a hardtop coupe, but Targa and

Prices are accurate at time of printing; subject to manufacturer's change.

Porsche 911 Carrera 4

Cabriolet versions are due to arrive early in 1990. The Carrera 4's permanently engaged 4-wheel-drive system normally sends 69 percent of the power to the rear wheels. When any of the wheels slip, more power is sent to those with traction. Other changes for this year are that anti-lock brakes and dual front airbags are standard across the board. Porsche thus becomes the first manufacturer to provide standard driver's- and passenger-side airbags for all its U.S. models. None of the 911 models had airbags last year and only the Carrera 4 had anti-lock brakes. The Carrera 2 also gets as standard this year the power steering system that debuted on the Carrera 4 last year, plus a similar coil-spring suspension instead of torsion bars. In addition, the Carrera 2 acquires the "4's" automatic rear spoiler, which extends above 50 mph to reduce lift and direct more air to the rear-mounted, air-cooled engine. Automatic climate control is now standard on all models. We haven't driven the current 911 models so we cannot comment on their performance.

Specifications

	2-door notchback
Wheelbase, in.	89.4
Overall length, in.	168.3
Overall width, in.	65.0
Overall height, in.	52.0
Turn diameter, ft.	39.2
Curb weight, lbs.	3031[1]
Cargo vol., cu. ft.	NA
Fuel capacity, gals.	20.3
Seating capacity	4
Front headroom, in.	37.5
Front shoulder room, in.	NA
Front legroom, max., in.	43.0
Rear headroom, in.	31.1
Rear shoulder room, in.	NA
Rear legroom, min., in.	19.0

1. 3252 lbs., Carrera 4.

Powertrain layout: longitudinal rear engine/rear-wheel drive or permanent 4WD.

Engines

	ohc flat-6
Size, liters/cu. in.	3.6/220
Fuel delivery	PFI
Horsepower @ rpm	247 @ 6100
Torque (lbs./ft.) @ rpm	228 @ 4800
Availability	S
EPA city/highway mpg	
5-speed OD manual	16/24
4-speed OD automatic	NA

Prices

Porsche 911 Carrera 2/4	Retail Price	Dealer Invoice	Low Price
Carrera 2 Coupe	$58500	—	—
Carrera 2 Targa	59900	—	—
Carrera 2 Cabriolet	66800	—	—
Carrera 4 Coupe	69500	—	—
Carrera 4 Targa	70900	—	—
Carrera 4 Cabriolet	77800	—	—

Dealer invoice, low price and destination charge not available at time of publication.

Standard equipment:

Carrera 2: 3.6-liter PFI 6-cylinder engine, 5-speed manual transmission, anti-lock 4-wheel disc brakes, power steering, driver and passenger airbags, automatic climate control, partial leather front bucket seats with power height adjustment, power windows and locks, alarm system, heated power mirrors, leather-wrapped steering wheel, tachometer, coolant temperature and oil pressure gauges, oil level gauge, voltmeter, trip odometer, cruise control, heated windshield washer nozzles, speed-dependent extendable rear spoiler, visor mirrors, power sunroof (Coupe), power top (Cabriolet), AM/FM cassette, rear defogger, tinted glass, fog lamps, 205/55ZR16 front and 225/50ZR16 rear tires on alloy wheels. **Carrera 4** adds: automatic 4WD, forged alloy wheels.

OPTIONS prices not available at time of publication.

Porsche 928

Porsche 928

What's New

Dual front airbags, a limited-slip rear differential, and a tire-pressure monitoring system are new standard features on the 928, Porsche's V-8-powered luxury/sports car. Porsche has made airbags for the driver and front passenger standard on all its 1990 U.S. models, the first manufacturer to do so. Anti-lock brakes have been standard on the 928 since 1986. The new limited-slip differential automatically transfers more torque to the wheel with the most traction based on wheel speed, slip, and lateral acceleration. The tire-pressure monitoring system alerts the driver when any of the tires drop below a pre-set level. The 928 comes with either a 4-speed automatic or 5-speed manual transmission at the same price, $74,545, which is unchanged from last year. However, with the 5-speed, horsepower from the dual-cam, 5.0-liter V-8 is rated at 326 this year; with automatic, horsepower is listed at 316. We haven't driven the current 928 so we cannot comment on its performance.

Specifications

	3-door hatchback
Wheelbase, in.	98.4
Overall length, in.	178.1

Overall width, in.	72.3
Overall height, in.	50.5
Turn diameter, ft.	38.4
Curb weight, lbs.	3505
Cargo vol., cu. ft.	NA
Fuel capacity, gals.	22.7
Seating capacity	4
Front headroom, in.	NA
Front shoulder room, in.	NA
Front legroom, max., in.	NA
Rear headroom, in.	NA
Rear shoulder room, in.	NA
Rear legroom, min., in.	NA

Powertrain layout: longitudinal front engine/rear-wheel drive.

Engines

	dohc V-8
Size, liters/cu. in.	5.0/302
Fuel delivery	PFI
Horsepower @ rpm	316 @ 6000[1]
Torque (lbs./ft.) @ rpm	317 @ 3000
Availability	S

EPA city/highway mpg

5-speed manual	13/19
4-speed automatic	15/19

1. 326 hp with 5-speed manual transmission.

Prices

Porsche 928	Retail Price	Dealer Invoice	Low Price
3-door hatchback	$74545	—	—

Dealer invoice, low price and destination charge not available at time of publication.

Standard equipment:

5.0-liter DOHC 32-valve PFI V-8, 5-speed manual or 4-speed automatic transmission (5-speed includes higher-output engine), anti-lock 4-wheel disc brakes, power steering, driver and passenger airbags, automatic climate control, leather power seats with 3-position driver's-side memory (includes mirrors), power windows and locks, alarm system, cruise control, heated power mirrors, tire-pressure monitoring system, driver information and diagnostic system, AM/FM cassette, tachometer, coolant temperature and oil pressure gauges, voltmeter, trip odometer, height-adjustable steering column and instrument cluster, remote hatch release, rear wiper/washer, heated windshield washer nozzles, power sunroof, visor mirrors, fog lights, 225/50ZR16 front and 245/45ZR16 rear tires on forged alloy wheels.

OPTIONS prices not available at time of publication.

Porsche 944 S2

What's New

The 944 S2 Cabriolet, announced as a 1989 model and priced at $52,650, never made it to the U.S. The good news is that the Cabrio will arrive this fall as a 1990 and the price will be lower, $48,600. It comes with Porsche's 208-horsepower 3.0-liter 4-cylinder engine. A manual folding top is standard and a power top is optional. Also standard are anti-lock brakes and dual front airbags, as they are on all of Porsche's 1990 U.S. models. Gone from the 944 lineup are the base 944 and its 162-horsepower 2.7-liter 4-cylinder engine and the 247-horsepower 944 Turbo. Besides the new Cabriolet, the only other 944 model is the $41,900 S2 Coupe. When the 944 was introduced in the U.S. as an early 1983 model, its base price

Porsche 944 S2

was $18,450. The "entry-level" 944 S2 also has the 208-horsepower 3.0-liter 4-cylinder; both 944 models come only with a 5-speed manual transmission. We haven't driven the current 944 models so we cannot comment on their performance.

Specifications	3-door hatchback	2-door conv.
Wheelbase, in.	94.5	94.5
Overall length, in.	168.9	168.9
Overall width, in.	68.3	68.3
Overall height, in.	50.2	50.2
Turn diameter, ft.	35.2	35.2
Curb weight, lbs.	2998	3109
Cargo vol., cu. ft.	18.3	NA
Fuel capacity, gals.	21.1	21.1
Seating capacity	4	4
Front headroom, in.	35.5	NA
Front shoulder room, in.	NA	NA
Front legroom, max., in.	48.5	48.5
Rear headroom, in.	32.0	NA
Rear shoulder room, in.	NA	NA
Rear legroom, min., in.	12.0	NA

Powertrain layout: longitudinal front engine/rear-wheel drive.

Engines

	dohc I-4
Size, liters/cu. in.	3.0/182
Fuel delivery	PFI
Horsepower @ rpm	208 @ 5800
Torque (lbs./ft.) @ rpm	207 @ 4100
Availability	S

EPA city/highway mpg

5-speed OD manual	17/26

Prices

Porsche 944 S2	Retail Price	Dealer Invoice	Low Price
3-door hatchback	$41900	—	—
Cabriolet 2-door convertible	48600	—	—

Dealer invoice, low price and destination charge not available at time of publication.

KEY: ohv = overhead valve; **ohc** = overhead cam; **dohc** = double overhead cam; **I** = inline cylinders; **V** = cylinders in V configuration; **flat** = horizontally opposed cylinders; **bbl.** = barrel (carburetor); **PFI** = port (multi-point) fuel injection; **TBI** = throttle-body (single-point) fuel injection; **rpm** = revolutions per minute; **OD** = overdrive transmission; **S** = standard; **O** = optional; **NA** = not available.

Prices are accurate at time of printing; subject to manufacturer's change.

Standard equipment:

3.0-liter DOHC 16-valve PFI 4-cylinder engine, 5-speed manual transmission, anti-lock 4-wheel disc brakes, power steering, driver and passenger airbags, automatic climate control, power windows and locks, alarm system, heated power mirrors, leatherette front bucket seats with power height adjustment, split folding rear seat (Cabriolet), leather-wrapped steering wheel, front center armrest with cassette and coin storage, tachometer, coolant temperature and oil pressure gauges, voltmeter, trip odometer, cruise control, remote hatch release, visor mirrors, power tilt sunroof (3-door), power top (Cabriolet), rear defogger and wiper/washer (3-door), AM/FM cassette, heated windshield washer nozzles, fog lamps, tinted glass, 205/55ZR16 front and 225/50ZR16 rear tires on pressure-cast alloy wheels.

OPTIONS prices not available at time of publication.

Range Rover

Range Rover

What's New

Anti-lock brakes are standard this year as the major change on Range Rover, the British-built, 4-wheel-drive luxury wagon. The new anti-lock system works on all four wheels. Four-wheel disc brakes have been standard, and now the front discs are ventilated. Other changes include standard leather upholstery for the base model, a compact disc player as part of a new optional 120-watt sound system, a center high-mounted stoplamp, and an automatically dimming inside rear-view mirror. The automatic mirror is available only on the top-line Country model with the optional power sunroof. The Country was introduced last spring sporting chrome bumpers, Connolly leather upholstery, and burl walnut interior trim. Cloth upholstery is available instead of leather on the Country. On both models, the speedometer and tachometer have new graphics and stronger lighting, and the central locking system now works from both front doors, not just the driver's side. Range Rover's 3.9-liter V-8 has a revised fuel injection system that has helped boost the EPA city fuel economy estimate to 13 mpg, one more than last year. The highway estimate is unchanged at 16. The aluminum V-8, adapted from a 1961 Buick design, is teamed with a 4-speed automatic transmission. Rover's permanently engaged 4WD system splits engine

---

KEY: ohv = overhead valve; **ohc** = overhead cam; **dohc** = double overhead cam; **I** = inline cylinders; **V** = cylinders in V configuration; **flat** = horizontally opposed cylinders; **bbl.** = barrel (carburetor); **PFI** = port (multi-point) fuel injection; **TBI** = throttle-body (single-point) fuel injection; **rpm** = revolutions per minute; **OD** = overdrive transmission; **S** = standard; **O** = optional; **NA** = not available.

---

torque evenly between the front and rear wheels at all times. Range Rover comes only as a 5-door wagon with a 2-way tailgate.

For

- 4WD traction • Acceleration • Anti-lock brakes
- Ride • Passenger room • Cargo space
- Trailer-towing ability

Against

- Fuel economy • Noise

Summary

While Range Rover is a compact 4WD vehicle based on exterior dimensions, it's in a class by itself based on price. If spending nearly $40,000 is within your means, then Range Rover has lots to offer. The high, boxy passenger compartment affords plenty of space despite the short wheelbase, and all passengers will enjoy a well-cushioned ride. We timed a 1989 model at 11.6 seconds to 60 mph, which is quite brisk for this type of vehicle. In our braking tests of the 1989 Range Rover, we recorded a commendable 156 feet from 60 mph, though we had to watch out for rear lockup. With anti-lock control standard this year, that problem should be solved. Towing capacity is 1650 pounds for trailers without brakes. For trailers with brakes, its a maximum of 7700 pounds, quite impressive. On the down side, we averaged 14.5 mpg in mostly highway driving, noise levels are too high for a luxury conveyance, and the Range Rover tends to get blown about by gusty crosswinds. Bottom line: Would we spend this much money on a 4WD wagon? No, despite Range Rover's good features. We'd save $10,000 or more by buying a Jeep Cherokee Limited or a Toyota 4Runner.

Specifications

	5-door wagon
Wheelbase, in.	100.0
Overall length, in.	175.0
Overall width, in.	71.4
Overall height, in.	70.8
Turn diameter, ft.	39.4
Curb weight, lbs.	4389
Cargo vol., cu. ft.	82.8
Fuel capacity, gals.	20.0
Seating capacity	5
Front headroom, in.	38.4
Front shoulder room, in.	58.3
Front legroom, max., in.	41.0
Rear headroom, in.	37.3
Rear shoulder room, in.	59.0
Rear legroom, min., in.	32.7

Powertrain layout: longitudinal front engine/permanent 4-wheel drive.

Engines

	ohv V-8
Size, liters/cu. in.	3.9/241
Fuel delivery	PFI
Horsepower @ rpm	178 @ 4750
Torque (lbs./ft.) @ rpm	220 @ 3250
Availability	S
EPA city/highway mpg	
4-speed OD automatic	13/16

Prices

Range Rover (1989 prices)

	Retail Price	Dealer Invoice	Low Price
5-door 4WD wagon	$35800	$29356	$31783
Destination charge	550	550	550

Standard equipment:

3.5-liter PFI V-8 engine, 4-speed automatic transmission, 2-speed transfer case, power steering, power brakes, air conditioning, self-leveling rear suspension, power front seats, power windows and door locks, power mirrors, heated windshield, heated windshield washer jets, asymmetrically split removable rear seat, cruise control, rear wiper/washer, rear defogger, tachometer, coolant temperature gauge, AM/FM ST ET cassette, trailer hitch, 205SR16 Michelin X M&S tires.

Optional equipment:

Leather upholstery	1125	900	988
Power sunroof	1375	1100	1207

Saab 900

1989 Saab 900 Turbo

What's New

Anti-lock brakes and a driver's-side airbag are new standard features on the 900 series models. Neither was available last year on the 900. The other major change for 1990 is that the fuel tank grows from 16.6 gallons to 18. Last year's lineup returns intact. The base 900 and the 900S come in 3-door hatchback and 4-door notchback styling with a 128-horsepower 2.0-liter 4-cylinder engine and a choice of 5-speed manual or 3-speed automatic transmissions. The 900 Turbo is available in the hatchback and notchback styling, plus as a convertible with a power top. Turbo models use a 160-horsepower 2.0-liter engine and are available with either a 5-speed manual or 3-speed automatic. At the top of the line is the 900 Turbo SPG, available only as a 3-door hatchback with the 5-speed manual. The SPG's 2.0-liter engine has a new Mitsubishi-made turbocharger that Saab says provides better response at low speeds. With the new turbocharger, the SPG gains 10 horsepower and is now rated at 175.

For

- Acceleration (Turbo) • Anti-lock brakes • Airbag
- Handling/roadholding • Passenger room • Cargo space

Against

- Manual shift linkage • Ride (Turbo)

Summary

The addition of anti-lock brakes (ABS) and a driver's-side airbag as standard equipment were necessary for the 900 to stay competitive in the premium sedan league. The absence of anti-lock brakes was especially noticeable last year, since ABS was available on some less-expensive rivals. The 900 already has one of the best records for occupant protection; ABS and the airbag should help make it even better. The basic design for the Swedish-built 900 is 20 years old, but these cars have aged well. The interiors have ample room for adults, who sit in comfortably upright, supportive seats; the narrow body makes it a squeeze to fit three people into the rear seat. Luggage space also is ample on the hatchback and 4-door sedan, thanks to folding rear seatbacks that create enough room to rival small station wagons. Turbo models provide exceptional acceleration and outstanding passing power, but the base models and 900S have leisurely acceleration by comparison. Turbo models have a stiffer ride than the others, with more tire thumping and suspension jiggling on broken pavement, but all 900 models have competent handling ability. Notchy, occasionally balky shift linkage makes the 5-speed manual clumsy to use at times, so we find the automatic easier to live with in urban driving. In addition, the ignition switch is mounted on the floor between the seats and you have to shift the 5-speed into Reverse to remove the key. Saab sales have been slipping, so this should be a good time to find a bargain on a 900 model.

Specifications

	3-door hatchback	4-door notchback	2-door conv.
Wheelbase, in.	99.1	99.1	99.1
Overall length, in.	184.5	184.3	184.3
Overall width, in.	66.5	66.5	66.5
Overall height, in.	56.1	56.1	55.1
Turn diameter, ft.	35.8	35.8	35.8
Curb weight, lbs.	2732	2787	2967
Cargo vol., cu. ft.	56.5	53.0	9.9
Fuel capacity, gals.	18.0	18.0	18.0
Seating capacity	5	5	4
Front headroom, in.	36.8	36.8	36.8
Front shoulder room, in.	52.2	53.0	52.2
Front legroom, max., in.	41.7	41.7	41.7
Rear headroom, in.	37.4	37.4	NA
Rear shoulder room, in.	53.5	54.5	NA
Rear legroom, min., in.	36.2	36.2	NA

Powertrain layout: longitudinal front engine/front-wheel drive.

Engines

	dohc I-4	Turbo dohc I-4	Turbo dohc I-4
Size, liters/cu. in.	2.0/121	2.0/121	2.0/121
Fuel delivery	PFI	PFI	PFI
Horsepower @ rpm	128 @ 6000	160 @ 5500	175 @ 5500
Torque (lbs./ft.) @ rpm	128 @ 3000	188 @ 3000	195 @ 3000
Availability	S[1]	S[2]	S[3]

EPA city/highway mpg

5-speed manual	22/28	22/29	21/28
3-speed automatic	19/22	19/23	

1. 900, 900S   2. Turbo   3. Turbo SPG.

Prices

Saab 900 (1989 prices)

	Retail Price	Dealer Invoice	Low Price
3-door hatchback	$16995	$14361	$14931
4-door notchback	17515	14800	15388
S 3-door hatchback	19695	16544	17257
S 4-door notchback	20245	17006	17739
Turbo 3-door hatchback	23795	19869	20792
Turbo 4-door notchback	24345	20328	21273

Prices are accurate at time of printing; subject to manufacturer's change.

	Retail Price	Dealer Invoice	Low Price
Turbo convertible	32095	26478	27892
Turbo SPG 3-door hatchback	26895	22323	23437
Destination charge	359	359	359

Standard equipment:

2.0-liter DOHC 16-valve PFI 4-cylinder engine, 5-speed manual or 3-speed automatic transmission, power steering, power 4-wheel disc brakes, air conditioning, tachometer, coolant temperature gauge, trip odometer, analog clock, rear defogger, intermittent wipers, power locks, tinted glass, driver's seat tilt/height adjustment, cloth heated reclining front bucket seats, folding rear seat, AM/FM ST ET, 185/65R15 SBR tires. **S** adds: cruise control, folding rear armrest, power windows and mirrors, AM/FM ST ET cassette, manual sunroof, alloy wheels. **Turbo** adds: turbocharged engine, sport seats, upgraded stereo with EQ; convertible has power top and leather interior. **Turbo SPG** has: higher-output engine, sport suspension, leather-wrapped steering wheel and shift knob, aero body addenda, wider tires.

Optional equipment:

3-speed automatic transmission(NA SPG) .	525	438	482
Metallic or special black paint	485	393	439
Leather Pkg., Turbos exc. conv.	1295	1049	1172

Saab 9000

1989 Saab 9000 Turbo

What's New

The Saab Direct Ignition system (SDI) is standard this year on the 9000 Turbo models, while a driver's-side airbag is standard on all 9000 models. SDI does away with the distributor and uses a separate ignition coil for each cylinder. Saab says SDI produces higher spark voltage and reduces radio interference. In addition, when the ignition key is first turned on each spark plug is fired about 50 times in a fraction of a second to clean and dry the electrodes for easier starting. Other changes to Turbo models include a new U.S.-made Garrett turbocharger that's supposed to improve low-speed response. Horsepower on the 2.0-liter turbo engine grows from 160 to 165. The naturally aspirated 2.0-liter engine used in the 9000S is unchanged at 130 horsepower. Last year Saab introduced the 9000 CD Turbo, a notchback 4-door sedan derived from the 9000 5-door hatchback. During the summer a naturally aspirated 9000 CD was added. This year, the 9000 Turbo 5-door gets the CD's softer suspension set-

---

KEY: **ohv** = overhead valve; **ohc** = overhead cam; **dohc** = double overhead cam; **I** = inline cylinders; **V** = cylinders in V configuration; **flat** = horizontally opposed cylinders; **bbl.** = barrel (carburetor); **PFI** = port (multi-point) fuel injection; **TBI** = throttle-body (single-point) fuel injection; **rpm** = revolutions per minute; **OD** = overdrive transmission; **S** = standard; **O** = optional; **NA** = not available.

---

tings, self-leveling rear shock absorbers, and narrower tires (195/65VR15 instead of 205/55VR15). All 9000 models have front-wheel drive. The naturally aspirated 9000 models have a new manual climate control system, instead of the previous fully automatic system, while the 9000 Turbos have a second-generation automatic system with a new "Off" switch and new temperature sensors. Other new features are a one-touch open feature for the driver's power windows for all 9000 models and headlamp washers for the CD. A driver's-side airbag became standard on Turbo models last spring; this fall it becomes standard on the 9000S models as well. Anti-lock brakes have been standard on all 9000 models since 1988.

For

- Acceleration (Turbo)
- Anti-lock brakes
- Airbag
- Handling/roadholding
- Passenger room
- Cargo space

Against

- Acceleration (9000S)

Summary

The 9000S offers the same capable handling, reassuring anti-lock brakes, roomy interior, and standard airbag as the Turbo models, but its 130-horsepower engine doesn't deliver the same kind of sparkling acceleration. While neck-snapping acceleration isn't all we're looking for, we expect more than the 9000S delivers for $25,000 or so. The 165-horsepower Turbo models deliver the kind of acceleration you expect in this price range—and more. At highway speeds, turbo boost is just a touch of the accelerator pedal away for an instant, smooth rush of power. Saab sales are suffering partly because the Swedish automaker only offers 4-cylinder engines at a time when premium-sedan buyers are demanding six cylinders or more. The 9000 is still a roomy, comfortable car with an impressive array of features and, on the Turbo models, strong engine performance. Slow sales put the buyer in the driver's seat in price negotiations.

Specifications

	4-door notchback	5-door hatchback
Wheelbase, in.	105.2	105.2
Overall length, in.	188.2	181.9
Overall width, in.	69.4	69.4
Overall height, in.	55.9	55.9
Turn diameter, ft.	NA	NA
Curb weight, lbs.	3022	3004
Cargo vol., cu. ft.	18.1	56.5
Fuel capacity, gals.	17.4	17.4
Seating capacity	5	5
Front headroom, in.	38.5	38.5
Front shoulder room, in.	NA	NA
Front legroom, max., in.	41.5	41.5
Rear headroom, in.	37.4	37.4
Rear shoulder room, in.	NA	NA
Rear legroom, min., in.	38.7	38.7

Powertrain layout: transverse front engine/front-wheel drive.

Engines	dohc I-4	Turbo dohc I-4
Size, liters/cu. in.	2.0/121	2.0/121
Fuel delivery	PFI	PFI
Horsepower @ rpm	130 @ 6000	165 @ 5500
Torque (lbs./ft.) @ rpm	128 @ 3750	195 @ 3000
Availability	S	S

EPA city/highway mpg	dohc I-4	Turbo dohc I-4
5-speed OD manual	21/28	20/26
4-speed OD automatic	18/24	18/24

Prices

Saab 9000 (1989 prices)	Retail Price	Dealer Invoice	Low Price
S 5-door hatchback	$24445	$20167	$21244
Turbo 5-door hatchback	30795	25406	26762
CD 4-door notchback (velour interior) . . .	30895	25488	28192
CD 4-door notchback (leather interior) . . .	31995	26396	29196
Destination charge	359	359	359

Standard equipment:

2.0-liter DOHC 16-valve PFI 4-cylinder engine, 5-speed manual or 4-speed automatic transmission, power steering, anti-lock braking system, 4-wheel disc brakes, automatic air conditioning, AM/FM ST ET cassette, power antenna, trip computer, trip odometer, tachometer, coolant temperature gauge, front and rear reading lights, reclining front bucket seats, driver's seat height/tilt, lumbar and lateral support adjustments, velour upholstery, emergency tensioning front seatbelt retractors, rear shoulder belts, telescopic steering column, power tilt/slide steel sunroof, 185/65R15 SBR tires on alloy wheels. **Turbo and CD** add: turbocharged engine, leather upholstery, power front seats, fog lights, power glass sunroof, upgraded stereo, 205/55VR15 tires (Turbo; CD has 195/65VR15).

Optional equipment:

4-speed automatic transmission	695	573	634
Leather Pkg., S	1595	1292	1444
Metallic or special black paint	485	393	439

Sterling 827

1989 Sterling 827SLi

What's New

Sterling will add an 827Si 4-door sedan to its fleet this year and all models will have a new automatic climate control system. The new Si will essentially take most of the standard equipment of the 827SL, which includes anti-lock brakes, and add new seats, a sport suspension, wider wheels and tires, and sportier exterior trim. The Si's suspension also becomes standard on the SLi 5-door hatchback. The SLi, introduced last year, this year gains a trip computer, a power front passenger seat, a heated driver's seat, and full leather upholstery instead of leather and suede. Sterling will install motorized front shoulder belts on its 1990 models to meet the federal passive-restraint requirement. The front-drive 827 is based on the same design used for the Acura Legend, but is built in England by the Rover Group rather than in Japan. Last year Sterling made the Legend's 160-horsepower 2.7-liter V-6 engine standard, but that didn't help sales, which slipped nearly 40 percent in the first eight months of 1989 to 4126 units.

For

● Acceleration ● Handling/roadholding ● Anti-lock brakes ● Ride (S, SL)

Against

● Driveability (automatic transmission)
● Instruments/controls

Summary

While the Acura Legend has been one of our Best Buys for years, the similar Sterling 827 has not. The main reason is that the Sterlings we've tested haven't been built as well as the Acuras. Among problems we've encountered on Sterlings are sloppy interior assembly, power sunroofs that didn't close snugly, cassette players that refused to eject tapes, and brakes that squealed incessantly. While none of these problems are major, we haven't encountered similar flaws on Japanese-made Legends. When we spend this much money on a car, or recommend how you spend yours, we tend to play it safe, so we endorse the Legend over the 827. It's only fair to point out that two 1989 827s we tested were well assembled and were probably the best cars we've seen from Sterling so far. Perhaps they've finally gotten the hang of building this car. Sterling offers the same brisk acceleration, capable handling, and commendable stopping ability as the Legend. As with the Legend, the automatic transmission tends to shift harshly under hard acceleration, but power delivery is otherwise responsive and smooth. Those who value crisp handling more than a comfortable ride should try the 827 Si or SLi hatchback; their firmer suspension and wider tires combine for cornering ability that's superior to the Legend's. Last year, the SLi's ride was stiff and jiggly on all but glass-smooth surfaces; this year, Sterling says the ride will be softer. Inside, we prefer Acura's dashboard and control layout to Sterling's. Legend's gauges are easier to read and the control placement and operation are more convenient. There is one big advantage to buying a Sterling: price. Legends usually sell close to suggested retail, while Sterling dealers are offering huge discounts.

Specifications

	4-door notchback	5-door hatchback
Wheelbase, in.	108.6	108.6
Overall length, in.	188.8	188.8
Overall width, in.	68.1	68.1
Overall height, in.	54.8	54.8
Turn diameter, ft.	36.5	36.5
Curb weight, lbs.	3097	3230
Cargo vol., cu. ft.	12.1	49.6
Fuel capacity, gals.	17.0	17.0
Seating capacity	5	5
Front headroom, in.	37.5	37.5
Front shoulder room, in.	54.9	54.9
Front legroom, max., in.	41.2	41.2
Rear headroom, in.	36.0	36.0
Rear shoulder room, in.	54.3	54.3
Rear legroom, min., in.	36.4	36.4

Powertrain layout: transverse front engine/front-wheel drive.

Prices are accurate at time of printing; subject to manufacturer's change.

Sterling ● Subaru

Engines

	ohc V-6
Size, liters/cu. in.	2.7/163
Fuel delivery	PFI
Horsepower @ rpm	160 @ 5900
Torque (lbs./ft.) @ rpm	162 @ 4500
Availability	S

EPA city/highway mpg

5-speed OD manual	19/24
4-speed OD automatic	18/23

Prices

Sterling (1989 prices)	Retail Price	Dealer Invoice	Low Price
827S 4-door notchback	$23300	$19572	$20415
827SL 4-door notchback	29675	24630	25860
827SLi 5-door hatchback	29675	24630	25860
827SL Limited Edition 4-door	30150	25025	26274
Destination charge	460	460	460

Standard equipment:

827S: 2.7-liter 24-valve PFI V-6, 5-speed manual transmission, power steering, 4-wheel disc brakes, self-leveling rear suspension, air conditioning, reclining front bucket seats, driver's seat height and lumbar support adjustments, cruise control, tilt steering column, tinted glass, tachometer, coolant temperature and oil pressure gauges, voltmeter, power windows, power locks with infrared remote, heated power mirrors, power moonroof, AM/FM ST ET cassette, security alarm, time-delay courtesy lights, rear reading lamps, right visor mirror, remote fuel door and decklid releases, 195/65VR15 tires on alloy wheels. **827SL adds:** 4-speed automatic transmission (5-speed manual may be substituted at no charge), anti-lock braking system, leather upholstery (cloth may be substituted at no charge), memory power front seats, power rear seat, heated driver's seat, upgraded audio system, automatic headlamps-off, trip computer, metallic paint, center console with armrest. **827SLi** deletes power passenger seat and adds: sport suspension, leather and suede upholstery, rear wiper/washer, 205/60VR15 tires. **827SL Limited Edition** adds: leather and suede upholstery, power rear recliner, green metallic paint.

Optional equipment:

4-speed automatic transmission, S	800	572	686
Anti-lock brakes, S	1225	1029	1127
Leather upholstery, S	1100	924	1012
Metallic paint, S	450	378	414
Power rear seat, SL	410	344	377

Subaru Justy

What's New

Big changes are planned for Subaru's smallest model, the Justy. The biggest change is that a 5-door hatchback body style has been added as a companion to the 3-door hatchback. Like the 3-door, the new 5-door is available with front-wheel drive or on-demand 4-wheel drive. The 5-door is built on the same 90-inch wheelbase as the 3-door. For 1990, all but the base models have multi-point fuel injection instead of

> **KEY: ohv** = overhead valve; **ohc** = overhead cam; **dohc** = double overhead cam; **I** = inline cylinders; **V** = cylinders in V configuration; **flat** = horizontally opposed cylinders; **bbl.** = barrel (carburetor); **PFI** = port (multi-point) fuel injection; **TBI** = throttle-body (single-point) fuel injection; **rpm** = revolutions per minute; **OD** = overdrive transmission; **S** = standard; **O** = optional; **NA** = not available.

1989 Subaru Justy GL

a 2-barrel carburetor. With injection, horsepower grows from 66 to 73 for Justy's 1.2-liter/73-cubic-inch 3-cylinder engine. Fuel-injected Justys also get an intermediate front drive shaft to reduce front torque steer (pulling to one side in hard acceleration). Subaru introduced its innovative Electronic Continuously Variable Transmission (ECVT) last year as an option on the front-drive Justy GL. This year it also becomes available on 4WD models, the first time Subaru has offered an automatic transmission on 4WD Justys. ECVT is different from conventional automatic transmissions in that it doesn't have three or four forward speeds, or gears. Instead, a metal belt connects two pulleys that continuously vary the ratio of engine speed to drive shaft speed. Subaru says this "gearless," infinite spread of ratios on the ECVT is like having a dimmer instead of a 3-way light switch. A 5-speed manual transmission remains standard in the Justy line. Also new is a "Fun Justy" appearance package, available on the 3-door. It includes special paint and custom interior trim.

For

● Fuel economy   ● 4WD traction   ● Maneuverability

Against

● Ride   ● Noise   ● Entry/exit

Summary

A round of applause, please, for still another technical first for Subaru. Not content to just offer 4WD in a tiny car like the Justy, Subaru now has combined 4WD with ECVT, a feature no other manufacturer offers in the U.S. The ECVT gets more performance out of the Justy's 3-cylinder engine than a conventional automatic ever could. We timed a 1989 model at 12.5 seconds to 60 mph time, which makes the ECVT model only slightly slower than a Justy with manual transmission (Subaru claims 12.3 seconds). With fuel injection, the 1990 models should be quicker still. Standing-start acceleration isn't everything, though, and the ECVT Justy has little zip in the 25-to-50-mph range. The transmission responds readily, but there's not enough torque for quick, safe passing on the flat and the ECVT Justy quickly loses momentum going uphill. Though it's easier to drive in stop-and-go congestion than a manual-shift Justy, the ECVT is more frustrating on freeways because the engine lags far enough behind your throttle foot so you can't move as quickly as the traffic flow. We averaged nearly 30 mpg with ECVT from a city/highway driving mix, which is fine by absolute standards, but nearly four mpg lower than we averaged with a Justy 5-speed. In most other categories, Justy is typical of low-priced minicompacts. ECVT is an interesting feature that produces mixed results, so the available 4WD remains Justy's principal advantage over small-fry rivals.

Specifications

	3-door hatchback	5-door hatchback
Wheelbase, in.	90.0	90.0
Overall length, in.	145.5	145.5
Overall width, in.	60.4	60.4
Overall height, in.	55.9	55.9
Turn diameter, ft.	32.2	32.2
Curb weight, lbs.	1745	NA
Cargo vol., cu. ft.	21.9	21.9
Fuel capacity, gals.	9.2	9.2
Seating capacity	4	4
Front headroom, in.	38.0	38.0
Front shoulder room, in.	51.9	51.9
Front legroom, max., in.	41.5	41.5
Rear headroom, in.	37.0	37.0
Rear shoulder room, in.	51.0	51.0
Rear legroom, min., in.	30.2	30.2

Powertrain layout: transverse front engine/front-wheel drive or on-demand 4WD.

Engines

	ohc I-3	ohc I-3
Size, liters/cu. in.	1.2/73	1.2/73
Fuel delivery	2 bbl.	PFI
Horsepower @ rpm	66 @ 5200	73 @ 5600
Torque (lbs./ft.) @ rpm	70 @ 3600	71 @ 2800
Availability	S	S

EPA city/highway mpg

5-speed OD manual	33/37	34/37
ECVT automatic		34/35

Prices

Subaru Justy (1989 prices)	Retail Price	Dealer Invoice	Low Price
DL 3-door hatchback	$5866	$5405	$5500
GL 3-door hatchback	7251	6512	6714
RS 4WD 3-door hatchback	8351	7482	7723

Destination charge varies by region.

Standard equipment:

1.2-liter 2bbl. 3-cylinder engine, 5-speed manual transmission, locking fuel door, reclining front bucket seats, one-piece folding rear seat, SBR tires. **GL** adds: rear defogger, tachometer, intermittent wipers, rear wiper, digital clock, AM/FM ST ET, 50/50 folding rear seat, luggage shelf, remote hatch release, all-season tires. **RS** adds: monochrome exterior, AM/FM ST ET, remote mirrors, carpet, digital clock, cloth and vinyl upholstery, graphic monitor, full wheel covers.

Optional equipment:

Electronic Continuosly Variable Transmission, GL	540	—	—
On-Demand 4WD, GL	700	—	—
Air conditioning	650	—	—
AM/FM cassette, base	250	—	—
Cassette deck w/console, GL & RS	230	—	—
Fog lights	80	—	—
Right remote mirror	75	—	—
Floormats	40	—	—

Subaru Legacy

Subaru Legacy L

What's New

Subaru introduced the Legacy 4-door sedans and 5-door wagons last spring as its new bread-and-butter models. Legacy is larger and more luxurious than the carryover Subaru Sedan/Wagon/Coupe, which continue for 1990 as the Loyale line. At 101.6 inches, Legacy's wheelbase is 4.4 inches longer than Loyale's, while its overall length is three to five inches greater, depending on model. While the Loyale models are subcompacts, Legacy is a compact, competing in the same league as the Honda Accord, Toyota Camry, Mazda 626, and others. Both the sedan and wagon come in base, L, and LS trim levels, and with either front-wheel drive or permanently-engaged 4-wheel drive. All models use a new 130-horsepower 2.2-liter flat (horizontally opposed) 4-cylinder engine with four valves per cylinder, mated to either a 5-speed manual or 4-speed automatic transmission. Models with the automatic transmission have a shift lock that requires applying the brake pedal before a drive gear can be engaged. Power steering and 4-wheel disc brakes are standard on all models. Anti-lock brakes were optional on 4WD LS models with automatic on early 1990 models; now they are also available with 4WD and the 5-speed manual transmission. Motorized front shoulder belts are standard to meet the federal passive-restraint rule; separate lap belts have to be buckled manually. Most Legacys are imported from Japan, but some sedans are built in Lafayette, Indiana, at a plant operated jointly by Subaru and Isuzu.

For

- Acceleration
- Anti-lock brakes
- Handling/roadholding
- 4WD traction

Against

- Fuel economy

Summary

Legacy's new 2.2-liter engine is stronger than the 1.8-liter engines used in the Loyale line and noticeably quieter. We timed an LS 4WD wagon with automatic, the heaviest Legacy model, at 10.2 seconds to 60 mph, an impressive showing. Our test wagon also had the optional anti-lock brakes, which helped stop the vehicle from 60 mph in just 123 feet, also quite impressive. Too bad fuel economy isn't any better than in the Loyale line; we averaged 18.3 mpg in urban driving. We highly recommend the anti-lock brakes for the safer stops

Prices are accurate at time of printing; subject to manufacturer's change

Subaru

they provide and are glad to see it available on cars in this price range. We also like Subaru's permanently engaged 4WD systems, which provide outstanding traction without requiring any input from the driver. Legacy can hold five adults, but four will be much more comfortable. Sedans have adequate trunk space, with little intrusion from the rear suspension, while the wagons have a long flat cargo area with the rear seatbacks folded down. The compact spare tire is below the storage shelf in the trunk, rather than under the hood as in most other Subarus. Legacy is a capable, mainstream, reasonably priced car that emerges as a good alternative to the Accord, Camry, and other compacts.

Specifications

	4-door notchback	5-door wagon
Wheelbase, in.	101.6	101.6
Overall length, in.	177.6	181.1
Overall width, in.	66.5	66.5
Overall height, in.	52.6	53.7
Turn diameter, ft.	33.5	33.5
Curb weight, lbs.	2620[1]	2750[2]
Cargo vol., cu. ft.	12.8	71.0
Fuel capacity, gals.	15.9	15.9
Seating capacity	5	5
Front headroom, in.	38.2	38.2
Front shoulder room, in.	54.1	54.1
Front legroom, max., in.	42.3	42.3
Rear headroom, in.	36.0	37.8
Rear shoulder room, in.	53.7	53.7
Rear legroom, min., in.	35.4	35.6

1. 2830 lbs., 4WD 2. 2960 lbs., 4WD.

Powertrain layout: longitudinal front engine/front-wheel drive or permanent 4WD.

Engines

	ohc flat-4
Size, liters/cu. in.	2.2/135
Fuel delivery	PFI
Horsepower @ rpm	130 @ 5400
Torque (lbs./ft.) @ rpm	137 @ 4400
Availability	S

EPA city/highway mpg

5-speed OD manual	23/30
4-speed OD automatic	21/28

Prices

Subaru Legacy	Retail Price	Dealer Invoice	Low Price
4-door notchback	$11299	—	—
L 4-door notchback	12499	—	—
LS 4-door notchback	14699	—	—
L 4WD 4-door notchback	13699	—	—
LS 4WD 4-door notchback	16499	—	—
5-door wagon	11849	—	—
L 5-door wagon	13049	—	—
LS 5-door wagon	15249	—	—

KEY: ohv = overhead valve; **ohc** = overhead cam; **dohc** = double overhead cam; **I** = inline cylinders; **V** = cylinders in V configuration; **flat** = horizontally opposed cylinders; **bbl.** = barrel (carburetor); **PFI** = port (multi-point) fuel injection; **TBI** = throttle-body (single-point) fuel injection; **rpm** = revolutions per minute; **OD** = overdrive transmission; **S** = standard; **O** = optional; **NA** = not available.

216

	Retail Price	Dealer Invoice	Low Price
L 4WD 5-door wagon	14249	—	—
LS 4WD 5-door wagon	17049	—	—

Destination charge varies by region. Dealer invoice and low price not available at time of publication.

Standard equipment:

2.2-liter SOHC 16-valve PFI 4-cylinder engine, 5-speed manual transmission, power steering, 4-wheel disc brakes, Hill-Holder, automatic front shoulder belts, outboard rear lap/shoulder belts, coolant temperature gauge, trip odometer, tinted glass, remote mirrors, center console, remote fuel door and decklid/liftgate releases, beverage holder, 175/70HR14 all-season tires. **L** adds: power windows and locks, power mirrors, spot lamps, tilt steering column, driver's-seat lumbar support adjustment, tachometer, intermittent wipers, AM/FM ST ET; wagon has cargo cover, 60/40 split rear seatback, rear wiper/washer. **LS** adds: air conditioning, air suspension (4WD automatic), cruise control, driver's-seat height adjustment, rear center armrest (4-door), trunk-through (4-door), variable intermittent wipers, power sunroof. **4WD** models have 185/70HR14 tires.

Optional equipment:

4-speed automatic transmission	750	—	—
Anti-lock brakes, LS 4WD automatic	1095	—	—
Value Plus Option Pkg., L	995	—	—
Air conditioning, AM/FM ST ET cassette w/EQ, cruise control.			
Metallic paint	120	—	—

Subaru Loyale

1989 Subaru Sedan

What's New

What used to be Subaru's highest-volume line, the subcompact Sedan/Wagon/3-Door Coupe trio, carries on for 1990 as the Loyale with fewer models and less emphasis, as Subaru shifts its focus to the newer Legacy. Three Loyale body styles are still offered, but the 5-door wagon gets most of the attention since it has been Subaru's best-selling model and the most popular wagon in the U.S. Gone are the previous DL, GL, and GL-10 trim levels, replaced by a single price series with standard equipment that falls between that of the old DL and GL. This serves to simplify model choices and reduce retail prices below that of comparable Legacy models. Prices weren't available in time for this issue, but Subaru has been indicating they will be lower than last year's. Two engines are available: a 90-horsepower 1.8-liter flat-4 and a 115-horsepower turbocharged version of the flat-4. As before, all body styles are available with front-wheel drive or 4-wheel-drive (either the on-demand type or permanently engaged 4WD).

CONSUMER GUIDE®

For

- 4WD traction • Cargo space • Handling/roadholding

Against

- Fuel economy (turbo) • Acceleration (non-turbo)
- Passenger room (Coupe)

Summary

Though eclipsed in size, acceleration, and features by the Legacy line, the Loyale models still offer Subaru's famed 4WD systems, all of which are convenient to use and provide great traction. If you don't really need 4WD, then save money and buy a front-drive model. You'll also save on fuel and gain a little acceleration to boot, because the front-drive models are lighter. If you do opt for 4WD, beware that the base 90-horsepower engine is strained by the extra weight, particularly with automatic transmission. Even the 115-horsepower turbocharged engine is no ball of fire off the line, though it provides good passing response. Fuel economy is mediocre with the turbo engine; we averaged 20.7 mpg with a 4WD wagon with automatic transmission and never exceeded 26.25 mpg, even on the highway. We drove that 4WD wagon more than 20,000 miles in a long-term test and the car required no mechanical repairs, an impressive performance. Interior room is sufficient on all models except the 3-door Coupe, which has a cramped rear seat. Cargo room is at least adequate on all models, and the wagon and coupe have folding rear seatbacks for additional luggage space. The 1990 price structure should make the Loyale line a little less expensive than before, and Subaru has been offering incentives to try to spur sales. Among Japanese rivals, Honda and Toyota offer small 4WD wagons, and Toyota also sells a 4WD Corolla sedan, so you don't have to limit your shopping to Subaru if you want all-wheel drive in a small package.

Specifications

	3-door hatchback	4-door notchback	5-door wagon
Wheelbase, in.	97.2	97.2	97.0
Overall length, in.	174.6	174.6	176.8
Overall width, in.	65.4	65.4	65.4
Overall height, in.	51.8	52.5	53.0
Turn diameter, ft.	34.8	34.8	34.8
Curb weight, lbs.	2280	2240	2370
Cargo vol., cu. ft.	39.8	14.9	70.3
Fuel capacity, gals.	15.9	15.9	15.9
Seating capacity	5	5	5
Front headroom, in.	37.6	37.6	37.6
Front shoulder room, in.	53.5	53.5	53.5
Front legroom, max., in.	42.2	41.7	41.7
Rear headroom, in.	35.8	36.5	37.7
Rear shoulder room, in.	52.8	53.5	53.5
Rear legroom, min., in.	32.6	35.2	35.2

Powertrain layout: longitudinal front engine/front-wheel drive, or on-demand or permanent 4WD.

Engines

	ohc flat-4	Turbo ohc flat-4
Size, liters/cu. in.	1.8/109	1.8/109
Fuel delivery	TBI	PFI
Horsepower @ rpm	90 @ 5200	115 @ 5200
Torque (lbs./ft.) @ rpm	101 @ 2800	134 @ 2800
Availability	S	S

Subaru

EPA city/highway mpg	ohc flat-4	Turbo ohc flat-4
5-speed OD manual	25/32	22/25
3-speed automatic	24/26	22/24
4-speed OD automatic		20/26

Prices

Subaru Sedan, Wagon & 3-door Coupe (1989 prices)	Retail Price	Dealer Invoice	Low Price
DL 4-door notchback	$9731	$8649	$8922
GL 4-door notchback	11521	14189	12481
GL-10 Turbo 4-door notchback	16401	14189	14850
DL 3-door hatchback	10031	8912	9196
GL 3-door hatchback	11821	10391	10783
RX 3-door hatchback	16361	14216	14843
DL 5-door wagon	10181	9044	9333
GL 5-door wagon	11971	10522	10919
GL-10 Turbo 5-door wagon	16851	14575	15255

Destination charge varies by region.

Standard equipment:

DL: 1.8-liter TBI 4-cylinder engine, 5-speed manual transmission, power steering and brakes, reclining front bucket seats, cloth upholstery, tinted glass, digital clock, rear defogger, remote fuel door and hatch/trunk releases, bodyside moldings, trip odometer, 50/50 folding rear seat (wagon), rear wiper (wagon), 155SR13 all-season SBR tires. **GL** adds: power mirrors, tachometer, power windows and locks, AM/FM stereo, memory tilt steering column, 50/50 folding rear seat (except 4-door), driver's seat lumbar support adjustment, 175/70SR13 tires. **GL-10 Turbo** adds: PFI turbocharged engine, 4-wheel disc brakes, variable intermittent wipers, power sunroof, air conditioning, cruise control, digital instruments with trip computer, upgraded stereo. **RX** adds: Continous 4WD, 5-speed dual-range manual transmission, upgraded suspension, white monochrome exterior treatment, analog instruments, performance tires.

Optional equipment:

3-speed automatic transmission, DL & GL .	560	—	—
4-speed automatic transmission, RX	760	—	—
On-Demand 4WD, GL	700	—	—
Continuous 4WD/5-speed, GL-10 Turbo . .	1600	—	—
Active 4WD/4-speed automatic, GL-10 Turbo	2360	—	—
Continuous 4WD Turbo/5-speed pkg., GL wagon	2475	—	—
Touring Wagon Pkg., GL	200	—	—
GL-10 Turbo	NC	—	—

Subaru XT

What's New

The XT coupe loses its 4-wheel-drive/4-cylinder models, but otherwise is unchanged for 1990. XT is due to be replaced in 1991 and rumors are that it will be a Giugiaro-designed 2-door with a multi-valve 6-cylinder engine capable of producing over 200 horsepower. The current range has a base front-drive model with a 97-horsepower 1.8-liter 4-cylinder engine and either a 5-speed manual or 4-speed automatic transmission. Heading the lineup is the XT6, powered by a 145-horsepower 2.7-liter 6-cylinder engine. A front-drive XT6 comes only with a 4-speed automatic transmission. The 4WD XT6 models have a permanently engaged 4WD system and either a 5-speed manual or a 4-speed automatic transmission. Like most of Subaru's engines, the two available in the XT have horizontally opposed cylinders, what is known as a "flat" engine, rather than an inline or V-type.

Prices are accurate at time of printing; subject to manufacturer's change

1989 Subaru XT6

For

- Acceleration (XT6) ● 4WD traction ● Maneuverability
- Handling/roadholding ● Fuel economy (4-cylinder)

Against

- Acceleration (4-cylinder) ● Passenger room
- Dashboard controls

Summary

If you want a sporty car with distinctive, flamboyant looks, the XT might strike your fancy. The mild-mannered 4-cylinder models are definitely for show rather than go, though they compensate with high fuel economy. The XT6 is a different animal, and a much better one if you rank performance above economy. The 6-cylinder engine is smooth and responsive, and works equally well with either automatic or manual transmission. The 4-cylinder, on the other hand, feels anemic with automatic. In addition, the 6-cylinder is much quieter. We also like the permanently engaged 4WD systems available on the XT6, which provide outstanding foul-weather traction instantly and without any input required from the driver. XT6 models are pricey, however, and 4WD adds hundreds more, so you're into all-wheel-drive Mitsubishi Eclipse/Eagle Talon territory. We like the Eclipse and Talon better overall, partly because they have a more sensible, more ergonomic control layout than the XT. The XT's dashboard is too complicated, too weird. Four buttons control the lights and five the wiper/washer functions. Heat/vent distribution controls are on the dashboard, but the temperature control and fan switch are mounted between the seats. We can only guess that three engineers designed the interior, but never talked to each other. If the interior controls aren't too weird for you and the rakish looks don't turn you off either, then an XT6 can be lots of fun to drive.

Specifications

	2-door notchback
Wheelbase, in.	97.0
Overall length, in.	177.6
Overall width, in.	66.5
Overall height, in.	49.4
Turn diameter, ft.	34.1
Curb weight, lbs.	2455
Cargo vol., cu. ft.	11.6
Fuel capacity, gals.	15.9
Seating capacity	4
Front headroom, in.	37.4

	2-door notchback
Front shoulder room, in.	52.8
Front legroom, max., in.	43.3
Rear headroom, in.	34.4
Rear shoulder room, in.	52.8
Rear legroom, min., in.	26.2

Powertrain layout: longitudinal front engine/front-wheel drive, or on-demand or permanent 4WD.

Engines	ohc flat-4	ohc flat-6
Size, liters/cu. in.	1.8/109	2.7/163
Fuel delivery	PFI	PFI
Horsepower @ rpm	97 @ 5200	145 @ 5200
Torque (lbs./ft.) @ rpm	103 @ 3200	156 @ 4000
Availability	S	O

EPA city/highway mpg		
5-speed OD manual	25/31	20/28
4-speed OD automatic	23/29	19/25

Prices

Subaru XT (1989 prices)	Retail Price	Dealer Invoice	Low Price
GL 2-door notchback	$13071	$11379	$11643
XT6 2-door notchback	17111	14735	15165

Destination charge varies by region.

Standard equipment:

1.8-liter PFI 4-cylinder engine, 5-speed manual transmission, power steering and brakes, cloth reclining front bucket seats, passive restraint system (automatic front shoulder and manual lap belts), console, Hill Holder, tinted glass, remote fuel door and trunk releases, dual spot lamps, memory tilt steering column, coolant temperature gauge, trip odometer, tachometer, digital clock, rear defogger, telltale graphic monitor, variable intermittent wipers, AM/FM ST ET, power windows and locks, power mirrors, driver's seat lumbar and height adjustments, one-piece folding rear seat, oil pressure gauge, voltmeter, 185/70HR13 all-season tires. **XT6** adds: 2.7-liter PFI 6-cylinder engine, 4-wheel disc brakes, air conditioning, fog lamps, cruise control, upgraded stereo with cassette and EQ, headlamp washers, trip computer, 195/60HR14 all-season tires on alloy wheels.

Optional equipment:

4-speed automatic transmission, GL	760	655	708
On-Demand 4WD, GL	700	604	652
Active 4WD/4-speed automatic	1660	1431	1546
Continuous 4WD/5-speed, XT6	840	700	770

Suzuki Sidekick and Samurai

What's New

The Sidekick 4-wheel-drive sport-utility vehicle, new in the U.S. last year, gets a 2-wheel-drive companion this year, and all models are powered by an 80-horsepower 1.6-liter 4-cylinder engine with single-point fuel injection. Sidekick came only with 4WD during 1989 and the Standard JA model used a 64-horsepower, carbureted 1.3-liter engine. This year's revised lineup has the JS as the base model, available only as a soft-top convertible with 2WD. The more expensive JX and JLX models come with either a soft top or hardtop with on-demand 4WD. Chevrolet dealers sell a nearly identical version of Sidekick as the Geo Tracker. General Motors owns an equity interest in Suzuki and the two companies are jointly

Suzuki Sidekick

operating a plant in Canada that produces Sidekicks and Trackers. While Sidekick gets more marketing emphasis this year, the smaller, older Samurai gets less. Samurai, which has on-demand 4WD, has been trimmed to a single price series from two and the slow-selling hardtop has been dropped, leaving the convertible. Samurai's 1.3-liter engine trades in its 2-barrel carburetor for fuel injection, gaining three horsepower in return.

For

● 4WD traction   ● Fuel economy

Against

● Ride   ● Noise   ● Rear seat room

Summary

With its greater power and weight, longer wheelbase, and broader stance, Sidekick is a much more substantial and comfortable vehicle than Samurai. However, that doesn't make Sidekick a high achiever. For example, 0-60 mph takes a leisurely 13.7 seconds—a lot better than the Samurai but hardly neck-snapping. Still, Sidekick's extra strength helps when merging onto fast-moving freeways. Where the Samurai works very hard to pick up speed, the Sidekick does it with far less strain. With either model, engine and road noise are prominent, but more so in Samurai. Sidekick is more stable in corners and on the highway, though the ride is still stiff and jiggly on rough surfaces. Despite the Sidekick's greater width, the rear bench seat holds only two adults, same as the Samurai's. The back bench is also hard, and there's little leg space with the front seats fully aft. Sidekick's convertible top is infuriating to put up and down—much worse than the Samurai's—because of a multitude of snaps, clips, cords, and fasteners. So, while Sidekick boasts significant improvements over Samurai, we don't see it as a good choice for an everyday vehicle. Samurai sales have never recovered from allegations in 1988 that the vehicle is prone to rolling over in quick directional changes. Suzuki has cut Samurai's base price $500 to $7999, but that still doesn't make it much of a buy.

Specifications

	Sidekick 2-door wagon	Samurai 2-door wagon
Wheelbase, in.	86.6	79.9
Overall length, in.	142.5	135.0
Overall width, in.	64.2	60.6
Overall height, in.	65.6	65.6
Turn diameter, ft.	32.2	33.4
Curb weight, lbs.	2134	2125
Cargo vol., cu. ft.	32.1	31.9

	Sidekick 2-door wagon	Samurai 2-door wagon
Fuel capacity, gals.	11.1	10.6
Seating capacity	4	4
Front headroom, in.	39.5	38.6
Front shoulder room, in.	52.1	48.5
Front legroom, max., in.	42.1	40.0
Rear headroom, in.	38.3	35.5
Rear shoulder room, in.	50.2	51.0
Rear legroom, min., in.	31.6	27.6

Powertrain layout: longitudinal front engine/rear-wheel drive or on-demand 4WD.

Engines

	ohc I-4	ohc I-4
Size, liters/cu. in.	1.6/97	1.3/79
Fuel delivery	TBI	TBI
Horsepower @ rpm	80 @ 5400	66 @ 6000
Torque (lbs./ft.) @ rpm	94 @ 3000	76 @ 3500
Availability	S[1]	S[2]

EPA city/highway mpg

5-speed OD manual	26/28	28/29
3-speed automatic	24/25	

1. Sidekick   2. Samurai.

Prices

Suzuki Sidekick	Retail Price	Dealer Invoice	Low Price
JS soft top	$9999	—	—
JX soft top	NA	—	—
JX hardtop	NA	—	—
JLX soft top	NA	—	—
JLX hard top	NA	—	—

Dealer invoice, low price and destination charge not available at time of publication.

Standard equipment:

JS: 1.6-liter TBI 4-cylinder engine, 5-speed manual transmission, folding canvas top, front bucket seats, trip odometer, center console, tinted glass, carpet, power mirrors, 195/75R14 tires. **JX** adds: part-time 4-wheel drive with 2-speed transfer case, rear defogger (hardtop), AM/FM cassette, tachometer, spare tire lock, 205/75R15 all-terrain tires. **JLX** adds: cloth seats, spare tire cover, individual reclining and sliding rear seats.

OPTIONS prices not available at time of publication.

Suzuki Samurai

KEY: ohv = overhead valve; **ohc** = overhead cam; **dohc** = double overhead cam; **I** = inline cylinders; **V** = cylinders in V configuration; **flat** = horizontally opposed cylinders; **bbl.** = barrel (carburetor); **PFI** = port (multi-point) fuel injection; **TBI** = throttle-body (single-point) fuel injection; **rpm** = revolutions per minute; **OD** = overdrive transmission; **S** = standard; **O** = optional; **NA** = not available.

Suzuki Samurai

	Retail Price	Dealer Invoice	Low Price
2-door convertible	$7999	—	—

Dealer invoice, low price and destination charge not available at time of publication.

Standard equipment:

1.3-liter TBI 4-cylinder engine, 5-speed manual transmission, part-time 4-wheel drive with 2-speed transfer case, folding canvas top, locking fuel cap, dual outside mirrors, vinyl reclining front bucket seats, trip odometer, intermittent wipers, 205/70R15 tires.

OPTIONS prices not available at time of publication.

Suzuki Swift

Suzuki Swift GT

What's New

Suzuki introduced the front-drive Swift for 1989 in 3- and 5-door hatchback body styles. This year, a 4-door notchback sedan with a regular trunk replaces the 5-door hatchback in the lineup. The 4-door shares the 93.1-inch wheelbase of the 5-door, but putting a trunk on the rear adds about 10 inches to the Swift's body, making the 4-door 160 inches overall. The 4-door is scheduled to go on sale by the end of December in three trim levels: GA, GL, and GS, with base prices ranging from $7399 to $8599. All will use a 70-horsepower 1.3-liter 4-cylinder engine; the GA will come only with a 5-speed manual transmission, the others with a choice of the 5-speed manual or extra-cost 3-speed automatic. The Swift 3-door hatchback comes three ways for 1990: A new $6399 GA is slotted at the bottom as the entry-level model; the plusher GL is the mid-level model; and the sporty GT is the top-line version. The sporty model was called "GTi" last year, but Suzuki ran into a legal problem over the name with Volkswagen, which has marketed its own "GTI" model in the U.S. for several years. The Swift GT uses a 100-horsepower, dual-cam 1.3-liter 4-cylinder, while the other hatchbacks use the 70-horsepower 1.3. The Geo Metro hatchbacks sold by Chevrolet are built from the Swift's design, but Chevy doesn't have a copy of the new 4-door or the GT.

For

● Fuel economy ● Acceleration (GT)
● Handling/roadholding (GT)

Against

● Noise ● Ride (GT)

Summary

We haven't driven the new 4-door, so our comments concern only the 3-door hatchback, whose diminutive proportions aren't suited for tall people. Six footers have adequate leg room in front, but their heads will be against the ceiling. In the rear seat, there's even less head room, while leg room is minuscule if the front seats aren't pushed well forward. A 1989 GTi we tested felt tinny and lacked good sound insulation, so a lot of engine and road noise invaded the interior. On the plus side, the dual-cam engine revved eagerly and provided quick acceleration without sounding or feeling like it was going to beat itself to death. Despite a lot of stop-go urban commuting, we still averaged a commendable 31.6 mpg. The 70-horsepower engine used in other Swifts isn't as frisky, but with the 5-speed manual it should be at least as economical. Our test of the GTi showed that the firm suspension and small proportions help Swift maneuver deftly through dense traffic and tear around tight turns with impressive agility, but we found the ride to be stiff and unyielding. Despite its low base prices, we just aren't real enthused about Swift. The same amount of money or a little more can buy cars such as the Honda Civic, Dodge/Plymouth Colt, Mazda 323, and Volkswagen Fox. Some Suzuki dealers have been offering rebates in the $1500 range on '89 Swifts, so you should be able to get a big discount on this year's models as well.

Specifications

	3-door hatchback	4-door notchback
Wheelbase, in.	89.2	93.1
Overall length, in.	146.1	160.4
Overall width, in.	62.0	63.0
Overall height, in.	53.1	54.3
Turn diameter, ft.	30.2	31.4
Curb weight, lbs.	1716	NA
Cargo vol., cu. ft.	15.4	NA
Fuel capacity, gals.	10.6	10.6
Seating capacity	4	4
Front headroom, in.	NA	NA
Front shoulder room, in.	NA	NA
Front legroom, max., in.	NA	NA
Rear headroom, in.	NA	NA
Rear shoulder room, in.	NA	NA
Rear legroom, min., in.	NA	NA

Powertrain layout: transverse front engine/front-wheel drive.

Engines

	ohc I-4	dohc I-4
Size, liters/cu. in.	1.3/79	1.3/79
Fuel delivery	TBI	PFI
Horsepower @ rpm	70 @ 6000	100 @ 6500
Torque (lbs./ft.) @ rpm	74 @ 3500	83 @ 5000
Availability	S	S[1]

EPA city/highway mpg

5-speed OD manual	46/50	40/44
3-speed automatic	38/39	31/34

1. GT only.

Prices

Suzuki Swift	Retail Price	Dealer Invoice	Low Price
GA 3-door hatchback	$6399	—	—
GA 4-door notchback	7399	—	—
GL 3-door hatchback	6799	—	—
GL 4-door notchback	7899	—	—
GS 4-door notchback	8599	—	—
GT 3-door hatchback	9399	—	—

Dealer invoice, low price and destination charge not available at time of publication.

Standard equipment:

GA: 1.3-liter TBI 4-cylinder engine, 5-speed manual transmission, cloth and vinyl reclining front bucket seats, split folding rear seat, trip odometer, 155/70R13 tires. **GL** adds: intermittent wipers, remote hatch release, velour carpet, door pockets. **GS** adds: tachometer, power mirrors. **GT** adds: DOHC 16-valve PFI engine, close-ratio 5-speed manual transmission, 4-wheel disc brakes, sport seats, AM/FM cassette, digital clock, 175/60R14 tires.

OPTIONS prices not available at time of publication.

Toyota Camry

Toyota Camry LE V6

What's New

The optional V-6 engine gains a knock sensor and three horsepower (to 156) as the major mechanical changes for the compact Camry, Toyota's most popular U.S. model. Last year's lineup returns. A front-drive 4-door sedan comes in base, Deluxe, and LE trim, and a front-drive 5-door wagon in Deluxe and LE trim. The All-Trac, a sedan with a permanently engaged 4-wheel-drive system, is available in Deluxe and LE guise. A 115-horsepower 2.0-liter 4-cylinder engine is the base engine and the 2.5-liter V-6 is optional on front-drive Deluxe and LE models. All Camry wagons and some sedans are imported from Japan. Toyota's Georgetown, Kentucky, plant is now at capacity, producing 200,000 Camry sedans per year for sale in the U.S. Other changes for 1990 are that Deluxe models with manual transmission have a tachometer as standard equipment (it was formerly optional) and 60/40 split, folding rear seatbacks are optional on Deluxe sedans. The optional Power Package has a new door unlocking system; one turn of the key unlocks the driver's door and a second turn unlocks the other doors. Camry's passive-restraint system consists of motorized front shoulder belts with manual lap belts. Anti-lock brakes are available on the LE sedan and wagon with the V-6 engine and the All-Trac LE.

For

- Acceleration (V-6)   • Anti-lock brakes
- 4WD traction (All-Trac)   • Passenger room

Against

- Driveability (automatic transmission)
- Engine noise (4-cylinder)

Summary

Camry's arch rival in the compact class, the Honda Accord, is new this year, offering a roomier interior and a significant improvement in acceleration over the previous version. However, Camry still offers some features not available on Accord, including the V-6 engine, 4WD, and a station wagon body

style. Accord's new 4-cylinder engine is more powerful and quieter than Camry's 4-cylinder, but the optional V-6 evens the score for Camry. The V-6 is smooth, eager to go, and commendably quiet. Unfortunately, it produces little power at low speeds, which hampers driveability with the automatic transmission. The automatic has electronic shift controls; in the Power mode, the transmission is too sensitive to the throttle and tends to hunt annoyingly between gears, while in the Normal mode it reacts too slowly when you need a quick burst of power. The V-6 is still a better match for the automatic transmission than the 2.0-liter four, which is even more gutless low down. Camry has several other virtues, such as ample passenger room, good assembly quality, a reputation for reliability, and good resale value, all of which help compensate for higher-than-average retail prices. Toyota dealers were offering substantial discounts on 1989 Camrys, so if that continues on the 1990 models, you should be able to buy one for well below suggested retail.

Specifications

Specifications	4-door notchback	5-door wagon
Wheelbase, in.	102.4	102.4
Overall length, in.	182.1	183.1
Overall width, in.	67.4	67.4
Overall height, in.	54.1	54.5
Turn diameter, ft.	34.8	34.8
Curb weight, lbs.	2690[1]	2910
Cargo vol., cu. ft.	14.6	65.2
Fuel capacity, gals.	15.9	15.9
Seating capacity	5	5
Front headroom, in.	37.9	38.2
Front shoulder room, in.	54.3	54.3
Front legroom, max., in.	42.9	42.9
Rear headroom, in.	36.6	37.7
Rear shoulder room, in.	53.7	53.7
Rear legroom, min., in.	34.4	34.4

1. 3086 lbs., All-Trac.

Powertrain layout: transverse front engine/front-wheel drive or permanent 4WD (All-Trac).

Engines

Engines	dohc I-4	dohc V-6
Size, liters/cu. in.	2.0/122	2.5/153
Fuel delivery	PFI	PFI
Horsepower @ rpm	115 @ 5200	156 @ 5600
Torque (lbs./ft.) @ rpm	124 @ 4400	160 @ 4400
Availability	S	O

EPA city/highway mpg

5-speed OD manual	26/34	19/26
4-speed OD automatic	24/31	19/25

Prices

Toyota Camry	Retail Price	Dealer Invoice	Low Price
4-door notchback, 5-speed	$11588	$9966	$10777
4-door notchback, automatic	12258	10542	11400
Deluxe 4-door notchback, 5-speed	12388	10555	11471

KEY: ohv = overhead valve; **ohc** = overhead cam; **dohc** = double overhead cam; **I** = inline cylinders; **V** = cylinders in V configuration; **flat** = horizontally opposed cylinders; **bbl.** = barrel (carburetor); **PFI** = port (multi-point) fuel injection; **TBI** = throttle-body (single-point) fuel injection; **rpm** = revolutions per minute; **OD** = overdrive transmission; **S** = standard; **O** = optional; **NA** = not available.

Prices are accurate at time of printing; subject to manufacturer's change

Toyota

	Retail Price	Dealer Invoice	Low Price
Deluxe 4-door notchback, automatic	13078	11142	12110
LE 4-door notchback, automatic	14658	12415	13536
All-Trac Deluxe 4-door, 5-speed	14168	12071	13119
All-Trac Deluxe 4-door, automatic	15058	12829	13943
All-Trac LE 4-door, automatic	16648	14101	15374
Deluxe 5-door wagon, automatic	13768	11730	12749
Deluxe V6 4-door notchback, 5-speed . . .	13698	11671	12684
Deluxe V6 4-door notchback, automatic . .	14388	12259	13323
LE V6 4-door notchback, automatic	16428	13915	15171
Deluxe V6 5-door wagon, automatic	15078	12846	13962
LE V6 5-door wagon, automatic	17218	14584	15901

Dealer invoice and destination charge may vary by region.

Standard equipment:

2.0-liter DOHC 16-valve PFI 4-cylinder engine, 5-speed manual or 4-speed automatic transmission, power steering, coolant temperature gauge, trip odometer, center console with storage, velour reclining front bucket seats with driver's-seat height adjustment, rear shoulder belts, remote fuel door and trunk releases, rear defogger, tinted glass, P185/70SR13 tires. **Deluxe** adds: 2.0-liter DOHC 16-valve PFI 4-cylinder or 2.5-liter DOHC 24-valve PFI V-6 engine, 4-wheel disc brakes (V-6), wide bodyside moldings, dual remote mirrors, tilt steering column, automatic-off headlamp feature, folding rear seatbacks (wagon), rear wiper/washer (wagon), digital clock, right visor mirror, cup holder. **LE** adds: air conditioning (V-6), power mirrors, tachometer, console armrest, multi-adjustable driver's seat, folding rear armrest, cargo cover (wagon), illuminated entry with fadeout, upper windshield tint band, AM/FM radio with power antenna. **All-Trac** models have full-time 4-wheel drive.

Optional equipment:

	Retail Price	Dealer Invoice	Low Price
Anti-lock brakes, LE All-Trac	1280	1024	1152
LE V6	1130	904	1017
Air conditioning (std. LE V6)	825	660	743
Power glass moonroof (NA base)	700	560	630
Cruise control, base	315	258	287
Deluxe & LE	210	168	189
Base includes tilt steering column.			
Power Pkg., Deluxe 4-door	620	496	558
LE	565	452	509
Deluxe wagon	570	457	514
Power windows and locks; Deluxe 4-door includes split folding rear seat; LE includes lighted visor mirrors.			
Power Seat Pkg., LE	230	184	207
Requires Power Pkg. or Value Pkg.			
Leather trim, LE 4-doors	1080	864	972
Includes power height adjustment for driver's seat; requires Power Pkg. or Value Pkg.			
Alloy wheels, LE 4-cyl.	390	312	351
LE V6	410	328	369
All-Trac LE	360	288	324
AM/FM radio, base & Deluxe 4-doors . . .	330	247	289
Deluxe wagon	360	270	315
AM/FM cassette, base & Deluxe 4-doors .	480	360	420
Deluxe wagon	510	382	446
LE	190	142	166
AM/FM cassette w/EQ, LE	470	352	411
Speaker upgrade, 4-doors	140	112	126
Deluxe wagon	170	136	153
Convenience Pkg., base	120	96	108
Conventional spare tire, digital clock.			
Fall 1990 Value Pkg., Deluxe 4-cyl.	1399	1259	1329
Deluxe V6, LE	1190	1008	1099
LE V6	650	551	601
Air conditioning, cruise control, AM/FM cassette, Power Pkg., floormats.			

> **KEY: ohv** = overhead valve; **ohc** = overhead cam; **dohc** = double overhead cam; **I** = inline cylinders; **V** = cylinders in V configuration; **flat** = horizontally opposed cylinders; **bbl.** = barrel (carburetor); **PFI** = port (multi-point) fuel injection; **TBI** = throttle-body (single-point) fuel injection; **rpm** = revolutions per minute; **OD** = overdrive transmission; **S** = standard; **O** = optional; **NA** = not available.

	Retail Price	Dealer Invoice	Low Price
Split folding rear seat, Deluxe 4-doors . . .	100	80	90
All Weather Guard Pkg., base	55	46	51
California emissions pkg.	70	59	65
Mudguards (std. All-Trac)	30	24	27

Toyota Celica

Toyota Celica GT

What's New

A redesigned Celica sports coupe debuts this fall with rounded, flowing styling aimed specifically at the U.S. market. In addition, two new engines are available and a driver's-side airbag is standard for all models. The wheelbase is the same as the 1986-89 generation's, 99.4 inches, while overall length grows about three inches. Choices in body styles are the same as before: A 2-door coupe and a Liftback 3-door hatchback, both of which go on sale in the fall; next spring, a convertible arrives. Besides the new exterior styling the biggest changes are under the hood. Base ST models, which previously came with a 115-horsepower 2.0-liter 4-cylinder, now have a 103-horsepower, dual-cam 1.6-liter engine with 16 valves, the same engine that powers most Corolla models. GT and GT-S models share a new 130-horsepower 2.2-liter 4-cylinder, also with dual cams and 16 valves. All these models have front-wheel drive and are available with either a 5-speed manual or 4-speed automatic transmission. The 4-wheel-drive Celica All-Trac retains a turbocharged 2.0-liter engine, but horsepower is rated at 200 this year, 10 more than in 1989. The All-Trac, whose 4WD system is permanently engaged, comes only with a 5-speed manual. Anti-lock brakes are optional on the All-Trac and will be available on the GT-S later in the year. Even with the standard airbag, a tilt steering column is available on Celica. A new 220-watt, 10-speaker sound system, called "System 10," with a cassette player and a compact disc player is optional on GT, GT-S, and All-Trac models. Complete price lists weren't available in time for publication, but the base Celica ST starts at $12,268, the GT at $13,938, and the GT-S at $16,268.

For

● Acceleration (except ST) ● Handling/roadholding
● Airbag ● Anti-lock brakes ● Fuel economy

Against

● Rear-seat room ● Entry/exit ● Engine noise

222
CONSUMER GUIDE®

Summary

We sampled the new Celicas at Toyota's preview and were surprised at how well the base ST accelerated with the 1.6-liter engine, at least with manual transmission. We weren't given the opportunity to try one with automatic, which we fear will sap some of the 1.6-liter engine's vigor, thus requiring a heavy throttle foot to keep up with traffic. The new 2.2-liter engine is stronger and more flexible, producing more torque at lower speeds than the 1.6. Even so, the 2.2—like most other multi-valve engines—produces the bulk of its power at higher speeds, which makes it better suited for use with manual transmission. For those who want automatic, the 2.2 will still deliver decent acceleration and fuel economy. The new Celica's interior design puts the gauges where they're easy to see and controls where they're easy to reach, and provides adequate room for adults in the front seats. As with most sports coupes, the rear seat is too cramped for all but kids. Toyota predicts the ST and GT will be the volume models, each accounting for about 45 percent of Celica sales. We prefer the GT for its stronger engine. Those who want more sporting handling should consider the GT-S, which has larger tires and a firmer suspension, and anti-lock brakes as an option. Celicas are pricey, but previous models have been reliable cars with good resale value.

Specifications

	2-door notchback	3-door hatchback
Wheelbase, in.	99.4	99.4
Overall length, in.	176.0	174.0
Overall width, in.	67.1	67.1
Overall height, in.	50.6	50.6
Turn diameter, ft.	36.1	36.1
Curb weight, lbs.	2500	2696[1]
Cargo vol., cu. ft.	12.6	24.7
Fuel capacity, gals.	15.9	15.9
Seating capacity	4	4
Front headroom, in.	37.7	37.7
Front shoulder room, in.	52.0	52.0
Front legroom, max., in.	42.9	42.9
Rear headroom, in.	34.5	33.0
Rear shoulder room, in.	49.2	49.2
Rear legroom, min., in.	26.8	26.8

1. 3272 lbs., All-Trac.

Powertrain layout: transverse front engine/front-wheel drive or permanent 4WD (All-Trac).

Engines	dohc I-4	dohc I-4	Turbo dohc I-4
Size, liters/cu. in.	1.6/97	2.2/132	2.0/122
Fuel delivery	PFI	PFI	PFI
Horsepower @ rpm	103 @ 6000	130 @ 5400	200 @ 6000
Torque (lbs./ft.) @ rpm	102 @ 3200	140 @ 4400	200 @ 3200
Availability	S[1]	S[2]	S[3]
EPA city/highway mpg			
5-speed OD manual	28/33	23/29	19/24
4-speed OD automatic	25/33	22/28	

1. ST   2. GT, GT-S   3. All-Trac.

Toyota Corolla

What's New

Toyota has dropped the 90-horsepower, carbureted 1.6-liter 4-cylinder that powered Corolla Deluxe, LE, and SR5 models

Toyota Corolla

last year in favor of a 102-horsepower, fuel-injected version of the same engine. Last year, the fuel-injected engine came only in the 4-wheel-drive All-Trac models. The sporty Corolla GT-S 2-door gains 15 horsepower from a higher compression ratio and a knock sensor. Its dual-cam 1.6-liter engine now pumps 130 horsepower. Corollas now come with front shoulder belts that can be left buckled for automatic deployment and knee bolsters under the dashboard. Models with automatic transmission have a shift lock that requires the brake pedal be applied to shift out of Park. The optional power door locks have a new feature; one turn of the key unlocks the driver's and a second turn unlocks the other doors. All Corollas have front-wheel drive except the All-Trac sedan and wagon, which have permanently engaged 4WD. Corolla 2-door coupes and 5-door wagons, and some 4-door sedans, are imported from Japan. The 4-door also is built at the New United Motor Manufacturing Inc. plant in California, where the similar Geo Prizm is built for Chevrolet.

For

- Fuel economy   • Acceleration (GT-S)
- 4WD traction (All-Trac)   • Ride

Against

- Engine noise   • Rear seat room

Summary

This year's change to fuel injection for all models not only adds 12 horsepower, but also should improve overall engine performance and perhaps fuel economy. Carbureted versions we tested suffered from flat spots and occasional hesitation. The GT-S 2-door coupe has become quite a hot number, packing 130 horsepower into its 97-cubic-inch engine, and it delivers much livelier acceleration than other Corollas, though it comes only with manual transmission. The GT-S also has a much firmer suspension than other Corollas, exacting a big toll in ride quality. The sedan and wagon, on the other hand, soak up rough roads with impressive resiliency. The sedan and wagon have roomier interiors than many rivals, but adults sitting in the upright rear bench will need to have the front seats moved well forward for adequate leg room. We rank the Corolla among the leaders in the subcompact class, along with the similar Prizm and the Honda Civic, which is slightly less expensive than a comparably equipped Corolla. There are much cheaper alternatives among subcompacts (such as the Hyundai Excel and Dodge Omni/Plymouth Horizon), and somewhat less expensive cars (Nissan Sentra, Dodge/Plymouth Colt), but Corolla's commendable reliability record and good resale value compensate in the long run.

Prices are accurate at time of printing; subject to manufacturer's change

Specifications

	2-door notchback	4-door notchback	5-door wagon
Wheelbase, in.	95.7	95.7	95.7
Overall length, in.	172.2	170.3	171.5
Overall width, in.	65.6	65.2	65.2
Overall height, in.	49.6	52.4	54.5
Turn diameter, ft.	31.5	31.5	31.5
Curb weight, lbs.	2414	2390[1]	2436[2]
Cargo vol., cu. ft.	11.7	12.7	64.5
Fuel capacity, gals.	13.2	13.2	13.2
Seating capacity	4	5	5
Front headroom, in.	37.9	38.4	39.6
Front shoulder room, in.	52.4	53.2	53.2
Front legroom, max., in.	42.9	40.9	40.9
Rear headroom, in.	35.3	36.4	39.3
Rear shoulder room, in.	51.0	52.7	52.7
Rear legroom, min., in.	25.8	31.6	31.6

1. 2650 lbs., All-Trac 2. 2736 lbs., All-Trac.

Powertrain layout: transverse front engine/front-wheel drive or permanent 4WD (All-Trac).

Engines

	dohc I-4	dohc I-4
Size, liters/cu. in.	1.6/97	1.6/97
Fuel delivery	PFI	PFI
Horsepower @ rpm	102 @ 5800	130 @ 6800
Torque (lbs./ft.) @ rpm	101 @ 4800	105 @ 6000
Availability	S	S[1]

EPA city/highway mpg

5-speed OD manual	28/33	25/31
3-speed automatic	26/29	
4-speed OD automatic	25/33	

1. GT-S.

Prices

Toyota Corolla	Retail Price	Dealer Invoice	Low Price
4-door notchback, 5-speed	$8748	$7786	$8267
4-door notchback, automatic	9218	8204	8711
Deluxe 4-door notchback, 5-speed	9488	8159	8824
Deluxe 4-door notchback, automatic	9958	8563	9261
LE 4-door notchback, 5-speed	10928	9365	10147
LE 4-door notchback, automatic	11598	9939	10769
Deluxe 5-door wagon, 5-speed	10128	8709	9419
Deluxe 5-door wagon, automatic	10598	9114	9856
All-Trac Deluxe wagon, 5-speed	11838	10189	11014
All-Trac Deluxe wagon, automatic	12608	10842	11725
All-Trac SR5 wagon, 5-speed	13238	11345	12292
All-Trac Deluxe 4-door, 5-speed	10758	9251	10005
All-Trac Deluxe 4-door, automatic	11528	9913	10721

Dealer invoice and destination charge may vary by region.

Standard equipment:

Base and Deluxe: 1.6-liter DOHC 16-valve PFI 4-cylinder engine, 5-speed manual or 3-speed automatic transmission, power brakes, cloth reclining front bucket seats (vinyl on wagons), split folding rear seatback (wagons), tinted glass, console with storage, door map pockets, cup holder, remote fuel door and decklid releases, trip odometer, coolant temperature gauge, 155SR13 tires. **LE** adds: 5-speed manual or 4-speed automatic transmission,

> **KEY: ohv** = overhead valve; **ohc** = overhead cam; **dohc** = double overhead cam; **I** = inline cylinders; **V** = cylinders in V configuration; **flat** = horizontally opposed cylinders; **bbl.** = barrel (carburetor); **PFI** = port (multi-point) fuel injection; **TBI** = throttle-body (single-point) fuel injection; **rpm** = revolutions per minute; **OD** = overdrive transmission; **S** = standard; **O** = optional; **NA** = not available.

tachometer, intermittent wipers, digital clock, AM/FM radio, 60/40 folding rear seatbacks, bodyside molding, remote mirrors, driver's seat height and lumbar support adjustments, upgraded trunk trim, 175/70SR13 all-season tires. **Deluxe All-Trac** models have permanent 4-wheel drive, 5-speed manual or 4-speed automatic transmission. **SR5 All-Trac wagon** adds: power steering, cruise control, digital clock, AM/FM radio, cloth upholstery, tilt steering column, remote mirrors, intermittent wipers, rear wiper.

Optional equipment:	Retail Price	Dealer Invoice	Low Price
Power steering, base & Deluxe	250	214	232
Air conditioning	775	620	698
Convenience Pkg., Deluxe	115	92	104
Remote OS mirrors, digital clock.			
Power sunroof, Deluxe & LE 4-doors	530	424	477
Cruise control & int. wipers (NA base)	210	168	189
Alloy wheels, LE 4-door	370	296	333
SR5 wagon	415	332	374
AM/FM radio w/4 speakers	330	247	289
AM/FM cassette, base & Deluxe 4-doors,			
All-Trac wagon	480	360	420
Deluxe wagons	380	285	333
SR5 wagon	190	142	166
LE	150	112	131
AM/FM radio w/2 speakers, Deluxe	210	157	184
Tilt steering column	85	73	79
Power Pkg., LE 4-door, SR5 wagon	570	456	513
Power windows and locks, power mirrors.			
Two-Tone Paint Pkg., SR5 wagon	320	256	288
Fabric seats, Deluxe wagon	70	60	65
Rear wiper, Deluxe wagon	135	111	123
Exterior Appearance Pkg., LE 4-door,			
All-Trac wagons	85	68	77
Upgrade Speaker Pkg., Deluxe All-Trac wagon	115	92	104
Rear overhead storage shelf, two rear speaker enclosures and wiring (speakers not included).			
Tachometer, 5-speed models	60	48	54
Fall 1990 Value Pkg., Deluxe 4-door	669	602	636
Power steering, digital clock, remote OS mirrors, AM/FM cassette, full wheel covers, floormats, 175/70R13 tires.			
Fall 1990 Value Pkg., LE 4-door	799	719	759
Air conditioning, AM/FM cassette, power windows and locks, power mirrors, color-coordinated bumpers, tilt steering column.			
Fall 1990 Value Pkg., Deluxe 2WD wagon	675	607	641
Deluxe 4WD wagon	659	593	626
Power steering, digital clock, remote OS mirrors, AM/FM cassette, full fabric seats, full wheel covers, 175/70R13 tires (2WD), floormats.			
All Weather Guard Pkg., Deluxe & LE	55	46	51
Base	160	130	145
California emissions pkg.	70	59	65

Toyota Corolla Sport	Retail Price	Dealer Invoice	Low Price
SR5 2-door notchback, 5-speed	$11068	$9485	$10277
SR5 2-door notchback, automatic	11738	10059	10899
GT-S 2-door notchback, 5-speed	13238	11318	12278

Dealer invoice and destination charge may vary by region.

Standard equipment:

SR5: 1.6-liter DOHC 16-valve PFI 4-cylinder engine, 5-speed manual or 4-speed automatic transmission, cloth reclining front bucket seats, trip odometer, coolant temperature gauge, tachometer, 175/70SR13 tires. **GT-S** adds: higher-output engine, power steering, split folding rear seat, driver's-seat lumbar support and cushion height adjusters, AM/FM radio, power mirrors, oil pressure gauge, voltmeter, tilt steering column, automatic headlights-off system, power mirrors, leather-wrapped steering wheel, intermittent wipers, 185/60R14 tires.

Optional equipment:

	Retail	Dealer	Low
Power steering, SR5	250	214	232
Air conditioning	775	620	698
Power sunroof	530	424	477
Cruise control & int. wipers	210	168	189

	Retail Price	Dealer Invoice	Low Price
Convenience Pkg., SR5	180	151	166
Digital clock, split folding rear seat, driver's-seat lumbar support and cushion height adjusters.			
Alloy wheels, SR5	370	296	333
GT-S	435	348	392
AM/FM radio, SR5	330	247	289
AM/FM cassette, SR5	520	390	455
AM/FM cassette w/EQ, GT-S	430	322	376
Tilt steering column, SR5	85	73	79
Power Pkg.	390	312	351
Power windows and locks.			
Sport seat, GT-S	180	144	162
Exterior Appearance/Convenience Pkg., SR5	355	291	323
Color-coordinated bumper, bodyside moldings, power mirrors, digital clock, driver's-seat lumbar support and cushion height adjusters, split folding rear seat.			
All Weather Guard Pkg.	55	46	51
California emissions pkg.	70	59	65

Toyota Cressida

Toyota Cressida

What's New

New last year, Cressida is unchanged for 1990. The rear-drive Cressida is still the top-shelf luxury sedan under the Toyota name, but it has been superseded in price and prestige by the Lexus LS 400, the flagship of Toyota's new upscale car division. Cressida comes only as a 4-door notchback sedan in one trim level. The powertrain consists of a 190-horsepower 3.0-liter 6-cylinder engine, derived from the engine used in the Supra sports car, and a 4-speed automatic transmission with electronic shift controls. A standard shift lock requires that the brake pedal be applied before the transmission can be shifted out of Park. Motorized front shoulder belts, with separate manual lap belts, are standard as Cressida's way of meeting the federal mandate for passive restraints. Anti-lock brakes are optional.

For

- Acceleration
- Anti-lock brakes
- Ride
- Quietness

Against

- Control layout

Summary

We clocked a 1989 Cressida at 9.3 seconds in the 0-60-mph test—more than competitive with rivals such as the Acura Legend and Nissan Maxima. The engine's not only powerful, but quiet as well, giving the Cressida a definite edge over the

Maxima in that department. The automatic transmission complements the engine with prompt, smooth shifts up and down the speed range. We averaged 22.3 mpg overall in our test, ranging from a low of 17 in the city to an impressive 29 mpg on the highway. Braking was exceptional with the optional anti-lock control. Our test car pulled down from 60 mph in just 119 feet, versus an absolute norm of about 150 feet. Cressida's ride is firm but supple, with good resistance to pitching and bouncing. In usable passenger room Cressida slightly trails the Mazda 929, another rear-driver, as well as the front-drive Legend and Maxima. The general ergonomics give little cause for complaint—with two exceptions. The automatic climate system has a motorized, slide-out auxiliary panel that holds manual fan-speed and mode buttons; trouble is, it can't extend or retract without the ignition on. Just as silly is the bank of duplicate radio/cassette controls just under the center dash vents, which are so close to the main controls that they're of little use. Visibility is excellent, thanks to tall windows and slim roof pillars. Cressida is a little cheaper than either the 929 or the base Legend sedan, but a couple of thousand above even the most expensive Maxima, which stands out as a bargain in this class. Cressida lacks the verve of the Legend and the Maxima SE, but appeals for its healthy helping of standard luxuries, reliability, and smooth performance.

Specifications

	4-door notchback
Wheelbase, in.	105.6
Overall length, in.	189.6
Overall width, in.	67.3
Overall height, in.	54.5
Turn diameter, ft.	32.8
Curb weight, lbs.	3417
Cargo vol., cu. ft.	12.0
Fuel capacity, gals.	18.5
Seating capacity	5
Front headroom, in.	38.4
Front shoulder room, in.	54.6
Front legroom, max., in.	42.8
Rear headroom, in.	37.1
Rear shoulder room, in.	54.4
Rear legroom, min., in.	35.0

Powertrain layout: longitudinal front engine/rear-wheel drive.

Engines	dohc I-6
Size, liters/cu. in.	3.0/180
Fuel delivery	PFI
Horsepower @ rpm	190 @ 5600
Torque (lbs./ft.) @ rpm	185 @ 4400
Availability	S

EPA city/highway mpg

4-speed OD automatic	19/24

Prices

Toyota Cressida	Retail Price	Dealer Invoice	Low Price
4-door notchback	$21498	$17628	$19563

Dealer invoice and destination charge may vary by region.

Standard equipment:

3.0-liter DOHC 24-valve PFI 6-cylinder engine, 4-speed automatic transmission, power steering, 4-wheel disc brakes, automatic climate control, reclin-

Prices are accurate at time of printing; subject to manufacturer's change

ing front bucket seats, rear shoulder belts, cruise control, variable intermittent wipers, trip odometer, coolant temperature gauge, tachometer, AM/FM cassette with EQ, power antenna, power windows and locks, heated power mirrors, tilt/telescopic steering column, 205/60R15 tires.

Optional equipment:	Retail Price	Dealer Invoice	Low Price
Anti-lock brakes	1130	904	1017
CD player	700	525	613
Power sunroof	810	648	729
Power Seat Pkg.	540	432	486
Leather/Power Seat Pkg.	1245	996	1121
California emissions pkg.	70	59	

Toyota Land Cruiser

Toyota Land Cruiser

What's New

The slow-selling Land Cruiser 4-wheel-drive wagon is unchanged for 1990, but a revamped model will be introduced next spring as an early 1991. We don't know how extensive the changes for 1991 will be. Land Cruiser is the oldest product in Toyota's U.S. line. It was last redesigned for 1981, but received a fairly extensive update for 1988. This included a new 155-horsepower 4.0-liter inline 6-cylinder engine, increased towing capacity (to 3500 pounds), a modified on-demand 4WD system, and adoption of "velocity-sensitive" shock absorbers that automatically stiffen on rough roads for better control. On smooth surfaces they operate in a "soft" mode for more ride comfort. The 4WD system has manual front hubs that have to be locked or unlocked by hand. A dashboard switch is used instead of the transfer-case lever to engage 4WD High; the driver can change in or out of 4WD High on-the-fly once the hubs are locked. 4WD Low is engaged by shifting the floor-mounted transfer-case lever when the vehicle is stopped. Land Cruiser comes only in a 5-door body style.

For

- 4WD traction
- Passenger and cargo room

Against

- Fuel economy
- Acceleration
- Ride

KEY: ohv = overhead valve; **ohc** = overhead cam; **dohc** = double overhead cam; **I** = inline cylinders; **V** = cylinders in V configuration; **flat** = horizontally opposed cylinders; **bbl.** = barrel (carburetor); **PFI** = port (multi-point) fuel injection; **TBI** = throttle-body (single-point) fuel injection; **rpm** = revolutions per minute; **OD** = overdrive transmission; **S** = standard; **O** = optional; **NA** = not available.

Summary

Those seeking a traditional 4×4 wagon will find the Land Cruiser a safe choice, thanks to Toyota's reputation for building reliable, durable vehicles. Life with Land Cruiser isn't a bowl of cherries, however. The steering is vague and over-assisted, the ride pitchy and choppy, even on roads that look smooth, despite the variable-rate shock-absorber damping. Fuel consumption is piggish—10.5 mpg in our test—no surprise with only 155 horses to move more than two tons of curb weight. Acceleration is mediocre: 15.4 seconds 0-60 mph. Worse, the engine sounds like it's working hard except in gentle cruising. On the plus side, passenger room is ample all around and the seats seem comfortable for long trips, while cargo space is bountiful. There's a slapdash look to some controls, but full instrumentation is standard, the interior has a sturdy, high-grade look, and body construction is solid and tight. That doesn't add up to outstanding value, though, with prices starting at around $21,000. That's steep for an old-fashioned 4WD wagon that lacks true shift-on-the-fly convenience. In market position Land Cruiser rivals the Jeep Cherokee Limited and Wagoneer, Mitsubishi Montero 5-door, and Range Rover. A 6-cylinder Cherokee/Wagoneer or Montero, or Toyota's own 4Runner, should serve most buyers just as well, and for the same amount of money or even less.

Specifications

	5-door wagon
Wheelbase, in.	107.5
Overall length, in.	184.0
Overall width, in.	70.9
Overall height, in.	68.9
Turn diameter, ft.	40.7
Curb weight, lbs.	4480
Cargo vol., cu. ft.	98.0
Fuel capacity, gals.	23.8
Seating capacity	5
Front headroom, in.	40.0
Front shoulder room, in.	59.5
Front legroom, max., in.	39.2
Rear headroom, in.	40.4
Rear shoulder room, in.	59.6
Rear legroom, min., in.	34.6

Powertrain layout: longitudinal front engine/rear-wheel drive or on-demand 4WD.

Engines

	ohv I-6
Size, liters/cu. in.	4.0/241
Fuel delivery	PFI
Horsepower @ rpm	155 @ 4000
Torque (lbs./ft.) @ rpm	220 @ 3000
Availability	S

EPA city/highway mpg

4-speed OD automatic	12/14

Prices

Toyota Land Cruiser	Retail Price	Dealer Invoice	Low Price
5-door wagon	$20898	$17450	$19174

Dealer invoice and destination charge may vary by region.

Standard equipment:

4.0-liter PFI 6-cylinder engine, 4-speed automatic transmission, freewheeling manual front hubs, power steering, cloth reclining front seats, tachometer, trip odometer, coolant temperature and oil pressure gauges, digital clock, remote fuel door release, AM/FM radio, voltmeter, locking fuel door, tinted glass, dual OS mirrors, tilt steering column, front tow hook, intermittent wipers, 225/75R15 M&S tires.

Optional equipment:	Retail Price	Dealer Invoice	Low Price
Air conditioning	890	712	801
AM/FM cassette	190	142	166
Power Pkg.	544	680	612
Power windows and locks, power mirrors.			
Two-tone paint	245	196	221
California emissions pkg.	70	59	65

Toyota MR2

1989 Toyota MR2

What's New

Mister Two, Toyota's 2-seat, mid-engine sports car, is skipping the 1990 model year. A new MR2 is scheduled to arrive next spring as an early 1991 model, so until then only leftover 1989 models will be available. We don't have the details on the 1991 model, but the new MR2 will be larger and will have Ferrari-like styling. It will be powered by Toyota's new 2.2-liter engine, used in the 1990 Celica GT and GT-S, and there will be a high-performance model with a turbocharged 2.2, perhaps with twin turbos. There is not expected to be a super-charged engine for 1991. The 1989 models came with either a 115-horsepower, twin-cam 1.6-liter 4-cylinder engine or a 145-horsepower supercharged 1.6. The naturally aspirated models were available with a fixed roof or a T-bar roof with removable panels, while the supercharged MR2 came with the T-bar roof.

For

● Acceleration ● Braking ● Fuel economy

Against

● Noise ● Cargo room ● Entry/exit

Summary

Hefty insurance rates and high suggested retail prices have slowed MR2 sales the past couple of years, but the new model is expected to have racier styling that will broaden its appeal. We've always been fond of the 1986-89 MR2 because it's so much fun to drive. The supercharged engine provides an instant, smooth rush of power, even at low speeds. By contrast, most turbo engines suffer a noticeable lag before delivering more power, which often comes in a big gob instead of a steady flow. You don't have to order the supercharged model to get good performance. The base engine delivers almost as much pleasure for substantially less money, with

a free-revving nature that is perfectly suited to a 2-seat sports car. Either engine will return commendable fuel economy. Our staff is split on the MR2's handling ability; some rate it excellent, others claim the MR2 feels loose in corners, lacks straight-line stability, and has vague steering. All our drivers agree that the brakes are strong and responsive. Though the interior is tight, most drivers find a workable position. The gauges are clearly marked and all controls are within easy reach, except for the low-mounted stereo. The ground-hugging build makes getting in or out a chore, and despite trunks in the front and rear, cargo space is minimal. However, MR2s are built for driving pleasure, not practical considerations. Check with your insurance agent before you buy.

1989 Specifications

	2-door notchback
Wheelbase, in.	91.3
Overall length, in.	155.5
Overall width, in.	65.6
Overall height, in.	48.6
Turn diameter, ft.	31.5
Curb weight, lbs.	2350[1]
Cargo vol., cu. ft.	7.8
Fuel capacity, gals.	10.8
Seating capacity	2
Front headroom, in.	37.4
Front shoulder room, in.	52.4
Front legroom, max., in.	43.0
Rear headroom, in.	—
Rear shoulder room, in.	—
Rear legroom, min., in.	—

1. 2493 lbs., Supercharged MR2.

Powertrain layout: transverse mid engine/rear-wheel drive.

Engines	dohc I-4	Supercharged dohc I-4
Size, liters/cu. in.	1.6/97	1.6/97
Fuel delivery	PFI	PFI
Horsepower @ rpm	115 @ 6600	145 @ 6400
Torque (lbs./ft.) @ rpm	100 @ 4800	140 @ 4000
Availability	S	S
EPA city/highway mpg		
5-speed OD manual	26/31	24/30
4-speed OD automatic	25/30	22/27

Prices not available at time of publication.

Toyota Supra

What's New

A driver's-side airbag is standard on Supra this year to meet the federal passive-restraint requirement. In addition, a padded knee bolster has been added to the driver's side of the instrument panel. The airbag is housed in a new 4-spoke steering wheel; the steering column retains its tilt and tele-scoping features. With the airbag, cruise-control switches have been moved from the steering wheel to a steering-column stalk. The rear-drive Supra comes in fixed roof or Sport Roof (with removable T-tops) guise with either a 200-horse-power 3.0-liter 6-cylinder or a 232-horsepower, turbocharged 3.0 six. Both engines now have a fully balanced crankshaft and hydraulic engine mounts, and the power steering system

Prices are accurate at time of printing; subject to manufacturer's change

Toyota Supra Turbo

has been revised to provide more feel at medium and high speeds. The standard power door locks have a new feature: turning the key once unlocks the driver's door and turning it a second time unlocks the passenger's door.

For

- Acceleration • Anti-lock brakes • Airbag
- Handling

Against

- Interior room • Fuel economy • Road noise
- Entry/exit

Summary

The current Supra was introduced as a late 1986 model, so it's an old-timer compared to its primary rival, the Nissan 300ZX, which was introduced last spring as an early 1990. Supra still has much to offer, including strong acceleration, tenacious handling ability, optional anti-lock brakes, an airbag, and a long list of standard comfort and convenience features. With a base curb weight of nearly 3500 pounds, Supra isn't nimble like an MR2, but its wide tires and low stance give it impressive cornering power, while the firm suspension confidently tackles demanding roads. In snow, however, the tires have poor traction, and it can be quite a challenge to keep a Supra on course. Engine and wind noise are low on the highway, but road noise is high, partly because of the aggressive tire tread. Supra has a tiny rear seat, but well-shaped, supportive front seats, a comfortable driving position, and simple, convenient controls. The cargo area is shallow, even with the rear seats folded down, while entry/exit is compromised by Supra's low build and wide doors that require a lot of space to be opened all the way. We've complained in recent years that Supra has become quite expensive, but a 300ZX Turbo now starts at $33,000, so everything's relative. In its favor, Supra also has proven to be a reliable and durable sports car.

Specifications

	3-door hatchback
Wheelbase, in.	102.2
Overall length, in.	181.9
Overall width, in.	68.7
Overall height, in.	51.2
Turn diameter, ft.	35.4
Curb weight, lbs.	3463
Cargo vol., cu. ft.	12.8
Fuel capacity, gals.	18.5
Seating capacity	4
Front headroom, in.	37.5
Front shoulder room, in.	52.5
Front legroom, max., in.	43.6

	3-door hatchback
Rear headroom, in.	33.9
Rear shoulder room, in.	50.5
Rear legroom, min., in.	24.7

Powertrain layout: longitudinal front engine/rear-wheel drive.

Engines	dohc I-6	Turbo dohc I-6
Size, liters/cu. in.	3.0/180	3.0/180
Fuel delivery	PFI	PFI
Horsepower @ rpm	200 @ 6000	232 @ 5600
Torque (lbs./ft.) @ rpm	188 @ 3600	254 @ 3200
Availability	S	S
EPA city/highway mpg		
5-speed OD manual	18/23	17/22
4-speed OD automatic	18/23	18/23

Prices

Toyota Supra	Retail Price	Dealer Invoice	Low Price
3-door hatchback, 5-speed	$22860	$18745	$20803
3-door hatchback, automatic	23610	19360	21485
w/Sport Roof, 5-speed	23930	19623	21777
w/Sport Roof, automatic	24680	20238	22459
Turbo, 5-speed	25200	20664	22932
Turbo, automatic	25950	21279	23615
Turbo w/Sport Roof, 5-speed	26220	21500	23860
Turbo w/Sport Roof, automatic	26970	22115	24543

Dealer invoice and destination charge may vary by region.

Standard equipment:

3.0-liter DOHC 24-valve PFI 6-cylinder engine, 5-speed manual or 4-speed automatic transmission, power steering, 4-wheel disc brakes, driver's-side airbag, automatic climate control, power windows and locks, heated power mirrors, two-can cupholder, tilt/telescopic steering column, fog lights, theft deterrent system, bodyside moldings, tachometer, coolant temperature and oil pressure gauges, voltmeter, trip odometer, variable intermittent wipers, cruise control, console with storage and padded armrest, cloth sport seats, driver's seat power lumbar and lateral support adjustments, folding rear seatbacks, lighted visor mirrors, remote fuel door and hatch releases, automatic-off headlight system, illuminated entry system, tinted glass, rear defogger, cargo cover, AM/FM cassette with EQ, diversity power antenna, 225/50VR16 Goodyear Eagle GT Gatorback tires on alloy wheels. **Turbo** adds: turbocharged, intercooled engine, speed-sensitive power steering, oil cooler, turbo boost gauge, limited-slip differential.

Optional equipment:

Anti-lock brakes	1130	904	1017
Power driver's seat	230	184	207
Sports Pkg., base	795	647	721
Turbo	360	288	324
Electronically modulated suspension, limited-slip differential, progressive power steering.			
White Exterior Appearance Pkg.	40	32	36
CD player	700	525	613
Leather/Power Seat Pkg.	1240	992	1116
California emissions pkg.	70	59	65

Toyota Tercel

What's New

The front-drive Tercel subcompact, Toyota's entry-level line, has a smaller roster for 1990. All 5-door hatchbacks are gone and so are the Deluxe 3-door hatchbacks. That leaves a 3-door hatchback in EZ and base trim levels, and a 2-door

Toyota Tercel

	2-door notchback	3-door hatchback
Turn diameter, ft.	31.2	31.2
Curb weight, lbs.	2020	1990
Cargo vol., cu. ft.	11.0	36.2
Fuel capacity, gals.	11.9	11.9
Seating capacity	5	5
Front headroom, in.	37.8	38.4
Front shoulder room, in.	51.5	51.5
Front legroom, max., in.	40.2	40.2
Rear headroom, in.	35.9	36.6
Rear shoulder room, in.	50.7	51.5
Rear legroom, min., in.	30.8	32.1

Powertrain layout: transverse front engine/front-wheel drive.

Engines

	ohc I-4
Size, liters/cu. in.	1.5/89
Fuel delivery	1 bbl.
Horsepower @ rpm	78 @ 6000
Torque (lbs./ft.) @ rpm	87 @ 4000
Availability	S[1]

EPA city/highway mpg

4-speed OD manual	31/36
5-speed OD manual	30/36
3-speed automatic	29/32

1. Calif. models with automatic transmission have multi-point injection.

coupe in base and Deluxe trim. The EZ 3-door comes only with a 4-speed manual transmission, the others with a standard 5-speed manual or optional 3-speed automatic. All models get automatic front shoulder belts, with manual lap belts, to satisfy the passive-restraint rule. Those with automatic transmission now have a shift lock that requires the brake pedal be applied to shift out of Park, plus the transmission must be in Park before the ignition key can be removed. Tercels are powered by a carbureted, 78-horsepower 1.5-liter 4-cylinder engine, except for California models with automatic transmission, which have fuel injection and 82 horsepower. The 2-door coupes gain remote trunk and fuel-door releases and a remote outside mirror as standard equipment, while the Deluxe 2-door also adds power steering as standard.

For

- Fuel economy
- Cargo room (hatchback)

Against

- Passenger and cargo room (coupe)
- Acceleration (automatic transmission)

Summary

As Toyota's smallest, least-expensive model, Tercel's mission is to lure buyers on a tight budget away from the Hyundai Excel, Nissan Stanza, Dodge Omni/Plymouth Horizon, and other low-cost, basic-transportation cars. Several rivals undercut Tercel in price, but few match its admirable record for reliability and durability. Fuel economy is good with automatic transmission, and outstanding with either manual transmission, both of which have overdrive top gears that help stretch a gallon of gas. Acceleration is adequate with manual shift and barely adequate with automatic. Models we've tested have suffered flat spots during acceleration that may be caused by the variable-venturi carburetor used on this engine. In addition, the air conditioner saps a lot of engine power. The coupe has minimal rear seat room, while the hatchback has enough space for two adults to sit in somewhat cramped fashion. Trunk space is modest on the coupe as well; the more functional hatchback has rear seatbacks that fold for more cargo room. Tercel is a competent small car, but neither its performance nor its price are exceptional. In today's competitive market, you might find a Toyota dealer who's willing to sell one at an attractive discount.

Prices

Toyota Tercel	Retail Price	Dealer Invoice	Low Price
Standard 2-door notchback, 5-speed	$7618	$6856	$7237
Standard 2-door notchback, automatic	8078	7270	7674
Deluxe 2-door notchback, 5-speed	9028	7763	8396
Deluxe 2-door notchback, automatic	9498	8168	8833
EZ 3-door hatchback, 4-speed	6488	5936	6212
Standard 3-door hatchback, 5-speed	7558	6878	7218
Standard 3-door hatchback, automatic	8028	7368	7698

Dealer invoice and destination charge may vary by region.

Standard equipment:

EZ: 1.5-liter 12-valve 4-cylinder engine, 4-speed manual transmission, locking fuel door, trip odometer, vinyl reclining front bucket seats, door pockets, folding rear seatback, 145/80SR13 tires on styled steel wheels. **Standard** adds: 5-speed manual or 3-speed automatic transmission, cloth seat inserts, cup holder, door-ajar light, bodyside moldings, rear ashtray. **Deluxe** adds: cloth seat trim, folding rear seatbacks, right visor mirror, rear defogger, tinted glass, 155SR13 tires.

Optional equipment:

Power steering, Standard	250	214	232
Air conditioning (NA EZ)	735	588	662
Rear wiper/washer, Standard hatchbacks	135	111	123
AM/FM radio	210	157	184
AM/FM cassette	480	360	420
Cargo deck cover, Standard hatchbacks	50	41	46
Convenience Pkg., Standard hatchbacks	280	225	253

Full wheel covers, intermittent wipers, remote OS mirrors, analog clock, remote fuel door and hatch releases, full fabric seats.

KEY: ohv = overhead valve; **ohc** = overhead cam; **dohc** = double overhead cam; **I** = inline cylinders; **V** = cylinders in V configuration; **flat** = horizontally opposed cylinders; **bbl.** = barrel (carburetor); **PFI** = port (multi-point) fuel injection; **TBI** = throttle-body (single-point) fuel injection; **rpm** = revolutions per minute; **OD** = overdrive transmission; **S** = standard; **O** = optional; **NA** = not available.

Specifications

	2-door notchback	3-door hatchback
Wheelbase, in.	93.7	93.7
Overall length, in.	166.7	157.3
Overall width, in.	64.0	64.0
Overall height, in.	51.8	52.6

Prices are accurate at time of printing; subject to manufacturer's change

	Retail Price	Dealer Invoice	Low Price
All Weather Guard Pkg., EZ & Std. 2-door .	90	77	84
Standard hatchback & Deluxe 2-door . .	55	46	51
California emissions pkg.	70	59	65

Toyota Van

1989 Toyota 4WD Van

What's New

There won't be a 1990 version of the Van, but a redesigned model will go on sale next spring as an early 1991. Until the 1991 models arrive, Toyota dealers will be selling leftover 1989s. We don't have much information on the 1991, but it will have more aerodynamic styling and will be designed specifically as a passenger vehicle for the U.S. market. The 1984-89 models were originally designed as commercial vehicles for the Japanese market, and were converted to passenger use in the U.S. as an answer to the Chrysler minivans. As with the previous models, the 1991 Van will be available with rear drive or 4-wheel drive and it will have a mid-engine design. However, the engine in the new model will reportedly be tilted to one side to allow walk-through space from the front seats to the rear of the vehicle. The engine in the 1984-89 Van is mounted upright between the front seats. The lineup at the end of 1989 included Deluxe and LE models in both rear- and 4WD configurations, all with a 101-horsepower 2.2-liter 4-cylinder engine.

For

• Passenger and cargo room   • 4WD traction

Against

• Handling/roadholding   • Entry/exit   • Driving position

Summary

We haven't driven the 1991 Van, so our comments are on the 1989 models. You should still be able to find '89s at most Toyota dealers, who should be willing to offer substantial dis-

---

KEY: ohv = overhead valve; **ohc** = overhead cam; **dohc** = double overhead cam; **I** = inline cylinders; **V** = cylinders in V configuration; **flat** = horizontally opposed cylinders; **bbl.** = barrel (carburetor); **PFI** = port (multi-point) fuel injection; **TBI** = throttle-body (single-point) fuel injection; **rpm** = revolutions per minute; **OD** = overdrive transmission; **S** = standard; **O** = optional; **NA** = not available.

---

counts. Our advice, though, is to look instead at the Dodge Caravan/Plymouth Voyager or the Mazda MPV, the leaders of the minivan class. If you're inclined to stick with Toyota, then hang on to your money until next spring, when the new model arrives. It's bound to be better than the '89 Van, whose short 88-inch wheelbase improves maneuverability, but also leaves excessive body overhang front and rear, which results in a lot of bouncing and pitching. In addition, the Van is taller than it is wide, so there's too much body lean around corners and the inside rear wheel tends to lift and lose traction on slippery roads. Traction improves greatly with the 4WD system, but that adds 400 power-robbing pounds to the Van's curb weight, which it can ill afford with only 101 horsepower. There's ample room inside for passengers to move around, but the engine placement forces the driver and front passenger to get out of the vehicle to get to the rear. The driver has little foot room and he's squeezed between the door and the engine compartment. Also, the steering wheel is too horizontal, as in a bus. To enter, you squeeze through narrow front doorways while stepping up into the tall interior; the driver has an even harder time since he has to slip under the steering wheel. The 1989 Van just has too many compromises to make it a good buy even with a hefty discount.

1989 Specifications

	4-door van
Wheelbase, in.	88.0
Overall length, in.	175.8
Overall width, in.	66.3
Overall height, in.	70.3
Turn diameter, ft.	30.2
Curb weight, lbs.	3038[1]
Cargo vol., cu. ft.	149.8
Fuel capacity, gals.	15.9
Seating capacity	7
Front headroom, in.	39.6
Front shoulder room, in.	54.9
Front legroom, max., in.	41.5
Rear headroom, in.	40.6
Rear shoulder room, in.	57.7
Rear legroom, min., in.	32.2

1. 3455 lbs., 4WD Van.

Powertrain layout: longitudinal mid engine/rear-wheel drive or on-demand 4WD.

Engines

	ohv I-4
Size, liters/cu. in.	2.2/137
Fuel delivery	PFI
Horsepower @ rpm	101 @ 4400
Torque (lbs./ft.) @ rpm	133 @ 3000
Availability	S

EPA city/highway mpg

5-speed OD manual	22/24
4-speed OD automatic	21/23

Prices not available at time of publication.

Toyota 4Runner

What's New

The 1990 4Runner sport-utility vehicle went on sale in late spring, and in the fall a rear anti-lock braking system (ABS) became standard on V-6-powered 4Runners and optional on 4-cylinder models. The ABS operates only when the vehicles

Toyota 4Runner 2WD

are in 2-wheel-drive; a load-sensing proportioning valve works on the rear brakes when 4-wheel drive is engaged. Unlike conventional ABS systems, which draw power from engine vacuum, Toyota's operates off the power steering pump. The 1990 4Runner comes in 3- and 5-door body styles with a choice of a 116-horsepower 4-cylinder engine or 150-horsepower V-6. Earlier versions were limited to a 3-door body and 4-cylinder engines. The 5-door is available with rear-wheel drive, but only with automatic transmission. Other models have on-demand 4WD. V-6 4×4 models come with 4WDemand, a system that allows changing in or out of 4WD on the move at speeds up to 50 mph. 4WDemand is optional on 4-cylinder models with the 5-speed manual transmission. Other 4×4 models have to be stopped to engage or disengage 4WD. The new 4Runner is still built on Toyota's pickup-truck platform, but now it has a full steel roof instead of the detachable fiberglass shell that previously had been used from the middle pillars rearward. All models have seats for five; some earlier 4Runners had only two front seats.

For

- Ride   • 4WD traction   • Anti-lock rear brakes
- Quietness (V-6)   • Passenger and cargo room

Against

- Fuel economy   • Acceleration (4-cylinder)

Summary

The new 4Runner boasts major improvements over its predecessor. The most obvious is the comfortable, stable ride, making the 4Runner much more carlike than before. Gone is the pounding, bouncing ride of before; instead, there's a softer ride that absorbs most bumps with little notice and still provides steady highway cruising. Of the two engines we much prefer the V-6; the four is overmatched with more than a couple of passengers aboard. The V-6 is no ball of fire, especially with automatic transmission, but it is a smooth, refined engine that generates little noise. Toyota claims that 4Runner is the quietest compact 4×4, and we're inclined to agree. Adding two side doors makes 4Runner much more of a family wagon than before, but it's a high step up into the cabin, even on 2WD models. This might limit some of its appeal as daily transportation. Head and leg room are good all around and there's generous cargo space. With its smooth ride, low noise levels, shift-on-the-fly capability, and 5-door body style, the new 4Runner has joined the leaders in the sport-utility pack. The Jeep Cherokee/Wagoneer offers more power, a full-time 4WD system, and 4-wheel anti-lock brakes, but the 4Runner has a better reputation for reliability.

Specifications

	3-door wagon	5-door wagon
Wheelbase, in.	103.3	103.3
Overall length, in.	176.0	176.0
Overall width, in.	66.5	66.5
Overall height, in.	66.1	66.1
Turn diameter, ft.	37.4	37.4
Curb weight, lbs.	3720	3760
Cargo vol., cu. ft.	78.3	78.3
Fuel capacity, gals.	17.2	17.2
Seating capacity	5	5
Front headroom, in.	38.7	38.7
Front shoulder room, in.	53.9	53.9
Front legroom, max., in.	41.5	41.5
Rear headroom, in.	38.3	38.3
Rear shoulder room, in.	53.7	53.9
Rear legroom, min., in.	31.6	31.6

Powertrain layout: longitudinal front engine/rear-wheel drive or on-demand 4WD.

Engines

	ohc I-4	ohc V-6
Size, liters/cu. in.	2.4/144	3.0/180
Fuel delivery	PFI	PFI
Horsepower @ rpm	116 @ 4800	150 @ 4800
Torque (lbs./ft.) @ rpm	140 @ 2800	180 @ 3400
Availability	S	S

EPA city/highway mpg

5-speed OD manual	19/21	16/19
4-speed OD automatic	17/19	15/19

Prices

Toyota 4Runner	Retail Price	Dealer Invoice	Low Price
4WD 3-door wagon, 5-speed	$16718	$14545	$15632
4WD 3-door wagon, automatic	17568	15284	16426
3-door wagon w/4WDemand, 5-speed	16918	14719	15819
4WD 3-door wagon, V6, 5-speed	18788	16252	17520
4WD 3-door wagon, V6, automatic	20018	17316	18667
2WD 5-door wagon, automatic	15498	13173	14336
2WD 5-door wagon, V6, automatic	17598	14870	16234
4WD 5-door wagon, 5-speed	16218	13785	15002
4WD 5-door wagon, automatic	17068	14508	15788
5-door wagon w/4WDemand, 5-speed	16418	13995	15207
4WD 5-door wagon, V6, 5-speed	18288	15453	16871
4WD 5-door wagon, V6, automatic	19518	16493	18006

Dealer invoice and destination charge may vary by region.

Standard equipment:

2.4-liter PFI 4-cylinder engine, 5-speed manual or 4-speed automatic transmission, reclining front bucket seats, coolant temperature gauge, trip odometer, power tailgate window, 225/75R15 tires. **V6** adds: 3.0-liter PFI V-6, 4WDemand (allows engagment of 4WD at speeds up to 50 mph), power steering, intermittent wipers, map lights, AM/FM radio, rear defogger, tilt steering column.

Optional equipment:

Anti-lock rear brakes, 4-cyl.	250	212	231
Requires power steering.			
Power steering, 4-cyl.	280	238	259
Air conditioning (NA 3-doors)	795	636	716
4WDemand, 4-cyl. w/automatic	200	170	185
w/alloy wheels	650	530	590
AM/FM radio, 4-cyl.	210	157	184
AM/FM cassette, 4-cyl.	540	405	473
V6	330	247	289

Prices are accurate at time of printing; subject to manufacturer's change

	Retail Price	Dealer Invoice	Low Price
AM/FM cassette w/EQ, 5-door V6	1370	1060	1215
3-door V6	1240	956	1098
AM/FM cassette w/EQ & CD, 5-door V6 . .	2070	1585	1828
3-door V6	1940	1481	1711

Audio systems with EQ include diversity antenna, power windows and locks, power mirrors; requires cruise control.

Power moonroof	700	560	630
Tilt steering column, 4-cyl.	120	102	111
Alloy wheels & 31" tires, 4WD V6	1262	995	1129
Alloy wheels	450	360	405
Steel wheels & 31" tires, 4WD V6	872	683	778
Chrome Pkg.	230	184	207
Rear wiper/washer	150	123	137
Cruise Control Pkg.	290	232	261
Power Pkg., 5-door 4-cyl.	655	524	590
5-door V6	720	576	648
3-door 4-cyl.	525	420	473
3-door V6	590	472	531

Power windows and locks, power mirrors, power antenna (V6); requires Cruise Control Pkg.

Rear heater	150	120	1
Front vent windows	60	48	

Volkswagen Cabriolet

1989 Volkswagen Cabriolet Wolfsburg

What's New

A driver's-side airbag becomes standard this year as the principal change on the Cabriolet, Volkswagen's front-drive convertible. The Cabriolet is the only U.S. Volkswagen model to get the airbag; other VWs use automatic front shoulder belts. Along with the new airbag, standard equipment now includes power front windows (a feature not previously available). The Cabriolet, sold in the U.S. since 1980, is based on the Rabbit design that preceded the current Golf. Cabriolet is powered by a 90-horsepower 1.8-liter 4-cylinder engine and comes with either a 5-speed manual or 3-speed automatic transmission. It comes with a manual folding top and integral roll bar.

For

- Acceleration ● Airbag ● Fuel economy
- Handling/roadholding

Against

- Rear seat room ● Cargo space ● Noise

Summary

Though more than 10 years old, Cabriolet hides its age well. It offers sporting handling and, with the 5-speed manual transmission, brisk acceleration. You'll lose some acceleration with

automatic transmission, and also some fuel economy. With the 5-speed, we consistently average 25 mpg or more in urban driving. Thanks to the integral roll bar, Cabriolet's body is more rigid than most ragtops', so you aren't constantly bothered by shakes and rattles. On the down side, though, the convertible top takes up a lot of rear seat room and reduces the trunk to a tiny cubicle with a small load opening. The rear seat folds down for extra cargo space, but it's hard to fit anything sizeable through the doors or the trunk. Wind noise is prominent at highway speeds, even with the top in place, so you have to crank up the stereo volume to enjoy tunes. Also, Cabriolet has historically been a favorite among stereo thieves, who only have to cut through the soft top to gain entry. That's something to keep in mind if you park outdoors most of the time. The Mazda Miata 2-seat roadster, the smash hit of the 1990 model year so far, is sure to steal some sales from Cabriolet. However, you'll pay a hefty premium above suggested retail price for a Miata, while you might be able to get a substantial discount below suggested retail on a Cabriolet.

1989 Specifications

	2-door conv.
Wheelbase, in.	94.5
Overall length, in.	153.1
Overall width, in.	64.6
Overall height, in.	55.6
Turn diameter, ft.	31.2
Curb weight, lbs.	2274
Cargo vol., cu. ft.	6.5
Fuel capacity, gals.	13.8
Seating capacity	4
Front headroom, in.	37.4
Front shoulder room, in.	51.9
Front legroom, max., in.	39.4
Rear headroom, in.	35.6
Rear shoulder room, in.	50.4
Rear legroom, min., in.	31.0

Powertrain layout: transverse front engine/front-wheel drive.

Engines

	ohc I-4
Size, liters/cu. in.	1.8/109
Fuel delivery	PFI
Horsepower @ rpm	90 @ 5500
Torque (lbs./ft.) @ rpm	100 @ 3000
Availability	S

EPA city/highway mpg

5-speed OD manual	24/27
3-speed automatic	22/24

Prices

Volkswagen Cabriolet	Retail Price	Dealer Invoice	Low Price
2-door convertible	$15485	—	—
Bestseller 2-door convertible	16180	—	—
Boutique 2-door convertible	16740	—	—
Destination charge	320	320	320

Dealer invoice and low price not available at time of publication.

Standard equipment:

1.8-liter PFI 4-cylinder engine, 5-speed manual transmission, power steering, driver's-side airbag, cloth reclining front bucket seats, tachometer, coolant temperature gauge, oil temperature and pressure gauges, voltmeter, trip odometer, AM/FM cassette, power windows, door pockets, remote mirrors, intermittent wipers, rear defogger, tinted glass, 185/70HR14 tires. **Bestseller** adds: sport seats, driver's-seat height adjustment, leather-wrapped steering wheel and shift knob, alloy wheels. **Boutique** adds: white leather seats, leatherette trim.

Optional equipment:	Retail Price	Dealer Invoice	Low Price
3-speed automatic transmission	505	—	—
Air conditioning	825	—	—
Cruise control	225	—	—
Metallic paint	165	—	—
California emissions pkg.	95	—	—

Volkswagen Corrado

Volkswagen Corrado

What's New

Billed as Volkswagen's "first full-blooded sports car," Corrado replaces the Scirocco in VW's North American lineup. Like Scirocco (discontinued here after '88), it's a front-drive, 4-seat hatchback. Corrado's main distinction is a new supercharged version of the familiar 1.8-liter 4-cylinder Golf/Jetta engine, teamed only with a 5-speed manual transmission. The 158-horsepower engine is called "G-Charger" because its crankshaft-driven supercharger is shaped like the letter G. The G-Charger employs a single-overhead-cam cylinder head with two valves per cylinder. Corrado is based on the current Golf/Jetta platform and has standard 4-wheel disc brakes with optional anti-lock control (VW expects 85 percent of U.S. models will be equipped with the anti-lock feature). Corrado is 6.3 inches shorter than Scirocco but nearly three inches longer in wheelbase, almost two inches wider, and some 450 pounds heavier. An unusual Corrado feature is a so-called "active" rear spoiler that extends automatically above 45 mph to reduce rear aerodynamic lift; it retracts below 12 mph. A dashboard switch allows manual extension for cleaning. Also included in the $17,900 base price are power steering, air conditioning, anti-theft AM/FM/cassette stereo, central locking, power windows and door mirrors, 65/35 split-folding rear seat, and motorized front shoulder belts.

For

- Acceleration
- Handling/roadholding
- Anti-lock brakes
- Cargo room

Against

- Visibility
- Noise
- Entry/exit

Summary

Corrado's G-Charger engine is a mixed blessing. It's potent for its size and delivers strong midrange pull, yet almost seems anemic off the line. VW claims 7.5 seconds for the benchmark 0-60-mph sprint, but that seems optimistic by the seat of our pants. Corrado's 2660-pound curb weight does nothing for acceleration, nor fuel economy, plus the engine needs premium fuel. The lack of an automatic transmission will be a drawback for some buyers, and there apparently won't be one soon. As for the manual transmission, it's way behind the best the Japanese offer and is occasionally obstructive. Other gripes include poor rearward vision (blame the high tail, thick rear pillars, and somewhat low driving position), limited head room for 6-footers (even in front), and a lot of engine noise. On the plus side, handling is crisp, cornering grip ample, body lean minimal, and the power steering is fluid, quick, and properly boosted. It all makes for a car that's really fun to drive on tight, winding roads. The ride is firm and well-damped but supple and comfortable, enhanced by a solid structure that minimizes rough-road shakes and rattles. We also like the shapely, comfortable front seats, ample cargo space, generally good ergonomics, and thorough workmanship. In all, Corrado strikes us as interesting, enjoyable, well-made, and relatively practical for a sports coupe, though it's not outstanding value. For similar money you can get better performance and 4-wheel drive in the Mitsubishi Eclipse GSX/Eagle Talon TSi.

Specifications

	3-door hatchback
Wheelbase, in.	97.3
Overall length, in.	159.4
Overall width, in.	65.9
Overall height, in.	51.9
Turn diameter, ft.	34.5
Curb weight, lbs.	2660
Cargo vol., cu. ft.	18.6
Fuel capacity, gals.	14.5
Seating capacity	4
Front headroom, in.	37.0
Front shoulder room, in.	53.8
Front legroom, max., in.	41.7
Rear headroom, in.	35.0
Rear shoulder room, in.	50.4
Rear legroom, min., in.	31.2

Powertrain layout: transverse front engine/front-wheel drive.

Engines	Supercharged ohc I-4
Size, liters/cu. in.	1.8/109
Fuel delivery	PFI
Horsepower @ rpm	158 @ 5600
Torque (lbs./ft.) @ rpm	166 @ 4000
Availability	S

EPA city/highway mpg

5-speed OD manual	21/28

KEY: ohv = overhead valve; **ohc** = overhead cam; **dohc** = double overhead cam; **I** = inline cylinders; **V** = cylinders in V configuration; **flat** = horizontally opposed cylinders; **bbl.** = barrel (carburetor); **PFI** = port (multi-point) fuel injection; **TBI** = throttle-body (single-point) fuel injection; **rpm** = revolutions per minute; **OD** = overdrive transmission; **S** = standard; **O** = optional; **NA** = not available.

Prices are accurate at time of printing; subject to manufacturer's change

Prices

Volkswagen Corrado

	Retail Price	Dealer Invoice	Low Price
3-door hatchback	$17900	—	—
Destination charge	320	320	320

Dealer invoice and low price not available at time of publication.

Standard equipment:

1.8-liter supercharged PFI 4-cylinder engine, 5-speed manual transmission, 4-wheel disc brakes, velour height-adjustable bucket seats, split folding rear seat, rear shoulder belts, air conditioning, cruise control, power windows and locks, power mirrors, AM/FM cassette, tachometer, coolant temperature and oil pressure gauges, voltmeter, trip odometer, tilt steering column, rear defogger, tinted glass, leather-wrapped steering wheel and shift knob, cargo cover, visor mirrors (lighted right), speed-activated retractable rear spoiler, fog lamps, intermittent wipers, rear wiper/washer, 195/60VR15 tires on alloy wheels.

Optional equipment:

Anti-lock brakes	835	— —
Leather interior	710	— —
Metallic paint	165	— —
Sunroof	695	— —
California emissions pkg.	100	— —

Volkswagen Fox

1989 Volkswagen Fox GL Sport

What's New

Motorized front shoulder belts are standard on all Fox models this year to meet the federal passive-restraint requirement. Separate lap belts have to be buckled manually. Other than the new passive restraints, last year's Fox lineup returns largely unchanged. A base 2-door sedan, GL 4-door sedan, and a GL 3-door wagon have an 81-horsepower 1.8-liter 4-cylinder engine and a 4-speed manual transmission. The GL Sport 2-door has the same engine, but a 5-speed manual transmission. In addition, the GL Sport has alloy wheels instead of steel wheels. Neither automatic transmission nor power steering is available. The front-drive Fox, built in Brazil, is 5.4 inches longer than the Volkswagen Golf hatchbacks,

---

KEY: ohv = overhead valve; **ohc** = overhead cam; **dohc** = double overhead cam; **I** = inline cylinders; **V** = cylinders in V configuration; **flat** = horizontally opposed cylinders; **bbl.** = barrel (carburetor); **PFI** = port (multi-point) fuel injection; **TBI** = throttle-body (single-point) fuel injection; **rpm** = revolutions per minute; **OD** = overdrive transmission; **S** = standard; **O** = optional; **NA** = not available.

---

but 8.3 inches shorter than the Jetta sedans. Fox rides a 92.8-inch wheelbase, 4.5 inches shorter than the Golf/Jetta wheelbase.

For

- Fuel economy ● Visibility
- Driveability (5-speed manual)

Against

- Passenger room ● Cargo space ● Noise

Summary

The base 2-door Fox offers the most value for the money if you're looking for basic transportation with a little more flair than the run-of-the-mill entry-level subcompact. There are some benefits to spending more money on a Fox, however. GL models come with larger tires for better handling, a tachometer that helps you get more out of the frisky engine, and nicer interior furnishings. GL Sport models have the 5-speed manual transmission, whose gearing makes Fox easier to drive in traffic. The 4-speed manual has a tall overdrive top gear that keeps the engine well below the 3250-rpm torque peak, making a downshift to third gear mandatory for passing power. Fuel economy is similar with either transmission (25-30 mpg in urban driving). While all models handle with agility, the manual steering is quite heavy at low speeds, requiring lots of muscle in tight parking spaces. Fox isn't wide enough to fit three people in the rear seat without serious cramping and head room is tight all around. The trunk on the sedans is shallow and a full-size spare tire—which is appreciated—takes up a lot of cargo space. The rear seat folds on the wagon to increase cargo room to nearly 62 cubic feet. A deep glove box provides ample storage space, plus there are door map pockets and a dashboard shelf. Few subcompacts under $10,000 are as fun to drive as Fox, though the lack of automatic transmission and power steering will turn off some shoppers.

1989 Specifications	2-door notchback	4-door notchback	5-door wagon
Wheelbase, in.	92.8	92.8	92.8
Overall length, in.	163.4	163.4	163.4
Overall width, in.	63.0	63.0	63.9
Overall height, in.	53.7	53.7	54.5
Turn diameter, ft.	31.5	31.5	31.5
Curb weight, lbs.	2126	2203	2203
Cargo vol., cu. ft.	9.9	9.9	61.8
Fuel capacity, gals.	12.4	12.4	12.4
Seating capacity	4	4	4
Front headroom, in.	36.6	36.6	36.6
Front shoulder room, in.	51.7	51.7	51.7
Front legroom, max., in.	41.1	41.1	41.1
Rear headroom, in.	35.4	35.4	35.8
Rear shoulder room, in.	52.1	51.1	51.5
Rear legroom, min., in.	30.2	30.2	30.2

Powertrain layout: longitudinal front engine/front-wheel drive.

Engines

	ohc I-4
Size, liters/cu. in.	1.8/109
Fuel delivery	PFI
Horsepower @ rpm	81 @ 5500
Torque (lbs./ft.) @ rpm	93 @ 3250
Availability	S

EPA city/highway mpg	ohc I-4
4-speed OD manual	25/30
5-speed OD manual	24/29

Prices

Volkswagen Fox	Retail Price	Dealer Invoice	Low Price
2-door notchback	$7225	—	—
GL Sport 2-door notchback	8595	—	—
GL 4-door notchback	8310	—	—
GL 3-door wagon	8550	—	—
Destination charge	320	320	320

Dealer invoice and low price not available at time of publication.

Standard equipment:

1.8-liter PFI 4-cylinder engine, 4-speed manual transmission, cloth reclining front bucket seats, left remote mirror, rear defogger, intermittent wipers, console with coin box and storage bin, analog clock, 155/80SR13 tires. **GL Sport 2-door/GL 4-door** adds: 5-speed manual transmission (2-door), upgraded carpet, velour upholstery, digital clock, door pockets, map light, tachometer, right visor mirror, tinted glass, wide bodyside molding, flip-out rear window, 175/70SR 13 tires, alloy wheels (2-door). **Wagon** deletes tachometer and digital clock and adds: folding rear seat, tonneau cover, analog clock.

Optional equipment:

Air conditioning	715	—	—
Heavy Duty Pkg.	90	—	—
Metallic paint	165	—	—
AM/FM cassette	300	—	—
Radio prep	130	—	—
Rear wiper/washer	150	—	—
Sunroof	300	—	—

Volkswagen Golf/Jetta

1989 Volkswagen Golf GL

What's New

The Golf GTI 16V and Jetta GLI 16V have a larger, more powerful engine this year as the top-shelf models in a revised lineup. The GTI 16V and GLI 16V trade in last year's 123-horsepower 1.8-liter 4-cylinder engine and return for 1990 with a 131-horsepower 2.0-liter 4-cylinder, derived from the base engine used in the Audi 80. Like the engine it replaces, the new 2.0-liter has two overhead cams and four valves per cylinder, and is available only with a 5-speed manual transmission. All Golfs and Jettas have non-motorized automatic front shoulder belts for 1990 to meet the federal passive-restraint rule; separate lap belts have to be buckled manually. Golf and Jetta are built on the same front-drive platform and differ only in body configuration. This year's lineup includes Golf GL hatchbacks and Jetta GL sedans powered by a 100-horsepower 1.8-liter 4-cylinder. Slotted above the GL models are the Golf GTI 3-door hatchback and the Jetta Carat 4-door sedan, both with a 105-horsepower version of the 1.8-liter engine. GL, GTI, and Carat models are available with a 5-speed manual or 3-speed automatic transmission. Rounding out the lineup are the Jetta GL Diesel and Carat Diesel, available only with a 5-speed manual transmission in the 4-door body. The diesel engine added last summer, uses a 52-horsepower 1.6-liter 4-cylinder. A 4-wheel-drive version of the GTI hatchback with the Corrado's supercharged, 158-horsepower engine may be introduced to the U.S. during 1990.

For

- ● Acceleration ● Anti-lock brakes ● Fuel economy
- ● Handling/roadholding ● Cargo space

Against

- ● Driveability (automatic transmission) ● Noise

Summary

Golf and Jetta are practical subcompacts that offer sporty handling and a taut, well-controlled ride even on the lowest-priced models. Anti-lock brakes, a safety feature we recommend, are available on Jetta Carat and GLI models, and may be offered soon on the Golf GTI. All three gasoline engines provide brisk performance and good fuel economy with the 5-speed manual transmission. The optional automatic transmission saps a lot of power and hurts economy, plus you have to tromp on the gas pedal to force the transmission to downshift for passing. In addition, the automatic lacks an overdrive top gear, which makes for noisier highway cruising. We haven't driven the new diesel model, but with only 52-horsepower it's clearly for those who prize fuel economy over acceleration. Golf and Jetta are compacts based on EPA interior volume, but subcompacts based on their 97.3-inch wheelbase. Even so, all models have ample room for four adults and generous cargo space. Golf hatchbacks have folding rear seatbacks and Jetta sedans a cavernous trunk that's wide, deep, and easy to load. A Jetta GLI 16V or a Carat with anti-lock brakes and other extras can be pricey, but a less-expensive GL model with fewer goodies is just as practical and nearly as much fun to drive. Volkswagen has cut some prices for 1990 to try to make its vehicles more competitive and is offering cash incentives to its dealers as well.

1989 Specifications	Jetta 2-door notchback	Jetta 4-door notchback	Golf 3-door hatchback	Golf 5-door hatchback
Wheelbase, in.	97.3	97.3	97.3	97.3
Overall length, in.	171.7	171.7	158.0	158.0
Overall width, in.	65.5	65.5	65.5	65.5
Overall height, in.	55.7	55.7	55.7	55.7
Turn diameter, ft.	34.4	34.4	34.4	34.4
Curb weight, lbs.	2305	2305	2194	2246
Cargo vol., cu. ft.	16.6	16.6	39.6	39.6
Fuel capacity, gals.	14.5	14.5	14.5	14.5
Seating capacity	5	5	5	5
Front headroom, in.	38.1	38.1	38.1	38.1
Front shoulder room, in.	53.3	53.3	53.3	53.3
Front legroom, max., in.	39.5	39.5	39.5	39.5
Rear headroom, in.	37.1	37.1	37.5	37.5
Rear shoulder room, in.	53.3	53.3	54.3	54.3
Rear legroom, min., in.	35.1	35.1	34.4	34.4

Prices are accurate at time of printing; subject to manufacturer's change.

Volkswagen

Powertrain layout: transverse front engine/front-wheel drive.

Engines	ohc I-4	ohc I-4	dohc I-4	Diesel ohc I-4
Size, liters/cu. in.	1.8/109	1.8/109	1.8/109	1.6/97
Fuel delivery	PFI	PFI	PFI	PFI
Horsepower @ rpm	100 @ 5400	105 @ 5400	123 @ 5800	52 @ 4800
Torque (lbs./ft.) @ rpm . . .	107 @ 3400	110 @ 3400	120 @ 4250	71 @ 2000
Availability	S¹	S²	S³	S⁴

EPA city/highway mpg

5-speed OD manual	25/34	25/34	22/29	37/43
3-speed automatic	23/28	23/28		

1. GL models   2. GTI, Carat   3. GTI 16V, GLI 16V   4. Jetta Diesel.

Prices

Volkswagen Golf/GTI

	Retail Price	Dealer Invoice	Low Price
GL 3-door hatchback	$8695	—	—
GL 5-door hatchback	8995	—	—
GTI 8V 3-door hatchback	9995	—	—
GTI 16V 3-door hatchback	12900	—	—
Destination charge	320	320	320

Dealer invoice and low price not available at time of publication.

Standard equipment:

GL: 1.8-liter PFI 4-cylinder engine, 5-speed manual transmission, velour height-adjustable reclining front bucket seats, folding rear seat, rear shoulder belts, tachometer, coolant temperature gauge, trip odometer, rear defogger, tinted glass, door pockets, right visor mirror, remote OS mirrors, intermittent wipers, rear wiper/washer, center console with storage, 175/70SR13 tires. **GTI 8V** adds: higher-output engine, power steering, sport suspension, sport seats, upgraded upholstery, 185/60HR14 tires on teardrop-style alloy wheels. **GTI 16V** adds: 2.0-liter DOHC 16-valve engine, 4-wheel disc brakes, Recaro front seats with power height adjustment, trip computer, visor mirrors (lighted right), leather-wrapped steering wheel, tilt steering column, 195/60VR15 tires on BBS alloy wheels.

Optional equipment:

3-speed automatic transmission	505	—	—
Power steering	275	—	—
Air conditioning	805	—	—
Cruise control	225	—	—
Tilt steering column	75	—	—
Metallic paint	165	—	—
Power Pkg.	605	—	—
AM/FM cassette	300	—	—
Sound II AM/FM cassette	450	—	—
Sunroof	395	—	—

Volkswagen Jetta

	Retail Price	Dealer Invoice	Low Price
GL 2-door notchback	$9995	—	—
GL 4-door notchback	10295	—	—
GL diesel 4-door notchback	10495	—	—
Carat 4-door notchback	10990	—	—
Carat diesel 4-door notchback	11190	—	—
GLI 16V 4-door notchback	13750	—	—
Destination charge	260	260	260

Dealer invoice and low price not available at time of publication.

> **KEY: ohv** = overhead valve; **ohc** = overhead cam; **dohc** = double overhead cam; **I** = inline cylinders; **V** = cylinders in V configuration; **flat** = horizontally opposed cylinders; **bbl.** = barrel (carburetor); **PFI** = port (multi-point) fuel injection; **TBI** = throttle-body (single-point) fuel injection; **rpm** = revolutions per minute; **OD** = overdrive transmission; **S** = standard; **O** = optional; **NA** = not available.

Standard equipment:

GL: 1.8-liter PFI 4-cylinder gas or diesel engine, 5-speed manual transmission, power steering, velour height-adjustable reclining front bucket seats, rear shoulder belts, tilt steering column, center console with storage, rear defogger, tinted glass, tachometer, coolant temperature gauge, trip odometer, door pockets, rear armrest with storage, right visor mirror, remote OS mirrors, 185/60HR14 tires. **Carat** adds: higher-output engine (gas model), power locks, upgraded upholstery, rear head restraints, time-delay interior light, visor mirrors (lighted right). **GLI 16V** adds: 2.0-liter DOHC 16-valve engine, 4-wheel disc brakes, sport suspension, Recaro front seats with power height adjustment, trip computer, leather-wrapped steering wheel, 185/55VR15 tires on BBS alloy wheels.

Optional equipment:

	Retail Price	Dealer Invoice	Low Price
3-speed automatic transmission	505	—	—
Anti-lock brakes	835	—	—
Air conditioning	805	—	—
Alloy wheels	365	—	—
Cold Weather Pkg.	365	—	—
Cruise control	225	—	—
Metallic paint	165	—	—
Power Pkg.	450	—	—
AM/FM cassette	300	—	—
Sound II AM/FM cassette	450	—	—
Sunroof	395	—	—
California emissions pkg.	95	—	—

Volkswagen Passat

Volkswagen Passat (European model)

What's New

Passat is a new front-wheel drive model that's already available in Europe and is scheduled to arrive in the U.S. in the first quarter of 1990. Volkswagen has informed its dealers that it plans to introduce Passat with a base price of $14,770. Passat is a well-known name in Europe, but has never been used in the U.S. before. The previous version was called Quantum in the U.S. and was VW's top-rung sedan from 1982 through 1988, essentially a restyled Audi 4000. The new Passat has much different styling than other recent Volkswagens, marked by a grille-less nose and rounded flanks. U.S. specifications weren't available, but European models have a wheelbase of 103.3 inches, six inches longer than the Golf/Jetta. Overall length is about 180 inches, giving Passat the dimensions of a compact, close to those of the Toyota Camry and Mitsubishi Galant. It will be available as a 4-door notchback sedan and a 5-door wagon. U.S. models will come with a 2.0-liter 4-cylinder engine, similar to the 108-horsepower 4-cylinder that's the base engine for the Audi 80. A 5-speed manual transmission will be standard on the sedan and a new 4-speed overdrive automatic transmission will be optional. The wagon will come only with the automatic. Eventually, Passat also may get the narrow-angle V-6 engine being developed by Volkswagen. Anti-lock brakes are expected to be optional on U.S. models. We haven't driven the Passat so we cannot comment on its performance.

Volkswagen Vanagon

1989 Volkswagen Vanagon Wolfsburg

What's New

Volkswagen's compact van sports minor exterior styling changes, but is otherwise unchanged from last year. Appearance changes for GL models include body-color bumpers, outside mirrors, and rocker-panel covers. All Vanagons are powered by a 90-horsepower 2.1-liter 4-cylinder engine mounted at the rear. Volkswagen offers a choice of rear-wheel drive or, on the Syncro models, a permanently engaged 4-wheel drive system. A 4-speed manual transmission is standard on all versions and a 3-speed automatic is optional on rear-drive models. Syncro's 4WD system sends 95 percent of the engine power to the rear wheels on smooth, dry pavement. If the wheels start to slip, the system automatically delivers enough power to the front wheels to stabilize traction. Once traction is stabilized, the system automatically reverts to sending 95 percent of the power to the rear. Vanagon is available in 7-passenger form or as the Camper, with seats for four, a 2-place bunk that pops out of the roof, a stove, refrigerator, and kitchen sink. Vanagon is the oldest compact van sold in the U.S. It was introduced in 1980 as the successor to the VW Microbus.

For

● Passenger room ● Cargo space
● 4WD traction (Syncro) ● Ride

Against

● Acceleration ● Fuel economy ● Entry/exit
● Driving position

Summary

Vanagon is not only the oldest compact van, but also the roomiest. Even the 7-passenger models still have 50 cubic feet of luggage space with all seats in place. With the rear and/or middle seats removed, Vanagon has a cavernous cargo area that easily tops all competitors. Camper models are uniquely outfitted as factory-built recreational vehicles that come with virtually everything, including the proverbial

kitchen sink. The 4WD Syncros deliver impressive traction when you need it, and you don't have to shift a transfer-case lever to get it; it arrives automatically. Vanagon is also one of the best riding vans, making it well suited to long-distance cruising. However, there are several drawbacks. Vanagon is the tallest compact van, which makes for a steep climb into the interior through the narrow front doors; we find it easier to enter through the sliding side door. The driving position is bus-like behind a fixed steering wheel, forcing most drivers to sit too close to the pedals. Vanagon's biggest drawback is lack of power, which is especially apparent on the Syncros because they weigh 320 pounds more than the rear-drive models. With only 90 horsepower for at least 3500 pounds of curb weight, there's too little engine for too much van. Mileage is no bargain either. The best we've ever seen on the highway is 19.2 mpg. The Syncro and Camper models offer the best features, but they also are the highest priced Vanagons.

Specifications

	4-door van	Syncro 4-door van
Wheelbase, in.	96.9	96.7
Overall length, in.	179.9	179.9
Overall width, in.	72.6	72.6
Overall height, in.	75.9	78.3
Turn diameter, ft.	35.8	35.8
Curb weight, lbs.	3460	3780
Cargo vol., cu. ft.	201.0	201.0
Fuel capacity, gals.	15.9	18.4
Seating capacity	7	7
Front headroom, in.	NA	NA
Front shoulder room, in.	NA	NA
Front legroom, max., in.	NA	NA
Rear headroom, in.	NA	NA
Rear shoulder room, in.	NA	NA
Rear legroom, min., in.	NA	NA

Powertrain layout: longitudinal rear engine/rear-wheel drive or permanent 4WD.

Engines

	ohv flat-4
Size, liters/cu. in.	2.1/129
Fuel delivery	PFI
Horsepower @ rpm	90 @ 4800
Torque (lbs./ft.) @ rpm	117 @ 3200
Availability	S

EPA city/highway mpg
4-speed OD manual	18/19
3-speed automatic	17/18

Prices

Volkswagen Vanagon	Retail Price	Dealer Invoice	Low Price
4-door van	$14080	—	—
Syncro 4-door van	17605	—	—
GL 4-door van	16490	—	—
Carat 4-door van	18670	—	—
Camper GL 4-door van	20990	—	—
Camper GL Syncro 4-door van	25575	—	—
Carat Camper 4-door van	20430	—	—
Destination charge	320	320	320

Dealer invoice and low price not available at time of publication.

Prices are accurate at time of printing; subject to manufacturer's change

Standard equipment:

2.1-liter PFI 4-cylinder engine, 4-speed manual transmission, power steering, tweed reclining front bucket seats, two rear-facing removable middle bucket seats, rear bench seat, rear defogger, right visor mirror, dual OS mirrors, intermittent wipers, 185/70R14 tires; Syncro has 4-wheel drive, locking rear differential. **GL** adds: air conditioning, center bench seat, rear head restraints, full carpeting, velour upholstery, tachometer, upgraded interior trim, front vent windows, rear wiper/washer, clearcoat metallic paint, 205/70R14 tires. **Carat** adds: 3-speed automatic transmission, cruise control, power windows and locks, two rear-facing removable middle bucket seats, folding table, five cupholders, alloy wheels. **Camper models** have pop-up top with double bed, rear clothes locker, privacy curtains, window and rear hatch screens, folding rear bench seat.

Optional equipment:	Retail Price	Dealer Invoice	Low Price
3-speed automatic transmission	515	—	—
Air conditioning	1030	—	—
Alloy wheels	365	—	—
Cold Weather Pkg.	365	—	—
Convenience Group	940	—	—
Cruise control	225	—	—
Metallic paint	390	—	—
Power locks	235	—	—
Power windows	235	—	—
AM/FM cassette	350	—	—
Rear wiper, washer	190	—	—
Tinted glass	100	—	—
Wheel covers	60	—	—

Volvo 240

Volvo 240

What's New

A driver's-side airbag and an under-dashboard knee bolster are new standard feature this year on all 240 models to meet the federal passive-restraint requirement. The GL price series has been dropped and a new base trim level has been added. Prices hadn't been announced for the new base 4-door sedan and wagon, but they will be slotted below the DL models and will have fewer standard features. Air conditioning, a stereo radio with cassette player, cruise control, and power windows, all of which are standard on the DL, are optional on base models. All 240 models have a 114-horsepower 2.3-liter 4-cylinder engine, available with either a 5-speed manual or 4-speed automatic transmission.

KEY: ohv = overhead valve; **ohc** = overhead cam; **dohc** = double overhead cam; **I** = inline cylinders; **V** = cylinders in V configuration; **flat** = horizontally opposed cylinders; **bbl.** = barrel (carburetor); **PFI** = port (multi-point) fuel injection; **TBI** = throttle-body (single-point) fuel injection; **rpm** = revolutions per minute; **OD** = overdrive transmission; **S** = standard; **O** = optional; **NA** = not available.

For

● Airbag ● Passenger room ● Handling ● Ride
● Visibility

Against

● Acceleration (automatic transmission)

Summary

The rear-drive 240 was introduced in 1975, which is ancient history in the auto industry, yet Volvo says these cars accounted for about 40 percent of the company's 1989 U.S. sales, a testament to its enduring popularity. And, Volvo says that despite rumors that a replacement is imminent, it will continue to offer the 240 "as long as it remains popular with the public." The 240 has a reputation for longevity and safety, and this year's standard airbag will provide even better occupant protection. The most recent insurance statistics support the 240's reputation for safety: the 4-door sedan has fewer injury claims than most mid-size cars, while the wagon has substantially fewer claims. However, the same is true of the Ford Taurus/Mercury Sable sedans and wagons, so you shouldn't limit your shopping to Volvos if safety is your priority. In addition, a driver's-side airbag and anti-lock brakes are optional on the Taurus/Sable this year, while anti-lock brakes aren't available on the 240. The 240 is still a competent, fairly roomy car that is worth considering. DL models are fully equipped, so there aren't expensive options that can push the prices up. The 114-horsepower 2.3-liter engine is adequate, though brisk passing response with automatic transmission requires a heavy throttle foot. Using the air conditioner also makes the engine sluggish, slowing acceleration. The 240 feels stable and confident on the road, and the suspension is firm without being stiff. Inside, there is ample head room all around and adequate leg room in the rear seat for adults. Four adults fit comfortably and a fifth can be squeezed in. Thanks to a high seat, thin roof pillars, and tall windows, the driver has an excellent view to all directions.

Specifications

	4-door notchback	5-door wagon
Wheelbase, in.	104.3	104.3
Overall length, in.	189.9	190.7
Overall width, in.	67.3	67.7
Overall height, in.	56.3	57.5
Turn diameter, ft.	32.2	32.2
Curb weight, lbs.	2919	3051
Cargo vol., cu. ft.	14.0	76.0
Fuel capacity, gals.	15.8	15.8
Seating capacity	5	5
Front headroom, in.	37.9	37.9
Front shoulder room, in.	NA	NA
Front legroom, max., in.	40.1	40.1
Rear headroom, in.	36.1	36.8
Rear shoulder room, in.	NA	NA
Rear legroom, min., in.	36.4	36.1

Powertrain layout: longitudinal front engine/rear-wheel drive.

Engines

	ohc I-4
Size, liters/cu. in.	2.3/141
Fuel delivery	PFI
Horsepower @ rpm	114 @ 5400
Torque (lbs./ft.) @ rpm	136 @ 2750
Availability	S

EPA city/highway mpg | | ohc I-4
5-speed OD manual 21/28
4-speed OD automatic 20/25

Prices

Volvo 240	Retail Price	Dealer Invoice	Low Price
DL 4-door notchback, 5-speed	$18450	—	—
DL 4-door notchback, automatic	19095	—	—
DL 5-door wagon, 5-speed	18940	—	—
DL 5-door wagon, automatic	19585	—	—
DL 4-door w/sunroof, 5-speed	18975	—	—
DL 4-door w/sunroof, automatic	19620	—	—
Destination charge	350	350	350

Dealer invoice and low price, and prices for base model not available at time of publication.

Standard equipment:

2.3-liter PFI 4-cylinder engine, 5-speed manual or 4-speed automatic transmission, power steering, 4-wheel disc brakes, driver's-side airbag, power locks, trip odometer, rear defogger, tinted glass, remote OS mirrors, reclining front bucket seats, driver's-seat height adjustment, rear head restraints, 185/70R14 tires (4-door), 185R14 tires (wagon). **DL** adds: air conditioning, AM/FM cassette, power windows.

Optional equipment:

Metallic paint	245	—	—
California emissions pkg.	125	—	—

Volvo 740/760/780

Volvo 740 GLE

What's New

A driver's-side airbag is standard across the board, 740 models get nose jobs, and turbocharged models have more power this year. A new base 740 sedan and wagon trim level has been added with a slightly lower price than the 740 GL. The major difference between them is that the GL's standard sunroof isn't available on the base. Last year, the GL was the only 700-Series model that didn't have a standard airbag; it has been made standard on the GL and base 740 for 1990. Aerodynamic halogen headlamps, new grilles, and integrated bumpers give the 740 models a new appearance at the front, while the 740 and 760 wear new taillamps that are similar to those on the 780. The 740 and 760 are built from the same rear-drive design and share 4-door sedan and wagon body styles, but different in standard features and available engines. The 780 is built on the same rear-drive chassis as the others, but comes only in 2-door coupe styling and is assem-

bled in Italy by Bertone rather than by Sweden-based Volvo. The 2.3-liter 4-cylinder engine used in the 740 Turbo and 760 Turbo have a smaller turbocharger, new exhaust manifold, and recalibrated fuel and ignition systems. Horsepower is up by two and torque by five pounds/feet, and Volvo says maximum turbo boost is now available at 1800 rpm for better low-speed performance. The 780 Turbo uses the same turbocharged engine, but with different electronic controls; this "Turbo +" engine gains 13 horsepower and 19 pounds/feet torque. The 780 rides on new 195/65HR15 tires. Anti-lock brakes are optional on the base 740 and 740 GL, and standard on all other 700-Series models.

For

- Acceleration (Turbos, V-6) ● Anti-lock brakes ● Airbag
- Handling ● Passenger room ● Cargo space

Against

- Acceleration (base 740, GL) ● Fuel economy (Turbos)
- Engine noise (Turbos)

Summary

The 700-Series offers luxury-car buyers a choice of three body styles, four engines, and a price spread that runs from $21,000 to $40,000. Unfortunately, you have to go above $25,000 before you get more than ordinary performance. The 114-horsepower engine used in the base 740 and GL is sturdy and economical, but you'll be dusted off by cars that cost half as much in the Stop Light Grand Prix. The 740 GLE has the dual-cam, 153-horsepower 4-cylinder, but even that engine doesn't have a lot of low-speed torque. The turbocharged engine provides good off-the-line acceleration and sensational passing power. While the V-6 lacks the turbo's Sunday punch, it is a smooth, refined engine with ample low-speed power, and much less noise than the turbo. The sedans and wagons are functional, roomy cars that easily hold five adults. In addition, sedans have a deep, wide trunk, while wagons have a long, flat cargo floor. The higher-priced 700-Series models are highly capable and enjoyable to drive, but we think there are better alternatives in this price range.

Specifications	780 2-door notchback	740/760 4-door notchback	740/760 5-door wagon
Wheelbase, in.	109.1	109.1	109.1
Overall length, in.	188.8	188.4	188.4
Overall width, in.	69.3	69.3	69.3
Overall height, in.	55.1	55.5	56.5
Turn diameter, ft.	32.2	32.2	32.2
Curb weight, lbs.	3415	2954	3082
Cargo vol., cu. ft.	14.9	16.8	74.9
Fuel capacity, gals.	21.0	15.8[1]	15.8
Seating capacity	4	5	5
Front headroom, in.	37.2	38.6	38.6
Front shoulder room, in.	NA	NA	NA
Front legroom, max., in.	41.0	41.0	41.0
Rear headroom, in.	35.8	37.1	37.6
Rear shoulder room, in.	NA	NA	NA
Rear legroom, min., in.	34.7	34.7	34.7

1. 21.0 gals., 760.

Powertrain layout: longitudinal front engine/rear-wheel drive.

Engines	ohc I-4	dohc I-4	Turbo ohc I-4	ohc V-6
Size, liters/cu. in.	2.3/141	2.3/141	2.3/141	2.8/173
Fuel delivery	PFI	PFI	PFI	PFI

Prices are accurate at time of printing; subject to manufacturer's change

	ohc I-4	dohc I-4	Turbo ohc I-4	ohc V-6
Horsepower @ rpm	114 @ 5400	153 @ 5700	162 @ 4800[1]	144 @ 5100
Torque (lbs./ft.) @ rpm ...	136 @ 2750	150 @ 4450	195 @ 3450[1]	173 @ 3750
Availability	S	S	S	S
EPA city/highway mpg				
4-speed manual + OD ...				20/25
5-speed OD manual	21/28	18/26		
4-speed OD automatic ...	20/26	18/24	18/21	17/21

1. 780 Turbo has 188 horsepower, 206 lbs/ft torque.

Prices

Volvo 740/760/780	Retail Price	Dealer Invoice	Low Price
740 4-door notchback, 5-speed	$20685	—	—
740 4-door notchback, automatic	21330	—	—
740 5-door wagon, 5-speed	21365	—	—
740 5-door wagon, automatic	22010	—	—
740 GL 4-door notchback, 5-speed ...	21700	—	—
740 GL 4-door notchback, automatic ...	22345	—	—
740 GL 5-door wagon, 5-speed	22380	—	—
740 GL 5-door wagon, automatic	23025	—	—
740 GLE 4-door notchback, 5-speed	25440	—	—
740 GLE 4-door notchback, automatic ...	25995	—	—
740 GLE 5-door wagon, 5-speed	26120	—	—
740 GLE 5-door wagon, automatic	26675	—	—
740 Turbo 4-door, 4-speed + OD	25775	—	—
740 Turbo 4-door, automatic	26330	—	—
740 Turbo 5-door, 4-speed + OD	26455	—	—
740 Turbo 5-door, automatic	27010	—	—
760 GLE 4-door notchback	33185	—	—
760 GLE Turbo 4-door notchback	33965	—	—
760 GLE Turbo 5-door wagon	33965	—	—
780 2-door notchback	38735	—	—
780 Turbo 2-door notchback	39950	—	—
Destination charge	350	350	350
Gas Guzzler Tax, 760/780 V-6	500	500	500
Anti-lock brakes, 740 base & GL	1175	—	—

Standard equipment:

740 base & GL: 2.3-liter PFI 4-cylinder engine, 5-speed manual or 4-speed automatic transmission, power steering, 4-wheel disc brakes, driver's-side airbag, air conditioning, cloth reclining front bucket seats, power windows and locks, tachometer, coolant temperature gauge, trip odometer, AM/FM cassette, sunroof (GL), 185/70R14 tires. **740 GLE adds:** DOHC 16-valve engine, anti-lock braking system, Supplemental Restraint System, cruise control, 185/65R15 tires on alloy wheels. **740 Turbo adds:** turbocharged, intercooled engine, 4-speed manual plus overdrive or 4-speed automatic transmission, power sunroof, power mirrors, velour and leather upholstery, 195/60R15 tires. **760 adds:** 2.8-liter PFI V-6 or 2.3-liter turbocharged 4-cylinder engine, 4-speed automatic transmission, independent rear suspension, automatic climate control, leather upholstery, power seats, tilt steering column, upgraded stereo with EQ, front map lights, rear reading lights (Turbo). **780 adds:** power moonroof, elm burl accents.

Optional equipment:

Leather upholstery, 240	895	—	—
Metallic paint, 740 base & GL	245	—	—
California emissions pkg.	125	—	—

Yugo GV Plus

What's New

Yugo America has been reorganized since the company declared bankruptcy last January and the new management

1989 Yugo GV

says it has big plans for 1990. Yugo America expects to be out of Chapter 11 bankruptcy proceedings by January 1990, when it will operate as a subsidiary of Zavodi Crvena Zastava, the Yugoslavian company that manufactures the car. Yugo says it still has about 260 U.S. dealers. First among new products is a convertible, promised as a 1989 model, which is now supposed to arrive this fall. It is based on the front-drive Yugo GVX, which includes a 1.3-liter 4-cylinder engine and 5-speed manual transmission. Yugo says the base price of the convertible will be "under $9000," including a standard power top. Then, the Yugo GV, GVL, GVS, and GVX models will be consolidated into one model—the GV Plus—and their 1.1-liter 4-cylinder will be traded in for the 1.3-liter four, which will have multi-point fuel injection instead of a 2-barrel carburetor. In addition, the 5-speed overdrive manual will replace a 4-speed direct-drive manual as standard. A Yugo spokesman said even with those changes, the base price will be "under $4500." Yugo didn't bring in 1989 models; base price of leftover 1988 GV models is $4349. Sometime in 1990, a Renault-built 3-speed automatic transmission is supposed to be available on both the hatchback and convertible.

For

● Fuel economy   ● Price

Against

● Resale value   ● Interior room   ● Noise   ● Ride
● Driving position

Summary

Yugo is promising a lot for 1990, but based on past performance we're not holding our breath. The Yugo GV started out as a great idea: a new car for the price of a used car, with great gas mileage to boot. Poor quality, however, is no bargain, and many owners were frequent visitors to the local Yugo franchise for repairs, where they often found that parts weren't readily available. Worse, there was almost no market for Yugos as used cars. How could there be when Yugo dealers were having trouble selling new ones for less than $3000? Yugo says all that's in the past and things are much different now. We'll see. And, we suggest you take the same attitude. Other than rock-bottom prices and commendable fuel economy, there's little else to recommend about the Yugo. A used Honda, Nissan, or Toyota subcompact sounds like a better bet than a new Yugo.

Specifications and prices not available at time of publication.

Prices are accurate at time of printing; subject to manufacturer's change

CONSUMER GUIDE®